HATE SPEECH FRONTIERS

No serious attempt to answer the question 'What is hate speech?' would be complete without an exploration of the outer limits of the concept(s). This book critically examines both the ordinary and legal concepts of hate speech, contrasting social media platform content policies with national and international laws. It also explores a range of controversial grey area examples of hate speech. Part I focuses on the ordinary concept and looks at hybrid attacks, selective attacks, reverse attacks, righteous attacks, indirect attacks, identity attacks, existential denials, identity denials, identity miscategorisations, and identity appropriations. Part II concentrates on the legal concept. It considers how to distinguish between hate speech and hate crime and examines the precarious position of denialism laws in national and international law. Together the authors draw on conceptual analysis, doctrinal analysis, linguistic analysis, critical analysis, and diachronic analysis to map the new frontiers of the concepts of hate speech.

ALEXANDER BROWN is Associate Professor of Political and Legal Theory in the School of Politics, Philosophy, Language and Communication Studies, University of East Anglia.

ADRIANA SINCLAIR is Lecturer in International Relations in the School of Politics, Philosophy, Language and Communication Studies, University of East Anglia.

HATE SPEECH FRONTIERS

Exploring the Limits of the Ordinary and Legal Concepts

ALEXANDER BROWN
University of East Anglia
ADRIANA SINCLAIR
University of East Anglia

CAMBRIDGE
UNIVERSITY PRESS

CAMBRIDGE
UNIVERSITY PRESS

Shaftesbury Road, Cambridge CB2 8EA, United Kingdom

One Liberty Plaza, 20th Floor, New York, NY 10006, USA

477 Williamstown Road, Port Melbourne, VIC 3207, Australia

314–321, 3rd Floor, Plot 3, Splendor Forum, Jasola District Centre, New Delhi – 110025, India

103 Penang Road, #05–06/07, Visioncrest Commercial, Singapore 238467

Cambridge University Press is part of Cambridge University Press & Assessment, a department of the University of Cambridge.

We share the University's mission to contribute to society through the pursuit of education, learning and research at the highest international levels of excellence.

www.cambridge.org
Information on this title: www.cambridge.org/9781009357104

DOI: 10.1017/9781009357111

First published 2024

A catalogue record for this publication is available from the British Library

A Cataloging-in-Publication data record for this book is available from the Library of Congress

ISBN 978-1-009-35710-4 Hardback
ISBN 978-1-009-35713-5 Paperback

For Eli, Delphine, and Milo

CONTENTS

ACKNOWLEDGEMENTS

We begin by paying thanks to our children, who motivate us to do and be better every day. Parts of Chapters 3 and 4 were presented at a workshop on hate speech hosted by the Karlsruhe Institute of Technology, February 2021. For their comments and suggestions, we thank Teresa Marques, Dirk Kindermann, Rae Langton, Katharine Gelber, Mari Mikkola, Mihaela Popa-Wyatt, Stefan Rinner, and Inga Bones. In researching Chapters 3 and 4, we also benefited greatly from a series of informal discussions with Facebook including Peter Stern, Niley Erdem, Hansa Kaul, Kim Malfacini, and David Inserra. We are immensely grateful for their transparency, time, and expertise. We would also like to express our sincere thanks to Tom Shakespeare and Chi-He Elder for their advice and guidance on certain examples of grey area hate speech. An early draft of Chapter 6 was presented at an international conference on hate speech at the University of Helsinki, in November 2016. We are also indebted to Stephanos Stavros for his excellent critical feedback on this chapter. In preparing Chapter 7, we received nuggets of wisdom from Raphael Cohen-Almagor, Stephanie Farrior, Alexander Tsesis, and Mike Whine. For help in proofreading and translations, we are grateful to Emma Wyatt and Marian Arribas-Tome. Finally, we would like to thank the three anonymous reviewers from Cambridge University Press for their support and pointers and Marianne Neild for managing the project so adeptly.

1

Conceptual Frontiers in the Understanding of Hate Speech

1.1 Introduction

No serious attempt to answer the question 'What is hate speech?' would be complete without an exploration of the outer limits of the concept(s). Is it hate speech to call someone 'fatty'? Is it hate speech to say 'Rapists should be hanged, but only the black ones'? Is it hate speech for a Black person to call a White person a 'honky' or 'white devil'? Is it hate speech to label someone a 'male chauvinist pig' or 'TERF' if doing so is righteous? Is it hate speech to use the slur 'poof' against a straight person? If so, who is the relevant victim? Is it hate speech to say 'homosexuality is disgusting'? Is it hate speech to declare 'Bisexuals do not exist'? Is it hate speech to assert 'Transwomen are not women' or 'Transwomen are men'? Is it hate speech to call someone a 'cisgender woman' if she identifies as simply a woman? Is it hate speech to perform blackface? If so, what about womanface? If Holocaust denial is hate speech, does the same apply to even bare denial of specific facts relating to the Holocaust? And, what about denial of genocide or other atrocity crimes in general? If defaming a group of people identified by their religion is hate speech, does the same apply to defamation of religion itself? Is using threatening words or behaviour with intent to cause people distress, alarm, or harassment based on their protected characteristic hate speech or hate crime? And, what about using threatening words or behaviour with intent to stir up hatred against people based on their protected characteristics?

These questions show how the frontiers of hate speech spread out in many directions and occur at different levels of analysis, all of which stand in need of exploration. This book explores several conceptual frontiers including grey area examples whose status as hate speech is marginal, uncertain, or subject to reasonable disagreement; differences between social media platform content policies on hate speech and hate speech laws; divergence between national and international hate speech laws; and the sometimes fuzzy boundary lines or penumbral zones where concepts of hate speech end and other concepts begin.

In this book we shall not rehearse longstanding debates about the rights and wrongs of enacting legislation to make hate speech unlawful.[1] Nor for that matter do we get into the weeds of more recent arguments for and against legislation requiring social media platforms to remove unlawful hate speech.[2] Instead, we provide a new conceptual analysis of the term 'hate speech' with a view to clearing up not only misconceptions about the core meaning of the term but also ambiguities that emerge at the edges of its application – both of which have a tendency to hinder the former debates.

This chapter establishes the context of our project and defends its theoretical and practical importance. Section 1.2 outlines the basic conceptual framework employed in the book, including the distinction between two concepts of hate speech and our twin-track approach to analysing them. We also highlight some of the pay-offs that flow from this conceptual framework. Section 1.3 explains what we mean by 'grey areas of hate speech', including identifying three underlying reasons or explanations why certain phenomena might end up falling into these areas, namely moral, semantic, and conceptual. We also try to motivate the significance and value of working to clear up the grey areas. Finally, Section 1.4 introduces and attempts to respond to the sceptical challenge that says, because the term 'hate speech' is linked to conceptual ambiguities, misleading connotations, an explosion of applications, and politicisation, it would be better to dispense with both the term and its concepts. We critically examine five main ways of responding to this sceptical challenge: rehabilitation, downsizing, abandonment, replacement, and enhanced understanding. We defend the final response as being the most promising and the overarching goal of the book.

1.2 Conceptual Framework

As much as the book is ultimately concerned with the question 'What is hate speech?', the more direct focus will be on these related questions: 'What is paradigmatic hate speech?', 'What is grey area hate speech?', and 'What is not hate speech at all?'. We take it as read that answering these questions requires techniques and approaches from several academic disciplines including law, hate studies, sociolinguistics, philosophy, semiotics, communication studies, internet studies, politics, and international relations. More specifically, in this book we employ conceptual analysis, doctrinal analysis, linguistic analysis, critical analysis, and diachronic analysis. Overlaying all of this is the particular conceptual framework we employ, namely a distinction between two concepts of hate speech and a twin-track approach to analysing them. This section explains and defends that framework in more detail.

Before doing so, however, we first need to make a wider point about the academic study of hate speech. In this book we follow customary practice among academic scholars of hate speech by explicitly mentioning particular examples including citing specific words that most reasonable people would find deeply offensive and hateful if used in other contexts and with different intentions and purposes.[3] Reading such words may be confronting for all readers, but for some readers it could trigger upsetting reminders of personal experiences of hate speech. Some readers may simply prefer not to read two White academics repeating the n-word, for instance, no matter the circumstances. We want to warn readers about these possibilities and apologise in advance for any distress caused. At the same time, however, we wish to express our allyship with all victims of hate speech through a rigorous and open academic exploration of the subject. Sometimes it is necessary to see words on the page in order to gain a proper sense of just how uncomfortable but also ambiguous they can be.

Of course, some scholars make a conscious decision not to cite well-known or widely recognised examples of hate speech or instead to replace some of the letters with hyphens so as not to repeat the offending words in full (e.g. 'N----r', 'The J-ps are coming'). Matsuda, for example, defends the latter approach as follows: 'to prevent desensitization to harmful words'.[4] However, the primary subject of this book is grey area examples of hate speech that are not well known. The secondary purpose is to interrogate how organisations and institutions handle these specific examples. As such, we believe it would be virtually impossible to write intelligibly about grey area examples of hate speech without citing them. This book represents a good faith attempt to explore the frontiers of concepts of hate speech. Our hope is that the reader will recognise this intention as well as critically engaging with our arguments. We also hope that the reader will not become desensitised to our examples and will not copy or misuse the examples for hateful purposes.

In light of the above, throughout the book we rely on the conventional distinction between citing or mentioning slurs or hate speech in an academic context, on the one hand, and using slurs or hate speech, on the other hand.[5] It is also worth emphasising that academic purposes are not the only prima facie legitimate reasons for citing specific examples of hate speech. Other prima facie legitimate reasons might include everything from judges iterating examples of hate speech when discussing the facts of legal cases; through to legislators mentioning especially notable examples of hate speech in parliamentary debates about whether to ban hate speech, what hate speech to ban, and how to draft sound legislation; to social media platforms citing examples of the sort of content they deem hate speech.[6]

1.2.1 *The Ordinary and Legal Concepts of Hate Speech*

Central to our analysis is the fundamental insight that there is not one but two concepts of hate speech: the ordinary concept and the legal concept.[7] As a rough preliminary characterisation, the ordinary concept is related to social norms, social rules, and social sanctions, such as social media platform content policies that disallow directly attacking people with racial slurs, for instance, whereas the legal concept is intimately bound up with legal norms, laws, and legal sanctions, such as criminal laws that ban incitement to hatred, discrimination, or violence on grounds of race, for instance. Meta (Facebook, Instagram) implicitly relies on this broad distinction within its operational structure and division of labour. Whilst its 'terms of use' and 'legal compliance' teams focus on unlawful hate speech within given jurisdictions, its global 'community standard', internal content policy, and content moderation teams concentrate on disallowed though lawful hate speech.[8] This distinction is also reflected in the mandate Facebook has given to its Oversight Board, namely to only deal with suspected cases of disallowed though lawful hate speech.[9] In a similar vein, in 2022 the Committee of Ministers of the Council of Europe distinguished between hate speech prohibited under criminal law, hate speech subject to civil or administrative law, and less grave forms of hate speech that call for alternative responses and measures, including but not limited to victim-support, education, and counterspeech.[10]

However, the above characterisation and illustrations only tell half the story. It is equally important to understand the genesis of the two concepts of hate speech and this has to do with semantics. The semantics of the term 'hate speech' are both non-compositional and polysemic in that its meaning is not divinable from the words out of which it is composed and it is a term with more than one meaning.[11] In its basic or original meaning, the term 'hate speech' relates to certain forms of unlawful speech, but it also conveys another, much wider meaning that captures lawful speech. To be more precise, during the late 1980s a group of legal academics and journalists began to use the neologism 'hate speech' to classify and make generalisations about a particular group of laws.[12] At first glance, it might seem a stretch to interpret Mari Matsuda's coinage of the term 'hate speech' as her introducing an exploratory concept since the laws and legal phenomena she was studying were far from new and had previously been discussed using terms like 'group defamation' and 'hate propaganda'.[13] However, Matsuda's focus on people's lived experience of hate speech both as victims and seekers of justice for victims almost certainly had 'net positive exploratory utility'.[14] At the very least, because of the work of legal scholars like Matsuda, the term 'hate speech' has now been taken up by lawmakers and legal professionals themselves more explicitly. But, and this next part of the story is crucial, the new bit of terminology was subsequently adopted by various other speakers and has 'taken on a life of its own'.[15]

The splitting of the general notion into two concepts of hate speech partly supervenes on divergence in the sorts of speakers who use the term 'hate speech'. Today the term continues to be used by legal scholars, legal journalists, lawmakers, legal professionals, and law enforcement officers who typically have the legal concept in mind. But the term is also used by political scientists, linguists, sociologists, philosophers, mental health professionals, journalists, politicians, activists, social commentators, artists, writers, film and television producers, diversity in the workplace trainers, business leaders, social media platforms, and ordinary members of the public. Of course, in some instances these people may also have the legal concept in mind. But sometimes they have the ordinary concept in mind.

In fact, social media platforms have played a significant role in popularising the term 'hate speech' in the sense that their adoption of this term has been pivotal in turning it from a niche bit of legalese into a commonplace and non-technical phrase that regularly crops up in the media, popular culture, and public discourse more generally. That social media platforms like Facebook have public-facing community standards disallowing 'hate speech' has helped to bring this term to the public's attention. Especially in an online environment, it is now almost as hard to avoid the term 'hate speech' as it is to avoid hate speech itself.

Importantly, the basic division of labour between legal systems and social media platforms in tackling hate speech has also helped to cement some of the differing social functions or purposes played by the two concepts. The term 'hate speech' in its ordinary sense implies, among other things, the moral objectionableness and social unacceptability of certain speech, as in, speech worthy of moral condemnation and social sanction. By contrast, the term 'hate speech' in its legal sense connotes, among other things, that there is a pro tanto reason for legal institutions and quasi-governmental agencies to prohibit or regulate certain speech, as in, speech that merits legal sanction. That said, some innovations in the legal field have challenged this basic division of labour, including the rise of internet regulations in Germany (NetzDG), France (Loi Avia), and more recently the United Kingdom (the Online Safety Act) and the European Union (the Digital Services Act), that create legal responsibilities on the part of social media platforms and other internet service providers to record and remove unlawful content.[16] However, even when platforms have legal responsibilities to record and remove unlawful hate speech, it is clear they will continue to operate their own content policies and remove disallowed though lawful hate speech.

We shall delve deeper into the distinction between the ordinary and legal concepts of hate speech in Chapter 5, including presenting a new theory of not only how they overlap and diverge but also how they relate to, or interact with, each other. However, it is perhaps worth making the point at this early stage that, when it comes to distinguishing the ordinary and legal concepts of hate speech, unfortunately we are not especially well served by the English language. The term 'hate speech' hides the fundamental ambiguity between the two different concepts and this occlusion has some interesting linguistic consequences. For example, researchers have recently uncovered a tendency among journalists to write stories about examples of speech in their local communities which they describe as 'not hate speech, but . . . '. They use this phrase partly because they recognise the speech in question is not unlawful but also partly because they see it as problematic and hate speechy.[17]

If a society or organisation were starting from scratch and creating a new vocabulary to capture the two concepts of hate speech, perhaps it would be wise to create two different terms or phrases. For example, it might propose the literal pairing 'lawful hate speech' and 'unlawful hate speech'. Then again, this might create uncertainty about which term to use if people want to refer to speech which is not currently but ought to be unlawful in their view. Perhaps a more eloquent pairing would be 'hate speech lite' and 'hate speech'. But this may convey the impression that the former is not as serious as the latter, which could call into question the legitimacy of social sanctions in the eyes of the public. Another option might be 'disallowed hate speech' and 'unlawful hate speech'. The former certainly speaks to the way in which certain forms of hate speech are disallowed by social media platforms. That said, the ordinary concept *hate speech* is not synonymous with the rules promulgated by such platforms, even though the latter significantly influence and shape the former. If the ordinary concept were synonymous with the rules promulgated by platforms, then it would be confusing to say something like 'Facebook allows this speech even though it is hate speech'. When reading Facebook's community standard on 'hate speech', it should always be borne in mind that the term means 'hate speech of the sort disallowed by Facebook'. Not all forms of hate speech in the ordinary sense of the term are disallowed by Facebook. For these reasons, we proceed with 'ordinary hate speech' and 'unlawful hate speech'.

What is the pay-off from distinguishing two concepts of hate speech? First, to say there is not one but two concepts is more faithful to the myriad and varied uses of the term 'hate speech' in contemporary societies. Second, distinguishing the ordinary and legal concepts of hate speech provides a framework with which to mark the different social functions or purposes a society and institutions and organisations can reasonably expect these concepts to play. Third, drawing the distinction may be needed to capture people's lived experiences, the fact that they experience certain words as hate speech even though the words are not unlawful. This is especially important in the current internet epoch – following the Internet of content, the Internet of services, the Internet of people, and the Internet of things – which many users experience as the Internet of hate.[18] Fourth, drawing the distinction can mitigate against the problem that focusing only on legal understandings of hate speech creates a tendency to work towards a more precisely and narrowly defined concept ignoring the relevance or social utility of having a concept that is less precisely defined and broader in scope but still meaningful. Finally, drawing the distinction may be indispensable to improving the quality of not only academic and legal argument but also public debate more broadly about the nature of the problem of hate speech and the rights and wrongs of using different measures to tackle it. For example, there may be some interests, rights, principles, and values that are better suited as reasons for and against using legal norms, rules, and sanctions to combat hate speech; and others that are more fitting as reasons for and against using social norms, rules, and sanctions to deal with hate speech.

1.2.2 Twin-Track Approach

Building on the distinction between the ordinary and legal concepts of hate speech, we develop a twin-track approach to analysing the two concepts. Beginning with the ordinary concept, in the past fifteen to twenty years there has been an explosion in the number and range of applications of the term 'hate speech' and this has created a vast system of examples.

Members of this vast system can be, and often are, connected to prototypes or exemplars of hate speech in the sense that they show a complex pattern of overlapping and criss-crossing similarities or family resemblance with the exemplars.[19] As a result, competent language users of various kinds are able to use the term 'hate speech' in ways their interlocutors can understand even without being able to articulate a formal definition.[20]

By analogy, think of the way objects in the solar system are composed of materials traceable to the solar nebular in the early life of the system but have varying degrees of similarity in composition to each other. To push the astronomy analogy even further, exemplars of hate speech, like Earth as a prototype for planets in our solar system, stick in the minds of competent language users and provide a basis for comparison. This is one of the reasons why ordinary people have a hard time thinking that Pluto is not a planet, even though the scientific community has downgraded it to the category of dwarf plant.[21] Just as the term 'planet' has the ordinary meaning 'something like the Earth', even though it also has a far more formal and detailed scientific definition, so the term 'hate speech' has the ordinary meaning 'something like calling Black people "niggers", comparing Jews to rats, or denying the Holocaust', even though it also has a more precise and narrow legal definition within given jurisdictions. In Part I of this book we shall argue that different examples of hate speech in the ordinary (nonlegal) sense of the term share a family resemblance based on the distinguishing qualities of target, style, message, act, and effect even though they lack a singular common feature, akin to the way different planets in the ordinary (nonscientific) sense of the term share a family resemblance when taking into account mass, density, size, orbit, and gravitational influence, even though they lack a singular common feature.

Of course, we do not mean to downplay the fact that just as it is useful for astronomers to more precisely define the term 'planet' and limit its scope of application, so it is useful for legislators to lend greater precision to the term 'hate speech' and to restrict the range of unlawful hate speech. But when it comes to the ordinary concept *hate speech*, part of its usefulness may rest in its imprecision and wide application.[22] It allows people to air grievances but also to disagree. The ordinary concept is useful precisely because its looseness provides a space for communication: a shared vocabulary yet with polymorphic semantics. If people can at least come together to talk about the 'hate speech' they see around them, then at least they are talking the same language, even if they are thinking about different examples or disagree about what the examples have in common with exemplars. In that sense the ordinary concept *hate speech* is an intercultural concept, namely the sort of concept that can serve as 'part of a contact language between groups'.[23]

This partly explains why there can be some shared understandings even between people who invoke the pejorative 'hate speech' to condemn certain things, on the one hand, and people who attack this condemnation, on the other.[24] For example, some people may denounce phrases like 'These women are sluts and whores' as hate speech because they see this language as seeking to control women's behaviour, but other people decry the very label 'hate speech' as itself a means by which mainstream culture seeks to control certain groups.[25] Religious speakers whose own words have been condemned for expressing hateful stereotypes or enacting forms of discrimination sometimes respond by using the label 'hate speech' to describe what they allege their critics are doing to them, namely expressing negative stereotypes or enacting forms of discrimination.[26] Here people are presupposing distinguishing qualities of the ordinary concept *hate speech* in the very act of rejecting or rearming that concept.

In short, we believe analysing the ordinary concept *hate speech* as a family resemblance concept with a wide scope of application not only lends meaning to the myriad and varied uses of the term but also better serves the range of social functions or purposes that a society can reasonably expect the ordinary concept to play. This includes everything from expressing moral condemnation and social disapproval towards certain forms of speech; through to voicing grievances about injustice and oppression; and to providing a vernacular for disagreement not dissimilar to other useful phrases in politics such as 'That's bullshit!' or 'That's propaganda!'.[27] In Chapter 5, we seek to uncover and distinguish the full spectrum of social purposes served by the ordinary and legal concepts of hate speech, respectively.

We also believe our analysis of the ordinary concept *hate speech* paves the way for a more balanced treatment of some of the most highly controversial and antagonistic areas of discourse today. As we shall try to show in Chapters 3 and 4, based on a family resemblance analysis, both the slurs 'tranny' and 'TERF' can be hate speech; both miscategorising people who identify as men as 'women' and miscategorising people who identify as just women as 'cisgender women' can be hate speech; both calling Black people 'niggers' and calling White people 'honkies' can be hate speech; and both stereotyping Mexicans as 'rapists' and stereotyping Trump voters as 'racists' can be hate speech.

In addition, this balanced treatment could help to mitigate what we call hate speech spirals or hatred feedback loops.[28] For example, when speakers say things like 'Transwomen are not women' or 'Transwomen are men', this can provoke the use of slurs like 'TERF' and 'Feminazi'. In turn, some people make generalisations about trans people such as that if you accidentally misgender trans people they will lose their temper and yell at you or that if you intentionally question whether trans people really are the gender with which they identity, then they will send you death threats. As a result, other people will accuse speakers who express these sorts of generalisations as peddling transphobic stereotypes. In response, some speakers will call it bigotry and intolerance to seek to misconstrue legitimate concerns about the behaviour of some trans people in yelling at women and sending them death threats as transphobia. In turn, some trans people may argue that it is a microaggression to ignore the fact that they experience generalisations made about them as hate speech or to downplay or minimise real hate speech as merely voicing legitimate concerns about trans people. In our view, analysing the ordinary concept *hate speech* as a family resemblance concept with a wide scope of application helps to put a different light on this sort of dispute. Perhaps we have antagonistic groups of people drawing on various different forms of hate speech to attack each other whilst simultaneously disagreeing about what hate speech is, all because the concept lacks a singular common feature. However, it would be wrong to see the lack of a singular common feature as the root problem. Indeed, the mere fact that the groups are able to communicate at all may be a good thing. If they consciously use the term 'hate speech' in its ordinary sense to voice their grievances, this could be at worst a pressure-valve and at best a gateway to further deliberation, mutual understanding, and even compromise.

Turning to the legal concept *hate speech*, it is associated with a smaller cohort of competent language users than the ordinary concept. Unsurprisingly, this alters how the term 'hate speech' is understood among those with the relevant competency. For example, Facebook[29] and Twitter[30] define hate speech in the ordinary sense of the term as a 'direct attack' against people based on protected characteristics, but it is far less common for legal scholars, legislators, and courts to define hate speech using this broad terminology. Ironically, when legal scholars do define hate speech as 'speech attacks' this is often for the polemical purpose of depicting a legal interpretation of hate speech so broad as to pose a significant danger to free speech and ultimately with the aim of rejecting the case for banning hate speech.[31] Of course, both Facebook and Twitter supplement their general definitions of hate speech with long lists of rules disallowing specific forms of hate speech, but even these forms are typically more expansive than the speech prohibited by hate speech laws.

Focusing on legal scholars for a moment,[32] some limit themselves to defining a specific legal concept *hate speech* that relates to a particular body of law and legal jurisdiction, such as the concept *the stirring up hatred offences in England and Wales.* Others describe a cluster concept associated with a particular class of hate speech laws, such as the concept *incitement to hatred laws.* Yet others characterise an umbrella legal concept *hate speech* that implicates a range of different clusters of hate speech laws, including laws criminalising group libel, laws disallowing insult or denigration, laws banning incitement to hatred, discrimination, or violence, civil rights laws prohibited discriminatory harassment, human rights laws disallowing group vilification, and tort laws relating to intentional infliction of emotional distress or injuria. Because these characterisations differ in terms of both which body of law is the focus and the levels of generality at which they operate, they often wind up saying different, often contradictory things about what hate speech is.

Techniques of conceptual jurisprudence can be used to analyse the legal concept(s) *hate speech* by investigating the language and content of given bodies of law, even if the laws do not themselves contain the term 'hate speech'. This could work by identifying certain common elements of the laws in question. In order to identify a relevant body of law in the first place, the researcher could search through statutes and case law looking for words that are indicative of, contiguous with, or serviceable proxies for the legal concept – for example, 'protected characteristics', 'hatred', 'contempt', 'enmity', 'racial superiority', 'racist propaganda', 'xenophobia', 'antisemitism', 'Islamophobia', 'homophobia', 'group defamation', 'vilification', 'insult', 'negative stereotypes', 'stigmatisation', 'humiliation', 'degradation', 'emotional distress', 'violation of dignity', 'threats', 'cross burning', 'racist fighting words', 'discriminatory harassment', 'hostile environment discrimination', 'advocacy, encouragement, or incitement to hatred', 'incitement to discrimination', 'incitement to violence', 'incitement to genocide', 'Holocaust denial', 'genocide denial'.[33]

Since the legal concept *hate speech* is not a hermetically sealed object, it may also be feasible to analyse the concept by studying other bodies of discourse besides law itself. However, the challenge in this sort of approach lies in selecting a corpus that allows researchers to reliably separate the ordinary and legal concepts of hate speech. For example, if the corpus is simply any journalistic news story containing the term 'hate speech', then it would be difficult to say for certain that the discourse provides a reliable guide to the meaning of the legal concept given that the journalists concerned may be switching seamlessly between the ordinary and legal concepts. But if the corpus is selected by the researcher using the more selective filter that the news story must be about relevant legislation or case law, then the researcher must rely on pre-theoretical assumptions about relevance, namely pre-theoretical assumptions about what makes something hate speech law as opposed to some other kind of law. These assumptions may reflect the researcher's own intuitions about the concept and create a confirmation bias in the results.

At any rate, the gold standard for conceptual jurisprudence at least in the analytic tradition is to try to clarify the meaning and extension of legal concepts by developing sets of necessary and sufficient conditions for appropriate application. These conditions might be supported in different ways. A condition might be descriptively grounded in relevant bits of legal text or legal practices. Also, it might be normatively justified by arguing the condition shows the concept in its best light. In this book we do not attempt to meet this gold standard and shall not provide a full and substantive definition of the legal concept(s) *hate speech* based on a complete set of necessary and sufficient conditions for its appropriate application. Nevertheless, in Chapter 5 we do outline several purposes that a society might reasonably expect the legal concept to play and contrast them with purposes associated with the ordinary concept. In addition, in Chapter 6 we provide a limited formal characterisation of the legal concept *hate speech* comprised of a single necessary condition, namely that, formally speaking, this concept only refers to laws which create bespoke crimes or other sorts of offences that do not have corresponding or parallel basic or base versions. This necessary condition for applying the legal concept *hate speech* is the mirror opposite of a well-established necessary condition for applying the concept *hate crime.*

The merits of this form of analysis include that it provides sufficient detail about the nature and extension of the legal concept *hate speech* as to establish a clear map of where this concept ends and where at least some other legal concepts begin without necessarily having to provide a full account of the disposition of this concept in relation to all concepts. Moreover, the analysis furnishes a characterisation of the legal concept *hate speech* that is still universal enough to be grounded and/or normatively justified in different ways, including being grounding in several different bodies of law and justified by the social functions or purposes a society can reasonably expect the legal concept to play. In addition to this, the analysis can be grounded in legal texts and legal practices at both the domestic and international levels. We attempt to demonstrate these merits in Part II of the book.

1.3 Grey Areas

Grey areas of hate speech are one of the main frontiers to be explored in the book. We use the term 'grey areas' in a broad way to mean examples that do not readily conform to classification. For example, examples can be hard to classify due to fundamental ambiguity at the conceptual level but also because of uncertainties based on limited information or reasonable disagreement about the examples. Grey area examples are not manifestly hate speech but could potentially be marginal hate speech or could turn out not to be hate speech pending further assessment. If paradigmatic examples of hate speech occupy space where the ordinary and legal concepts of hate speech overlap with each other, then marginal hate speech can be found at the outer edges of both concepts. These sorts of grey areas represent penumbral zones where concepts of hate speech overlap with other sorts of concepts. That said, an example might fall into a grey area simply because people do not know enough about the example or because the moral quality of the example is the subject of reasonable disagreement. In other words, cutting across different grey area examples is a further distinction between different underlying reasons or explanations for why certain types of words, signs, or behaviours might end up falling into grey areas of hate speech. We propose three main reasons: moral, semantic, and conceptual.

1.3.1 Moral Uncertainty and Disagreement

One reason for an example falling into a grey area of hate speech is moral uncertainty and disagreement. One of the many social purposes served by the term 'hate speech' in its ordinary sense is to express moral condemnation and social disapproval of certain forms of speech and by implication the speaker.[34] The term is in that sense a pejorative, but more than merely expressing disapproval, the term also conveys (expresses, implies, presupposes, infers) ideas about why certain things deserve disapproval. The ordinary concept *hate speech* is a thick normative concept combining description with moral evaluation. The concept says something not only about the basic semantic and/or pragmatic features of the speech to which it refers (e.g. related to protected characteristics, related to messages of hatred, contempt, and prejudice, related to the performance, justification, and perpetuation of subordination, misrecognition, and marginalisation) but also about its moral quality (e.g. wrong, unjust, bad, harmful, reprehensible, or otherwise morally objectionable), and the way moral quality relates to basic features (e.g. morally objectionable because related to protected characteristics, because related to hatred, contempt, and prejudice, and because related to subordination, misrecognition, and marginalisation).[35] However, if part of what is conveyed by the term 'hate speech' in its ordinary sense is a moral evaluation of the speech and the speaker, then this opens up the possibility of moral uncertainty and disagreement.

One source of moral uncertainty and disagreement has to do with ambiguity about the object of the moral evaluation. For instance, is the use of racial slurs morally objectionable due to the immoral ideas conveyed, due to the immoral sentiments expressed, due to the immoral act of communicating the ideas or expressing the sentiments to others, due to some kind of immoral act that is performed over and above the act of simply using the slur, due to its immoral effects, or due to a combination of some or all of these things? There may be uncertainty and disagreement over the status of a particular racial slur as hate speech because people have in mind different things about the slur that are morally objectionable.

In addition to this, moral uncertainty and disagreement could be rooted in fundamental differences of opinion about what the relevant immorality or moral objectionableness of hate speech consists in (e.g. bad intentions, violation of dignity, psychological damage, acts of subordination, misrecognition, and marginalisation, consequences for society including threats to public order or undermining democracy and legitimacy), the hierarchy between different forms of moral objectionableness, and the application of aspects of moral objectionableness to concrete circumstances. The upshot is that there could be dispute about whether certain words qualify as hate speech because people reasonably disagree about whether the words are morally objectionable all things considered. This is especially prominent in cases of what we call righteous attacks such as calling someone a 'male chauvinist pig' or 'TERF', to be discussed in Chapter 3. In one sense calling someone a 'TERF' might be a righteous thing to do but in another sense it might be harmful.

Furthermore, it goes without saying that whether speech is morally objectionable all things considered may be contextually dependent including both the specific conversational context and the wider social context. As a result, some forms of moral uncertainty and disagreement about the status of given bits of language as hate speech may reflect imperfect information or differences of interpretation about the relevant context as well as differences of opinion about how far context should in fact matter to moral evaluation.

1.3.2 Semantic Ambiguity

Another reason for an example falling into a grey area of hate speech has to do with semantic ambiguity (and, in the case of signs, symbols, or gestures, semiotic ambiguity); which is to say, the expressive, communicative, or performative phenomena purported to be hate speech may be such that they have more than one meaning or convey different content. For example, there might be ambiguity in the intended target or subject and ambiguity in what is being said about the target or subject. In these sorts of cases, the status of something as hate speech changes dramatically depending on what content is conveyed, and this can lead to significant uncertainty and disagreement among competent users of the term 'hate speech'.

In some instances, semantic ambiguity can result from the relevant words being ambiguous words such as homonyms or polysemes, where the words have multiple basic or literal meanings. Consider the following example.

(1) The Jews in my town always like to visit the bank at the weekend.

Here whether statement (1) is a candidate for being labelled 'hate speech' depends to a large extent (although not fully) on which sense of 'bank' is intended.

(1a) *The Jews in my town always like to visit the financial institution at the weekend.*

(1b) *The Jews in my town always like to visit the land near the river at the weekend.*

In other instances, semantic ambiguity can result from words or whole sentences being associated with different kinds of conveyed content. In this book we use the phrase 'conveyed content' in a deliberately broad way so that it might capture some or all of: literal meaning; conventional meaning; expressive meaning; implied meaning or implicature (including speaker implicature, conversational implicature, and sentence implicature); presuppositional content; inferred content; the speaker's intended meaning or encoded content; receiver understandings or decoded content; speaker and hearer negotiated meaning; use-conditional content; and contextually dependent content.[36] Consider another example.

(2) They are very hard working for black people.

The ambiguity of (2) lies in the fact that it conveys not only a literal meaning but also further conveyed content (implicature) that is not part of what is directly expressed.

(2a) *They are more hard working than other black people.*
(2b) *Black people tend not to be hard working all because they are black.*

Perhaps the semantic ambiguities in (1) and (2) are not especially difficult to resolve by looking at one or a combination of the words used, the speaker, the recipients, and the context including the conversational context, social practices and conventions, wider social and political circumstances, and cognitive environment including beliefs and assumptions. However, other examples may be trickier, as we shall now try to demonstrate.

First, consider phrases or statements containing words that are semantically ambiguous as between referring to a country and referring to its people. One such example has recently been reviewed by Facebook's Oversight Board.[37]

(3) Sout ta-yote [Burmese].

During the case, Facebook explained to the Board that, according to its interpretation, the Burmese word 'ta-yote' contained in (3) 'is perceived culturally and linguistically as an overlap of identities/meanings between China the country and the Chinese people'.[38] Facebook also explained that because in its view the user did not 'clearly indicate that the term refers to the country/government of China', it determined that 'the user is, at a minimum, referring to Chinese people'.[39] As a consequence, Facebook removed the post under its community standard on hate speech. However, the Board took a different view as follows.

> As the same word is used in Burmese to refer to a state and people from that state, context is key to understanding the intended meaning. A number of factors convinced the Board that the user was not targeting Chinese people, but the Chinese state.[40]

Second, consider compound sentences containing independent clauses that include references to countries but other independent clauses that refer to a people but no direct and explicit link is drawn between what is being said about the country and what is being said about the people.

(4) Think about their attitudes about eating whale meat—I hate Japan.
(5) I abhor what they are doing in Xinjiang—death to China!
(6) Israel is a fascist state—these people are scum.
(7) COVID-19 originated in China—they all deserve to get sick and die.

In the case of both (4) and (5), the second independent clause in the sentence contains an attack in the relevant sense (e.g. a vilificatory or threatening remark), but it is about a specific country not a people, whereas the first independent clause contains a pronoun referring to a people but it is not explicit to whom it refers and it may not be an attack in the relevant sense. In the case of (6) and (7) the situation is reverse, the first independent clause relates to a specific country but may not be an attack in the relevant sense, whereas the second independent clause contains an attack in the relevant sense but it is not explicit to whom it refers. A strict approach to interpreting these compound sentences might be to insist that they cannot be labelled 'hate speech' because the attack and the pronoun do not occur together in the same independent clause and so the sentences remain ambiguous. A more nuanced interpretive approach might be to say there could be co-referencing exhibited in these sentences based on reading across between the independent clauses. On this approach, if any part of the sentence is referring to a people and any part of the sentence is an attack in the relevant sense, then the entire sentence can be classified as hate speech even if the reference and the attack occur in different clauses, provided that it is clear from the sentence, the speaker, and the context that the overall conveyed content does incorporate an attack on a people. Dispute about whether to classify these compound sentence as hate speech may well result from reasonable disagreement about which interpretive approach is correct.

Third, consider statements that directly attack a property, identity, or characteristic, but do not explicitly attack the people who possess that characteristic.

(8) Homosexuality is disgusting.
(9) Transgenderality is a fraud.

Focusing on the literal meanings of statements (8) and (9) might lead a society or organisation to conclude these statements are not hate speech, especially if they embrace a rule of thumb that says hate speech is a direct attack on people as opposed to properties, identities, or characteristics. However, looking at the non-literal content conveyed by these statements, such as the implicature or inference that homosexuals are disgusting or that transgender people are frauds, could lead a society or organisation to conclude these statements are hate speech. Here the dispute about appropriate classification rests on disagreement about which is the most relevant form of conveyed content. We shall investigate these sorts of cases more fully in Chapter 4.

Fourth, consider hybrid slurs which, like personal insults, are typically used to attack specific individuals, but, like prototypical hate speech, also seem to attack the groups to which targeted individuals belong.

(10) She is a fucking bitch.

Disputes about whether (10) counts as hate speech may reflect differences in how men and women typically understand the connotations of terms like 'bitch'. However, these differences are not simply a matter of the qualities or traits being attributed to the targets. In a 1978 participant experiment study asking 168 American college students their opinion on what they thought a person generally means when describing another person as a 'bitch', the researchers found that the top four traits most closely associated with the term 'bitch' by men were 'Critical', 'Stubborn', 'Inconsiderate', and 'Dominant', whereas the top four traits most closely associated with the term 'bitch' by women were 'Inconsiderate', 'Critical', 'Insincere', and 'Deceitful'.[41] This difference might predict that men are more likely to classify 'bitch' as hate speech than women, but in reality the opposite seems to be true. Perhaps the more significant difference is that men are more likely to interpret 'bitch' as merely a personal insult, whereas woman are more likely to interpret it as a group-based attack and, therefore, hate speech. We shall return to these issues in Chapter 3.

Finally, consider statements that attack a group but are ambiguous as to scope, as in, it is unclear if they attack all, most, or some of the group. Some statements might be hate speech in a straightforward way because they involve unqualified behavioural statements about the whole group and because the message conveyed is clearly defamatory or vilificatory. Other statements may be manifestly not speech because they involve qualified behavioural statements about only a small proportion of a group and because they appear to be grounded in historical facts, for instance. However, another class of statements fall into a grey area because, even though they involve qualified statements about members of a group, it is unclear what proportion of the group is being attacked and because they convey stereotypes that go beyond the mere statement of historical facts. Compare the following examples.

(11) All Russians are war criminals and they commit war crimes because they are Russians.
(12) Some Russian soldiers have committed war crimes in the past.
(13) More Russian soldiers are war criminals than is true of other nationalities.

In a recent Facebook Oversight Board case involving a user who had posted a poem about Russian soldiers,[42] Facebook provided a strong suggestion as to how it would classify statements such as (11) and (12). Whilst statements like (11) would be treated as Tier 1 hate speech by virtue of being dehumanising attacks on people based on their nationality, statements like (12) would be deemed to be not hate speech in that sense.[43] This reflects the fact that Facebook would consider the group of people referred to by the noun-phrase 'some Russian soldiers' in (12) as a 'non-protected group' under Tier 1 of its community standard due to these people 'representing less than half of a group'.[44] We shall critically examine this rule in Chapter 3. However, this still leaves a question mark surrounding statement (13). The question is whether the noun-phrase 'Russian solders' is correctly interpreted as referring to all, most, or only some Russian soldiers, and this remains semantically ambiguous. After all, even if statement (13) is true, it is compatible with several different inferences.

(13a) *All Russian soldiers are war criminals.*
(13b) *The majority of Russian soldiers are war criminals.*
(13c) *Only a small minority of Russian soldiers are war criminals.*

If there is dispute about whether to classify statement (13) as hate speech, this might reflect disagreement about whether to focus only on the literal meaning of (13) or also to consider inferred content, disagreement about whether to look at any inference (13) could invite a receiver to make or only some inferences, and, ultimately, disagreement about whether (13) infers (13a), (13b), or (13c). We shall explore the status of selective attacks in Chapter 3.

In addition to this, dispute about whether (13) counts as hate speech might also be a function of disagreement about whether stereotypes can still be classified as hate speech if grounded in reliable statistics. Interestingly, Facebook's community standard on hate speech does not disallow stereotypes per se but does disallow 'harmful stereotypes' which it defines as 'dehumanising comparisons that have historically been used to attack, intimidate or exclude specific groups, and that are often linked with offline violence'.[45] We shall scrutinise this sort of conceptual linkage between hate speech and harmfulness in various chapters of the book. For now, however, we simply point out that other social media platforms do not appear to make the qualification that only harmful stereotypes may count as hate speech. Twitter's hateful conduct policy, for example, refers instead to 'content that intends to degrade or reinforce *negative or harmful* stereotypes about a protected category'.[46] This divergence between Facebook and Twitter speaks to a third reason for examples falling into a grey area of hate speech, to which we now turn.

1.3.3 *Conceptual Confusion and Contestedness*

The third reason for an example falling into a grey area of hate speech relates to conceptual confusion and contestedness, namely lack of precision in, and contest over, the meaning of the term 'hate speech' itself. This can take different forms. For one thing, an example may appear to fall into a grey area due to a failure to disambiguate the ordinary and legal concepts of hate speech. Thus, certain people may deny that something counts as hate speech because they have in mind the legal concept, whereas other people may believe it is hate speech due to the fact that they are thinking about the ordinary concept.

Some social media platforms have not done enough to eliminate this confusion. Arguably, Facebook's community standard on hate speech is more complex, detailed, considered, coherent, responsive to feedback, evolving, transparent, reflective of its authoritative internal policy, and subject to independent oversight than any comparable public-facing hate speech code of any social media platform in existence globally. Ironically, because Facebook has put its head above the parapet it has often faced the heaviest criticism; and sometimes entirely justified criticism. As we shall argue in Chapters 3 and 4, Facebook's community standard is full of ambiguities, inconsistencies, and blind spots – which is perhaps inevitable given its complexity. However, there is one area of conceptual confusion created by the wording of the standard that is easily avoidable. Nowhere in the standard itself does Facebook clarify that the standard is about defining hate speech in the ordinary sense of the term as opposed to defining hate speech in the legal sense of the term, as in, the sort of unlawful hate speech recognised in national and international hate speech laws.

Furthermore, even without conflating the two concepts of hate speech, there can be contests among competent users over the extension of each concept. Some contests concern which particular styles of speech ought to count as hate speech. Consider the disagreement between certain Muslim states and the rest of the world as to whether defamation of religion is a form of unlawful hate speech.[47] Other contests relate to whether particular characteristics and groups are properly considered 'protected'. Consider disagreement among some legal scholars about whether sexist speech targeting women should be considered hate speech in the legal sense of the term.[48] Similar disagreements occur in relation to the ordinary concept *hate speech*, such as policy differences between Facebook, TikTok, and Twitter over whether, in relation to hate speech, age should be treated as a primary or secondary protected characteristic and whether hate speech includes or excludes targeted misgendering.[49]

At a deeper level, there may be differing views over whether hate speech should be specified in objective or subjective ways. Some people might think it right to specify hate speech based not on the personal feelings or opinions of either the speaker or target but instead on widely accepted norms or commonly recognised standards concerning what is taboo. However, other people might insist such an approach is flawed for the reason that these norms and standards can be themselves discriminatory. For example, to live in a society in which there is a widely accepted norm that treats the word 'nigger' as hate speech but not the term 'fatty' may be experienced by some people as discrimination through misrecognition of an identity they affirm (*fat and proud*) and believe ought to be protected (*don't call be 'fatty'*). Kylie Weston-Scheuber makes a similar point about gendered slurs. 'Unlike words such as "nigger" or "Paki" which automatically trigger an adverse response in the public domain and are commonly recognised as racial slurs, words used to and about women are not recognised as gendered epithets.'[50] This differentiated taboo status cannot be easily justified by differences in the proportions of derogatory and non-derogatory (reclaimed) uses of the terms 'nigger' and 'bitch', for example. Both words can be, and often are, used with reclaimed meanings,[51] but it is not obviously the case that 'bitch' is disproportionately used with its reclaimed meaning; it very frequently retains is patriarchal, oppressive, and subordinating meanings.[52] We shall return to these arguments in Chapter 3.

A connected reason people may have to reject an over-reliance on widely accepted norms or commonly recognised standards is that such norms and standards can mask variations in the language different groups find acceptable or unacceptable and ignore the extent to which social taboos disproportionately reflect the views of powerful or dominant groups. Interestingly, in 1987 Preston and Stanley undertook a large-scale participant experiment asking 164 American college students to give their opinion on the question of what is the worst thing people could say about other people, and found that on average 'bitch' came out as the top answer to the question 'What is the worst thing a man can call a woman?' and to the question 'What is the worst thing a woman can call a woman?'.[53] However, breaking down the results by the gender of the respondent, 'the men were likely to say that the worst thing a man could say about a woman was "lesbian", whereas the women chose words such as "bitch" or "mean"'.[54] This suggests social taboos may be unreliable guides to what should count as hate speech. Similar observations apply to dictionary definitions of slurs, for example. The precise ways in which words are defined as slurs can reveal the attitudes of the majority culture – attitudes that may be implicitly biased against minority groups. For example, if dictionaries define the meaning of certain slurs as *derogatory* or *disparaging*, this could place emphasis or blame on the persons doing the disparaging. By contrast, if dictionaries define the meaning of certain slurs as *insulting* or *offensive*, this could implicitly place the emphasis or blame instead on the persons who are targeted. Ironically, to define certain words as insulting or offensive may signal ambivalence towards the targets and could even be tantamount to blaming the victim: that somehow the true source of 'the problem' lies in how certain groups of people react to words. Furthermore, this asymmetry in the definition of slurs may reveal an implicit racial bias if divergent patterns of dictionary definitions consistently track along racial lines, so that slurs against White people are defined as disparaging, but slurs against Black people as merely offensive.[55]

Based on all this, some people may gravitate back to specifying hate speech in subjective ways. But once again this is likely to be contested ground. A definition of hate speech can be subjective in stronger or weaker ways. A definition of hate speech is strongly subjective if it defines hate speech simply as whatever the targets of speech are disposed to call 'hate speech'.[56] Yet some people may reject that sort of definition, especially as a definition of hate speech in the legal sense of the term, on the grounds that it arbitrarily privileges the personal feelings or opinions of the targets over those of the speaker or of an impartial third party. It effectively gives victims a sort of discursive veto, namely the power to classify as hate speech any mode of expression or message they do not like. By contrast, a definition of hate speech is weakly subjective if it defines hate speech in terms of a set of objective criteria – such as language that carries a message of racial inferiority, is persecutorial, hateful, and degrading, or is intended to demean – but then gives priority to the perspective of the victim when it comes to understanding whether a given bit of language satisfies the relevant criteria.[57] But even here some people may refuse this definitional approach, especially as applied to the legal concept, on the grounds that it incorrectly assumes that members of a victim group will reliably and accurately know degrading speech, for instance, when they see it, and, moreover, will have uniform understanding.[58]

Yet another form of conceptual confusion and contestedness comes to the fore when hate speech is conceptualised not using a set of criteria but instead by affirming that it is a family resemblance concept. As explained above, we believe the ordinary concept *hate speech* is a family resemblance concept and that its proper use is based on nuanced assessment of complex patterns of overlapping and criss-crossing similarities between examples. In Chapter 2, we identify a set of prototypes or exemplars of hate speech, and in Chapters 3 and 4 we assess the extent to which a range of grey area examples resemble these exemplars. However, it is possible that some uncertainty or dispute about whether to classify a given grey area example as hate speech may result if the example is similar or alike in some ways to exemplars of hate speech but also dissimilar or unalike in other ways.

Therefore, at the end of Chapter 2 we seek to mitigate this source of ambiguity by providing an account of the five main distinguishing qualities of hate speech in the ordinary sense of the term, namely target, style, message, act, and effect, and by drawing a distinction between partial and global resemblance. Whereas a particular example might have a partial resemblance if it shows at least some similarities with exemplars of hate speech, the global resemblance test involves an overall assessment of whether the range, extent, degree, and salience of the similarities between the example and exemplars of hate speech across at least four out of five of the main distinguishing qualities justifies classifying the example as hate speech on the basis that it resembles the exemplars of hate speech as closely as the exemplars resemble each other. Moreover, according to our normative conceptualisation of the ordinary concept *hate speech*, the global resemblance test must itself reflect the functions or purposes a society and its major organisations can reasonably expect this concept to play.

1.3.4 Why Clearing Up Grey Areas Matters

It is important to clear up grey areas of hate speech both in the ordinary and legal senses of the term for several reasons. First, clearing up grey areas can serve to clarify the general positions that different sides take on how strictly to interpret the word 'speech' in 'hate speech'. For example, some people argue the use of racial slurs on college campuses is paradigmatic hate speech that transgresses civility norms, norms of public discourse, or ideals of deliberative democracy.[59] Other people are more ambivalent about applying the label 'hate speech' to such cases and argue it is much harder to justify campus codes if the problem they are supposed to tackle is classified as transgressive speech. They argue it is more appropriate and powerful to classify the problem as transgressive behaviour or 'discriminatory harassment'.[60] Social media platforms also appear to take different positions on the speech versus behaviour dilemma. It is not merely a superficial difference that Facebook has a community standard on 'hate speech', whereas Twitter has a policy on 'hateful conduct'. These labels provide clues to substantive differences in the definitions they each provide: Facebook's standard underscores dehumanising speech and imagery, generalisations that state inferiority, and harmful stereotypes,[61] whereas Twitter's policy highlights these things plus inciting others to spread fear, to harass, or to discriminate.[62] We believe some grey areas provide interesting test cases for these positions. Consider blackface, blackfishing, and womanface. They typically involve a combination of speech and behaviour. Clearing up whether these really are hate speech and, if so, what makes them hate speech, can involve taking a position on whether the salient features are dehumanising speech and harmful stereotypes, or some sort of immoral behaviour such as epistemic injustice or exploitation, or all of the above. We discuss this further in Chapter 4.

Second, clearing up grey areas can provide a response to the familiar slippery slope objection made against the label 'hate speech' itself and hate speech laws and codes: that if society accepts what seem to be not obviously unacceptable applications of the label 'hate speech' and not obviously unacceptable hate speech laws and codes at the current time, then it is stepping onto a slippery slope that will carry it towards a set of obviously unacceptable practices in the future.[63] Slippery slope objections have been made against both the ordinary and legal concepts of hate speech. For example, in spring of 2022 the Canadian Liberal MP Ya'ara Saks gave a speech during a parliamentary debate on the Emergencies Act in which she claimed that the catchphrase 'honk honk' used by participants in the Freedom Convoy was in fact a dog whistle commonly used by neo-Nazis as code for 'Heil Hitler'. Some critics took to social media to reject her analysis based on the following slippery slope objection.

> Where it started: 'Holocaust denial' is hate speech. Where it is now: 'Honk honk' is hate speech. Where it's going: 'I'm not voting Liberal' is hate speech.[64]

In a similar vein, speaking at an international conference on hate speech in Budapest in April 2006, the then US ambassador to the Organization for Security and Cooperation in Europe (OSCE), Julie Finley, raised the following slippery slope objection to hate speech laws.

> Efforts to restrict hate speech represent a clear and present danger to robust political debate. Once we start down the slippery slope, trying to define a nebulous term like 'hate speech,' we are heading for the potential for abuse.[65]

A common denominator to slippery slope objections is the assumption that certain terminus points are obviously unacceptable but once on the slippery slope it is hard or impossible to avoid ending up at those points. Grey areas of hate speech can be invoked in slippery slope objections as either terminus points or steps along the way. For example, some people might make the slippery slope objection that if today social media platforms classify as hate speech the phrase 'Death to Jews', then in the future they will have to classify as hate speech the hyperbolic phrase 'Death to Liberals'. This sort of hybrid attack is a grey area of hate speech because though the attack uses violent language and is group-based, the relevant group is identified by political beliefs and affiliations rather than the standard protected characteristics of race, ethnicity, nationality, religion, gender, sexual orientation, and so on. We believe clearing up whether hybrid attacks really are hate speech and, if so, what makes them hate speech, can provide an answer to this slippery slope objection. If 'Death to Liberals' turns out to be hate speech and for good reason, then the terminus point may not be as unacceptable as it first appears. Then again, if it turns out not to be hate speech and major institutions and organisations are able to reflect this in their hate speech laws and policies, then the alleged slippery slope is not so slippery after all. We shall say more about this grey area in Chapter 3.

Third, clearing up grey areas could help to defuse social tensions between groups over highly contentious language. Uncertainty about whether particular language is hate speech can lead groups to enter into a war of words that can escalate into violence. For example, members of a minority group may end up labelling language that attacks core aspects of their identity (e.g. atrocity denials) as 'hate speech'. The minority group might respond angrily to the criticism by using their own violent language or threats against the group to which the speakers belong. The minority group might fail to recognise its own language as hate speech because it regards itself as speaking in self-defence (e.g. righteous attacks). All of this can further inflame tensions and increase the risk of violence. However, using robust and credible conceptual analysis to clarify to both sides whether these grey areas of language really are hate speech might hold out a slim chance of creating common ground and deescalating the war of words. We shall discuss righteous attacks in Chapter 3 and denialist speech in Chapter 7.

Fourth, clearing up grey areas could be a way of answering complaints against institutions and organisations of the sort that can be corrosive of trust and legitimacy if left unanswered. For example, some people complain that the way hate speech laws and codes are drafted and enforced involves a double-standard, namely that they crack down on conventional hate speech against minorities but turn a blind eye to reverse hate speech against White people and men, for example. Sometimes these complaints are made in good faith; other times they are more cynical. But either way, these complaints can be corrosive if left unanswered insofar as they undermine people's belief that the relevant institutions or organisations can be trusted to do the right thing and even the belief that the relevant laws or codes are legitimate. Clearing up uncertainty as to whether reverse attacks are actually hate speech, one way or the other, provides a response to these complaints that could mitigate these corrosive effects. On the one hand, if it can be shown that reverse attacks are not hate speech, then it draws the sting from the complaint. On the other hand, if it turns out that reverse attacks are hate speech, then it can provide an impetus for institutions and organisations to work harder to ensure there is no double standard in either the drafting or enforcement of the relevant laws and codes. We shall say more about this in Chapter 3.

Finally, clearing up grey areas is important not only to improve the quality of hate speech laws and codes but also the depth of public understanding, both of which are important for protecting human rights. If institutions and organisations get it wrong about particular grey areas of hate speech, they can end up not merely failing to punish or remove content that really is hate speech but also restricting language that is not hate speech. Along similar lines, if the general population gets it wrong about examples, this can lead to language not being countered even though it is hate speech or alternatively people coming under social pressure to remain silent even though they are not hate speakers. Cancel culture is a contemporary phenomenon often associated with college campuses and social media but it is simply the most recent incarnation of a much older phenomenon J. S. Mill called 'the tyranny of the majority'. To name and shame, censure, call out, revoke invitations to speak, or participate in a pile on against someone for hate speech can inflict real reputational cost. The fear of being cancelled and the self-censorship this fear creates can have as great a chilling effect on people's speech as oppressive laws and codes. Given the stakes are so high for misapplications of the label 'hate speech', clearing up grey areas is paramount.

1.4 What Use Is the Term 'Hate Speech' Anyway?

A final way of motivating the importance of this book and the project of conceptual analysis in which it is engaged is to try to answer the following sceptical question. What is so useful about the term 'hate speech' that cannot be achieved using different terminology? One answer to that question is that the term serves as a vehicle for expressing moral condemnation and social disapproval against certain forms of speech.[66] Then again, it might be countered that the job of expressing disapproval against speech is performed by many terms besides 'hate speech' – for example, 'impolite speech', 'ill-considered speech', 'transgressive speech', 'disrespectful speech', 'unjust speech', 'dangerous speech', 'harmful speech', 'irresponsible speech'. So, what is so special about the term 'hate speech'?

Part of the answer is surely that the term 'hate speech' seems to be particularly powerful in the present climate. People often reserve the term for forms of speech which are especially problematic or divisive within diverse societies, as in, societies made up of groups who are identified by, and identify with, protected characteristics. This perhaps explains why people engaged in hotly contested debates surrounding institutional racism, religious intolerance, sexual and transgender politics, and national identity and immigration, to name but a few examples, sometimes resort to accusing the other side of engaging in 'hate speech'.

However, this answer only invites additional challenges. For one thing, the term 'hate speech' is not merely ambiguous as between two concepts but can also be associated with the myth of hate, the misleading connotation that all examples of hate speech are intimately bound up in some way with thoughts, feelings, emotions, or sentiments of hate or hatred.[67] Reflection on competent usage of the term 'hate speech' shows that not everything appropriately labelled 'hate speech' is connected with mental states of hate or hatred. In a similar vein, looking at competent usage of the term 'microaggression' reveals that not everything appropriately labelled 'microaggression' involves actual aggression or aggressive behaviour (in fact very few microaggressions are actually aggressive). But insofar as terms like 'hate speech' and 'microaggression' can have misleading connotations, this raises a question as to their suitability as categories used in discussions about what we owe to each other and what should be allowed or disallowed in matters of interpersonal communication. It is also ironic that one of the ambiguities surrounding the term 'hate speech' is whether microaggression can count as hate speech or whether these are mutually exclusive concepts.

Furthermore, as we have repeatedly emphasised in this chapter, the term 'hate speech' has undergone a significant expansion in applications since the late 1980s. This expansion has caused some scholars to signal a note of caution about its social utility. In the words of the political scientist Katharine Gelber: '[The term "hate speech"] is used in such a wide variety of contexts that the distinction between hate speech and other types of speech has been elided, and it is losing its traction as a specific claim that speech that can harm in a specific way and to a sufficient degree to warrant government regulation.'[68]

In addition to this, the term 'hate speech' has become highly politicised. For example, in disputes over immigration controls the pejorative 'hate speaker' has become a sort of trump card (excuse the pun). Moreover, even though many political actors use this pejorative on a principled basis, others use it for purely instrumentalist reasons. For them, it has become an opportunistic or go-to move in rhetorical combat – a move that is capable of packing a punch, cutting through the white noise, and being used either offensively or defensively depending on the need.[69] Of course, because no side has a monopoly on this pejorative, it is frequently used tit for tat, with both sides trading the accusation 'hate speaker!'[70] The fact that the proper meaning of terms like 'hate speech' and 'hate speaker' is not simply the subject of reasonable disagreement but also highly politicised has led some scholars to raise doubts over its social utility. As David Boromisza-Habashi observers, invoking a different meaning has become 'an "easy out" to speakers publicly accused of "hate speech"'.[71] If '[o]ne challenge for antiracist rhetoric is to identify evaluative terms for communicative conduct that can be used to persuasively portray racist or discriminatory talk as a norm violation', then at least in some countries this challenge cannot be easily met by the term 'hate speech' insofar as its semantic contestedness renders it unpersuasive.[72]

Given the conceptual ambiguities, misleading connotations, expansion of applications, and politicisation associated with the term 'hate speech', and in the light of the myriad functions or purposes a society might reasonably expect this general kind of term to fulfil, would it not be better to simply abandon the term 'hate speech' altogether? Rather than analyse it, why not bury it in the graveyard of useless or defunct concepts? In other words, assuming Matsuda had, in effect, introduced a new exploratory or experimental concept, has the time now come to declare the experiment a failure and to cut our losses?

We believe there are five main ways of responding to this sceptical challenge: rehabilitation, downsizing, abandonment, replacement, and enhanced understanding. In this final section of the chapter we critically examine each of these different responses, and having ruled out the first four, defend the final response as the most promising.

1.4.1 *Rehabilitation*

The first response to the sceptical challenge argues that the myth of hate is itself a misnomer and that in fact hate is essential to the meaning of the concept *hate speech*. The first step in this rehabilitationist project is to see hate as potentially connected with different kinds of mental states (e.g. beliefs, perceptions, prejudgments, evaluations, appraisals, episodic emotions, motivations, action tendencies, prescriptive judgments). The next step is to use the label 'hatred' or 'hate sentiments' to pick out a particular combination or set of these mental states as being essential to hate. For example, Robert Sternberg analyses the concept *hatred* in terms of (i) anger, (ii) contempt, and (iii) disgust.[73] Teresa Marques associates the concept *hate sentiments* with (i) negative appraisals of outgroup members as malevolent or malicious just by being members of that group, (ii) action tendencies that go from revenge, social exclusion, or attacks to the destruction of the target group, and (iii) motivation goals such as the desire to harm, humiliate, or even kill the target.[74] The final step is to claim that all proper applications of the concept *hate speech* refer to speech that is connected with one such set of mental states, whether hatred or hate sentiments.[75]

However, this rehabilitationist project has several flaws. For one thing, without drawing on a plausible account of how competent users actually employ the term 'hate speech' and of the social purposes the concept *hate speech* can be reasonably expected to play, the choice of one set of mental states over another to stand as the essential characteristics of hatred or hate connected with hate speech looks arbitrary.

Moreover, it is not obvious that all meaningful uses of the term 'hate speech' by competent language users refer to forms of speech that are in fact connected with one or other of these sets of mental states. For example, ordinary people might label statements as 'hate speech' simply due to them expressing stereotypes, generalisations, or false beliefs of a descriptive nature. Consider these statements.

(14) All African Americans are brawny.
(15) All Jews are money lenders.
(16) All Muslim men rape young girls.

Competent language users may be perfectly willing to label statements (14)–(16) as 'hate speech', and to do so properly and meaningfully, even if the sets of mental states labelled 'hatred' and 'hate sentiments' are not involved when the relevant speakers make these statements, and even if competent users do not assume that these mental states are involved.

In addition, the rehabilitationist project is partially eliminativist in that the terms 'hatred' and 'hate sentiments' are used as placeholders for more sophisticated mental phenomena – more sophisticated than the mental states associated with the term 'hate' in folk psychology. Looking carefully at the sets of mental states proffered by Sternberg and Marques respectively, neither of them include ordinary hate, as in, a state of intense dislike that most people associate with the term 'hate'. In the process of rehabilitating the concept *hate speech* it appears ordinary hate has been eliminated from the picture. If hate is essential to the meaning of the term 'hate speech', then it is not hate as most people understand it.

Finally, in order to sustain the dogma that every instance of hate speech involves hatred or hate sentiments one could, through stipulation, keep expanding the meanings of the terms 'hatred' or 'hate sentiments' to swallow up putative counter-examples to the dogma. For example, if competent language users would call something 'hate speech' that involves not anger, contempt, and disgust but instead ridicule and grievance, then one could simply redefine the term 'hatred' to mean *either anger, contempt, and disgust or ridicule and grievance.* Alternatively, if competent language users would call something 'hate speech' that involves not negative appraisals, action tendencies, and motivation goals but instead descriptive beliefs and prejudgments, then one could simply redefine the term 'hate sentiments' to mean *either negative appraisals, action tendencies, and motivation goals or descriptive beliefs and prejudgments.* Such a process could go on indefinitely, so as to deal with emerging counter-examples. But this appears to be an ad hoc approach without intrinsic conceptual merit. It does not posit a fixed essence that supports sound and reliable inferences to new examples.[76]

1.4.2 Downsizing

The second main response to the sceptical challenge attempts to relaunch the term 'hate speech' with a new slimline semantics. This downsizing strategy involves turning back the clock so that the term 'hate speech' reverts to its original legal meaning. This confronts the 'problems' of the systematic ambiguity and expansion of applications of the term 'hate speech' by advocating that henceforth it is used only in the legal sense. For example, Gelber advocates that society and its institutions should stick with the term 'hate speech' for the legal concept but use some other term(s) for what we call the ordinary concept.[77]

However, there are once again important weaknesses in this response. For one thing, when it comes to applications of the term 'hate speech', once the genie is out of the bottle it cannot easily be put back in. Words and concepts are living things that are born, live, and die through the practices of people, societies, and organisations. Practices are difficult to shape and even harder to stop. Other things remaining equal, it is easier to coin a new piece of terminology than it is to kill it off. A neologism can appear overnight and its use grow rapidly, but its demise can take much longer. It is one thing for a neologist or conceptual inventor to inspire others with the words, 'And I call this "hate speech"'; it is quite another for someone to change or reverse linguistic practices with the slogan '"Hate speech" should only mean unlawful hate speech and no more'.

Part of the reason for this is that linguistic norms, like other norms, require sufficiently widespread adherence to become embedded and internalised. In the case of the term 'hate speech', downsizing the term would require buy-in not simply from ordinary language users but also from major internet companies like Meta, Alphabet, and ByteDance (the owners of Facebook, Instagram, YouTube, and TikTok respectively). However, these companies have invested heavily in the terminology 'hate speech' over many years or even decades in some cases. This terminology figures prominently in everything from the wording of their content policies; to the training they provide to their moderators around the world; through to the setting up of oversight boards; to public engagement with their users and the media; and on to significant collaboration with quasi-governmental agencies, civil society organisations, academics, and other stakeholders. To expect these companies to switch terminology seems unrealistic given the lost investment and costs of change management involved.

More importantly, so long as the term 'hate speech' and the ordinary concept to which it refers serve social purposes or functions, people and organisations are unlikely to commit to the downsizing strategy; and rightly so. We shall say more about the different social purposes served by the ordinary and legal concepts of hate speech in Chapter 5, but we make two additional points here simply about the social utility of the term 'hate speech' itself. One is that even if it were true that the term 'hate speech' has lost traction as a designation for the legal concept (or could lose traction) because of the explosion of people using it in the ordinary sense, this might be offset by the social utility of having a term that can refer not only to the legal concept but also to a category of speech that is broadly harmful or wrongful but not unlawful (the ordinary concept). In other words, the social utility of retaining the term 'hate speech' in all of its capacious glory ought to be assessed in the round, just as the social utility of sticking with terms like 'fraud' is evaluated taking into account the fact that they can be ambiguous between ordinary and legal meanings. If a society or its institutions were to insist on downsizing every bit of terminology that has come to have both ordinary and legal meanings, there would be a vast downsizing project afoot. Furthermore, in the case of ambiguous terms, it is not clear why the legal meanings should be automatically privileged, rather than, say, saving the ordinary meanings and calling on lawmakers and legal professionals to simply come up with different words (legalese) for the things they justifiably need to legally restrict. Just because the term 'hate speech' originally had only a legal meaning, this does not mean the law has an automatic right to custody.

In addition, it is not obvious that the term 'hate speech' has lost traction as a specific claim about speech of the sort that can harm in such a way as to warrant legal restriction. The fact is that advocacy groups, lawmakers, courts, and international organisations from across the globe continue to debate, agree on obligations regarding, enact, repeal, revise, apply, and either widen or limit the scope of hate speech laws in countless ways, on the basis of myriad reasons, arguments, and principles, and typically in response to a body of commissioned reports, public consultations, and inputs from experts, most of which touch on the issue of harmfulness – and they manage to do all of this whilst still using the term 'hate speech'. We believe they can do this because they are also capable of making it clear both to each other and to the wider public that they have the legal concept in mind. Consider once again the Recommendation of the Committee of Ministers to member States on combating hate speech cited above, which explicitly and directly distinguishes between hate speech prohibited under criminal law, hate speech subject to civil or administrative law, and forms of lawful yet harmful hate speech that should be tackled in other ways.[78]

Of course, that institutions should be working towards improving their definitions of the legal concept(s) *hate speech*, such as by making hate speech laws more precisely and narrowly defined, is a point well taken.[79] To serve legal purposes, concepts should be capable of standing as public legal norms, as in, norms that are both justiciable through the work of lawmakers, law enforcement agencies, and courts and also understandable by those members of the public subject to them. But it is not clear that the explosion of popular discourse employing the term 'hate speech' makes it significantly harder for the legal concept(s) *hate speech* to play this role. The vast majority of hate speech laws do not actually contain the term 'hate speech'. So, the mere fact that this term is used not only by lawmakers and legal professionals but also by ordinary people and social media platforms need not be an impediment to lawmakers and legal professionals doing their job. After all, ordinary people use the word 'fraud' all the time and with countless nonlegal meanings, but this does not prevent lawmakers and legal professionals from devising precise and narrow definitions of fraud offences. In fact, during the period that has seen an explosion in usage of the term 'hate speech', arguably hate speech laws have become more, not less, precise and narrow, largely due to the work of legislatures and courts. In England and Wales, the newer stirring up hatred offences contained in Part 3A of the Public Order Act 1986 are narrower than the older offences in Part 3; in Spain the Holocaust denial offence set out in Art. 607.2 of the Criminal Code was replaced with a narrower offence in Art. 510(1)(c); and in South Africa the hate speech offences established under s. 10 of the Promotion of Equality and Prevention of Unfair Discrimination Act 2000 (PEPUDA) have recently been declared unconstitutionally overbroad by the Constitutional Court in *Qwelane v South African Human Rights Commission and Another* [2021] ZACC 22 – to cite just three examples.

1.4.3 Abandonment

The third main response to the sceptical challenge argues that the challenges faced by the term 'hate speech' in terms of conceptual ambiguities, misleading connotations, expansion, and politicisation are overwhelming and clearly point in the direction of abandoning the term altogether even if there is no obvious replacement. This is not a matter of arguing for an alternative that is like the term 'hate speech' but minus its problems. Rather, it is a case of abandoning having language and concepts that do the sorts of things that the term 'hate speech' and its allied concepts do. The claim being that society simply does not need that sort of language or conceptual framework.

However, to argue successfully for straight abandonment would be difficult, especially if the acid test would involve showing that some people would be better off and nobody would be worse off without the term 'hate speech' *or something like it*. We believe the argument cannot be made. In Chapter 5 we shall set out the various valuable social functions played by the ordinary and legal concepts of hate speech. That is our primary reply to the abandonment project. Even so, we shall supplement that reply with some observations immediately. These observations are intended to show not only that some of the features of these concepts are typical of normative concepts as a broader category of concepts but also that taking the abandonment response seriously could suggest abandoning all normative concepts (reductio ad absurdum).

As explained earlier in the chapter, the ordinary concept *hate speech* is a thick normative concept that combines description and normative evaluation. The term 'hate speech' is also a pejorative conveying a negative connotation about its objects. Interestingly, the concept *slur* and term 'slur' also share these qualities.[80] These shared qualities may partly explain why ordinary language users are pre-programmed to accepting slurs as paradigmatic hate speech; other reasons being cross-over in the targets of many slurs and hate speech in general (see Chapter 2). Like many terms that refer to thick normative concepts, the terms 'hate speech' and 'slur' are subject to dispute concerning the extensions of the concepts they represent. However, few people seriously argue that society should kill off the concept *slur* or that nobody would be worse off and some people would be better off if society abandoned the term 'slur'. Partly this is because the term 'slur' plays a useful role in picking out forms of speech that are typically derogatory and group-based. Surely a similar story can be told about the term 'hate speech'.

Another feature of the term 'hate speech' is that, at least in its ordinary meaning, it designates a family resemblance concept. But, once again, this feature is hardly unique among thick normative concepts. Various such concepts have been analysed as family resemblance concepts – for example, *objectification*,[81] *power*,[82] *exploitation*,[83] and *fascism*.[84] This in turn can mean that, as Ann Garry puts it, some '[f]amily resemblances can be much messier and more politically laden than Wittgenstein's own examples of games or numbers.'[85] The ordinary concept *hate speech* is no different. It has become a political football reflecting the values, goals, and ideologies of different interest groups. Some groups will see a family resemblance between given words and exemplars of hate speech that other groups may not see and *vice versa*. For example, Democrat voters think the term 'hate speaker' befits Trump due to his racist and xenophobic dog whistles, whilst Maga voters apply the same term to Trumphobic detractors but not to Trump himself.[86] Then again, abandoning the term 'hate speech' for these reasons would also seem to imply abandoning a slew of other terms including 'objectification', 'power', 'exploitation', and 'fascism'.

Now it is also true that the term 'hate speech' can convey different kinds of negative connotations depending on its occurrence alongside different bodies of collocates ('semantic prosody').[87] Within public discourses associated with the alt-right but also civil libertarianism and certain forms of feminism, the term 'hate speech' often occurs alongside words like 'censorship', 'political correctness', 'merely offensive', 'words people dislike', 'dogma', 'victim culture', 'competitive victimhood', 'no platforming', 'snowflake generation', 'wokeness', 'closing down options', 'a form of tyranny', and 'yet another means of subordinating women'. Here the negative connotation attaches to the term 'hate speech' itself. Within public discourses associated with liberalism, progressivism, critical race theory, and LGBTQIA+ doctrine, by contrast, the term 'hate speech' typically occurs alongside words like 'racism', 'xenophobia', 'homophobia', 'transphobia', 'TERF', 'historically oppressed groups', 'prejudice', 'discrimination', 'climate of hatred', 'incitement', 'violence', and 'genocide'. Here the negative connotation attaches to the objects of the term 'hate speech' (i.e. things that are hate speech). But once again the term 'hate speech' does not seem unusual in this regard; many other terms in public life convey different connotations depending on linguistic environment. Consider the term 'discrimination' which has different connotations when it occurs alongside words like 'positive', 'affirmative', and 'reverse', compared to when it occurs alongside words such as 'racial', 'gender', and 'unfair'.

Nevertheless, given the politically laden nature of the ordinary concept *hate speech*, has the term 'hate speech' now become a liability? If both sides use it to attack each other, and attach different meanings and connotations to it, how can using it do any good or move disputes forward? However, our reply to this sceptical challenge is twofold. We have already touched on the first. It is that the term 'hate speech' is far from unique in being weaponised in this way. Such weaponisation is an occupational hazard for any thick normative concepts and family resemblance concepts used in political speech and public discourse. Recall the old adage that in politics 'one person's terrorist is another person's freedom fighter'. Likewise, the pejoratives 'bullshit' and 'propaganda' are traded back and forth between political parties. None of this means, however, it would be better not to have such terms. Indeed, it would be hard to think of an agreed list of neutral descriptive terms that political antagonists could agree on as a replacement lexicon. Furthermore, it is no coincidence that terms which are prevalent in political speech and public discourse are typically contested. Part of their social purpose is to provide expressive outlets for fundamental disagreements about what the other side has done, about what matters, and about what should happen in the future. They provide a language for non-violent disagreement if not always an avenue for actual compromise. Thus, the pejorative 'hate speaker' might be a fixture of political rhetoric not in spite of but because of its heterogeneous, capacious, and contested nature.

Second, it is important to see that the pejorative 'hate speaker' is not a personal insult akin to 'asshole' much less an evaluative similar to the thin normative concept *wrongdoer*. According to our normative conceptualisation, the pejorative 'hate speaker' is not a blank canvass onto which a speaker can paint almost whatever meaning he or she chooses and still be using it properly; not, that is, when it is being used at its best. Precisely because the ordinary concept *hate speech* is a family resemblance concept, a given application of the concept is only appropriate if it satisfies the global resemblance test meaning that the speech to which it refers must resemble exemplars as closely as they resemble each other. We believe it does not take much comparative reflection to see that calling detractors of Trump 'hate speakers' fails the global resemblance test. We shall also argue in Chapter 3 that the pejorative 'hate speaker' itself is insufficiently similar to exemplars of hate speech to be considered hate speech; if that were not the case, perhaps it might be curtains for the concept.

1.4.4 Replacement

The fourth main response to the sceptical challenge argues for replacing the term 'hate speech' with something else. For example, Dirk Kindermann accepts that the 'political, legal and epistemic importance' of the term 'hate speech' in 'public discourse, in linguistics, the humanities and social sciences, and in the legal domain' 'can hardly be overstated' but at the same time argues for its replacement with a term and concept that is better.[88] The replacement project is importantly different to an abandonment project. The former does not suggest that society and its institutions do not need a term like 'hate speech'. Instead, the replacement project must simply show that society would be better off with an alternative term. Then again, this is still a tall order. The test is partly whether the replacement term can perform all of the valuable social functions already performed by the term 'hate speech', the same or better, as well as serving other valuable social functions better than the term 'hate speech'. In addition, even if the replacement term is better in its own right, it must be worth the costs and risks of change. After all, sometimes the perfect is the enemy of the good.

We believe that no version of the replacement project can pass this twin test. Starting with the second part of the test, there is significant existing utility in the fact that people are familiar with and roughly understand the term 'hate speech'. Because the groundwork has already been laid, people can communicate using this term with a fair chance of mutual comprehension even if there may be reasonable disagreement as well. Depending on which replacement term is chosen, to replace a known term with something else could mean restarting the process of comprehension-building and this potentially means the loss of valuable communication during the transition period. There is also an opportunity cost to replacing existing terminology: a potentially significant amount of attention, effort, and money is expended on making the switch that could be better spent on embedding the original term within society and supporting the work of institutions and organisations in combating the problematic phenomena to which the term refers. Risks of change include the possibility that having convinced society to jettison the original term, there is a lack of consensus over the replacement term and society ends up without a replacement, just a jumble of different words used by different people, in different ways, and without resemblance. The net result of this would be the absence of a single unifying point of linguistic contact between different groups in society. The worst-case scenario could be that, in the absence of this unifying discursive framework, the amount and severity of speech hitherto referred to as 'hate speech' grows. If there is no agreed label for the speech in question, speakers might be emboldened since there is no longer a banner around which a coalition of the concerned can gather to call out the speech and to coordinate a collective response. The collective response might include developing a coherent division of labour between social media platforms and legal institutions, for example. A precautionary principle might suggest that it is better to stick with the devil you know.

Turning to the second test, one of the benefits of the term 'hate speech' is precisely its ambiguity, namely that it can refer to both ordinary and legal concepts. Kindermann focuses on the functions a society can reasonably expect the legal concept *hate speech* to play and argues another concept (*discriminatory speech*) would do a better job.[89] Even if he were right about that (and we remain unpersuaded as we shall explain below), it ignores the key point that the term 'hate speech' also refers to an ordinary concept that serves a set of non-equivalent but no less valuable social functions (see Chapter 5). This cannot be ignored when deciding whether to replace the term 'hate speech'. The ordinary concept *hate speech* has taken on its own life beyond the law and is used by people to refer to a diverse range of expressive, communicative, and performative phenomena. Imprecision and breadth are strengths of the ordinary concept even if they would be weaknesses of the legal concept if it were similarly conceptualised. What is more, one of the strengths of the term 'hate speech' is that it can facilitate a certain type of useful read across between ordinary and legal meanings. For example, there may be utility in social media platforms disallowing a category of speech that is broadly harmful or wrongful but not unlawful, and using the familiar term 'hate speech' to refer to that special category of speech. Doing so may increase the chances that users will have at least a broad understanding of roughly what sort of speech is at stake (publicity), an appreciation of why disallowing it may be justified (salience), and a basic disposition to follow the rules (compliance). These benefits could potentially outweigh any disbenefits of users failing to properly grasp some of the important differences between hate speech disallowed by social media platforms and hate speech that is unlawful.

However, the fundamental flaw in the replacementist project is the lack of a worthy replacement for the term 'hate speech'. There is no suitable replacement for the term 'hate speech' in the English language that is without similar or other sorts of problems. For example, the term 'hate speech' is itself only one term in a longer lineage of comparable terms including 'group libel' and 'hate propaganda'.[90] Yet these terms are much narrower than the term 'hate speech' and refer to specific styles including defamatory statements, statements inciting hatred or discrimination, and statements expressing racial superiority. Historically, they have tended not to refer to other styles such as slurs, stereotypes, and genocide denial, for example. This is one reason Matsuda coined the term 'hate speech'.

Are there any other alternatives? In the 1950s Gregory Allport invented the term 'antilocution' to describe the first stage in his scale of prejudice; a model that seeks to explain the social processes that lead up to genocides. Antilocution is speech against an out-group, especially by political figures, that is subsequently followed by 'avoidance', 'discrimination', 'physical attack', and 'extermination'.[91] Once again, however, this term only refers to certain styles, such as negative comments about an out-group that are not directly addressed to the subjects of those comments. Matsuda introduced the term 'hate speech' so as to capture another important part of the victim's story, namely the experience of being directly addressed or targeted with racist hate messages, threats, slurs, epithets, and disparagement, and the ways this direct targeting 'wounds' its victims.[92]

Around the time Matsuda introduced the term 'hate speech', several other scholars used the alternative 'assaultive speech' also to capture this idea of wounding and to underscore not merely the analogies but also the overlaps between physical and verbal assault.[93] This term may be especially apt when describing some of the personal damage done by words including inflicting emotional distress, knocking people's confidence or self-esteem, intimidating or shocking people into silence, and causing people medium- to long-term emotional, psychological, and even physiologically harm. However, one of the strengths of the term 'hate speech' – one of the things that renders it so useful – is that it also refers to expressive phenomena where the metaphor of assault seems far less fitting such as in the case of statements that damage reputation, bring people into contempt, misrecognise identity, undermine civic dignity, rank people as inferior, or incite hatred or discrimination.

More recently, some scholars have used the term 'offensive public speech' to refer to people's experiences of racist speech directly addressed to them in public places and the silencing effect of such speech (i.e. the way fear of violence causes them not to 'talk back').[94] However, the term 'offensive public speech' may convey a misleading impression that what is distinctive or problematic about the speech in question is that people targeted find it offensive or are offended by it. This misleading impression, even if not one that is intended by the scholars concerned, risks minimising the grave nature of the speech and implicitly puts the blame onto victims for the fact of being offended, as though these issues could be easily resolved simply by greater effort on their part not to be offended.

Other alternatives avoid this misleading impression by describing the speech in question in such a way as to make the grave nature of the speech unmistakable and by implicitly conveying the idea that the fault lies with the speaker and society, not the victim. Examples include 'extreme speech',[95] 'dangerous speech',[96] and 'atrocity speech'.[97] However, these terms are poor replacements for the term 'hate speech'. On the one hand, the terms 'extreme speech' and 'dangerous speech' fail to convey the idea of speech targeting certain groups identified by protected characteristics (as opposed to any group of human beings), dissimilar to the way the term 'hate speech' is ordinarily used. They also potentially cover a category of speech that is far broader than is ordinarily captured with the term 'hate speech' insofar as they cover statements that espouse terrorist ideology or incite or glorify terrorism, and forms of child pornography. On the other hand, not all speech that is referred to using the term 'hate speech' is extreme or dangerous or related to atrocities in the specific sense of speech that incites violence or atrocities or significantly increases the risk that its audience will participate in violence or atrocities against members of another group.

Other terminology, such as 'bigoted speech',[98] 'prejudiced speech',[99] 'discriminatory speech',[100] and 'subordinating speech',[101] certainly does convey the idea of speech targeting certain groups identified by protected characteristics, similar to the term 'hate speech'. However, these terms also have other weaknesses. For one thing, the term 'discriminatory speech' suggests speech that enacts, facilitates, perpetuates, legitimates, or incites discrimination, or speech that itself relies on, reproduces, or is a product of, discrimination, where this connection with discrimination is enough to warrant legal restriction. Although this term might be useful for speaking about the sort of speech that should be made unlawful, it misses another useful social function served by the term 'hate speech' in its ordinary sense, namely to speak about the sort of speech that is broadly harmful or wrongful but not discriminatory in a specific sense that might warrant legal restriction. Consider reverse attacks (e.g. 'honky', 'white devil') that do not enact or rely on discrimination against historically vulnerable groups. Or consider righteous attacks (e.g. 'male chauvinist pigs') that at least in one possible sense do not enact unfair discrimination. Part of the value of the term 'hate speech' lies in the fact that it discursively equips a society and its major organisations to condemn or even disallow such attacks without subjecting them to legal sanctions (see Chapter 3). Similarly, the term 'subordinating speech' might be understood in a more restrictive way to mean speech that has a special force to subordinate certain groups, that has this force because of a background of structural inequality and oppression (or 'systemic discrimination'[102]), and that involves subordination *qua* harm that is sufficiently grave to warrant legal restrictions. But once again, the term 'hate speech' can also imply these things with the added bonus of also referring to forms of speech that are broadly harmful or wrongful but not necessarily in the aforementioned way. Indeed, the term 'subordinating speech' might convey the idea that the speech in question is a mere symptom of the real problem (e.g. a background of structural inequality and oppression) and not a fundamental or intrinsic problem in its own right. The advantage of the term 'hate speech' is that it can imply or presuppose that the speech is itself a fundamental problem, and this makes it more versatile, enabling it to be applied to reverse attacks and righteous attacks, for instance. Of course, defenders of the term 'subordinating speech' might see this versatility as a weakness and insist that it is absurd to apply the label 'hate speech' to reverse attacks and righteous attacks (reductio ad absurdum). But in Chapter 3 we shall argue that this reaction would be hasty and that reverse attacks and righteous attacks share sufficient similarities with exemplars of hate speech across the distinguishing qualities of target, style, message, act, and effect to justify using the label 'hate speech', at least in its ordinary (nonlegal) sense.

Furthermore, terms like 'bigoted speech' and 'prejudiced speech' may harbour misleading connotations analogous to those of the term 'hate speech'. Just as the term 'hate speech' may convey the misleading connotation that the relevant speech is necessarily connected with mental states of hate or hatred, so the terms 'bigoted speech' and 'prejudiced speech' may imply that the relevant speech is necessarily connected with mental states of bigotry and prejudice.[103] Now clearly some of the speech in question is connected with mental states of bigotry and prejudice, but not all the speech referred to using the original term 'hate speech' is connected with these mental states just as not all the speech referred to using the original term 'hate speech' is connected with mental states of hate or hatred.

In summary, it appears there is no suitable term in the English language that could provide not merely a replacement but a worthy replacement for 'hate speech', namely no term that means something like what 'hate speech' means, that can better serve the various social purposes the latter serves or else better serve other social purposes, that does not suffer the same or similar problems of conceptual ambiguity, misleading connotations, expansion, and politicisation, that does not have different but equally significant problems, and that is sufficiently better to justify the costs and risks associated with going through the process of replacement. So long as there is no superior alternative, all things considered, the remaining alternative is to stick with the term 'hate speech' but to improve conceptual understanding of it both among the general public and institutions and organisations.

1.4.5 Enhanced Understanding

The final response to the sceptical challenge (our preferred response) is to stick with the term 'hate speech' and to recognise rather than minimise or ignore its ambiguities, misleading connotations, expansion, and politicisation, but at the same time to shed greater light on its meanings so as to enhance understanding. This is by no means a perfect solution, but we believe it is the least bad of the five main responses we have explored.

We believe the goal of enhancing understanding is served by providing a rigorous, credible, and constructive analysis of the term 'hate speech'. This conceptual project should not be complacent or biased towards the status quo. The term 'hate speech' and the concepts it designates must earn their keep. Also, it must be clear how conceptualising the term 'hate speech' in a given way helps to serve the purposes a society can reasonably expect it to serve. Of course, to make an argument that certain terms and associated concepts have particular social purposes is also part of the analysis. In that sense, the overarching aim of our normative conceptualisation is to achieve coherence between meanings and purposes.

To give an example, we believe recognising that the term 'hate speech' is ambiguous between ordinary and legal concepts and showing how these concepts serve different social functions may in turn help to improve the quality of public discourse about hate speech. It might help lawmakers and legal professionals come to see that ordinary people interpret the term 'hate speech' in ways that reach beyond the scope of law, and appropriately so. It could also provide an impetus for the former to be even clearer about what they are doing and why, such as to explain to the public why they seek to define hate speech laws even more precisely and narrowly. Conversely, it could drive both ordinary people and major organisations like social media platforms to be more explicit about when they are using the term 'hate speech' in the nonlegal sense, and why they are doing so.

As well as giving stakeholders a nudge to clarify which of the two concepts of hate speech they are talking about, enhancing understanding could also have more practical benefits in terms of tackling the problem of hate speech. For one thing, it could help people to see that the law is not the only source of order in the field of interpersonal communication. The Internet has become a site of contestation, including both hate speech itself and debates over where to draw the line between acceptable and unacceptable speech. Understanding that lawmakers and legal professionals do not have a monopoly on the term 'hate speech' might be helpful to these debates. When a social media company publicises the fact that disallowed hate speech will be removed, made subject to reduced distribution, or amended with warning labels, it serves to highlight the impact of social norms, social rules, and social sanctions on our everyday lives. If relatively few people would consider going to the police with a complaint about hate speech they have experienced, perhaps they would be more willing to report cases to social media platforms or to trusted flagger organisations. Coming to understand that the term 'hate speech' does not simply refer to unlawful hate speech but also to broadly harmful or wrongful yet lawful hate speech might provide the information people need to come forward and report cases, a crucial step in tackling the problem.

Now it is one thing to say the ordinary concept *hate speech* serves a range of social functions; it is another thing to provide a conceptualisation of that concept which explains how it can best serve those social functions. If the ordinary concept *hate speech* were so utterly vague and unendingly capacious that it could be meaningfully applied to almost any speech whatsoever, then it would struggle to serve its purposes. It is likely competent users would vote with their feet and stop using it, perhaps jumping onto the next exploratory concept that looks more favourable.

We suggest that the ordinary concept *hate speech* is able to serve myriad social functions and that competent language users continue to buy into the concept (at least for now) precisely because it is a family resemblance concept. People implicitly understand the similarities between its exemplars. This makes a practical difference to how far the concept can be stretched. It means, for example, that competent language users can see the many important dissimilarities between the terms 'hate speaker' and 'hater', based on the differences in target, style, message, act, and effect of the speech in question.[104]

In short, we believe that enhanced understanding is the most promising response to the sceptical challenge. The remainder of the book is an attempt to fulfil that promise. In particular, we shall focus on examples that stress test our conceptual framework, namely grey areas of hate speech. The goal is to provide a system of conceptualisations that can shed light on, and wherever feasible resolve, the grey areas (as being hate speech, marginal hate speech, or not hate speech at all) and in a way that is consistent with the purposes that a society and its institutions and organisations can reasonably expect the term 'hate speech' to play.

PART I

The Ordinary Concept

2

Prototypical Examples of Hate Speech

2.1 Introduction

In our view, posing and answering the questions 'What is hate speech?' and 'Is x hate speech?' is not only a socio-linguistic practice based on conventions or rules but also a normative enterprise rooted in the justification of the relevant conventions or rules based on valuable social purposes or functions. We believe the ordinary concept *hate speech* is at its best when five key steps are respected or worked through: first, establishing specific conventions or rules identifying a set of exemplars of hate speech (prototypical examples of hate speech); second, developing general conventions or rules of thumb that articulate dimensions of similarity between the prototypical examples which help to explain and justify why they are exemplars (rules of thumb may uncover distinguishing qualities or clusters of features exhibited by the exemplars); third, analogical reasoning pointing out similarities between a new example whose status as hate speech is uncertain (grey area examples) and prototypical examples of hate speech (including invoking distinguishing qualities); fourth, adopting further general conventions or rules according to which a new example falls under the ordinary concept *hate speech* only if it has enough similarities with the prototypical examples; and, finally, reflecting on and adjusting all of the above in the light of the various social functions or purposes a society can reasonably expect the concept to serve. The overall aim of these steps is to achieve coherence between meanings and purposes.

This chapter identifies prototypical examples of hate speech and seeks to explain what makes them such. Chapters 3 and 4 then apply this analysis to ten grey area examples of hate speech in the ordinary sense of the term. In Chapter 5 we distinguish the social functions of the ordinary and legal concepts. The remainder of this chapter proceeds as follows. Section 2.2 lists the original examples of hate speech cited in Mari Matsuda's seminal article on the legal concept. We then explain how, even though the ordinary and legal concepts of hate speech share paradigmatic examples, the ordinary concept now has its own extended body of exemplars. Section 2.3 attempts to plot the complex pattern of overlapping and criss-crossing similarities among these exemplars. We highlight similarities based on five distinguishing qualities (or clusters of features): target, style, message, act, and effect. Section 2.4 looks in more depth at one of the paradigmatic examples of hate speech, namely racial slurs such as 'nigger'. We highlight similarities it shares with other prototypical examples of hate speech. Finally, Section 2.5 defends a particular account of what it means for a new example to have enough similarities with exemplars to count as hate speech. Here we rely on the general rule that if a new example resembles prototypical examples as closely as prototypical examples resemble each other, then the new example is also hate speech. In addition, we explain that resemblance is constituted by an overall assessment of the range, extent, degree, and salience of the similarities between a new example and prototypical examples of hate speech. If there are enough similarities across at least four out of five of the distinguishing qualities of target, style, message, act, and effect, then this conceptually justifies applying the phrase 'x is also hate speech' to the new example. We dub this penultimate stage in the practice the global resemblance test.

2.2 Matsuda's Examples and Beyond

Usage of the term 'hate speech' can be traced back to its origins in the late 1980s,[1] including when Matsuda cited several examples of what she called 'hate speech'.[2]

(1) [A group of White oil rig worker address African-American co-workers as 'niggers'.]

(2) [An African American family enters a coffee shop in a small Texas town. A White man places a card on their table that reads 'You have just been paid a visit by the Ku Klux Klan.']

(3) [White Americans hurl the slur 'Jap' at Japanese and Asian people in the street.]

(4) [White students put up a sign on a Black student's bedroom door consisting of a caricature picture of a Black person with a red diagonal line across it.]

(5) [Posters stating 'Asians Out or Racial War'.]

(6) [An anonymous note sent through an office internal mail system to a Black employee reading 'The only good nigger is a dead nigger.']

(7) [A noose placed in an office supply room used by African American employees.]

(8) [People making the verbal taunt to Jews that 'Hitler still lives'.]

(9) [Books, postcards and other published material portraying Jews as animal-like (e.g. as pigs, snakes, mice, or rats) and requiring extermination.]
(10) [The wearing of symbols, uniforms, or other regalia that in the context of history carry a message of threat, hatred, and persecution towards minority racial groups.]
(11) [A sign in a store window that reads 'No blacks allowed'.]
(12) [Public dissemination of ideas based on racial superiority or hatred, incitement to racial discrimination, as well as incitement to acts of violence against any race or group of persons of another colour or ethnic origin.]
(13) [The publication or distribution of written material or the use of language in a public place to incite genocide of the Jews.]
(14) [The publication or distribution of written material or the use of language in a public place to deny the existence of the Holocaust.]

This is a heterogeneous family of expressive phenomena, displaying multiple dissimilarities.[3] Despite the dissimilarities, however, we suggest Matsuda's original examples of hate speech also exhibit several dimensions of similarity based on five main qualities (or clusters of features) that serve to identify them as hate speech and distinguish them from other forms of speech, namely target, style, message, act, and effect. The target of hate speech relates to the persons or groups the speech is about, addressed to, the objects of, or attacked with (e.g. Asians, African Americans, Jews). The style of hate speech has to do with the form, manner, mode of deliver, or type of presentation (e.g. a slur, a strategically placed noose, denial of atrocities). The message of hate speech is constituted by the propositions, ideas, opinions, sentiments, meanings, or contents that are expressed, communicated, or conveyed (e.g. the idea of the racial inferiority of African Americans, the sentiment that Asians are not welcome). The hate speech act is what is done with the words, as in, the speech acts performed with hate speech (e.g. inciting racial hatred against Jews). The hate speech effect is what impact the relevant words or speech acts have on the world, including on the interlocutor, the target (if not the same as the interlocutor), and society in general (e.g. that Asians are continuously forced to think about whether insults they receive are racist or simply rudeness, that Asians experience feelings of exclusion, inadequacy, fear, and intimidation, that Asians are hated, held in contempt, or mistrusted, that society is divided along racial lines). The message, act, and effect roughly correspond to the Austinian distinction between locutionary, illocutionary, and perlocutionary force.[4]

The story does not end there, however. Even though Matsuda's initial examples involve racist hate speech, she also makes it clear that, based on her understanding of the concept, this is not the only form of hate speech.

She also mentions 'misogynist propaganda'[5] and 'anti-gay and anti-lesbian hate speech'.[6] Indeed, in her later work she characterises homophobic discourse as 'the semiotic motherlode, the paradigm binary, the place we learn about hate, disgust, fear, inside, outside, retribution'.[7] It is as though Matsuda is saying: 'These and similar things are called "hate speech" and I intend them to be part of the rules governing the social practice of using this term.'[8] Many other legal scholars have subsequently joined and extended this practice, whether ultimately to defend hate speech laws or to challenge and reject them as unconstitutional. Indeed, as we have explained elsewhere, '[b]ecause of the work of legal scholars like Matsuda, the term 'hate speech' has now been taken up legislators and legal professionals themselves more explicitly.'[9]

More importantly for Part I of our book, however, this new bit of terminology has now 'taken on a life of its own'.[10] New flowerings of the term 'hate speech' have bloomed across various fields of discourse including in the media, politics, the arts, popular culture, and public discourse in general. Like Matsuda, philosophers have also sought to define hate speech based on proffered lists of paradigmatic examples.[11] But by far the most influential and certainly the most enforced definitions of hate speech in the ordinary (nonlegal) sense of the term belong to the major social platforms. Facebook's community standard on hate speech, for example, begins with the following general definition.

> We define hate speech as a direct attack against people – rather than concepts or institutions – on the basis of what we call protected characteristics [...]. We define attacks as violent or dehumanising speech, harmful stereotypes, statements of inferiority, expressions of contempt, disgust or dismissal, cursing and calls for exclusion or segregation. We also prohibit the use of harmful stereotypes, which we define as dehumanising comparisons that have historically been used to attack, intimidate or exclude specific groups, and that are often linked with offline violence.[12]

Twitter likewise offers this general definition of what it calls 'hateful conduct'.

> You may not directly attack other people on the basis of race, ethnicity, national origin, caste, sexual orientation, gender, gender identity, religious affiliation, age, disability, or serious disease. [...] We prohibit targeting individuals or groups with content that references forms of violence or violent events where a protected category was the primary target or victims, where the intent is to harass.[13]

These social media definitions paint hate speech or hateful conduct as 'direct attacks against people', but what becomes clear from the examples they provide and how they enforce their policies is that such attacks are interpreted as coming in all manner of different forms. Hate speech in the ordinary sense of the term can include words, signs, symbols, images, pictures, cartoons, memes, videos, GIFs, flags, logos, uniforms, clothing, statues, monuments, gestures, bodily movements, mannerisms, and behaviours.

If Matsuda's examples of hate speech are prototypes for the legal concept *hate speech*, they have been supplemented with yet further examples of hate speech selected by the major social media platforms. Furthermore, the various general definitions and lists of specific examples promulgated by these platforms themselves form part of an even larger body of socio-linguistic conventions and rules surrounding the term 'hate speech' that includes the definitions and lists issued by media companies, including television broadcasters and newspapers, colleges and universities, and many other companies and organisations, public and private. Layered on top of these definitions and lists of examples is countless other discourses about the nature, types, and harms of hate speech; discourses found in political debate, popular culture, public discourse, and academic research including in philosophy, politics, linguistics, sociology, media studies, and hate studies. Together this new repertoire of examples constitutes an extended body of archetypes for the ordinary concept *hate speech.*

We maintain that these archetypes also exhibit the five distinguishing qualities associated with Matsuda's original examples. However, and this is crucial, the specific features that instantiate these abstract qualities will vary between the ordinary and legal concepts. These variations, along with key differences in ontology, orientation, and social purposes, suffice to distinguish the concepts (see also Chapter 5). The main aim of this chapter is to look for complex patterns of overlapping and criss-crossing similarities among the examples comprising the expanded repertoire of the ordinary concept *hate speech.* These similarities are then utilised in Chapters 3 and 4 to assess whether certain grey area examples exhibit enough similarities (global resemblance) with the archetypes to count as hate speech.

2.3 Five Distinguishing Qualities of Hate Speech in the Ordinary Sense of the Term

The distinguishing qualities and specific features of examples of hate speech found in the expanded repertoire are what might be called the observable characteristics or traits of the ordinary concept *hate speech.*

It would be wrongheaded to call these phenotypes, since in biology a phenotype is the product of genotype plus environmental factors and examples of hate speech lack genetic constitution. Nevertheless, like phenotypes, examples of hate speech have qualities and features that are observable traits. That said, because the ordinary concept *hate speech* is a family resemblance concept, these qualities and features are not identical across every example (see Section 2.5). We shall not attempt to provide a comprehensive or exhaustive list of all the specific features associated with each of the distinguishing qualities (clusters of features). This is partly because we do not believe the ordinary concept *hate speech* admits of a definition, or even a disjunctive definition, of this sort; it is not that kind of concept. Contrast this with a concept like *cousin*, for example, which can be defined disjunctively as *the son or daughter of an uncle or aunt*. Nevertheless, we do think it is possible to illustrate the five distinguishing qualities.

2.3.1 Hate Speech Targets

The first distinguishing quality is the target, namely the persons or groups who are spoken about, subject to, the objects of, or attacked with hate speech. In her seminal article, Matsuda focuses on historically oppressed racial or ethnic groups, including African Americans, Asian Americans, Jewish Americans, and Latino Americans. But she also mentions other 'forms of hate speech' including 'misogynist propaganda'[14] and 'anti-gay and anti-lesbian hate speech'.[15] More importantly, following its splintering from the legal concept, the ordinary concept *hate speech* has evolved to encompass an even wider array of groups and associated protected characteristics. Surveying discourses on hate speech found in the content policies promulgated by the major social media platforms, discriminatory harassment policies instituted by universities and colleges across America, as well as in news reporting, political debate, popular culture, public discourse, and the large body of academic literature,[16] a very long, aggregated list of protected characteristics emerges.

(i) Colour, race, ethnicity, ancestry, descent, origin, tribe, nationality, homeland, place of birth, cultural heritage, regional identity including sub-national and trans-national region, language status, mother tongue, dialect, accent.
(ii) Citizenship status, immigration status, legal relationship to a state.
(iii) Religion including religious beliefs, practices, or affiliations, as well as lack thereof.

(iv) Sexual orientation.
(v) Sex, gender, gender identity, gender expression, gender performance.
(vi) Caste, class, social status, social origin.
(vii) Disability, including mental and physical disability, atypical ability, neuro-diverse ability, and atypical physical anatomy or appearance.
(viii) Medical status including serious illness or disease.
(ix) Age, age expression, age performance.
(x) Physical appearance when not already included under race and disability, such as body weight, skin quality, hair colour, facial configuration, and other bodily features.
(xi) Political beliefs, activities, affiliations, or ideological commitments.
(xii) Conduct, behaviour, ways of living, lifestyle, cultural performance, experiences, and victim status when not already included above, such as benefits dependency, breastfeeding, criminal record, drug or alcohol dependency, education status, employment status, itinerant lifestyle, marital status, occupation or profession, parental status, sexual practices, preferences, and proclivities, veteran status or war record, and being victims of a major violent event or atrocity and their family.

This is a highly variegated list of characteristics including as it does attraction or patterns thereof (e.g. sexual orientation); affiliations relating to communities, cultures, social groups, or families (e.g. ethnicity, language, nationality, marital status, victims of violent events and their family); attitudinal dispositions, beliefs, or ways of thinking (e.g. religious beliefs, political beliefs); biological, genotypic, physiological, or physical characteristics or attributes (e.g. race, sex, disability, physical appearance); conduct, behaviour, performance, or ways of living (e.g. gender performance, war record). This list of characteristics also displays other potentially salient dimensions of similarity and dissimilarity. For example, some of the characteristics seem to be deeply personal, private, internal, central to identity, unchosen, related to being, immutable, natural, and universal; whilst others seem to be more impersonal, external, peripheral, chosen, related to lifestyle, constructed, and idiosyncratic.

Within some discourses, as we move towards the bottom of the list of protected characteristics the association with the ordinary concept *hate speech* becomes more tenuous and controversial. For example, clearly there are people who would never associate the concept with slurs attacking others simply based on their political views or affiliations; other people may take the different view that insofar as attacking members of a political minority with slurs (e.g. 'commie') can have prototypical hate speech effects, then it can make sense to categorise the attacks as hate speech. Furthermore, there are internet companies, such as YouTube,[17] for whom characteristics like age and veteran status are primary protected characteristic, whereas for other platforms, notably Meta (Facebook, Instagram), characteristics such as age, veteran status, and occupation are secondary or dependent protected characteristics (or 'quasi-protected' as Meta calls them) in the sense that content attacking people based on secondary characteristics only counts as hate speech when the content also attacks people based on at least one primary protected characteristic at the same time.[18] We return to investigate all of these complications in Chapter 3.

2.3.2 *Hate Speech Styles*

A second distinguishing quality has to do with the style, as in, the form, manner, mode of delivery, or type of presentation. A hate speaker's selection of particular combinations of words, symbols, or other expressive behaviours, as well as the adoption of specific modes of delivery, is often linked to social groups or practices (sociolects), ideologies, viewpoints, or stances. For example, a hate speaker may be conforming to the vocabulary or rhetorical performance of a particular group or ideology, or publicly signalling association with an in-group or disassociation with an out-group. Among the styles of hate speech associated with the ordinary concept can be found the following.

(i) Slurs, epithets, insults, or otherwise harsh, abusive, aggressive, coarse, or offensive names, phrases, statements, gestures, images, or memes (e.g. calling someone a 'nigger' in an abusive manner as opposed to an affiliatory way or resignified as a positive affirmation).
(ii) Negative stereotypes, generalisations, or typecasts (e.g. describing a person or group as typically being lazy, stupid, promiscuous, animalistic, aggressive).
(iii) Disparagements, vilifications, or otherwise derogatory or highly unfavourable judgments, evaluations, or appraisals (e.g. declaring a person or group to be uncivilized, abnormal, deviant, criminal, pathological, unclean, diseased, unwanted, not belonging, Other, fake, untrustworthy, disloyal, cowardly, wicked, dangerous, irritating, vile, disgusting, contemptible, despicable, repugnant, objectionable, condemnable, contemptible, despicable, good-for-nothing, worthless, inferior, second-class, subordinate, natural born slaves, enemies, lacking human dignity).
(iv) Group libels, false rumours, or disinformation about a group or class of persons that has the intention or likely effect of damaging their reputation or bringing them into contempt in the eyes of others (e.g. untrue and unfounded allegations that members of the group have committed rapes or murders).

(v) Dehumanising words, images, or portrayals (e.g. comparing persons or groups to non-human entities such as animals, insects, aliens, lumps of flesh, inanimate objects, property, commodities, robots, viruses, diseases, rubbish, dirt, or excrement; referring to persons using pronouns such as 'it' in contexts where such pronouns are normally reserved for non-human animals or objects and doing so implies inhumanity).

(vi) Caricatures, architypes, or stock characters that constitute exaggerated or ridiculous facsimiles of a person or group, typically in a manner that highlights, mimics, or mocks their physical characteristics or aspects of identity, and also in ways that are unflattering, disrespectful, or demeaning (e.g. blackface).

(vii) Expressions, articulations, or self-admissions of adverse emotions, feelings, sentiments, beliefs, attitudes, or patterns of thinking towards a person or group (e.g. intense dislike, hatred, loathing, contempt, disdain, extreme aversion, callous indifference, anger, indignation, resentment, fear, alarm, disgust, revulsion, disapproval, abhorrence, scorn, ridicule, envy, pity, superiority, profound disrespect, bigotry, prejudice, intolerance, rejection, exclusion, discrimination).

(viii) Coded, subtle, implicit, veiled, indirect, or dog whistle messages, as well as microaggressions that have a dual meaning (e.g. code words that refer to groups in derogatory ways the meaning of which is non-literal and may not be widely understood; giving backhanded compliments or expressing positive stereotypes that on the surface appear inclusive but beneath the surface pigeonhole people or hold them to unequal standards; asking strangers or mere acquaintances very personal questions about, say, their hair texture, skin colour, place of origin, physical appearance, or surgical status, in ways that presuppose or imply not merely that the questioners have the right to ask such questions but also that the questionees are in some way exotic, foreign, curiosities, oddities, abnormal, or Other; comments that minimise or brush under the carpet people's lived experiences of bigotry and discrimination in ways that implicitly invalidate those realities; histories that omit key aspects of the identity of victims of mass killings for propaganda purposes; using metaphors such as being born in the wrong body to describe the experiences of an entire group of people without making an effort to check whether those metaphors chime with how specific members of the group in fact understand and narrate their own unique experiences; using trigger words whilst at the same time ignoring, failing to understand, or refusing to acknowledge the history, significance, and conventional meaning of those words as slurs or stereotypes).

(ix) Propaganda, rhetoric, invective, or ideology that incorporates or embodies ideas or theories of social or moral hierarchy (e.g. racist hate propaganda that proclaims people of colour as being socially inferior and having lower fundamental moral worth or dignity compared to White people).

(x) Words or other expressive behaviour that are intended or have the likely effect of being provoking, antagonising, threatening, intimidating, menacing, ominous, frightening, disturbing, distressing, alarming, harassing, or otherwise a violation of privacy and safety (e.g. aggressive or angry tones, inflections, or postures; violent metaphors; symbolically violent gestures, symbols, or objects such as hanging a noose or burning a cross; encroachment on personal space; repeatedly sending people private messages or showing up at their homes or places of work uninvited; doxing or outing; threats of murder, rape, and other violent crimes).

(xi) Images, symbols, or words associated with hate groups, regimes, or ideologies associated with bigotry, discrimination, intolerance, or violence towards a target group (e.g. spray painting a Nazi Swastika on the walls of a synagogue).

(xii) Statements denying, trivialising, or glorifying mass killings, acts of terror, genocide, ethnic cleansing, mass expulsions, or other atrocities (e.g. Holocaust denial).

(xiii) Public statements or other expressive behaviour used for the purposes of voicing support for, legitimating, advocating, stirring up, or inciting hatred, discrimination, segregation, exclusion, violence, or genocide against a group or class of persons (e.g. a poster put up outside a public library that reads 'Don't be scared to express how you really feel about these disgusting Muslims').

(xiv) Words, signs, or symbols that enact discriminatory, exclusionary, or segregationist policies or practices (e.g. a sign in a store window that reads 'No blacks, no Irish').

This list of styles is intended to be neither exhaustive nor mutually exclusive. One piece of hate speech may combine two or more styles at the same time. For instance, the expression of adverse sentiments such a prejudice, hatred, and contempt can often be done using coded language; hate propaganda based on ideas of moral inferiority often contains dehumanising imagery; insults, stereotypes, caricatures, and group defamation are among the modes of communication often used by hate speakers to incite hatred against a target group. In Chapter 3 we focus on grey areas of hate speech involving slurs, but Chapter 4 opens out the discussion into various other prototypical hate speech styles, including hybrid styles.

2.3.3 *Hate Speech Messages*

A third distinguishing quality concerns the message, namely the propositions, ideas, opinions, sentiments, meanings, or contents that are expressed, communicated, or conveyed. We use the phrase 'conveyed content' in a deliberately broad way so that it might capture one or more of the following forms: literal meaning, expressive content, implied content or implicature, presuppositional content, and inferential content. In fact, it is not uncommon for a particular piece of hate speech to have more than one form of conveyed content. This is true not simply of metaphors, code words, dog whistles, and microaggressions but also of slurs like 'nigger'.[19]

What distinguishes hate speech messages in terms of substance as opposed to form? In her seminal article, Matsuda suggested that hate speech of the sort that ought to be legally restricted shares 'three identifying characteristics': '1. The message is of racial inferiority; 2. The message is directed against a historically oppressed group; and 3. The message is persecutorial, hateful, and degrading.'[20] We believe Matsuda probably intended the three characteristics not only to define the legal concept *hate speech* but also to be read conjunctively, meaning that a given piece of speech must share all three characteristics to be legally restricted. This helps to prevent the legal concept from becoming overbroad. However, although the ordinary concept *hate speech* shares Matsuda's original examples, it now has its own extended corpus of examples and associated cluster of messages. Moreover, a given example need only exhibit one message from the cluster to be a candidate example of hate speech in the ordinary sense of the term. Consider these familiar messages.

(i) Messages that the speaker has loathing, hatred, contempt, disdain, fear, anger, resentment, grievance, separation, disinterest in getting to know, or cruel indifference towards a target group.
(ii) Messages that the speaker has affinity, solidarity, or approval of hate groups, regimes, or ideologies associated with bigotry, prejudice, discrimination, intolerance, or violence towards a target group.
(iii) Messages that a target group are lazy, filthy, ignorant, aggressive, dishonest, criminals, disloyal, ill-intentioned, greedy, sexually promiscuous, degenerate, retarded, mentally unstable, deranged, or violent.
(iv) Messages that a target group are a disease, animals, sub-human, abnormal, inhuman, or mere objects.
(v) Messages that a target group are held in contempt, unwanted, Other, vile, disgusting, despicable, repugnant, despicable, good-for-nothing, worthless, inferior, low types, second-class, subordinate, natural born slaves, enemies, lacking human dignity, or a danger to society.
(vi) Messages that a target group do not exist.
(vii) Messages that a target group have not been the victims of mass killings or other atrocities.
(viii) Messages that it is of no consequence, normal, unregrettable, desirable, deserved, righteous, or legitimate if a target group are brought low, threatened, intimidated, harassed, excluded, shunned, segregated, marginalised, cast out, boycotted, discriminated against, physically attacked, or killed.

(ix) Messages that there are certain actions, strategies, policies, or other practical steps that may permissibly be taken, that the speaker intends to take, or that the speaker advocates others take to ensure that a target group are brought low, threatened, intimidated, harassed, excluded, shunned, segregated, marginalised, cast out, boycotted, discriminated against, physically attacked, or killed.

Given the nature and variety of this non-exhaustive list of archetypical hate speech messages, it is perhaps unsurprising they contain some ambiguities and contradictions. For example, it is one thing to convey the idea that a group of people are held in contempt or unwanted by a society or deserve this contempt or social exclusion or are incapable of being held in high regard or being wanted; it is surely less grave to suggest that a group of people are unpopular or controversial. It is unclear in the case of (v) whether the relevant sorts of hate messages stretch to the latter sorts of suggestions. Furthermore, whilst most of the messages listed above boil down to the thought that the target group are inherently bad and should have bad things done to them, such as with messages (iii), (iv), (v), (ix), and (x), some of the messages convey the different thought that the target group either does not exist or has not had bad things done to them, but also that they would deserve it if they did have bad things done to them, such as with messages (vi), (vii), and (viii).

However, in our view the mere presence of these ambiguities and contradictions is not grounds to abandon ordinary usage of the term 'hate speech'. There is no reason to suppose that instantiations of the ordinary concept *hate speech* must be unambiguous and hang together in a coherent manner. The concept can still serve important social functions even with these frailties, as we shall try to show in Chapter 5.

2.3.4 Hate Speech Acts

A fourth distinguishing quality involves the things speakers do with words, namely the sorts of illocutionary and perlocutionary acts identified by speech pragmatics. Looking at the content policies promulgated by the major social media platforms, as well as campus speech codes in the United States, media discourse, political debate, popular culture, public discourse in general, and the academic literature on hate speech,[21] the following acts are frequently highlighted.

(i) Insult, derogate, disparage (judge or present as being less estimable), vilify, discredit, ridicule, mock, malign, stigmatise, defame, turn people against, bring into contempt, demonise.

(ii) Caricature, pigeonhole, essentialise (deindividualise), stereotype, prejudge (epistemically wrong), misrecognise, pathologise.
(iii) Degrade (rank as fundamentally inferior), infantalise, turn into second-class citizens, subordinate, dehumanise, Other.
(iv) Psychologically hurt, distress, dishearten, traumatise, gaslight, treat cruelly, humiliate (disparage or degrade in front of others).
(v) Provoke, taunt, antagonise, back into a corner.
(vi) Threaten, intimidate, frighten (make feel insecure), alarm, disturb, bully, harass, terrorise.
(vii) Oppress, discriminate against, persecute, disempower (deprive of rights and powers), censure, punish, control, dominate, silence, steal from, exploit, segregate, exclude, reject, alienate, marginalise, isolate, shun, exclude, drive out, banish, ostracise.
(viii) Justify, condone, glorify, minimise, trivialise, wish for, deny, perpetuate, reinforce, reproduce, endorse, legitimate, act as a negative role model in relation to, miseducate others about, promote, incite, encourage, call for, demand, order, aid, abet, allow (make permissible), facilitate (make possible), orchestrate, instigate, partake of, perform, enact – where such acts are done in relation to fear, anger, resentment, contempt, hatred, discrimination, segregation, exclusion, violence, genocide, crimes against humanity, or other atrocities.

Competent users of the term 'hate speech' in its ordinary sense may have in mind one or more of these speech acts or other similar speech acts not listed above. Indeed, it is possible that when people think about hate speech in the ordinary sense of the term, they are more likely to have in mind some speech acts (core) than others (peripheral). Moreover, the speech acts which spring to mind first may vary between the ordinary and legal concepts *hate speech*.

However, a more pressing issue is how speech acts associated with the ordinary concept *hate speech* are successfully performed. Interestingly, the following speech acts are among the most frequently highlighted in the philosophical literature on hate speech: oppression including enacting policies of discrimination against or marginalising the targeted group;[22] subordination in the sense of ranking members of the targeted group as inferior, legitimating discrimination, and depriving them of rights and opportunities;[23] and vilification including insulting, defaming, or inciting hatred, discrimination, or violence against the targeted group.[24] This is a heterogeneous collection, but one thing all these acts have in common is that the felicity conditions for their successful performance seem to require the speaker to have obtained some degree of power, authority, or audience uptake.

Hate speakers may obtain the requisite capacity to perform acts of oppression, subordination, and vilification in different ways. Of course, most ordinary users of the term 'hate speech' may be unable to articulate definitive lists of archetypal hate speech acts much less all the ways hate speakers obtain the requisite capacity to perform these acts, but they can still use the term meaningfully. Even so, possible sources may include the following.

(i) Speakers can successfully perform hate speech acts against members of targeted groups by occupying positions of formal authority such as the authority that comes with having a role or position in an institution.[25]

(ii) Speakers can successfully perform hate speech acts against members of targeted groups by means of the state, and particularly the decisions it reaches and communicates over the prohibition or non-prohibition of hate speech, lending or devolving to them an authority to perform those acts.[26]

(iii) Speakers can successfully perform hate speech acts against members of targeted groups by holding certain types of informal authority such as the authority that comes from having a high status, power, or influence within a social group.

(iv) Speakers can successfully perform hate speech acts against members of targeted groups by means of bystander silence granting them a general authority or licence to perform those acts.[27]

(v) Speakers can successfully perform hate speech acts against members of targeted groups by means of bystander silence combined with speakers mirroring or giving voice to bystanders' discriminatory attitudes against the targeted group granting them a specific authority to perform those acts.[28]

(vi) Speakers can successfully perform hate speech acts against members of targeted groups if speakers simply presuppose they have the authority to perform those acts and this presuppositional authority goes uncontested or unchallenged by listeners (so-called accommodation).[29]

(vii) Speakers can successfully perform hate speech acts against members of targeted groups by dint of partaking in patterns of speech that over time and in a cumulative fashion constitute the performance of the relevant acts,[30] especially where the patterns of speech are dominant and become a collective enterprise.

(viii) Speakers can successfully perform hate speech acts against members of targeted groups by virtue of being participants in rule-governed activities of discrimination which are partly composed of rules (i.e. 'general rules') of the sort that give speakers the power to perform those acts (e.g. enact 'specific rules' of discrimination).[31]

(ix) Speakers can successfully perform hate speech acts against members of targeted groups in the absence of resistance such as if the targeted groups are victims of background discrimination, oppression, and inequality, and thereby less capable of blocking the relevant acts, whether through raising objections, counterspeech, or reclaiming the meanings of the relevant words.[32]

However, such background power, authority, or audience uptake is not necessarily required for the performance of every kind of hate speech act.

In Austinian terms, some hate speech acts are 'exercitives' and 'verdictives': they involve the *giving of a decision in favour of or against a certain course of action, or advocacy of it,* and the *issuing of verdicts*, respectively.[33] This almost certainly makes them 'authoritatives', meaning a type of act that can only be successfully performed by a person with some form of authority. By contrast, other hate speech acts seem to be 'expressives', 'assertives', or 'behabitives': they have to do with *expressing*, *asserting*, or *adopting* feelings, ideas, or attitudes.[34] These are non-authoritatives in the sense that the speaker can perform them even without having authority. Non-authoritative kinds of hate speech acts might include *prejudging*, *stereotyping*, *essentialising*, *stigmatising*, or *misrecognising*.

2.3.5 *Hate Speech Effects*

A final distinguishing quality relates to the effects of speech, which has to do with its actual or likely impact on the interlocutor, the target person or group, and society in general. The idea of harmful effects, or the risk of harmful effects which is itself a harm, is part of the folklore of the ordinary concept *hate speech*, even if people may not have the same effects in mind and develop their thinking based on different sources of information. For example, stories and anecdotes circulating within peer groups, in popular culture, and online, as well as the moderation decisions and communications of internet companies, may be more prominent sources of the ideas younger people form about hate speech effects than the texts produced by legal institutions (e.g. parliaments, courts, the police), quasi-governmental agencies (e.g. regulators), international organisations, civil society groups, news journalists, and academics.[35] At any rate, reflecting on how the ordinary concept *hate speech* is framed across various fields of discourse, several types of harmful effects are highlighted, many of which overlap with effects associated with the legal concept.

(i) An increase in the sense of righteousness, superiority, power, or grievance felt by the speaker and the in-group.
(ii) Distress, alarm, anxiety, hurt, shame, uncertainty, worry, fear, exclusion, loneliness, or other sorts of episodic yet adverse psychological or emotional states felt by victims.
(iii) Medium- and long-term psychological and physiological effects including feeling unwanted or alienated, low self-esteem, raised background levels of stress, anxiety, hypervigilance, fear, anger, fatigue, mood swings, bouts of depression, high blood pressure, and increased rates of alcoholism, self-harm, or suicide.

(iv) Internal insecurity including a reduction in confidence in the important dimensions of physical and political security.
(v) Dignitary effects including a reduction in the target group's sense of assurance that they enjoy good standing in society as equal citizens, or even a reduction in their sense of worth as human beings.
(vi) Entrenchment, reinforcement, or growth in unempathetic, contemptuous, hateful, prejudiced, bigoted, discriminatory, intolerant, or violent social attitudes toward the target group, including but not limited to among the in-group.
(vii) De facto segregation including lower rates of intermarriage, residential integration, and social and professional intermingling.
(viii) Creation or maintenance of climates of hatred which predict a higher risk of oppression, persecution, exclusion, segregation, discrimination, and violence.
(ix) Creation or maintenance of climates of intimidation, fear, and exclusion which predict the target group's withdrawal from public life including from political positions and offices, public discourse, and democratic decision-making, which in turn can damage democratic legitimacy (the democratic authorisation of laws and institutions) and political legitimacy (the normative justification of laws and institutions).
(x) A general sense of disillusionment with social media and society in general, whether a sense that it is no longer safe or inclusive or a sense that it is no longer a place of freedom of thought and expression.
(xi) Lessening of public trust in basic political, social, and legal institutions over time, among both the in-group and the out-group, and in extreme cases a reduction in the stability of those institutions.
(xii) Community tensions, damage to social cohesion, reduced intercultural communication, public disturbances, breaches of the peace, a general breakdown in law and order, mass civil disobedience, election violence, civil war, and even genocide.

Many users of the term 'hate speech' in its ordinary sense will have at least some degree of appreciation of the fact that which type of harmful effect is in play, the degree of harm, and the extent of the risk of harm, will vary across different targets and styles of hate speech, as well as between different sorts of speakers, audiences, and social and political contexts. They might also have an implicit sense of the background circumstances that could shape these differential effects, even if they cannot give a definitive list of the circumstances. At any rate, background circumstances that are sometimes associated with the ordinary concept, as well as the legal concept, include but are not limited to the following.

(i) The past experiences or emotional vulnerability of individual victims.
(ii) The historical and ongoing oppression, discrimination, and violence perpetrated against the targeted group, as well as their collective memory of these things.

(iii) The authority, power, and influence of the speaker.
(iv) The degree of alignment in ideology and prejudices between the speaker and the audience.
(v) The size of the reach or audience that speech has, especially online.
(vi) The extent to which the target group and concerned third parties are capable of preventing or mitigating the relevant effects not merely through social and legal sanctions but also through counterspeech, allyship, counselling, and resilience building.
(vii) The background level of social and political division within the society including ideological polarisation, the prominence of extremist political parties, the tone of public debate, culture wars, and so on.
(viii) Social and economic conditions in the country including levels of prosperity, the extent of economic inequality, demographics, levels of immigration, the degree of ethnic and religious diversity, and so on.

Having opened out the discussion to give an overview of the ordinary concept *hate speech*, we shall now try to focus down again to provide some finer detail. We do this by exploring the semantics and pragmatics of the racial slur 'nigger'.

2.4 Slurs

Most competent users of the term 'hate speech' in its ordinary sense may not be able to give a precise or analytical definition of it, but if pressed many would probably say, 'I know it when I hear it or read it or see it.'[36] It is hard to imagine a word more likely to trigger the 'That's hate speech!' response than the word 'nigger'. It is certainly one of the prototypical examples of hate speech established by Matsuda. But what is it about the word 'nigger' that makes it a clear-cut example of hate speech? Is it simply because it is a slur? If so, are all slurs hate speech? Or is 'nigger' hate speech because it relates to race or because it targets an historically oppressed group or because it is a group-based slur? Indeed, what makes something a group-based slur and are group-based slurs always hate speech? Finally, what role does the semantics and pragmatics of the slur 'nigger' play in qualifying it as hate speech? It is to these questions that we now turn. We shall consider grey areas involving slurs which target groups that are not historically oppressed in Chapter 3.

2.4.1 *The Group-Based Nature of Slurs*

Scholars of hate speech and slurs typically classify racist slurs like 'nigger' as hate speech.[37] But what is it about this and similar slurs that make them hate speech? Consider two approaches. The first is analytical and says simply that the term 'hate speech' semantically encodes the following inference: that if something is a direct attack against people based on protected characteristics, then it is hate speech, a slur is such an attack, therefore a slur is hate speech. However, this approach expects the terms 'hate speech', 'direct attack', and 'slur' to admit of precise definitions (specification of a set of necessary and sufficient conditions) and this expectation may be unreasonable if these concepts are able to serve a variety of social purposes precisely because they do not readily admit of such definitions. Of course, if an internet company wishes to create a social rule disallowing certain content on the platform, then it may seek to give a precise definition of the term 'hate speech'. Like the legal concept, sometimes conceptualising the ordinary concept *hate speech* in a precise way can have the virtues of publicity and predictability. However, even though the ordinary concept *hate speech* is influenced by the content policies adopted by internet companies, it is not synonymous with the narrower concept *disallowed hate speech on social media*.

A second approach is more substantive and attempts to uncover features of slurs that can explain and justify the social practice of classifying them as hate speech in the ordinary sense of the term. This involves identifying dimensions of similarity between slurs and other members of the family. One obvious similarity has to do with the target of slurs. Slurs are group-based in the sense they attack people based on their membership or perceived membership of a group, class, category, or set of people. Indeed, academic research suggests not simply that slurs are derogatory, insulting, and offensive but also that the derogatory component 'is not so easily separable from the predication of group membership.'[38] Perhaps it is inherently insulting for a speaker to derogate people simply for being members of a group.[39] Maybe the targets see themselves as separate persons or individual human beings and so resent being put into categories. Alternatively, some people might understand themselves or their personal identity as being partly constituted by the relevant group identity in the sense that they identify with the group being derogated by the slur. It is natural to experience attacks on one's identity as insulting and offensive.

This group-based dimension comes out in Facebook's community standard on hate speech which contains a Tier 3 rule disallowing 'Content that describes or negatively targets people with slurs, where slurs are defined as words that inherently create an atmosphere of exclusion and intimidation against people on the basis of a protected characteristic, often because these words are tied to historical discrimination, oppression, and violence'.[40] The word 'nigger' would seem to be an exemplar case of a word that inherently creates an atmosphere of exclusion and intimidation against people on the basis of a protected characteristic and which is tied to historical discrimination, oppression, and violence. By contrast, if the more neutral term 'African American' is not an insulting label for one's race, then it is unlikely to be inherently exclusionary.

In fact, group-based slurs exhibit several features that both distinguishes them from general insults, say,[41] and shed light on what makes them similar to other prototypical examples of hate speech. First, even when a speaker hurls a slur like 'nigger' at a particular individual, there remains an emphasis on the group to which the speaker perceives the addressee to belong.[42] Slurring uses of the term 'nigger' do not derogate individuals whilst only coincidentally mentioning their race; the slur is closely connected to, or intimately bound up with, a group membership or status that is based on race. This can take different forms – for example, the speaker picked out or selected the individual to call the slur because of the individual's membership of the group or because the speaker perceived the individual to exemplify qualities, attributes, or characteristics the speaker associates with the group; the speaker is using the slur to claim or affirm that the individual is a member of the group including to transpose qualities of the group to the individual or conversely to generalise from qualities of the individual to the group; the slur refers to the individual in their capacity as a member of the group; the slur is being used to convey a derogatory message about the group; the slur is being used to demarcate boundaries and an order of hierarchy between groups; or the slur is being used to perform other illocutionary or perlocutionary acts against the group.

This close connection between the slur and the group distinguishes slurs like 'nigger' from general insults or personal pejoratives such as 'dickhead', which otherwise share some semantic similarities.[43] As Mihaela Popa-Wyatt puts it, '[t]here is no reasonable sense in which we could say that ["You dickhead!"] derogates the group of all dickheads, in the way that ["Faggot!"] derogates all the gay people.'[44] The pejorative 'dickhead' is more a commentary on the addressee displaying the quality of dickheadedness than on the group of all the dickheads. This explains why it is easier to identify the neutral counterpart for the slur 'nigger' (i.e. 'African Americans', 'people of African descent', 'Black people') than for the personal pejorative 'dickhead'.[45] In the case of group-based slurs like 'nigger', the accusation that certain undesirable qualities are possessed by all or nearly all members of the group is part of the internal motivation and semantics of the slur. By contrast, when it comes to general insults or personal pejoratives like 'dickhead' or 'asshole', the fact that other people possess the quality of dickheadness or arseholishness is an incidental fact. It would make sense to call someone an 'asshole' even if the class of assholes only consisted of one individual, in a way that would not make sense for slurs like 'nigger'. Note, this feature may also have implications for whether grey areas involving slurs that pick out only a subset of a group should count as hate speech. We discuss these selective attacks in Chapter 3.

Second, speakers who use group-based slurs typically do so on the basis of at least some *a priori* beliefs, attitudes, or sentiments towards the relevant group or class of persons – what can be called prejudices.[46] For example, people who use racial slurs like 'nigger' typically have preconceived ideas or preconceptions that are formed and conveyed without sound and reliable knowledge of African Americans as a group and prior to getting to know, or getting to know fully, the particular individuals being addressed with the slur. By contrast, speakers who hurl general insults or personal pejoratives at particular individuals typically do so on the basis of at least some *a posteriori* beliefs, opinions, or impressions about those individuals. These opinions can be based on differing degrees of experience, of course. Compare the motorist who is cut up by another motorist, winds down the window and yells 'Asshole!' with the disgruntled employee who fires these parting words at a boss she has known for a decade, 'The main problem I have with you David is that you're an incurable asshole'. But to use the insult or pejorative competently the speaker must be familiar enough with the individual to feel confident that he or she has exhibited a behaviour or character trait that justifies the insult or pejorative. Contrast this with paradigmatic uses of the slur 'nigger' in which the speaker might know only the colour of the target's skin but nothing of their behaviour, much less the content of their character.

Third, group-based slurs identify shared characteristics or attributes that are anchor points for the ascription of a set of further qualities or traits, where the former are supposed to explain the presence of the latter. For example, some uses of the slur 'nigger' identify a group or class of persons based on being African American, of African descent, or Black, and then ascribes to them certain traits (e.g. *lazy*, *stupid*, *promiscuous*, *animalistic*, *aggressive*) that are supposedly the result of the anchor characteristics. By contrast, general insults or personal pejoratives like 'dickhead' or 'asshole' are more semantically basic: there is an implicit attribution of certain undesirable traits (e.g. *stupid, inconsiderate, rude*) to the addressee without conveying, implicating, or presupposing any explanatory content about some prior characteristic (anchor characteristic) being responsible for those traits.

Finally, group-based slurs typically convey a proportionate balance of descriptive, explanatory, evaluative, and prescriptive content concerning the target group. By contrast, general insults or personal pejoratives tend to be disproportionately weighted to one kind of content. For example, the insults 'dickhead', 'twerp', and 'scumbag', although to some extent descriptive,[47] manifest a high proportion of evaluative content (e.g. *irritating, annoying, condemnable*). By comparison, the pejoratives 'pencil pusher' and 'freeloader', although to some degree evaluative,[48] are heavily balanced towards descriptive content (e.g. *a person whose job involves a lot of tedious and repetitive paperwork, someone who is economically or materially dependent on others without giving in return*).

2.4.2 The Semantics of 'Nigger'

Aside from the target ultimately being a group, another dimension of similarity between slurs like 'nigger' and other prototypical examples of hate speech is message. Teasing out this message, however, requires careful analysis. Slurs are syntactically interesting because they can be used as both nouns and adjectives such as in the following set of examples.

(15) You are some dumb ass niggers.
(16) Jake is a Kike.
(17) Muzzies are terrorists.
(18) I hate spics.
(19) These folks have nigger habits.

Accordingly, some sociolinguists and philosophers of language argue that slurs exhibit two semantic features: first, a reference to a group or class of persons, typically the persons referred to by the slur's neutral counterpart (actual, imaginary, or possible counterpart), which in the case of 'nigger' is usually 'African Americans', 'people of African descent', or simply 'Black people'; second, some sort of description of, expression of feeling, sentiment, or attitude towards, or evaluation or appraisal regarding, the target which embodies and explains the derogatory force or insultingness of slurs.[49] We shall not seek to directly challenge that conventional wisdom in this book but at the same time we will not be slavish to it. For instance, some scholars argue that even terms lacking obvious neutral counterparts, such as 'bitch' and 'slut', can be slurs, and that even for paradigmatic slurs like 'nigger' identifying a neutral counterpart is not always a straightforward exercise for some of its uses.[50] We are sympathetic to this nonconventional view, even though we shall not attempt to defend it here in any systematic way. In Chapter 3, for example, we too argue that 'bitch' and 'slut' can be slurs and hate speech; and we do so by emphasising the fact that the implicated or presuppositional content it conveys includes ideas based on bigotry and gender bias.

In our view, not merely is the term 'hate speech' polysemic but also prototypical examples of hate speech like 'nigger' can be polysemic, in the sense they can convey different contents or messages depending on the speaker, recipients, and context. Consider once again some of the concrete examples of hate speech cited above.

(1) [A group of White oil rig worker address African-American co-workers as 'niggers'.]
(6) [An anonymous note sent through an office internal mail system to a Black employee reading, 'The only good nigger is a dead nigger.']
(15) You are some dumb ass niggers.
(19) These folks have nigger habits.

Or take this further example.

(20) [Two White racists are talking together on the street one morning whilst looking across at some African American youths. The first White racist turns to the other and says, 'Would you just look at those god damn niggers jumping around and hollering!']

In examples (1), (6), (15), (19), (20) and similar sorts of examples, the term 'niggers' may convey content in different ways including being encoded, expressed, implied, presupposed, or inferred. Furthermore, the term 'niggers' may convey slightly different contents or messages depending on which particular example one is assessing.

Below we provide a list of contents or messages that could be conveyed by such uses of the slurs 'nigger' and 'niggers' and that bear similarities with messages of hatred, bigotry, threat, discrimination, intolerance, or violence conveyed by other prototypical examples of hate speech. We do not include reclaimed, resignified, or restaged uses of the term 'niggers' which convey positive messages. Once again, this is intended to be an illustrative as opposed to exhaustive list.

(1a) *African Americans (or people of African descent or Black people) have a tendency to be lazy, stupid, raggedy, promiscuous, aggressive, animalistic, non-rational, childlike, poor, unemployed, devoid of moral agency or conscience, immoral, criminal, unpatriotic, etc. (one or more of a constellation of stereotypical traits*[51]*), due to the fact of being African Americans.*[52]

(1b) *African Americans (or …) are repugnant, contemptible, despicable, good-for-nothing, inhuman, worthless, inferior, second-class, subordinate, natural born slaves, Other, enemies, a danger to society, lacking human dignity, etc. (one or more) whether simply due to the fact of being African Americans or because of their possession of stereotypical traits.*[53]

(1c) *The speaker has entrenched feelings, attitudes, or sentiments towards African Americans, such as hatred, contempt, superiority, callous indifference, disgust, resentment, fear, anger, grievance, suspicion, etc. (one or more), due to the speaker's endorsement of stereotypes about and adverse appraisals or evaluations of African Americans, and the speaker typically intends to express these feelings, attitudes, or sentiments*[54] *(although not always*[55]*).*

(1d) *The speaker is demonstrating a commitment to a perspective on African Americans (or …) central to which is the idea that the mere possession of certain descriptive features (e.g. skin colour) explains the presence of further stereotypical traits (e.g. laziness), makes certain appraisals or evaluations of African Americans appropriate (e.g. contemptible), and justifies holding certain feelings, attitudes, or sentiments towards African Americans (e.g. contempt).*[56]

(1e) *The speaker intends to indicate or signal that he or she is uninterested in seeing any particular African Americans (or …) as distinct individuals and does not care to get to know them in any meaningful way as separate persons, but is instead dedicated to forming opinions about them simply based on their membership of a racial group.*

(1f) *The speaker intends to signal an affiliation with an in-group of White people (or a subgroup of White people such as working class White people or socially conservative White people), a group which the speaker deems to be not merely different to African Americans (or …) (due to possessing different characteristics, traits, or qualities) but also superior to them, a group that has the convention of using the word 'nigger' to express contempt for African Americans, and a group that sees its common attitudes towards African Americans as both shaping its social identity and warranting having its own distinct name for African Americans ('nigger').*[57]

(1g) *The speaker is signalling commitment to the idea that it is justifiable to use the term 'nigger' to derogate African Americans (or …) based on the speaker's sentiments towards, or perspectives on, this group of people, and thereby to participate in practices of discrimination including the very act of derogating such people.*[58]

(1h) *The speaker believes it is justified for other people to have certain negative feelings, attitudes, or sentiments towards African Americans (or …), such as hatred, contempt, disdain, repulsion, resentment, etc., and that it is also right for other people to use the term 'nigger' to express these feelings, attitudes, or sentiments.*[59]

(1i) *The speaker presupposes not only that targeting African Americans (or …) with the derogatory term 'nigger' can be a way of treating them with contempt but also that other people share the disposition to treat African Americans (or …) with contempt in this way, and that doing so, therefore, is perfectly normal or natural.*

(1j) *The speaker directs other people to hold certain negative feelings, attitudes, or sentiments towards African Americans (or …) (e.g. hatred, contempt, anger, resentment) and to adopt the practice of calling them 'niggers'.*[60]

(1k) *The speaker presupposes that it is fitting, permissible, and incumbent on everybody to stereotype African Americans (or …) (e.g. lazy, stupid), to adversely appraise or evaluate African Americans (on the basis of stereotypical traits) (e.g. despicable, contemptible), to have negative feelings, attitudes, or sentiments towards African Americans (e.g. hatred, contempt, anger, resentment, etc.), and to exclude or discriminate against African Americans in a range of ways (not limited to targeting them with derogatory language).*[61]

(1l) *The speaker prescribes that African Americans (or …) ought to be the subject of various forms of discrimination, oppression, and persecution.*[62]

(1m) *The speaker intends to send a message of advocacy, justification, and support for people, organisations, and institutions engaged in subjecting African Americans (or …) to various forms of discrimination, oppression, and persecution.*[63]

(1n) *The speaker (and also the receiver) understands that certain uses of the term 'niggers' are conventionally understood to be insulting, offensive, or distressing to African Americans (or …), and typically the speaker intends these effects (although not always or necessarily).*[64]

(1o) *The speaker draws the receiver's attention to the fact that the speaker wants to convey a message, the receiver then forms a belief that the speaker has called certain people 'niggers', the receiver also accesses relevant beliefs and contextual assumptions about how 'niggers' is usually understood, namely, as a derogatory expression for African Americans (or …), and the receiver infers that the speaker has derogated African Americans.*[65]

(1p) *The use of the term 'niggers' is generally understood to be morally objectionable (a morally bad way to refer to non-White people) and typically the speaker (and also the receiver) is aware of this conventional understanding, but the speaker is intentionally seeking to either transgress or challenge this conventional wisdom (although not always or necessarily) by using the term 'niggers' in a way that is not merely derogatory but also, in the speaker's mind, deservedly or justifiably applied to African Americans (or …) and, therefore, not morally bad.*

We believe the slur 'niggers' is and should be counted as an exemplar of hate speech partly because it conveys the above sorts of messages and because of similarities between these messages and the messages (Section 2.3.3) conveyed by other prototypical examples of hate speech (Section 2.2). Compare two of the examples cited by Matsuda.

(1) [A group of White oil rig worker address African-American co-workers as 'niggers'.]

(4) [White students put up a sign on a Black student's bedroom door consisting of a caricature picture of a Black person with a red diagonal line across it.]

At first glance, examples (1) and (4) seem to convey similar messages of hatred, bigotry, discrimination, and intolerance.

But what, more precisely, is it about these messages that qualifies them as prototypical hate speech messages? We proffer several reasons. First, most competent users tend to reserve the term 'hate speech' for speech which is ultimately about a group or class of persons. Even if words are targeted at a particular individual, competent users label something 'hate speech' when they perceive the individual is targeted on the basis of membership of a group.[66] Conveyed contents or messages (1a)–(1p) all seem to fit this use-condition or common understanding of the ordinary concept *hate speech*.

Second, when people think about hate speech in the ordinary sense of the term, they often have in mind language that attributes certain undesirable traits or features to a group of people and contains some sort of adverse appraisal or evaluation of the group, all based on the attribution of some basic characteristic such as race. The slur 'niggers' certainly seems to do these things, especially in terms of conveyed contents (1a)–(1d).[67]

Third, a literalist analysis of the ordinary concept *hate speech* assumes that something is hate speech only if it expresses the speaker's feelings, attitudes, or sentiments of hatred towards a particular group or class of persons.[68] Conveyed content (1c) is certainly consistent with that literalist analysis.[69] Then again, sometimes hate speech expresses contempt as opposed to hatred.[70] Nevertheless, a more flexible analysis states that hate speech is a family resemblances concept that can be but is not necessarily associated with hatred.[71] Conveyed content (1c) is also consistent with that more flexible analysis since it is drawn widely enough to capture the expression of any one of a collection of mental states including not only hatred but also contempt and many other things besides.[72]

Fourth, if one reverts to the original examples of hate speech articulated in Matsuda's seminal article, it is clear many of them convey negative stereotypes about the target groups, one example being (4). Therefore, the very fact that the slur 'niggers' might itself encode content (1a) (i.e. negative stereotypes) shows a direct similarity with other exemplars and further cements its position as hate speech.

Fifth, one intuition people seem to have about hate speech is that it is associated with bigotry and prejudice.[73] This intuition is borne out in many of the above conveyed contents or messages and as such provides further grounds for seeing the slur 'niggers' as an exemplar of hate speech. For one thing, arguably (1a) stereotypes, (1b) attributions of typical traits, (1c) entrenched feelings, attitudes, or sentiments, and (1d) rigid explanatory perspectives are each forms of prejudice about the relevant group. Furthermore, in the case of (1e), the speaker who uses the slur 'niggers' intends to indicate his or her commitment to the defining idea of prejudice, namely that it is unnecessary to have any direct familiarity with, or personal knowledge about, individuals aside from their membership of a group in order to make evaluative judgments about them. By contrast, the neutral counterpart 'African American people' is less likely to convey the speaker's intention to signal his or her commitment to prejudiced evaluations.

Finally, another folk platitude that surrounds the ordinary concept *hate speech* is that it picks out forms of speech that are morally wrong or objectionable.[74] Much the same can be said for the concept *slur*.[75] Indeed, it is worth noting that conveyed content (1p) assumes that the use of the term 'niggers' is conventionally understood to be morally objectionable, even if the speaker also intends to transgress or challenge that way of thinking. Of course, it is one thing to say that both 'hate speech' and 'slur' are thick evaluative terms which imply or presuppose that the speech in question is morally wrong or objectionable; it is another thing to explain the source or grounds of the suggested immorality, which might differ for hate speech and slurs (hence why these terms are not synonyms). Even so, the broad similarity could also help to explain and justify the position of slurs as exemplars of hate speech.

2.4.3 *The Pragmatics of 'Nigger'*

Yet further similarities between slurs like 'nigger' and other prototypical examples of hate speech can be seen in the distinguishing qualities of act and effect. Many scholars understand hate speech to be not simply communicative but also performative or 'speech plus': that hate speech involves doing something to people (pragmatics) over about simply saying something (semantics).[76] Indeed, it is telling that in the first collected volume on hate speech, Matsuda and her co-authors begin with the following description: 'This is a book about [...] words that are used as weapons to ambush, terrorize, wound, humiliate, and degrade.'[77] It is also revealing that although Facebook addresses the issue through its community standard on 'hate speech', it defines hate speech as 'an attack'.[78] Furthermore, other platforms explicitly address the issue as a performative phenomenon. Consider the fact that Twitter has a 'hateful conduct' policy[79] and TikTok has a community guideline on 'hateful behaviors'.[80]

Below we describe several different action-types and effects that we believe are associated with commonplace uses of the racial slur 'nigger' and that render such uses similar to other prototypical examples of hate speech. Importantly for the aims of Part I of this book, we also believe these action-types and effects are highly relevant when assessing the ten grey areas of hate speech to be discussed in Chapters 3 and 4.

First, the use of group-based slurs like 'nigger' may constitute epistemological wrongdoing – or what Miranda Fricker calls 'epistemic injustice'[81] – by virtue of *prejudging* other people. This can involve saying things about other people that are rooted in *a priori* assumptions as opposed to *a posteriori* judgments or, perhaps more often, 'judgment[s] made or maintained without proper regard to the evidence'.[82] As messages (1a)–(1e) show, group-based slurs like 'nigger' may convey generalisations or prejudgments about a particular group or class of persons based on limited knowledge of, or direct familiarity with, members of the group. As Fricker puts it, 'for this reason we should conceive of prejudice generally as something epistemically culpable'.[83] Consider a conversation between two White racists about the problems faced by their city, during which one turns to the other and delivers the following one-liner without further elaboration or challenge.

(21) This city sure has its big problems, and to see why you don't need to look no further than niggers.

The statement may convey the following content or message.

(21a) *This city faces problems of high crime, drug use, unemployment, moral decay, and corruption; all/most African Americans are involved in crime, drug use, unemployment, immorality, and corruption, and this is due to the fact of them being African Americans; therefore, African Americans are responsible for the big problems this city has.*

No doubt this statement can be morally objectionable for many different and serious reasons, but one of the reasons is surely that it commits an epistemic injustice against its targets.[84] Arguably, this general kind of action-type (Section 2.3.4) can also be seen in other prototypical examples of hate speech (Section 2.2).

Similarly, even when slurs like 'nigger' are hurled at a single individual, they can convey shorthand or fast track opinions based on epistemically culpable prejudices. They can be a way of taking the measure of an individual prior to actually getting to know them, or without getting to know them in a proper way – a public form of prejudgment or summary verdict. Consider a conversation between two bigoted, White interviewers about a job applicant they have just met for the first time, in which one says to other.

(22) This guy is a nigger, that's all you need to know about him.

The slur may convey this unspoken logical inference or implied syllogism.

(22a) *African Americans tend to be lazy, stupid, promiscuous, animalistic, aggressive, etc. (some or all); this guy is African American; therefore, this guy is probably lazy, stupid, promiscuous, animalistic, aggressive, etc.; moreover, there is no need to get to know this guy in order to feel justified in believing that he is probably lazy, stupid, promiscuous, animalistic, aggressive, etc.*

Here the slur conveys a preconceived idea of the stranger based on his African descent, without any real experience or knowledge of that person, and in the absence of any serious attempt to learn about and consider his track record, qualifications, character references, and so on. It is an act of racial discrimination built on the foundations of an epistemic wrong.

Of course, sometimes speakers use slurs to refer to individuals they know quite well but nonetheless manifest prejudgment in the way they draw spurious causal connections between different features, attributes, or characteristics without proper regard to evidence. Consider a conversation between two prejudiced White teachers, in which one says to the other the following.

(23) She is quite terrible at maths, poor girl, but she is a nigger after all.

Arguably, this statement does not merely convey a value-laden description of African Americans but also offers a ready-made explanation for why the girl is not good at maths.

(23a) *African Americans are not good at maths due to the fact of being African Americans, and so naturally this girl is not good at maths on account of being African American.*

The prejudgment lies not merely in invoking a spurious explanatory connection between race and predisposition to mathematical ability (or inability)[85] but also in making assumptions about the girl without further investigation into her particular circumstances or considering other possible reasons for her apparent difficulties with maths (if indeed she is having difficulties). Such lack of interest in undertaking proper inquiry into the persons one is evaluating seems especially morally culpable among teachers.

In addition to the epistemic injustice, the teachers' use and tacit acceptance of the slur may also be morally objectionable insofar as it additionally signals a commitment to the prejudiced idea or perspective that it is appropriate to have lower expectations of Black pupils and ultimately reasonable to show them less care and attention, treating them as lost causes. After all, (23) might also express, imply, or presuppose the following message.

(23b) *In the future let's not waste time giving extra help to the nigger child.*

This is morally repugnant because it condones, legitimises, and in the context even directly enacts a form of educational discrimination. Insofar as it signals a justification for, and intention to, discriminate against the child, it performs another action-type (Section 2.3.4) of the sort that can also be seen in other prototypical examples of hate speech (Section 2.2).

Second, the use of slurs, like other prototypical examples of hate speech, may enact forms of misrecognition.[86] To use the slur 'nigger' can be to *misrecognise* African Americans in several ways including: *oppressive ascription of identity*,[87] in that the slur externally, non-consensually, and insensitively imposes an identity onto African Americans; *tarnishing identity*, in that the identity imposed on its targets is synonymous with what is bad (e.g. *lazy*, *raggedy*, *animalistic*, *non-rational*, *childlike*, *aggressive*); and *oversimplifying identity*, meaning that the multiple, complex, and idiosyncratic concatenations of identities that people of African descent actually create for themselves can be reduced to a single identity, *the nigger*.[88] Arguably, messages (1a) and (1e) lend themselves easily to these performative speech acts of ascription, tarnishing, and oversimplification.

In addition, some uses of the slur 'nigger' can enact a form of what we have elsewhere called 'existential misrecognition'.[89] This can involve *denial* of key elements of the cultural identity of targeted individuals and the groups with which they identify. Suppose a White racist historian and slavery revisionist publishes a book containing this statement.

(24) The enslaved niggers of America were better off than the working poor in the old world as at least they had enough food to eat and a place to lay their heads at night, and for the most part they were treated with almost maternal kindness by their slave masters, which explains why they were happy to remain in place, and why so many of them chose to fight alongside their white brothers in the Confederate army.

Statement (24) is not simply at odds with the facts but in a more meaningful sense *contradicts*, *rejects*, and *denies* fundamental aspects of African American identity – in particular, the cultural memory of widespread malnutrition, systematic violence and cruelty, routine use of locks, chains, and slave catchers, and the experiences of Black slaves forced to cook and clean for Confederate soldiers. In general, cultural memory encompasses the store of experiences and narratives passed between generations of a community – memories embodied and protected in oral histories, texts, monuments, museums, special holidays, and practices of remembrance. Cultural memory is something that binds members of the community and furnishes them with important aspects of their identity. There are obvious parallels here with acts of existential misrecognition associated with Holocaust denial, another prototypical example of hate speech (Section 2.2). 'Holocaust denial may constitute an existential threat to the cultural identity of living Jews, by denying the memories that are partly constitutive of their identity as members of Jewish cultural communities.'[90]

Third, the slur 'niggers' can be used in some contexts to *dehumanise* the targeted individuals or group. This might include: *portraying* them as not human or lacking in human qualities; *denying* they are humans, have human qualities, or possess human dignity; and *legitimating*, *condoning*, or *justifying* the treatment of them in ways that would befit creatures or things that lack humanity or human dignity. Consider once again this example.

(20) [Two White racists are talking together on the street one morning whilst looking across at some African American youths. The first White racist turns to the other and says, 'Just look at those god damn niggers jumping around and hollering!']

If the speaker is using 'niggers' to convey messages like (1a) and (1b), the speaker could be *dehumanising* African Americans by implicitly *portraying* them as animalistic, non-rational, devoid of moral agency or conscience, or effectively *denying* their humanity or human dignity. Similarly, by using the slur 'niggers' to convey messages (1k), (1l), and (1m), the speaker may also be *legitimating*, *condoning*, or *justifying* acts of oppression, discrimination, exclusion, segregation, or violence against African Americans by presupposing their lack of humanity or human dignity. Compare this with another two of Matsuda's examples.

(4) [White students put up a sign on a Black student's bedroom door consisting of a caricature picture of a Black person with a red diagonal line across it.]

(9) [Books, postcards and other published material portraying Jews as animal-like (e.g. as pigs, snakes, mice, or rats) and requiring extermination.]

Arguably, these other prototypical examples of hate speech may also involve *dehumanising* their targets. If there is a close resemblance between the acts of dehumanisation performed in (20), (4), and (9), this can help to explain and justify why racial slurs count as hate speech.

Fourth, group-based slurs can be used to perpetuate, facilitate, or even enact forms of oppression and subordination and, importantly, they seem to share this action-type in common with other prototypical examples of hate speech.[91] Consider the following example.

(25) [A White employee of a cardboard box factor turns to his White co-workers in the canteen and says, 'Hey, the next time that nigger gets on the tannoy let's just ignore him.' His fellow workmates do not object, and when the Black foreman gets on the tannoy and says, 'All packers are to be advised that there is no more cardboard glue in the ground floor dispenser', there is no uptake of his warning because people carry on as though he didn't say anything.][92]

Here the slur 'nigger' is used to deprive the foreman of his ability to do his job, even if temporarily. Such enactment of oppression or subordination is often associated with other prototypical examples of hate speech including the following example from Matsuda's list.

(11) [A sign in a store window that reads, 'No blacks allowed'.]

Indeed, Mary Kate McGowan argues not only that examples like (11) are exemplars of hate speech precisely because they enact oppression but also extends this analysis to new examples involving yet more complex forms of oppression.[93] Similarly, Rae Langton has identified hate speech with various subordination-typical acts. According to Langton, public signs of the sort that read 'No blacks allowed' can serve to 'rank blacks as having inferior worth', 'legitimate discriminatory behavior on the part of whites', and 'deprive blacks of some important powers: for example, the power to go to certain areas'.[94] This resemblance in action-types further solidifies the position of slurs like 'nigger' as hate speech.

Finally, it is widely held that hate speech can be causally or otherwise explanatorily linked to further harmful effects suffered by its targets.[95] For example, it is claimed hate speech can contribute to adverse perceptions of target groups and that these perceptions predict experiences of oppression, subordination, and social hierarchy insofar as audiences regard and treat target groups in accordance with what the hate speech says about them.[96] Clearly, when the slur 'niggers' is used to convey messages like (1a)–(1d), this can have the effect of reinforcing adverse perceptions of African Americans and normalising the unequal power relations to which the targets are subjected, especially when the messages chime with the prejudices of in-groups and are internalised by out-groups.[97] As Robin Jeshion puts it, 'the manifestation of contempt is a central fulcrum of in-group/out-group construction' and 'the formation of [...] social hierarchies' because when the manifestations 'are shared and are common knowledge, they naturally spawn shared identities amongst the contemnors as superior'.[98] Indeed, a 2009 experimental study of slurs found that exposure to basic slurs (defined as low complexity in the cognitive representations of the target groups that are encoded in the slurs) predicts higher discriminatory ('exclusionary') dispositions towards target groups compared to exposure to complex slurs.[99] Basic slurs like 'nigger' may resemble (4) (a caricature picture of Black people) in terms of these predicted effects.

2.5 The Global Resemblance Test

To say that the ordinary concept *hate speech* is a family resemblances concept is to say there is not an essential feature or common quality shared by all examples of hate speech but instead a series of distinguishing qualities with each quality possessed by some and not other examples. No one quality is common to all examples of hate speech, yet nevertheless examples display a complex pattern of overlapping and criss-crossing similarities, or global resemblance. So far we have suggested there are five distinguishing qualities (or clusters of features) associated with the ordinary concept *hate speech*: target, style, message, act, and effect. However, this still leaves some unanswered questions. For example, are prototypical examples defined as such only if they exhibit all five distinguishing qualities? If not, how many of the five qualities must they exhibit? In addition, what kind of resemblance must grey area examples share with prototypical examples to also count as hate speech? The aim of this final section is to provide answers to these questions. Then, in Chapters 3 and 4, we apply the global resemblance test to a total of ten different grey area examples of hate speech.

2.5.1 *Only Four Out of Five of the Distinguishing Qualities*

Like other concepts, there is a danger that the ordinary concept *hate speech* could end up with an indefinitely extending range or wide open texture depending on how it is conceptualised. Since any bit of speech will be in some ways similar to any other, there seems to be a risk that any bit of speech could fall within the extension of the ordinary concept *hate speech*. However, this danger is mitigating by saying that only *some* distinguishing qualities are relevant to the extension of the concept. In fact, we have said there are five distinguishing qualities associated with the ordinary concept *hate speech*, reflecting prototypical examples. Because the extension of the concept is fixed by a determinate or finite range of qualities, this lessens the risk of a wide open texture. On our interpretation, so long as the list of qualities stays the same, this indicates the persistence of the concept over time, even if more examples are gobbled up by the concept or the extension of the concept grows over time. By contrast, if the list of qualities significantly changes in quality or number, this would signal a significant shift in meaning, transforming hate speech into a different concept, so to speak.[100]

Although we have said there are five distinguishing qualities associated with the ordinary concept *hate speech*, we do not mean to suggest competent users of the term 'hate speech' will light upon a single definition of hate speech. Hate speech in the ordinary sense of the term is not that kind of concept. One user of the phrase 'x and y are hate speech' may have in mind a different collection, configuration, or set of the five distinguishing qualities to that which a second user of the phrase has in mind. To be more precise, we propose that prototypical examples of hate speech need exhibit only four out of five of the distinguishing qualities to count as exemplars. Likewise, even if a new example comes along, such as a grey area example, which exhibits only four out of five of the distinguishing qualities, then it could also count as hate speech provided it is similar enough to the prototypical examples. By contrast, if a bit of speech exhibits merely three out of five of the qualities, then it is a penumbral case, meaning it falls just outside of the concept. Examples that exhibit only one or two of the qualities may be clear-cut examples of non-hate speech.

There is, however, a further complication. Qualities are themselves general or abstracts sorts of things that can admit of a variety of particular or concrete instances. In other words, the five distinguishing qualities are themselves clusters of more specific features. Therefore, even if two users have in mind the same quality-type (e.g. target), they might also be thinking of different features-tokens (e.g. people of colour, homosexual people). Furthermore, specific features within a cluster can be more or less similar to each other. As a result, prototypical examples of hate speech may have differing degrees of resemblance at the level of features. This reintroduces the risk that the ordinary concept *hate speech* has a wide open texture. Yet despite this risk, it is evident that competent users are still able to make and understand meaningful utterances like 'x and y are hate speech'.

According to the global resemblance test, a grey area example counts as hate speech in the ordinary sense of the term only if it also exhibits at least four out of five of the distinguishing qualities and provided that it is similar enough to prototypical examples of hate speech to warrant its classification as hate speech. In a moment we shall explain what we mean by 'similar enough'. Before doing so, however, we need to address several initial objections that might be levelled at the approach we have outlined.

One objection is essentially that the list of five distinguishing qualities is suspiciously neat and speaks to an overly narrow or small concept. This conceptualisation might befit the legal concept, the objector might allow, but not the ordinary concept, which seems capable of serving myriad social purposes only because it is neither a neat nor a small concept. In response to this objection, however, we reiterate the point that each quality is itself a cluster made up of a larger number of specific features (Section 2.3). Once this additional complexity is taken into account, we believe our conceptualisation presents the ordinary concept *hate speech* as neither suspiciously neat nor overly narrow or small.

A second objection targets the 'only four out of five qualities' caveat. Why four out of five rather than five, three, or even two out of five qualities? Without a compelling conceptual and/or normative reason for lighting upon four, the approach seems arbitrary. Our answer to the arbitrariness objection is essentially that the caveat is not only true to what kind of concept the ordinary concept *hate speech* is (a family resemblance concept) but also strikes a reasonable balance. In particular, the list of five distinguishing qualities allied to the 'only four out of five qualities' caveat enables the ordinary concept *hate speech* to serve various functions or purposes a society might reasonably expect it to serve (one desiderata of an adequate conceptualisation). Alternatively, to insist that examples exhibit five out of five qualities to count as hate speech or, in the other direction, to say that examples need only display a couple of qualities to count as hate speech, may inhibit the concept from serving the full range of morally desirable purposes a society might reasonably expect it to serve, such as by rendering the ordinary concept either overly narrow or excessively broad.

A third objection picks up on this last point and insists that the caveat lowers the bar for something to count as hate speech and risks leaving the concept too bloated or capacious to serve some valuable social functions. For example, if social media platforms adopted the caveat as part of their hate speech content policies, they could end up removing more content than is desirable, especially if it looks as though the policies are being used simply to remove words that companies who buy advertising space on the platforms hate to see alongside their adverts. However, even though the caveat could mean, if implemented by social media platforms, the removal of more content, that is not necessarily a bad thing and does not automatically mean that commercially driven censorship is afoot. Perhaps content that only exhibits four out of five of the distinguishing qualities of hate speech really ought to be removed, such as if it is harmful to users and society at large, irrespective of the issue of advertising revenues. Furthermore, the desiderata for a good or adequate theory of the ordinary concept *hate speech* are not exhausted by enabling the concept to serve as a plausible basis for social media platform content policies. Conceptualising hate speech in the ordinary sense of the term using the 'only four out of five qualities' caveat might also be compatible with that concept playing its social role in supporting people's sense they have equal standing in society, for example.[101]

A fourth objection highlights what the caveat means for speech that may lack prototypical hate speech effects. Conceptually speaking, how could something be plausibly counted as hate speech if it lacks such effects? Surely competent language users are more likely to apply the label 'hate speech' to speech they perceive to have harmful effects than speech that does not. Indeed, if part of the social function of the ordinary concept is to highlight forms of harmful speech,[102] as well as to serve as a touchstone for the momentous decisions taken by internet companies in removing content,[103] then arguably these functions could not be performed by a conceptualisation of hate speech that permits content to be flagged as hate speech even if it lacks harmful effects. Yet this is exactly what the 'only four out of five qualities' caveat appears to allow. However, the objection conflates harmful effects and harmfulness or wrongfulness in general. Not all harms or wrongs take the form of harmful effects. Some prototypical hate speech acts constitute harms or wrongs in themselves quite apart from any further effects they may have or lack. In many instances, speakers who use the term 'hate speech' in its ordinary sense may not pause to pinpoint the harmfulness or wrongfulness they have in mind, but it may be evident that the speech they are referring to is harmful or wrongful due to its illocutionary force as opposed to perlocutionary effect. Furthermore, the major social media platforms typically do not rely on a general definition of hate speech as 'harmful attacks' and a harm condition is not built into most of the specific rules disallowing forms of hate speech. Instead, they tend to reserve a harm condition for a limited number of specific rules. Consider Facebook's hate speech content policy which combines a general definition of hate speech as 'a direct attack against people' with a large number of specific rules disallowing forms of hate speech. The following rule is unusual because it references harm in a way that the majority of the specific rules do not: 'Content attacking concepts, institutions, ideas, practices or beliefs associated with protected characteristics, which are likely to contribute to imminent physical harm, intimidation or discrimination against the people associated with that protected characteristic.'[104]

A final objection concerns the possibility that, under the 'only four out of five qualities' caveat, something could be counted as hate speech even though it does not exhibit the quality of directly attacking a person or group based on protected characteristics. At first glance, this runs contrary to a folk platitude about hate speech that seems to exist in various fields of discourse,[105] and which is embodied in the general definitions of hate speech promulgated by Facebook[106] and Twitter,[107] namely that hate speech is a direct attack against people based on protected characteristics. However, the objection is built on false premises. For one thing, at least in its bare form Holocaust denial is a prototypical example of hate speech (as understood by Matsuda and most of the major social media platforms) which does not directly attack a person or group. It is merely saying that certain events did not happen. Its subject is events and what it directly attacks is facts, information, and beliefs about the Holocaust. Similarly, a speaker who asserts that homosexuality is disgusting may be engaged in hate speech even though they are not directly attacking a person or group. We shall return to consider this sort of example in Chapter 3. Furthermore, as a distinguishing quality of hate speech, *target* can be read in narrower or broader ways. The objection assumes a narrower reading, but target might also mean either *directly or indirectly* attacking people based on protected characteristics.

Thus, even bare forms of Holocaust denial may be indirectly attacking people killed in the Holocaust by saying either they were not killed by the Nazis or that they simply never existed. What is more, such people are identified by the primary protected characteristic of being Jewish allied to the characteristic of being victims of atrocities. Interestingly, Facebook disallows 'Statements denying existence' under Tier 1 of its community standard on hate speech, which covers content targeting a person, groups of people, and all subgroups of people, based on protected characteristics, including therefore the subgroup *Jews killed in the Holocaust*. Tier 1 also includes a specific rule disallowing 'Holocaust denial'.[108] For its part, YouTube's hate speech policy cites 'victims of a major violent event and their kin' in its list of protected characteristics. It also contains a specific rule disallowing the following content: 'Deny or minimise a well-documented, major violent event or the victimhood of such an event.'[109]

2.5.2 *Similar Enough*

We have analysed the ordinary concept *hate speech* in terms of a combination of linguistic conventions or rules and normative justifications for those conventions or rules. We have identified a convention manifest across several fields of discourse of applying the label 'hate speech' to an extended body of exemplars. We believe these exemplars share a complex pattern of overlapping and criss-crossing similarities based on several distinguishing qualities (or clusters of features). In our view, it may be appropriate to count grey area examples as hate speech in this ordinary sense provided they also display at least four out of five of the distinguishing qualities and are similar enough to the exemplars to warrant that label (the global resemblance test). But what does 'similar enough' mean here? Is it sufficient simply that the grey area examples display at least four out of five of the distinguishing qualities or is similarity also needed at the level of specific features? Moreover, is similarity measured by degree, quality, or both? Does the same level of similarity need to hold across the distinguishing qualities? Must the similarity between the grey area examples and the prototypical examples of hate speech match the similarity held among the prototypical examples or can it be a different level of similarity?

Beginning with the last of these questions, we appeal to H. H. Price's general rule of matching resemblance: that if a new example resembles the prototypical examples as closely as the prototypical examples resemble each other, then the new example is also a member of the category.[110] Then again, what does resemblance among the prototypical examples look like? Consider the following formal representation of resemblance among prototypical examples based on the distinguishing qualities of target, style, message, act, and effect.

(P1) T, S, M, A, but not E.
(P2) S, M, A, E, but not T.
(P3) T, M, A, E, but not S.
(P4) T, S, A, E, but not M.
(P5) T, S, M, E, but not A.

There is a sense in which prototypical examples (P1) to (P5) all have the same degree of resemblance to each other. First, they share the condition that they each exhibit at least four out of five of the distinguishing qualities T, S, M, A, and E. Second, for any two prototypical examples, they possess three qualities that are the same. For instance, prototypes (P1) and (P3) each possess the three qualities T, M, and A, prototypes (P2) and (P4) each possess the three qualities S, A, and E, and so on. Thus, according to the general rule of matching resemblance, if a grey area example of hate speech (G1) exhibits at least four out of five of the distinguishing qualities, and if (G1) also possesses three qualities that are the same as those possessed by any given prototypical example (P), then (G1) resembles the prototypical examples as closely as they resemble each other and, therefore, (G1) is also hate speech.

However, as highlighted above, the qualities are themselves abstract types that are instantiated in different specific features. So, the question arises what concatenation of specific features are similar enough to warrant applying the label 'hate speech' to a grey area example? Once again, we appeal to the general rule of matching resemblance, meaning that the resemblance in qualities and features between the grey area example and the prototypical examples must be as close as the resemblance in qualities and features among the prototypical examples. But what does it mean for one resemblance to be 'as close as' another resemblance once specific features are factored into the conceptual equation? We propose that resemblance, viewed as an ideal type, is a function of several different forms of similarity including range (diversity in the quality of similarities), extent (the number of similarities), degree (how similar within each dimension of similarity), and salience (the noticeability and importance of each similarity).[111]

How far real-world social practices associated with the ordinary concept *hate speech* in fact adhere to this ideal type of resemblance is an open question. Our working assumption is that competent users of the term 'hate speech' in its ordinary sense look for similarities between grey area examples and existing prototypical examples of hate speech to judge whether the former really are hate speech. Moreover, we take it as read that when ordinary people think of hate speech they are more likely to think of prototypical examples of hate speech than grey area examples and are likely to recognise as hate speech the prototypical examples more quickly than grey area examples – these being features of cognitive processes related to similar concepts studied in experimental psychology.[112] We are not aware, however, of any studies in experimental psychology that have looked in detail at the ideas or psychological representations in the minds of competent users of the ordinary concept *hate speech*, including the roles played by range, extent, degree, and salience of similarity. Likewise, we assume that the content policy teams and human moderators working for the major social media platforms also look for similarities between grey area examples and existing designated examples of disallowed hate speech under the relevant content policies to judge whether the former should also be designated as hate speech. But this is also only a working assumption because hitherto the major social media platforms have tended not to share detailed information with the public or academic researchers on the forms of analogical reasoning and deliberation utilised by their content policy teams and human moderators.[113] Therefore, in the absence of evidence to the contrary, we assume for the purposes of our conceptualisation that each of the different forms of similarity associated with conceptual resemblance as an ideal type figure to some extent in how ordinary people and social media platforms, for example, assess similarities between grey area examples and prototypical examples of hate speech.

Take the issue of salience. Perhaps people will take resemblance in some distinguishing qualities to be a more noticeable or important indicator of whether a grey area example really is hate speech than resemblance in other qualities. This unequal weighting or ranking of qualities is likely to depend on the context and on the particular social purpose being served by a particular conceptualisation of *hate speech*. For example, an internet company may place an emphasis on signalling to users that they are equal members of society in good standing, but may also want to send a message that it does not apply double standards in the decisions it takes about removing or reducing the distribution of content. As such, the internet company might place special weight on resemblance in target when assessing grey area examples. Furthermore, if target is an especially salient distinguishing quality, then the internet company may be more likely to assess examples like bare Holocaust denial or descriptions of homosexuality as disgusting as borderline examples. The internet company might then look to see if there is sufficiently high resemblance in message, act, and effect, for example, to offset low resemblance in target, despite the greater salience of the latter. Understanding the decisions of internet companies in such terms may have explanatory power – for example, it might explain why Facebook was for many years reluctant to designate Holocaust denial as disallowed hate speech and why in the case of 'content attacking concepts, institutions, ideas, practices or beliefs associated with protected characteristics' Facebook requires that the content is 'likely to contribute to imminent physical harm, intimidation or discrimination against the people associated with that protected characteristic' in order to classify it as disallowed hate speech on the platform.[114]

The broader point is that the global resemblance test must factor in the prototypical examples, the various distinguishing qualities, and the different kinds of similarity among specific features to form a judgment of global resemblance. The upshot is that different grey area examples could satisfy the global resemblance test in different ways. So, for example, a reverse attack (e.g. 'honky', 'white devil') could be strongly similar to prototypical examples of hate speech in its message, but moderately similar in its act and only minimally similar in its target and effect; whilst identity denials (e.g. 'Transwomen are not women') might be similar to prototypical examples of hate speech in precisely obverse ways. Such examples testify to the fact that global resemblance can embody what Wittgenstein called a 'complicated network of similarities overlapping and criss-crossing: similarities in the large and in the small'.[115]

That said, some people might be sceptical at this stage about how reverse attacks, for example, could conceivably pass the global resemblance test given the high salience of target when determining what counts as hate speech and given the fact that reverse attacks cannot be highly similar to prototypical examples of hate speech insofar as the latter typically involve attacks against historically oppressed groups. We shall discuss reverse attacks in more detail in Chapter 3, but we end this chapter by making two points. The first is that grey area examples need only exhibit four of five of the distinguishing qualities to potentially count as hate speech in the ordinary sense of the term. The second is this: the fact that reverse attacks target people based on their protected characteristics is at least one similarity they share in common with prototypical examples of hate speech and this fact combined with stronger similarities in act and message may be enough to satisfy the global resemblance test.

3

Attacks against Groups

3.1 Introduction

In Chapter 2 we listed exemplars of hate speech that featured in Matsuda's seminal article and that are shared by both the ordinary and legal concepts of hate speech, as well as an extended body of exemplars of the ordinary concept found in various fields of discourse. In Chapters 3 and 4 we examine a series of grey area examples and how they are classified under the content policies promulgated by Facebook and other major social media platforms. In this chapter we look at examples that fall into a grey area either because of who the target is or because of who the speaker is, including speaker motivation, the common denominator being an attack on groups. To maintain consistency with Chapter 2, we once again concentrate on slurs. More specifically, we investigate hybrid attacks (e.g. 'fatty', 'bitch'), selective attacks (e.g. 'I love black people, I hate niggers'), reverse attacks (e.g. 'honky', 'white devil'), righteous attacks (e.g. 'commie', 'male chauvinist pig', 'TERF', 'ex-con'), and indirect attacks (e.g. 'retard', 'poof').

This chapter makes the case for classifying each of these kinds of attacks as hate speech in the ordinary sense of the term based on similarities with exemplars of hate speech under the global resemblance test (Chapter 2), and in the light of reasonable expectations about the important social functions or purposes of the concept (Chapter 5). We also argue that Facebook's community standard on hate speech is ambiguous, inconsistent, and incomplete in relation to the aforementioned attacks. Thus, we recommend specific reforms of the standard to address these problems. Section 3.2 looks at hybrid attacks, which we classify as words that, like personal insults, target specific individuals, but, like prototypical hate speech, also attack the groups to which targeted individuals belong and, what is more, go beyond standard protected characteristics. Section 3.3 investigates selective attacks, which we understand as derogatory or insulting words that refer to only a subset of a group or else to an amalgamated set of people who belong to multiple groups. Section 3.4 scrutinises reverse attacks, which involve words used by members of groups typically perceived as victims against groups more usually considered perpetrators. Section 3.5 examines righteous attacks, which we associate with attacks in pursuit of some righteous cause. Finally, Section 3.6 assesses indirect attacks, wherein the speaker intentionally uses a derogatory word to address or target someone whom the speaker knows or presumes to be not a member of the group referred to by the word under its literal or primary meaning.

3.2 Hybrid Attacks

Hybrid attacks are hybrid in two respects: first, like personal insults, they are typically used to attack specific individuals, but, like prototypical hate speech, they also attack the groups to which targeted individuals belong; and second, although they are partly group-based, the relevant groups either are not identified by the standard protected characteristics of race, ethnicity, religion, gender, and sexual orientation, or are identified by combinations of standard protected characteristics and other characteristics.[1]

Hybrid attacks may take different linguistic forms but in what follows we shall focus on pejoratives and slurs. The sociolinguistics literature has identified a range of hybrid slurs including relating to gender (e.g. 'bitch', 'slut', 'ice queen'); physical appearance (e.g. 'fatty', 'shorty', 'ginger'); lifestyle (e.g. 'wino', 'druggie', 'scrounger', 'fitness fanatic'); sexual desires, preferences, or activities, or lack thereof ('swinger', 'frigid', 'cold fish'); political or ideological beliefs and affiliations (e.g. 'commie', 'tree hugger', 'Tory scum', 'feminazi'); and age (e.g. 'crone', 'codger').[2] Although these tend to be addressed to particular individuals, there is a sense in which they also speak to entire groups or classes of persons.

3.2.1 *The Hybrid Attacks Challenge*

Hybrid attacks pose a challenge to any society or specific organisation that wishes to develop a coherent picture of the ordinary concept *hate speech* because they seem to both invoke and test the limits of the following intuitive rule about this concept.

(R1) Hate speech is group-based.

Hybrid attacks test the limits of (R1) by inviting two hard questions. Can pejoratives used to target specific individuals still count as group-based slurs? Do group-based slurs always count as hate speech irrespective of what sort of group is being attacked? Together these questions comprise what we call the hybrid attacks challenge.

We believe there are just three sensible ways of responding to this challenge, none of which involve abandoning (R1). The first is to deny that hybrid attacks are group-based in the strict sense and, therefore, to deny that hybrid attacks can be hate speech. The second is to affirm that hybrid attacks can be counted as group-based slurs and, moreover, to hold that all group-based attacks automatically qualify as prima facie hate speech regardless of the group. The third is to allow that hybrid attacks can be counted as group-based slurs whilst also insisting that hybrid attacks only qualify as hate speech if they satisfy the global resemblance test, that is, if they display sufficient similarities with exemplars of hate speech taking into account the five distinguishing qualities of target, style, message, act, and effect. In what follows we shall defend the third response.

3.2.2 *The Complexity of Hybrid Slurs*

Like general insults or personal pejoratives targeted at individuals (e.g. 'dickhead'), hybrid slurs (e.g. 'fatty', 'bitch') derogate people on the basis of traits or behaviours the speaker associates with the targeted individual. Speakers who use hybrid slurs do so on the basis of at least some *a posteriori* impressions of the targeted individuals, meaning the speaker has enough familiarity with the relevant people to feel justified in derogating them personally. Moreover, a hybrid slur is intended to derogate the targeted person *for a reason* and is not a random verbal attack in that sense.

However, like group-based slurs, hybrid slurs say something derogatory or insulting not only about the specific targeted individual 'but also about other people who have similar features, and so may be identified as part of a group.'[3] As with group-based slurs, hybrid slurs are in one sense a verbal assault on someone who is seen as a mere representative or stand-in for an entire group or class of persons. If the addressee is interchangeable, then the slur is really about the group.[4] Furthermore, the speaker's reason for picking out the targeted individual is partly that the target belongs, or is perceived to belong, to some group or class of persons. Typically, this reason has something to do with the speaker's hostility, prejudice, bigotry, hatred, contempt, fear, and so on. These attitudes in turn are likely to be shared with others and connected with wider practices and institutions. As Hess puts it,

> [slurs] exist as part of a broader context of bigoted attitudes, practices and institutions. If not for this context, slurs could not be any different than general insults—'motherfucker', while a vicious insult, is not a slur,

> because there aren't practices and institutions of discrimination towards a group of people routinely referred to as 'motherfuckers'.[5]

That said, hybrid slurs are not identical to paradigmatic group-based slurs like 'nigger', for example. As David Partlett explains, '[t]he fat, the short, and the ugly may all suffer unfocused defamation, but not for one moment do we treat these matters as we do race.'[6] However, it would be wrong to deduce from this that words such as 'fatty' are equivalent to general insults like 'motherfucker'. Part of the reason is that terms like 'fatty' are hybrid slurs and, therefore, partly group-based. Moreover, we may not treat terms like 'fatty' exactly as we do terms like 'nigger' but that does not necessarily mean the former are not hate speech.

Interestingly, Kent Greenawalt claims instead that the personal insult 'You are a fat slob' 'is not cast in terms of group membership at all'.[7] However, this is disputable, and it certainly cannot be inferred simply from the fact that it is addressed to specific individuals. Arguably, there are contexts in which the term 'fat slob' *is* also about a group of persons identified in terms of being overweight, obese, or plus size (or perceived as such), and does derogate members of that group, such as by conveying the attribution of further traits (e.g. *lazy*, *slovenly*) and adverse evaluations (e.g. *disgusting*, *contemptible*). As Popa-Wyatt puts it: 'If someone is overweight, calling them "fatso" is certainly targeting them as an individual, but it is again by implicitly expressing a negative attitude towards all people who are overweight.'[8]

At any rate, we shall assume for the sake of argument there is a class of slurs (hybrid slurs) that are like personal insults but also say something about groups. But does this suffice to qualify hybrid slurs as hate speech in the ordinary sense of the term? Do all hybrid slurs count as hate speech simply in virtue of being partly about groups as well as individuals? We believe not. To count as hate speech, hybrid slurs need to share further distinguishing qualities with paradigmatic slurs like 'nigger' in addition to simply being partly group-based. It is to the assessment of these similarities, as in, the global resemblance test, that we now turn.

3.2.3 *The Targets of Hybrid Slurs*

Does a hybrid slur about *any* group whatsoever count as hate speech? Customary practice or linguistic convention would suggest otherwise. According to Justina Diaz Legaspe, for example, '[m]ost commonly, slurs target people in virtue of their race, ethnicity, religion, nationality, gender or sexual orientation.'[9] Likewise, when it comes to the broader category of hate speech, a common assumption across various fields of discourse is that hate speech targets people in virtue of certain 'protected characteristics'. Although different lists of relevant characteristics are posited, they often, although not always, overlap Legaspe's list.[10]

What makes something a protected characteristic? When this question is about the legal concept(s) *hate speech*, it is not so difficult to frame the answer. It is a matter of identifying those characteristics that either are already protected under hate speech laws in given jurisdictions or for which there is a pro tanto case for making them legally protected. This pro tanto case might be made by appealing to more general claims about the fundamental purpose of hate speech laws, for example.[11]

What about the ordinary concept *hate speech*? Here the pressing question is not whether a characteristic is or should be protected under the law. Rather, the analogue question is whether a characteristic is or should be recognised and shielded by society in general. This may include being shielded indirectly via the development and internalisation of inclusive social attitudes and cultural norms or directly via widespread participation in practices of allyship and solidarity such as by ordinary people frowning on, publicly condemning, counter-speaking against, and seeking to block speech attacking people based on the characteristic; being shielded by social movements, political campaigns, and advocacy groups that work to highlight and combat the problem of speech attacks based on the characteristic; being shielded by particular civil society institutions and commercial organisations such as by universities and internet companies disallowing speech attacks based on the characteristic; and in general terms whether the characteristic is deemed by society to be worthy of being recognised and shielded in these ways. Because the ordinary concept *hate speech* serves myriad purposes,[12] and relates to countless modes of social protection, it might be even more complicated to say which characteristics ought to be protected as compared to the legal concept(s). We shall say more about these differences between the ordinary and legal concepts of hate speech in Chapter 5.

Nevertheless, we believe the correct benchmark of whether a hybrid slur attacks people on the basis of protected characteristics that are relevant to the ordinary concept *hate speech* is to look for similarities with exemplars of hate speech. Consider these examples involving hybrid slurs.

(1) Fatties deserve to die.
(2) I hate gingers.
(3) Frigids shouldn't be allowed on dating apps.

Do these words attack people based on characteristics which are sufficiently similar to the sorts of characteristics associated with exemplars of hate speech to make it credible to call them hate speech as well? As explained at the end of Chapter 2, we take it as read that resemblance as an ideal type is a function of the range, extent, degree, and salience of the similarities.

With regard to salience, relevant similarities may include anything that could explain why the relevant characteristics are or should be considered worthy of social protection. Among the features that could make some characteristics more fitting candidates for social protection than others are whether they relate to groups or classes of people that are widely recognised as facing forms of institutional, structural, or social discrimination, oppression, subordination, and disadvantage, for example.[13] Another relevant feature may include certain formal properties that some characteristics may exhibit, or partake of, including but not limited to being immutable, unchosen, or central to identity. Consider the words of the model Lily Cole recounting her painful experiences of being targeted with the slur 'ginger' as a child.

> I think it's really problematic because it's the kind of slur that's largely overlooked by teachers because it's not really politically incorrect. It's not a racial slur but it's also not dissimilar because it's something a child can't change about themselves, short of dyeing their hair.[14]

Cole is not suggesting a sameness between racial and non-racial slurs, but she is suggesting they are comparable in at least one respect. Of course, not every derogatory label that pertains to physical appearance and natural-born characteristics qualifies as a hybrid slur and as hate speech.[15] But, as we read it, Cole's comparison does not, and is not intended to, capture an essence or necessary feature of hate speech in the ordinary sense of the term. Rather, it is simply the intuition of a competent speaker that some racial and non-racial slurring terms share a similarity in that they target physical appearance and natural-born characteristics.

In fact, the literature on hate speech has spawned a whole set of formal distinctions between, on the one hand, characteristics that are thought to be deeply personal, private, internal, central to identity, unchosen, related to being, immutable, natural, universal, and, therefore, prima facie worthy of protection, and on the other hand, characteristics that are perceived to be impersonal, external, peripheral to identity, chosen, related to lifestyle, constructed, and idiosyncratic, and as such potentially unworthy of protection.[16] Provided a given slurring term targets people based on a characteristic that has a level of similarity with characteristics associated with exemplars of hate speech that matches the level of similarity that the latter characteristics have among each other, then the ordinary concept *hate speech* may be in play; or should at least be in the conversation. However, whether the slur qualifies as hate speech in the final analysis will depend on whether it also shares similarities with exemplars of hate speech based on the other distinguishing qualities of style, message, act, and effect.

In what follows we examine these other qualities. Before doing so, however, we first need to make the practical point that when social media platforms create and enforce content policies on disallowed hate speech, it is customary for them to make public the relevant protected characteristics. This is done for the sake of transparency and to give users predictability. However, it is important to critically evaluate these lists, including identifying potential inconsistencies or arbitrariness in the underpinning decisions to include or omit given characteristics.

When comparing the lists promulgated by the major social media platforms, it is evident that although there are some differences, there is also striking overlap. Consider Meta's (Facebook, Instagram) community standard on hate speech which specifies the 'protected characteristics' of 'race, ethnicity, national origin, disability, religious affiliation, caste, sexual orientation, sex, gender identity and serious disease';[17] Twitter's hateful conduct policy which lists the 'categories' of 'race, ethnicity, national origin, caste, sexual orientation, gender, gender identity, religious affiliation, age, disability, or serious disease';[18] TikTok's community guideline on hateful behaviour which enumerates the 'protected attributes' of 'caste, ethnicity, national origin, race, religion, tribe, immigration status, gender, gender identity, sex, sexual orientation, disability, serious disease';[19] Snap Inc.'s (formerly Snapchat) community guideline on terrorism, hate groups, and hate speech which itemises the protected characteristics of 'race, colour, caste, ethnicity, national origin, religion, sexual orientation, gender identity, disability or veteran status, immigration status, socio-economic status, age, weight or pregnancy status';[20] YouTube's hate speech policy which lists the 'attributes' of 'age, caste, disability, ethnicity, gender identity and expression, nationality, race, immigration status, religion, sex/gender, sexual orientation, victims of a major violent event and their kin, veteran status';[21] and WeChat's 'objectionable content' rule on hate speech which specifies 'race, ethnicity, national origin, religion, sexual orientation, physical or mental disabilities'.[22]

Nevertheless, a noticeable feature of these content policies is that, with one exception, they omit several potentially protection-worthy characteristics and, therefore, fail to disallow associated hybrid slurs. These omissions include: physical appearance (e.g. 'fatty', 'shorty', 'ginger'); occupation (e.g. 'blood sucking banker', 'ambulance chaser'); lifestyle (e.g. 'wino', 'druggie', 'scrounger', 'fitness fanatic'); sexual preferences or lack thereof (e.g. 'swinger', 'cold fish', 'frigid'); and political or ideological beliefs (e.g. 'commie', 'tree hugger', 'Tory scum'). The one exception is Snap Inc.'s community guideline which does list 'weight'.

On the one hand, these omissions echo the state of play of hate speech laws in most jurisdictions,[23] although again with some exceptions.[24] On the other hand, these omissions are also perhaps surprising given that social media platforms often emphasise the fact that content policies are not intended to track hate speech laws.[25] This separation of purpose in theory gives platforms greater scope to recognise a much wider variety of hate speech both in terms of forms of speech and protected characteristics. Moreover, the fact that social media platforms have a far more detailed, accurate, and real-time understanding of the sort of hate speech circulating on their platforms would seem to point in the direction of a much longer list of protected characteristics. Likewise, the fact that social media platforms mete out what are essentially social sanctions (e.g. content removal, reduced distribution of content, account suspension or deletion) rather than legal sanctions (e.g. fines, prison sentences, community service orders, damages), might also suggest the suitability of a wider scope of protected characteristics.

More importantly, these omissions can be open to criticism based on similarities between the omitted characteristics and the sorts of characteristics that are protected by these platforms and are associated with exemplars of hate speech. Consider three examples. First, an absence of sexual attraction (e.g. being asexual) is a characteristic that shares some notable similarities with sexual orientation (e.g. being homosexual) including being the subject of forms of social discrimination and, in terms of its formal properties, being unchosen and typically being unchanging, although with exceptions. Second, political or ideological beliefs, like religion, nationality, and gender identity, can be sources of institutional, structural, and social discrimination and, what is more, can be central to some people's identities, although not for everybody. Third, people's physical appearance can be associated with many forms of discrimination and, in addition, can be a deeply personal, sensitive, and private feature of who people are or how they see themselves but at the same time shaped by the external world including social attitudes and structures: arguably this complex property is also shared by people's physical and mental capacities.

Notwithstanding these points, one notable point of divergence among the social media platforms listed above is the fact that age and immigration status appear in roughly half of the hate speech content policies. This picture is further complicated by the fact that Facebook handles these characteristics in a unique way, neither including them in the core list of protected characteristics nor excluding them entirely from the community standard. Facebook's nuanced inclusion of age and immigration status merits further attention not least because it creates several anomalies.

Facebook's community standard on hate speech in effect describes four different varieties of protected characteristics, distinguishable in terms of both how they relate to each other and how they relate to the three types or Tiers of hate speech outlined in the standard, as in, Tier 1 (e.g. violent speech, speech about inhumanity), Tier 2 (e.g. speech expressing hatred or contempt), and Tier 3 (e.g. speech calling for exclusion).[26] The first variety is what we shall call Tier-insensitive primary protected characteristics (e.g. race). These characteristics are primary or independent in the sense that if the relevant type of content is attacking people based on these characteristics, then this may count as hate speech irrespective of whether the content is simultaneously attacking people based on other characteristics; and they are Tier-insensitive because they are protected whichever type or Tier of hate speech is involved. The second variety is Tier-sensitive primary protected characteristics (e.g. immigration status). These characteristics are also primary, but they are Tier-sensitive meaning they only qualify or operate as primary protected characteristics when a particular Tier of hate speech is in play (namely Tier 1). The third variety is Tier-insensitive secondary protected characteristics (e.g. age). These characteristics are secondary or dependent (or 'quasi-protected' as Facebook calls them) in the sense that content attacking people based on these characteristics only counts as hate speech when the content also attacks people based on at least one primary protected characteristic at the same time; and they are Tier-insensitive because they are always secondary protected characteristics whichever Tier of hate speech is involved. The fourth variety is Tier-sensitive secondary protected characteristics (e.g. occupation, veteran status). These characteristics are also secondary, but they are Tier-sensitive, meaning they only qualify or operate as secondary protected characteristics when a particular Tier of hate speech is in play (namely Tier 1).

This complex structure of rules creates several anomalies. In the case of age, for example, one obvious anomaly is the fact that, based on its community standard, Facebook would probably treat as hate speech a hybrid attack on people based on their age plus gender, for example, but would not treat as hate speech a similar attack purely based on age, unlike Twitter, YouTube, and Snap Inc, who would treat the latter as hate speech because they designate age a primary protected characteristic. Consider this pair of examples.

(4) I hate old men.
(5) I hate old bastards.

Based on the standard, Facebook would probably treat (4) as disallowed hate speech because it is based on a primary and Tier-insensitive secondary protected characteristic, but would not treat (5) as disallowed hate speech because it is only based on a secondary protected characteristic. Yet we believe both (4) and (5) ought to be treated as potential hate speech in the ordinary sense of the term because they involve attacks based on the characteristic of age (whether chronological age, biological age, or age presentation) and because of similarities with other standard protected characteristics such as sex, gender identity, and gender presentation. For one thing, both age and sex or gender can be, and often are, associated with widely recognised forms of discrimination such as discrimination in the workplace. These characteristics also share several formal similarities. For one thing, both sex at birth and chronological age are beyond people's control, although with the differences that people can seek to change some features of their sex but nobody can change their chronological age purely of their own volition, and all people experience changes to their chronological age beyond their control but only a small minority of people experience changes to their sex beyond their control (e.g. people with diverse sex development). Moreover, both gender identity and biological age may exhibit some features that reflect or result from personal choices as well as some features that are ascriptive and unchosen. Finally, both gender presentation and age presentation can be central to people's identity in the sense of being intimately bound up with sense of self.

A second anomaly relates to immigration status. Based on its community standard, Facebook treats attacks on people purely based on their immigration status as hate speech only if they involve Tier 1 type attacks, whereas TikTok and YouTube do not distinguish in this way. Consider this pair of examples.

(6) Immigrants deserve to drown like vermin.
(7) I hate all immigrants including the so-called dreamers, aka anchor babies.

Facebook would probably treat (6) as disallowed hate speech because it is Tier 1 hate speech, but not (7) because it is not Tier 1 hate speech. But we believe (6) and (7) are equally strong candidates for classification as hate speech because they attack people based on immigration status, and this characteristic shares some notable similarities with archetypal protected characteristics like nationality. Once again, both types of characteristics are associated with other forms of discrimination besides the hate speech itself. Furthermore, both share certain formal properties. For example, both nationality and immigration status can be matters that juxtapose where people happened to have been born with where they now live but can also be things that, during their lives, people may seek to change or can be forced to change through no fault of their own. In addition, both characteristics can be either central or peripheral to identity depending on the person concerned.

A third anomaly relates to veteran status. Based on its community standard, Facebook treats attacks based on people's veteran status as hate speech only if they are combined with at least one primary protected characteristic and involve Tier 1 type attacks, as contrasted with YouTube's policy, at least as written, which protects veteran status across the board. Consider this pair of examples.

(8) Suicide is too good for male Vietnam veterans; let's napalm these men to see how they like it.
(9) Vietnam vets are violent criminals.

Facebook would most likely treat (8) as disallowed hate speech because it is combined with gender and involves Tier 1 hate speech, but would not disallow (9) because it is not combined with a primary protected characteristic even though it is a Tier 1 type attack. Once again, we believe both (8) and (9) are apt to be considered hate speech because the characteristic of veteran status bears a resemblance to archetypal protected characteristics such as religion. Veteran status, like religion, has been a basis of institutional, structural, and social discrimination in many countries at different times. Furthermore, veteran status and religion share a number of formal similarities. For example, both religion and veteran status may relate to behaviours that can be in one sense chosen yet in another sense unchosen. For instance, both things done in the name of religion and in the name of war can be done by individuals operating within the commands and structures of religious and military institutions. Moreover, both religion and veteran status can be sources of pride or guilt and also central to the self or peripheral to the self, depending on the person concerned.

3.2.4 *The Message of Hybrid Slurs*

Some hybrid slurs convey negative stereotypes on a par with how paradigmatic examples of hate speech such as 'nigger' can convey negative stereotypes, as described in Chapter 2. Consider hybrid slurs relating to women.

(10) Bitch.
(11) Slut.

Depending on the speaker, context, and recipients, these hybrid slurs may convey the following messages.

(10a) *A malicious, spiteful, or overbearing woman.*
(11a) *A promiscuous woman.*

Interestingly, hybrid slurs like (10) and (11) can also express, imply, presuppose, or infer standards or norms that the women concerned fail to live up to. In the words of Diane Felmlee et al.,

> Calling a woman a 'bitch' in an aggressive message, for example, implies that she is not conforming to the expectations that she should be 'sugar and spice and all things nice.' Identifying a woman as a 'whore' or 'slut' means that she falls far out of line with the norm of sexual inexperience.[27]

These are instances of a more general type of slur that Legaspe calls 'normalizing slurs'.[28]

As outlined in Chapter 2, paradigmatic group-based slurs operate most frequently as nouns occurring in place of the name of a person or group, but they can also sometimes occur as adjectives referring to properties or qualities. Therefore, we believe it is telling that gendered hybrid slurs like 'bitch' can also play the same syntactical roles as paradigmatic group-based slurs. Compare these examples.

(12) He is a nigger.
(13) I hate niggers.
(14) I would hate to be a nigger.
(15) I would hate to have nigger genes.
(16) He has a nigger state of mind.
(17) She is a bitch.
(18) I hate bitches.
(19) I would hate to be a bitch.
(20) I would hate to have bitch chromosomes.
(21) She has a bitch state of mind.

If, despite these similar syntactical roles, certain people in society or particular social media platforms are more likely to recognise 'nigger' as hate speech than 'bitch', then in some instances this may say more about their level of gender awareness than it does about how these slurring terms are actually used and the meanings they convey in the relevant social contexts, especially if other members of society and other platforms recognise both slurs as prima facie hate speech.

We note with interest that Facebook's Tier 3 category of hate speech disallows 'Content that describes or negatively targets people with slurs, where slurs are defined as words that inherently create an atmosphere of exclusion and intimidation against people on the basis of a protected characteristic, often because these words are tied to historical discrimination, oppression, and violence'.[29] Yet there is evidence to suggest that although Facebook treats 'nigger' as a designated slur within at least some of its 'markets' (given parts of the world for moderation purposes), it does not treat gendered slurs like 'bitch' and 'slut' as designated slurs, that is, as insulting labels for women as a group. The evidence includes Facebook Oversight Board case decisions relating to the slurs 'son of a bitch', 'fag', and 'nigger', in which the Board explains how Facebook officials clarified to the Board that 'fag' and 'nigger' are designated slurs in the relevant markets, but at the same time the Board says nothing about Facebook treating 'bitch' as a designated slur.[30] Moreover, a recent study of Facebook's removal practices, reveals that the terms 'bitch' and 'slut' are not always removed by Facebook but sometimes removed and sometimes left depending on the context.[31] Therefore, it is likely that Facebook would treat (12)–(16) as disallowed hate speech but not (17)–(21).

Instead, Facebook's community standard lists 'bitch' as an example of the sort of language that is disallowed under its Tier 2 category of hate speech in the event that it qualifies as: 'Profane terms or phrases with the intent to insult, including, but not limited to: fuck, bitch, motherfucker.'[32] In other words, under Facebook's standard, although the word 'bitch' is not in itself hate speech since it is not treated as an insulting label (slur) for women as a group on a par with the designated slur 'nigger', the word 'bitch' is disallowed if it is used to insult women or any group identified by a protected category, and if the group has already been independently picked out by another word in the sentence, thus making 'bitch' on a par with the general insult 'motherfucker'.[33] Therefore, Facebook would almost certainly deem the following as disallowed hate speech.

(22) All women are motherfuckers.
(23) All women are bitches.
(24) All men are motherfuckers.
(25) All men are bitches.

By contrast, most probably Facebook would not deem the following to be disallowed hate speech.

(26) All bitches are motherfuckers.
(27) All bitches are cunts.

However, we believe this way of categorising 'bitch' has the (unintended) effect of overlooking a major semantic ingredient of many uses of the word, namely that it is a derogatory description of women or a derogatory label for the property of being a woman or a norm-violating woman. To clarify, we are not suggesting the word 'bitch' always semantically encodes these derogatory descriptions and labels. Even so, we are saying that typically the word at least either implies, presupposes, or infers these descriptions and labels. To focus exclusively on encoded meaning and to ignore implied, presuppositional, and inferential content is arbitrary from a semantic as well as social and moral point of view. Furthermore, we are not singling out Facebook for special criticism. Other social media platforms may also fail to recognise 'bitch' as a slur and prima facie hate speech, but their acts of misrecognition can be even less transparent because they do not provide to the public as many concrete illustrations of disallowed hate speech as Facebook does. The lack of recognition or awareness of 'bitch' as a gendered slur is also echoed in some courtrooms, for example.[34] Nevertheless, we believe it matters that Facebook seems to have analogised the term 'bitch' not to the slur 'nigger' but to the general insult 'motherfucker'.

It matters because slurring terms are widely recognised as paradigmatic examples of ordinary hate speech in a way that general insults are not. As explained in Chapter 2, we believe this has something to do with the group- and identity-based nature of slurs. General insults like 'asshole' and 'motherfucker' typically do not derogate the group of all the assholes or the group of all the motherfuckers, and are not tied to fundamental aspects of people's identities, such as aspects of the self they identify with. Slurs like 'nigger' and 'fag' are a different kettle of fish precisely because they do derogate all African Americans and all homosexual people, and because they can implicate aspects of identity, as in, characteristics that victims may understand as being important parts of who they are and worthy of protection. Of course, people targeted with these slurs tend not to identify as 'nigger' or 'fag' as these carry derogatory connotations. But they do typically identify with the groups referred to by the neutral counterparts of these terms, to wit, 'African Americans' and 'homosexual people'.

As mentioned above, part of Facebook's differentiated treatment of 'bitch' and 'nigger' may have to do with its implicit reliance on the distinction between encoded or expressed meaning, on the one hand, and other sorts of implied, presuppositional, or inferential content, on the other hand. However, that might not be the only thing going on here. Perhaps Facebook's content policy teams and moderators are also making an assumption (which may or may not be correct) that the word 'bitch' is referentially restrictive in a manner they think 'nigger' is not. For example, maybe Facebook presumes that 'bitch' refers in a derogatory way to a subcategory or subset of women or is an insulting label for the qualified property of being a specific type of woman – for example, *uppity women* or *being an uppity woman not just any woman* – whereas 'nigger' refers in a derogatory way to *all African Americans* or is an insulting label for the unqualified property of *being lazy, stupid, and aggressive, all because of being African American.* We shall discuss these sorts of selective attacks in Section 3.3.

However, we believe this assumption might be not merely incorrect in its own terms but also misses the real point about gendered slurs. Even using 'bitch' to refer to a subset of women presupposes that this subset fails to live up to a norm of expected behaviour for the larger group or class, namely, *women.* This presuppositional content is itself bigoted and controlling. In other words, such uses clearly pertain to the group identity, or social status, of targeted individuals *qua* women. A particular woman or even a subset of women are attacked for failing to live up to gender norms about how women as an entire group or class of persons should behave or comport themselves.

We believe similar analyses apply to 'slut'. On the surface, 'slut' might appear closer to being a general insult because it relates to sexual behaviour. Indeed, Facebook's Tier 2 category of hate speech lists 'slut' as an example of '[d]erogatory terms related to sexual activity', on a par with 'pervert'; both of which can be disallowed hate speech when targeted at an independently identified group based on protected characteristics.[35] This means Facebook would regard the following as hate speech.

(28) Women are sluts.

But, assuming Facebook does not treat 'slut' as a designated slur, Facebook would almost certainly not view the following as disallowed hate speech.

(29) I hate sluts.

Once again, this might be because Facebook would treat 'sluts' as referring to a subgroup or subset (*promiscuous women*) and not to a whole group, based on protected characteristics. Importantly, Facebook's Tiers 2 and 3 of hate speech do not contain all subgroups catchalls, unlike Tier 1 ('including all groups').[36] However, we believe even if promiscuous sexual behaviour is one of the main descriptive properties conveyed by the term 'sluts', another main part of its implied content, presuppositional, or inferential content is a bigoted message about women in general. The idea of promiscuous *women* is not incidental or tangential to the conveyed content of 'sluts'.[37] Contrast this with the general insult 'She is a motherfucker', concerning which the gender of the person targeted with the slur is typically accidental or tangential to the core message. In other words, being about promiscuous people may be a key part of the encoded meaning of 'slut', but being about women is also a main part of the implied, presuppositional, or inferential content of 'slut'. By contrast, being about women is at most merely a contingent part of the content of 'She is a motherfucker'.

On the basis of these analyses, we would classify both 'bitch' and 'slut' as slurring terms and potentially hate speech depending on other aspects of the global resemblance test. Perhaps a defender of Facebook's position, however, would insist that context is king and that sometimes people call men, including gay men, 'bitches' and 'sluts'; and sometimes this could be hate speech. Consider these statements.

(30) Gay men are bitches.
(31) Men are sluts.

Even so, it is important to understand the multiple ways (30) and (31) could be hate speech; first, (30) and (31) may be hate speech because in a literal sense they say something derogatory or insulting about groups (gay men, men) who are identified on the basis of protected characteristic (gender, sexual orientation); second, because they indirectly convey (express, presuppose, imply, or infer) messages that are derogatory about a different protected group, namely women. These examples fall into a category of grey area hate speech we call indirect attacks, to be discussed in Section 3.6.

3.2.5 *The Acts Performed by Hybrid Slurs*

Another key to determining whether hybrid slurs count as hate speech is to consider whether they are typically used to perform paradigmatic acts associated with the ordinary concept *hate speech* (pragmatics).[38] In Chapter 2 we provided a long list of acts associated with the ordinary concept *hate speech* across various fields of discourse. In some of the academic literature, for example, hate speech is analysed in terms of one or more of the following sorts of acts: *disparage* (*judge or present as less estimable*), *degrade* (*rank as fundamentally inferior*), *dehumanise* (*judge or present as non-human or less than fully human*), *humiliate* (*disparage or degrade in front of others*), *prejudge* (*making assumptions about, stereotype, caricature, misrecognise*), *disempower* (*deprive of rights and powers*), *discriminate* (*enact a discriminatory policy or practice*), *marginalise* (*make others feel unwelcome, excluded, or Other*), and *turn people against* (*reinforce, perpetuate, legitimise, or incite bigotry, hatred, contempt, discrimination, or violence against*).[39] It is not difficult to link group-based slurs like 'nigger' with the performance of these paradigmatic hate speech acts. What then about hybrid slurs?

According to the feminist activist Joreen, there are clear overlaps between the kinds of acts carried out by people using the prototypical racial slur 'nigger' and what we have called the hybrid slur 'bitch'. As she puts it, '[l]ike the term "nigger," "bitch" serves the social function of isolating and discrediting a class of people who do not conform to the socially accepted patterns of behavior'.[40] We believe the same overlaps exist for other hybrid slurs as well, such as slurring terms relating to physical size and weight such as 'fatty', 'fatso', 'lard ass', and 'salad dodger'. These words can be, and often are, used to *disparage*, *humiliate*, *discriminate*, *marginalise*, and *turn others against* overweight people and, therefore, clearly bear some of the hallmarks of fatist hate speech.[41]

That said, whether or not a speaker has the power or authority to perform paradigmatic hate speech acts may depend on one or more of several different types of background circumstances (or felicity conditions) outlined in Chapter 2. So, if these background circumstances are not present or are only partly present, a speaker may be less likely to have the relevant power or authority, and as a result may be less likely to successfully perform the relevant acts. In that event, the speaker might still use the slurring term, but the usage might not rise to the level of hate speech, at least in terms of the paradigmatic hate speech acts, based on the global resemblance test. For example, as Katharine Gelber argues, the question of whether the pejorative 'fatty' counts as hate speech in general may partly depend on extra-linguistic facts about whether overweight people and third parties engage in counterspeech against the pejorative, whether overweight people have been able to rehabilitate and reclaim the meanings of terms like 'fatty' through fat and proud campaigns, say, and whether overweight people are victims of what she calls 'systemic discrimination'.[42]

However, it is also important to distinguish between the general power any speaker might have to use a word like 'fatty' to perform paradigmatic hate speech acts within a society, and power that particular speakers might obtain at the subsocietal level, that is, within specific situational contexts and subcommunities. Suppose a group of adolescents are picking teams for an informal football match during lunchbreak and one of the team captains says the following, to which nobody in the group objects.

(32) Of course, I'm not gonna pick fatty over here so instead I'll pick John.

Within this particular communicative setting or situational context, the speaker may successfully use the word 'fatty' to perform acts of *social discrimination*, *humiliation*, and *marginalisation*, irrespective of whether or not it is true that overweight or obese people face systemic discrimination in society in general.

We have discussed the case of fat-shaming insults *qua* hybrid slurs and hate speech, but what about insults targeting people due to their thinness (e.g. 'skinny', 'scrawny') or other aspects of physical appearance such as nose size (e.g. 'gonzo', 'big nose'), hair colour (e.g. 'ginger', 'carrot top'), eye shape (e.g. 'bug eyes'), height (e.g. 'shorty', 'beanpole'), or even eyebrow shape (e.g. 'beetle-browed', 'monobrow')? Applying the global resemblance test to these other sorts of insults once again involves an assessment of whether there are sufficient similarities between such words and exemplars of hate speech, including but not limited to assessing whether the words are at least partly cast in terms of group membership (hybrid slurs), whether they convey prototypical hate speech messages, and whether speakers have the power (generally or situationally) to use the words to perform paradigmatic hate speech acts such as to *derogate*, *disparage*, *dehumanise*, *humiliate*, *prejudge*, *disempower*, *discriminate*, *marginalise*, or *turn others against* the targeted individuals.

These determinations may be more straightforward for some words than others. Take derogatory labels for people with bushy eyebrows or bulbous eyes. Intuitively, insults like 'monobrow' and 'bug eyes' do not seem to be hate speech and the resemblance approach might explain this as these words not being cast in terms of group membership and also speakers lacking power to perform paradigmatic hate speech acts partly because the targeted individuals are typically able to engage in counterspeech and blocking, and are not subject to systemic discrimination, for example.[43] When it comes to other labels for physical appearance, however, the picture can be mixed. To give one illustration, there may be societies in which having less common hair colour or nontypical height predicts forms of societal discrimination (e.g. marital prospects, social capital) but does not necessarily predict that targets experience higher barriers to executing counterspeech and blocking.[44] Here the question 'How alike is this to standard hate speech?' may partly rest on socio-linguistic analyses of the relative power of speakers (generally or situationally) to use these words to perform paradigmatic hate speech acts given the presence of some felicity conditions but the absence of others.

However, there also remains a conceptual ambiguity, over and above the empirical challenges. What if there are societies in which speakers typically lack the requisite power to use a given set of slurring terms to perform certain acts associated with Matsuda's original list of examples of hate speech (e.g. *disempower*, *discriminate*, *turn people against*) but nonetheless are in a position to use these same slurs to perform other acts associated with these original examples and the extended body of exemplars linked to the ordinary concept *hate speech* (e.g. *prejudge*, *disparage*, *humiliate*)? Would this still be hate speech? This is a genuine dilemma, and we believe it stems from the fact that the ordinary concept *hate speech* is a family resemblances concept.

Even so, we believe the question 'Is this hate speech?' is answerable by drawing reasonable pairwise comparisons. So, if there are societies in which the term 'carrot top' shares in common with 'nigger' not only that it *derogates* on the basis of a group identity but also that it can be used by speakers to *prejudge* or *stereotype* people with ginger or red hair (e.g. as being *fiery*, *supernaturally endowed*, *weird looking*, or *sexually voracious*), and that it can be used by speakers to *marginalise* others, for example, then this term could potentially count as hate speech. Likewise, if there are societies in which the derogatory label 'shorty' shares in common with 'nigger' not only the fact that it is cast in terms of group membership but also that it can be used by speakers to *pigeonhole* people who are below average height (e.g. as *lower status*, *less capable*, *less masculine*, *less athletic*, *less attractive*, *funny looking*, or *ridiculous*), and that it can be used by speakers to *humiliate* others, for example, then this term could also potentially qualify as hate speech.

At this point it might be objected that the analysis is in danger of making the ordinary concept *hate speech* too capacious. But we believe the analysis does not render the ordinary concept too large to be able to perform the myriad social purposes a society can reasonable expect it to perform (see Chapter 5). Moreover, this analysis does not manufacture capaciousness but accurately reflects and explains it. Usage of the term 'hate speech' across media, popular culture, and public discourse is broad, and it is broad because competent users are in the habit of analogising.

The idea that slurs targeting people with ginger or red hair qualifies as hate speech is commonplace in popular culture. Consider three examples. In a 2005 episode of *South Park*, Cartman, a character partly defined by his racist, xenophobic, and misogynist attitudes, gives a student presentation about 'ginger kids', who he claims are 'disgusting', suffer from an incurable disease called 'gingervitis', have 'no souls', are 'like vampires', and 'could envelope our lives in blackness for all time'. Another character, Kyle, objects, 'That's not a lecture, it's a hate speech.'[45] This scene is a satire about people who harbour prejudices, showing how irrational, stupid, or ridiculous they can become. But within the scene there is no attempt to deny or diminish the existence of gingerism itself. Indeed, one of the other children in class frankly admits to also being 'creeped out' by gingers.[46] Gingerism is being analogised to racism. And on this basis, anti-ginger speech is being analogised to racist speech. As a result, 'even if there is something humorous about the scene, the use of the term "hate speech" does not seem unintelligible'.[47]

Second, consider this tweet from the Simply Red frontman Mick Hucknall from 2011: 'Let's play a game: whenever you read 'ginger' try replacing it with 'black' or 'asian' and see how it reads.'[48] Hucknall is explicitly asking people to reflect on patterns of similarity between anti-ginger speech and canonical hate speech relating to race and ethnicity.

Third, consider instances where the slurs 'nigger' and 'ginger' are used to convey derogatory ideas about targets being ugly or repulsive, or possessing supernatural powers such as the stock characters of the redheaded witch or the magical negro in popular culture. Based on these messages, both slurs can be used not merely to *stereotype* but also to *dehumanise* the target groups.

3.2.6 *The Effects of Hybrid Slurs*

A further line of comparison important for assessing whether hybrid slurs can qualify as hate speech is to ask whether the use of hybrid slurs is likely to have the same or similar effects to those associated with exemplars of hate speech. In Chapter 2, we provided a long list of such effects including not merely psychological, emotional, and dignitary harms but also an increased risk of bigotry, discrimination, and violence, and adverse societal consequences such as damage to social cohesion, public disorder, and even democratic and political delegitimisation. We do not suggest that all of these or similar effects are present for every hybrid slur, but we do believe if a hybrid slur can be associated with at least one effect similar to the effects of paradigmatic slurs like 'nigger', then this matters for global resemblance.

Consider derogatory words relating to people's physical size or weight such as 'fatty'. As already mentioned earlier in the chapter, Greenawalt distinguishes insults hurled at overweight people from slurs and epithets relating to race, ethnicity, religion, sexual orientation, and gender. He notes the latter may 'reinforce prejudices and feelings of inferiority',[49] underpin 'social patterns of domination',[50] 'injure the status and prospects of members of groups',[51] and 'contribute to structural subordination'.[52] But when it comes to the insult 'You fat slob', he contends 'the effect of most such insults is contained and dissipates fairly quickly'.[53]

However, this fails to recognise that, partly because words like 'fatty' can carry messages and perform acts somewhat similar to those associated with 'nigger', the former also has the potential to produce effects somewhat similar to the latter. Suppose the society is one in which overweight people face not only widespread negative judgment (e.g. anti-fat attitudes) and prejudiced cultural norms (e.g. beauty industry norms) but also institutional discrimination (e.g. employment, income, and career advancement prospects) and societal discrimination (e.g. marital prospects, social capital). Against this general backdrop, it is not difficult to see how, for example, a boss repeatedly calling an employee 'fatty' could trigger acts of discrimination in that particular workplace. To give another example, suppose a group of people are connected on social media, whether formally through a private Facebook group or informally as people who all happen to follow the same person on Twitter, partly because they respect or value the opinions of the person who set up the Facebook group or of the social influencer they are following on Twitter. Suppose this 'trusted source' labels someone a 'salad dodger' and other group members and followers do not counter it. This could perpetuate and reinforce negative attitudes and prejudiced norms within these social networks and could make overweight people feel worthless, humiliated, and shamed, and even isolated, excluded, and unwelcome. Indeed, insofar as social media in general is a context in which physical appearance is valorised above all else, in which beauty norms create impossible expectations and can evince self-loathing, and in which overweight people are socialised to believe they fall below the expected norms and are less estimable, then it is not hard to see how the slur 'fatty' could produce in some ways similar effects to those associated with slurs like 'darky', 'inky', 'spook', 'tar baby', 'choco', 'blick', and 'shitskin' which play on racist beauty norms around skin colour, including harm to self-esteem and potentially an increase in self-destructive behaviours.[54]

Usage of the gendered slur 'bitch' can also have perlocutionary effects in some ways like those associated with paradigmatic slurs like 'nigger'. As Keith Allan explains, the slur 'bitch' 'typically ascribes the female human being as aggravating (i.e. of confrontational, disagreeable or malicious character)'; moreover, when it is used in confrontational speech situations as an insult, a speaker calling someone a 'bitch' can have 'the perlocutionary effect (perhaps realizing the agent's perlocutionary intention) of demeaning someone and/or of affronting or outraging them by manifest arrogance, scorn, contempt, or insolence'.[55] Similarly, in their recent analysis of Incel discourse, including the prevalent use of the slur 'bitches' and similarly gendered expressive attacks, Tranchese and Sugiura argue that 'Incel misogyny is a speech act whose perlocutionary effect is to silence women, police their behavior and, ultimately, harm them'.[56] These effects are often the reverse of those experienced by hate speakers who 'experience a perlocutionary effect of feeling superior to their target'.[57] This seems especially true of Incel usage of misogynistic slurs like 'bitch'; part of the psychological purpose of which is to make male Incels feel better about themselves, as though filling an emotional void or soothing insecurity.

Interestingly, the potential adverse effects on women of certain (although not necessarily all) uses of gendered slurs like 'bitch' echo the rationale given by Facebook for having a community standard on hate speech in the first place.

> We believe people use their voice and connect more freely when they don't feel attacked on the basis of who they are. That is why we don't allow hate speech on Facebook. It creates an environment of intimidation and exclusion, and in some cases may promote offline violence.[58]

This serves, once again, to underscore the anomaly that Facebook treats 'nigger' as a designated slur in various markets but not 'bitch'. Indeed, even in countries whose highest courts have adopted aggressive freedom of expression protecting doctrines such as the United States, the courts have sometimes recognised the pernicious discriminatory effects on women wrought by uses of the slur 'bitch'.[59]

Turning to a final set of examples, is it plausible to classify as potential hate speech even hybrid slurs targeting individuals on the basis of their political or ideological beliefs (e.g. 'commie', 'Repuglican' [*sic*], 'Tory scum', 'tree hugger', 'feminazi', 'gammon', 'pro-deather') partly on account of having the same or similar harmful effects as paradigmatic racial or religious slurs, for example?[60] We take this to be as much an empirical question as a conceptual one. Surely part of the answer lies in a careful exploration of history and context. Have there been times when being labelled a 'commie' or 'red', for example, has had dire consequences for the intended targets of these political slurs, such as a heightened risk of falling prey to social and professional discrimination and even to authorisations of official persecution, on a par with the devastating effects of being labelled with religious slurs at certain moments in history such as being called a 'marrano' in Spain during the middle ages, especially when used by persons in positions of institutional or judicial authority? The McCarthy era in the United States would seem to demonstrate there have been.[61]

More generally, do political slurs reflect a characteristic that has in the past been a source of social friction or even schism of the sort that, like a powder keg, can explode into breakdowns in social cohesion, civil strife, civil disobedience, election violence, or even civil war, when ignited by this sort of inflammatory language, especially by political leaders?[62] The history of human conflict would certainly put political or ideological beliefs into this category. In the words of Geoffrey Nunberg:

> For one thing, a derogative word qualifies as a slur only when it disparages people on the basis of properties such as race, religion, ethnic or geographical origin, gender, sexual orientation or sometimes political ideology—the deep fatalities that have historically been the focus of discrimination or social antagonisms that we see as rents in the fabric of civil society. Sailing enthusiasts deprecate the owners of motor craft as 'stinkpotters,' but we probably wouldn't call the word a slur—though the right-wingers' derogation of environmentalists as 'tree-huggers' might qualify, since that antipathy has a partisan cast.[63]

This last point is perhaps evidenced in the skirmishes and public disturbances that have arisen in the UK in recent years involving Extinction Rebellion and Insulate Britain activists and ordinary members of the public, especially around attempts by the former to block major transport links such as tube lines and motorways. This is not to suggest that every instance of a member of the public calling an environmental campaigner 'A bloody tree hugger!' will lead to a confrontation that ends in blows. But what it does suggest is that in general the use of slurs based on the characteristic of political and ideological beliefs, affiliations, or activities must be assessed as posing some risk of public disturbance, although the extent of risk depends on context.

Similarly, usage of terms like 'feminazi', particularly when combined with other provocative behaviours, has also had paradigmatic hate speech effects in the UK. Consider the heated verbal exchanges and ensuing physical confrontations between participants in LGBTQIA+ marches and counter-demonstrators exemplified at the London Pride event in 2018.[64] Just as the use of homophobic and transphobic slurs could potentially pose a threat to public order and security (including not only external security but also people's internal sense or feeling of security), so usage of anti-feminist slurs may do the same in some contexts. Generally speaking, it is not difficult to see how terms like 'feminazi' and 'TERF' might feed into climates of hatred, hostility, fear, mistrust, and resentment between different communities divided along intersecting lines of gender, politics, and ideology, analogous in some ways to slurs that speak to divisions along lines of religion, politics, and ideology.[65]

Indeed, it is common for slurs to derogate people based on multiple intersecting identities, including ethnic, religious, geographic, cultural, political, and ideological.[66] For example, in India, the term 'urban Naxal' is a derogatory label for a putative group of people who are cultural communists (Marxists or Maoists) and part of an insurgency of traditionally rural communists into urban areas as a launchpad for overthrowing the government, or simply any persons who are on the left of Indian politics and critical of the ruling Indian People's Party (BJP). In Turkey, encouraged by President Erdogan, various sections of Turkish society, government, and media use the derogatory acronym 'FETÖ' ('Fethullahist Terrorist Organisation') as a stand-in for the Hizmet (Gülen) movement, and the term '*FETÖ'cü*' ('FETÖists') for its leaders, participants, and supporters, terms which intersect aspects of religious, spiritual, political, cultural, and ideological identity. In Kenya, the term '*kihii*' ('uncircumcised male') is used in some public discourse as a derogatory label for politicians, members, and supporters of particular ethno-political coalitions and the ethno-political constituencies they represent or advocate on behalf of.[67] In Ethiopia, the term '*Woyane*' ('rebellious') was used self-referentially for decades by the minority ethnic Tigrayan people to describe their aspiration for self-determination, but when the Tigray People's Liberation Front (TPLF) became the country's ruling party in the early 1990s, other ethnic groups began to use the term as a catchall ethno-political epithet for Tigrayan people.[68] In all of these contexts, the usage of the relevant slurs can have paradigmatic hate speech effects.

To conclude this section, we have argued that hybrid slurs, depending on the context, may display enough similarities with exemplars of hate speech across the dimensions of target, style, message, act, and effect (at least four out of five) to support the conclusion that such slurs can qualify as hate speech, at least in the ordinary sense of the term.

3.3 Selective Attacks

Another cluster of grey area cases involves speech that refers to only a subset of a group or else to an amalgamated set of people who belong to multiple groups. Such language still identifies people based on protected characteristics, but it does so in referentially restrictive ways such as by picking out only subgroups of people who possess the relevant characteristic or by picking out larger groups whose members are selected on the basis of possessing two or more characteristics combined. We call these selective attacks.[69] Selective attacks may manifest different styles including slurs, stereotypes, vilification, false rumours, disparagements, dehumanising comparisons, threats, incitements, and so on, but for the sake of consistency we shall continue to cite examples of selective attacks in which slurs figure.[70]

In one mode of selective attack, the speaker uses a numerical or existential quantifier that clearly limits the number of people in the group being attacked. This mode can be illustrated with the following anti-Semitic statement.

(33) There are certainly a few Jews I wouldn't mind being wiped from the face of the Earth.

In other instances, a speaker might use language in a more subtle or oblique way to narrow down a subset of people to be attacked, such as by drawing a distinction between a group and a subgroup without explicitly specifying the basis of the distinction. Consider what are, at least on the surface, expressions of hatred towards only some African Americans, only some men, and only some women respectively.[71]

(34) I love black people, but I hate niggers.
(35) I prefer real men, I can't stand pansies.
(36) I don't hate all women, just the stuck-up bitches.

Another type of selective attack involves a speaker explicitly referring to a subgroup who possess a mash up of different characteristics, where each characteristic is directly signposted in the speech. Of the following three examples, the first involves an attack based on two classic protected characteristics (race, gender), and the others involve attacks based on a mixture of classic protected characteristics and sometimes non-protected characteristics, depending on the society or specific social media platform (sexual orientation, gender expression or presentation).

(37) I hate black women.
(38) It is the uppity white women I would shoot first.
(39) I despise butch lesbians; you'd think as women they'd know what it's like to be on the receiving end of toxic masculinity.

Alternatively, a speaker might implicitly refer to a subgroup who possess a combination of different characteristics, where each characteristic is not directly mentioned or spelled out separately but is implied or indirectly conveyed. Consider these examples, with the implied characteristics spelling out in brackets.

(40) Coconuts are race traitors and should be shunned from our black community [*race, racial sympathies or loyalties*].
(41) I hate bible-bashers [*religion, aggressive proselytising*].
(42) Whenever I come across Southern fairies I just wanna smack them in the mouth, I just can't help myself [*regional identity, effeteness or pretentiousness*].
(43) Ice queens have no right to be on this Earth [*gender, asexuality*].

3.3.1 *Selective Attacks and the Goldilocks Problem*

Selective attacks do not directly or obviously violate the rule of thumb about hate speech cited earlier in this chapter.

(R1) Hate speech is group-based.

But they do pinpoint an ambiguity in the term 'group-based' since this can be interpreted in more or less inclusive ways resulting in the following three variants.

(R1.1) Hate speech is group-based but relates to whole groups only.
(R1.2) Hate speech is group-based and relates to both whole groups and all subgroups.
(R1.3) Hate speech is group-based and relates to both whole groups and some subgroups but not all.

One of the central problems in figuring out which groups can fall within the orbit of bona fide hate speech is to find the golden mean between including too few and including too many groups, as in, the golden middle path between underinclusivity and overinclusivity. Call this the goldilocks problem.

To illustrate the problem, endorsing (R1.1) and saying that hate speech only relates to whole groups risks including too few examples under the category of hate speech (underinclusivity). Consider the following examples.

(44) I hate black people.
(45) I hate black youths.
(46) I hate black footballers.

Intuitively, it seems arbitrary to treat (44) but not (45) and (46) as examples of hate speech. There seems to be hatred and bigotry in all these examples.

Conversely, embracing (R1.2) and saying that hate speech relates to both whole groups and all subgroups risks including too many examples under the category hate speech (overerinclusivity). Consider another trio of examples.

(47) Uncle Toms are race traitors.
(48) I despise Guidos.
(49) I hate the sort of woman who dates you for a couple of weeks and then ghosts you.

To automatically count (47), (48), and (49) as examples of hate speech simply because they refer to subgroups defined partly by membership of at least one whole group linked to a protected characteristic – namely, African Americans ('Uncle Toms'), Italian Americans ('Guidos'), and women ('the sort of woman who…') – would be to ignore potentially salient differences among these examples and between these examples and paradigmatic examples of hate speech. After all, in the case of 'Uncle Tom', being Black is extremely important to the meaning of the slur in the sense that it is always part of the derogatory message. But in the case of 'Guido', although being Italian American is connected to the meaning of the word, there could be instances in which it is not the most salient part of what the speaker is saying. Finally, when it comes to 'the sort of woman who…', being a woman is clearly part of the meaning of the phrase, but it may or may not be part of the core message and its salience is highly dependent on the speaker and the circumstances of speech. Therefore, a blanket rule that counts (47), (48), and (49) as hate speech is highly questionable.

A related consequence of embracing (R1.2) is that it would seem to imply that something counts as hate speech no matter how many different characteristics are mashed together in the target group. This could mean that even descriptions that refer to microgroups of only a single individual may count as hate speech.

(50) I hate the black woman who stands across the street from my house on Friday mornings wearing her pink dressing gown and slippers, whistling the theme tune from *Casablanca* and puffing away on her Lucky Strike.

Despite the target being both Black and a woman and, therefore, implicating two protected characteristics, statement (50) seems much closer to an expression of personal antipathy than to a hate speech. This may have something to do with the fact that it refers to a subgroup of one. Moreover, to label this statement hate speech would seem to depend crucially on the state of mind and intention of the speaker. It is the sort of thing a racist would say and, if so, may imply, presuppose, or infer a disparaging commentary on Black people in general. Yet it is also something that a nonracist could say and, if so, perhaps it simply mentions rather than invokes the woman's race.

What, then, of falling back onto (R1.3) and the idea that hate speech relates to both whole groups and some subgroups but not all? This looks promising but notice that it does not in itself solve the goldilocks problem. After all, the problem then becomes how to identify the relevant subgroups. Without properly explaining and justifying the grounds for the distinction, (R1.3) could seem arbitrary. For example, it might be intuitive to distinguish an example like (50) from the following statement.

(51) I have nothing but contempt for these Uncle Toms who are so obedient and servile to white people, all the while betraying their own kind.

Suppose for the sake of argument that such uses of 'Uncle Tom' could be classified as hate speech under (R1.3). The question is: what is it about (51) that makes it correct to treat it as hate speech but not (50)? It is fair to say (51) is about a subset of African Americans, but then again, so is (50), strictly speaking. So, why is an attack on the referents of the term 'Uncle Tom' the sort of attack, and by implication the sort of subgroup, appropriately connected with the ordinary concept *hate speech*?

Perhaps terms like 'Uncle Tom' in a literal sense refer to a subgroup but implicitly or indirectly speak to or provide disparaging commentary on the larger, whole group. For example, 'Uncle Tom' might imply that people who are referred to by this term possess an undesirable trait that is in fact possessed to some degree by all African Americans. Or perhaps the term presupposes the idea of a latent potentiality that is present in all African Americans, even though it is not widely prevalent in the group. Alternatively, it might presuppose some norm concerning how true or good African Americans are supposed to behave or carry themselves that people who are labelled 'Uncle Tom' fail to live up to or violate ('normalizing slurs'[72]).

In fact, 'Uncle Tom' seems to be an example of a broader category of speech that we shall call archetypes or stock character labels. This also includes terms like 'Guido', 'Mammy', 'Picaninny', 'Jezebel', 'Sapphire', 'Pocahontas', and 'Karen' but also 'welfare queen' and 'angry black woman'. Of course, not all uses of archetypes or stock character labels will necessarily count as slurring uses or hate speech. Consider the following use of the term 'Guido' between a speaker and his friend who are both Italian Americans.

(52) You are a true Guido.

In the case of (52), 'Guido' may consciously refer to some but not all Italian Americans (and not only Italian Americans) who exhibit a type of Guido culture based on clothing, behaviour, attitudes, and so on. Moreover, in this speech context, the meaning of 'Guido' is (re-)claimed as something positive; as an identity not only set apart from standard Italian American identity and the wider White Anglo-Saxon Protestant (WASP) identity of North-eastern America but also as something to be proud of and aspire to. Indeed, it may even signify a discrete ethnic group separate from the group Italian American.[73]

Nevertheless, there may be other derogatory or slurring uses of 'Guido' that do implicitly say something about all Italian Americans. Consider this statement.

(53) I despise these Guidos in Jersey who walk around with muscle T-shirts and gold jewellery like they own the place.

If spoken by an Italian American, (53) might presuppose a norm concerning how true or good Italian Americans are supposed to behave or carry themselves. If so, then the utterance of (53) may constitute an attempt to *censure*, *stigmatise*, or even *control* the behaviour of others – both those who do and those who do not currently conform to the norm. These acts may replicate or be close cousins of prototypical hate speech acts. Alternatively, if (53) is spoken or received by someone who is prejudiced against Italian Americans in general, then the speaker's meaning or received meaning could be a message about what to some extent all Italian Americans are like. In that scenario, 'Guido' is an allusion to extreme or striking examples of undesirable traits allegedly shared by every Italian American to greater or lesser degrees.

We shall discuss archetypes or stock character labels in greater length in Chapter 4 (as forms of what we call identity attacks), including when and why they might count as hate speech. However, at this stage we want to make the broader point that (R1.3) can provide a solution to the goldilocks problem but only when it is combined with a plausible set of reasons for distinguishing between those selective attacks on subgroups that are and those that are not covered under the ordinary concept *hate speech*. In what follows we attempt to furnish such reasons once again appealing to the global resemblance test. Before doing so, however, we shall first provide an illustration of how Facebook has struggled with the goldilocks problem.

3.3.2 Selective Attacks under Facebook's Community Standard on Hate Speech

We suggest the history of Facebook's evolving community standard on hate speech over the last decade or so can be interpreted in one sense as an unfolding series of attempts to solve the goldilocks problem. It is a story of shifting perceptions both within Facebook and from society at large that its standard was at first underinclusive then became overinclusive and is now either just right or back to underinclusive again. It also serves as a cautionary tale of how, in the absence of coherent and well-thought-out reasons for drawing distinctions between different subgroups, definitions of hate speech can very quickly seem anomalous and arbitrary.

Prior to 2011, Facebook's content policy on hate speech was briefly mentioned in its Statement of Rights and Responsibilities shared with users. 'You will not post content that: is hateful, threatening, or pornographic; incites violence; or contains nudity or graphic or gratuitous violence.' What qualified as hateful content remained opaque. Therefore, even when users had content removed under the rules specified in the Statement, they could only guess at what it was about the content that qualified as hateful. This situation improved somewhat in 2011 when Facebook made public on its platform several 'community standards' relating to disallowed content including hate speech. The community standard provided a more detailed description of what Facebook deemed hate speech, although it did not amount to a carbon copy of its authoritative internal content policy and enforcement guidelines on hate speech. Facebook also issued ad hoc public statements from time to time hinting at key parts of the internal policy. However, in June 2017 the investigative news agency *Pro Publica* published a bombshell report on Facebook's internal policy on hate speech. The report highlighted the following anomalies.

> Facebook deletes curses, slurs, calls for violence and several other types of attacks only when they are directed at 'protected categories'—based on race, sex, gender identity, religious affiliation, national origin, ethnicity, sexual orientation and serious disability/disease. It gives users broader latitude when they write about 'subsets' of protected categories. White men are considered a group because both traits are protected, while female drivers and black children, like radicalized Muslims, are subsets, because one of their characteristics is not protected.[74]

The report was picked up by tech journalists and social commentators alike, who opined that these sorts of examples demonstrated how 'bad' Facebook was at moderating hate speech on its platform.[75]

Setting aside the public shaming of Facebook and how this might have subsequently played into its evolving standard, it is worth reflecting on the different sorts of anomalies that could result from limiting the definition of hate speech to only attacks on entire characteristics and whole groups. Consider the following pairs.

(54) Muslims should be hunted down and killed.
(55) Radicalised Muslims should be hunted down and killed.
(56) Blacks are apes.
(57) Black children are apes.
(58) Females are inferior.
(59) Female drivers are inferior.

At first glance, it seems arbitrary from a moral and conceptual point of view to define hate speech such that (54), (56), and (58) count as hate speech but not (55), (57), and (59). Arguably, although these examples have differences, there may be sufficient similarities between the target, style, message, act, and effect of these examples to warrant calling them all hate speech. Interestingly, similar sorts of debates are echoed in courtroom interpretations of the legal concept(s) *hate speech*, such as whether using threatening words to stir up hatred against only radicalised Muslims should still count as illegal hate speech under offences of stirring up religious hatred.[76]

More importantly, there was nothing in Facebook's general definition of hate speech back in the 2010s ('we define the term to mean direct and serious attacks on any protected category of people based on their race, ethnicity, national origin, religion, sex, gender, sexual orientation, disability or disease'[77]) that would seem to justify the drawing of distinctions between attacks based on entire categories and attacks based on subcategories. Of course, Facebook has a principled commitment to defending the freedom of self-expression of, and social connection among, its users, and this might provide a general rationale for distinction-drawing of this kind. But arguably, these broad principles do not in themselves justify drawing the line in the specific ways Facebook seemed to be doing in the 2010s. In other words, protecting self-expression may explain the general practice of distinguishing examples, but it underdetermines the justifiability of specific distinctions in the absence of a particular doctrine or rule about what protecting self-expression actually demands.

At any rate, in April 2018 Facebook took the unprecedented step of sharing with the public an expanded community standard on hate speech that would, in its own words, 'closely mirror' its existing internal policy and enforcement guidelines.[78] This move was unprecedented among major social media platforms operating hate speech codes at the time. (Even now, other platforms do not match the detail and comprehensiveness of Facebook's public-facing community standard on hate speech.) Speaking at a launch event for the roll out, Facebook's Vice President of Global Product Management, Monika Bickert, directly addressed the issue of subsets. She was reported to have confirmed that, under the platform's evolving public standard and internal policy, the characteristic of being Black children, for example, 'would be protected' from attacks on the platform: the implication being that statements like (57) would be treated as an attack on people based on the combination of a primary and secondary protected characteristic ('quasi-protected characteristic'), namely race combined with age, and, therefore, would be deemed disallowed hate speech and would be subject to removal if detected or reported.[79]

However, the community standard was far more complicated than Bickert's comment to journalists implied. In reality, at that time, attacks against Black children would only be disallowed if they took the form of Tier 1 hate speech within the standard. For example, the 25 May 2018 version of Facebook's standard stated:

> Tier 1 attacks, which target a person or group of people who share one of the above-listed characteristics or immigration status (including all subsets except those described as having carried out violent crimes or sexual offenses)[80]

This clarification about Tier 1 attacks carved out an 'all subsets' catchall protection, although also exempted certain subsets. The upshot was that, at the time, the following would be treated as hate speech under Tier 1.

(60) Black children should be drowned at birth.

However, attacks against Black children falling under Tier 2 (e.g. speech expressing hatred or contempt), and Tier 3 (e.g. speech calling for exclusion), would not have been treated as disallowed hate speech under the standard, at that time.

Perhaps reflecting this anomaly, the 26 March 2020 version of the standard communicated to users the fact that age had been raised to an even higher protection level such that it would be treated as a secondary protected characteristic across all three Tiers of hate speech. This meant that if any relevant mode of attack, even a Tier 2 or 3 attack, targeted a person based on a combination of age and at least one primary protected characteristic, then it would be deemed hate speech under the policy.[81] This meant the following would be deemed hate speech.

(61) I hate black youths.
(62) Old women should be cast from society.

However, other secondary protected characteristics remained Tier-sensitive. So, for example, the 28 January 2021 version mentioned 'occupation' as a concrete example of the sort of secondary protected characteristic that might be in play under the Tier 1 'all subsets' catchall.[82] And so the following would be treated as hate speech.

(63) Death to female doctors!

But an attack against female doctors falling under Tier 2 or Tier 3, would not be treated as hate speech.

Subsequently, the 24 November 2021 version added a further exemption to the Tier 1 'all subsets' (now 'all groups') catchall, this time exempting Tier 1 attacks on subgroups 'representing less than half of a group'.[83] Under a strict reading of this exemption, content is only exempted if it contains a clear or semantically explicit reference to the size of the group along the lines of a numerical or existential quantifier like 'a few', 'a small number', 'a minority', 'forty-nine percent', or 'less than half of'. However, the following would qualify as hate speech.

(64) The majority of Muslims are terrorists.

In one sense, the 'less than half of a group' exemption represented a shift away from overinclusivity and back towards the golden mean or perhaps towards underinclusivity depending on one's perspective.

Now it is an open question what was driving these changes. Possible explanations include everything from a shift in internal politics resulting in the ascendancy of self-expression doves; through to a hard-nosed business decision based on internal market research about what users wanted and expected; to a knee-jerk response to bad publicity caused by public shaming by tech journalists. A more charitable reading would be that Facebook was responding in a reasonable and ethically responsible way to normal and appropriate feedback. In Facebook's own words, taken from an April 2018 press release on its community standards.

> It's important to note that our standards do evolve—in some cases, changes are prompted by input we receive from external stakeholders; in

> others, we make changes to account for the way language is used; in still others, a change is necessitated by a gap in existing policy. This process will continue—and with it, future updates to our standards.[84]

Nevertheless, it would not seem unfair to describe Facebook's evolving community standard on hate speech as a series of unsystematic and partial steps taken over a period of time. Then again, the community standard is at best only a rough approximation of the internal policy. So, at any given moment it is unclear whether changes in the community standard simply reflect changes in how Facebook has decided to present and explain its internal policy to the public or instead actual shifts in the internal policy itself. Moreover, given that Facebook's declared strategy is responsiveness – responsiveness to the external opinions of stakeholders and its independent oversight board, responsiveness to changes in how language is used, and responsiveness to closing gaps in existing policy – then perhaps it is inevitable that the evolution of the internal policy and community standard over time will have the appearance of putting out fires here and there as opposed to a systematic root and branch rethink of its fundamental understanding of what hate speech is. Indeed, it has been suggested that some hate speech laws have also evolved in piecemeal fashion,[85] so in that sense the evolution of Facebook's standard is not usual.

However, in this chapter we are more interested in the substance of the evolution than its causes. The upshot of the series of ad hoc changes made by Facebook over the past six years or so in response to the anomalous examples first reported in 2017 is twofold: the persistence of a few of those anomalous examples; and the creation of a set of new anomalous examples. Here are a few illustrations of content we believe Facebook would probably *not* treat as disallowed hate speech.

(65) Women who swear and burp like men are disgusting.
(66) The ugly transwomen make me want to throw up, the good looking ones not so much.
(67) I hate black inner city thugs, but the white ones are fine by me.
(68) Violent criminals should be torn limb from limb, if they are black.
(69) Black convicted rapists deserve to die horrible deaths, but not the white ones.
(70) Female drivers should not be allowed!
(71) There are a few Jews who deserve to be shot in the back of the head.
(72) Nobody can deny that at least a small number of black people are in fact subhuman.
(73) Nearly half of all gypsies, I would say around forty-nine percent, are petty thieves and should be shipped out of the country.

(74) Slightly less than half of all gay men are sexual predators who pose a threat to children.

(75) I would say that a little less than half of all Uyghurs are worthy of extermination.

3.3.3 *Similarities Between Selective Attacks and Exemplars of Hate Speech*

Faced with these sorts of anomalies, we believe Facebook would do better to directly entertain pair-wise comparisons between examples it already treats as disallowed hate speech and grey area examples involving selective attacks whilst also keeping in mind its own rationale for having a content policy on hate speech in the first place. In the remainder of this section, we present four model comparisons.

First, the current version of Facebook's community standard on hate speech creates Tier-sensitive secondary protected characteristics. In fact, the Tier 1 'all groups' catchall opens up the possibility of an (almost) unlimited number of Tier-sensitive secondary protected characteristics, provided they are not one of the exempted characteristics relating to 'non-protected groups'. Whilst occupation is explicitly mentioned in the standard, this is intended for illustrative purposes only and is non-exhaustive. Other characteristics might include, for example, hobbies or interests, social attitudes or political views, sexual preferences or proclivities, physical appearance or size, health status (other than serious disease which is a primary protected characteristic), and criminal record (other than violent crimes or sexual violence which are exempted). By contrast Tiers 2 and 3 do not contain the 'all groups' catchall, and so only Tier-insensitive secondary protected characteristics (e.g. age) apply. In light of this, consider the following pair of examples.

(76) Women who want to drive cars have no place in our society, they should be violently beaten by their husbands to uphold family honour.

(77) Women who want to drive cars have no place in our society, they should be expelled from their families and from our society.

Under Facebook's policy, at least as described by the current community standard on hate speech, (76) would be deemed hate speech because it is based on a combination of primary and secondary characteristics and because it is a Tier 1 type attack, but (77) would not be deemed hate speech because even though it is also based on the same combination of characteristics, it is a Tier 3 type attack and so the 'all groups' catchall does not apply.

What underlying general principle or rule of thumb would justify the creation of Tiers and ultimately the differential treatment of these examples? Previously, Facebook has made explicit its rule of thumb that the difference between Tiers 1, 2, and 3 is a difference of 'severity'.[86] However, the notion of severity is underspecified as a rule of thumb. What, more exactly, makes Tier 1 attacks more severe examples of hate speech than Tier 2 and 3 attacks? For instance, is there something more socially unacceptable or taboo, more wrongful or harmful, or simply more hate speechy about Tier 1 hate speech as compared to Tiers 2 and 3?

In fact, even assuming there is some real difference in degree of severity or seriousness between Tiers 1, 2, and 3, could this be enough to justify the tiered classification and differential treatment of examples? Are there some clear-cut, obvious, and non-arbitrary thresholds of severity that distinguish Tiers 1, 2 and 3? If not, then the significance of the Tiers arguably rests more in how they mark differences in semantics (different messages) and pragmatics (different acts and effects). In which case, what makes the three categories of hate speech so different as to justify the creation of Tier-sensitive secondary protected characteristics? And, ultimately, what could warrant treating (76) as disallowed hate speech but not (77)?

To try to answer this question, one might reflect on Facebook's rationale for having a community standard on hate speech in the first place. This rationale is articulated in the preamble of the current version of the standard as follows.

> We believe people use their voice and connect more freely when they don't feel attacked on the basis of who they are. That is why we don't allow hate speech on Facebook. It creates an environment of intimidation and exclusion, and in some cases may promote offline violence.[87]

Arguably, however, this rationale fails to warrant the creation of Tier-sensitive secondary protected characteristics and, therefore, the differential treatment of examples (76) and (77). Why so? Because if what ultimately qualifies any content as hate speech, according to Facebook, is that it makes people feel attacked on the basis of who they are and consequently can threaten their real freedom of voice and connectivity, and if who people are can be defined by a combination of primary and secondary characteristics, then it seems hard to justify the creation of Tier-sensitive secondary protected characteristics.

Indeed, presumably Facebook has created a class of Tier-*in*sensitive secondary protected characteristics (e.g. age), precisely because attacking people based on a combination of their age plus another primary protected characteristic threatens their real freedom of voice and connectivity, whether the attack falls under Tier 1 (e.g. violent speech, speech about inhumanity), Tier 2 (e.g. speech expressing hatred or contempt), or Tier 3 (e.g. speech calling for exclusion). But what makes age so different? Surely other secondary features of identity such as occupation and interests also play a key role in some people's sense of who they are. If people can be attacked on the basis of these other features of identity, and these attacks also threaten their real freedom of voice and connectivity, then there is a prima facie reason to consider such attacks as hate speech, whichever of the Tiers they fall under.

Ultimately, classifying hate speech should be primarily about looking at pairwise examples to see if they exhibit sufficient similarities based on target, style, message, act, or effect. Arguably, examples (76) and (77) are similar enough to both be considered hate speech in the ordinary sense of the term, partly because they share the same target and a similar sort of style but also because they are intended to stigmatise, discriminate, intimidate, marginalise, silence, and exclude women, and because they can have the effect of making women feel stigmatised, discriminated against, intimidated, marginalised, silenced, and excluded.

Turning to a second pairwise comparison, although Facebook's current standard on hate speech describes an 'all groups' catchall protection under Tier 1, it also carves out an exemption for certain characteristics related to non-protected groups including groups described as having carried out violent crimes or sexual offences. This means that if an attack is made against a subgroup identified by a combination of one of these exempted secondary characteristics plus any primary characteristic, then it does not count as hate speech, even if it is a Tier 1 type attack. Consider the following pair of examples.

(78) Even nonviolent criminals deserve to die a horrible death, if they are black.
(79) Violent criminals deserve to die a horrible death, if they are black.

Based on the standard, (78) would be deemed hate speech because it combines primary and secondary characteristics and qualifies under the 'all groups' catchall associated with Tier 1, but (79) would not be deemed hate speech because it relates to one of the exempted secondary characteristics (violent criminals) that define non-protected groups (as we read the community standard).

What general principle or rule of thumb would justify the creation of these exempted secondary characteristics related to non-protected groups and ultimately the differential treatment of (78) and (79)? There is nothing clear and obvious in the preamble to Facebook's community standard on hate speech that would provide a clue to the logic behind the exemption. No doubt there is a reason. Perhaps it has something to do with a policy goal of protecting the safety and dignity of victims of violent crimes and sexual offences. Facebook might reason that to classify as hate speech and remove content which attacks people described as having carried out violent crimes or sexual offences could unintentionally provide a cloak of protection to such people and may result in making victims and potential victims less safe. Maybe Facebook considers such attacks to be varieties of alarm bell or watchdog speech, and of especially high value, partly because of the seriousness of the crimes. However, this rationale at best speaks to why being described as having carried out violent crimes or sexual offences is not a primary protected characteristic. The present question is about what justifies Facebook in exempting being described in this way as a potential secondary protected characteristic in cases involving content that is simultaneously attacking people based on other primary protected characteristics.

Perhaps Facebook would defend this exemption on the following additional basis. It would be inconsistent (Facebook might argue) to hold that extreme invective against people described as having carried out violent crimes or sexual offences should not be classified as hate speech because alarm bell or watchdog speech is a high value category of speech; but at the same time, to also hold that similar invective against people that have been described as both being Black and having carried out violent crimes or sexual offences ought to be categorised differently, namely as hate speech. After all, if the general category of speech (alarm bell or watchdog speech) is considered especially high value and, therefore, should never be labelled 'hate speech', then by definition the subcategory of speech (alarm bell or watchdog speech about Black people) must also be especially high value.

However, this putative justification for treating (78) and (79) differently misses the crucial point that when the element of race is added into the picture, this fundamentally changes the character of the content, meaning that the subcategory of speech becomes significantly different in meaning and significance to the general category of speech. Just like (78), statement (79) expresses profoundly prejudiced and discriminatory attitudes (unfair prejudgment). If racial profile does not in itself provide a valid reason for differential attitudes towards and treatment of subgroups of violent criminals, then the picking out of just Black violent criminals for expressive attack is not impartial but grounded in an inherent antipathy or racial bias towards Black people. Putting this another way, the message of bigotry conveyed in (78) is part of what makes it a candidate for classification as hate speech and is surely one reason why Facebook would deem it as such. Yet the same or very similar message of bigotry is conveyed in (79). Arguably, it is not the case that if a speaker expressively attacks people based on them being violent criminals or sex offenders, then anything goes vis-à-vis attacking only a subgroup of such people simply based on the colour of their skin. Even in the case of groups who do not in themselves merit protection (because of the high value of alarm bell speech), it is still hate speech if a subgroup is attacked based on their race and if race is not rationally related to the reason for attacking the whole group; or, to be more precise, it is hate speech precisely because members of the subgroup are attacked based on grounds of race in an unfair way.[88]

A third pairwise comparison relates to another exemption that Facebook's current standard on hate speech carves out from the 'all groups' catchall protection under Tier 1, namely the exemption for Tier 1 content attacking subgroups 'representing less than half of a group'. Consider the following pair of examples.

(80) Exactly half of all Muslims are terrorists.
(81) Slightly less than half of all Muslims are terrorists.

Based on a strict reading of the standard, (80) would be deemed hate speech because it relates to a subgroup that qualifies under the 'all groups' catchall associated with Tier 1, but (81) would not be deemed hate speech because it relates to a subgroup that falls under the 'less than half of a group' exemption to the 'all groups' catchall associated with Tier 1 content.

What could be the justification for drawing this sort of distinction? Once again, the preamble of Facebook's standard on hate speech provides no clue to the internal policy debates and reasoning that might have led to the adoption of the 'less than half of a group' exemption. Perhaps it was assumed that attacks on groups representing less than half of a group are less likely to be indirectly talking about or providing a commentary on the whole group based on speaker meaning and received meaning. Or maybe the assumption was instead that attacks on groups representing less than half of a group are more likely to be fair and accurate. However, such assumptions would only be valid grounds for this policy if they were based on hard evidence and perhaps only legitimate if Facebook were willing to share its evidence with its users and the wider public. Moreover, even if the likelihoods are as described, it is far from obvious why representing less than half of a group should be the optimum cut-off point given that the relevant likelihoods are almost certainly matters of degree. As it stands

Facebook's choice of threshold looks arbitrary. After all, both (80) and (81) could be indirectly saying something about the whole group, as well as not saying something fair and accurate, and, therefore, both equally deserve to be counted as hate speech.

Moreover, the problem of arbitrariness is not resolved simply by lowering the threshold, such as to subgroups representing less than a third of a group. Consider another pair of examples.

(82) Exactly a third of women remain childless throughout their lives and this subset of women deserve to be euthanised because they fulfil no natural purpose.

(83) A little less than a third of women remain childless throughout their lives and this subset of women deserve to be euthanised because they fulfil no natural purpose.

Changing the threshold so that (82) counts as hate speech but not (83) seems no less arbitrary than sticking with the current threshold.

More importantly, applying the global resemblance test, it seems there are enough similarities between (80) and (81) and between (82) and (83), along the lines of target, style, message, act, and effect, to mean (81) and (83) ought to count as hate speech if (80) and (82) count as hate speech. For example, examples (80) and (81) both equally convey messages of hatred and bigotry against Muslims. Likewise, they both equally commit acts of epistemic injustice against Muslims, assuming there is no epistemically credible basis for the claims they each make about what proportion of Muslims are terrorists. Moreover, they seem to carry a similar risk of harmful effects. No doubt strong similarities exist between (82) and (83) as well.

A final pairwise comparison concerns the special status of slurs in Facebook's standard. In general, the standard does not prohibit Tier 2 and 3 attacks against subgroups identified by combinations of secondary and primary protected characteristics, except for age which is a Tier-insensitive secondary protected characteristic. Yet the standard also appears to give slurs a special status all of their own, and this opens up the possibility that referentially restrictive uses of slurs would be deemed hate speech. As mentioned above, Tier 3 contains a specific rule disallowing 'Content that describes or negatively targets people with slurs, where slurs are defined as words that inherently create an atmosphere of exclusion and intimidation against people on the basis of a protected characteristic, often because these words are tied to historical discrimination, oppression, and violence'.[89] Under one possible reading, an attack against people using a slurring term is automatically violative of Facebook's standard, unless it falls under one of the usage exceptions described in the standard, such as when a slurring term is being used to raise awareness about and/or condemn the use of the term or is used in an empowering way by the group.[90]

If designated slurs are automatically violating (unless usage exceptions apply), then this has two important consequences. First, it means referentially restrictive derogatory phrases which just happen to include slurs would be deemed hate speech even if the same phrases would be treated as not hate speech if they omitted the slur. Compare these examples.

(84) Inner city niggers should be denied access to public services to teach them a lesson; let them shoot each other and not be picked up by municipally-operated ambulances.

(85) Inner city black people should be denied access to public services to teach them a lesson; let them shoot each other and not be picked up by municipally-operated ambulances.

Based on the standard, it seems Facebook would deem (84) as hate speech because even though the phrase 'inner city niggers' relates to the combination of a primary protected characteristic and a Tier-sensitive secondary protected characteristic, and even though (84) is a Tier 3 attack, and Tier 3 lacks an 'all groups' catchall, statement (84) nevertheless contains the designated slur 'niggers'. By contrast, (85) would not be deemed hate speech insofar as the aforementioned also holds but it does not contain a designated slur.

A second consequence is that Facebook might end up declining to designate certain terms as slurs even though they share important similarities with paradigmatic slurs. Consider the slur 'Uncle Toms' which picks out a subgroup of African Americans. If Facebook has an internal policy or enforcement guideline (which it may or may not have) that declines to designate terms like 'Uncle Tom' as slurs partly on the grounds they are referentially restrictive and pick out only subgroups, then this would create yet another anomalous pairwise comparison.

(86) I love black people, but I hate niggers.

(87) I love black people, but I hate Uncle Toms.

Based on the standard, it seems Facebook would probably treat (86) as hate speech (assuming 'niggers' is a designated slur in the relevant market), but it may not treat (87) as hate speech in the event 'Uncle Toms' is not a designated slur (assuming it does not designate as slurs referentially restrictive terms). This is because (87) is a Tier 2 attack and Tier 2 lacks an 'all groups' catchall.

How could Facebook justify these anomalous consequences? Starting with the first consequence concerning (84) and (85), maybe Facebook takes the view some words are so toxic for people's self-respect and damaging to social harmony, for instance, that they should be almost always classified as hate speech. But then again, if toxicity and damage are the touchstones, and if these are both matters of degree, then it is hard to see why the threshold of toxicity and damage is obviously met by (84) but not (85). Arguably, a better test is whether there are enough similarities between (84) and (85) in terms of target, style, message, act, and effect. We think it highly likely that in most contexts (84) and (85) would meet the global resemblance test and are both hate speech.

Turning to the second consequen ceconcerning (86) and (87), if Facebook treats 'niggers' as a designated slur but not referentially restrictive terms like 'Uncle Toms', then this seems arbitrary based on reasonable ideas about what a slur is. Consider the conventional wisdom among sociolinguists that a slur is a derogatory or insulting label for a group of people usually applied either to members of the group or to the group in general, and which typically has a neutral counterpart.[91] Arguably, the word 'Uncle Toms' is derogatory or insulting (partly because it conveys both negative stereotypes and adverse evaluations[92]) and is group-based. Perhaps its neutral counterpart is something like 'Black people who are consciously subservient to White people'. Of course, it is a live question how neutral this sort of counterpart really is, but no doubt the same could be said of supposedly neutral counterparts of 'nigger'. At any rate, the mere fact that the relevant group is a subgroup of Black people does not seem to disqualify 'Uncle Toms' as a slur based on conventional wisdom.

As with other selective attacks, we believe terms like 'Uncle Toms' share enough similarities with exemplars of hate speech such as 'niggers' across the key dimensions of target, style, message, act, and effect (at least four out of five) to qualify as hate speech. Both target groups. Both to a greater or lesser extent embody the style of invoking archetypes or stock characters. Both convey the racially biased message that we must understand what it means to be a Black person in terms of how Black people orientate their behaviour towards the opinions, fears, and expectations of White people, irrespective of the cruelty and injustices perpetrated by White people. Both can be, and often are, used to *prejudge*, *stereotype*, *stigmatise*, *misrecognise*, and *control* people, for example. We also believe these similarities in act can transcend the contextual question of whether the speaker is White or Black, even if these terms may end up have differential effects, depending on the context.[93] In short, (86) and (87) are similar enough to each other and to exemplars of hate speech to be both classified as hate speech.

To conclude this section, we have argued selective attacks are capable of passing the global resemblance test even if they are not disallowed by Facebook. At this stage, however, defenders of Facebook might argue it has other reasons not to classify selective attacks as disallowed hate speech despite similarities with prototypical hate speech. Perhaps Facebook believes there are strong countervailing reasons in play for keeping selective attacks on the platform (as a form of *allowed hate speech*), such as to do with protecting self-expression, connectivity, and user-safety (e.g. alarm bell speech). But if that is the distinction being drawn, it is not made explicit or transparent in the current community standard. In the conclusion of the book (Chapter 8), we recommend Facebook is clearer about this with the public.

3.4 Reverse Attacks

A further cluster of grey area cases involve speech *by* members of groups more typically represented as victims of hate speech and other forms of oppression *against* groups more usually considered perpetrators. We shall call these reverse attacks. One familiar way of framing this grey area is in terms of anti-white slurs such as 'pinky', 'paleface', 'pastyface', 'honky', 'white devil', and 'blue-eyed devil'. In the words of Delgado and Stefancic: 'As a threshold question, one might ask whether it is even conceptually meaningful to speak of hate speech against whites.'[94] However, reverse attacks can be based on any protected characteristics, not just race. Consider reverse slurs relating to gender such as 'creepy guy', 'man-child', and 'cis folk', and reverse slurs relating to sexuality and lifestyle choices like 'breeder'.

Reverse attacks may be couched in various styles of hate speech besides slurs and epithets, including negative stereotypes, vilification, false rumours, threatening or intimidating words or behaviour, and statements advocating or inciting hatred, discrimination, or violence. Nevertheless, for the sake of consistency with the approach taken in this chapter, we shall focus primarily on slurs.

3.4.1 The Reverse Attacks Trilemma

At first glance, reverse attacks call into doubt the following rule of thumb about hate speech in the ordinary sense of the term.

(R2) Hate speech is by definition a type of one-way or unidirectional speech meaning that it is only ever an attack of the powerful against the powerless, the dominant against the subordinate, the oppressor against the oppressed, the advantaged against the disadvantaged, the well protected

> against the vulnerable, those with status, authority, and influence against those lacking in, or subject to, that status, authority, and influence.

Support for (R2) may stem from a normative view that says the term 'hate speech' ought to apply not to any speech that attacks persons on the basis of protected characteristics but, more specifically, speech attacking members of historically oppressed groups.[95] On this view, when it comes to prototypical examples of hate speech such as a White racist calling a Black person 'nigger' or an anti-Semite calling a Jewish person a 'kike', the most salient feature is that these are not attacks on the basis of race simpliciter but attacks against people based on the subcharacteristics of being Black and Jewish respectively. People who hold this view accept that speech attacking White people might be 'hateful' but insist that such attacks are not properly called 'hate speech'.[96] In fact, this view can be traced back to the very first uses of the term 'hate speech' found in the work of Matsuda, and in particular her insight that when it comes to 'the worst, paradigm example of racist hate messages' of the sort that ought to be legally restricted, '[t]he message is directed against a historically oppressed group'.[97]

On further reflection, however, the rule of thumb (R2) can be rendered more exact in different ways depending on the point of emphasis. One relevant distinction is between target-focused and speaker-focused definitions. A target-focused definition might state that something can be hate speech only if the target group are subject to background oppression or subordination. By contrast, a speaker-focused definition might insist that something can be hate speech only if the speaker is a member of a group that perpetrates and/or is the beneficiary of background oppression or subordination. Another distinction is between relational and correlational descriptions of the connection between hate speech and background oppression or subordination. A correlational description states that something can be hate speech only if it occurs alongside or together with background oppression or subordination, but is silent on how, if at all, the speech and these background phenomena interrelate or interact. The relational description, by contrast, says that something can be hate speech only if there exists some substantive relationship or interaction between the speech and these background phenomena. The relationship might be retro-facilitative (the speech is facilitated or made possible by background oppression or subordination), antero-facilitative (the speech facilitates, perpetuates, or incites oppression or subordination), interpolative (the speech inserts or imposes background oppression or subordination into the moment of speech in some way), interpellative (the speech is a materialisation or product of background oppression or subordination), or constitutive (the speech constitutes oppression or subordination).

At any rate, reverse attacks put pressure on the unidirectional view of hate speech because, on the one hand, reverse attacks are not messages directed against historically oppressed groups, but, on the other hand, they seem to share other things in common with paradigmatic hate speech. For one thing, like prototypical examples of hate speech, reverse slurs such as 'honky' and 'cracker' are partly based on the possession or perceived possession of protected characteristics (e.g. race). Moreover, reverse slurs are group-based in the sense they say something derogatory or insulting not merely about the particular targeted individual but also about everyone who shares the relevant characteristic (e.g. being White). In other words, reverse slurs are a verbal assault on someone who is seen as a mere representative of an entire group or class of persons; it just so happens that the group is powerful or dominant in society. In addition, like the paradigmatic racial slur 'nigger', reverse slurs such as 'honky' and 'cracker' seem to convey (express, imply, presuppose, or infer) attributions of certain stereotypical traits (e.g. difficult, entitled, heartless, bigoted, have an air of superiority) and adverse appraisals or evaluations (e.g. despicable, vile, odious), all because of targets possessing certain physical characteristics (e.g. being White).[98] Furthermore, like all slurs, reverse slurs are derogatory or insulting, typically because of painting targets in a bad light, expressing antipathy, contempt, or disrespect, conveying adverse appraisals or evaluations, or simply because of giving and being intended to give offence.[99]

At first glance, these basic similarities between reverse slurs and exemplar slurs like 'nigger' seem to merit provisionally treating reverse slurs as hate speech; or, at the very least, lifts them into a grey area of hate speech. Consequently, they pose the following trilemma for any society or specific organisation that sees itself as having a coherent and fair understanding of the ordinary concept *hate speech*. Either the society or organisation sticks to (R2) and treats reverse attacks as not hate speech, in which case this could smack of double standards or moving too far in the direction of tolerating attacks perpetrated by intolerant minorities. Or the society or organisation sticks to (R2) and treats reverse attacks as hate speech in disguise, in which case the notion of background oppression or subordination must work extra hard and might be stretched to breaking point. Or the society or organisation simply jettisons (R2) and treats reverse attacks as potential hate speech, in which case there is a danger that it will lose its grip on the ordinary concept and open the floodgates to accusations of hate speech whenever any group of people are verbally attacked, which could trigger a descent into competitive victimhood. On the face of it, none of these outcomes seem appealing. Call this the reverse attacks trilemma.

Broadly speaking, we believe the best way to escape the trilemma is to show that it is not really a trilemma after all. In fact, we point to five different options or pathways out of the trilemma, which together can be organised under two main responses. The first response is sceptical: it claims reverse attacks do not in fact call (R2) into doubt. This can be based on different grounds including that reverse attacks are not good candidates to be considered hate speech because they are dissimilar in kind to exemplars of hate speech in terms of semantics, derogatory force, or offensiveness (first option) or dissimilar in effect to prototypical hate speech such as in terms of quality and degree of harm (second option); or that what appear to be reverse attacks on closer examination turn out not to be reverse attacks and so the relevant examples adhere to (R2) after all, whether this is due to the complex nature of oppression (third option) or to the presence of situationally reversed power dynamics (fourth option).

The second response (our proposed response) claims that reverse attacks not only demonstrate the falsity of (R2) but also demonstrate that hate speech is in fact bidirectional or multidirectional in nature (fifth option). This line of response appeals to the following alternative rule of thumb about hate speech.

(R3) Hate speech is a two-way or multidirectional type of speech meaning that in some instances it can be an attack of the powerful against the powerless but in other instances it can be an attack of the powerless against the powerful, or both.

There can be different ways of supporting (R3) depending on how hate speech is further conceptualised. For example, if hate speech is defined, in a universalist or essentialist way, as necessarily about the expression of emotions, feelings, attitudes, or sentiments of hatred[100] – or about appraisal states of hatred[101] – then it would seem to follow that hate speech is a multidirectional category of speech, and, therefore, slurs like 'honky' could be hate speech. After all, members of oppressor groups do not have a monopoly on the expression of hatred – or appraisal states of hatred.[102] However, one can concede that reverse attacks undermine (R2), and as a result embrace (R3), without also adopting a universalist or essentialist definition of hate speech. For example, we believe the ordinary concept *hate speech* is a family resemblance concept and we also embrace (R3). Indeed, a key implication of recognising hate speech in the ordinary sense of the word as a heterogeneous collection of expressive, communicative, and performative phenomena is that diverse forms of speech can be understood as hate speech based on other shared similarities besides simply whether or not they happen to be attacks against the powerless.

Below we shall argue that the first four options are untenable and unworkable: the key arguments either do not stack up or are incomplete. Instead, we shall defend the second main response, which involves consciously abandoning (R2) and embracing (R3), the idea that hate speech is multidirectional (fifth option). We aim to show how this fifth option may draw on the best, most plausible insights of the other four options, once freed from the baggage of (R2). More importantly, we argue that recognising hate speech as multidirectional need not amount to opening the floodgates to baseless accusations precisely because a complex patchwork of similarities helps to distinguish the concept and limit its extension. Before making these arguments, however, we shall first illustrate the practical dimensions of the reverse attacks trilemma once again using Facebook as a case study.

3.4.2 Reverse Attacks under Facebook's Community Standard on Hate Speech

As already noted in this chapter, Facebook's standard contains the following general definition: 'We define hate speech as a direct attack against people [...] on the basis of what we call protected characteristics.'[103] At face value, then, the standard, and the underpinning internal content policy it describes, seems to be bidirectional or multidirectional in the sense that it applies to relevant sorts of attacks based on protected characteristics, irrespective of whether they are attacks against oppressed or subordinated groups or attacks against oppressor or subordinating groups. Nevertheless, at the time of writing, Facebook has not made a definitive public statement to the effect that the internal policy is unidirectional or multidirectional. Moreover, although the Meta (Facebook/Instagram) Oversight Board has recently ruled on a pair of cases of putative reverse attacks against men involving content that was initially removed by Meta as violating its community standard on hate speech, the Oversight Board held that the cases were not hate speech attacks after all but instead allowable content that condemns or raises awareness of gender-based violence against women (Case decisions 2023-002-IG-UA and 2023-005-IG-UA, 12 July 2023).

On the one hand, it may seem reasonable to infer that the standard is multidirectional simply based on the plain wording of the standard allied to the fact that Facebook has not explicitly stated the policy is unidirectional.

Likewise, the standard does not explicitly exclude or rule out the possibility of reverse attacks counting as hate speech, and the aforementioned pair of cases of putative reverse attacks against men clearly show that Meta does recognise some reverse attacks as hate speech. On the other hand, none of the illustrations of hate speech set out in Facebook's standard amount to reverse attacks. For example, the Tier 1 list of disallowed hate speech includes 'Dehumanising speech or imagery' illustrated in term of comparisons between 'Black people and apes or ape-like creatures', 'Jewish people and rats', 'Muslim people and pigs', 'Mexican people and worms', and in terms of 'women as household objects or property or objects in general' and 'Black people as farm equipment'. It does not mention dehumanising speech or imagery relating to White people, White Anglo-Saxon Protestants, or men. To give another example, the Tier 2 list of hate speech includes: 'Generalisations that state inferiority [...] [such as] Derogatory terms related to sexual activity, including but not limited to: "whore" [...] "slut" [...] [and] Other statements of inferiority, which we define as: [...] Expressions about being better/worse than another protected characteristic, including, but not limited to: "I believe males are superior to females".' The standard does not refer to generalisations that state the inferiority of men, however. Furthermore, the Tier 3 list of hate speech includes 'Content that describes or negatively targets people with slurs'. Yet it does not provide any illustrations of slurs and, therefore, no examples of reverse slurs.[104]

Therefore, if Facebook's internal policy on hate speech really is multidirectional, what explains the omission of reverse attacks from the extensive illustrations of hate speech included in the public-facing community standard? In the case of slurs, the omission is easy to explain: since the standard does not include any concrete illustrations, it provides examples of neither reverse slurs nor ordinary slurs. In this way there is parity. But this is not true of the other Tiers where only reverse attacks are absent from the illustrations. So, how can this absence be made consistent with the assumption that the internal policy is multidirectional?

Here are some possible explanations. One is simply that this is a coincidence. The absence of reverse attacks does not reveal something important about the internal policy but is simply an unintended quirk of the public-facing community standard. The internal policy is multidirectional, but it just so happens that the standard does not contain any examples of reverse attacks. There is no underlying agenda on the part of Facebook that could explain the omission, and no deliberate strategy at play. A second explanation is that Facebook's community standard is designed to communicate to users what are some of the most common and clear-cut forms of hate speech circulating on the platform. If the standard is designed more for user education and awareness than for providing a definitive statement of the internal policy, then it might make sense to focus on common and clear-cut examples rather than unusual and ambiguous examples. Even if the internal policy is multidirectional, focusing on unidirectional examples may best serve the intended educational purpose. A third explanation might be less flattering. Facebook has an incentive to manage public information about its internal policy on hate speech in a way that maintains favourable or positive public perception of the platform. So, even if the internal policy is in fact multidirectional, and applies to examples of reverse attacks, to include such examples in the public-facing community standard could result in bad publicity, such as if tech journalists report that Facebook's policy 'protects the strong from being attacked by the weak'. Of course, there is also a risk of bad publicity if certain groups complain that Facebook operates a double standard and does not recognise anti-white invective as being hate speech. But perhaps Facebook performs a calculation based on a balance of risks and the sorts of public perceptions it is most anxious to support, such as based on the values and concerns of its users and, importantly, the businesses paying for advertising on the platform. A final explanation is that the absence of reverse attacks reveals an underlying feature not of the internal policy but of the enforcement guidelines or actual enforcement practices. It could be an implicit admission that Facebook's moderators and algorithms will tend to treat reverse attacks as less egregious examples of hate speech; or that they will be more lenient and less rigorous in the enforcement of the policy as applied to reverse attacks. In other words, the absence could be indicative of there being de facto unidirectional enforcement of what is ostensibly a de jure multidirectional internal policy. This could happen if the team editing the public-facing community standard take advice from the moderation teams or simply end up reflecting actual patterns of enforcement.

Clearly, to reach any definitive conclusions about which, if any, of these explanations is correct would require Facebook to give academic researchers permission to interview staff on the record and to provide access to the internal policies, enforcement guidelines, and datasets of enforcement decisions. Nevertheless, there are other sources of evidence that can shed light on the plausibility of at least some of these explanations. For example, in terms of the final explanation, one real-world stress test of enforcement practices occurs when, even though the internal policy is multidirectional, there is public pressure on the platform to operate unidirectional enforcement. If the platform resists that pressure, then it seems less likely the final explanation holds. By way of illustration, there is at least anecdotal evidence to suggest that in the wake of the #MeToo movement and public pressure on Facebook to ease up on removing attacks against men, Facebook nevertheless persisted in the removal of misandrist statements of inferiority (e.g. 'all men are pigs', 'men are trash', 'men are scum', 'men are garbage', 'men are excrement', 'kill all men'). In that sense it continued to uphold multidirectional enforcement of a multidirectional policy despite some public criticism for doing so.[105]

More recently, *The Washington Post* has reported on a series of high-level debates within Facebook about whether to adopt a strategy of unidirectional enforcement, in which posts that breach community standards on hate speech are more actively and aggressively identified and removed (including with automation tools) if they attack oppressed groups than if they do not. Initially, there were indications that Facebook had undertaken a major trial of this new enforcement strategy and would be adopting it going forward: '"We know that hate speech targeted towards underrepresented groups can be the most harmful, which is why we have focused our technology on finding the hate speech that users and experts tell us is the most serious," said Facebook spokeswoman Sally Aldous.'[106] However, within a year it was being reported that Facebook had taken a step back from this policy allegedly on the basis of 'the potential for backlash from "conservative partners"'.[107]

Whatever the correct explanation is for the absence of concrete illustrations of reverse attacks within Facebook's community standard, Facebook is certainly not alone among social media platforms in facing the reverse attacks trilemma. Indeed, a similar trilemma is faced by lawmakers, law enforcement agencies, and courts in terms of drafting and applying hate speech laws.[108]

3.4.3 First Option: Reverse Attacks as Dissimilar in Kind to Prototypical Hate Speech

The first of the four (R2)-preserving pathways out of the reverse attacks trilemma maintain that reverse attacks are dissimilar in kind to exemplars of hate speech and as such are not good candidates to be considered hate speech after all. If this is right, then in fact there is no double standard to worry about and (R2) is not put under serious doubt. Of course, 'dissimilar in kind' is an ambiguous phrase. Therefore, below we assess three versions of what this phrase could mean: non-equivalent semantics; unequal derogatory force; and unequal insultingness or offensiveness. However, we will argue that none of these versions holds up under scrutiny.

3.4.3.1 Non-Equivalent Semantics

One version of this strategy challenges assumptions about a semantic equivalence between slurs such as 'nigger' and 'honky'. In 1969, for example, the American educationalist Frederick David Erickson proffered the following definition of 'honky' based on his first-hand experiences of teaching in inner city public schools:

> HONKY, HONCKY (háwnkee), n. sing. A white man, more especially a stupid, racist white man. Black dialect equivalent of wh. dial, nigger. Poss. der. from wh. dial. Hunky (from wh. dial. Bohunk, from stan. Eng. Bohemian).[109]

Arguably, however, 'honky' is not semantically equivalent to 'nigger', in the sense that 'honky' does not mirror or correspond with the meaning of 'nigger'. After all, 'nigger' does not typically convey (encode, imply, presuppose, or infer) the converse idea of a stupid racist black man. Instead, as discussed in Chapter 2, its meaning is more often encapsulated in stereotypes about African Americans as lazy, stupid, aggressive, animalistic, or childlike, for example.[110]

Furthermore, reverse attacks are often oriented more towards attacking structures, institutions, and practices than attacking people, even if they do both, whereas exemplars of hate speech tend to be directed more towards attacking people. Consider terms used by some people with disabilities in reference to nondisabled people such as 'TABS', 'people with abilities', 'normals', and 'ables'. Arguably, these words are not primarily or actively hostile toward nondisabled people, although they might also convey an idea that nondisabled people lack understanding, empathy, or humility toward people with disabilities, are ignorant about disability discrimination, have a sense of superiority, or assume that only they are normal. Instead, the main semantic thrust of these words is directed towards challenging assumptions about the nature of disability and highlighting disablist discrimination itself. The same might be true for the reverse slur 'cis folk'.

In addition to this, reverse attacks often have a reflexive nature that prototypical hate speech lacks. As Embrick and Henricks explain:

> Expressions like 'beat whitey' are as much a criticism of white racism as they are a call for minorities to legitimize their own self-image (i.e. similar to the cultural movement of 'black is beautiful'). [...] The discursive deployment of whitey, to say it another way, is not a straightforward racial insult like the terms cracker or honky but a complex slur carrying simultaneous meanings.[111]

On this analysis, expressions like 'beat whitey' convey (express, imply, presuppose, or infer) self-reflections on the subordinate position of Black people and an injunction to Black people to disabuse themselves of the anti-black racial stereotypes they may have internalised. Perhaps these or similar ideas might figure in the semantics of 'nigger' when used by educated or socially conscious Black people when referring to Black people in general. But these ideas are rarely part of the semantics of 'nigger' when used by White racists to slur people of colour.

Moreover, reverse attacks are more likely to be referentially restrictive than standard hate speech (see also Section 3.3). Embrick and Henricks again: 'Whereas *nigger* and *wetback* are terms typically attached to all members of each respective group, some of the most popular white slurs, especially honky and cracker, have historically been reserved for segments of the white population.'[112] Likewise, Delgado and Stefancic claim that 'whites as a rule are not collectively implicated by negative stereotypes such as *trailer park trash, Southern cracker*, or *angry white man*.'[113] Indeed, anti-white insults tend to presuppose a positive stereotype of White people in general as being well-off, educated, and fair-minded and, therefore, presuppose the opposite stereotype of Black people. As Thomas Grey puts it, 'in its usual sense, the term ['white trash'] is implicitly racist toward people of color – with its implication of surprise that a white person would be "trash".'[114] These observations need not be limited to racial slurs. Intersectional slurs portraying White women in a derogatory manner, for example, tend to demarcate exceptions to a positive caricature of White women as nice or pleasant, whereas slurs portraying Black women in a derogatory manner carry an implied generalisation that all Black women are unpleasant to which there are only some exceptions. Thus, the insult 'Karen' picks out a small subset of White women and in many instances is not intended and not received as a commentary on White women in general.[115] By contrast, the stereotype of the angry Black woman almost always speaks to or conveys an assumption about all Black women. The same goes for other slurring terms relating to gender. For example, the term 'himbo' attacks a subclass of men and typically conveys the idea they are not like most men. Yet when a sexist or misogynist person uses 'bimbo', more often than not this conveys the idea that all or most women are to some degree shallow, vacuous, and dumb, as though bimbos exemplify a trait hardwired into women in general and that all women exhibit to some extent.

There is also a possible difference in the average constituency or composition of speakers of reverse attacks, on the one hand, and the users of prototypical hate speech, on the other hand. For example, it is overwhelmingly men who call women 'bimbos', but the reverse insult 'himbo' is typically used by women and men alike. This nonparallel speaker composition may in turn predict differences in speaker meaning. For example, in one sense it is unsurprising that 'himbo' would be used to similar extents by both women and men because it is not referring to all men but a narrow subset of men; thus, ordinary men would not view it as self-referential. By contrast, most women, as well as most men, understand 'bimbo' to indirectly convey a derogatory message or negative stereotype about all women. Indeed, the fact that both men and women use 'himbo' predicts a further aspect of ordinary usage, namely that the term is often used in a positive way.[116]

Finally, evidence from experimental studies indicates that observers of hate speech will typically attribute greater prejudice (having a negative attitude towards a group of people) to a speaker who derogates the capabilities of members of less empowered groups than to a speaker who derogates the capabilities of members of more empowered groups.[117] This asymmetry in attributed prejudice might be at least partly explained by an asymmetry in the semantics of standard and reverse attacks.

However, on closer examination, we believe none of these observations can justify the blanket rule that reverse attacks are not hate speech. Take the observation that reverse attacks typically lack equivalent meanings to corresponding standard hate speech. Even if this observation is correct, it does not follow that the former cannot be hate speech. Consider anti-white slurs vilifying all White people as racists or Black nationalist propaganda that spreads negative stereotypes about White people as difficult, arrogant, and impossible to live with. Whilst not semantically equivalent to anti-black slurs and White nationalist propaganda, the messages conveyed may be similar enough to count the former as well as the latter as hate speech.

We are similarly sceptical towards the suggestion that reverse attacks are not hate speech simply because they have a different emphasis to prototypical hate speech. Even if it were true that the principal emphasis or central theme of reverse attacks is condemning discriminatory institutions, structures, and practices, and there is only a secondary focus on attacking people, whereas the pattern for prototypical hate speech is weighted more toward attacks against people, once again this does not entail that reverse attacks cannot be hate speech. If in fact the secondary meaning of reverse attacks does involve derogating people based on group membership, this alone might be sufficiently similar to prototypical hate speech to make it coherent for competent language users to call reverse attacks 'hate speech'. If speakers use the terms 'TABS' and 'normals', for example, to caricature nondisabled people as lacking humility or human empathy, this may qualify as hate speech, even if not the main theme.

What about the further suggestion that reverse attacks are more semantically complex and contain reflexive content that prototypical hate speech lacks? Even assuming for the sake of argument that expressions like 'beat whitey', and perhaps also some uses of 'cis folk', are complex because they direct Black people and transgender people to take pride in themselves and not get beaten down by others, this does not take away from the fact that they may also convey derogatory messages about White people and cisgender people based on group membership. And these derogatory messages may be sufficiently similar in kind to messages conveyed by prototypical hate speech to make it plausible to acknowledge reverse attacks as hate speech. Of course, the complexity of language might be salient for assessing what counts as hate speech all things considered, such as if this complexity predicts certain audience effects. For example, it is possible that exposure to more complex slurs, including the degree of self-reflexivity encoded in the slurs, predicts lower discriminatory dispositions towards the targets of the slurs among the audience, compared to exposure to more basic slurs.[118] But this is a matter of differentiating reverse attacks from prototypical hate speech based on perlocutionary effects not semantic complexity per se. We shall return to these effects in Section 3.4.4.

Consider also the contention that reverse attacks are more likely to be referentially restrictive. The evidence is inconclusive on this score. For example, the term 'honky' may convey the idea of a *stupid racist white person*, so in that sense refers to a subset of White people. But arguably the term 'nigger' may itself convey the idea of a *lazy, stupid, raggedy, promiscuous, or aggressive black person*, so also ostensibly picks out a subset of Black people. It is precisely this meaning that middle- and upper-class African Americans rely on when they call poorer African Americans 'niggers'. Likewise, the slur 'Southern cracker' may have similarities to 'black hoodlums' in terms of picking out subgroups of White and Black people respectively. Of course, sometimes caricatures only appear to be referentially restrictive on the surface but indirectly provide commentary on the entire group. Then again, this seems true of both standard and reverse caricatures. Consider racial stereotypes or caricatures of the angry White man or the demanding White women. They may operate in similar ways to prototypical racial stereotypes of the angry Black man and the uppity nigger. Such stereotypes or caricatures might be superficially referentially restrictive but underneath convey ideas about the nature of all White or Black people.

The questionable assumption that anti-white slurs are disproportionately referentially restrictive might also be partly based on misnomers about the type of protected characteristics involved. In particular, it might be based on the conflation of race and ethnicity. Consider putative reverse slurs like 'redneck', 'cracker', and 'hillbilly'. Just as not all Black people in America are of African descent so not all White people are white, rural, working class, conservative, southern, mountain-dwelling. So, in one sense, slurs like 'redneck', 'cracker', and 'hillbilly' are referentially restrictive slurs picking out a subset of a wider racial group (White people). However, it is more likely these slurs pick out groups based on ethnicity rather than race. In other words, they might be attacks not against racial subgroups but attacks against discrete and whole ethnic groups identified by degrees of shared ancestry, language, cultural traditions, beliefs, practices, and geographical locations.

Furthermore, even if the slur 'white trash' is referentially restrictive and conveys the idea that only a subgroup of White people are low types (i.e. poor White people), it does not follow from this that the slur is not hate speech. It is still stigmatising for the subgroup being attacked to be depicted as low types (e.g. poor, uneducated, uncivilised), even if the grounds for the attack are an admixture of the protected characteristics of race and class. The metaphor of trash is both dehumanising and a familiar style of hate speech. Therefore, 'white trash' bears some important hallmarks of hate speech in terms of target, style, and message.[119] Turning back to Facebook's standard for a moment, we note that although the Tier 2 category mentions 'Physical deficiencies' related to 'Hygiene' as a form of hate speech, the list of illustrations includes 'filthy, dirty, smelly' but not 'trash'.[120] Given the familiar trope related to 'white trash', this once again highlights the omission of illustrations of well-known reverse attacks within the standard (see also Section 3.4.2).

Finally, we turn to the idea that reverse attacks are not hate speech because they have on average a different speaker constituency and evince lesser prejudice attribution on the part of observers. There may be differences in the average speaker constituency of the terms 'bimbo' and 'himbo' but these differences do not necessarily strip the latter portmanteau of its derogatory meaning across a wide range of different uses. 'Himbo', like the antediluvian slur 'milksop' (*cowardly male*), is still capable of conveying a disparaging message about beautiful yet vacuous men. Indeed, like the caricature of the bimbo, the himbo may be an example of what we call an archetype or stock character style of stereotype (see Chapter 4). At any rate, we believe the term 'himbo', qua stereotype, can still rise to the level of hate speech in the ordinary sense of the term even though it is used by both men and women. By analogy, 'nigger' can be used in a derogatory way by both White people and middle- and upper-class African Americans but arguably retains its status as hate speech across these speaker constituencies. That said, in circumstances where reverse slurs are referentially restrictive and do have nonparallel speaker constituencies, this could impact the illocutionary force and even the perlocutionary effects of the slurs, which we shall discuss in Section 3.4.4. Similarly, it might be true that observers attribute greater prejudice to a speaker who derogates the capabilities of members of less empowered groups than to a speaker who derogates the capabilities of members of more empowered groups, but it is also true that the attribution of prejudice remains present to some degree in both scenarios suggesting that observers view both standard attacks and reverse attacks as expressing or embodying prejudice. Once again, asymmetry does not by itself demonstrate a difference in kind.[121]

3.4.3.2 Unequal Derogatory Force

Another potential argument for denying that reverse attacks are hate speech has two steps. The first starts with the general observation that not simply do slurs have non-equivalent semantics but also some slurs have less derogatory force than others.[122] Could it be that reverse attacks cast targets in a less bad light, portray them not quite as low, and express a lesser form of contempt compared to prototypical hate speech? This is certainly the view of some writers. In the words of Robin Lakoff, 'While there do exist epithets to be hurled at males and whites ("phallocrat," "honky"), they lack the sting of slurs against women, blacks, Latinos, and Asians.'[123] The second step in the argument is to claim that because reverse slurs lack the same derogatory force, weight, or sting as prototypical hate speech slurs, they are not hate speech at all.

We are sceptical about the second step in this argument. However, before explaining this scepticism, it is important to say more about the first step. What could justify the claim that reverse attacks lack the same derogatory force as prototypical hate speech? Consider three possible justifications. The first appeals directly to the wider social context of oppression and discrimination associated with hate speech. For example, the slurring term 'nigger' may carry special derogatory force due to its reference to a group of people who have been slaves, segregated, subject to lynching, disproportionately incarcerated, disadvantaged economically and educationally, and so on, and due to the fact that 'nigger' expresses prejudiced attitudes towards the group that has been oppressed in these ways (see Chapter 2). Of course, when the word 'nigger' is mentioned by socially conscious Black people to describe the plight of 'their own' people, the aim can be to highlight this oppression. But when used by a White racist against a Black person, the intended meaning can be that the oppression of Black people is fitting or somehow deserved. Since the slurs 'honky' or 'whitey' do not pick out these sorts of oppressed groups and do not express negative attitudes towards, and adverse evaluations of, people that have been victims of historical oppression, they lack the same derogatory force (so the argument runs).[124]

A second justification makes the related point that prototypical hate speech slurs have been around much longer than reverse slurs. In the words of Delgado and Stefancic, 'only in the last few decades have whites actually been subjected to one of the more dramatic forms of minority hate speech, that of Black nationalists, while some minority groups have been publicly and privately castigated for centuries.'[125] No doubt there is a public-private dimension to this observation. Even if anti-white hate speech is also centuries old, it may have languished in hushed tones, private spaces, and coded vernacular. Among the many historical privileges afforded to White people by their position of power and dominance has been the freedom to use racist speech out in the open and without fear of reprisals. Arguably, this privilege was challenged through the expansion of hate speech laws during the twentieth century.[126]

A third justification affirms that prototypical hate speech slurs are more disparaging about their targets than reverse slurs. For example, the slur 'nigger' speaks to powerlessness in a way anti-white slurs do not. As Delgado and Stefancic put it, '"cracker", although disrespectful, still implies power, as does "redneck".'[127] The point is that even when slurring terms for White people convey negative stereotypes, these are often stereotypes about the power as well as brutality of White people.[128] Moreover, derogatory uses of 'nigger' usually assign extremely negative attributes (e.g. aggressive, animalistic, childlike, devoid of moral agency or conscience) and egregiously bad evaluative properties (e.g. despicable, good-for-nothing, inhuman, worthless, inferior, second-class, lacking human dignity). By contrast, derogatory uses of 'honky' and 'whitey' typically assign somewhat less negative attributes (e.g. troublesome, cruel, or bigoted) and less egregious properties (e.g. a nuisance, unlikeable).[129] Indeed, anti-black discourse is more likely than anti-white discourse to employ dehumanising comparisons and hate propaganda. For example, whereas terms like 'ape' and 'monkey' draw comparisons between Black people and animals, the term 'white devil' speaks to a clever and unscrupulous exploiter and oppressor of Black people. Likewise, the slur 'nigger' can convey the idea that Black people have lesser cognitive or moral capacities and so have lower dignitary worth such that the success or failure of their lives matters less. It can also paint Black people as deserving of the structural discrimination they face, as though the current state of affairs is natural because Black people are racially inferior.[130] On the other hand, anti-white slurs often convey ideas about White people merely acting in morally bad ways towards Black people (as opposed to lacking in moral capacity). Furthermore, whereas the slurring term 'nigger' can often convey vertiginous contempt or scorn for its targets, in many instances the words 'honky', 'whitey', and 'white folks' signal a sort of fear or warning shared between the speaker and other people of colour, as though the speaker is saying, 'Watch out, trouble is coming!'

Based on these justifications, there is evidence to support the following general rule.

(R4) Reverse slurs are less powerful in their derogatory force than prototypical hate speech slurs.

Then again, it is arguable that some prototypical hate speech slurs like 'chink' may also have less derogatory force than the most derogatory hate speech slurs such as 'nigger'.[131] Moreover, it is not immediately obvious that a reverse slur like 'honky' has significantly less derogatory force than the slur 'chink'. Therefore, it might be more realistic to view the rule of thumb (R4), if true, as being at most a generalisation that speaks to averages whilst allowing for outlier cases.

(R4.1) Reverse slurs are on average less powerful in their derogatory force than prototypical hate speech slurs.

However, the principal weakness of the present argument for denying that reverse attacks are hate speech is that it is a non-sequitur. Even if it is the case that some slurs carry less derogatory force than others and, in particular, that reverse slurs are on average less powerful in their derogatory force than prototypical hate speech slurs, it does not follow from this that reverse slurs are not hate speech. By analogy, racial slurs and other forms of racial hate propaganda that speak to the fundamental inferiority of certain groups might be more egregiously derogatory forms of hate speech, but it does not mean that other less egregious forms of speech (e.g. racial stereotypes) are not hate speech. At most these examples serve to underline the fact that it is possible to draw many subtle distinctions between members of the ordinary concept *hate speech* precisely because it is a heterogeneous collection of expressive phenomena.[132]

Likewise, it might be true that the number of decades or centuries different groups have been subjected to public hate speech is not the same. Indeed, some forms of hate speech may depend on this historical fact. Consider microaggressions that take the form of brushing under the carpet people's lived experiences of bigotry and discrimination or that involve using racial trigger words whilst at the same time ignoring or refusing to acknowledge the historical meaning of those words as slurs. However, this difference is not in itself definitive proof that reverse slurs cannot be hate speech. Hate speech can include the new as well as the old.

One factor that could potentially mark out duration as a salient difference between reverse attacks and prototypical hate speech is the extent to which hate speech attains certain forms of illocutionary and perlocutionary force due to the accumulation of hate speech over time. However, it is one thing to recognise the importance of accumulation in the performance or realisation of prototypical hate speech acts and effects;[133] it is quite another to say that reverse slurs are associated with insufficient accumulation even to qualify as the performance of prototypical hate speech acts and effects. In Section 3.4.6 we shall look at how even speech repeated over a short period of time can be sufficient to lend it illocutionary and perlocutionary force in the context of particular speech situations.

3.4.3.3 Unequal Offensiveness

A third, albeit similar, possible argument for the claim that reverse slurs are a different kind of speech and, therefore, not hate speech is couched not in terms of a rule of thumb about the unequal derogatoriness of reverse slurs but as a rule about unequal insultingness or offensiveness.[134]

(R5) Reverse slurs are on average less insulting or offensive than prototypical hate speech slurs.

What, in general, qualifies a slur as insulting or offensive? In one sense this is simply a matter of the slur giving and being intended to give insult or offence. But in a deeper sense it may also have to do with the slur being socially unacceptable, as in, taboo in a given society.[135] Either way, the third argument assumes on the strength of (R5) that reverse slurs are not hate speech.

However, we are sceptical about both steps of this argument. Starting with the first step, at present the evidence for (R5) is weak. Results from participant experiments reveal there is no significant variation in the perceived offensiveness of anti-black and anti-white slurs.[136] Furthermore, if historically dominant social groups feel increasingly threatened by the social and economic advancement of formerly oppressed groups, arguably this could lead to reverse slurs becoming perceived to be more not less offensive among members of historically dominant social groups, irrespective of whether they have reasonable grounds to feel threatened. Furthermore, an important part of the semantics of reverse slurs like 'honky' and 'redneck' is that they convey caricatures of White people as being arrogant and racist. To attribute these traits to a group of people may become increasingly offensive within a society where anti-racism norms are becoming more prevalent. Being called a 'honky' or 'redneck' may be extremely offensive to White people who understand the meanings these words convey. What is more, they will probably find this offensive even if they are in fact prejudiced or unconsciously biased against non-White people.

Turning to the second step, even if there is some difference in degree of offensiveness between reverse slurs and standard slurs, this does not necessarily mean the former are not hate speech. There is no evidence of a generally accepted rule among competent users of the ordinary term 'hate speech', whether explicitly or implicitly, that says all slurs which count as hate speech – or, for that matter, all forms of speech that count as hate speech – must be equally offensive. A degree of difference in offensiveness does not automatically equate to a difference in kind. Moreover, one feature of the term 'hate speech' that distinguishes it from 'offensive speech', is that the former is reserved for speech that is more than merely offensive and exhibits distinguishing qualities of target, style, message, act, and effect.

3.4.4 Second Option: Reverse Attacks as Dissimilar in Effect to Prototypical Hate Speech

A second pathway out of the reverse attacks trilemma argues that irrespective of whether reverse attacks are similar or dissimilar in kind to prototypical hate speech in the ways outlined above, they typically have differential effects (are less harmful), so once again there is no double standard in denying they are hate speech. What are these differences? For one thing, when speakers of slurring terms and other reverse attacks are themselves members of oppressed or powerless groups, they may be less likely to have their words interpreted in the ways they intend,[137] and also less likely to be heard, to be seen as credible, and to be winners in the marketplace of ideas.[138] And so their attempts at derogating their targets may lack the same ideational effect.

Another differential effect might be the quantity and intensity of emotional distress caused by reverse attacks. In the words of Greenawalt and Popa-Wyatt respectively:

> [T]hose who are secure in a favored status can accept denigrating terms that apply to their privileged position with less distress than can those who know the terms reflect a wider dislike of their group. For example, in most contexts in our society, 'honky' hurts a lot less than 'nigger.'[139]

> An utterance of 'Nigger' will typically cause considerably worse psychological and social damage than an utterance of 'honky' in part because the former occurs against the background of current widespread racism, history of slavery, and historical civil rights struggles for African-Americans, and nothing comparable for Caucasians.[140]

Why so? Perhaps it is because reverse attacks like 'honky' are on average less likely to find the relevant targets in vulnerable states of mind as compared to people on the receiving end of prototypical hate speech slurs like 'nigger', and for various reasons. For one thing, people of colour are more often targeted with racist slurs than White people, which can happen almost at any time and in any place,[141] and have less access to spaces and interactions that carry little or no chance of being victimised. Furthermore, some victims may have lower psychological resilience or endurance to hate speech due to underlying personality traits or behaviours, such as a tendency to pessimism, unhealthy forms of emotional suppression, or self-isolation from social and family networks,[142] and those traits and behaviours may in turn be partly shaped by their personal and inherited experiences of racism including being targeted with racial slurs, for example.[143] Indeed, part of White privilege may include a greater opportunity to nurture and hold onto resilience or endurance to hate speech. For example, White people may be more able to cognitively deflect or disassociate themselves from slurs that refer to their race.[144] This could explain why, as Delgado and Stefancic put it, '[v]ituperation aimed at blacks [...] is individually wounding in a way that finds no ready analog with respect to whites'.[145]

As well as these immediate differential effects, differences in people's formative and ongoing experiences of racism, including being frequently targeted with racist slurs like 'nigger', might cause members of oppressed groups to suffer a build-up of emotional hurt from which more indirect or diffuse psychological effects could flow. The indirect effects of cumulative exposure to hate speech emerge over the medium- and longer-term, especially when combined with more general experiences of other forms of racism. Potential effects of cumulative exposure to racism include not merely raised background levels of stress, anxiety, hypervigilance, fear, anger, fatigue, mood swings, or bouts of depression[146] but also the more insidious dismantling of a person's sense of self-respect such as through a gradual internalisation of negative stereotypes leading to self-hatred.[147] Since White people are far less likely to be victims of repeated racist abuse and racism in general, they may be at a lower risk of these effects.

Both kinds of differential effects may also be exacerbated by some of the non-equivalent semantics highlighted in Section 3.4.3.1. For one thing, reverse slurs often convey a message of disparagement (that the targets are less estimable), whereas standard slurs are more likely to convey a message of degradation (that the targets are fundamentally inferior). It may be harder to psychologically cope with the former than the latter. Similarly, if reverse slurs are directed more towards a structure, institution, or system than against individuals, this may enable targets to disassociate themselves from the slur. More generally, members of non-oppressed groups may have a greater resilience to being slurred not merely if reverse slurs are more ambiguous concerning who or what is being attacking but also if the former have a cognitive bias toward interpreting ambiguous information positively. For example, there is less risk of cognitive dissonance if the slur 'honky' is interpreted by the target as not in fact a personal attack. Ironically, there is evidence to suggest that people with underlying stress, anxiety, or depression may have a bias toward interpreting ambiguous information negatively,[148] and regularly being the target of hate speech can be a source of such stress, anxiety, or depression. Likewise, if terms like 'cracker' and 'honky' refer to racial subgroups, namely to *poor White people* or to *stupid racist White people*, rather than to all White people, then individual White people who are targeted with these slurs may not be stung or hurt by them insofar as they do not see themselves as belonging to the relevant subgroups. To avoid cognitive dissonance between a positive self-conception and the accusation conveyed in the slur, the target might simply interpret the slur as mistaken (e.g. *The person who called me a 'cracker' wrongly thinks I'm poor*), based on ignorance (e.g. *The person doesn't know me well enough to call me a 'cracker'*), or referring to someone else (e.g. *The person who yelled 'honky' in my direction can't possibly have been yelling at me because I'm not a racist*).

Another differential effect might be the quality or kind of emotional distress caused by reverse attacks. For example, it is likely that the sort of generalised discomfort or diseuphoric feeling that a White person might potentially experience as a result of being called 'honky', including any shame that might come from being implicitly cast as a *stupid racist white person*, is incomparable with the singularly excruciating hurt of being called 'nigger' and reminded of the history of oppression of Black people and being told that this is how things ought to be. As Delgado explains, 'words such as "honky," "cracker," and "redneck" are insulting for white individuals, but nonetheless lack the socially and politically laden and corrosively dispiriting quality of words such as "nigger," "wop," "spic," "chink," or "kike"'.[149]

Furthermore, it is possible that reverse attacks do not produce the same level of fear or insecurity about physical safety as prototypical hate speech.[150] Similarly, perhaps reverse attacks are not as undermining of people's personal sense of confidence in their socio-legal status or standing in a country as standard hate speech.[151] In the words of Greenawalt and Sunstein respectively:

> Epithets used against members of oppressed groups may reinforce feelings of inferiority and fear of violence in a way not characteristic of epithets used against groups that have been dominant historically.[152]

> It is only obtuseness—a failure of perception or emphatic identification—that would enable someone to say that the word 'fascist' or 'pig' or 'communist,' or even 'honky,' produces the same feelings as the word 'nigger.' In view of our history, invective directed against minority groups, and racist speech in general, create fears of violence and subordination—of second-class citizenship—that are not plausibly described as mere offense.[153]

The uniting theme is that the psychological and emotional toll on people wrought by reverse attacks is qualitatively distinct from the effects of standard hate speech. Clearly there are parallels here with jurisprudential arguments concerning the legal concept(s) *hate speech* and, specifically, debates about potential qualitative differences between the effects of reverse attacks and the effects of standard forms of hate speech, as regards justifying the use of legal sanctions.[154]

In addition to differential psychological and emotional damage, according to Embrick and Henricks, 'racial epithets directed toward whites are unlikely to affect their life chances in the same way that racial epithets directed toward minorities do.'[155] How so? For one thing, at various stages in American history, the term 'nigger' has been used by people and institutions as a designation with the power to either de jure or de facto change a person's social and legal status, in many instances with devastating and life-changing effects, including enslavement, incarceration, segregation, unemployment, and homelessness.[156] By contrast, the term 'honky' has lacked such life-changing effects. If the conveyed meaning of 'honky' is *stupid racist white person*, it might in certain situations embarrass the target, but this effect is many orders of magnitude lower than the social and legal consequences of being categorised as 'nigger'. This in turn might account for why on average 'honky' has lower derogatory force compared to 'nigger'. As Hess puts it, '[n]o one really cares much if they're called a 'honky', because it doesn't much matter'.[157]

Similarly, according to Matsuda, '[r]acist speech is particularly harmful because it is a mechanism of subordination, reinforcing a historical vertical relationship'.[158] Slurs like 'nigger', for instance, serve to perpetuate social hierarchies, reinforce patterns of inequality and disadvantage, and support institutional and structural discrimination. '[I]t works in concert with other racist tools to keep victim groups in an inferior position'.[159] The same cannot be said of anti-white slurs (so the argument runs) because they cannot be used to perpetuate forms of oppression and structural discrimination against White people if those forms do not exist in the first place.[160]

A related way in which the harmful effects of prototypical hate speech might not be replicated by reverse attacks has to do with how the use of the former is a catalyst for further hate speech. As Popa-Wyatt explains, the flagrant use of egregious racial slurs like 'nigger' can 'make it more permissible for others to give voice to their bigotry'.[161] Yet if racial slurs achieve the illocutionary effects of *inciting*, *legitimating*, or *(mis)educating* other people in the use of hate speech[162] only by tapping into public and widespread anti-black racist social attitudes, then in societies where White people are a powerful majority, it is likely that Black people will be less able to use anti-white slurs with these effects since there may not be the same attitudes against White people to tap into. Indeed, the common thread in the current path out of the reverse attacks trilemma might be summed up with Popa-Wyatt's suggestion that 'it is socially acceptable to slur the powerful, precisely because they are powerful, and it does them no harm'.[163] Once again, these sorts of assumptions are echoed in policy debates concerning the legal concept(s) *hate speech*.[164]

However, there is an obvious flaw in the current pathway. Sometimes the use of reverse attacks can harm the powerful. Indeed, this is among the reasons why oppressed groups use them, although not the only reason.[165] Just as it is unhelpful to ignore general societal differences that predict dissimilar harmful effects of reverse attacks and prototypical hate speech, so it is unhelpful to ignore situational contexts which might predict more similar harmful effects. To recycle Sunstein's words, it is a failure of perception to see how in discursive microenvironments anti-white slurs can be used in such a way as to produce prototypical hate speech effects. To give one example, when a lone White employee in a Black-owned vehicle repair shop is greeted day after day with discriminatory harassment, through constant racial slurs against his Whiteness, this may have a cumulative psychological effect, even if viewed simply on an individual and isolated level. Sometimes reverse attacks can also be socially laden and corrosively dispiriting, such as in the context of a hostile work environment.

Now it may also be a safe to assume that members of dominant majority groups on average have greater access to exit as well as voice in the face of racist slurs against them, meaning that in the normal course of events they tend to be neither a captive audience nor silenced. As Matsuda puts it, '[t]he dominant-group member hurt by conflict with [members of a subordinate group] is more likely to have access to a safe harbor of exclusive dominant-group interactions'.[166] Nevertheless, there may be specific situations where a dominant group member lacks possibilities of exit and voice. What is more, differing individual circumstances may mean that not all dominant-group members have access to positive relationships and, therefore, opportunities for '[r]etreat and reaffirmation of personhood'.[167] Suppose an African American woman brings her White boyfriend to a family barbeque at which he is the only White person present. Imagine if several family members pull the boyfriend aside and call him a 'white boy' with intent to derogate him and ultimately to make him feel unwelcome, marginalised, and excluded. What if the boyfriend feels trapped by the situation and feels unable to leave the barbeque or stand his ground verbally? And, what if the boyfriend is not especially close to his own family, meaning that he cannot retreat to them to reaffirm his White personhood?

Similar observations apply to hate speech that is used to *threaten* other people. It might be the case that, generally speaking, '[r]acial or ethnic insults directed at non-Jewish White Americans simply do not have the same capacity as insults directed against subordinated groups', as Steven Shiffrin puts it.[168] Nevertheless, as Shiffrin also recognises, there may also be specific situations in which an anti-white verbal insult is 'delivered in a way that might be reasonably interpreted as a threat'.[169] The family barbeque may be a case in point. In other sorts of situations, the use of 'honky' could produce more visceral fears of violence. Ironically, this slur may be capable of triggering these fears not merely because of the speech context but also because of the effects of anti-black racism. If, for example, White people learn about people of colour through negative stereotypes in the media, and from hate propaganda posted on social media platforms, they may be socialised into fearing them as violent, criminal, or animalistic. Harbouring such prejudices, it is not difficult to see how the use of 'honky' by a group of Black students towards a lone White student on campus late at night could evince fears of violence, for example. Nevertheless, if it is plausible to label a slur like 'nigger' as hate speech partly because of its capacity to cause genuine fear of violence in certain situations, then something similar would seem to be true of 'honky' in situations where it is also intended to cause or has the foreseeable consequence of causing fear of violence.

Furthermore, when slurs are used by elites, such as powerful or influential politicians, this can socially speaking 'make it more permissible for others to give voice to their bigotry', and this seems true even if the politician is a member of a minority ethnic group and only holds relevant power and influence among the minority. Consider the example of reverse hate speech used by elites in Kenya, for example.[170] The point is that speech intended to incite hatred or acts of violence may still achieve these effects in some audiences even if the target of the incitement is a dominant group. If ethnic prejudices and hostilities are distributed evenly across a society, then they can be stirred up, enlivened, or magnified either by reverse attacks or by prototypical hate speech. Insofar as some paradigmatic hate speech effects depend on incendiary styles of hate speech, then a slur, a false rumour, or a bellicose oration, for example, might still provide the spark to ignite the powder keg despite targeting the group in power.[171]

Notwithstanding all this, a defender of the current pathway out of the reverse attacks trilemma might counter that even where reverse attacks do produce harms, they are less frequent and less severe. However, once again this generalisation does not bear scrutiny. The comparative lower frequency of harms flowing from reverse attacks does not entail the non-existence of such harms, and under the right circumstances, reverse attacks can be extremely severe.[172] Furthermore, even if on average the harmful effects of reverse attacks are together quantitatively and qualitatively lesser than the harmful effects of prototypical hate speech, it does not follow from this that reverse attacks cannot be hate speech. By analogy, suppose it happens to be true (and we are not saying it is) that on average the harms of racist slurs are lesser than the harms of racist hate propaganda, that the harms of racist hate speech are lesser than the harms of racist-misogynistic hate speech, or that the harms of religious hate speech are lesser than the harms of racist hate speech. This would not by itself indicate that racist slurs are not hate speech, that racist speech in general is not hate speech, or that religious expressive attacks are not hate speech.

To be clear, we do not intend to deny, or downplay the moral significance of, what are real differences in harmful effects between reverse attacks and prototypical hate speech. Indeed, Louise Richardson-Self plausibly argues that to egregiously deny or downplay the differential harmful effects of reverse attacks and prototypical hate speech could amount to not merely an epistemic injustice but an act of racial misrecognition.[173] What is more, insofar as such an act of denialism or downplaying would constitute an act of racial misrecognition or even a racial microaggression, then it might itself count as being hate speech (see also Chapter 2).

Rather, what we are pointing out is that the ordinary concept *hate speech* has a wide extension – wider than the legal concept, for example – and that competent language users can, and often do, apply the term 'hate speech' to phenomena that have varying levels of harmfulness. Clearly, some people may choose to deploy the term 'hate speech' when they intend to speak about harmful effects of the sort highlighted by Matsuda, Lawrence, and Delgado, such as anxiety and self-hatred. Other people may have a different point of emphasis, such as a climate of fear. Yet more people may have in mind social divisions and a breakdown in public order. Finally, when a competent language user applies the label 'hate speech' to the slur 'white devil' they may have in mind different kinds of harm but also lower degrees of the same kinds of harm. The label 'hate speech' is both coherently and meaningfully applied to reverse attacks precisely because this ordinary concept serves myriad purposes including speaking to different kinds and degrees of harm.[174]

3.4.5 *Third Option: Reverse Attacks as Oppression*

A third potential solution to the reverse attacks trilemma is to insist that what at first glance appear to be reverse attacks by oppressed groups against their oppressors, on closer examination almost always turn out to be prototypical hate speech against oppressed groups. If in fact there exists very few, if any, bona fide reverse attacks, then the reverse attacks trilemma disappears and the general rule of thumb (R2) that hate speech is the speech of the oppressor against the oppressed remains uncontested (so the solution claims). In fact, there are two versions of this third solution worth exploring: the first is that certain forms of speech are constitutive of oppression such that to be the subject of a reverse attack is itself to be oppressed; the second is that due to intersectionality, most people are members of groups exemplifying multiple characteristics, so reverse attacks almost always pick on groups that are oppressed in some respects. We shall argue that both versions fail, however.

3.4.5.1 Racist Speech as Constitutive of Oppression

The first version starts from the premise that the link between hate speech and oppression is not simply correlational, as in, things that merely occur together. Rather, it assumes there is a constitutive relationship between hate speech and oppression: specifically, that the former constitutes a form of the latter. After all, any society or organisation could accept that reverse attacks are hate speech whilst at the same time clinging on to the rule of thumb (R2) by stipulating that the mere use of racist speech, for example, constitutes a form of oppression, irrespective of whether the target of the speech is Black or White people. Imagine a society or social media platform in which there is widespread social practice of using racist slurs and that this practice spans the racial divide, meaning that Black people are just as likely to use anti-white racial slurs as White people are to use anti-black racial slurs. If both practices are defined in the society or by the relevant social media platform as constituting a form of oppression, then using any of these racial slurs becomes simultaneously racist, oppressive, and hate speech. For example, it may be that within this society or social media platform any unjust or discriminatory treatment of groups of people is considered to be oppression.[175]

However, what justifies the stipulation that social practices of racist speech are partly constitutive of oppression? One answer could be that social practices of racist speech constitute oppression when the targets of the racist speech are an oppressed group. But what is an oppressed group? The answer to this question cannot appeal to the concept of hate speech itself; otherwise, the line of argument becomes circular: *Hate speech is whatever speech attacks an oppressed group; an oppressed group is a group attacked with hate speech.* Another answer is slightly more granular and analyses oppression in terms of any unjust or discriminatory treatment of a group of people. But what constitutes unjust or discriminatory treatment of a group of people? Once again, the answer to this question cannot appeal to the concept of hate speech itself, as this would also be circular: *Hate speech is whatever speech constitutes oppression; oppression is any unjust or discriminatory treatment of a group of people; unjust or discriminatory treatment of a group of people includes hate speech.*

Of course, a more substantive answer could be that racist speech is unjust or discriminatory treatment of a group of people insofar as it carries messages of bigotry towards, and has certain harmful effects on, the relevant group. But then this begins to contradict the spirit if not the letter of (R2). Recall that (R2) describes hate speech as a type of one-way or unidirectional speech involving attacks by the powerful against the powerless. On the current analysis, however, even the powerless can be hate speakers provided what they say carries messages of bigotry towards, and has certain harmful effects on, a group of people. On closer examination, therefore, the current analysis is either circular or at risk of dissolving into (R3) and the idea of hate speech as multidirectional (fifth option).

3.4.5.2 Hate Speech and Intersectionality

The second version of the third solution takes a different tack. It starts with the premise that various features or determinants of being oppressed can be relied upon to help fix the meaning and extension of the concept *oppressed group* even without reference to whether members of the group are subject to racist speech, for example. Lack of political voice and influence, absence of social mobility, subjection to various types of social and institutional discrimination, being victims of systemic exploitation, poverty, and violence – these are among the possible determinants. Importantly, seeing oppression as complex and multidimensional means not only that the extension of the concept *oppressed group* needs to be handled on a group-by-group basis but also that some groups could be ultimately judged to be oppressed despite appearing at first glance not to be oppressed, provided the judgment is based on valid grounds, that is, reflects the relevant facts or credible evidence of the facts.

Insofar as this second version of the current solution to the reverse attacks trilemma rests on complex determinations of who is oppressed and who is an oppressor, this may be viewed as a strength or weakness of the approach depending on which purpose the ordinary concept *hate speech* is intended to play.[176] Note, similar controversies surrounding what constitutes an oppressed group crop up in scholarly debates about how best to define the legal concept(s) *hate speech*.[177]

At any rate, one immediate upshot of adopting this approach is that the category of oppressed groups may be wider than first appears, and so putative reverse attacks may turn out to be attacking oppressed groups after all. For example, it may be that poor rural White people are victims of class-based oppression. If so, then certain uses of slurring terms like 'cracker' and 'white trash' may be derogatory attacks on members of oppressed groups and, therefore, prototypical hate speech (on the current analysis). Of course, whether these slurring terms are currently considered to be hate speech by the major social media platforms is another matter. Comparing the lists of protected characteristics contained in the hate speech content policies of Meta,[178] Twitter,[179] TikTok,[180] Snap Inc.,[181] and YouTube,[182] whilst 'caste' is universally present, 'class' is absent except for Snap Inc.'s policy which includes 'socio-economic status'. Similarly, according to Thomas Grey, one of the chief authors of the Stanford University discriminatory harassment code, 'calling a white student "white trash" would not constitute harassment' under the code because '[i]n its commonly understood meaning, the term [...] is derogatory to the poor whites of the rural South by virtue of their class, not their race'.[183] Likewise, it is a further issue whether class currently is or ought to be considered a protected characteristic as far as the legal concept(s) *hate speech* is concerned.[184] Nevertheless, the current analysis certainly points in the direction of incorporating slurs based on race and class within the scope of the ordinary concept insofar as race and class can be identifiers of an oppressed group.

It is also an open question whether other complex identities can be considered identifiers of an oppressed group and, therefore, slurs based on these identities counted as hate speech under the current analysis. Consider 'peckerwood', 'redneck', 'hillbilly', and 'white nigger'. These slurs might refer not merely to race/ethnicity (being a White person) but also to wealth (poor, low income), profession and employment status (unskilled work, manual labour, unemployed), class (working class, under class), education (not college educated, perhaps lacking high school diploma), intelligence (unintelligent, backwards), housing conditions (poor quality housing, wood cabins, trailers), geographic area (rural, hills), geographical location (the Southern States, Appalachia and the Ozarks), criminality (participation in criminal activities), but also partly social attitudes (racist, conservative), political views (right-wing), and lifestyle (high alcohol consumption, outdoor pursuits, gun ownership, self-reliance, strong kin networks, intergroup violence, prevalence of incest). If these complex identities can be seen as representing oppressed groups, then the current analysis would suggest that the slurs 'peckerwood', 'redneck', 'hillbilly', and 'white nigger' are targeted at oppressed groups and, therefore, count as hate speech in the ordinary sense of the term.

Arguably, some groups of White people could be classified as discrete ethnic groups when the group is also formed around shared ancestry, language, culture, attitudes, and geographical location, and this opens up the possibility of oppressed White ethnic groups. Anthony Harkins, for example, identifies mountain dwelling White Americans as an ethnic group. He also observes that '"hillbilly" continued to be a vital actor on the American cultural stage throughout the last three decades of the twentieth century, long after similar stereotypes for other racial and ethnic groups had become unacceptable'.[185] Interestingly, all of the aforementioned social media platforms recognise ethnicity as a protected characteristic within their hate speech content policies. Thus, depending on thorough empirical assessments, it might be credible to view mountain dwelling White Americans as an oppressed group and, therefore, to recognise slurs like 'hillbilly' as perpetuating that oppression.[186]

What about 'redneck'? Patrick Huber underscores how the term 'redneck' is associated as much with White people who hold particular social and political attitudes as with poor rural White people. 'For approximately the last one hundred years, the pejorative term redneck has chiefly slurred a rural, poor White man of the American South and particularly one who holds conservative, racist, or reactionary views.'[187] Here the question of whether the term picks out an oppressed group is much harder to answer because of the complex nature of the group, such as if the group is economically oppressed but not politically or socially oppressed, for example. Nevertheless, if there are plausible grounds to count the group picked out by the slur 'redneck' as an oppressed group, then this suggests the slur is hate speech, consistent with (R2).

However, the current pathway out of the reverse attacks trilemma suffers from three major weaknesses. First, the idea that putative reverse attacks count as hate speech only if, on closer inspection, they target people who belong to an oppressed group seems to place too much weight on a single point of similarity. Suppose there is a business in which the people in positions of power (high paid owners, managers, supervisors) are all White men, who do not suffer any recognisable forms of oppression, save for the fact that a subset of these men are subject to intolerant, bigoted, or prejudiced speech attacks based on their being *bald White men*. Suppose the people performing these speech attacks are all Black women and in lower positions (low-paid employees) and themselves suffer a range of recognised forms of oppression. Think of scenarios in which a White bald supervisor is in the work canteen when several Black women start to make rude jokes about his White bald head ('cue ball'). Leaning on an independent account of what it means to be oppressed could point in the direction of saying the White bald men are not oppressed, and so the prejudiced speech is not hate speech. But the prejudiced speech seems to have important semantic similarities with hate speech, as in, it carries a similar enough message to make appear hate speechy. Furthermore, it also bears similarities with prototypical hate speech in terms of act and effect, such as if the jokes are an act of cruelty and make the supervisor feel publicly disparaged or humiliated. In this scenario refusing to see the prejudiced speech as hate speech seems hard to justify. It also reintroduces the first horn of the trilemma: if reverse attacks are dismissed as not being hate speech, this could smack of double standards.

A second, related flaw in the current approach is that it lacks explanatory power. Put simply, it is hard to believe nearly all real-world examples of reverse attacks dissolve into prototypical hate speech on closer inspection, or that there is no such thing as a genuine reverse attack. Take the slur 'honky'. Where is the intersectionality in that term? If it means *stupid racist white person*, to what oppressed group do such people belong? Of course, some individuals may perceive 'honky' to be an attack on an oppressed group based on their own political or ideological worldview. For example, members of alt right organisations maintain that White people are being replaced by non-whites in America and some White students believe not merely that they are a demographic minority on their college campus (that the sum of ethnic minorities outnumber White people) but also that they are being discriminated against by university authorities in the awarding of degree places, scholarships, housing bursaries, and other benefits. Such people might fail to comprehend 'honky' as a reverse slur, if 'reverse slur' means a verbal attack against an oppressor group. They may view 'honky' as a prototypical racist attack on an oppressed group.[188] However, on the current approach, it would seem to follow that if members of a group have no valid grounds, that is, no basis in fact or credible evidence of fact, to regard themselves as oppressed, then they are not oppressed and any slurs targeting them are reverse slurs. A defender of the current approach would be forced to draw the conclusion that 'honky' is not hate speech. But once again that reintroduces the first horn of the trilemma: a blanket and peremptory refusal to consider as hate speech even words that may in fact bear several semantic and pragmatic similarities to prototypical hate speech can smack of double standards.

A third weakness lays the foundation for a fourth response to the reverse attacks trilemma. It is that typically where members of oppressed groups verbally attack their oppressors in ways that seem like hate speech, there is something about the situational context that explains the hate speechiness as opposed to the targets turning out to be members of oppressed groups after all. Consider an affluent young White tourist from suburban America who stumbles into a predominantly Black area of the capital city and is surrounded by a group of Black locals who tell him this:

(88) Go home, you don't belong around here, whitey.

If (88) has potential to be hate speech and, what is more, if its counting as hate speech partly has something to do with power, then it seems far more likely to be because there is a momentary reversal of power than because the White tourist is a member of an oppressed group. In other words, the correct way out of the trilemma is not to reclassify targeted people as members of oppressed groups but instead to identify highly contextual, and often transitory, reversals of the normal power dynamics that exist between the speaker and people who are otherwise members of oppressor groups (fourth option).

3.4.6 Fourth Option: Reverse Attacks as Dependent on Situational Power Dynamics

Let us turn then directly to the fourth pathway out of the reverse attacks trilemma, namely to detach the ordinary concept *hate speech* from the idea of attacks against people who are oppressed or powerless in general, and focus instead on situational power dynamics. In 1992 Thomas Grey wrote: 'As best I can see, there are no epithets in this society at this time that are "commonly understood" to convey hatred and contempt for whites as such.'[189] Even as it stands, the statement is highly questionable. But if one were to add the universal quantifier 'in any situation', then the statement becomes demonstrably false. The key flaw in Grey's statement is that the scope of 'in this society' is much too broad to be determinative when analysing putative hate speech. The analysis must pay as much attention to particular speech situations or discursive microenvironments as to the general societal context. As Delgado and Stefancic put it, 'nothing that minorities can say can be considered hate speech, except, perhaps, in those relatively rare situations (a prison, an inner-city classroom) where blacks are in the majority and whites have something to fear from them'.[190]

The fourth option does not necessarily mean rejecting out of hand Matsuda's insight that in the case of paradigmatic hate speech '[t]he message is directed against a historically oppressed group',[191] but it does involve interpreting the insight in an importantly different way. The kernel of truth in Matsuda's insight (so the argument runs) is that in the case of hate speech there is a power dynamic, pecking order, control imbalance, or asymmetric vulnerability. This unequal power may follow a conventional pattern, but it can also take an atypical form, such as a highly contextualised and temporary reversal of the normal power dynamic or societal hierarchy. In short, the fourth option is to substitute (R2) with the following.

(R2.1) Hate speech is by definition a type of one-way or unidirectional speech in the sense that it is only ever the speech of persons who either generally or in particular situations occupy positions of relative power, dominance, control, or protection, against persons who either generally or in particular situations find themselves in positions of powerlessness, subservience, lack of control, or vulnerability.

The key difference between (R2) and (R2.1) is that the former restricts the scope of the ordinary concept *hate speech* to attacks against generally oppressed groups whereas the latter interprets the concept as having a wider scope such that it covers both standard attacks rooted in background oppression and reverse attacks based on situational power dynamics. Affirming (R2.1) means treating the claim that hate speech involves attacks against historically oppressed groups as an empirical generalisation as opposed to a formal rule or necessary condition. Of course, there are at least some specific hate speech acts that could only be performed against historically oppressed groups. For example, a White racist might use the slur 'nigger' to *cruelly remind* Black people of their lower place in a general or widespread social hierarchy; *derogate* Black people by telling them that having a lower place is something they deserve; *condone* this hierarchy as natural and beneficial; *hark back to* or *glorify* a time when the hierarchy was enforced through permissible segregation and discrimination; and *express regret* that further attempts are being made to question and dismantle the social hierarchy. But none of these specific hate speech acts could be performed by a Black nationalist using the slurs 'whitey' or 'honky' given facts about the background social hierarchy.[192] Nevertheless, defenders of the fourth option might insist that reverse slurs can be used to perform somewhat similar acts. For example, a leader of a Black nationalist movement could use the slur 'honky' to *derogate* White people by telling his audience that all Whites are racists; *agitate* for policies including the expropriation of White land and Black separation; and *express regret* that White people have not been the subject of lynching, to teach them a lesson about cruelty.

Notwithstanding these examples, how could members of an oppressed group successfully perform a range of other speech acts commonly associated with the ordinary concept *hate speech* that seem to rely on the exercise of oppressive power? Consider this statement.

(89) Go back to where you came from, you're not welcome here.

Depending on the context, (89) could be used to perform a prototypical hate speech act, namely to *marginalise* the targeted people. In Austinian terms, this might be an illocutionary act (exercitive or verdictive), such as if there is an existing convention that uttering (89) counts as *marginalising*, or even a perlocutionary act, such as if making persons feel marginalised is part of the real effects of telling them (89).[193] But, at first glance, it is hard to see how a Black person could utter (89) in such a way as to *marginalise* White people (illocutionary force) or to go one step further and *make White people feel marginalised* (perlocutionary effect). Jon Gould makes a similar sceptical point about anti-white slurs: '[a]bsent some other threat, no reasonable recipient of the slur ['dumb honky'] would believe himself in danger of marginalization or worse'.[194]

However, just as standard power dynamics exist at the wider societal level and can be relied on in the moment of speech,[195] so sometimes atypical power dynamics exist at the level of discursive microenvironments and can also be relied on in the moment of speech. In other words, certain types of speakers can obtain the power to perform prototypical hate speech acts if only within a particular domain of influence or communicative jurisdiction.[196] Consider again the earlier example in which an African American woman brings her White boyfriend to a family barbeque. Suppose her uncle, whom the boyfriend knows is held in high esteem within the family, pulls the boyfriend aside and, with grim faced sincerity, drops the following bombshell.

(90) Just so you know whitey, we don't want your kind here.

Surely it is conceivable that, within this situation or discursive microenvironment, the uncle could successfully use his utterance of (90) to *marginalise* the boyfriend (illocutionary force) and *make him feel marginalised* (perlocutionary effect). Of course, it is quite possible that the boyfriend carries a life of racial privilege into the situation, including a sense of security or confidence about the value of his White ethnicity, and that the uncle for his part may carry at least some baggage of internalised stereotypes, self-doubt, and experiences of racism. This background social hierarchy cannot be wiped entirely from the moment of speech. But facts on the ground may play an even bigger role in shaping the speech pragmatics because they are more immediate and visceral. Facts on the ground might include, for example, the boyfriend's sense of unease at being the only White person at the gathering and the uncle's position as an esteemed family member.

However, it is one thing to claim that even members of oppressed groups might have access to discursive microenvironments in which they, as speakers, have power to perform prototypical hate speech acts; it is quite another thing to explain how.[197] By what mechanism(s) do members of oppressed groups obtain the requisite power or authority to perform certain acts within the relevant microenvironments? Defenders of the fourth pathway out of the reverse attacks trilemma could perhaps point to the various mechanisms we outlined in Chapter 2 (Section 2.3.4), including formal authority, devolved authority, informal authority, licensed authority, presuppositional authority, special authority, cumulative force, rule-governed practices of discrimination, and lack of resistance. Although we do not have space to discuss this in more detail here, perhaps under the right set of circumstances one or more of these mechanisms could be applicable to reverse attacks. For now, we shall point out one potential benefit of this approach but also a significant residual problem.

The benefit of saying that historical oppression can help to explain the nature of hate speech in general terms but that the situational context of speech may also reveal other power dynamics that facilitate hate speech acts even in the case of reverse attacks is that individual human beings are not permanently fixed into roles as hate speakers and victims of hate speech. If these roles can be seen as reversible, this may be symbolically important not merely to challenge stereotypes but also to promote mutual understanding and even reconciliation. A similar sort of benefit might apply to the legal concept(s) *hate speech* and, in particular, hate speech laws that identify Black and White speakers alike as potentially unlawful hate speakers.[198]

However, the main residual problem with this pathway out of the reverse attacks trilemma is that it focuses too much on power. It still assumes that wielding some form of power (whether background oppression or situational authority or power) is a necessary condition for something to count as hate speech. But in plain terms this assumption seems false based on a broader analysis of the pragmatics of exemplars of hate speech. No doubt power can help to explain why some reverse attacks count as hate speech, such as when even members of oppressed groups find themselves in situations where they can perform authoritative acts like *marginalising other people* or *ranking other people as inferior*. Yet speakers can also use reverse attacks in the performance of other sorts of archetypal hate speech acts, such as *prejudging*, *stereotyping*, *misrecognising*, or *essentialising*, that are not authoritative acts (see also Chapter 2).

It is also worth noting here that Facebook's community standard on hate speech includes within its general definition 'expressions of contempt, disgust or dismissal', 'statements of inferiority', and 'harmful stereotypes'.[199] Yet the standard contains no clause or caveat stating that the hate speaker must occupy a position of power (oppression or authority). Moreover, the standard does not explicitly exclude or rule out the possibility of reverse expressions of contempt, disgust or dismissal, reverse statements of inferiority, or reverse harmful stereotypes. Arguably, at least some of these kinds of reverse attacks are made possible precisely because they do not require authority or power as a necessary condition of performance (felicity condition). That said, we do not mean to suggest archetypal hate speech acts like *prejudging*, *stereotyping*, *misrecognising*, or *essentialising* are part of some essence of the ordinary concept *hate speech* (i.e. necessary conditions for something to count as hate speech). To repeat, we do not believe the ordinary concept has an essence in that or any other way.

3.4.7 *Fifth Option: Similarities Between Reverse Attacks and Exemplars of Hate Speech*

Based on the above, we favour a fifth option to resolve the reverse attacks trilemma, which is to reject both (R2) and (R2.1) and instead embrace (R3), the rule of thumb that hate speech is a multidirectional type of speech. According to the fifth option, any attack, whether a conventional attack or a reverse attack, could potentially count as hate speech depending on its global resemblance to exemplars of hate speech based on the distinguishing qualities of target, style, message, act, and effect. The fifth option involves being a pluralist about hate speech. In answer to the question 'What reasons might we have to treat reverse attacks as hate speech?' the pluralist says, in effect, 'all of the above'. For example, a reverse attack could be hate speech partly because it shares a different, but still sufficiently similar, message to prototypical hate speech (Section 3.4.3); because it has sufficiently similar effects as prototypical hate speech (Section 3.4.4); or because it involves the performance of sufficiently similar acts as prototypical hate speech, where this performance could be made possible because it is conventional hate speech in disguise (attacks an oppressed group) (Section 3.4.5) or because, given the situational context, it involves reverse power dynamics (Section 3.4.6), or because, even in the absence of reverse power dynamics, it involves the performance of non-authoritative hate speech acts.

But what, then, of the second horn of the reverse attacks trilemma, that treating reverse attacks as hate speech risks opening the floodgates to limitless applications of the term 'hate speech'? We believe that, even though the ordinary concept *hate speech* has 'taken on a life of its own'[200] separate to the legal concept, this does not mean there is literally nothing the term cannot be applied to. On the contrary, there are sensible limits to ordinary uses of the term 'hate speech', even if such uses are more diverse and numerous. These limits are marked by the logic of resemblance, namely that reverse attacks, for example, must resemble exemplars of hate speech as closely as the exemplars resemble each other and that closeness of resemblance is a function of the range, extent, degree, and salience of similarities (see Chapter 2). Such resemblance embodies what Wittgenstein calls 'a complicated network of similarities overlapping and criss-crossing'.[201] Complexity is not the same thing as randomness. Moreover, we believe the study of complexity in ordinary usage of the term 'hate speech' can be as detailed and rigorous as the search for essences or universal definitions.[202] Part of a rigorous analysis involves uncovering some of the different points of similarity in play and explaining and justifying what overall similarity can and should look like.

What, then, about highly controversial uses which appear to show the term 'hate speech' can be applied to almost anything? Think about when President Trump referred to his critics as 'anti-Trump haters'.[203] Or consider the moment in a White House press conference when Trump was asked by an African American journalist if he thought his calling himself a 'nationalist' during the midterm elections in 2018 was 'emboldening' White nationalists and he retorted, 'I don't know why you'd say that, it's such a racist question'.[204] Or think about when the journalist Tom Switzer opined this about anti-Trump rhetoric: 'The irony here is that although Trump is all too often accused of creating a climate of fascism, the kind of vitriol he regularly evokes from the left creates a climate of hate.'[205] According to Gelber, these sorts of examples 'attest to a lack of clarity around what "hate speech" is in public debate'.[206]

However, we believe there is another way to look at these examples. If these examples are relatively rare and strike most competent language users as not simply marginal but in fact nonsensical uses or egregious misuses of the term 'hate speech', they may testify to a concept that has limits after all. In other words, widespread rejection of what are viewed as nonsensical uses or egregious misuses of the term may be evidence of some degree of shared public understanding of what is or is not hate speech in the ordinary sense of the term. Aside from the practices of competent language users, including their informal corrections of transgressive users, another thing constraining ordinary (nonlegal) usage of the term 'hate speech' is the interventions of authoritative or trusted sources of information about hate speech including social media platforms and even academic researchers. When platforms and academics alike make it clear that anti-Trump haters are probably not hate speakers in any coherent or meaningful sense of that term, this may help to limit ordinary usage.

3.5 Righteous Attacks

Yet another set of grey area cases involve speakers who launch expressive, communicative, or performative attacks against another person or group but in pursuit of some righteous cause. For example, they may be speaking up for others or speaking up for themselves in calling out the bad behaviour or attitudes of another person or group (as they see it). Call these righteous attacks.

Righteous attacks may take different linguistic forms but once again we shall focus on pejoratives and slurs. As with other grey areas, righteous attacks may derogate people on the basis of combinations of characteristics including but not limited to race, social attitudes, and behaviour (e.g. 'white folks', 'white racist', 'white nationalist', 'redneck', 'race traitor', 'Uncle Tom'); race and lifestyle (e.g. 'wigga'); ethnicity, nationality, ideology, and behaviour (e.g. 'Ruscist', '*Moskal*' [Slavic] ('Russian invader')); ethnicity, age, and social attitudes (e.g. 'old white men'); physical and mental capacities and social attitudes (e.g. 'TABs', 'normals'); class, social attitudes, and behaviour (e.g. 'toff', 'upper class twit', 'posh twat', 'filthy one-percenter'); race and profession (e.g. 'white cop'); race and criminal behaviour (e.g. 'black hoodlum', 'gang banger'); criminal record (e.g. 'ex-con'); profession or work-based behaviour (e.g. 'ambulance chaser', 'scab'); political views or affiliations (e.g. 'terrorist', 'facho', 'far right', 'Repuglican' [*sic*], 'basket of deplorables', 'Tory scum', 'class enemy', 'commie', 'socialist', 'liberal elite', 'woke brigade', 'thought police'); religion and religio-political views and associated behaviour or affiliations (e.g. 'extremist Muslims'); sexual preferences, proclivities, or practices (e.g. 'peeping tom', 'modeliser', 'unicorn hunter', 'dirty old man', 'dinge queen', 'frigids'); gender and behaviour (e.g. 'deadbeat dad', 'gold digger'); gender presentation, sex, and lifestyle (e.g. 'transtrender'); gender and social attitudes (e.g. 'arrogant prick', 'male chauvinist pig', 'phallocrat', 'gender traitor', 'anti-feminist', 'feminazi', 'cis folks', 'TERF'); race, gender, class, and social attitudes (e.g. 'Karen', 'white bitch'); and social attitudes towards LGBTQIA+ education and related civil rights (e.g. 'groomer').

An important preliminary question is whether a given righteous attack can be considered possible hate speech even before its righteousness is factored into the equation. Suppose for the sake of argument competent language users would be more likely to call something 'hate speech' if it appears to be attacking people based on a protected characteristic. If so, then certain righteous attacks could strike some people as not being hate speech because those people assume the underlying characteristic is non-protected.

Consider slurs like 'upper class twit', 'frigids', 'scab', 'Tory scum', 'feminazi', and 'TERF' which partly concern class, sexual preferences and extent of sexual attraction including asexuality, profession or work-based behaviour, political views or affiliations, and social attitudes respectively. Some people may think it odd to call such attacks 'hate speech', and this may have something to do with the nature of the characteristics involved.[207]

However, one or both parts of this presumption might be unsound and for three reasons. First, even if people assume that certain characteristics are not primary protected characteristics, on closer reflection they may yet accept them as secondary protected characteristics, meaning characteristics that become protected when combined with primary protected characteristics. Facebook's community standard on hate speech, for example, recognises age as a Tier-insensitive secondary protected characteristic.[208] We believe there may be a strong case for increasing the number of Tier-insensitive secondary protected characteristics (see also Section 3.2). If so, this would open up the possibility of recognising the following as potential hate speech.

(91) It's the Tory scum who are black that I despise the most.
(92) These men-hating feminazi women are first class cunts.
(93) Firemen who cross picket lines are scabs and so shouldn't receive hospital treatment if they get injured at work, they don't deserve it.

Second, it is an open question whether competent users of the term 'hate speech' do in fact take as read the relatively narrow list of primary protected characteristics promulgated by Facebook and other major social media platforms. At least the public-facing lists of primary characteristics tend to omit such characteristics as sexual preferences and extent of sexual attraction including asexuality, political views or affiliations, and social attitudes, for example, but that is not to say the majority of competent language users do the same. Perhaps some, or even many, people would be willing to at least consider applying the label 'hate speech' to the following.

(94) Rape the frigids.
(95) Socialists should have no place in our society.
(96) Many of the best wheelchair rugby league players in the world are non-disabled and nobody so much as bats an eyelid about that, but dare to mention a trans swimmer doing well and TERFs are apoplectic. The main difference is that basically these TERFs have a prejudice against trans women, and that makes them irredeemable shitheads as far as I'm concerned.

Third, even if people's gut instinct about whether to call something 'hate speech' rests on whether they think the relevant words are an attack based on a protected characteristic, this intuition itself is likely to depend on whether they evaluate the relevant characteristic as being worthy of protection, and this evaluation in turn may reflect not so much their moral appraisal of the characteristic considered in the abstract but more the people who possess it, and this is where the righteousness of the attack re-enters the picture. If people are unsure about whether to call certain pejoratives 'hate speech', then it may be because of adverse social attitudes towards the targets of those pejoratives. Perhaps people think that the targets are morally objectionable and do not deserve protection from verbal abuse.

This alternative explanation of the hesitancy some people might have in labelling certain words 'hate speech' shall be the focus of this section. Suppose the derogatory term 'modelisers' refers to men who only date models, 'feminazis' denotes a particular type of radical feminist who is glad to see large numbers of abortions carried out, believes that men are at best inferior and at worse unnecessary, and considers transwomen to be sinister, freakish, and simply men in disguise, and 'Karens' picks out a stereotypical White, middle-class woman who is unreasonable when little things do not go her way and talks in an aggressive and demeaning way to non-white members of staff essentially because she is arrogant, entitled, and racist. Perhaps it is a widely held view that the people described by these words in fact deserve moral condemnation because of what they think and how they behave. That is why there are no societies for the protection of Karens, for instance. If so, then maybe it is also no surprise that some competent language users should be ambivalent about calling these words 'hate speech'. It is because they find verbal attacks on such people to be righteous.[209]

Then again, some competent language users might reflect further on these sorts of pejoratives and slurs and come to see them as essentially linguistic fantasies or grotesque caricatures that do not correspond to any real individuals.[210] It is the very fact that they derogate a vague group of people without accurately representing or describing any actual people that makes them candidates for being classified as hate speech. After all, this is precisely the sort of thing that hate speech does.

We believe it is this tension between gut instinct and more considered reflection that explains why righteous attacks fall into a grey area of hate speech. Nevertheless, we also need to reemphasise that any given grey area example may fall into more than one of the grey area categories discussed in this chapter. A given slur or derogatory term might be viewed as a grey area example of hate speech for the combined reason that it is a hybrid attack, a selective attack, a reverse attack, and a righteous attack, for example. This may be true of several of the above-listed illustrations of righteous attacks. Part of the hallmark of real-world language is that words are rarely mono-categorisational and analytically discrete. Even so, in this section we shall try to focus on the narrower question of whether or not, if certain words are righteous attacks, this provides a sound reason *in itself* to discount them as being hate speech. Before moving directly to this conceptual problem, however, we first need to say more about what unites examples of righteous attacks, as this is an important first step to understanding why they fall into a grey area.

One common feature of righteous attacks is that the relevant speakers usually see themselves as well-intentioned, civic-minded, good Samaritans, heroic defenders or otherwise virtuous; or else as injured parties, good people forced to say bad things, or in the role of David against Goliath. Furthermore, the relevant speakers tend to assume their words serve a higher purpose or are crucial in the performance of some righteous action. For example, people may see themselves as speaking up for the vulnerable, condemning perpetrators of injustice, or signalling solidarity with victims. Alternatively, people may have the sense that they are speaking up for a vulnerable group they themselves belong to, reacting to provocation, acting out of self-defence, engaging in just retaliation, raising the alarm, protesting against injustice, speaking truth to power, dissenting against stifling orthodoxy, voicing legitimate grievances, raising consciousness, or performing a legitimate act of defiance or civil disobedience.

In many instances of putative righteous attacks, speakers feel morally justified in talking in a derogatory or even violent way about another person or group because the speaker believes the target has done something despicable, or poses an imminent threat of doing something despicable, and so has the attack coming to them. There is then a live question as to whether the attack ought to count as hate speech. Consider Facebook's temporary adjustment to its community standard on hate speech in Ukraine during early 2022 with regard to Tier 1 attacks against Russian soldiers. 'As a result of the Russian invasion of Ukraine we have temporarily made allowances for forms of political expression that would normally violate our rules like violent speech such as "death to the Russian invaders".'[211] In one sense, arguably this was merely a context-specific interpretation of Facebook's existing exemption from the Tier 1 'all groups' catchall in the case of attacks against 'non-protected groups described as having carried out violent crimes or sexual offences'.[212] Perhaps Facebook was merely making public that it would interpret the term 'invaders' as implying a description of violent crimes. Or else it was indicating that, under the internal policy, the general category of non-protected groups is larger than the illustration listed in the public-facing community standard (i.e. 'groups described as having carried out violent crimes or sexual offences'), such that non-protected groups also includes groups described as having carried out a violent and illegal invasion of a sovereign country. Either way, Facebook has not publicly revealed its internal rationale or justification for introducing the non-protected groups exemption. Nevertheless, one potential reason could be that it implicitly regards statements like 'death to the Russian invaders' as righteous attacks and, therefore, not hate speech in its view.

However, not all righteous attacks, on closer analysis, are really about people, even if the literal meaning does refer to people. In some instances, speakers may be more intent on condemning structures, institutions, and practices than expressing anger, hostility, or contempt towards the individuals who benefit from those structures. Consider an example due to Embrick and Henricks:

> In one situation Jose, a Mexican route driver in his mid-forties, and Terrance, a newly hired Black man in his forties, were having lunch at a local Mexican restaurant. Jose, quick to point out white favoritism in the company, asks, 'Why does Paul have a twelve thousand dollar route when mine is barely running seven thousand?' Terrance replied, 'He's a white man. Gotta take care of the whitey.' Jose then remarked, 'That's a bunch of bullshit. All of the whites get the better routes. I want a route like Lawrence's with only three stops. I'm tired of having to do all these schools.' In this case, 'whitey' refers to a work relation between whites and minorities at Whitebread. Terrance and Jose use the term to criticize Whitebread's racialized division of labor and their own subordinate position within it. The slur is as much of a disguised release of powerlessness as it is a demarcation of whiteness.[213]

Perhaps this attack, assuming it is an attack, feels righteous in the mind of the speaker partly because of the injustice being pointed out, and also partly because the intention is to attack not White people as such but the system of workplace discrimination from which they benefit. Nevertheless, the question is whether it is less credible to classify this use of 'whitey' as hate speech because it is righteous.

Even in circumstances where a speaker does seem to be attacking people, the speaker might feel justified in saying something apparently hateful if she is telling it like it is or speaking truth to power, especially if this seems a courageous thing to do. Consider the rhetoric of Sister Souljah. In a 1992 interview with the *Washington Post*, she is reported to have said the following about Black-on-White violence during the Los Angeles riots of that year.

> I mean, if black people kill black people every day, why not have a week and kill white people? You understand what I'm saying? In other words, white people, this government and that mayor were well aware of the fact that black people were dying every day in Los Angeles under gang violence. So if you're a gang member and you would normally be killing somebody, why not kill a white person? Do you think that somebody thinks that white people are better, or above dying, when they would kill their own kind?[214]

On the one hand, these words seem to be hate speech insofar as they normalise or legitimate violence against White people, or incite Black people already engaged in an uprising against White authority to escalate their protest through more serious acts of violence. On the other hand, perhaps some competent language users would be hesitant to call this 'hate speech' if they perceive that Sister Souljah was using this language as a way of pointing out the hypocrisy and cruel indifference of White Americans towards the fact that Black Americans are disproportionately victims of violent murder. But once again it is open to debate whether this hesitancy is credible because of the righteousness of the speech.

In addition to voicing home truths about how an oppressed group has been treated, the use of apparently hateful language can sometimes constitute an act of defiance directly in the face of discrimination. Suppose Jesiah lives in a small town in Tennessee in the 1950s. A White woman is sexually assaulted. She did not see her attacker's face but assumes he was Black. This is all the local sheriff needs to justify his rounding up of several Black males including Jesiah. He is unable to provide an alibi and is found guilty by a White jury and sentenced to thirty years in prison by a White judge. In a final act of defiance, he utters these parting words.

(97) Go to hell, you white devils! I shall not go gentle into that long night.

On the one hand, statement (97) might resemble hate speech on account of expressing hatred or anger towards White people. On the other hand, perhaps some competent language users might deem (97) to be something less than hate speech because they see it as a heroic act of insubordination, a rallying call for other victims of racism to rage against injustice.

In other circumstances, the use of racially charged language by an oppressed group might be an act of self-expression or self-realisation. In the words of Matsuda: 'While white-hating nationalist expressions are troublesome both politically and personally, I would interpret an angry, hateful poem by a person from a historically subjugated group as a victim's struggle for self-identity in response to racism.'[215] Without context, someone using poetry to express their hatred and anger towards another ethnic group resembles hate speech whether the target is a majority or minority group. But if the poem expresses anger at a group which the author believes is responsible for perpetrating a genocide against his or her own kind, for example, then in some people's eyes the poem will look less like hate speech and more like the blameless expression of collective memory or performative catharsis.

Whilst our focus in this chapter is grey area examples of the ordinary concept *hate speech*, it is worth noting, as Matsuda's intervention demonstrates, that similar debates about the status of righteous attacks figure in the literature on the legal concept(s).[216] That said, there is a mismatch between Matsuda's idealised legal concept *hate speech* which excludes righteous attacks and most real-world legal concepts which do not.[217] That said, in some jurisdictions courts have paid close attention to the re-active nature of speech in the wider social context of racism as a potential mitigating circumstances at sentencing.[218] This reflects a contextualist approach to penalising righteous attacks endorsed by some legal scholars.[219]

Returning to the ordinary concept, it also bears emphasis that righteous attacks are by no means limited to race. Consider an example concerning gender. In October 2017, amid the #MeToo movement, the TV writer Nicole Silverberg shared on the Facebook page of her friend and comedian, Marcia Belsky, a series of hateful and threatening comments the former had received from men following the publication of her op-ed piece listing some of the concrete ways she believed men could treat women better. In the comments section below Silverberg's post, Belsky wrote, 'Men are scum'. Facebook subsequently contacted Belsky to notify her that the comment had been removed due to violating its community standard on hate speech and that her account would be suspended for 30 days. At first glance, arguably Belsky's words did violate the standard which disallows, for example, 'Content targeting a person or group of people [...] on the basis of their aforementioned protected characteristic(s) [...] with [...] Dehumanising speech or imagery in the form of comparisons, generalisations or unqualified behavioural statements (in written or visual form) to or about: [...] Filth, bacteria, disease and faeces.' However, Belsky Tweeted her dismay at the decision: '"Men are scum" in response to threats got me banned from @facebook for 30 days.'[220] In her view, words posted in response to, and highlighting the problem of, threats of violence against women by men, should not be deemed hate speech. Perhaps she had not intended 'Men are scum' to literally mean 'all men'. At any rate, a month later Belsky reported that Facebook had sent her multiple messages saying the removal of her 'Men are scum' post had been 'a mistake'. To which she replied: 'WHoaaaa @facebook just reversed my ban [...] What about [...] all of the other ppl flagged for "reverse hate speech?".'[221] Nevertheless, pace Belsky, perhaps Facebook overturned its own decision not because 'Men are scum' is reverse hate speech but because a human moderator reinterpreted the words as righteous indignation.

Importantly, in some instances speakers use what appears to be hate speech when responding to what they see as the hate speech of others. For example, speakers may see themselves as having been provoked by, or as speaking in self-defence or retaliation against, the hate speech of others targeting them.[222]

(98) How dare you call me 'nigger' you piece of white trash.

In other situations, speakers may be engaged in condemning or censuring hate speakers but in the course of expressing their moral or social disapprobation they themselves resort to hate speech.[223]

(99) You have absolutely no right to repeat hateful myths and stereotypes about transgender women you feminazi!

Similarly, speakers engaged in acts of counterspeech against hate speakers might themselves lapse into using hate speech.[224]

(100) [Cartman] Because their skin is so light, ginger kids must avoid the sun, not unlike vampires. [Kyle] That's not true fat ass. I have red hair and I don't have to avoid the sun.[225]

Likewise, speakers attempting to block hate speakers from derogating or degrading other people with implied meanings, may themselves end up hate speaking.

(101) You just said, 'Martin works so hard, it's unbelievable; he's not like other black people'. You do realise this implies that all black people are lazy right? I can't let that stand; everyone in this room needs to understand what these words mean. It's so racist what you said, it's exactly the sort of garbage white folks come out with.

No doubt these examples are subtly different and could potentially trigger varying intuitions across competent language users when deciding whether to label them hate speech. Then again, arguably they share in common a putative quality of righteousness that deserves further exploration as a possible hate speech frontier.

However, to clarify, the righteousness that characterises what we are calling righteous attacks does not depend solely on the speaker's perspective. It is not enough that speakers happen to believe or assume what they are saying or doing is merited or justified. We believe competent language users have no difficulty in calling faux righteous attacks 'hate speech'. As we shall define it, therefore, true righteousness is a function of the speaker saying and doing things reasonably, in good faith, and proportionately. First, they must have reasonable grounds on which to believe both that the message conveyed is accurate and that what they are saying or doing serves a legitimate purpose. Second, they must be acting in good faith when taking on the role of being the person to say or do what needs to be said or done. Third, what they are saying or doing must be proportionate to the legitimate purpose. Putative examples of righteous attacks must satisfy all three conditions if they are to count as truly righteous.

To expand on the first condition, we propose that reasonableness partly depends on speakers acting in epistemically responsible ways. Suppose a speaker thinks a group of Democrat congresswomen have the subversive goal of establishing communism in America. The speaker might use the slur 'little commie bitches' to disparage such people. Let us assume for the sake of argument this slur might relate to primary characteristics or a combination or primary and secondary protected characteristics. However, the question of whether this is a righteous attack and, therefore, potentially disqualifies as hate speech does not rest on whether the speaker merely believes the derogation is merited. Rather, it depends on whether the speaker has credible reasons or grounds for holding the belief and making the allegation based on standards of epistemic responsibility that are widely held in the relevant society. Of course, the relevant norms and expectations may vary between examples and contexts. Nevertheless, some standards might be universal including accuracy, due diligence, and fairness. Reasonableness also depends on the speaker having a legitimate purpose. Suppose a Black speaker calls a group of White people 'racist southern crackers'. The speaker might be correct to assume this phrase accurately describes what the people have said and done, or what they think. Nevertheless, to count as righteous the speaker must also have a legitimate purpose in using this phrase, meaning a goal that falls under a general category of purpose that other people in the society could not reasonably reject,[226] such as saying something that needs to be said in order to end oppression or that needs to be said for the rescue or betterment of society as a whole.

Second, acting in good faith is about the speaker having the right sort of intention in taking on the role of saying or doing what needs to be said or done. Suppose a speaker believes a certain group of people are responsible for the historical oppression of another group. The speaker might use the derogatory term 'honkies' to convey this message. The question of whether this is a righteous attack must also depend on whether the use of the term in the context was honest and sincere. For example, if the speaker only used the term as a cynical ploy to further his own personal interests and was not really intended to serve and not likely to serve the interests of members of the oppressed group, and the speaker was aware of this but was not honest and upfront about his true agenda, then this would be acting in bad faith. Similarly, if the use of a derogatory term like 'greedy one-percenter' is in fact merely virtue-signalling, as in, based on vanity and excessive concern with how one is viewed by others rather any genuine concern for the well-being of the poorest in society, then once again this would be bad faith. In such scenarios the use of the term could not count as a righteous attack, as we understand the category.

Third, proportionality is a matter of the speaker saying and doing things in proportion to the legitimate purpose. Suppose a group of students launch a series of campus protests using graffiti, posters, and social media messages that read 'TERFS Out!' and that they feel justified in doing so as a means of protecting trans students. They may have credible reasons to believe what some professors have written about sex and gender identity creates an unsafe environment for trans students. Even so, the righteousness of these words and of what the students do when they use them must also depend on whether what they are saying and doing is in balance with the gravity of the specific issues being addressed whilst also taking into consideration the possible effects of what they are saying and doing. For example, an expressive attack might be irresponsible or reckless with regard to unintended consequences, and in that sense disproportionate, if the words could foreseeably incite acts of violence or themselves create a hostile environment in which people feel bullied and harassed.

Of course, there may be reasonable disagreement in a society about whether the use of certain words, that would otherwise be classified as hate speech, is itself credible and serves a legitimate purpose (reasonableness), is honest and sincere (good faith), and is proportionate to the legitimate purpose given the context (proportionality). Nevertheless, we believe reflecting on such aspects of righteousness allows most competent language users to spot at least some allegedly righteous attacks for what they really are, namely hate speech operating under a veil of unjustified, disingenuous, or disproportionate anger. That said, this still leaves all those examples of attacks that really are righteous or that are not obviously unrighteous. So, the pressing question is whether they count as hate speech.

3.5.1 *The Righteous Attacks Problem*

Part of the problem posed by bona fide righteous attacks is that they may convey (express, convey, presuppose, or infer) an adverse moral evaluation of the targeted group that is itself reasonable, such as if it fits the targeted group. In that scenario, some people may instinctively feel it strange or inappropriate to call the attack 'hate speech'.[227] However, the issue of righteousness is more complex than simply the moral guilt of the targets. To qualify as righteous attacks, words must be reasonable, in good faith, and also proportionate. Nevertheless, righteous attacks even defined in this more careful way still pose a problem for competent users of the term 'hate speech'. Consider the following rules of thumb.

(R6) Hate speech is morally objectionable speech.
(R7) Righteous attacks are not morally objectionable speech.

If (R6) and (R7) are true, then the following rule seems to follow as a conclusion.

(R8) Righteous attacks can never be hate speech.

Although these rules may appear harmless enough, they could have perverse implications. In particular, there is a danger that even some exemplars of hate speech could end up qualifying as righteous attacks, which would result in the counter-intuitive judgment that some exemplars of hate speech are not hate speech. Suppose a white nationalist police officer uses the epithet 'nigger' to convey what he believes is an uncomfortable truth the public needs to hear that African Americans are more likely to have a criminal record than other groups. Depending on how broadly righteousness is understood, this usage could end up qualifying as a righteous attack and, if (R8) is true, then such usage could not count as hate speech. Call this the righteous attacks problem.

Roughly speaking, there are two main lines of response to the righteous attacks problem. The first accepts (R6), (R7), and (R8) but seeks to block counter-intuitive judgments about specific examples. It does this by showing that, despite how they might appear on the surface, exemplars of hate speech are never epistemically responsible and, therefore, cannot count as righteous attacks. The second response accepts (R6) but rejects (R7) and (R8). In particular, it claims that the status of an attack as hate speech is based on a range of similarities with exemplars of hate speech across the dimensions of target, style, message, act, and effect. Therefore, contrary to

(R8), righteous attacks can still be hate speech. In addition, it affirms that the overall moral status of an attack is not determined simply by its status as righteous or unrighteous. Indeed, any attacks can be morally objectionable precisely because they are hate speech. Therefore, contrary to (R7), even righteous attacks can be morally objectionable (because still hate speech).

In what follows, we argue that the first response may be fitting and workable in many instances, but there remain a stubborn set of examples for which there is a danger that they could end up being classified as righteous attacks and, therefore, not hate speech even though this would be a counter-intuitive judgment. Problem examples may include slurs or other sorts of invectives directed against people with criminal records or against transgender women based on generalisations about threats to public safety that might be rooted in putatively reasonable prejudices – for example, the speaker has a precautionary or safety-first reason to believe the slur or invective fits the target group and serves a legitimate purpose. The invective might be a righteous attack in one sense but intuitively it also resembles exemplars of hate speech.

Following on from this, we shall defend the second line of response which is to claim that even righteous attacks can be hate speech based on the global resemblance test. As a result, we endorse this alternative rule of thumb.

(R9) Righteous attacks can be hate speech but not always or necessarily.

We also consider whether embracing (R9) could generate additional counter-intuitive judgments, including the paradoxical result that even the pejorative 'hate speaker' could count as hate speech. However, we show (R9) avoids this result by virtue of its stipulation that just because righteous attacks can be hate speech it does not mean they are always or necessarily hate speech. In particular, we argue the sorts of things that speakers typically say and do with the pejorative 'hate speaker' are *not* similar enough to exemplars of hate speech across the distinguishing qualities of target, style, message, act, and effect to count as hate speech.

3.5.2 First Response: Attacks Based on Unreasonable Prejudice Can Never Be Righteous

The first main line of response to the righteous attacks problem seeks to block counter-intuitive outcomes in which exemplars of hate speech turn out to be classifiable as righteous attacks and, according to (R8), not hate speech by claiming that because such examples are typically rooted in forms of illegitimate, unfair, or unreasonable prejudice, they cannot be righteous attacks after all.[228]

As discussed in Chapter 2, archetypally racist uses of the epithet 'niggers', for example, not merely refer to African Americans or people of African descent but also convey a set of ascriptive, explanatory, justificatory, and/or prescriptive attitudes and perspectives. So, in some contexts the epithet may have the following conveyed meaning.

(102) You are all just niggers at the end of the day.
(102a) *The speaker is expressively demonstrating a commitment to a perspective on African Americans central to which is the idea that the mere possession of certain descriptive features (e.g. skin colour, African descent) explains the presence of further stereotypical traits or attributes (e.g. lazy, stupid, criminal), makes certain evaluations of African Americans appropriate (e.g. contemptible), and justifies holding certain feelings or attitudes towards African Americans (e.g. contempt).*

Racist uses of 'niggers' may also convey a further attitude to the effect that targeting members of this group with slurring terms is a justifiable thing to say and do.

(102b) *The speaker is signalling commitment to the idea that it is justifiable to use the slurring term 'nigger' to derogate the group of people who are the targets of the term based on the speaker's perspective on this group of people, and thereby to participate in practices of discrimination including the very act of derogating such people.*

However, because there is no credible epistemic basis for the sorts of attitudes exemplified in (102a) and (102b), as in, they are illegitimate, unfair, or unreasonable, such uses of the word 'nigger' cannot be righteous. In this case the current line of response claims to have aligned with linguistic intuitions by showing why these terms are in fact non-righteous and hate speech.

Importantly, the current line of response also seeks to avoid counter-intuitive outcomes in relation to attacks on people who really are morally objectionable and about whom reasonable prejudices could be conveyed. Contrast a slur like 'nigger' with terms like 'Nazi', 'child molester', and 'mass murderer'. What is the unreasonable or epistemically unjust attitude conveyed by the latter terms? If the answer is 'none', then these sorts of attacks could be righteous and, according to (R8), not hate speech. Here the current line of response claims to have aligned with linguistic intuitions precisely by showing why these terms are not hate speech.

However, the story is a little more complicated than may first appear. After all, what if the basis for the negative moral evaluation conveyed by terms like 'Nazi', 'child molester', and 'mass murderer' were simply the brute fact of group membership without consideration as to the context of what it means to be a member of the group or what a person must do to qualify as a member? In that scenario the attitude might smack of bigotry: if the attitude concerns the targeted person's possession of the purely formal characteristic *being a member of the the relevant out-group*, this could suggest unfair prejudice.[229]

Nevertheless, arguably when it comes to pejoratives like 'Nazi', 'child molester', and 'mass murderer', the negative evaluation is partly rooted in a contextual assessment of what persons must be or do to qualify as members of the group.[230] In some contexts, the pejorative 'mass murderer' might convey the following content.

(103) This person is a mass murderer at the end of the day.

(103a) *The speaker is expressively demonstrating a commitment to a perspective on people that have murdered lots of other people central to which is the idea that being a murderer of lots of people makes certain evaluations of being this sort of person appropriate (e.g. wicked, despicable), and justifies holding certain feelings or attitudes towards such persons (e.g. abhorrence).*

(103b) *The speaker is signalling commitment to the idea that it is justifiable to use the pejorative term 'mass murderer' to derogate the group of people who are the targets of the term based on the speaker's perspective on this group of people, and thereby to participate in practices of discrimination including the very act of derogating such people.*

Perhaps (103) is a righteous attack and, according to (R8), not hate speech (under the current line of response) because it conveys a reasonable prejudice, namely that the target really ought to be negatively evaluated and derogated precisely because of what a person must be or do to be classified as a mass murderer.

Interestingly, Facebook's community standard on hate speech would also seem to disqualify some posts involving the pejoratives 'mass murderers' and 'child molesters' from being counted as impermissible hate speech (although not all such posts). For one thing, the standard does not include among its primary protected characteristics things like violent behaviour or criminal record. Moreover, even in the case of Tier 1 hate speech that covers 'all groups' (i.e. all subgroups) attacked on the basis of a combination of primary and secondary protected characteristics, an exception is carved out for 'those who are considered non-protected groups described as having carried out violent crimes or sexual offences'.[231] As such, the following examples are highly unlikely to be deemed hate speech under Facebook's policies.

(104) I hate mass murderers.
(105) All Russian commanders who are responsible for mass murders in Ukraine are animals.

So far so good, then, for the current line of response. However, there are other sorts of invective that might be classifiable as righteous attacks even though it would seem conceptually incoherent to disqualify them from being considered hate speech. Not all prejudices are the same and some might be reasonable given widely shared norms and expectations about what it means to be epistemically responsible. Consider what we shall call precautionary prejudices. In the case of a precautionary prejudice, a speaker holds the view that certain deeds are so bad or unconscionable that it is always better to err on the side of caution when it comes to the group that contains perpetrators of such deeds. This could mean responding to what limited evidence is available to form provisional attitudes (generalisations, stereotypes, prejudices) about a group of people – attitudes the speaker holds until such time as conclusive evidence comes along showing the attitudes to be mistaken. Perhaps it is a truism of human psychology that, as Leslie puts it, '[e]xtreme and aberrant actions of the few can thus lead to conclusions concerning the group at large, and these conclusions will influence judgments concerning a newly encountered member of the group'.[232] But it does not necessarily follow that a disposition to generalise from limited evidence to attitudes about the entire group is thoughtless or irrational. Even if the actions of a few members of the group are not prevalent across the whole group and so statistically speaking the chances of other members acting in the same way are low, maybe the harm is so extreme or severe that a precautionary attitude might be not merely understandable on a human level but also epistemically reasonable.[233] Consider the following statements expressing precautionary prejudices.

(106) Ex-cons should never be fully trusted, just look at the high rates of recidivism; it shows that in general the leopard does not change its spots.
(107) No goddam trannies should be allowed to enter bathrooms used by our wives, daughters, and mothers; you hear stories about some of these people that would give anyone the shivers, it's just not worth the risk.

In the case of (106) and (107), the speaker's precautionary attitudes may provide a bridge from the neutral counterparts of the relevant slurring terms (e.g. having a criminal record, being a transgender woman) to the further attribution of undesirable traits or attributes (e.g. poses a risk to others) and on to the implied negative moral evaluation (e.g. despicable, dangerous) and the resulting prescription (e.g. society should not trust, should not allow the same freedoms). The connections between these different components may be tenuous but, depending on the context, could turn out to be epistemically reasonable (at least in a minimal sense).

To explain, in the case of the slurring term 'ex-con', a speaker's precautionary attitude might involve both a presumption that a criminal record indicates a risk that endures beyond the point of prison release (such as if the speaker has in mind statistics about high recidivism rates) and a commitment to thinking and acting on the strength of this presumption in the absence of strong counter-evidence. In the case of 'tranny', a speaker's precautionary attitude might involve both an assumption that a person being a transgender woman increases the level of threat they pose to others within certain enclosed environments (such as if the speaker has in mind statistics showing that a higher percentage of sexual assaults committed in public bathrooms are carried out in unisex bathrooms compared to single sex bathrooms or statistics suggesting that of the sexual assaults carried out in women's prisons a disproportionately high percentage are carried out by transgender inmates relative to transgender inmates as a proportion of the women's prisons inmate population) and a commitment to working with this assumption unless and until proven inaccurate or unreliable. In some contexts, it might be reasonable (in a minimal sense) to operate with these sorts of prejudices such as if doing so falls under the old maxim that it is better to be safe than sorry. This in turn could qualify (106) and (107) as righteous attacks and, according to (R8), not hate speech (under the present line of response).

Then again, many competent users of the term 'hate speech' may be inclined to call out statements (106) and (107) as hate speech even if they are righteous attacks in one sense. In our view, the main driver of this linguistic inclination stems from obvious similarities between these statements and exemplars of hate speech. One similarity is how (106) and (107) use derogatory epithets ('ex-cons', 'trannies') rather than neutral descriptors to pick out the people they are discussing – the rhetorical technique of priming the audience to think badly of the group of people the speaker is about to warn, advise, or instruct them about is a familiar feature of hate speech including racist and homophobic slurring terms such as 'niggers' and 'fags', for example. A second similarity is the way (106) compares people with criminal records to an animal ('the leopard') with a bad reputation (e.g. dangerous, unchanging), and the way (107) expresses physical unease or revulsion towards transgender women ('shivers') – both of which are also familiar tropes of hate speech. A third similarity, and perhaps the crucial similarity, is how (106) and (107) make generalisations about entire groups of people based on the behaviour of only some members of the group – acts of stereotyping, essentialising, and misrecognising are once again commonplace within the pragmatics of hate speech. Therefore, the current line of response to the righteous attacks problem does seem in danger of producing counter-intuitive results.

However, perhaps the current line of response has reserves of explanatory power we have overlooked. Maybe it can explain why righteous attacks constitute grey area cases in the first place. For one thing, righteous attacks might encode prejudices that seem both fair and unfair based on different sorts of credible reasons. For example, the fact that people have a criminal record might be a reasonable basis for negative appraisal, in one sense, if it reflects the speaker's precautionary attitude. But, in another sense, forming a negative judgment of a person solely based on something they may have done only once, a long time ago, and when they were young is unfair. Indeed, terms like 'ex-con' and 'jail bird' abstract from the mitigating circumstances and miscarriages of justice that can surround criminal convictions as well as ignore people's varying capacities to become reformed characters. Such terms may also be disproportionate if they imply or presuppose that it is somehow fair to discriminate against people with criminal records in matters of housing, employment, and voting for the remainder of their lives.

Righteous attacks might also fall into a grey area due to the shifting circumstances of the targeted group. Consider in the Ethiopian context the anti-Tigrayan epithet '*Woyane*'.[234] On the one hand, people who use this derogatory epithet may believe it is a righteous attack on a group of people who have historically occupied positions of power and authority and who have in the past exploited their positions to oppress the very groups using the epithet against them. On the other hand, some people might insist that circumstances have changed and that it is Tigrayans who are now marginalised and relatively powerless. Indeed, younger Tigrayans might argue that it is unreasonable to vilify them for the crimes of previous generations of Tigrayan people and that the former dominant position of their ethnic group cannot perpetually justify attacks against them as righteous.

In addition, righteous attacks could fall into a grey area based on reasonable disagreement within a society about whether religious beliefs, for example, are a source of credible opinions about the reprehensibility of targeted groups. Thus, religiously conservative speakers might sometimes use terms like 'homo', 'deviant', and 'pervert' to derogate gay and lesbian people based on what they see as unnatural or ungodly sexual preferences and sinful sexual behaviours. They may deny this is hate speech but instead a sort of righteous attack. However, because the view that religious beliefs are reasonable sources of expressive attacks is not universally shared, it is likely that other sections of society, including not only members of LGBTQIA+ communities but also religious moderates, agnostics, and liberals, may be more inclined to view this language as unrighteous and, therefore, potentially hate speech. Note, similar debates about religiously motivated expressive attacks are a fixture of the academic literature on the legal concept(s) *hate speech*.[235]

However, assuming these illustrations are representative of the wider class of speech, then it is quite possible that many or even most putative righteous attacks will end up permanently residing in a grey area of hate speech. This is because many or most of these examples may be subject to unresolvable reasonable disagreement about whether they are in fact righteous. As a result, even if one accepts in principle that righteous attacks can never be hate speech as per (R8), for many or most putative righteous attacks, it will remain fundamentally ambiguous whether they are hate speech precisely because their status as righteous remains unresolvable.

We believe that on balance this result is more of a weakness than a strength of the current response. The ordinary concept *hate speech* is a purposive concept, meaning society shapes its rough contours and articulates different conceptions of it based on the different functions or purposes society has in mind for it.[236] These purposes can be many and varied (see also Chapter 5). But as the Facebook community standard ably demonstrates, one mainstream purpose is as a standard that can be used to sift out the sort of language that should not be allowed to cast a pall over public discourse in diverse societies. In other words, the ordinary concept *hate speech* can be, and often is, used by organisations to make important editorial and content moderation decisions, including decisions about removing, adding warning labels to, or reducing the distribution of content. Therefore, it might be more helpful, at least in terms of this particular purpose (although by no means all purposes), if decisions about whether words qualify as hate speech are not tethered to potentially unresolvable, albeit reasonable, disputes of a moral, political, and cultural variety about whether the words are righteous.

We believe this unhelpful result is avoidable and that in fact putative righteous attacks are not essentially ambiguous even if they are the subject of unresolvable reasonable disagreement as outlined above. In the next subsection we shall defend a second line of response to the righteous attacks problem, namely that if such attacks share sufficient similarities with exemplars of hate speech, then they are hate speech, irrespective of whether in fact they are righteous, unrighteous, or else the subject of unresolvable reasonable disagreement as to their righteousness.

3.5.3 *Second Response: Even Righteous Attacks Can Still be Hate Speech*

The second line of response (our proposed response) to the righteous attacks problem parts company from the first response in its reaction to the above-listed rules.

(R6) Hate speech is morally objectionable speech.
(R7) Righteous attacks are not morally objectionable speech.
(R8) Righteous attacks can never be hate speech.

Whereas the first line of response accepts these rules and fights a rear-guard action to try to block any counter-intuitive implications that might flow from such acceptance, the second line of response accepts only (R6) and rejects (R7) and (R8).

Its main grounds for rejecting (R8) is that even righteous attacks can have significant similarities with prototypical hate speech in terms of target, style, message, act, or effect and that to ignore these similarities is arbitrary from a conceptual, moral, and social point of view. More specifically, the suggestion that righteous attacks can never be hate speech conflates two different sorts of questions: the first is about the legitimacy, justification, or righteousness of using certain speech in given circumstances; the second is about what category of speech is in play. It might be legitimate, justifiable, or righteous for Black people to use the expression 'white devils' in a derogatory way, for example, such as to convey ideas about the bigoted attitudes and air of superiority adopted by some or even many White people, given that Black people are often on the receiving end of these sentiments. But that does not in itself show that 'white devils' does not fall under the ordinary concept *hate speech*. The issue of whether a given piece of language counts as hate speech in the ordinary sense of the term is not reducible simply to facts about whether the message accurately describes the target group or whether the speaker is in the right or has moral standing to make the attack. Rather, it depends on a complex pattern of overlapping and criss-crossing similarities with exemplars of hate speech, which are in turn to be considered in the light of the various social purposes or functions people can reasonably expect the concept to play.

Unfortunately, the English language does not serve us well here. There is no obvious term which is both in public circulation and refers in a restricted way to language that, at lexical, semantic, and pragmatic levels, falls under the category hate speech but which also differs from other sorts of hate speech in being used righteously. If we were to invent such a term, we might propose 'mitigated hate speech', 'excusable hate speech', 'merited hate speech', 'victimless hate speech', or simply 'righteous hate speech'. But the fact that the qualified term does not currently exist is not a reason to disapply the label 'hate speech' to such language.

By way of clarification, however, we do not mean to suggest that the righteousness of attacks is completely irrelevant or makes no difference. For one thing, if the similarities between certain words and exemplars of hate speech are already very thin or tenuous, then righteousness could conceivably make a difference at the margin, such as if a significant dissimilarity in the righteousness of the words grounded on the behaviour of the relevant targets tips the balance towards withholding the label 'hate speech'. Furthermore, even if it fails to make a difference in the first way, righteousness could still mark an important distinction between different forms of hate speech – with implications for what organisations and society as a whole decides to do. An organisation might decide to disallow hate speech in general but allow righteous hate speech, for instance. Instead, we are saying that the overall similarity or global resemblance between righteous attacks and exemplars of hate speech cannot be a function of just one dimension of comparison.

In the remainder of this section, we want to set out some key similarities between righteous attacks and exemplars of hate speech in terms of target, style, message, act, or effect. To do this we shall revisit several of the above examples. Starting with message, it can be relatively easy to spot whether the term 'nigger' is being used to convey derogatory generalisations about African Americans based on the speaker and context. But we believe the same may be true of some righteous attacks. Consider once again the act of court room defiance mentioned above.

(97) Go to hell, you white devils! I shall not go gentle into that long night.

This use of 'white devils' shares several lexical and semantic similarities with paradigmatic racist uses of the slur 'nigger'. First, it is group-based. Second, it conveys the attribution of undesirable traits (e.g. exploiter, oppressor) but also negative moral evaluations (e.g. evil), partly based on the possession of a physical characteristic (i.e. white). Third, and relatedly, it attacks persons based on a protected characteristic (race). Fourth, it is derogatory and insulting and intended to be so. Fifth, it wears its derogatory force on its sleeve, in the sense that it is not a coded or veiled attack.

Moreover, there may be other discursive contexts in which what speakers are doing by using slurring terms like 'white devils' or by using generics like 'That's typical of white folks' could also constitute the performance of prototypical hate speech acts. So, for example, to call people 'white devils' or to express the generalisation 'That's typical of white folks' could be to *stereotype*, *prejudge*, *essentialise*, *misrecognise*, and *stigmatise* such people. These are prototypical hate speech acts in part because they involve abstracting from the individuality and complex identities of real people and reducing them to a single undesirable identity, typically prior to getting to know or finding out information about them as separate persons.

We believe this holds true even if words are used righteously (at least in one sense of righteousness). Consider a situation in which the speaker seeks to block anti-black racist language but also makes a dig at White people in the process.

(108) It is clear that public discourse around black anger has been used for centuries to covertly stereotype and disparage African Americans and that this linguistic strategy is typical of white folks.

An analysis of (108) may suggest it too conveys a derogatory generalisation about all White people. It associates White people with using coded racist language and being closet racists. Of course, the ambiguity in locutions of the form 'typical of white folks', much like the ambiguity in public discourse about Black anger, may give the speaker an opportunity to deny using bigoted speech. It enables a speaker to make the argument (a form of occlusion) that he was not suggesting White people's adoption of the linguistic strategy is literally true of all White people or statistically true of the majority of White people or a characteristic of White people as a kind or a propensity ingrained into White people or part of what it means to be a true White person.[237] When pressed to explain what he was in fact saying, if not a derogatory generalisation, the speaker might protest that he was merely pointing out a striking linguistic technique used by a certain type of White person against Black people. Yet even the conjuring up of a White archetype can be a form of stereotyping. It might not be an embodied archetype like the term 'Karen' (see Chapter 4) but it operates in a similar way by creating a simplistic image or oversimplified representation of an entire group of people based on a certain type. If competent language users would be willing to classify Black archetypes, such as the archetype of the angry Black man, as hate speech, this may support applying the same label to White archetypes given the parallel message, even if the attack is righteous.

Of course, we do not mean to say that all generics do the same things, much less that they are always used to perform the most serious or egregious hate speech acts. In the case of stereotypes about historically oppressed groups, for example, these can be more than simply essentialising and stigmatising, they can also be controlling, that is, 'used to maintain social hierarchies and, often, to promote domination.'[238] Nevertheless, the key point is that even righteous attacks can be used to perform at least some acts commonly associated with exemplars of hate speech, such as to *stereotype, prejudge, essentialise, misrecognise*, or *stigmatise* people.

We believe it is possible to draw similar comparisons between many other examples of righteous attacks and exemplars of hate speech keeping in mind the message and the act. Consider the following examples.

(109) #cancelwhitepeople.
(110) Why not kill a white person?
(111) Men are scum.
(112) Say no to transwomen, say no to trans-predators.
(113) Ex-cons can never be trusted.
(114) Gold diggers have no soul.

Even if one assumes for the sake of argument that each of these examples could be a righteous attack under the right sort of circumstances, they might nevertheless share several key similarities with exemplars of hate speech that might go some way at least to warranting the label 'hate speech'.

Rather than providing pairwise comparisons for each of these examples, we shall limit ourselves to using (114) as an illustration of our broader point about family resemblance. Compare the following statements uttered by an avowed misogynist.

(114) Gold diggers [*certain women*] have no soul.
(115) Birds [*all women*] have no sexual morals.

Even if (114) turned out to be a righteous attack on a certain kind of woman as righteousness is defined at the start of Section 3.5 (which it may or may not be), arguably (114) might still share important similarities with (115), such as in terms of target, style, and message, for example. We assume (115) is an exemplar of hate speech. First, each of these statements picks out the intended targets, explicitly or implicitly, at least partly based on their sex or gender. Second, they each use loaded expressions or slurs in place of neutral descriptors. Third, they attribute further undesirable traits that are, at least in the mind of the speaker, closely related to sex or gender. Fourth, they encode some form of adverse normative appraisal or express negative feelings or attitudes towards the target group. Finally, they might also convey (imply, presuppose, or infer) explanatory and justificatory content along the lines that the relevant sex or gender characteristic explains the presence of the undesirable traits, and together this justifies the adverse normative appraisal or negative feelings or attitudes.

Now it might be objected at this stage that 'birds' is a more clear-cut example of a group-based slur than 'gold diggers'. However, we believe 'gold diggers' is at least a hybrid slur on a par with 'bitch' (see Section 3.2). This is because the targeted people can experience these slurs as attacks both against themselves as individuals and against the group or class of people to which they take themselves to belong or with which they identify. This identification may or may not be as strong as someone who vigorously identifies as 'gay and proud', for instance. Even so, if a woman recognises being sexually active primarily or exclusively with wealthy men as part of her social or group identity and reasonably expects not to be spoken to in a demeaning way in virtue of that identity, then the slur is partly group-based.

In addition to similarities in target, style, and message, arguably (114) could also be used to perform prototypical hate speech acts. Like the gendered slur 'birds', terms like 'gold diggers' could be used to *stereotype*, *prejudge*, *essentialise*, *misrecognise*, or *stigmatise* a group of people, despite the term 'gold diggers' potentially being a righteous attack (at least in a minimal sense). Furthermore, under the right circumstances, like (115), statements such as (114) could be used to *disparage*, *degrade*, or even *dehumanise* a group of people. It might also be used to *control* or *disempower* the target group. And it could even be used to *legitimate* or *incite hatred*, *discrimination*, *or violence* against the target group.

Furthermore, it is possible that, if certain background conditions obtain, the use of statements like (114) could have prototypical hate speech effects, even if (114) also happened to be a righteous attack. For example, such statements could make women feel marginalised, perpetuate sexist norms, and could even contribute to forms of gender discrimination or violence. The archetype of the gold digger (typically a woman) may be responsible for perpetuating sexist norms and gender roles in society – for example, by presupposing that it is the role of men to be financially independent and the role of women to be helpless; by assuming that women are not allowed to place too much emphasis on the financial status of their partners even though men may place as much importance as they like on the physical appearance of their partners; and by endorsing the idea that a woman should never take advantage of a man whereas a man may take advantage of a woman. There is also evidence that the gold digger stereotype has been used as a weapon against women in alimony negotiations in the context of divorce proceedings.[239]

Because of the many and varied similarities – what we call global resemblance – that can obtain between examples of righteous attacks and exemplars of hate speech, we reject (R8), namely the rule that righteous attacks can never be hate speech. That said, there may be examples of righteous attacks that display significant dissimilarities to classic hate speech in terms of target, style, message, act, or effect. Therefore, we endorse this alternative rule of thumb.

(R9) Righteous attacks can be hate speech but not always or necessarily.

So far, we have explained and defended one important aspect of the second response (our proposed response) to the righteous attacks problem, which is the rejection of (R8) in favour of (R9). But what about the other two rules of thumb, (R6) and (R7), mentioned at the start of the section? It is to these rules that we now turn.

3.5.4 Hate Speech and Morality

What is the connection between righteous attacks and morality and, more generally, between the ordinary concept *hate speech* and morality? We believe it is an oversimplification to say that righteous attacks cannot be morally objectionable simply because they are righteous. Therefore, we also reject this rule of thumb.

(R7) Righteous attacks are not morally objectionable speech.

We reject (R7) on the grounds there is more to the moral status of an expressive attack than its righteousness. Even righteous attacks can be morally objectionable for other reasons. For example, they may be instances of *dirty hands*, namely doing what is in one sense morally objectionable to do what is in another sense right.[240] More specifically, righteous attacks can be morally objectionable partly as a result of being hate speech. And they are hate speech based on a global resemblance with exemplars of hate speech. Therefore, our proposed response to the righteous attacks problem, like the first response, is consistent with the folk platitude captured in the following rule of thumb.

(R6) Hate speech is morally objectionable speech.

Importantly, we believe the objectionableness of hate speech depends on a complex range of reasons including not merely the objectionableness of attacking the target (which may be absent in the case of righteous attacks) but also the objectionableness of the style, message, act, or effect of hate speech.

On closer examination, there are two ways of reading (R6). On the one hand, it could be understood as a justified true belief that ordinary people have about hate speech based on their assessments of the moral objectionableness of exemplars of hate speech, as in, a credible normative generalisation about the moral status of things that fall within the extension of the concept. On the other hand, it might also be understood as a statement about the conventional meaning of the term 'hate speech', as in, a sociolinguistic claim about what people mean when they use the term 'hate speech' in its ordinary sense. We believe the former is the more plausible reading since we reject the view that the ordinary concept *hate speech* has an essence.

The fact that the objectionableness of hate speech depends on a range of reasons is important not least because this can be used to contest or challenge certain applications or non-applications of the label 'hate speech'. Sometimes people may fail to apply the label 'hate speech' to particular words because they have overlooked one or more of the relevant reasons. For example, the moral attitude of the speaker and society in general towards the targets of words like 'white folks', 'race traitor', 'filthy one-percenter', 'Tory scum', 'gold digger', 'ex-con', 'tranny', 'TERF', and 'Karen', cannot by itself determine the appropriateness of applying or disapplying the label 'hate speech' to these words. An assessment of not only the target but also the style, message, act, and effect might show that the use of these words is morally objectionable even if they are righteous attacks.

In summary, we believe the second response to the righteous attacks problem is superior to the first response on two counts. For one thing, the second response provides a richer or more complete account of the relationship between the ordinary concept *hate speech* and morality. The second response recognises that the moral status of expressive attacks depends on a range of moral reasons including but not limited to righteousness, whereas the first response conceives of moral status exclusively in terms of righteousness. Furthermore, the second response has greater explanatory power than its rival. In particular, the second response not only helps to explain why righteous attacks might appear to be grey area examples of hate speech but also helps to resolve or clear up the ambiguity. At first glance, an attack might seem to be not hate speech in one aspect, such as if it is an act of self-defence, a means of highlighting social injustice, or righteous in some other way; but it might also seem to be hate speech in another aspect, such as if it says or does some of the things that exemplars of hate speech say and do. Therefore, it can appear as though the attack is not hate speech and hate speech at the same time. The second response resolves this ambiguity by distinguishing between two issues: justificatory and conceptual. An attack might be justified (to a greater or lesser extent) because it is a righteous attack; but it might still count as hate speech because of its global resemblance with exemplars of hate speech. By contrast, because the first response tethers the classification of words as being or not being hate speech to the righteousness of those words, it can leave the ambiguity unresolved, such as if there is unresolvable reasonable disagreement about the righteousness of the words.

3.5.5 Hypocrisy and Paradox

Having defended the second line of response to the righteous attacks problem, we must now face some potential counter-examples of our own. No doubt how well the second response handles these additional problem cases is just as important as its handling of the more straightforward cases discussed already.

The first set of problem cases involve speakers who target people precisely on the grounds that the speaker believes they hold prejudiced or bigoted views and are engaged in unfair, socially divisive, or discriminatory practices including using hate speech. Consider pejoratives like 'white racist', 'basket of deplorables', 'male chauvinist pig', 'transphobe', 'transmisogynist', 'feminazi', and 'TERF'. If our analysis of what counts as hate speech is correct, then the determiner is not whether the use of such words is righteous under the circumstances. Rather, what matters is whether this usage shares sufficient similarities with exemplars of hate speech.[241] In the event the use of this language does qualify as hate speech, then speakers using this language could be guilty of the very thing they are (righteously?) attacking other people for doing, namely holding prejudiced or bigoted views and using hate speech to express those views. Call these examples hypocritical attacks.

Do hypocritical attacks demonstrate there is something awry with the second line of response? We believe not. There is nothing peculiar about pointing out the existence of language that is both hate speech and hypocritical. Suppose some feminist women use derogatory language about members of the transgender community that constitutes the performance of prototypical hate speech acts including *expressing hostility, anger, or contempt* towards transgender people, *essentialising* and *stereotyping* transgender people, or even *denying or miscategorising the identity* of transgender people (see Chapter 4). Suppose also a second group of speakers use slurs such as 'transmisogynists', 'feminazis', and 'TERFs' in a shotgun manner to attack a range of feminist women, whom they perceive as likely to be prejudiced and prone to using hate speech all because they are members of that general group. In doing so, the second group might be themselves performing certain kinds of prototypical hate speech acts including *stigmatising, prejudging*, and *stereotyping* members of the target group. We believe it would be perfectly consistent to conclude that both groups of people are using hate speech and that the second group of people are both hate speakers and hypocrites. What is more, this holds true irrespective of whether the first group, the second group, or both groups are engaged in righteous attacks. Note also, the acts performed by the two groups might not be identical, equally egregious, or morally equivalent, but they may be sufficiently similar to exemplars of hate speech to qualify as hate speech.

The same analysis is applicable to other examples of hypocritical attacks. For example, like the bimbo, the male chauvinist pig is a stock character or archetype (see also Chapter 4). He is a misogynist and anti-feminist male who revels in boorish sexist joke that are designed to degrade but also shock and insult women.[242] On the one hand, the male chauvinist pig uses jokes about bimbos to pigeonhole women. These jokes attribute certain undesirable traits or behaviours and explain the possession of these in terms of female sex or gender. Such jokes also convey a general normative evaluation of women as ridiculous, stupid, or inferior. On the other hand, the speaker who uses the pejorative 'male chauvinist pig' is herself invoking a stock character or archetype and, therefore, is exploiting a similar rhetorical technique to that which she is in effect accusing men of exploiting. Superficially, 'male chauvinist pig' is a selective attack on a subset of men but under the surface it says something about or stereotypes all men, just as the archetype of the bimbo is an implicit commentary on the nature and propensities of all women or what it really means to be a woman. The stereotype of the male chauvinist pig also contains a dehumanising comparison to an animal that is perceived as disgusting or inferior. Interestingly, this sort of comparison is a prototypical style of hate speech (see also Chapter 2) and is explicitly recognised as such in Facebook's community standard on hate speech,[243] Twitter's hateful conduct policy,[244] and TikTok's community guideline on hateful behaviour.[245] Once again, we believe there is nothing contradictory in labelling as hate speech both the stereotype of the bimbo and the stereotype of the male chauvinist pig, and, furthermore, nothing incoherent in calling out people who use the latter stereotype as culpable of both hate speech and hypocrisy. Furthermore, we believe this holds true even if the latter also qualifies as a righteous attack in a way the former does not (righteous in calling out sexism).

A second set of potential problem cases involve speakers who are even more explicit in attacking the speech of racists, sexists, transphobes, and so on, by directly calling them 'hate speakers'. Suppose the term 'hate speaker' attributes undesirable traits or behaviours and conveys a negative moral evaluation based on those attributions. As David Boromisza-Habashi puts it: 'An alleged speaker of hate speech is portrayed as someone who has violated deeply held norms of a society and as someone with a flawed (hateful, prejudiced, racist, homophobic, sexist, authoritarian, etc.) personality that prompts her or him to perform hate speech.'[246] Does that mean the term 'hate speaker' could qualify as hate speech? If so, then this could generate what we shall call the hate speech paradox: namely that if the ordinary concept *hate speech* is conceptualised in a certain way, then the term 'hate speaker' could end up being hate speech itself. Arguably, this outcome would be not merely paradoxical but also detrimental to continued use of the term 'hate speaker'. It would mean that nobody could call another person a hate speaker without becoming a hate speaker themselves. Indeed, if hate speech tends to be morally objectionable speech, and if the term 'hate speaker' is hate speech, then the term 'hate speaker' may be itself morally objectionable speech. This would be a detrimental outcome given that part of the social purpose of the ordinary concept *hate speech* is an appropriate tool for calling out morally objectionable speech.

Perhaps the defender of the first line of response to the righteous attacks problem could try to avoid this paradox by claiming that when people call others 'hate speakers' they do so righteously, and, according to (R8), such attacks cannot be hate speech (under the first response). However, this strategy is unavailable in cases where calling people 'hate speakers' is not righteous such as in circumstances where the label is unreasonable, not in good faith, or disproportionate. At least in these cases, the hate speech paradox re-emerges as a problem for the first response.

Nevertheless, we believe the second response (our proposed response) does not fall foul of the hate speech paradox and for an importantly different reason to the one just proffered. Crucially, what matters on our analysis is whether 'hate speaker' shares sufficient similarities with exemplars of hate speech across the distinguishing qualities of target, style, message, act, and effect. And we suggest that the pejorative 'hate speaker' fails to satisfy the global resemblance test, irrespective of whether it is used righteously or unrighteously in any given case.

Now perhaps in relation to the target it is at least arguable that the pejorative 'hate speaker' attacks people based on a protected characteristic, either because it is fitting to classify something like attitudes and behaviours as a secondary protected characteristic (e.g. 'white hate speakers') or because it is appropriate to treat attitudes and behaviours as itself a primary protected characteristic (e.g. 'death to hate speakers'). Maybe some people would accept this line of argument; maybe others would be more sceptical, preferring a parsimonious list of protected characteristics. Even if this argument were plausible, however, we believe there are other important ways in which 'hate speaker' is dissimilar to exemplars of hate speech.

For one thing, the pejorative 'hate speaker' does not look like a group-based attack, in contrast to 'bitch', 'hillbilly' and even 'fatty', for example, that are typically meant as group-based slurs. In the latter cases speakers seem to have in mind not merely the individuals they are addressing but also the group of people to which the addressees belong. Similarly, targeted individuals tend to think of 'bitch', 'hillbilly' and 'fatty' as slurs picking them out not merely as individuals but as members of groups. Moreover, individual targets may regard the feature they share in common with other targets as being constitutive of a social or group identity with which they identify in the sense of seeing it as part of their own identity and as something worthy of protection (e.g. *hillbilly proud*). By contrast, the term 'hate speaker' seems more like an attack on the individual akin to general insults like 'asshole', 'potty mouth', and 'bully'. When a speaker attacks someone using these general insults, he or she is typically saying something derogatory about that person as opposed to a group of people. Furthermore, few targets of general insults identify with or see their own identities as being partly constituted by a social or group identity, such as all the assholes. Returning to Boromisza-Habashi's characterisation of the term 'hate speaker', he talks about the term as referring to '*someone* with a flawed [...] personality that prompts her or him to perform hate speech' (emphasis added). In terms of his use of 'someone' rather than 'a member of a group', we suggest this characterisation reveals something about the fundamental lexical and semantic nature of the term 'hate speaker' that distinguishes it from classic hate speech, namely it is not group-based.

3.6 Indirect Attacks

A final set of grey area cases relate to familiar hateful words used in referentially non-conventional ways. In conventional instances of hate speech involving slurring terms, for example, the speaker intentionally uses the slur to address or target persons whom the speaker knows or presumes to be members of the group referred to by the slur under its literal or primary meaning (i.e. the group picked out by the neutral counterpart of the slurring term in its standard sense).[247] Consider a speaker who calls someone they know to be African American a 'nigger'. In the case of referentially non-conventional uses of slurring terms, by contrast, the speaker intentionally uses the slur to address or target a person whom the speaker knows or presumes is *not* a member of the group referred to by the slur under its literal or primary meaning. Consider a speaker who calls someone they know to be White a 'nigger'; brands someone they know to be straight a 'fag', 'gay', 'poof', or 'homo'; labels someone they know to be non-Jewish a 'Jew'; calls someone they know to be not disabled or suffering genetic conditions a 'midget' or 'spastic'; addresses someone they know to be not suffering any learning difficulties or neurodivergent conditions as a 'retard' or 'mong'; refers to someone they presume to be not suffering any mental illnesses as a 'psycho' or 'schizo'; or dubs someone they presume to be a man a 'bimbo', 'bitch', or 'slut'. Potentially, even these referentially non-conventional uses of slurring terms also attack members of the group referred to by the slur under its literal or primary meaning. We shall call these indirect attacks.

Indirect attacks can take different forms, but for the sake of consistency we shall once again focus on slurring terms. Referentially non-conventional uses of slurring terms have the following distinguishing qualities. First, when a speaker uses a slurring term in a non-standard way, this is not a case of mistaken identity. The speaker using the slurring term knows or presumes that the targeted person is not a member of the group referred to by the slur under its literal or primary meaning, but the targeted person is the intended target nonetheless. Second, the targeted person does not perceive themselves to be a member of the group conventionally referred to by the slurring term. Third, the speaker believes the targeted person is a member of a group referred to by the slurring term under a figurative or secondary meaning and uses the slurring term in a way that conveys (expresses, implies, presupposes, or infers) this further belief. Finally, the group of people picked out by the slurring term under its figurative or secondary meaning is not coextensive with the group that is the subject of the slurring term under its literal or primary meaning.

Now referentially non-conventional uses of slurring terms could count as hate speech in at least two different ways. First, they could involve hate speech against the group referred to by the slurring term under its literal or primary meaning. We plan to focus exclusively on the issue of whether these sorts of indirect attacks qualify as hate speech. However, for the sake of completeness it is also worth noting that referentially non-conventional uses of slurring terms might potentially qualify as hate speech in a second way, namely as direct attacks on the people the speaker intended to target with the slurring terms. For example, a speaker might employ the slur 'gay' in a non-conventional way to directly attack a group of men who, although not homosexual and not perceived to be homosexual, are targeted based on some other protected characteristic, such as class or gender performance (e.g. upper class men, effeminate men). For reasons of space, we shall not discuss this issue here.

3.6.1 The Indirect Attacks Conundrum

The idea that some referentially non-conventional uses of slurring terms might involve indirect attacks and rise to the level of hate speech poses a challenge to the following rule of thumb often associated with the ordinary concept *hate speech*.

(R10) Hate speech is only speech which directly attacks people on the basis of protected characteristics.

A society or organisation seeking to develop a coherent and plausible conception of hate speech in the ordinary sense of the term must decide how to classify indirect attacks. If it simply denies that referentially non-conventional uses of slurring terms can qualify as hate speech, this upholds (R10) yet seems counter-intuitive and dogmatic. Alternatively, if it accepts that such uses can sometimes qualify as hate speech against the intended targets but never hate speech against the unintended targets, this could create a double standard. And if it goes a step further and concedes that such uses can in some instances involve hate speech against the intended targets and in some instances hate speech against the unintended targets (indirect attacks), this means abandoning (R10), but could risk over-enlarging the concept depending on the purpose it is being used for. Call this the indirect attacks conundrum.

There are two main ways of responding to this conundrum, each associated with various more specific options. The first main response is to defend (R10) even in the face of alleged counter-examples. One version of the response is stipulative: it involves simply assuming that (R10) is correct and inferring from this that indirect attacks cannot be hate speech purely based on the definition of hate speech contained in (R10). Another version of the response is more substantive and says that referentially non-conventional uses of slurring terms never attack the group referred to by the slur under its literal or primary meaning, whether directly or indirectly, because they always fall under other recognised categories of non-hate speech.

The second main response to the indirect attacks conundrum is to accept the force of the counter-examples and jettison (R10) for this alternative rule.

(R11) Hate speech can involve direct or indirect attacks against people on the basis of protected characteristics.

The motivation for this response may stem from the intuition that slurring terms based on protected characteristics are inherently derogatory and, therefore, almost every usage of the slur carries derogatory force. So, even using a slurring term in a referentially non-conventional way, such as by calling a White person a 'nigger' or a straight person a 'faggot', does not entirely get rid of the derogatory force. This is because the derogatory force possessed by the slur is present in every occurrence whether in basic or residual form. However, to be successful this response must also provide a plausible account of the nature of that derogatory force, of how slurring terms continue to be derogatory towards the group referred to under the literal or primary meaning of the slurring terms even when addressed to non-members, and of why this derogatory force qualifies such uses of slurring terms as hate speech.

Below we argue that the first response is unsustainable in either of its iterations, for reasons of question-begging and limited applicability respectively. Following on from that, we once again apply the global resemblance test and argue that indirect attacks share sufficient similarities with exemplars of hate speech across the distinguishing qualities of target, style, message, act, or effect to justify applying the label 'hate speech' to them. Before running through these arguments, however, we first look at how Facebook has confronted the indirect attacks conundrum.

3.6.2 Indirect Attacks under Facebook's Community Standard on Hate Speech

Facebook's public-facing community standard on hate speech offers this general definition: 'We define hate speech as a direct attack against people—rather than concepts or institutions—on the basis of what we call protected characteristics.'[248] Taken at face value, this definition seems to disqualify indirect attacks against people as hate speech since they are by nature not direct attacks. On closer examination, however, the position may be more nuanced. For one thing, the reference to 'a direct attack against people' could be designed to contrast attacks against people (direct attacks) from attacks against things like identities, qualities, and characteristics (or 'concepts') related to people (indirect attacks), as opposed to the different distinction, which is the focus of our discussion, between referentially conventional uses of slurring terms (direct attacks) and referentially non-conventional uses of slurring terms (indirect attacks). We shall return to discuss attacks against identities, qualities, and characteristics in Chapter 4. The upshot is that, because the phrase 'a direct attack' is itself ambiguous, it is not possible to read from this phrase alone whether Facebook's content policy applies to indirect attacks in the latter sense.

Therefore, it is necessary to examine each of the specific rules on disallowed hate speech described in the community standard. Suppose someone posts the following about Elon Musk whilst being fully aware that Musk is not in fact a Jew.

(116) Elon Musk is such a Jew. Not satisfied with controlling the market in electric cars and space rockets, now he wants to control Twitter. He won't stop until he is running the world.

If (116) were interpreted by Facebook moderators as being not merely a personal attack on Elon Musk but also an attack on Jews in general, this statement would seem to violate Facebook's Tier 1 category of hate speech which explicitly disallows 'claims that Jewish people control financial, political, or media institutions'.[249]

In addition to this, Facebook's Tier 3 category of hate speech includes a specific rule disallowing slurs: 'Content that describes or negatively targets people with slurs, where slurs are defined as words that inherently create an atmosphere of exclusion and intimidation against people on the basis of a protected characteristic, often because these words are tied to historical discrimination, oppression, and violence.'[250] Facebook also adds the following explanation: 'They do this even when targeting someone who is not a member of the PC group that the slur inherently targets.' This explanation makes it clear the policy applies to both referentially conventional and non-conventional uses of slurs. In fact, the wording of the rule seems consistent with the policy that designated slurring terms are by default violating. In operational terms, this policy would mean that whenever there is an attack using a designated slurring term based on a protected characteristic, then it is deemed prima facie hate speech (unless it falls under one of the usage exceptions described in the community standard, such as when a slurring term is being used to raise awareness about and/or condemn the use of the term, or is being used in an empowering way by the group[251]). If this accurately reflects Facebook's authoritative internal policy on hate speech, and if the word 'nigger', for instance, is treated as a designated slur under the internal policy as applied in specific parts of the world ('markets') such as in North America, then logging on Facebook to call an Italian American a 'white nigger' or calling any White American a 'nigger' would be considered disallowed hate speech by default (unless one of the usage exceptions applied), even if these are referentially non-conventional uses of the term.

However, since Facebook does not publish its authoritative internal content policy on hate speech, it is unclear whether the policy really is as described in the previous paragraph (i.e. it is unclear whether designated slurs are by default violating). Moreover, since the public-facing version of the policy (the community standard) only provides a general definition of the term 'slurs' and not concrete illustrations of actual designated slurs, it is not known for certain whether Facebook treats 'nigger', 'faggot', and 'gay' as designated slurs, for instance. This is further complicated by the possibility that Facebook has different iterations of its internal policy and moderation guidelines for each of its markets (different parts of the world for content moderation purposes). Facebook's internal lists of designated slurs are likely to vary according to market in a way that reflects not merely different cultural meanings attached to given words but also different social, political, and cultural attitudes towards the appropriate balancing of free speech and other considerations. Indeed, one practical reason why Facebook might be reluctant to publish concrete examples of designated slurs as part of its public-facing global community standard on hate speech is that there may be relatively few words that the company's content policy and moderation teams treat as designated slurs in every single one of its markets. It may also reflect ambivalence towards publishing designated slurs that might themselves be frequently subject to the relevant usage exceptions under the content policy as applied.

Fortunately, however, Facebook's Oversight Board has provided a useful window into the company's internal content policies through its published case decisions. Based on some of these decisions, there is evidence that the word 'nigger' does appear on Facebook's internal list of designated slurs in at least some markets. Consider the Oversight Board case decision 2021-011-FB-UA.[252] Here the Board explained how it took evidence from Facebook that the words 'kaffir' and 'nigger' appear on the company's internal list of designated slurs for the sub-Saharan market. There is also anecdotal evidence to suggest that the word 'nigger' is included on the comparable list for the North American market based on users' reported experiences of Facebook removing this word. Likewise, a recent study of Facebook's removal practices within the United States revealed that the term 'faggot' was removed by Facebook every time it was reported as part of the study, but 'homo' was not removed.[253] Although the sample size was too small to support any robust conclusions, the findings of the study are at least consistent with the hypothesis that the term 'faggot' is treated as a designated slur by Facebook in its North American market.[254]

More importantly, in the Oversight Board case decision 2021-010-FB-UA, the Board explains how it received a crucial further clarification from Facebook about its moderation approach to referentially non-conventional uses of slurring terms in general and of the slur 'fag' in particular. [255] In May 2021, the Facebook page of a regional news outlet in Colombia shared a post by another Facebook user without adding any additional caption. The original post contained a short video showing a street protest against the Colombian president. As part of their chant, the protesters call the president '*hijo de puta*' and use the phrase '*deja de hacerte el marica en la tv*'. Facebook translated these words as 'son of a bitch' and 'stop being the fag on TV' respectively. It is widely assumed in Colombia that the president is heterosexual and there is no suggestion the protestors thought any differently. The Decision explains that Facebook removed the content because it contained the designated slur '*marica*' ('fag'). There is no mention of 'bitch' being a designated slur. But the key clarification on Facebook's moderation approach to referentially non-conventional uses of designated slurs is described in the Decision as follows.

> The word 'm**ica' has been designated as a slur by Facebook on the basis that it is inherently offensive and used as an insulting and discriminatory label primarily against gay men. [...] Facebook explained to the Board that neither the sexual orientation nor the public figure status of the target is relevant to the enforcement of this policy. As discriminatory slurs are inherently offensive, the use of slurs is not allowed unless a policy exception applies.[256]

This suggests that Facebook's general response to the indirect attacks conundrum is to accept that even referentially non-conventional uses of designated slurring terms (indirect attacks) can qualify as disallowed hate speech.

In Section 3.6.4, we seek to provide a deeper conceptual justification for this response based on applying the global resemblance test. Before doing so, however, we make the following three recommendations on how Facebook should revise its public-facing community standard on hate speech to better reflect what is evidently the authoritative internal policy. First, Facebook's community standard should include an example of a word that it treats as a designated slur in virtually all its markets or else a series of words including at least one example for each market.

Second, Facebook should update its definition of 'slurs' to make clearer the extent and scope of the policy on designated slurs. The definition currently says this: 'Content that describes or negatively targets people with slurs, where slurs are defined as words that inherently create an atmosphere of exclusion and intimidation against people on the basis of a protected characteristic, often because these words are tied to historical discrimination, oppression, and violence.'[257] And this: 'They do this even when targeting someone who is not a member of the PC group that the slur inherently targets.' We propose Facebook make explicit which specific designated slurs (e.g. 'nigger', 'retard', 'poof') are by default violating because inherently exclusionary and intimidatory, whether used in referentially conventional or non-conventional ways.

Third, Facebook should either change or further clarify its general definition of hate speech which currently refers to 'a direct attack against people'.[258] It could drop the qualifier 'direct' or else replace it with 'direct or sometimes indirect'. Or it could retain 'direct' but provide a further sentence explaining that its distinction between direct and indirect attacks is not intended to refer to the distinction between referentially conventional and non-conventional uses of hateful words.

Whilst we have focused on Facebook's community standard on hate speech, we do not mean to imply that it is the only platform to face the indirect attacks conundrum or that its handling of it is worse than that of other platforms. On the contrary, one of the plusses for Facebook is that its decision to set up and adhere to the decisions of an independent oversight panel has provided an extra level of transparency and clarification regarding its internal policies. This is over and above the fact that its community standard is already the most comprehensive and detailed attempt to describe to the public its internal policy of any major social media platform. In these respects, Facebook's community standard is both best in class and imperfect.

3.6.3 *First Response: Indirect Attacks as Forms of Non-Hate Speech*

The first main response to the indirect attacks challenge is to deny that such attacks can be hate speech. One iteration of this response is simply to stipulate that hate speech only involves direct attacks, as per (R10). However, this approach begs the question at hand. It fails to provide a good reason – moral, conceptual, or social – why the ordinary concept *hate speech* should be conceptualised in such a narrow way, especially in the face of counter-examples.

Another iteration says that indirect attacks can never be hate speech because they always fall under other recognised categories of non-hate speech. For example, it might be claimed that pejoratives like 'retard' and 'moron' are more akin to general insults, which attack individuals, than to group-based or even hybrid slurs, which also attack an entire group or class of persons. Whereas slurs like 'nigger' target a group referred to by the neutral counterpart 'African Americans', perhaps this is not so of pejoratives like 'retard' and 'moron'. In the words of Anderson and Lepore: 'one who uses "moron" needn't be slurring every mentally disabled person'.[259]

However, this argument conflates the direct and indirect victims of slurring terms. A speaker who calls someone a 'retard' or 'moron' might be directly attacking the intended target only with a personal insult rather than a group-based slur. But arguably the speaker may also be indirectly attacking people who do have learning difficulties, intellectual disabilities, or neurodivergent conditions. Moreover, if the indirect attack carries a message of derogation, bigotry, and contempt based on a protected characteristic, then surely it is a slur and potentially hate speech.

Then again, a staunch defender of (R10) might appeal to a general distinction between hate speech modes of slur usage and non-hate speech modes of slur usage and argue that the latter category includes people using slurs within the context of friendly banter between equals or within the context of historically oppressed groups reappropriating or resignifying slurs as a form of self-empowerment.[260]

However, this response has limited applicability. When a sexist speaker calls certain men 'sluts', for example, this could potentially occur in a context of friendly banter between men. Yet the (unintended) indirect attack on promiscuous women/women in general is unlikely to qualify as a context of friendly banter between men and women as equals. Furthermore, when a speaker condemns certain men for being 'sluts' in a serious-minded way, this is unlikely to be a context in which he is drawing on a wider reappropriation of the word 'slut' whereby it carries a positive connotation.

On the contrary, this usage may presuppose a sexist norm that women ought to be chaste. This is not to suggest it is impossible for traditional slurring terms to be successfully reappropriated. People who self-label as 'queer', for example, may experience a sense of empowerment that is also recognised by other members of society resulting in the term being perceived to have lesser derogatory force.[261] Even so, attempts at reappropriation do not always succeed in fully ridding historically slurring language of stigmatising connotations, especially when used by people who are not members of the relevant group.[262] More importantly, not all referentially non-conventional uses of slurring terms can be neatly fitted into the reappropriation model. Many indirect attacks rely on the original meaning of slurs, even if the speaker's intention is to insult someone who is not a member of the group picked out by that original meaning.

3.6.4 Second Response: Similarities Between Indirect Attacks and Exemplars of Hate Speech

In the case of referentially non-conventional uses of slurring terms, typically speakers convey (imply, presuppose, or infer) a comparison between the intended target and the group referred to by the slur under its literal or primary meaning. The suggestion tends to be that the target shares certain stereotypical traits in common with the group that is referred to by the slurring term under its literal or primary meaning and, by inference, that the target deserves the same or similar negative evaluation and treatment as members of the latter group. In this way, even referentially non-conventional uses of slurring terms convey similar messages of derogation, bigotry, and contempt and perform similar acts of *stereotyping* and *subordinating* to referentially conventional uses of the same slurring terms.

In what follows we illustrate this analysis with three pairwise examples involving referentially conventional and non-conventional uses of common slurring terms. First, suppose a speaker holds bigoted attitudes towards people with Down syndrome and both says and conveys the following about his neighbour's son whom he knows has this syndrome.

(117) David is a retard, god help him.

(117a) *The speaker knows that David has Down syndrome and several learning difficulties. The speaker holds that David shares in common with other people with Down syndrome possession of certain traits such as being slow, dim-witted, naive, etc. And the speaker evaluates such people as being lesser, inferior, or pitiable by dint of possessing the aforementioned traits and ultimately because they have Down syndrome, and intends to express this evaluation.*

Now consider the message conveyed by the same speaker when he uses the slur 'retard' in a referentially non-conventional way, namely against someone he knows or presumes does not have any learning difficulty, intellectual disability, or neurodivergent condition.

(118) John is such a retard.

(118a) *The speaker knows or presumes that John does not have any learning difficulties, intellectual disabilities, or neurodivergent conditions. Nevertheless, the speaker also believes that John shares in common with people who do have such difficulties, disabilities, or conditions the possession of certain traits such as being slow, dim-witted, naïve, etc. And the speaker evaluates both people like John and people with genuine difficulties, disabilities, or conditions as being lesser, inferior, irritating, or pitiable by dint of being slow, dim-witted, naive, etc., and intends to express this evaluation.*

We believe there are sufficient similarities between parts of the respective messages contained in (117a) and (118a) to suggest at least a partial resemblance. Whether (117) and (118) pass the global resemblance test also depends on an assessment of the target, act, and effect. But it is hard to deny at least the partial resemblance.

To give a second example, suppose a speaker holds sexist views and both says and conveys the following about women.

(119) These women are sluts.

(119a) *The speaker believes that a certain group of women are sexually promiscuous and fail to live up to a social norm that says women should be sexually chaste, the sort of norm that the speaker believes is fitting for women's behaviour just because they are women. The speaker also believes that the women concerned are reprehensible because they fail to live up to this norm, and wishes to publicly articulate this judgment.*

Now consider what may be conveyed by the same speaker who uses the slurring term 'slut' against certain men.

(120) These men are sluts.

(120a) *The speaker believes a certain group of men are sexually promiscuous and that, in this regard, they are similar to promiscuous women. The speaker presupposes the appropriateness of certain norms of sexual behaviour that typically apply to women and apply to women just because they are women. The speaker also believes that the men concerned are reprehensible because they fail to live up to a norm that says men should not act like promiscuous women, and that the norm holds just because men are men and women are women, and wishes to publicly articulate this judgment.*

Once again, we believe part of the message contained in (120a) shares sufficient similarities to part of the message contained in (119a) to suggest at least a partial resemblance. At first glance, (120) might appear to challenge double standards about how men and women are supposed to behave sexually – the double standard that the more sexual partners a man has the more revered he is, but the more sexual partners a woman has the more reviled she is. The speaker seems to be holding men to the same norm of sexual abstinence as women are held to. But even this non-standard use of 'slut' may be an indirect attack on women, and hate speech, insofar as it implicitly conveys the core sexist attitude that certain norms of sexual chastity ought to apply to women just because they are women.

In some contexts, statement (120) may also perform paradigmatic hate speech acts and produce paradigmatic hate speech effects. First, partly owing to the literal or primary meaning of the word 'slut', as articulated in (120a), even the non-conventional use of the word 'slut' exemplified in (120) may amount to *normalising* or *legitimating* sexist norms. Second, upon being exposed to this sort of non-conventional usage of 'slut', some men might experience a sort of surprise, scepticism, or even mild amusement at the notion that a man could be judged negatively for being sexually promiscuous, and this might only serve to perpetuate the double standard. The same may be true of the word 'manslut'. The very fact that the prefix 'man' needs to be added to 'slut' to make calling a man a 'slut' comprehensible, might not merely presuppose but also reinforce a social practice in which norms of sexual abstinence are disproportionately applied to women.

Turning to a third example, suppose a speaker holds homophobic attitudes and both says and conveys the following about gay men.

(121) I despise faggots.

(121a) *The speaker holds that gay men possess one or more stereotypical traits including being effeminate, unmasculine, superficial, emotional, physically weak, submissive, sexually deviant. The speaker also believes that gay men fail to live up to social norms about ways of being, mannerisms, behaviour, interests, and attitudes that apply to men just because they are men. The speaker also evaluates gay men as contemptible, ridiculous, inferior, and repugnant, due to the possession of these traits and a failure to live up to masculinity norms, and intends to express this negative evaluation.*

Now suppose the same speaker both says and conveys this about a group of men whom he knows or presumes are not gay.

(122) Some of the guys who work in the admin office are such faggots; they are a fucking disgrace.

(122a) *The speaker holds that a certain group of men are not gay but nevertheless possess certain traits including being unmasculine, superficial, and*

> *physically weak, the sort of traits that the speaker associates with gay men. The speaker also believes that this group of men, like gay men, fail to live up to masculinity norms. The speaker also evaluates this group of men, in addition to gay men, as contemptible, ridiculous, inferior, and repugnant, due to the possession of these traits and a failure to live up to masculinity norms, and intends to express this attitude.*

Once again, parts of the message contained in (122a) mirrors parts of the message contained in (121a), suggesting at least a partial resemblance. More specifically, both (122a) and (121a) contain negative stereotypes about, and the expression of contempt for, gay men. Thus, even though the shift from (121) to (122) represents a change in target from homosexual men to straight men, the shift nonetheless leaves the anti-gay message in play.

Moreover, in certain contexts, the public statement of (122), given the ideational content it conveys, could constitute one or more paradigmatic homophobic acts, such as the act of *demeaning* gay people or *reinforcing* the social stigma attached to being gay. In terms of effects, there is also potential for referentially non-conventional uses of homophobic slurs like 'faggots' to be as destructive or undermining of the social standing of homosexual men as more conventional uses of such slurs that directly attack gay men, as with (121), and that are usually recognised as hate speech. How so? Insofar as non-standard slur usage does not present as obvious hate speech, it may appear innocent, normal, or unremarkable, thus rendering it an insidious form of hate speech. The bigoted messages conveyed may be internalised all the more easily because what the speaker says is not a direct attack on gay men and so does not seem so outrageous or hate speechy.[263] What is more, both referentially conventional and non-conventional uses of homophobic slurs may have similarly diffuse effects such as in terms of emasculating gay men and contributing to a climate of homophobia in which acts of violence against gay men are normalised; in which people do not feel deterred from, or culpable for, beating up gay men because they do not see them as 'real men' in the first place.

For these reasons, we believe referentially non-conventional uses of slurring terms like 'faggot' can constitute indirect attacks on gay men and may rise to the level of hate speech depending on the context of speech and the wider social context, and on a comprehensive application the global resemblance test. It is a further question – one we do not have space to address here – whether the term 'faggot' also carries a residue of its archaic meaning (*troublesome woman*), and thereby also constitutes an indirect attack on women.

We believe a similar analysis is applicable to referentially non-conventional uses of 'poof', 'homo', and 'gay'. If these uses directly attack straight men but in doing so also convey (express, imply, presuppose, or infer) negative stereotypes about homosexual men, convey the idea that homosexual men fall short of masculinity norms, and convey attitudes that being a homosexual man is a bad thing, then they can be indirect attacks on homosexual men and may qualify as hate speech.

Part of the reputational damage caused even by referentially non-conventional uses of these slurs may be a function of how the audience processes the ideational content. Assuming words like 'faggot', 'poof', 'homo', and 'gay' convey a sort of ideational residue left over from conventional attacks on homosexuals, in some circumstances the audience may end up recalling only the residue and not the non-conventional usage. Consider an analogy to how ordinary language users cognitively process the meaning of negations. There is evidence from linguistic psychology that when hearing a negation such as a flat denial ('I did not say those words'), people typically think about the accusation first (he said the words), then tag on the extra notion that the accusation is being denied (he claims he did not say the words).[264] This in turn means that when listeners are distracted or not fully paying attention or when listeners are ill-disposed towards the denier, they could be left remembering only the accusation, with the negation (the denial) being forgotten over time. Turning to referentially non-conventional uses of homophobic slurs (and other hate slurs), it is possible that audiences think about the core derogatory stereotype first (homosexual people are unmasculine), then tag on the extra notion that the derogation is being used against someone who is not homosexual (This person is not homosexual but is unmasculine). Where the audience is distracted or not fully paying attention, or already harbours certain prejudices towards homosexuals, they may be left remembering only the core derogatory stereotype, with the non-standard slur usage fading from memory.

Interestingly, a similar psychological process might be involved in some selective attacks of the sort discussed in Section 3.3. Consider these statements.

(123) Of course, some black people are not gangbangers and criminals.
(124) Not all Muslims are terrorists.

Where the audience is distracted or not fully paying attention, or already harbours certain prejudices towards Black people and Muslims, they may be left recalling only the core derogatory stereotype, with the referentially restrictive nature of the statements falling away from their minds. Indeed, there is some evidence from experimental psychology to suggest that statements like (123) and (124), even when the speaker intends to be supportive of Black people and Muslims, may in fact reinforce stereotypes and increase people's support for discriminatory policies that depend on such stereotypes.[265] This underscores how hate speech can be unintentional as well as indirect in nature.

4

Attacks on the Identities of Groups

4.1 Introduction

In Chapter 3 we considered examples that fall into a grey area of hate speech largely due to either who the target is or who the speaker is. In this chapter we shall focus on examples that fall into a grey area more because of the content of the speech and especially what is said about or done to people's identities. In order to do this, we move beyond slurs and pejoratives. Various styles of speech are addressed including some that are closely related to what are referred to in the psychology literature as microaggressions.[1] More specifically, we look at identity attacks (e.g. 'Homosexuality is disgusting'), existential denials (e.g. 'Bisexuals do not exist'), identity denials (e.g. 'Transwomen are not women'), identity miscategorisations (e.g. 'Transwomen are men'), and identity appropriations (e.g. blackface).

This chapter defends classifying each of these kinds of attacks as hate speech in the ordinary sense of the term based on similarities with exemplars of hate speech under the global resemblance test (Chapter 2), and in the light of reasonable expectations about the important social functions or purposes of the concept (Chapter 5). We shall also critically examine Facebook's community standard on hate speech in relation to its handling of these kinds of attacks, and make specific recommendations to address relevant weaknesses. Section 4.2 looks at what we call identity attacks, which include ascribing a protected characteristic to people even though not overtly attacking them, attacking a protected characteristic, or attacking a symbolic figure (real or fictional) who exemplifies a protected characteristic. Section 4.3 investigates existential denials, namely statements denying the very existence of people identified by a protected characteristic. Section 4.4 scrutinises identity denials, by which we mean statements denying that certain people are who they take themselves to be, based on protected characteristics. Section 4.5 examines identity miscategorisations, which go one step further and attribute identities to people that do not match the identities they take themselves to possess, based on protected characteristics. Finally, Section 4.6 assesses identity appropriations, wherein people adopt elements of the identities of other people, based on protected characteristics, but without claiming to possess the relevant identities.

4.2 Identity Attacks

The first cluster of grey area examples to be discussed in the chapter involves attacks against people's identities. Although these cases might be superficially similar to exemplars of hate speech insofar as they can be construed as attacks on the basis of protected characteristics, they also differ in the style of the attack, namely the particular way in which they attack people's identities. This difference is sufficient to place them into a grey area of hate speech. We call these identity attacks.

Identity attacks as we shall understand them include three main types. The first involves attacking people's identities either by simply ascribing a protected characteristic to people, even though not directly or overtly attacking them, or else by ascribing a protected characteristic to people and also overtly attacking them but without explicitly drawing a connection or association between the ascription and the attack. Consider the following two statements.

(1) These people are black.
(2) These people are black, and they are despicable.

Statement (1) ascribes a racial characteristic (being a Black person) to certain people but without overtly attacking them, that is, without explicitly saying anything further that is derogatory. In turn, statement (2) ascribes a racial characteristic to certain people and overtly attacks them but does not explicitly draw a connection or association between the ascription and the attack. Statements (1) and (2) are examples of what we shall call ascriptive identity attacks.

A second type of identity attack involves attacking people's identities either by ascribing a protected characteristic to them and attacking the characteristic but without explicitly drawing a connection or association between the ascription and the attack, or else by explicitly or implicitly attacking a protected characteristic even though not directly or overtly attacking people. Consider these further examples.

(3) These people are homosexuals, and homosexuality is disgusting.
(4) Homosexuality is disgusting.
(5) I hate the thing that makes homosexuals who they are.

Statement (3) ascribes a sexual orientation to certain people and attacks that orientation but does not explicitly draw a connection or association between the ascription and the attack. Moreover, statement (4) attacks the sexual orientation without directly or overtly attacking people, and statement (5) implicitly attacks the sexual orientation and once again without directly attacking people. We call these descriptive identity attacks.

A third type of identity attack involves attacking people's identities by ascribing a protected characteristic to a symbolic figure (real or fictional) who represents a group of people and attacking that symbolic figure on account of possessing the characteristic but without explicitly drawing a connection or association between the symbolic figure and a group of people. Take the following example.

(6) The prophet Muhammad was a rapist, a paedophile, and a war criminal all because he was Muslim.

Statement (6) ascribes the characteristic of being Muslim to the prophet Muhammad and attacks Muhammad on this basis, but it does not explicitly draw a connection or association between the prophet Muhammad and Muslims. We call these symbolic identity attacks.

4.2.1 *The Identity Attacks Quandary*

In Chapter 3 we discussed the general idea that hate speech involves attacks against people, an idea that is embedded in two competing rules of thumb.

(R10) Hate speech is only speech which directly attacks people on the basis of protected characteristics.
(R11) Hate speech can involve direct or indirect attacks against people on the basis of protected characteristics.

Yet this general idea creates uncertainty over how to define examples involving identity attacks because they seem to test the limits of what could be plausibly defined as 'an attack against people'. We call this the identity attacks quandary.

There are three variations of the identity attacks quandary relating to the three types of identity attacks outlined above. The first variation concerns ascriptive identity attacks such as (1) and (2). In order that something may qualify as an attack against people in a sense relevant to the ordinary concept *hate speech*, what must it do? On the one hand, a society or organisation might set the bar relatively high such as by embracing something like the following rule of thumb.

(R12) To count as hate speech, it is not enough merely to ascribe the possession of a protected characteristic to people or even both to ascribe the characteristic and to derogate those people.

However, accepting (R12) seems to rely on an overly restrictive interpretation of the general idea that hate speech has to do with attacks against people based on protected characteristics. In particular, we believe ordinary language users may be willing to countenance calling something 'hate speech' even if it did no more than ascribe a protected characteristic to certain people and derogate those people such as in the case of (2) and perhaps even if it only ascribed the characteristic as with (1).

On the other hand, if a society or organisation sets the bar lower, then it probably means rejecting (R12) and potentially accepting that ascriptive identity attacks could be counted as hate speech. Yet in order to motivate the rejection of (R12) and justify the classification of examples like (1) and (2) as potential hate speech, a further rationale or justification is needed such as showing there are sufficient similarities with exemplars of hate speech. But what are the similarities between (1) and (2) and exemplars of hate speech that makes this classification plausible?

The second variation of the identity attacks quandary relates to descriptive identity attacks such as (3), (4), and (5). The quandary is whether to classify these sorts of statements as hate speech given that they do not look like straightforward attacks against people. One way to deal with the uncertainty is to claim that descriptive identity attacks are not hate speech on the grounds that they are attacks against things other than people. This appeals to the following rule of thumb.

(R13) Hate speech attacks people as opposed to things other than people such as characteristics, concepts, ideas, beliefs, practices, institutions, or symbols.

Yet this resolution of the quandary may be implausible insofar as statements (3), (4), and (5) at the very least do seem to be indirect attacks against people. It is worth noting here that the quandary of how to handle these sorts of statements has been replicated in cases relating to the legal concept *hate speech*, including in legal cases where a speaker has declared homosexuality or, more precisely, 'sexual deviation', to be 'disgusting' without directly calling homosexuals disgusting.[2]

Following on from this, another way of dealing with the quandary is to argue that descriptive identity attacks are indirect attacks against people and, therefore, potentially hate speech based on (R11). However, this option might be unappealing to people who are sceptical of (R11). They might fear almost anything could be treated as hate speech if this concept includes indirect as well as direct attacks against people.

The third variation of the identity attacks quandary has to do with symbolic identity attacks such as (6). The quandary is whether to classify (6) as hate speech given that it does not look like a prototypical attack against a group of people. One way to deal with the uncertainty is to claim that symbolic identity attacks are not hate speech on the grounds they are attacks against symbolic figures as opposed to groups of people, in accordance with (R13). But this putative solution may seem counter-intuitive for the simple reason that, other things being equal, attacking a symbolic figure on account of possessing a particular characteristic seems tantamount to attacking the wider group of people who also possess that characteristic, especially if those people regard both the symbolic figure and the characteristic as part of who they are.

The alternative is to say that symbolic identity attacks are indirect attacks against people and, therefore, potentially hate speech based on (R11). But once more there may be reticence about taking this path if it means allowing things to be classified as hate speech in a way that could signal a material expansion of the ordinary concept *hate speech* that is both irreversible and socially undesirable.

In general, there are two main ways of responding to the identity attacks quandary (encompassing all three variations). The first response is to insist that identity attacks are not hate speech because, on a very strict reading of both what these attacks are and what hate speech is, these attacks are against things other than people. We believe this response crumbles under the weight of a careful analysis of these examples and that it errs in assuming that something can be hate speech only if it is a direct attack against people. The second response (our proposed response) is to insist that identity attacks ought to be considered prima facie hate speech in the ordinary sense of the term because on closer examination they do in fact involve attacks against people, whether based on their non-literal meanings or based on their being indirect attacks against people. Moreover, accepting these outcomes need not expand the ordinary concept to a point where it is conceptually incoherent or lacking social purpose. Before discussing these responses in more detail, however, we shall first exemplify the quandary using the example of Facebook's community standard on hate speech.

4.2.2 *Identity Attacks under Facebook's Community Standard on Hate Speech*

Facebook's community standard on hate speech begins with this general definition: 'We define hate speech as a direct attack against people – rather than concepts or institutions – on the basis of what we call protected characteristics'.[3] But what does 'a direct attack against people [...] on the basis of [...] protected characteristics' actually mean? Assuming they have discretion, Facebook's policy teams and moderators could interpret this in more or less restrictive ways. On the one hand, they could interpret it in a less restrictive way so that it applies even to content that falls short of directly and explicitly attacking people, including the three types of identity attacks outlined above. In that event, Facebook could deem the following, previously cited examples to be at least potential hate speech.

(1) These people are black.
(2) These people are black, and they are despicable.
(3) These people are homosexuals, and homosexuality is disgusting.
(4) Homosexuality is disgusting.
(5) I hate the thing that makes homosexuals who they are.
(6) The prophet Muhammad was a rapist, a paedophile, and a war criminal all because he was a Muslim.

On the other hand, Facebook could choose to interpret its general definition in a strict way such that examples (1)–(6) could not be deemed as hate speech. Instead, the policy would only disallow the following sorts of statements.

(7) These people are niggers.
(8) These people are black, and they are despicable because of it.
(9) Homosexuals are disgusting.
(10) I hate everything about homosexuals.
(11) Muslims are terrorists.

Statements (7)–(11) directly and explicitly attack people in a way (1)–(6) do not.

The identity attacks quandary poses various practical challenges for Facebook given other aspects of its community standard on hate speech. For one thing, in order to interpret identity attacks as hate speech, it might be necessary for Facebook's staff to evaluate statements not simply on the basis of their literal meanings. For example, if descriptive identity attacks such as (4) are to be counted as a 'direct attack against people', Facebook would need to consider the non-literal content conveyed. Perhaps it could read (4) as expressing, implying, presupposing, or inferring the following.

(4a) *The speaker holds that homosexuals are disgusting, and intends to publicly articulate that view.*

But embracing this sort of interpretive approach may pose enormous challenges for Facebook in terms of being able to operationalise it through existing automated hate speech detection algorithms, machine learning tools, and AI models. Because of the well-documented technical limitations of these models,[4] increasing interpretive sophistication almost inevitably means decreasing accuracy. And so, it might fall on Facebook's human moderators, policy teams, and ultimately the Oversight Board to make all of the tough calls, drawing on insights from linguistic experts and other stakeholders. This human labour would be required at least in the short-term to build up a corpus of examples large enough to feed into new AI models.

As a matter of principle, we suggest this sort of interpretive sophistication would not be a quantum leap for the platform. After all, Facebook's community standard already makes it plain that in some instances the platform is willing to look beyond literal meanings: 'Sometimes, based on local nuance, we consider certain words or phrases as frequently used proxies for PC groups.'[5] Perhaps Facebook could also interpret statements like (4) as code for conveyed content like (4a) depending on the speaker, context, and receiving audience. Then again, how far is Facebook willing to go with this interpretive sophistication? If all words and phrases are to be evaluated as potential hate speech off the back of not only literal meanings but also the non-literal content conveyed, then potentially vast amounts of content on the platform might ultimately need to be looked at by human beings. The financial costs of this may be incompatible with the platform's business model.

Another practical dimension of the quandary is how far Facebook should depart from its general definition of hate speech. Whilst Facebook defines hate speech 'as a direct attack against people',[6] the standard also contains specific rules seemingly disallowing attacks on things other than people. For example: 'Content attacking concepts, institutions, ideas, practices or beliefs associated with protected characteristics, which are likely to contribute to imminent physical harm, intimidation or discrimination against the people associated with that protected characteristic.'[7] But if harm prevention is so important, why is harmfulness not mentioned in the general definition of hate speech? The omission suggests Facebook's policy disallows some forms of hate speech that are not imminently harmful. On the other hand, if the policy disallows some forms of hate speech that are not imminently harmful, then why not also disallow content attacking concepts, institutions, ideas, practices, or beliefs associated with protected characteristics regardless of whether they are likely to contribute to imminent harm?

In addition, the aforementioned exception to the general definition refers to 'Content attacking concepts, institutions, ideas, practices or beliefs associated with protected characteristics'. But what does 'associated with' mean? Perhaps the test is whether the association is so close as to make it extremely difficult to draw a line between, on the one hand, content attacking the concept, institution, idea, practice, or belief associated with the protected characteristic or indeed content attacking the protected characteristic itself, and, on the other hand, content attacking the people who possess or are perceived to possess the protected characteristic. Then again, what qualifies as indistinguishable? Would a constitutive association qualify such as if the people concerned are partly constituted by the concept, institution, idea, practice, belief, or characteristic, meaning that an attack on the latter is an attack on them? Or, would a subjective association qualify such as if the people concerned identify with the concept, institution, idea, practice, belief, or characteristic so closely that they experience an attack on the latter as an attack on them? Facebook's community standard fails to provide explicit answers to these questions.

Yet another practical dimension of the quandary relates to the fact that Facebook's community standard makes no reference to what are among the most high-profile and controversial grey area examples of hate speech today, especially in the Muslim world, namely content derogating, ridiculing, defaming, or otherwise attacking religious prophets, such as cartoons depicting the prophet Muhammad as a suicide bomber. Interestingly, in its Q3 2022 Quarterly Update on the Oversight Board (November 2022), Meta explains that it submitted the following case for the Board to consider: 'A Facebook page shared a video that showed a former spokesperson of the ruling Indian political party (Bharatiya Janata Party) criticizing the Prophet Muhammad. We took no action on the content as we concluded that it did not violate the Hate Speech policy.' This suggests that Facebook does not treat symbolic identity attacks as hate speech.

Importantly, however, Facebook's community standard does include a specific Tier 1 rule disallowing 'Dehumanising speech or imagery in the form of comparisons, generalisations or unqualified behavioural statements (in written or visual form) to or about: [...] Harmful stereotypes historically linked to intimidation, exclusion or violence on the basis of a protected characteristic, such as Blackface'.[8] Let us suppose for the sake of argument that Facebook's staff in the North American market would deem it hate speech to post an image or video of a White person appearing on stage as the character Jim Crow, an exaggerated archetype or stereotype of African American people, unless one of the usage exceptions applies (e.g. condemning blackface). Let us also suppose they would treat this as hate speech partly because portraying Jim Crow as a limping, drinking, and singing buffoon is in effect to caricature all Black people as buffoons. In which case, why not also disallow depictions of the prophet Muhammad as a suicide bomber on the grounds that they in effect caricature all Muslims as terrorists?

4.2.3 First Response: Identity Attacks as Attacks against Things Other than People

The first main response to the identity attacks quandary is to insist that identity attacks are not hate speech because, on a very strict reading of both what these attacks are and what hate speech is, these are not attacks, not attacks on the basis of protected characteristics, or else attacks against things other than people. There are different iterations of this response corresponding to the three types of identity attacks outlined above.

One iteration focuses on ascriptive identity attacks, which it says are not hate speech due to the fact that they are, literally speaking, either statements simply ascribing protected characteristics to people, or statements ascribing protected characteristics to people and also overtly attacking those people but without explicitly drawing a connection or association between the ascription and the attack. If (R12) is correct, then these sorts of attacks are not hate speech (according to the first response).

However, we believe there are two decisive shortcomings with this iteration of the first response. For one thing, there is more to the content conveyed by statements than the literal meanings they encode. Statements can also express, imply, presuppose, or infer non-literal content. Consider once again the following statements.

(1) These people are black.
(2) These people are black, and they are despicable.

Looking at the speaker intent, the context in which the statements are made, and how they are received, they could convey the following content.

(1a) *The speaker holds that these people are lazy, stupid, raggedy, promiscuous, aggressive, animalistic, non-rational, childlike, poor, unemployed, devoid of moral agency or conscience, immoral, criminal, unpatriotic, etc., all due to the fact of being black, and intends to publicly articulate that view.*
(2a) *The speaker holds that these people are black, that they are despicable, and that they are despicable all because of being black, and intends to publicly articulate that view.*

If (1a) and (2a) accurately capture the conveyed content of (1) and (2), then it would seem (1) and (2) would qualify as hate speech, even if one accepts (R12), not least because (1a) and (2a) display prejudice and bigotry towards Black people.

Furthermore, even if one focuses on the literal meanings of ascriptive identity attacks, it might still be implausible to discount them as potential hate speech. Contrary to (R12), it is far from obviously correct to say that (1) and (2) cannot be hate speech simply by dint of the fact that statement (1) ascribes a racial characteristic (being Black) to certain people but without overtly attacking them, and statement (2) ascribes a racial characteristic to certain people and overtly attacks them but does not explicitly draw a connection or association between the ascription and the attack. Arguably, there can be something oppressive and essentialising about even these ascriptive identity attacks and that marks them out as hate speech. We shall present relevant similarities with exemplars of hate speech in Section 4.2.4.

A second iteration of the first response relates to descriptive identity attacks, which it says are not hate speech because they are, at face value, either statements ascribing a protected characteristic to people and attacking the characteristic but without explicitly drawing a connection or association between the ascription and the attack, or else statements just attacking a protected characteristic and not directly or overtly attacking people. If (R13) is correct, such attacks are not hate speech.

However, once again we maintain that this iteration of the response ultimately fails. First of all, descriptive identity attacks may convey non-literal content which is plausibly classified as hate speech. Consider once again the following examples.

(3) These people are homosexuals, and homosexuality is disgusting.
(4) Homosexuality is disgusting.
(5) I hate the thing that makes homosexuals who they are.

Dependent on the speaker, context, and receiving audience, it is possible these statements convey the following content.

(3a) *The speaker holds that these people are homosexuals and, because of the speaker's perspective that homosexuality is disgusting, that these people are disgusting, and intends to publicly articulate that view.*
(4b) *The speaker holds that homosexuality is disgusting and that, therefore, all homosexuals are disgusting, and intends to publicly articulate that view.*
(5a) *The speaker intends to express hatred for homosexuality and also for homosexuals.*

In addition, even sticking with the literal meanings of statements (3), (4), and (5), arguably it is not credible to simply say that descriptive identity attacks are not direct attacks against people and, therefore, cannot be hate speech. We believe most competent language users would regard such attacks as being at least indirect attacks against homosexuals. After all, what is it to be a homosexual if not to possess the characteristic of homosexuality? And, what is it to attack homosexuality if it is not either equivalent or tantamount to an attack against homosexuals? Even if descriptive identity attacks are not identical to attacks against people, arguably they are equivalent to attacks against people precisely because they are attacks on identity and attacks on identity can be on a par with attacks on people with that identity. Likewise, descriptive identity attacks may be tantamount to attacks against people insofar as they have the same effect or result, namely the relevant people feel as though they are being indirectly attacked. And this surely has a bearing on whether there is a prima facie case for classifying such attacks as hate speech.

A third iteration of the first response pertains to symbolic identity attacks, which it says are not hate speech because they are, strictly speaking, attacks against symbolic figures who happen to possess protected characteristics as opposed to attacks against people, namely the groups of people who possess the relevant characteristics. If (R13) is correct in affirming that an attack on a symbol (or symbolic figure) is not hate speech, then these sorts of identity attacks are not hate speech.

However, for similar reasons as above, we believe this response is ultimately untenable. Once again, symbolic identity attacks may convey non-literal content which is plausibly classified as hate speech. Reconsider the following example.

(6) The prophet Muhammad was a rapist, a paedophile, and a war criminal all because he was a Muslim.

It is conceivable that someone who posts (6) on social media may convey the following non-literal content.

(6a) *The speaker holds that Muslims are rapists, paedophiles, and war criminals all because they are Muslims, and intends to articulate that view.*

Furthermore, even if one focuses on the literal meanings of symbolic identity attacks, such attacks can be considered at least indirect attacks on people, and so potential hate speech. The speaker might or might not intend the symbolic figure to be a proxy, stand in, or place holder for the larger group of people who also possess the same characteristic. This ambiguity in speaker intent is reflected in the literal meaning of the words. But what about the standing of the symbolic figure in the minds of members of the group? What if it is part of their identity to regard the symbolic figure as representing the best of them or an essence of who they are? What if it is a common belief or practice among members of the group to look upon the symbolic figure as an embodiment or extension of their identity? Surely in that scenario an attack on the symbolic figure is on a par with an attack against people insofar as an attack on their identity is for all intents and purposes an attack against them. Such an attack may also be tantamount to an attack against people if it shares the similar effect of making people feel as though they have been indirectly attacked.

4.2.4 *Second Response: Similarities between Identity Attacks and Exemplars of Hate Speech*

Building on the above arguments against the first response to the identity attacks quandary, the second response (our proposed response) affirms that identity attacks can be hate speech, although in the final analysis this is dependent on the global resemblance test, whilst also taking into account the social purpose or function of the ordinary concept *hate speech*. Once again, there are alternative iterations of this response corresponding to the three types of identity attacks outlined above.

4.2.4.1 Ascriptive Identity Attacks

The first iteration concerns ascriptive identity attacks, which we claim can be hate speech. In fact, we believe there are two compelling justifications for this claim. The first looks beyond the literal meanings of such attacks to focus on the non-literal content they might convey. Consider once again the following statements.

(1) These people are black.
(7) These people are niggers.

Perhaps there are circumstances in which both (1) and (7) convey a very similar message such as along the following lines.

(1a)/(7a) *The speaker holds that these people are lazy, stupid, raggedy, promiscuous, aggressive, animalistic, non-rational, childlike, poor, unemployed, devoid of moral agency or conscience, immoral, criminal, unpatriotic, etc., all due to the fact of being black, and intends to publicly articulate that view.*

If (1) and (7) do indeed convey the same content, then surely both must be hate speech or neither hate speech. Indeed, it would be hard not to classify (1) as hate speech if it conveyed (1a). After all, (1a) contains a litany of stigmatising stereotypes about Black people that seem to be paradigmatic messages of prejudice and bigotry, thus exhibiting the closest possible family resemblance with what is likely to be conveyed by (7).

The second justification for the claim that ascriptive identity attacks can be hate speech reverts back to focusing on the literal meanings of such attacks. Even if the term 'black' is not a recognised or designated racial slur, and even if (1) in its literal meaning does no more than ascribe a protected characteristic to certain people (or even a category, status, or identity), we contend that (1) can still qualify as hate speech.

One key similarity between (1) and (7) is that both involve acts of misrecognition. One relevant act of misrecognition is what we have elsewhere called 'oppressive ascription of identity'.[9] This is a matter of 'oppressively ascribing an identity to, or arbitrarily imposing an identity upon, individuals.'[10] What qualifies such ascriptions as being morally wrong and potential hate speech is twofold:

> First, this is a matter of that identity being ascribed externally (by other agents, institutions, structures) against the will of the person, meaning that it is an identity that people have not chosen and would not chose to adopt if they had been given the choice. Second, the content of an identity can be oppressive if it forecloses the possibility of other joint identities that someone might want to adopt; that is to say, if it closes down rather than opens up the possibility of other, elective identities.[11]

Therefore, whilst classifying certain people as 'black' (Black people) may not carry the same derogatory force as classifying them using the slur 'niggers', the ascription of the former characteristic (or category, status, or identity) might nevertheless be an act of misrecognition in the aforementioned sense of ascribing to people an identity against their will and one that may foreclose other identities they would favour or would choose for themselves.[12]

Ascriptive identity statements like (1) may also involve another form of misrecognition we call 'oversimplifying the cultural identity of the individual'.[13] Such misrecognition has to do with attributing a basic identity to an individual 'when in fact he or she may partake of a multitude of cultural identities, to differing degrees and in idiosyncratic concatenations'.[14] Statements like (1) can be reductionist and essentialist both in the sense of relying on simplistic and overgeneralised ideas of what it means to be a Black person and in the sense of reducing individual human beings to 'uniform specimens' of the relevant racial or ethnic categories.[15] These processes ignore or misrecognise the individuality of personal identity – individuality both in terms of the ways individuals see themselves as possessing their own special combinations of group identities and in terms of how individuals interpret those group identities in their own distinctive ways. This capacity for individuality in personal identity may be partly what makes individuals unique in comparison to each other but also partly what makes them human beings. Paradoxically, there is also a risk of reductionism and essentialism when people seek to block, counter-speak, or legislate against hate speech, without giving proper space for the individuality of victims of hate speech.[16]

To avoid falling into ascriptive identity attacks, and potential hate speech, we do not claim that it is necessary for speakers to entirely ignore the fact that individuals may possess certain protected characteristics or have group identities. Indeed, identity denial may be a form of hate speech itself, as we shall discuss in Section 4.4. Rather, what matters is listening to, and asking people about, how they wish or need to be classified, and recognising that the particular content of personal identity or self-identification is not merely a whim or inconsequential preference but typically a matter of deep personal conviction about who or what one is. There should be a profound recognition of 'the personalized way in which the individual construes his or her own identity partly in relation to group identities.'[17] At minimum, respect for the autonomy and individuality of personhood means treating people as being capable of playing a part as co-authors in collaborative processes of their identity creation; an idea to which we will return also in Section 4.4.

4.2.4.2 Descriptive Identity Attacks

Turning next to descriptive identity attacks, once again there are different ways of making the case they are hate speech. The first is to look beyond the literal meanings of descriptive identity attacks and focus on the non-literal content they may express, imply, presuppose, or infer. Even if a statement does not explicitly refer to people, it can still imply, presuppose, or even produce an inference in the minds of the receiving audience, that it is about people. Consider the following statements.

(4) Homosexuality is disgusting.
(12) Retardedness is an abomination.
(13) Untouchableness is a punishment for sins of a past life.
(14) To be *Buraku* [Japanese] ('of a village') is to be uncivilised.
(15) I hate transgenderality.

It is possible that, dependent on the speaker, context, and receiving audience, these statements could convey the following content.

(4a) *The speaker holds that homosexuals are disgusting.*
(12a) *The speaker holds that retards are an abomination.*
(13a) *The speaker holds that untouchables are suffering a punishment for sins of a past life.*

(14a) *The speaker holds that Burakumin are uncivilised.*
(15a) *The speaker hates transgender people.*

We suggest one mechanism by which descriptive identity attacks can convey non-literal content that itself constitutes an attack against people has to do with the nature of the characteristics they are attacking and the relationship between the characteristics and the people who possess them. For example, the term 'homosexuality' contained in (4) conventionally refers to properties, qualities, or characteristics that are possessed by homosexual people. Suppose a speaker understood and intended the term 'homosexuality' to refer to an *orientation*, specifically, *a tendency or enduring pattern of being sexually attracted solely to people of one's own sex*. Let us assume for the sake of argument this is a universal and unique property of homosexuals, meaning that it is possessed by all homosexuals and is only possessed by homosexuals. In that event, it may be more likely, although not guaranteed, that the speaker who states (4) also conveys the non-literal content (4a), namely the idea that homosexuals are disgusting. By contrast, suppose a speaker meant the term 'homosexuality' to refer only to a *practice*, namely, *a practice of regularly engaging in sexual intercourse with people of the same sex*. This is a non-unique but typical characteristic of homosexual people, as in, a characteristic that is possessed by many homosexual people but is not universal to all homosexual people (e.g. celibate homosexuals) and is also possessed by some non-homosexual people (e.g. some bisexuals, some pansexuals, some heterosexual porn stars, some heterosexual rent boys). In that scenario, it may be less likely, although not impossible, that the speaker who states (4) conveys the non-literal content (4a).

Another mechanism is if the speaker uses a descriptive identity attack that triggers in the receiver a chain of inferences or syllogism that builds from a series of premises to the conclusion that the speaker is engaged in an attack against people. Thus, (4) might trigger the following inference in the receiving audience.

(4b) *The speaker holds that all homosexuals possess the characteristic of being sexually attracted solely to people of their own sex, that this characteristic (homosexuality) is disgusting, that this is a defining characteristic in the sense that it speaks volumes about what people are and is an appropriate basis for the evaluation of people, that anyone who possesses a defining characteristic that is itself disgusting is themselves disgusting and that, therefore, all homosexuals are disgusting.*

A third mechanism is if the term 'homosexuality' has only the formal appearance of an adjective referring to properties, qualities, or characteristics, but semantically functions in a different way. In some contexts, a speaker may be intending to use the term 'homosexuality' with the semantic function of a definite description (noun-phrase) that refers to a unique group of people, namely *the group of people who are sexually attracted solely to people of their own sex*. In which case, (4) would convey the following content.

(4c) *The speaker holds that people who are sexually attracted solely to people of their own sex are disgusting.*

Notwithstanding these points about the non-literal content possibly conveyed by descriptive identity attacks, we maintain that it still makes sense to classify such attacks as hate speech even when focusing on literal meanings. We believe most competent language users would, or should, consider them to be at least indirect attacks against people. This is because even though descriptive identity attacks are not exactly the same as attacks against people, it is arguable that descriptive identity attacks are for all intents and purposes attacks against people.

To explain, we propose there is a metaphysical linkage between attacking a characteristic and attacking people who possess the characteristic. The linkage is formed of two main links: the first between characteristics and identity; the second between identity and people. Starting with the first link, if protected characteristics are attributes, qualities, properties, or features shared by people, what is the relationship between these characteristics, on the one hand, and ontological categories, social statuses, group memberships, and identities, on the other hand? We suggest people fall under categories, have statuses, belong to groups, and acquire identities partly by virtue of their possession or perceived possession of characteristics. In that case, even though a characteristic is not the same thing as an identity, for example, characteristics are a part of what gives people their identities. Of course, the term 'identity' is notoriously ambiguous. In the impersonal sense of 'identity', the term can refer to either natural or social rules and conventions, formal or informal, concerning who or what people are, and a person has no direct control over those rules and conventions, hence 'impersonal'. In the personal or subjective sense of 'identity', by contrast, the term refers to who or what a person takes themselves to be or how they see themselves, where this is largely governed by a person's self-perception, hence 'personal'. Furthermore, characteristics can be related to identity in different ways. Some characteristics can be peripheral to an identity, others more central or integral. Some characteristics can be merely correlated with an identity, whilst others are constitutive. Nevertheless, in general terms characteristics are a part of what identifies a person as similar or different to others and part of what forms an impression of that person whether presented by others or by that person.

Addressing the second link, clearly there is a difference between a person and their identity in the sense they are not one and the same thing. But even though they are discrete in one sense, they can also be intimately connected with each other such as if a person is partly constituted by their identity or if personhood supervenes on identity. If a descriptive identity attack targets an identity that is intimately connected with people, then it would seem to follow that an attack on the identity can be equivalent and tantamount to an attack against people with that identity. This is to say that an attack on an identity can be on a par with an attack against people and that the targets of the attack are likely to feel as though *they* are being attacked.

We propose that, due to the metaphysical linkage between characteristics, identities, and people, an attack on a characteristic can be reasonably considered at least an indirect attack against people, and that this has a positive bearing on any preliminary or initial credibility of calling descriptive identity attacks 'hate speech'. Consider once again the following statements.

(4) Homosexuality is disgusting.
(5) I hate the thing that makes homosexuals who they are.
(9) Homosexuals are disgusting.
(10) I hate everything about homosexuals.

In one sense these statements are distinguishable insofar as (9) and (10) directly attack homosexuals whereas (4) and (5) appear to be attacks on homosexuality. Nevertheless, we maintain that in another sense these statements share a commonality of target understood in terms of the metaphysical linkages introduced above. Arguably, they are all attacks against people, even though (9) and (10) are direct attacks whereas (4) and (5) are indirect attacks. Interestingly, this insight is mirrored in some legal analyses of unlawful hate speech involving descriptive identity attacks.[18]

That said, in our view whether ultimately statements like (4) and (5) are hate speech in the ordinary sense of the word depends on the global resemblance test. It is not enough simply to identify metaphysical linkages between characteristics, identities, and people. It must also be shown that descriptive identity attacks share sufficient similarities with exemplars of hate speech across the dimensions of target, style, message, act, and effect. However, we believe sufficient similarities do exist. For one thing, there is a similarity in the indirect nature of the attack on the target, in the sense that descriptive identity attacks involve indirect attacks against people based on protected characteristics just as there are exemplars of hate speech that also involve indirect attacks against people based on protected characteristics. Consider Holocaust denial as an indirect attack on Jews (see Chapter 2). Indeed, there are other grey areas of hate speech that we have already argued pass the global resemblance test despite being indirect attacks against people. Consider the act of calling a straight person a 'poof', which is a direct attack on the target but an indirect attack against homosexuals (see Chapter 3).

In addition, there are notable similarities between descriptive identity attacks and exemplars of hate speech in terms of style, message, act, and effect. For example, like (10), (5) expresses the speaker's hatred. And like (9), (4) conveys a message of prejudice and intolerance, even though the literal meanings differ. Moreover, like (9) and (10), (4) and (5) could be used to *normalise*, *justify*, or *incite hatred, discrimination, and violence* against people who are homosexual. All of these statements could also have the effect of Othering and marginalising homosexuals including making them feel as though they are different and unwelcome.

Notwithstanding these comparisons, it might be objected at this point that identities are, in one sense, concepts, implying that an attack on an identity is an attack on a concept. Consider the following examples.

(16) Transgenderality is a pernicious social construct leading to delusion and anguish.

(17) Ukrainian-ness is a disorder of the mind.

If (16) and (17) are in fact attacks on identities *qua* concepts (*transgenderality*, *Ukrainian-ness*), and if rule (R13) is correct in declaring that an attack on a concept is not hate speech, then this entails that (16) and (17) cannot be hate speech (so the objection runs).

However, we believe this objection both proves too little and proves too much. On the one hand, even if one accepts the premise that (16) and (17) involve attacks on concepts, it does not follow from this that they cannot also be indirect attacks against people, namely people who identify as being transgender and people who identify as being Ukrainian respectively. On the other hand, there is surely a sense in which *people* and *personhood* are also concepts. So, if the current objection is accurate, then it also seems to entail that an attack against people cannot be hate speech because *people* is a concept. But this is surely counter-intuitive. Thus, both this objection and (R13) need to be taken with a pinch of salt.

4.2.4.3 Symbolic Identity Attacks

A final iteration of our proposed response to the identity attacks quandary concerns symbolic identity attacks. Once again, there are different ways of showing they can be hate speech. The first way involves a shift of emphasis from the literal meanings of such attacks to the non-literal content they convey. Consider the following examples.

(6) The prophet Muhammad was a rapist, a paedophile, and a war criminal all because he was a Muslim.
(18) The Guido is a poster child for toxic masculinity, and his behaviour is a product of being Italian-American.
(19) Pocahontas paid the ultimate price for her sexual avarice, and she alone is to blame for what happened to her because she was a disloyal member of the First Nation peoples.
(20) Fethullah Gülen is a terrorist, and we know this because he is a FETÖist personified.

The symbolic figures represented in these statements include religious prophets, stock characters, real people, and sometimes more than one of these things at the same time. One basis for classifying these statements as hate speech involves identifying circumstances in which, due to the speaker, context, and receiving audience, they convey non-literal content along the following lines.

(6a) *The speaker holds that Muslims are rapists, paedophiles, and war criminals all because they are Muslim.*
(18a) *The speaker holds that Italian American men demonstrate toxic masculinity and that this is a consequence of being Italian-American.*
(19a) *The speaker holds that there is an inevitability about the demise of any member of the First Nation peoples who sell out their culture for their own ends and that ultimately it is the sell outs and not the Europeans who are responsible for that demise.*
(20a) *The speaker holds that people who support Fethullah Gülen and FETÖism are terrorists in virtue of being FETÖists (or Gülenists).*

This type of content says something derogatory and contains a message of prejudice and bigotry about the wider group for which the figure is symbolic or who are represented by the figure, most notably about how the bad nature or worst excesses of the figure reveal something as to the nature of the group. We believe there are striking similarities here with exemplars of hate speech, not least negative stereotypes, group defamation, and hate propaganda (see Chapter 2).

However, even focusing on the literal meanings of symbolic identity attacks, we propose such attacks can be plausibly classified as hate speech on a different but equally valid basis. It is that attacks against symbolic figures based on protected characteristics can be equivalent or tantamount to attacks against the entire group of people who share that characteristic. Akin to our analysis of descriptive identity attacks in Section 4.2.4.2, we suggest this has to do with a metaphysical linkage between attacking a symbolic figure and attacking the people for whom the figure is symbolic. This is composed of a link between the symbolic figure and identity and a further link between identity and people. In terms of the first link, consider the role of Muhammad in Muslim identity. In the impersonal sense of identity, a society may ascribe Muslim identity to people partly based on whether those people believe God sent Muhammad as the final prophet but also based on whether they revere Muhammad and uphold him as a representation of who they are when they are at their best. Likewise, in the personal sense of identity, it may be part of the self-identification of many Muslims to regard Muhammad as a symbol of what it means to be a good Muslim or part of the essence of who they are as Muslims. It may even be a common practice among Muslims to look upon Muhammad as an embodiment or extension of their identity, and this in turn may lead to a further practice of protesting cartoons denigrating the prophet. Likewise, clearly there are Italian Americans to whom society may ascribe an identity that contains as a core element the stock character of the Guido. And there are also some Italian Americans who are self-identified Guidos, who regard the archetype of the Guido as something to be proud of and aspired to.[19] Historically, some native American tribes (First Nation peoples) have revered the real historical figure *Amonute* (also known as 'Pocahontas'), even though this reverence has been undermined over time by stigmatising portrayals of the character of Pocahontas in American popular culture.[20] Part of this reverence may include an identification with Amonute as a symbol of who they are, not least the struggles they have faced. Similarly, there have been and continue to be Turks who do not merely revere Fethullah Gülen and see him as speaking for them but also view Gülen as an embodiment of their identity as Gülenists and perhaps even Sunni Muslim Turks in general.

The second link is between identity and people. As stated in Section 4.2.4.2 above, if there is an intimate connection between an identity and a person, then it would seem to follow that an attack on an identity can be equivalent and tantamount to an attack against people with that identity. This means that (6), (18), (19), and (20) can be on a par with attacks on Muslims, Italian American men or perhaps Italian Americans in general, disloyal Native American women or perhaps Native Americans in general, and Gülenists or even Sunni Muslim Turks as a group, respectively. Moreover, it means that such statements can be experienced by the targets as attacks against *them*. In other words, such people may experience these statements as symbolic threats to them and not simply as attacks on their identity.

Because of this metaphysical linkage, we believe it is credible to view descriptive identity attacks as potential hate speech. But once again whether they qualify as hate speech in the final analysis depends on the global resemblance test. We note that numerous scholars have considered the question of whether denigrating the prophet Muhammad, for instance, can amount to, if not group defamation *senso stricto*, then at least negative stereotyping, maligning, vilifying, or ridiculing Muslims as a group, and, therefore, hate speech. The consensus, although with some exceptions,[21] is that this type of attack can be a form of hate speech, although there is disagreement about whether it does and should rise to the level of illegal hate speech.[22]

In our view, messages and acts of stereotyping are a key similarity between symbolic identity attacks and exemplars of hate speech. Islamophobic hate speech, for instance, often typecasts Muslims as lovers of violence, oppressors of women, and people with divided loyalties. Getting other people to accept and internalise this stereotype, when allied to 'the representativeness bias' (the psychological tendency people have of evaluating new people and events based on their similarities with models or stereotypes of existing people and events as a sort of heuristic or mental short-cut to cope with either limited or complex information), may increase the likelihood that those people will prejudge any new Muslims they come across as fitting the stereotype simply due to being Muslim.[23] Since Muhammad was the first Muslim, he provides an obvious baseline for the representativeness bias, meaning ideas about him could serve as the original stereotype of the Muslim. Hence, if speakers can use statements like (6) to successfully stigmatise Muhammad, that creates the archetype against which all other Muslims are evaluated in the minds of the receiving audience.[24] In these ways symbolic identity attacks are closely associated not only with stereotyping but also with acts and effects of stigmatisation, prejudice, and marginalisation – all things associated with exemplars of hate speech.

At this stage, however, we face several counter-arguments. That said, we believe none of these counter-arguments holds water. One counter-argument might be that there is a fundamental difference between statements (6), (18), and (19), which are attacks based on the protected characteristics of ethnicity or religion, and statements such as (20), which are attacks based on the intersecting characteristics of religion and political beliefs and affiliations – the significant difference being that the latter is not a protected characteristic (so the counter-argument runs). Whilst we concede that, as defined by the major social media companies, political beliefs and affiliations are not primary protected characteristics, Facebook at least recognises this as a secondary protected characteristic, meaning it can be protected from Tier 1 attacks when targeted in combination with primary protected characteristics.[25] Moreover, platform-definitions of hate speech exert a lot of influence over but are not identical with the ordinary concept *hate speech*, which is a product of many types of organisations as well as public discourse and popular culture in general. Moreover, as discussed in Chapter 3, there are examples of attacks against people on the basis of political beliefs and affiliations that may pass the global resemblance test given the wider context, such as the slur 'commie' during the McCarthy era in America. Therefore, the mere fact that statement (20) is partly based on a contested protected characteristic should not automatically disqualify it from being hate speech.

A second counter-argument is that statement (6) is the only credible example of hate speech among the list because Muhammad has consistently been a symbolic figure for Muslims across cultures and spanning centuries. By contrast, Gülen's position as a symbolic figure is potentially only transitory. However, it is an open question what Gülen's legacy will be and whether he will endure as a symbolic figure for Sunni Muslim Turks in the way Atatürk, say, has endured as a symbolic figure for Turks in general. More importantly, we submit that the transitory nature of a symbolic figure does not in itself undermine or detract from the existence and significance of the metaphysical linkage outlined above. Indeed, for people whose identity is bound up with a symbolic figure at any given moment, they are unlikely to view attacks on that figure as any less indirect attacks on them simply because there is a chance that the figure may not endure (even if they could conceive of that possibility). More generally, it is one thing to point out that statements which are hate speech today might not be in the future because identities are not static; it is quite another to try to argue that they were never hate speech in the first place.

A third counter-argument relates to symbolic identity attacks in general. It is that humans do not and cannot substitute their own identities in entirety for the identities of other persons, even religious prophets or leaders. And so, attacks on Muhammad or Gülen, for example, are not one and the same thing as attacks on the identities of people who self-classify as Muslims or Gülenists. Not merely are there many facets to Muslim identity besides the prophet and many aspects of Gülenist identity aside from

Gülen but there are also many elements to each person's identity besides being Muslim or Gülenist. Even people who deeply revere and connect with Muhammad or Gülen have other dimensions to their identities, as exemplified by self-identified British Muslims or self-proclaimed pro-Gülenist Turkish-Americans. Thus, an attack on Muhammad or Gülen is at most only an attack on part of a person's identity and, therefore, cannot be hate speech (according to the current counter-argument). However, whilst we concede the premise, we reject the conclusion of this counter-argument on the grounds that it is a non sequitur. After all, it might be true of even exemplars of hate speech such as the slur 'nigger' that they only attack one feature of a person's identity (i.e. being an African American), but that does not debar them from being classified as hate speech. Surely what matters for determining if an identity, and persons with the identity, is being attacked is whether the bit of identity that is being attacked has significance and consequence, whether that is measured by how society perceives and treats persons or by how persons see themselves.

A fourth counter-argument seeks to show that it would be absurd to treat symbolic identity attacks as hate speech given the sheer number of figures who might be symbolic for at least one group of people. As mentioned above, one practical way of teasing out whether an attack on a symbolic figure (real or fictional) is equivalent or tantamount to an attack on a larger group of people is by looking at the degree to which the figure serves as an archetype such that depicting the figure in a negative light is in effect stereotyping the entire group. Therefore, as the set of examples being assessed as potential hate speech expands from statements maligning Muhammad, the Guido, Pocahontas, and Gülen to statements disparaging Jesus, Mary, the wives of Muhammad, Shylock, the Ayatollah Khomeini, Putin, Beyoncé, the Sapphire, and even Donald Trump, for example, it is also possible that these figures can and do serve as archetypes of Christians, Muslims, Jews, Iranians, Russians, African Americans, and some right-wing Americans respectively. According to the current counter-argument, it would be absurd to consider vilification of these figures as hate speech. However, we reject that assumption on the grounds that even statements attacking these figures could conceivably qualify as hate speech *if* they pass the global resemblance test. Moreover, we are not suggesting that literally every public figure is a symbolic figure. A symbolic figure is more than someone who is famous or powerful; they must also serve, and be widely known to serve, as the epitome of the relevant group of people. It is a sociological as much as a linguistic question whether the figures just listed are symbolic and for which groups.

A fifth counter-argument is that identities, at least in the personal sense of the term, are merely self-perceptions or reflexive beliefs, implying that an attack on someone's personal identity, including an attack on a symbolic figure, is at heart an attack on a perception or belief. And if (R13) is correct in saying that an attack on a perception or belief is not hate speech, then this would seem to entail that symbolic identity attacks are not hate speech. However, we believe this counter-argument is unsound because built on false premises. Even if symbolic identity attacks are in one sense attacks on a perception or belief, this does not necessarily disqualify them as hate speech, contrary to what (R13) may suggest. As the British intercultural theorist Tariq Modood argues, the idea that groups of people identified by certain characteristics such as race or religion should be protected against hate speech but attacks on people's beliefs should always be fair game 'does not hold' for 'beliefs which form the self-definition of a group'.[26] In the case of Muslims, identity-defining beliefs could include the five pillars of Islam, not least the pillar that Muhammad is the Messenger of God as articulated in the Islamic oath the *Shahadah*. Moreover, there are countless other ways the figure of Muhammad is integral to Muslim identity besides perception or belief, including through various cultural practices and rituals.[27] Muslim identity as embodied in these practices and rituals would be an entirely different thing without the prophet Muhammad. It is hardly surprising, therefore, that cartoons depicting him as a suicide bomber are perceived by many Muslims, and by many competent language users, as being attacks on them as Muslims and, therefore, potentially hate speech at least in the ordinary sense of the term and in some cases even in the legal sense of the term.[28]

A final counter-argument is that the relationship between Muslims and Muhammad is special and that other symbolic figures are not as prominent within the corresponding identities. On this view, only (6) could be hate speech because the symbolic figures of the Guido, Pocahontas, and Trump, for example, are not as prominent within the wider identities of Italian Americans, Native Americans, and right-wing Americans. However, surely this depends on which particular subgroups of Italian Americans, Native Americans, and right-wing Americans one is talking about. After all, it would be hard to deny there is a cult of personality surrounding Trump among some people on the political right in America. The perception or belief that Trump is a central part of who they are not merely as voters but as people has become for some on the right not merely a peripheral belief but a core tenet. That Trump is central to their personal identity is something they publicly espouse through the name emblazoned on their baseball caps and T-shirts, almost branding their own bodies with their identity as Trumpists. In their eyes, being Trumpist would be totally different, unimaginable, if it did not mean seeing Trump as an extension of their own identity. Therefore, statements calling Trump a devil are taken extremely personally, and as an attack on them, their identity, and their personhood – all on the basis of the putative protected characteristic of political beliefs and affiliations. For these die-hard supporters, anti-Trump(ist) hate speech is real, even though paradoxically some of them would also reject in general terms concepts of *hate speech* as part of a liberal conspiracy to silence right-wing discourse.[29]

All of that said, we believe the credibility of applying the ordinary concept *hate speech* to symbolic identity attacks depends on the global resemblance test, based on similarities of target, style, message, act, and effect, and ultimately on the social purposes or functions a society or organisation can reasonably expect the concept to play. When such attacks are directed at Trump, for example, the wider circumstances of American social, economic, and political life may be such that there are insufficient similarities between these attacks and exemplars of hate speech across the dimensions of target, act, and effect to warrant the label 'hate speech', all things considered, even if there are similarities in message and style, for instance.

4.3 Existential Denials

Another cluster of grey area cases of hate speech involve negative existence statements, namely statements denying the very existence of certain people identified by protected characteristics. We call these existential denials. Like other grey area examples, existential denials refer to people on the basis of their possession of protected characteristics, but what makes existential denials unique is that the relevant attack consists in the denial that such people even exist. Moreover, unlike microaggressions that take the form of snubbing or acting as though people do not exist – consider a White hotel receptionist who carries on as though a Black guest is invisible or does not exist – negative existence statements take a more overt or explicit form, actively declaring that a group or class of persons do not exist.

Existential denials are in one sense the most fundamental sort of attack a speaker could launch against other people. After all, asserting that people do not exist seems to preclude, if true, anything else that could be said about them, whether positive or negative. It also opens the door to almost any sort of harmful institutions or practices. If in fact people do not exist, they cannot be discriminated against or murdered. Consider the following statements when spoken by bigots who do not mean them in an ironic way and are not seeking to empower or defend their targets.

(21) Jewish Holocaust victims have never existed.
(22) Bisexuals do not exist.
(23) Transgender people do not exist.

At first glance, it might be tempting to assume that targets of existential denials, at least in the case of (22) and (23), do not really care about these sorts of expressive attacks and that what they really find hurtful is statements containing stigmatising stereotypes and abuse along the following lines.

(24) Bisexuals are promiscuous.
(25) Transgender people are disgusting.

However, there is evidence to suggest some people do experience attacks like (22) and (23) as every bit as damaging to their sense of dignity and corrosive of their well-being as (24) and (25).[30] Indeed, this is partly evidenced in people's willingness to counter-speak against negative existence statements such as through the collective practice of Bi Visibility Day and Trans Day of Visibility.

Of course, as a general category, existential denials have notoriously tricky semantics (truth conditions). If such statements are true, then the people to which they refer do not actually exist, in which case the statements could not have said anything about existent people, but if a statement does not say anything about existent people, then it may seem counter-intuitive to think it could be true.[31] We intend to bracket off the issue of truth conditions and focus instead on the question of whether existential denials can count as hate speech. That said, we shall consider whether there is a valid truth defence against the charge that existential denials amount to hate speech. If the denial is true and the people concerned do not exist, how could the denial qualify as an attack and hate speech? However, it turns out the truth defence is invalid for several reasons, to be set out further below.

Existential denials can take many different forms. Sometimes they occur in explicit form, such as with (21), (22), and (23). Even so, not all uses of the phrase 'x do not exist' necessarily amount to existential denials. Much may depend on differences between the literal meaning, speaker meaning, and receiver or inferred meaning, for instance. Consider the following assertion made by a misogynist.

(26) Honest women don't exist.

The literal meaning could be something along these lines.

(26a) *Honest women lack the property of existence.*

But, depending on the context, the speaker's intended meaning could be one or more of the following.

(26b) *The property of being honest is not instantiated by any women.*
(26c) *Women are not honest.*
(26d) *All women are liars.*

Furthermore, the presence of the phrase 'do not exist' is not a necessary condition for existential denials. In some instances, the denial is not explicitly encoded in the statement but is part of the expressive, implied, presuppositional, or inferential content. Take the following examples.

(27) There is no such thing as bisexual people.
(28) The Holocaust did not happen, Jewish Holocaust victims are fictional.
(29) God doesn't make mistakes, you can't be born in the wrong body, transgender people aren't real just like changelings aren't real.

In certain contexts, statements (27), (28), and (29) may convey the following content.

(27a) *The speaker holds that people are either straight or gay people and that, therefore, bisexual people do not exist.*
(28a) *The speaker holds that there was no systematic mass murder of Jews across German-occupied Europe between 1941 and 1945, that since these events did not take place, Jewish Holocaust victims are fictional, and that, therefore, such people do not exist and have never existed.*
(29a) *The speaker holds that people cannot be born with an innate gender identity that differs to the sex they were born with naturally, that so-called transgender people are not real, and that, therefore, transgender people do not exist.*[32]

In addition to this, existential denials can take absolute forms as in the case of (21), (22), and (23), but also qualified forms. Consider qualified existential denials relating to certain geographical areas or locations such as a particular locality, country, or region.

(30) In this country, there is no such thing as homosexuality and homosexuals, unlike in your country.
(31) There is no history of transgender people in the Middle East.

Or consider qualified negative existence statements that assert the non-existence of certain people within particular abstract domains or realms, or that limit the existence of certain people to only abstract domains or realms.

(32) In our culture, bisexuals do not exist.
(33) The Jews do not exist outside of the sphere of their own imagination.
(34) Homosexuals do not exist in the Bible.
(35) Transgender people do not exist in Orthodox Judaism.
(36) Gypsies do not exist in the universe of moral concern.
(37) Bisexuals do not exist in the real world.
(38) Transgender men do not exist save for as a disorder of the mind.
(39) South Sudanese people do not exist other than as social constructs.
(40) The Ukrainian people do not exist except in their own myths and propaganda.

Or consider qualified negative existence statements that allege the non-existence of certain people when it comes to particular modes of existence or ways of being, such as human, moral, physical, material, spiritual, real, or as a discrete group.

(41) Jews do not exist in human form.
(42) Russians do not exist as human beings.
(43) The white man does not exist in the form of a being with a soul.
(44) Gypsies do not exist as moral entities.
(45) The uneducated are incapable of existing in the world of transcendental experiences.
(46) Transgender men do not exist in physical form.
(47) White people do not exist in material form.
(48) Gentiles do not exist in spiritual form.
(49) Ukrainians do not exist in real form.
(50) South Sudanese do not exist as a discrete group.

Or consider negative existence statements that are qualified in terms of degree of existence.

(51) Western Saharans exist only to some degree.
(52) There has only ever existed a single transwoman, Eve, no other trans-women exist.

Or consider existential denials that are qualified by the degree of certainty with which they are asserted.

(53) I guess bisexual people don't really exist.
(54) On the balance of probabilities, I would say transgender people do not exist.

Furthermore, some existential denials do not directly deny the existence of certain people identified by protected characteristics. For example, some statements deny the existence of the characteristics themselves.

(55) Homosexuality does not exist.
(56) Bisexuality does not exist.
(57) Transgenderality does not exist.

Other statements deny the existence of a people, community, or nation.

(58) The Jewish people do not exist.
(59) There are people who live in Western Sahara, but the community of Sahrawi people does not exist.
(60) There is no such thing as the Ukrainian nation, it does not exist.

We believe all the examples listed above potentially fall into a grey area of hate speech, although some existential denials may share greater similarities with exemplars of hate speech than others. Indeed, like all other grey areas of hate speech, the speaker, the context, and the receiving audience are crucial factors in determining what the conveyed content is. Thus, in some instances, it will be clear from these factors that the intended meaning is something other than hateful. Like a speaker who mentions racist slurs in order to highlight the problem of hate speech itself, sometimes negative existence statements might be used to point out the injustices faced by a group. Consider the following statement and the content it might convey when spoken by a gay rights activist.

(61) Homosexuals do not exist in Iran.
(61a) *The speaker has an insight that homosexuals are not officially recognised in Iran and that this facilitates the unjust persecution of homosexuals through the penal code, and the speaker intends to express that insight.*

Similarly, a speaker might utter a negative existence statement in order to highlight and reject the essentialisation of people who identify with protected characteristics. Consider these words and conveyed content when spoken by a gay person.

(62) The gay community does not exist.
(62a) *The speaker has a perspective that homosexuals do not form a single community in the sense of having a shared set of practices, beliefs, narratives, values, interests, and goals and that to talk in terms of a gay community risks essentialising people who happen to be gay, and the speaker intends to express that perspective.*

We take it as read that if (61) and (62) in fact convey (61a) and (62a), then they are not hate speech. We note also that Facebook carves out similar sorts of exemptions within in policy on hate speech. For example: 'speech that might otherwise violate our standards can be used self-referentially or in an empowering way.'[33]

4.3.1 *The Existential Denials Dilemma*

Existential denials pose a dilemma for any society or organisation seeking to appropriately conceptualise hate speech in the ordinary sense of the term precisely because existential denials are both like and unlike exemplars of hate speech. Such denials refer to people or groups based on protected characteristics, but at the same time the act of denying existence is unlike other sorts of attacks associated with paradigmatic hate speech. Call this the existential denials dilemma.

In fact, the dilemma can take several forms depending on which aspects of existential denials are being considered. One form of the dilemma concerns the issue of truth. Does classifying a negative existence statement as hate speech depend on making a further assumption that the statement is not true? On the one hand, if a society or organisation answers this question in the affirmative, then it seems to be tethering the classification of hate speech to the prior question of truth. It means accepting something like the following irreconcilabilist rule.

(R14) Classifying statements as being hate speech is irreconcilable with also accepting that those same statements are true or that the speaker has reasonable grounds on which to believe they are true, and so speaking the truth is a knock-down defence against an accusation of hate speech.

Accepting (R14) might be appealing because it enables a society or organisation to explain why the following statement is not hate speech.

(63) Changelings do not exist.

Since changelings are fictional beings and do not actually exist, presumably it would be absurd to judge that (63) is hate speech. However, accepting (R14) might also generate counter-intuitive outcomes precisely because it effectively analogises all hate speech to libel and ignores other similarities between existential denials and exemplars of hate speech.

On the other hand, if a society or organisation answers the aforementioned question in the negative, then it means affirming a reconcilabilist rule.

(R15) Classifying statements as being hate speech is reconcilable with also accepting that those same statements could be true or that the speaker has reasonable grounds on which to believe they are true, and so speaking the truth is not a knock-down defence against an accusation of hate speech.

Yet in order to motivate (R15) and justify the classification of existential denials as potential hate speech, one has to provide a good account of why such a classification is morally and conceptually fitting (and without relying on the assumption that existential denials are not true). But what are the similarities between existential denials and exemplars of hate speech that makes this classification plausible?

Another form of the existential denials dilemma relates to dissimilarities between the sorts of properties attributed or de-attributed to people by existential denials as compared to exemplars of hate speech. As illustrations, consider the following statements.

(22) Bisexuals do not exist.
(64) Bisexuals are oversexed.

On first appearances, whereas (64) asserts that bisexuals possess the hybrid descriptive-evaluative property of being oversexed, (22) makes a very different kind of assertion, to wit, that bisexuals possess the descriptive property of non-existence or that they lack the descriptive property of existence. The dilemma is whether or not to classify both (22) and (64) as hate speech given this notable difference. One horn of the dilemma involves accepting the following rule of thumb.

(R16) The mere attribution or de-attribution of descriptive properties to people identified by protected characteristics is never hate speech.

If (R16) is accepted, then it would follow that (22) cannot be hate speech. Then again, this may seem dogmatic if it ignores other sorts of similarities between (22) and exemplars of hate speech besides the kinds of properties they attribute to target groups. This also overlooks examples of hate speech that do seem to involve the mere attribution or de-attribution of descriptive properties to relevant groups, such as attributing physical properties to a race of people.

The second horn of the dilemma involves embracing the opposite rule.

(R17) The mere attribution or de-attribution of descriptive properties to people identified by protected characteristics is always hate speech.

Embracing (R17) would enable a society or organisation to say that attributing the descriptive property of non-existence or de-attributing the descriptive property of existence to people identified by protected characteristics is hate speech. However, the problem is that embracing (R17) might also commit a society or organisation to judging the following as hate speech.

(65) Bisexuals have sexual attraction towards and typically a desire to engage in sexual behaviour with both people of their own sex and people of the opposite sex.

In a very straightforward sense, statement (65) attributes a descriptive property to people identified by a protected characteristic. Yet to claim that (65) is hate speech seems counter-intuitive. It looks far more like a bland tautology than a hate speech.

A final version of the existential denials dilemma stems from the attempt to compare negative existence statements to exemplars of hate speech in terms of both literal and non-literal meanings. On the one hand, looking at the non-literal meanings of existential denials opens up further possibilities for drawing comparison between them and exemplars of hate speech. Then again, do all existential denials convey non-literal meanings that are highly similar to messages associated with exemplars of hate speech? Alternatively, if existential denials are a sui generis form of hate speech based on their literal meanings, as in, an existential denial is a particular type of hate speech message in its own right, what makes existential denials hate speech and not some further discrete category of problematic speech? What else do they have in common with paradigmatic forms of hate speech?

In general, there are two main ways of responding to the existential denials dilemma (covering its various forms). The first response is to claim that existential denials are never hate speech because on closer inspection they do not involve attacks against people. This response has several variants corresponding to some of the different forms of the dilemma. These variants include the claim that if negative existence statements are true, then they cannot be hate speech, based on the irreconcilabilist rule (R14); the claim that such statements constitute denials of people's beliefs rather than attacks against people and therefore cannot be hate speech, in compliance with rule (R13); the claim that such statements constitute assertions about concepts with null extensions and/or uninstantiated properties rather than attacks against people and therefore cannot be hate speech, also in compliance with rule (R13); and the claim that existential denials involve the attribution or de-attribution of descriptive properties (i.e. non-existence, existence) and, therefore, are not classifiable as hate speech, according to rule (R16). However, we shall argue that this first response fails because these various claims are either inherently unsound or not applicable to all relevant examples of existential denials.

The second response (our proposed response) is to maintain that existential denials do involve attacks against people and can be hate speech based on the global resemblance test. Once again, there are different variants of this response. One variant puts an emphasis on the non-literal content conveyed by existential denials and on the similarities between these sorts of messages and exemplars of hate speech. Another variant focuses instead on the literal meanings of existential denials and argues that these meanings constitute a sui generis form of hate speech message. We argue that each variant is appropriate for different existential denials. As regards the issue of truth, we argue that speaking the truth is not a knock-down defence against an accusation of using hate speech. As discussed in Chapter 2, there are paradigmatic examples of hate speech whose classification as hate speech seems immune to the truth defence. Precisely for this reason, we reject the irreconcilabilist rule (R14) and endorse instead the reconcilabilist rule (R15). Moreover, we argue that even if there is a sense in which existential denials are denials of people's beliefs or assertions about concepts with null extensions and/or uninstantiated properties, they can still constitute an indirect attack on people and, therefore, can qualify as hate speech, based on (R11). Furthermore, contrary to both (R16) and (R17), we believe the binary choice between never and always classifying as hate speech the mere attribution or de-attribution of descriptive properties to people identified by protected characteristics is a false choice. Sometimes this is hate speech (e.g. non-existence, existence), but sometimes it is not. Most importantly, adopting this second main response to the existential denials dilemma is closely connected with our general theory of the ordinary concept *hate speech* as a family resemblance concept. This means that whether existential denials count as hate speech depends on whether they have sufficient similarities with exemplars of hate speech across the distinguishing qualities of target, style, message, act, and effect, given reasonable expectations about the social functions or purpose of the concept. Below we discuss these two main responses in more detail, but before doing so we shall first provide an illustration of the existential denials dilemma in action, once again in the shape of Facebook's community standard on hate speech.

4.3.2 Existential Denials under Facebook's Community Standard on Hate Speech

Facebook's community standard on hate speech appears to confront the existential denials dilemma head on by adopting the second response outlined above, namely that existential denials can be hate speech. After all, the standard contains the following specific Tier 1 rule disallowing 'Statements denying existence (including but not limited to: "[protected characteristic(s) or quasi-protected characteristic] do not exist", "no such thing as [protected characteristic(s) or quasi-protected characteristic]")'.[34]

On the one hand, Facebook is alone among the major social media platforms in making public a specific rule disallowing existential denials. Then again, this is partly a function of the fact that these other platforms do not publish comprehensive versions of their authoritative internal policies on hate speech. For example, both Twitter's hateful conduct policy[35] and YouTube's hate speech policy[36] provide lesser detail about what they mean by 'hate speech' including only a small number of illustrative examples. Neither of these public-facing hate speech standards contains specific prohibitions on existential denials, but this is not to say the relevant internal policies at Twitter and YouTube do not in fact disallow existential denials. This is uncertain precisely because they fail to publish their internal policies in full. Even Facebook's community standard on hate speech is at best only a rough approximation or description of its authoritative internal policy.

On the other hand, the fact that Facebook treats existential denials as hate speech in the ordinary sense of the term is not entirely unheard of or unprecedented. If we compare this situation with the legal concept(s) *hate speech*, some notable international organisations have adopted a similar position. For example, in 2005 the Committee on the Elimination of Racial Discrimination (CERD) recognised what it called 'Systematic official denial of the existence of particular distinct groups' as one of the indicators of patterns of systematic and large-scale racial discrimination.[37]

Notwithstanding these points, there are also several ambiguous, unexplained, and potentially anomalous features of Facebook's Tier 1 rule disallowing 'Statements denying existence' that illustrate the existential denials dilemma. For one thing, the rule categorises statements denying existing under the general heading of 'dehumanising speech'.[38] Yet neither the community standard nor Facebook's numerous public statements concerning the standard provide any explanation or justification for why existential denials are deemed instances of dehumanising speech as opposed to instances of other forms of hate speech or being a unique form of hate speech in its own right. As such, we can only conjecture as to Facebook's thinking.

Perhaps Facebook is relying on the assumption that negative existence statements are typically used to convey non-literal content that itself obviously constitutes dehumanising speech such as content denying the humanity of the targets or content comparing targets to animals or objects, for instance. Then again, it seems hard to believe that all negative existence statements convey this sort of figurative content. Surely sometimes speakers mean exactly what they say when they make statements denying existence. Furthermore, would there be any limits to the kinds of inferences about non-literal content that a statement could invite the receiving audience, and Facebook's AI models and moderators, to construct based on their background information and perspectives and, therefore, any limits to what could be interpreted as conveying dehumanising speech?

What are the limits? Without a good answer to that question, taking into account non-literal meanings risks giving carte blanche to unlimited interpretations. The dilemma is whether to draw the line at literal meanings or instead to embrace an expansive conceptualisation of hate speech that includes non-literal meanings.

Alternatively, maybe Facebook is adopting an analytical position about dehumanising speech. In other words, Facebook is simply stipulating that for a user to post a statement that certain people do not exist is a designated form of dehumanising speech, simply based on literal meanings. But then again, if Facebook is merely stipulating that existential denials are dehumanising speech, such statements are quite unlike other forms of dehumanising speech recognised by Facebook, including comparing people to insects or animals; calling them filth, bacteria, a disease or faeces; labelling them as subhuman; referring to them as mere objects; and describing them as violent or sexual criminals.[39] So where does Facebook draw the line between what does and does not constitute a form of dehumanising speech? For example, is Facebook's underpinning assumption that existence is among the fundamental qualities or basic prerequisites of being human, such that statements denying existence count as dehumanising on that basis? Then again, as just mentioned, Facebook also counts as dehumanising speech statements describing people identified by protected characteristics as violent or sexual criminals.[40] So what makes such descriptions dehumanising? Surely Facebook is not assuming that not being a violent or sexual criminal is a prerequisite of being human.

Reflecting on this dilemma, we propose the following practical solution. Facebook should re-write its community standard on hate speech (and its internal policy assuming they mirror each other) so that existential denials are listed as a distinct form of hate speech under Tier 1, as opposed to being included simply as an instance of 'dehumanising speech'. Facebook could then defend that position both internally and externally by drawing comparisons between existential denials and other forms of disallowed hate speech that it also recognises, especially within Tier 1. We shall present exactly these sorts of comparisons in Section 4.3.4.

Turning to a second ambiguity, Facebook's rule on existential denials leaves room for uncertainty about what exactly users are not permitted to deny the existence of. For instance, the rule contains not merely a general specification but also an explanatory clause in brackets as follows: 'Statements denying existence (including but not limited to: "[protected characteristic(s) or quasi-protected characteristic] do not exist", "no such thing as [protected characteristic(s) or quasi-protected characteristic]").'[41]

Based on the grammatical structure of the illustrative examples contained within the brackets and other examples featured elsewhere in the standard including '"All [protected characteristic or quasi-protected characteristic] are 'criminals'"',[42] and also based on the standard's general definition of hate speech, it is more likely than not that the schema '"[protected characteristic(s)...]"' is not intended by Facebook to be read as a simple placeholder for the protected characteristics themselves (e.g. bisexuality). Instead, the schema '"[protected characteristic(s)...]"' is probably intended as a complex placeholder for people identified by protected characteristics (e.g. bisexuals). Therefore, we read Facebook's policy as disallowing statements denying the existence of people identified by protected characteristics but not disallowing statements denying the existence of the protected characteristics themselves. Consider two examples cited above.

(22) Bisexuals do not exist.
(56) Bisexuality does not exist.

As we read Facebook's rule on existential denials, the rule would disallow (22) but not (56).

If this reading is correct, however, then it creates a dilemma. After all, it is possible that someone who posts (56) could in fact convey (express, imply, presuppose, or infer) the following non-literal content that is very close to (22).

(56a) *The speaker affirms that bisexuality does not exist and that, therefore, bisexuals do not exist.*

In that case, the dilemma for Facebook is whether to stick rigidly to the literal meaning of (56), which might suggest non-removal, or instead to make its determination about (56) based on the non-literal content it conveys including potentially (56a), which may suggest removal. Alternatively, Facebook could embrace a broad understanding of 'statements denying existence' so that the rule automatically covers statements denying the existence of protected characteristics themselves as well as statements denying the existence of people identified by protected characteristics. Although there might be good reasons to take this path such as if victims tend to experience (22) and (56) as almost equally hate speechy, doing so would lead Facebook even further from its general definition of hate speech ('a direct attack against people').

Similar dilemmas emerge if statements denying existence can be interpreted as conveying other sorts of non-literal content. Consider once again the following statement.

(23) Transgender people do not exist.

Perhaps Facebook's moderators would disallow (23) simply on the grounds that literally speaking it denies the existence of people identified by a protected characteristic. Then again, depending on the speaker, context, and receivers, (23) could convey one or more of the following things.

(23a) *The speaker is denying the existence of people who identify as transgender.*
(23b) *The speaker is denying the existence of people who have a gender that differs from the sex that they were assigned at birth.*
(23c) *The speaker is denying the existence of transgender people as a group.*
(23d) *The speaker is denying the existence of the quality or property of transgenderality or being transgender.*
(23e) *The speaker is denying the existence of the right to identify as transgender.*
(23f) *The speaker is denying the existence of being transgender as something that has equal socio-legal status and is a protected characteristic in a given society.*

In this event, Facebook faces a dilemma about whether to make its determinations about (23) based on non-literal content it conveys and, if so, to decide which, if not all, of the conveyed content (23a)–(23f) it would disallow under the standard and why.

A third source of uncertainty concerns how Facebook draws a line between unqualified negative existence statements such as (22) and (23) and qualified negative existence statements. Consider the following examples of the latter.

(66) Transwomen do not exist in material form.
(67) Transwomen do not exist in physical form.
(68) Transwomen do not exist in real form.
(69) Transwomen do not exist in women form.

All of these statements involve denials of existence and relate to a protected characteristic, and so Facebook's community standard on hate speech is potentially in play. Yet these statements do not claim transwomen do not exist at all. Rather, they deny transwomen possess particular modes of existence, and this might be consistent with them existing in other ways. For example, statements (66), (67), and (68) are consistent with transwomen existing in the form of ideas, concepts, or pretence and (69) is consistent with transwomen existing in male or transgender form.

How might Facebook handle these sorts of qualified negative existence statements? One possibility is for Facebook's moderators and policy teams to look beyond the literal meanings of these statements and identify the potential non-literal content that is conveyed. For example, they might interpret these statements as expressing, implying, presupposing, or inferring non-literal content having to do with the property of womanhood such as the claim that transwomen do not exemplify the property of womanhood. Following on from this, they might choose to classify these statements as not attacks against people and, therefore, not hate speech. Perhaps this could be justified by saying that it is important to allow public debate including wrangling over the extension of properties like womanhood.

However, it is quite possible that Facebook may also be reticent about this way of thinking and on various grounds. For one thing, to assume that comments on properties can never be hate speech seems dogmatic given that some comments on properties can be experienced by people as indirect hate speech against them, such as if they take themselves to exemplify, or partake of, those properties. Thus, even if the non-literal content conveyed by statements (66)–(69) turns out to be simply a rejection of the claim that transwomen exemplify, or partake of, the property of womanhood, this may yet be experienced by transwomen as an indirect attack against them. The present point is not limited to existential denials attacking transwomen. Consider once again the following statements.

(40) The Ukrainian people do not exist except in their own myths and propaganda.
(49) Ukrainians do not exist in real form.

It seems likely that people who identify very strongly as being Ukrainian may experience (40) and (49) as attacks against them. Arguably, this would hold true even if the non-literal content conveyed by these statements turns out to be an attack on the concept of the Ukrainian people or nation or the property of Ukrainianness, such as an allegation that the Ukrainian nation or people or the property of Ukrainianness are inventions or social constructs that do not relate to a people with specific and separate historical land, ethnicity, and genetics but merely reflect an arbitrary set of political aims and shifting geographical boundaries.

It is also worth recalling at this stage that Facebook's standard contains a specific rule disallowing 'Content attacking concepts, institutions, ideas, practices or beliefs associated with protected characteristics, which are likely to contribute to imminent physical harm, intimidation or discrimination against the people associated with that protected characteristic'.[43] It is quite possible that Facebook's moderators and policy teams may decide that in certain contexts statements such as (40) and (49), and perhaps also statements (66)–(69), would fall under this rule.

Furthermore, Facebook might err on the side of sticking with literal meanings wherever possible since classifying existential denials as hate speech simply based on the non-literal content conveyed potentially opens a Pandora's box. Following on from this, a second possibility is for Facebook to stick with the literal meanings of statements like (66)–(69) but draw a distinction between, on the one hand, unqualified existential denials and certain kinds of qualified existential denials, which are to be classified as hate speech, and, on the other hand, other kinds of qualified negative existence statements, which are deemed not hate speech. Then again, to make it work Facebook would need to have a compelling set of principles underpinning the distinction. For example, Facebook could opt to classify as hate speech both unqualified existential denials like (22) and (23) and qualified existential denials which deny certain people exist in 'material form', 'physical form', or 'real form' such as (66), (67), and (68). In turn it could deem as not hate speech other qualified negative existence statements which deny certain people exist 'in women form' such as (69). What could justify drawing the line in this way? Perhaps Facebook could stipulate that when a speaker denies that certain people exist in material, physical, or real form, this is especially egregious or dehumanising, whereas when a speaker merely denies that certain people exist in women form, say, then this is less egregious or dehumanising. But would this stipulation be rational and reasonable? What is unique about denying material, physical, or real modes of existence as opposed to denying other modes of existence or forms of being? What evidence is there for saying transwomen would experience (66), (67), and (68) as existential threats but not (69)? Alternatively, is there something especially important about allowing public debate about whether transwomen exist in women form as compared to allowing public debate about whether transwomen exist in material, physical, or real form? Without proper answers to these questions, the distinction would look arbitrary from a moral, conceptual, and social point of view.

4.3.3 First Response: Existential Denials as Not Attacks against People

The first main response to the existential denials dilemma is to maintain that these grey area cases are not hate speech because after careful semantic inspection they do not involve attacks against people. There are alternative variants of this response each drawing on slightly different analyses of what existential denials are if not attacks against people. Nevertheless, each of the variants involves looking beyond the literal meanings of statements denying existence and focusing instead on the expressive, implied, presuppositional, or inferential content of such statements.

The first variant analyses at least some negative existence statements as being incapable of conveying attacks against people on the basis that, if the statements are true, then there are no people to be attacked. Compare these statements.

(23) Transgender people do not exist.
(70) Therians do not exist.
(71) Psychics do not exist.

According to the first variant, the correct way to analyse these statements is to set aside the following simplistic literal meanings.

(23a) *The speaker is denying the existence of people who identify as transgender.*
(70a) *The speaker is denying the existence of people who identify as therians.*
(71a) *The speaker is denying the existence of people who identify as psychics.*

After all, if (23), (70), and (71) conveyed only the literal meanings (23a), (70a), and (71a), then they would be straightforwardly false statements, since even a rudimentary look at the world shows that in fact there are people who identify as transgender, therians, and psychics respectively. Therefore, (23), (70), and (71) should be interpreted as conveying non-literal content such as the following.

(23b) *The speaker is denying the existence of people who have a gender that differs from the sex that they were assigned at birth.*
(70b) *The speaker is denying the existence of beings who appear to be human but in fact who are non-human animals or have the mind, spirit, or souls of animals.*
(71b) *The speaker is denying the existence of people who have extrasensory perception.*

The next step in the first variant says that if statements like (23), (70), and (71) convey the non-literal content (23b), (70b), and (71b), and if they are in fact true, then they cannot be attacks against people, because no such people exist to be attacked, and, therefore, they cannot be hate speech. Interestingly, when it comes to the legal concept *hate speech*, at least some domestic hate speech laws include truth defences,[44] but this remains an uncommon feature of hate speech law in general.[45]

We believe the current variant of the first response to the existential denials dilemma fails on several grounds, however. For one thing, and as already mentioned above, it is quite possible that negative existence statements cannot be true because they are self-refuting. To explain, such statements assert that certain people lack the property of existence or possess the property of non-existence. But if these statements are true, then this robs these statements of a subject to which properties can be attributed or not attributed. And without speaking *of* a subject, it is hard to see how they could be true. Of course, various philosophers have furnished ingenious solutions to the problem of how to explain the truth conditions of negative existence statements,[46] but if none of those solutions work, then the current variant fails.

In addition, the current variant assumes that the non-existence of the subject is a block to statements counting as hate speech. However, as a generalisation about hate speech this seems straightforwardly mistaken. After all, there are exemplars of hate speech that, according to one coherent line of analysis, refer to non-existent or fictional people, but which are still regarded as hate speech by competent language users. For example, according to Hom and May,[47] the best way to understand the semantics of racial slurs like 'nigger' is to interpret them as referring to fictional groups of people. Nevertheless, being about people who do not actually exist does not debar such slurs from being classified as paradigmatic hate speech.

Another flaw in the current variant is that it is only applicable to negative existence statements that are true. And this means the proffered analysis would disapply to a statement like (23) should they turn out to be false. More generally, because the proffered analysis ties its fate to the truth defence against accusations of hate speech, it may have limited applicability in a world where a great many negative existence statements are not true (or lack credible epistemic grounds).

A second variant of the first response analyses existential denials as conveying not attacks against people but attacks on people's beliefs. Consider once again the following statements.

(21) Jewish Holocaust victims have never existed.
(58) The Jewish people do not exist.

According to the current variant, these statements may in fact convey the following content.

(21a) *The speaker understands that there are people who believe in the existence of Jewish Holocaust victims, but the speaker asserts that this is a false belief since from the speaker's perspective the Holocaust did not happen, and if an event did not happen it cannot have victims.*

(58a) *The speaker understands that there are people who believe in the existence of the Jewish people as a racial, ethnic, or ethno-national group, but the speaker asserts that this is a false belief since from the speaker's perspective Jews are at most a group identified by a common religion.*

Moreover, the current variant accepts the following rule of thumb mentioned above.

(R13) Hate speech attacks people as opposed to things other than people such as characteristics, concepts, ideas, beliefs, practices, institutions, or symbols.

Based on its interpretation of (21) and (58) as conveying (21a) and (58a), and given its acceptance of (R13), the current variant judges that (21) and (58) are not hate speech.

However, this variant is fundamentally flawed. For one thing, (R13) is oversimplistic in that it fails to recognise the blurring of the lines between attacks against people and attacks on people's beliefs, most notably when beliefs are constitutive of people's identity. For many Jews, holding justified true beliefs about the existence of Jewish Holocaust victims, and the practice of passing on this knowledge to the next generation of Jews and to the non-Jewish world, is partly constitutive of their Jewish identity. From their perspective, an attack on this belief and practice, such as statement (21) when it conveys (21a), is an attack on who they are and, therefore, an attack against them as they see it (see also Section 4.2).

The situation may be more complicated when it comes to the belief that Jews are members of a racial, ethnic, or ethno-national group. For some Jews, this belief might also be partly constitutive of their Jewish identity, but for others it may not be. Indeed, for some Jews, enthusiastic adherence to the opposite belief – the belief that Jews are *not* a racial, ethnic, or ethno-national group – is part of what it truly means to be Jewish. However, this does not necessarily preclude statement (58), when it conveys (58a), from being hate speech. Perhaps it is an attack on the identity of some Jews and, therefore, a selective attack against some Jews (see also Chapter 3).

Another variant of the first response analyses negative existence statements as conveying not attacks against people but claims about the null extension of concepts or the uninstantiation of properties. Reconsider the following statements.

(21) Jewish Holocaust victims have never existed.
(23) Transgender people do not exist.

According to the current variant, these statements typically convey (express, imply, presuppose, or infer) something like the following content.

(21b) *The speaker holds that the concept of Jewish Holocaust victims is an empty concept that is not instantiated by the deaths of actual Jews.*

(23g) *The speaker holds that the property of being born into the wrong body is not possessed by any real or actual people, it is an uninstantiated property.*

Moreover, the current variant also accepts (R13) which includes the assumption that commentary on concepts or properties is not hate speech. Based on its interpretation of (21) and (23) as conveying (21b) and (23g) respectively, and given its acceptance of (R13), the current variant judges that (21) and (23) are not hate speech.

However, the current variant is flawed for similar reasons to the previous variant. Put simply, (R13) overestimates the sharpness of the distinction between attacks against people and attacks on concepts or properties, most notably when the latter are partly constitutive of people's identity. Thus, even if an negative existence statement conveys a claim about a concept having a null extension or a property being uninstantiated, certain receivers may still interpret the statement as an indirect attack against them if they see themselves as falling under the concept or as instantiating the property.

A final variant of the first response claims that existential denials cannot be hate speech because, unlike exemplars of hate speech, they involve the mere attribution or de-attribution of descriptive properties (i.e. non-existence, existence), and as such cannot be considered hate speech, in accordance with rule (R16). We believe this variant is unsound for the simple fact that sometimes the mere attribution or de-attribution of a descriptive property to people identified by protected characteristics can be hate speech. Consider the following statements.

(72) Black people are brawny.
(73) Homosexuals are not masculine.

These statements smack of hate speech partly because they convey stereotypes. Then again, having said that the mere attribution or de-attribution of descriptive properties can be hate speech, we believe it would be wrong to make the further claim that such attribution or de-attribution is always hate speech. As discussed in Section 4.3.1, rule (R17), which is the mirror opposite of (R16), seems equally implausible.

Now the correct solution to this form of the existential denials dilemma might seem obvious. It is to adopt the following amended rule.

(R17.1) Whilst the mere attribution or de-attribution of descriptive properties to people identified by protected characteristics can be hate speech, it is not always or necessarily hate speech.

That said, adopting (R17.1) requires an independent account of why the relevant types of attribution or de-attribution sometimes do count as hate speech (e.g. non-existence, existence) but also sometimes do not count as hate speech. We believe this is where the second response to the existential denials dilemma comes into its own.

4.3.4 *Second Response: Similarities between Existential Denials and Exemplars of Hate Speech*

The second response to the existential denials dilemma (our proposed response) affirms that negative existence statements can constitute attacks against people and can be hate speech in the ordinary sense of the term. Once again, there are alternative variants of this response each drawing on different analyses of the semantics of negative existence statements. One variant treats some negative existence statements as figurative language. This involves looking beyond the literal meaning of such statements to uncover any expressive, implied, presuppositional, or inferential content which itself has similarities with exemplars of hate speech.

We believe this variant can help to resolve the above-mentioned dilemma that negative existence statements involve the attribution or de-attribution of a descriptive property (i.e. non-existence, existence), whereas exemplars of hate speech typically attribute either purely evaluative properties (e.g. contemptible, disgusting) or hybrid descriptive-evaluative properties (e.g. criminal, oversexed). However, even though a statement that certain people do not exist might be descriptive in its literal meaning, it could also be used in an evaluative way or convey evaluative content due to the normative commitments of the speaker.[48] And in that scenario the statement might be classifiable as hate speech. Consider once again the following statement.

(21) Jewish Holocaust victims have never existed.

It is conceivable that when making statement (21) the speaker conveys the following non-literal content.

(21c) *The speaker is committed to the idea that Jews invented the Holocaust simply in order to attract sympathy, resources, and power.*

We suggest there are obvious similarities in message between this content and exemplars of hate speech. After all, the message contained in (21c) is that Jews are scheming, dishonest, and power hungry, a familiar trope of anti-Semitic hate speech in general. It is a message of disparagement, vilification, and group defamation.

If (21) is similar to exemplars of hate speech based on the non-literal content it conveys, namely (21c), how far does this similarity stretch? Do other negative existence statements also convey messages of disparagement, vilification, group defamation, or similar hate speech messages? Reconsider the following statements.

(22) Bisexuals do not exist.
(53) I guess bisexual people don't really exist.

Given the right sort of speaker, context, and receiving audience, perhaps these statements might convey the following non-literal content.

(22a) *The speaker is committed to the idea that people who identify as bisexual are either lying to themselves about their true sexuality as a form of repression or else lying to other people in order to manipulate them.*
(53a) *The speaker does not actually know anyone who is bisexual and assumes that being bisexual is just another name for a person who hasn't yet come to terms with being homosexual and is on the path to finally admitting to themselves and others their true sexual orientation as homosexual, and the speaker thinks it is appropriate to express this idea even without really knowing anything about bisexuals.*

It is certainly arguable that (22a) conveys messages of disparagement, vilification, group defamation, or other prototypical hate speech message. Likewise, it would seem that (53a) presents not merely a message of disparagement but also one of prejudice and bigotry: the message that it is acceptable to prejudge people based on labels without getting to know them as individuals and appropriate to form an unflattering opinion of an entire group or class of persons without proper regard to the evidence. The utterance of (53), when conveying content (53a), may constitute not merely an act of 'epistemic injustice',[49] as Miranda Fricker calls it, but also prototypical hate speech acts of *essentialising*, *misrecognising*, and *pathologising*.

Depending on the speaker, context, and receiving audience, other negative existence statements might convey non-literal content that shares different similarities with exemplars of hate speech. Consider the following statements.

(74) Women do not exist.
(75) Homosexuals do not exist.
(76) Ukrainians do not exist.

Perhaps there are circumstances in which the conveyed content of (74), (75), and (77) is something along the following lines.

(74a) *The speaker has a feeling, attitude, or perspective that women are worthless or beneath consideration and intends to express that perspective.*

(75a) *The speaker views homosexuals as being disgusting such that he cannot even bear to think about them or bring himself to acknowledge their existence, and the speaker intends to communicate that attitude.*

(76a) *The speaker has a perspective that existence is a precondition of the right to be treated as human beings, that Ukrainians do not exist, and that, therefore, Ukrainians are not human beings and so do not need to be treated as such.*

It seems fair to say that (74a), (75a), and (76a) present messages of contempt, disgust, and dehumanisation toward their targets, and that they share these or similar sorts of messages in common with exemplars of hate speech (see Chapter 2).

To give a different example, consider once again the following geographically qualified negative existence statement.

(30) In this country, there is no such thing as homosexuality and homosexuals, unlike in your country.

Suppose the speaker is a homophobe and uses (30) in a figurative, rather than a literal, way, such that it conveys the following content.

(30a) *The speaker understands that, in his country, the people and its government do not tolerate the presence of homosexuality and homosexuals and from his point of view this a good thing, and he intends to publicly express that view to others.*

Arguably, (30a) is a paradigmatic message of hatred, prejudice, and intolerance. Moreover, for certain speakers within certain contexts, to assert (30) with the intended figurative meaning (30a), might constitute the performance of one or more prototypical hate speech acts, such as *marginalising* and *Othering*, or even *justifying, legitimating*, or *normalising acts of hatred, discrimination, and violence.*

Notwithstanding the differences between these examples, the unifying feature of the current variant of the second main response to the existential denials dilemma is that it is possible to find hateful messages lurking within the non-literal meanings of existential denials. If this is true, however, then might it prove too much? After all, it seems to suggest that although existential denials appear to be a grey area of hate speech, they are in fact paradigmatic forms of hate speech in disguise.

We believe there would be nothing inherently paradoxical about solving the dilemma in this way. Indeed, the status of negative existence statements as a grey area would be left untouched in one sense. After all, on this reading, existential denials are ambiguously hate speech because, on the one hand, their literal meanings are unlike those of exemplars of hate speech, but, on the other hand, their non-literal meanings are directly comparable with exemplars of hate speech.

Nevertheless, we believe it would be wrong to conclude from the above discussion that somehow the literal meanings of negative existence statements could not be appropriately classified as hate speech messages in their own right. On the contrary, we think they can. Therefore, a second variant of our proposed response to the existential denials dilemma – which we view as a supplement rather than an alternative to the first variant – presents the literal meaning of an existential denial as a sui generis hate speech message. As previously noted, Facebook's community standard on hate speech contains a specific Tier 1 rule disallowing 'Statements denying existence'.[50] We believe another way to justify this rule is by recognising the literal meanings of statements denying existence as distinct hate speech messages.

That said, we do not mean to suggest that the literal meanings of negative existence statements always and necessarily constitute hate speech messages. Consider the following statements concerning people identified by a combination of characteristics including at least one protected characteristic.

(77) Black geniuses do not exist.
(78) Peace-loving Muslims do not exist.
(79) Honest men do not exist.
(80) Female firemen do not exist.

Whereas statements (77), (78), and (79) clearly come across as hate speechy, the nature of statement (80) seems far more uncertain. After all, a speaker might make a statement like (80) in order to challenge stereotypes about fire fighters and to reject the old fashioned and sexist use of the label 'firemen', for example. This may have an empowering as opposed to subordinating effect on women as a group.

Therefore, if a negative existence statement is to qualify as hate speech it cannot simply be based on its literal meaning alone. What matters is whether there are sufficient similarities between existential denials and exemplars of hate speech across the distinguishing qualities of target, style, message, act, and effect. We believe many (although not all) existential denials pass this global resemblance test. One similarity is that both existential denials and some exemplars of hate speech (i.e. bare forms of Holocaust denials) share the stylistic form of being denials, even if the ostensible subjects of the denials may differ (e.g. denials of the existence of people versus denials of the existence of historical events involving people). A further important similarity is that both existential denials and exemplars of hate speech target people, whether directly or indirectly, on the basis of their protected characteristics.

The importance of these similarities can be underscored by asking a slightly different question. What makes existential denials such as (21), (22), and (23), or even (77), hate speech but not other statements that have a similar style? As already stated above, it would be counter-intuitive to class the following as hate speech.

(63) Changelings do not exist.

So, what is the difference? Moreover, can the difference be explained without relying on the fact that (63) is a true statement (assuming changelings do not actually exist)? The answer surely is that changelings are a (fictional) group of people not identified by a protected characteristic. Race, for example, is a protected characteristic, but it refers to groupings into which human beings are divided on the basis of physical characteristics or shared genetic ancestry. Changelings are not a race in that sense because they are not human beings, not even fictional human beings.

Of course, calling people 'changelings' could be hate speech if those people are themselves identified by protected characteristics. Consider this statement.

(81) Jews are changelings.

However, the characteristic of being a changeling (i.e. a non-human life-form pretending to be a human or having been left in place of a human[51]) is not itself a protected characteristic. No doubt it is not a protected characteristic precisely because it is an uninstantiated characteristic in the real world and so it does not need to be protected by social, moral, and legal norms on hate speech. Nevertheless, the reason why it is an unprotected characteristic is distinct from the fact of its being so.

Another important similarity between existential denials and exemplars of hate speech is that both can be used not only to perform similar acts but also can have similar effects, something that also relates to who the targets are. For example, there may be circumstances in which negative existence statements like (21), (22), and (23) can be used to *condone*, *legitimate*, or even *incite hatred, discrimination, or violence* against Jews, bisexuals, and transgender people, just as statements expressing false rumours and negative stereotypes about these groups can be used to perform such acts (see Chapter 2). Or consider once again the following statements.

(40) The Ukrainian people do not exist except in their own myths and propaganda.
(49) Ukrainians do not exist in real form.

History shows that statements like (40) and (49) are often used to perform the prototypical hate speech act of *paving the way for genocide*. These sorts of statements may also be used to *deny* the very fact that a genocide has happened or that it is currently underway (see also Chapter 7).

Perhaps another part of what makes existential denials hate speech is the fact that making such statements is not only bitterly ironic but especially cruel. To explain, arguably there is something particularly callous about denying the existence of people who are at the same time the victims of various forms of hatred, discrimination, and violence. To deny the existence of certain LGBTQIA+ groups, for example, creates a double-bind: it effectively means that such people are both targets of hate crimes because of their identity and targets of hateful denials of the very existence of that identity. Then again, we also believe it would be dogmatic to assume that existential denials targeting groups of people who are not historically oppressed cannot be hate speech (see also Chapter 3). Perhaps then the more accurate thing to say is that it is particularly callous to deny the existence of people whenever such denials either reinforce existing forms of hatred, bigotry, and prejudice or contribute to the creation of new forms of hatred, bigotry, and prejudice.

Speakers who make negative existence statements may also be performing another type of prototypical hate speech act, what we have elsewhere called 'existential misrecognition'.[52] To the extent that the existence of a group of people and its group identity is dependent on its cultural memory and narratives, including the many personal stories based on first-hand experiences that its members pass on to the next generation, statements like (21) may perform an existential misrecognition of victims of the Holocaust and the group identity of Jews in general.[53]

Perhaps the same may be said about other existential denials. Consider once again the following geographically qualified negative existence statements.

(30) In this country, there is no such thing as homosexuality and homosexuals, unlike in your country.
(31) There is no history of transgender people in the Middle East.

Depending on the speaker and context, to make statements like (30) and (31) could constitute acts of existential misrecognition against gay and trans people: namely, a refusal to recognise the cultural memory of a group, with its own experiences of living in a country or being part of a regional culture, and thereby the denial of the existence of a group identity. Statements like (30) and (31) *un*-acknowledge everything from the childhood memories of gay and transgender people living in the community, sometimes in secret; through to their experiences of hate crime; and on to official records and deeply personal recollections of interactions with providers of medical or spiritual diagnoses, services, and treatments, including things like gay conversion therapy and the misdiagnosis of gender dysphoria as depression or teenage hysteria. In some regions, statements denying the existence of certain LGBTQIA+ groups would also *un*-acknowledge countless museums, archives, monuments, memorials, parades, marches, rallies, commemorations, and national days of visibility.

4.4 Identity Denials

Another crop of grey area cases of hate speech involve negative being statements, namely statements denying certain people are who they take themselves to be, denying they possess the properties they understand themselves to possess, denying they are members of the groups they see themselves as belonging to, or otherwise denying they are what they identify as, where the denials are based on protected characteristics. Such denials typically juxtapose the two senses of identity already mentioned in Section 4.2.4.2: identity in the impersonal sense of natural or social rules and conventions, formal or informal, governing who or what people are, and identity in the personal or subjective sense of who or what a person takes themselves to be or how they see themselves. The denials give priority to, or privilege, people's impersonal identities over their personal identities. We call these identity denials.[54]

Identity denials come in various forms. For example, they can take a targeted form, in which specific individuals are picked out, as with the following examples.

(82) This Mulatto is not white.
(83) This Igbo is not a Jew.
(84) This mystic is no Muslim.
(85) John is not the bisexual he claims to be.
(86) Susan identifies as a woman, but clearly is not a woman.

But they can also take a general form, which directly and explicitly speak to an entire group or class of persons.

(87) People with a drop of black blood are not white.
(88) Igbo Jews are not Jews.

(89) Sufi Muslims are not Muslims.
(90) Transwomen are not women.

This parallels a broader distinction conventionally drawn in the literature on hate speech between targeted and generalised iterations of hate speech.[55]

In addition, identity denials can take a basic or bare form comprising simply the denial, but they can also take a more expansive or elaborate form, such as by combining the denial with further explanations, evaluations, or assessments of the people concerned and/or arguments, prescriptions, or suggestions about how the people ought to be treated, as with the following statements.

(91) John is not the bisexual he claims to be; this is simply an outpouring of repressed homosexuality.
(92) This square jawed 6-foot-5 inch tall trans person identifies as a woman, but frankly it's just weird to go around dressed like that when everyone knows this person is not a woman.
(93) So-called transwomen are not merely deluded; they are being deliberately deceitful because deep down they know they are not really women.
(94) Of course transwomen should be denied access to women only spaces whatever the context; they are not women for God's sake!

Without prejudging at this stage whether identity denials are in fact hate speech, it is interesting to note that the distinction between basic and elaborate identity denials also mirrors a distinction commonly drawn in the literature between basic, coldblooded, or softcore forms of hate speech, on the one hand, and more elaborate, hot-blooded, or hardcore forms of hate speech, on the other hand.[56]

Moreover, identity denials can be explicit and overt, as exemplified in statements (82)–(94) above, but they can also be implicit or covert, as shown in the following pairings of statements and expressed, presupposed, implied, or inferred content.

(95) People are either gay, straight, or lying.
(95a) *People who claim to be bisexuals are not actually bisexual.*
(96) This person is a womxn.
(96a) *This person is not a woman.*
(97) A woman is an adult human female.
(97a) *A woman is an adult human female, someone who is not an adult human female is not a woman, transwomen are not biologically female, and therefore transwomen are not women.*
(98) Women are people who from early childhood are socialised to play the role of a woman.
(98a) *Women are people who from early childhood are socialised to play the role of a woman, transgender women have not from early childhood been socialised to play the role of a woman, and therefore transgender women are not women.*

(99) Women's experience of oppression is based on their being oppressed simply due to their female biology and this essential feature of being a woman can't be replicated through gender reassignment surgery.

(99a) *Women's experience of oppression is based on their being oppressed simply due to their female biology and this essential feature of being a woman can't be replicated through gender reassignment surgery, transwomen lack experience of being oppressed simply due to their female biology and so lack an essential feature of being a woman, and therefore transwomen are not women.*

(100) Yes, transwomen are like women, but I'm not going to sit here and say that transwomen are women; however, what I think we can all agree on is that women are women and transwomen are transwomen.

(100a) *Transwomen are not women.*

Once again, the wider literature on hate speech also draws a similar distinction between explicit or overt hate speech, on the one hand, and implicit, covert, sneaky, implied, sanitised, coded, or dog whistle hate speech, on the other hand.[57]

However, we take it as read that although a statement such as (90) is an identity denial in the straightforward sense that it denies transwomen are women, it falls short of explicitly misgendering transwomen. Statement (90) does not directly assert that transwomen are men. Of course, there might be elaborate forms of identity denials that do indeed express, imply, presuppose, or infer that transwomen are men. Consider the following pairings of statements and conveyed content.

(101) Transwomen are not women, it is obvious what they are.

(101a) *Transwomen are not women, they are men.*

(102) Call transwomen what you like but they are not women: male people are male people are male people.

(102a) *Transwomen are not women, they are male people.*

However, we shall not try to argue that all identity denials convey this sort of content. Instead, we reserve discussion of misgendering and other kinds of what we call identity miscategorisations until Section 4.5.

4.4.1 *The Identity Denials Conundrum*

Identity denials are a conundrum for any society or organisation wishing to develop a coherent picture of the ordinary concept *hate speech* because identity denials seem to both invoke and test the limits of rules of thumb that say hate speech is an attack against people on the basis of protected characteristics, as per rules (R10) and (R11). Like hate speech, identity denials refer to people or groups of people in relation to protected characteristics, but at the same time the act of denying that people possess a particular protected characteristic is unlike other sorts of attacks associated with hate speech. The question of how to classify identity denials is confusing and difficult precisely because identity denials are both similar and dissimilar to exemplars of hate speech. We call this the identity denials conundrum.

In general, there are two main ways of responding to this conundrum. The first is to argue that, on closer examination, identity denials are not hate speech because they fall short of being blanket denials of identity (i.e. denials that people possess any identity whatsoever). However, we believe this response sets the bar unrealistically high in terms of what it would take for identity denials to count as hate speech. The second response (our proposed response) is to affirm that identity denials should be considered a sui generis form of hate speech but at the same time to underscore the similarities with exemplars of hate speech. These similarities are not exhausted by the fact that identity denials refer to people or groups on the basis of protected characteristics, nor by the fact that they can take targeted or general forms, basic or elaborate forms, and explicit or implicit forms. Importantly, we believe there are sufficient similarities with exemplars of hate speech across the dimensions of target, style, message, act, and effect. Before running through these responses, however, we shall first demonstrate the conundrum in action, sticking with Facebook's community standard on hate speech.

4.4.2 Identity Denials under Facebook's Community Standard on Hate Speech

Facebook's community standard on hate speech comprises a general definition and list of specific rules. The general definition refers to 'a direct attack against people [...] on the basis of what we call protected characteristics',[58] but this is sufficiently vague to make it unclear whether identity denials count as hate speech. Moreover, the main body of the standard omits a specific rule explicitly disallowing identity denials. But since the public-facing standard is only an approximation of the authoritative internal policy, this omission is not decisive. The internal policy or moderation guidelines might or might not contain a specific rule disallowing identity denials, although if it does contain such a rule it is unclear why the public-facing standard would omit that rule.

At any rate, Facebook's staff face a dilemma about whether or not to treat identity denials as hate speech. They could choose to interpret and classify them in several ways. On the one hand, they could class them as attacks against people and hate speech based on either their literal meanings or the non-literal content they convey. If so, they might adopt the following policy approaches.

(i) Identity denials encode an explicit meaning that constitutes a unique form of attack against people and are hate speech, even though they are not currently included in the list of specific rules on hate speech.
(ii) Identity denials express, imply, presuppose, or infer content that constitutes a direct attack against people that falls under one or more of the existing specific rules on hate speech, such as the rule disallowing statements denying existence.

On the other hand, Facebook's staff could class identity denials as being not direct attacks against people and, therefore, not hate speech based on Facebook's general definition of hate speech, and once again this could be on the strength of either literal meanings or the non-literal content conveyed.

(iii) Identity denials encode or convey content that constitutes not a direct attack against people but instead an attack on people's beliefs, and so are not hate speech.
(iv) Identity denials encode or convey content that constitutes not a direct attack against people but instead an attack on people's assumptions about identity, and so are not hate speech.
(v) Identity denials encode or convey content that constitutes not a direct attack against people but instead a commentary on the nature and extension of qualities, properties, ontological categories, social statuses, concepts, or characteristics, and so are not hate speech.

Applying these different policy approaches (i)–(v) to concrete examples could lead Facebook's staff to interpret the same words in quite different ways. Consider an illustration of the varying interpretations to which these approaches might lead.

(90) Transwomen are not women.
(90a) *Transwomen are not women* [(i)]
(90b) *Transwomen do not exist* [(ii)].
(90c) *Transwomen believe they are women, but this is a false belief* [(iii)].
(90d) *Transwomen assume that transwomanhood identity is a subidentity of womanhood identity, but this is a false assumption* [(iv)].
(90e) *Transwomen do not exemplify, or partake of, the quality or property womanhood* [(v)].
(90f) *The ontological category woman does not include transwoman as a subcategory* [(v)].
(90g) *The social status woman does not include the social status transwoman* [(v)].
(90h) *The concept woman does not incorporate the concept transwoman* [(v)].
(90i) *The protected characteristic of being a woman is not possessed by transwomen* [(v)].

However, each of these approaches has its potential problems. One hesitancy Facebook's staff might have in treating identity denials as direct attacks against people and hate speech, as per approach (i), is that doing so requires acknowledging a new form of hate speech and expanding what is already a long list of disallowed hate speech. They might also worry that it would lead to an absurd situation in which whenever someone denies that a group of people are something this counts as hate speech. We shall address this worry in more detail below.

With regard to approach (ii), an obvious problem is that not all identity denials can be plausibly interpreted as conveying non-literal content that falls under one or more of the existing specific rules on hate speech. It seems doubtful that speakers who make statements like (90) always mean to express existential denials such as (90b) or some other form of hate speech already acknowledged by Facebook. Moreover, Facebook staff may prefer to avoid making classifications based on the non-literal content conveyed as opposed to literal meanings, wherever possible.

That said, Facebook's staff may be reluctant to adopt approaches (i) or (ii) if they instead find it more intuitive or more straightforward to interpret identity denials as attacks against beliefs or assumptions about identities, as per approaches (iii) and (iv), or as statements about the nature and extension of qualities, properties, ontological categories, social statuses, concepts, or characteristics, as with approach (v). Accordingly, Facebook's staff might seek to interpret (90) as conveying one or more of the non-literal content (90c)–(90i). As a result, they may also feel more justified in determining that (90) is not in fact an attack against people and, therefore, not hate speech. This impulse might reflect a commitment to a literalist reading of the general definition of hate speech set out at the start of the community standard. More specifically, Facebook might take the view that it is not hate speech to question what people believe or the assumptions they make about their identities; not hate speech to say something about the extension of the property womanhood or even to say this property is exemplified by some people but not by others; and not hate speech to discuss the limits of even controversial concepts like *woman*. After all, Facebook presumably believes it is fair game to discuss the limits of other controversial concepts including the ordinary concept *hate speech*.

However, approaches (iii)–(v) also have some serious weaknesses. One reason against adopting these approaches, and against interpreting (90) as conveying one or more of non-literal content (90c)–(90i), is that this is likely to be plausible only in a very limited range of circumstances. Surely there are going to be many situations in which the speaker states (90) and is not making an epistemological point about what transwomen believe or about the assumptions transwomen make about gender identity. Rather, the speaker intends to make a metaphysical point about what transwomen are not. Moreover, in many instances, if a speaker states (90), they really do mean to be saying something mainly about transwomen, as opposed to saying something mainly about the property of womanhood or the concept *woman*.

Given the limitations of approaches (ii)–(v), perhaps the obvious move would be for Facebook's staff to revert back to the more prosaic approach (i), which concentrates on the literal meanings of identity denials. Focusing on the literal meaning (90a), it is surely much harder to maintain that (90) is not a direct attack against people and not hate speech. Indeed, in our view, Facebook should build into its internal policy, and mirror this in the community standard under Tier 2, that identity denials are a sui generis form of hate speech. We defend this view in Section 4.4.4. However, the question then becomes what makes identity denials similar enough to the various other specific forms of hate speech already disallowed by Facebook to warrant counting identity denials as a form of hate speech as opposed to merely offensive speech. This is the other side of the identity denials conundrum.

Furthermore, if they adopt approach (i), Facebook's staff may then face a further challenge of how to determine the relevant protected characteristic (or subcharacteristic) on the basis of which people are being attacked by identity denials. A potential danger might be that they beg the gender question or even misgender people. On the one hand, if Facebook's staff interpret (90) not merely as an attack against people on the basis of sex or gender identity but specifically as an attack against men, then that would be to assume transwomen are men, and to concede that (90) is true. In which case, the speaker might insist that (90) cannot be hate speech if it is actually true. Then again, many targeted individuals are likely to continue to interpret (90) as hate speech and may even regard the proposed interpretation that (90) is an attack against men to be itself a form of misgendering. On the other hand, if Facebook's staff treat (90) as an attack against women, then that would be to assume transwomen are women, and to judge that (90) is false. In that event, targeted individuals may feel justified in calling for the content to be removed as hate speech. But speakers might complain that Facebook's staff are inappropriately and dangerously adopting the position of arbiters of truth on matters of gender. Either way, staff would be making decisions about what qualifies as gendered hate speech based on their own factual or metaphysical views about the nature of gender.

Of course, Facebook's staff could adopt a more neutral approach of interpreting (90) as an attack against people on the basis of sex or gender identity, and more specifically, as an attack against transgender women. This would be a neutral approach in the sense of enabling staff to determine whether (90) is hate speech without formally taking sides in the gender debate. But then that still leaves the conundrum of whether or not to classify (90) as hate speech. So let us now turn to consider the two main responses to that conundrum.

4.4.3 *First Response: Identity Denials as Falling Short of Blanket Denials of Identity*

The first main response to the identity denials conundrum opines that identity denials cannot constitute hate speech because of what they fall short of saying. Typically, identity denials do not take the form of blanket denials of identity. Clearly the following two statements are non-equivalent.

(90) Transwomen are not women.
(103) People who self-identify as transwomen are not women, they are not transwomen, they are not men, they are not human, they are not anything.

Whereas (90) is a limited negative being statement involving the denial of being women, (103) is a comprehensive negative being statement because it involves the denial of being anything.

Now we certainly accept the premise that comprehensive negative being statements can qualify as hate speech. It seems intrinsically dehumanising to assert that a person or group do not possess any characteristic, fail to belong to any group, do not fall under any ontological category, and lack any identity. Such statements may be on a par with existential denials discussed in Section 4.3. However, we reject the inference that identity denials which are non-comprehensive cannot be hate speech. Statement (90) is a limited negative being statement but can still constitute hate speech even on that basis. For one thing, it would be peculiar to suggest (90) is not an identity denial. After all, it is a denial of a particular gender identity (women), and for many people their gender identity is an integral part of their personal identity, that is, a fundamental part of who they think they are.[59] Moreover, reflecting our general theory of hate speech in the ordinary sense of the word, in Section 4.4.4 we seek to demonstrate that identity denials can share sufficient similarities with exemplars of hate speech to warrant also being labelled 'hate speech'.

Notwithstanding these points, the first response is not done yet. Another way of arguing that identity denials are not hate speech is by means of the strategy *reductio ad absurdum*, namely by supposing for the sake of argument that identity denials are hate speech and proceeding by a series of reasonable steps to a consequence that is itself counter-intuitive or absurd. Consider once again the following canonical examples of identity denials.

(87) People with a drop of black blood are not white.
(88) Igbo Jews are not Jews.
(89) Sufi Muslims are not Muslims.
(90) Transwomen are not women.

If these statements are identity denials and hate speech, then what about the following statements?

(104) People with pets are not homosexuals.
(105) Sikhs are not shorthaired people.

Surely it would be absurd to think that (104) and (105) are hate speech, in which case (according to the first response) the premise that identity denials can be hate speech cannot be true after all.

However, this particular argument only works if it is impossible to draw a distinction between statements (87), (88), (89), and (90), on the one hand, and the further statements (104) and (105), on the other hand. But surely there is an obvious distinction. On the one hand, the targets of (87), (88), (89) and (90) are people who possess protected characteristics (or subcharacteristics), namely, race/ethnicity (being Black), ethnicity (Igbo Jews), religion (Sufi Muslims), and sex or gender identity (transwomen). Moreover, these statements deny these groups possess a further protected characteristic (or subcharacteristic), namely, race/ethnicity (being White), race/ethnicity/religion (being Jews), religion (being Muslims), and sex or gender identity (being women). On the other hand, even though statement (104) is denying that a group of people possess a protected characteristic (or subcharacteristic), namely, sexual orientation (being homosexuals), it is not a statement made about people who are identified by their possession of a protected characteristic (or subcharacteristic). This is because the characteristic of having a pet is not protected. Conversely, whilst (105) is attacking a group of people who are identified by their possession of a protected characteristic (or subcharacteristic), namely, religion (Sikhs), it is not denying they possess a protected characteristic (or subcharacteristic). This is because the characteristic of being shorthaired is not protected. At first glance, identity denials are statements that explicitly or implicitly attribute the possession of a protected characteristic (or subcharacteristic) to certain people but then deny they possess a further protected characteristic (or subcharacteristic).

We believe this way of thinking about identity denials also provides a way of dealing with another set of potential banana skin examples.

(106) Psychics are not really people with extrasensory perception.
(107) Therians are not really people who are animals or have the mind, spirit or souls of animals.
(108) People who identify as Jedi are not really people who can feel the force.

It would be absurd to classify statements (106), (107), and (108) as hate speech. Fortunately, this absurd consequence can be avoided by pointing out that, unlike typical examples of hate speech, these statements are not doubly associated with protected characteristics (or subcharacteristics). It may be true, or at least arguable, that (106), (107), and (108) refer to people identified by a protected characteristic, specifically the protected characteristic of religion and spirituality, broadly construed. It is also the case that (106), (107), and (108) deny that these people possess further qualities or properties, namely, having extrasensory perception, being animals or having the spirit or souls of animals, and being able to feel the force. But these further properties are not protected characteristics. Whereas religion and spirituality might be a protected characteristic, supernaturality and non-human animality are not. Therefore, to deny that psychics, therians, and people who identify as Jedi possess supernaturality or non-human animality is not the same thing as to deny that Sufi Muslims are Muslims, say.

This line of analysis also helps to explain why certain other statements denying people the possession of similar sorts of speculative properties do not seem to qualify as hate speech in and of themselves. Consider the following statement.

(109) Jews are not the chosen people.

Whilst (109) picks out a group of people on the basis of a protected characteristic (or subcharacteristic), namely, religion (Jews), and also denies that this group of people possess a further property, specifically the property of being in a covenant with God, this further property is not a protected characteristic per se. There is a difference between the various religious beliefs or practices that distinguish religion as a protected characteristic and the metaphysical property of being the chosen people.

Nevertheless, defenders of the first response to the identity denials conundrum may yet have another argument up their sleeves. For, they might point to examples that do not intuitively qualify as hate speech, even though they both identify a person or group based on a protected characteristic (or subcharacteristic) and deny possession of a further protected characteristic (or subcharacteristic). Consider the following example.

(110) This white guy is not black, so he can't fully know what it's like to be the victim of anti-black racism in this country, and so it was ignorance to say what he said.

If (110) is an identity denial, but does not intuitively seem to be hate speech (if anything, it seems to be counterspeech), why not draw the conclusion that no identity denials are hate speech?

We reject that conclusion, but we do so with caution. There are several ways of drawing a distinction between statement (110) and standard identity denials such as (87), (88), (89), and (90), but we believe some distinctions do need to be ruled out. First, people might suppose it makes a difference that (110) is an attack on a White person and, therefore, against a member of a powerful group. However, as we argued in Chapter 3, even reverse attacks can be hate speech. Second, statement (110) may strike people as not hate speech because it serves to empower Black people, to articulate the experiences and injustices faced by Black people, and even to counter anti-black hate speech. But, as we also argued in Chapter 3, even righteous attacks can still qualify as hate speech. Third, suppose the speaker of (110) is speaking the truth. Some people may assume identity denials cannot be hate speech if they are true. To make this assumption would be to embrace the irreconcilabilist rule (R14). However, as discussed in Section 4.3.1, we reject (R14) and instead endorse the reconcilabilist rule (R15), which affirms that a statement could be hate speech even if it is true or the speaker has reasonable grounds on which to believe it is true.

Nonetheless, we believe there is an alternative basis on which to distinguish statement (110) from standard identity denials such as (87), (88), (89), and (90). Identity denials properly called are statements that explicitly or implicitly attribute the possession of a protected characteristic (or subcharacteristic) to a person or group but then deny they possess a further property they take themselves to possess, deny they have a social status they take themselves to have, deny they are members of a group they take themselves to belong to, or deny they have some other identity marker they take themselves to have, where the property, status, group, or identity marker is associated with a protected characteristic (or subcharacteristic).

What matters is not whether the denial is objectively true or false, but rather whether the denial stands in opposition to or contradicts the way in which the targeted people see themselves. Therefore, if the subject of statement (110) himself identifies as White and does not identify as Black, then statement (110) is not an identity denial properly called, and the absurd outcome that (110) is hate speech fails to materialise.

Then again, together the foregoing points raise this pressing question: Why does it constitute an attack against people and potentially hate speech to say they are not who they think they are or not what they take themselves to be? In the next section, we shall propose several points of similarity between identity denials and exemplars of hate speech that could justify treating the former as hate speech in the ordinary sense of the term.

4.4.4 *Second Response: Similarities between Identity Denials and Exemplars of Hate Speech*

When weighing up identity denials as potential hate speech, it might be tempting to piggyback off related concepts. For example, an organisation might propose that hate speech includes statements expressing bigoted, intolerant, exclusionary, or discriminatory attitudes such as transphobia, say, and then define transphobia as an attitude towards trans people that includes amongst other things denial that transgender people possess the gender identity they take themselves to possess.[60] However, this definitional approach merely postpones the conceptual controversy because it remains an open question why transphobia should be defined in this particular way.

Instead, we submit that identity denials ought to be classified as a sui generis form of hate speech but also that identity denials are sufficiently similar to exemplars of hate speech to warrant this classification. For one thing, they share in common the target: identity denials, like exemplars of hate speech, are attacks against people on the basis of protected characteristics. There is also a stylistic similarity between identity denials and some exemplars of hate speech, specifically Holocaust denial, in that they both take the form of denials, even though the subject of the denial can differ. This stylistic similarity is also shared with existential denials. In terms of message, one notable similarity between identity denials and standard forms of hate speech such as stereotypes, caricatures, and group defamations – claiming that a certain group of people are criminals, for instance[61] – is that they all portray an image of people that misaligns in important respects with how they see themselves.

But what else? What about acts and effects? We shall now present six prototypical hate speech acts and/or effects potentially performed by identity denials. The first point of similarity is that identity denials can *misrecognise* targeted people by *oversimplifying their identities*, which is a paradigmatic hate speech act.[62] Consider once again identity denials that take a general form.

(87) People with a drop of black blood are not white.
(88) Igbo Jews are not Jews.
(89) Sufi Muslims are not Muslims.
(90) Transwomen are not women.

These statements essentialise White identity, Muslim identity, Jewish identity, and womanhood identity in ways that exclude allegedly peripheral or non-standard modes of being White, Muslim, Jewish, or a woman. In the case of gendered identity denials like (90), the words could convey a particular perspective along the following lines.

(90j) *The speaker intends to express the perspective that, in terms of the identity markers of being a woman that really count, transwomen are not women.*

Content (90j) says that some kinds of sex or gender identity markers are the be all and end all (e.g. biological sex, assigned sex, pubescent hormones, formative gender experiences, childhood socialisation including exposure to certain subordinating or oppressive gender norms) and devalues, ignores, or deprioritises other markers (e.g. gender self-identification, gender presentation, adult hormones, post-transition gender experience, delayed socialisation and exposure to gender norms).[63]

The oversimplification of identity can also occur in relation to identity denials that take a targeted form. Consider the following comment.

(111) Ok yes, you are a 'trans woman', and I guess you are a 'good mother' to your boys, and you are a member of the Women's Institute, and no doubt you are good at knitting as well, but the bottom line is that clearly you're not actually a woman because you weren't born a woman biologically.

This comment oversimplifies the targeted individual's personal identity, boiling it down to a single thing. Yet for many transwomen their identity is multifaceted, ranging from being a transwoman and a woman; through to presenting as a woman perhaps using feminine dress, behaviour, mannerisms, and comportment; to navigating the norms and customs associated with being a woman including sometimes performing roles deemed by society to be women's roles; to doing and being countless things that have nothing at all to do with being a woman. Targeted identity denials like (111) reduce the target's multifaceted identity to one thing, namely sex assigned at birth. This analysis also bears comparison with Everett Hughes' notion of 'master status' introduced in the 1940s in connection with race: 'the tendency of observers to believe one label or demographic category is more significant than any other aspect of the observed person's background, behavior or performance'.[64]

A second, although closely related, point of similarity is that identity denials can *misrecognise* targeted people through an *oppressive withholding of identity*. Conventional hate speech attacks people partly by *oppressively ascribing* the possession of a characteristic, group membership, ontological category, social status, or identity to a person or group in order to attack the targets (see Section 4.2).[65] In a similar, although opposite, way, identity denials *misrecognise* people by *oppressively withholding* a characteristic, group membership, ontological category, social status, or identity that they take themselves to possess. Ascribing or withholding identity is oppressive when done externally to, against the will of, and in the absence of due regard for the thoughts, feelings, convictions, and lived experiences of the targeted people. Consider the following examples.

(112) If God gave you a penis, then you're not a woman. Stop thinking you are smarter than almighty God or that you can change what God made you.

(113) Transmen identify *with* men, in the sense that they see themselves as similar to men, portray themselves as men, act like and want to become more like men, in the sense that they believe becoming more manlike would be marvellous, and would bring them great happiness, and in the sense they think that not being men would be extremely detrimental, but transmen do not in fact identify *as* men because, either consciously or subconsciously, they know they are not actually men.

A statement like (112) can be oppressive not simply because it asserts that if people are born with certain physical attributes, then they must remain classified under a particular sex category or gender identity, and cannot transition away from or leave behind that category or identity, but also because it involves a refusal to show due regard for the thoughts, feelings, convictions, and lived experiences of people who do in fact transition away from the sex or gender they were given at birth. We believe statement (113) also involves oppressive misrecognition because of a lack of due regard for the thoughts, feelings, convictions, and lived experiences of transmen who do in fact identify *as* men. Just as most people who identify as homosexuals believe they are homosexuals as opposed to believing they are merely similar to homosexuals or aspirant homosexuals, so many transmen who identify as men take themselves to be men as opposed to merely being similar to men or aspirant men. In other words, for many transmen, their subjective gender identity is a matter of them seeing themselves as being men alongside other people who are more traditionally defined as men. Their mode of gender self-identification is not merely one of close affinity, qualitative similarity, and aspiration, without actually being men, as though they simply possess manhood traits but not manhood itself. Therefore, the way in which (113) construes transgender identity to mean 'identify *with*' flies in the face of, and fails to show due regard for, not only the maleness of many transgender men but also the particular mode of transgender identity, namely, 'identify *as*', that is itself an integral part of many transmen's everyday lives.

A third point of similarity is that identity denials can *degrade* people by being *condescending* or *patronising* towards them or else by *belittling* or *stigmatising* them. For example, statement (113) implies that transgender men are confused or in denial about the true nature of their own self-identification. Statement (113) also implies that transmen deep down know they do not self-identify *as* men but are dependent on other, more insightful and rational people to point this out to them, and may even imply transmen are suffering from some sort of pathology. Moreover, statement (113) betrays both a double standard and an attitude of epistemic superiority, which are also familiar features of hate speech (see Chapters 2 and 3). Few people would ascribe the 'identify *with*' model of gender self-identification to cisgender people. For example, nobody seriously suggests that cisgender men typically have a gender self-identification that consists in a belief that they are merely similar to men and aspirant men. So, what justifies applying that particular model of gender self-identification to transmen? Insofar as the model is not an accurate characterisation of the form of gender self-identification that is actually experienced by many transmen, ascribing the model to them and not to cisgender men smacks of a double standard. The typical driver of applying different standards to groups who deserve to be subject to the same standard is bias and prejudice, as evidenced in the double standard behind the term 'slut', for example. But in this particular case it must ultimately stem from a deep-seated belief (epistemic arrogance?) on the part of the speaker that only they (and not transmen) fully comprehend why transmen are not actually men, on a par with a prototypical hate speaker who promulgates stereotypes about Muslim women because the speaker believes only they (and not Muslim women) fully comprehend why all hijab-wearing Muslim women are oppressed.

A fourth point of similarity is that identity denials can *dehumanise* people by *disregarding their capacity for autonomous self-identification*, specifically by treating persons as though they lack the capacity to shape their own identities. Perhaps human beings are unique in not merely having self-awareness and personal identity but also a capacity to form complex ideas about and conceive the content of their own identity. In turn, personal identity is valuable because it furnishes people with self-understanding and a strong sense of connection to self. It is also an important source of meaningful choices and valuable ways of life. In its strongest form, the capacity to shape one's own identity is the power of sole authorship, meaning complete personal control or autonomy over one's subjective identity. This strong form of self-identification makes each person the absolute sovereign or the sole agent in charge of their own identity.[66] Some elaborate identity denials disregard this capacity for autonomous self-identification. Consider the following examples.

(114) People with a drop of black blood are not white; even if they happen to identify as white, that does not give them a magic power to confer on themselves white identity.
(115) Igbo Jews lack the genetic markers of the Jewish race; so despite their adoption of Jewish practices, they cannot become Jews simply by an act of self-proclamation.
(116) Messianic Christians are not Christians; it is not up to them to define themselves as Christians just because they hold a few core Christian beliefs.
(117) Transwomen are not women; you don't get to just wake up one morning and decide you are a women.

These statements disregard the capacity for autonomous self-identification by withholding an identity from targeted individuals against their will. In its strongest form, the capacity to shape one's own identity implies that if anyone is to withhold an identity from an individual, it must be solely the decision of that individual.

Nevertheless, some people might object to this way of interpreting the capacity to shape one's own identity on the grounds that it is overblown. It is unreasonable to expect (so the objection runs) that people should be recognised as possessing an absolute sovereignty over their own identity, such that merely to express a view that a person acting alone does not get to decide if they are White, Jews, Christians, or women constitutes a dehumanising attack against them and hate speech. On this view, if statements (114), (115), (116), and (117) do count as hate speech, then it should not be because of the elaborate way in which they deny people's identity.

We take this objection seriously and so we shall recast what is dehumanising about identity denials as follows. What is really dehumanising about identity denials is that they can reject an egalitarian form of the capacity to shape one's identity, specifically the capacity to act as a co-author of, or equal participant in, the social creation of identity. This line of analysis presents identity-creation not as an individualistic enterprise but as a mutual, joint enterprise typically involving processes of dialogue and negotiation. So, the question becomes whether certain speech acts show due regard for people's capacity to participate as equals in creating a collaborative-identification. Arguably, some identity denials have the potential to *dehumanise* people in the sense of *failing to treat them as equals* in these processes of dialogue and negotiation. Consider the following two examples.

(118) Jews can convert to Christianity and start to believe Yeshua and not the Halakha is their saviour, but what they don't get to do is identify as Jews; it doesn't work like that. Being a Jew is being situated in Jewish cultural history and Messianic 'Jews' fall outside of that history and do not have the same identification rights as those who do. This is not something that is settled by negotiation with them.

(119) Women belong to a social group who share a long history of interpreting what it means to be women in certain ways, and other people can't just come along and claim membership of that group willy nilly. It is about acknowledging the special position of the genealogy of female identity and understanding who are the true inheritors of women's culture, both of which evolve over time but are also distinct from the identity and culture of transwomen. Transwomen are not women just because they say they are. It's not up to them but up to actual women to decide this. This is not something that gets decided through dialogue with transwomen.

Statements (118) and (119) are verdictives, delivering an unofficial finding both that certain people are not who they take themselves to be and that those people lack the standing to be part of any negotiation or dialogue over their identity. In this sense statements (118) and (119) are *dehumanising*.

Our proposed analysis assumes that identity creation involves human fellowship. The term 'identity' references not simply narratives and images of the self as a member of a group but also narratives and images that are mutually created over time. The very idea of mutually created identity assumes people are capable of taking part in the creation of their identity alongside others; it views them as jointly sovereign over their identity along with other people. Elaborate identity denials like (118) and (119) reject the idea that Messianic Jews and transwomen enjoy equal status alongside Jews and women as co-authors of, or equal participants in, collaborative shaping of their identity through dialogue and negotiation. Importantly, statements (118) and (119) work by implying or presupposing that certain people are non-members. Identity denials replace dialogue and negotiation with monologue and verdict. They seek to reserve the creation of identity only for true members. For many people their religious and gender identity are among the most central and intimate aspects of their identity. Thus, being treated as equals in the production of collaborative-identification takes on an extra special importance in these areas. To not be treated as an equal within the identity community, to be subordinated or excluded in that sense, cuts deep. It may even be felt as dehumanising insofar as fellowship is part of the human experience.

This account of how identity denials may exhibit paradigmatic hate speech acts strikes a compromise between some trans activists and some feminists over gender identity. *Some* feminists see gender as created socially and reject the idea that an individual's gender identity is something that could be created purely through the self-identification of the individual concerned. However, *some* trans activists accuse such feminists of excluding from this picture the voice or role of the individuals concerned, individuals who self-identify with a gender other than the one given to them by society. They feel as though denials of who trans people take themselves to be are not merely exclusionary but oppressive and degrading.[67] Conversely, *some* trans activists see gender as purely a matter of the self-identification of the individuals concerned. Yet *some* feminists argue that this elides a key element of gender identity: that it is created socially not individually. They feel as though there is something coercive about self-identification, in the sense of trans people forcing others to accept their self-identification without their consent. Our compromise position interprets gender identity as created socially but in a way that is also collaborative, meaning the individuals concerned are co-authors of their own gender identity. This means that the construction of womanhood identity is the product of an ongoing dialogue and negotiation that includes both cisgender and transgender women. Collaborative-identification is negotiated not in the sense of an obstacle that a person must negotiate – in the way many people have to negotiate discriminatory attitudes in the workplace, for example. Rather, collaborative-identification is negotiated in the sense that it is a product of discussion, compromise, and collaboration between equal participants. It is the denial of a person's capacity to act as an equal participant in the joint production of their identity that is oppressive.

Nevertheless, it might be further objected at this stage that because identity negotiation typically involves a degree of conflict or a battle of wills,[68] it would be more appropriate to look on identity denials not as oppressive speech acts but as simply part of the discourse that feeds into the social creation of identity. According to this objection, far from being engaged in oppressive attacks against transgender people and, therefore, hate speech, people who make identity denials are simply operating as equal participants in the dialogue and negotiation that surrounds gender identity. To classify such statements as exclusionary or oppressive is to place speakers in the position of gender overlords (or sorting hats), which is unrealistic.

However, an obvious response to this objection is to insist that some identity denials do indeed involve speakers casting themselves in that type of position and so classifying such statements as exclusionary or oppressive is entirely realistic. For example, the speaker who makes statement (119) may exclude or oppress the intended targets precisely by issuing a verdict not only that transwomen are not women but also that transwomen have no standing to be co-partners in the social formation of their gender identity.

That said, how do speakers of elaborate identity denials obtain the power needed to successfully issue the verdicts they contain? As previously described in Chapter 2, speakers may obtain this power in a variety of different ways, with or without formal authority. In informal contexts, a speaker may acquire this power through the silence of bystanders. Suppose a White patron of an officially segregated 'Whites Only' public swimming pool turns to someone whom he suspects of not being allowed and says the following, loudly enough for everyone else to hear.

(120) You shouldn't be in this pool; and it makes no blind bit of difference if you claim you're white because you have no say in that matter, we all know you ain't white.

If both the intended target of (120) and the other people in earshot are cognisant of what has been said but do not protest or challenge the assertion (such as by remaining silent), this may 'license' the speaker, as Ishani Maitra puts it, in the sense of granting him the linguistic power to successfully perform the dual speech acts of *denying another's racial identity* and *setting aside another's capacity to be an equal participant in the social creation of their own racial identity* in that context.[69]

Alternatively, a speaker might gain linguistic power, as Rae Langton explains, by means of merely presupposing they have the authority to perform hate speech acts, which they thereby obtain if this authority goes uncontested or unchallenged.[70] Suppose someone turns to a transwoman and says the following.

(121) Only we women get to decide if you are a women, and we decide you aren't a woman, you know that, right?

Imagine the speaker presupposes she has the authority to give verdicts both on who is a woman and on who gets to decide. In the absence of the target or bystanders protesting or challenging this authority ('Who the hell are you to tell me I'm not a woman?', 'Who are you to tell her she has no say on whether she is a women or not?'), the authority is obtained and speaker can perform the dual speech acts of *denying another's gender identity* and *disregarding another's capacity to be an equal participant in the social creation of their own gender identity.*

A fifth point of similarity is that identity denials can be used to *subordinate* people by *ranking them as inferior*, which is another prototypical hate speech act.[71] Consider the following statements.

(122) Homosexual men are not real men.
(123) Transgender women are not real women.

Looking beyond the literal meanings, there may be circumstances in which statements (122) and (123) express, imply, presuppose, or infer the drawing of distinctions between different kinds of men and women based on a hierarchy of worth or value along the following lines.

(122a) *The speaker holds that homosexual men are inferior to heterosexual men.*
(123a) *The speaker holds that transgender women are inferior to ciswomen.*

In circumstances where statements (122) and (123) convey (122a) and (123a) respectively, they demean their targets by attacking their social standing or rank, by suggesting they have lesser value, or by proclaiming they are morally or socially inferior, second-class, or third-rate men or women.

A similar analysis might be applied to elaborate identity denials that invoke the distinction between fake and authentic being. Consider the following statement.

(124) Transwomen lack the distinguishing biological traits of women such as a uterus and menstruation, the beautiful bodies of women such as the particular proportions between waist and hips, and the emotional depth and maternal instincts of women, and because they cannot do and be all the things women can do and be, they are not authentic women.

Arguably, statement (124) does not merely deny the authenticity of transgender women but also questions their equal worth. Depending on the speaker, context, and receiving audience, statement (124) could convey the following content.

(124a) *The speaker holds that transgender women are not as good as cisgender women.*

If statement (124) conveys (124a), then it ranks transgender women as inferior to cisgender women. It is worth noting at this stage that Facebook's community standard on hate speech explicitly disallows, under Tier 2, 'statements of inferiority', including 'Expressions about being less than adequate [...] worthless, useless' and 'Expressions about being better/ worse than another protected characteristic, including, but not limited to: "I believe males are superior to females"'.[72]

Clearly there are similarities here with other forms of hate speech that rank people as inferior. Consider hate propaganda that is based on ideas of the superiority and inferiority of certain races, 'normalizing slurs' that attack people for deviating from the norms presupposed by the speaker that govern what it means to be a good woman, for example,[73] and 'controlling images' that simultaneously define social roles for certain groups and deride some individuals for failing to fulfil said roles.[74]

A final point of similarity is that identity denials, especially in elaborate or hot-blooded forms, can be used to *enact*, *facilitate*, or else *legitimate*, *promote*, or *incite hatred, discrimination, and violence*, which are yet more paradigmatic hate speech acts.[75] With regard to *enacting discrimination*, in contexts where the speaker has formal authority, identity denials could have the perlocutionary effect of depriving people of rights. Consider the following example.

(125) [Gender denial during a wedding ceremony: A registrar strictly interprets linguistic rules on using the terms 'husband' and 'wife' during wedding ceremonies and insists the words used must match a person's sex as listed on their birth certificate. At the end of the ceremony, he declares 'I now pronounce you man and wife' and in doing so calls a transgender man 'wife'.]

In the context of the wedding ceremony, by insisting on calling a transgender man 'wife', the wedding official could be accused of enacting a discriminatory policy, namely preventing transmen but not cisgender men from getting married *as husbands*. Of course, the transman could apply to have his birth certificate updated with the gender he identifies with. But suppose for the sake of argument the process for this is unreasonable or unfair. In that scenario, arguably the registrar *unfairly* discriminates against the transman by insisting on calling him 'wife'.

Identity denials may also *facilitate discrimination* against the people targeted by them. Consider once again the following statements.

(87) People with a drop of black blood are not white.

(90) Transwomen are not women.

Denying that a group of people have the status of being White or women respectively, could be used as a basis on which to perform further acts of discrimination. For example, widespread use of statement (87) could lay the groundwork for the discrimination enacted by 'Whites Only' signs by sorting people into categories of Black and White and thereby making some people vulnerable to discrimination. Katharine Jenkins provides a parallel analysis of how gender denials can facilitate discrimination against trans people (i.e. making them vulnerable to 'being subjected to a set of social constraints and enablements that is wrongful').[76] She cites the issue of transwomen being denied access to women only spaces.[77] Suppose a leisure centre employee is asked by her boss to enforce a 'Women Only' sign which is pinned to the door of one of the changing rooms. She asks her boss what counts as a woman and the boss replies by declaring (90). There is a sense in which by uttering (90) in this context, the boss facilitates a form of discrimination against transwomen.[78]

Identity denials can also be used either intentionally or with the likely effect of *normalising, legitimating, promoting,* or even *inciting hatred, discrimination, or violence* against the targeted people. Consider the following elaborate identity denials.

(126) These people are not white as defined by the laws of nature, and they should be treated accordingly.
(127) Of course Igbo Jews should be denied the right of immigration into Israel; they are not Jews!
(128) Sufi Muslims are not Muslims, and they know it. How can you trust people who set out to deceive others about their true identity?
(129) Transwomen are not women, so don't ever be fooled by them. They pose an inherent threat to vulnerable women and young girls and should be dealt with by any means necessary, castrate them if you have to.

Statements (126) and (127) might be used in some circumstances to perform acts of *justifying or legitimating discriminatory practices* against certain groups by implying that it is appropriate or even required to treat them in accordance with norms or conventions of impersonal identity. In some contexts, statements (128) and (129) may *legitimate, promote,* or *incite hatred, discrimination, or violence* against certain groups by portraying them as deceptive and dangerous.[79]

Furthermore, statements like (129) can create what we call a transgender trap. Even if the audience rejects the statement in its literal sense, there can remain a residual implicature that transwomen are somehow abnormal or different to real women (cisgender women), and this might serve to stigmatise transwomen as Other. But if the audience accepts the statement as true, then this could, depending on the circumstances, serve to legitimate physical attacks against transwomen. For one thing, some in the audience might believe it more acceptable to physically attack men than women. Furthermore, if the audience accepts the statement as true and reads it as implying that transwomen are being deceptive about their gender, this might incite hatred or violence on the presumption that deception is always a signpost to evil intent (e.g. gaining access to women only spaces in order to commit sexual assaults). In whichever way the audience receives statement (129), it traps transwomen by reinforcing prejudiced attitudes and even legitimating hate crimes against them.

4.4.5 Defences against the Charge That Identity Denials Are Hate Speech

Having outlined a range of similarities between identity denials and exemplars of hate speech, we shall now turn to consider potential dissimilarities. In particular, we want to look at three bases on which people making identity denials might dispute accusations of hate speech. We shall argue, however, that ultimately these bases are unsound and do not justify disapplying the ordinary label 'hate speech'.

The first basis on which speakers might reject comparisons between identity denials and exemplars of hate speech is if they are engaged in public discourse, specifically if they are intending to contribute in good faith to the formation of public opinion in the public sphere and on a subject of public concern.[80] For example, a speaker might insist that to deny certain people belong to the group Jews or to deny some people fall under the ontological category women is unlike paradigmatic forms of dehumanising speech because in the case of the group Jews and the category women, in contrast to the characteristic of being human, there is reasonable disagreement in the public sphere about the nature of Jewishness and womanhood, and these are matters of public concern that are far from being settled.

However, there are two problems with this defence. For one thing, in reality identity denials often take elaborate forms that exceed public discourse. When people use language that is abusive, menacing, threatening, belittling, or ridiculing, for example, they move beyond public discourse and travel further into the terrain of hate speech.[81] Consider comments made by the feminist and public intellectual Germaine Greer to BBC's the *Victoria Derbyshire Show* in October 2015.

> Just because you lop off your dick and then wear a dress doesn't make you a fucking woman. I've asked my doctor to give me long ears and liver spots and I'm going to wear a brown coat but that won't turn me into a fucking cocker spaniel. [...] A man who gets his dick chopped off is actually inflicting an extraordinary act of violence on himself.[82]

This statement conveys ridicule (comparing transwomen to someone pretending to be a dog), disgust (graphic imagery of chopping off genitalia), aggression (the use of 'fucking'), and connotations of abnormality ('an extraordinary act of violence on himself') – all points of similarity with exemplars of hate speech (see Chapter 2).

Furthermore, we disagree that merely intending to participate in public discourse is sufficient to disqualify words from being hate speech. Even in situations where a speaker uses basic, sober, and toned-down language both to pass comment on the nature and extension of the ordinary concept womanhood and to assert that transwomen are not women, for example, this does not necessarily mean they are not engaging in hate speech. Basic identity denials can be hate speech whilst also qualifying as public discourse. The same is true of some exemplars of hate speech, including basic Holocaust denial, for example. The key point here is that hate speech and public discourse are not mutually exclusive concepts, especially if one is referring to the ordinary concept *hate speech.*[83] Even basic identity denials can share similarities with paradigmatic hate speech in terms of target, style, message, act, and effect. It matters, for example, what acts it performs and what effects it can have on transwomen (or transmen) to be the subject of statements denying they are women (or men).

A second basis on which speakers might reject comparisons between identity denials and exemplars of hate speech is if the former are being used in the service of a righteous cause. For example, it might be objected that it would be unreasonable, even oppressive or subordinating, to expect feminist speakers to temper the manner of their speech, especially on matters of sex and gender identity. In the case of women speakers in particular, they belong to a group that has historically and continues to face various forms of silencing by men and patriarchal structures, including, but not limited to, being chastised for using coarse, vulgar, aggressive, uncivilised, emotional, or unladylike language. In some circumstances, women may deliberately use transgressive modes of language to directly challenge gendered norms about how women are supposed to speak, as a protest against gender injustice and an act of feminist empowerment. What could be a more righteous cause than that?

We do not disagree with the basic premise of this analysis. Clearly it would be an injustice if society more frequently or disproportionately labels women as 'hate speakers' even when they use the same or similar language to men. Whether men or women make identity denials, this should be viewed similarly by society and organisations. By the same token, however, it does not follow from this that what *some* women say about transgender people is not hate speech. In making this point we are not relying simply on the fact that both women and transgender people are historically oppressed, subordinated, and marginalised groups. Rather, we are relying on a complex pattern of overlapping and criss-crossing similarities between identity denials and exemplars of hate speech under the global resemblance test. Moreover, as discussed in Chapter 3, we accept there is such a thing as righteous hate speech. Greer's comments may be a case in point. But the righteousness of words does not remove the imprint of hate speech: that words belong to the category of hate speech is a separate matter from whether the speaker is using the words in a righteous way.

We believe the same goes for basic identity denials. Consider once again the following example.

(90) Transwomen are not women.

Suppose a speaker posts (90) as a rejection of what he sees as coercively imposed gender revisionism. He invokes a concept *womanhood* rooted in antediluvian examples of women (i.e. cisgender women) precisely because he objects to what in his view is a rising tide of compulsory political correctness that makes it difficult to make even the most basic statements about who or what people are. Or suppose another speaker posts (90) because she has thought very carefully about the important functions served by the concept *womanhood* in an unjust world. She intends to express her view that the extension of the property of womanhood is fixed by the quality of being born with a cervix and uterus and growing up having to confront everything this means both in terms of biological and physiological experiences and in terms of constraining and subordinating social norms and customs that are constructed on the basis of bodily features, and her view that *this* property is not exemplified by transwomen on account of the fact that they are not born with a cervix and uterus and do not grow up having to confront everything this means both bodily and socially. She is also defending a concept *womanhood* that she sincerely believes is more legitimate not because more closely aligned to a natural kind but because in her view it better serves the purpose of having sex and gender concepts, namely to highlight social injustices and promote positive change in people's lives.[84] This speaker may view herself as a bulwark against what she believes are regressive reimaginings of the concept *womanhood* that set back the cause of women's rights and safety in regrettable ways. Even if these are examples of righteous hate speech as defined in Chapter 3, however, righteous hate speech remains hate speech. In other words, it might be true that some speakers combine identity denials with a perspective that is in some ways righteous, but this does not in itself make identity denials any less hate speech if they share sufficient similarities with exemplars of hate speech across the dimensions of target, style, message, act, and effect.

We are not suggesting hate speech is or should be treated as a purely descriptive or non-normative concept. On the contrary, ordinary usage of the term 'hate speech' often includes the assumption that it is morally objectionable speech. Instead, what we are saying is that examples of hate speech can be simultaneously morally objectionable and in some ways righteous. We believe this complexity in the ordinary concept adds to rather than takes away from its social usefulness. Indeed, although Facebook does specify some exemptions to its community standard on hate speech including 'speech that might otherwise violate our standards can be used self-referentially or in an empowering way',[85] there is nothing to suggest Facebook is keen to venture deep into the ethical weeds of distinguishing between the righteous and the unrighteous when it comes to determining what should or should not count as disallowed hate speech.

A third basis on which speakers might try to resist comparisons between identity denials and exemplars of hate speech is if the denials are true or speakers have reasonable grounds on which to believe them to be true. To support this argument, a speaker might endorse the irreconcilabilist rule (R14) set out in Section 4.3.1 of this chapter (that classifying statements as being hate speech is irreconcilable with also accepting that those same statements are true or that the speaker has reasonable grounds on which to believe they are true). Let us grant for the sake of argument that at least in the case of some identity denials a speaker could in theory have reasonable grounds on which to believe them to be true. According to the present line of thought, speaking the truth in this way would be a knock-down defence against an accusation of hate speech.

However, as discussed in Chapter 2, there are exemplars of hate speech from which it would be highly unusual for ordinary language users to withhold the label 'hate speech' simply on the strength of a viable truth defence. It is precisely for this reason that we endorse the reconcilabilist rule (R15). Therefore, it is not evident that mounting a truth defence of identity denials would be enough to lift them out of the category of hate speech.

Furthermore, there are certain kinds of identity denials concerning which a truth defence may not even be possible, let alone effective. So far we have focused on identity denials which take the form of a speaker giving absolute priority to identity in the impersonal sense over identity in the personal or subjective sense. But there are other identity denials which take the form of a speaker denying even the basic fact that the target has a particular subjective identity or sees themselves a certain way. We call these fundamental identity denials. We submit that fundamental identity denials are also hate speech and, moreover, that it is difficult to see how even in principle such denials could benefit from a truth defence. Consider the following discursive exchange between a transman [Person A] and an identity denier [Person B].

(130) [Person A] I am a man.
(131) [Person B] You are not a man.
(132) [Person A] Yes I am a man, well, at least in the subjective sense.
(133) [Person B] You are not a man even in the subjective sense.

Let us assume for the sake of argument that person A is speaking in good faith meaning that person A sincerely believes they are speaking the truth when they state (132). In that scenario, how could person A possibly be wrong about their subjective identity in such a way as to make person B's statement (133) true?

However, the defender of the truth defence might respond by insisting that person B has reasonable grounds on which to believe person A is not a man in the subjective sense. One possibility is that (133) implies or presupposes the following content in addition to its literal meaning.

(133a) *The speaker holds that transgender men's subjective sense that they are men is not innate.*

Perhaps person B thinks the development of a transgender man's subjective sense that they are a man is influenced by various contingent biological and environmental factors, meaning that nobody could credibly claim this sense is innate.[86] After all, a person born female but who as a young person identifies as a man and opts to undergo transitioning procedures could later decide they are a woman and elect to detransition.[87] However, considered in its own right, content (133a) fails to provide reasonable grounds to support the truth of (133). On the contrary, content (133a) seems to concede the point that transgender men do indeed identify as men. The mere susceptibility to change over time of a transgender man's subjective sense they are a man does not demonstrate that a person is not in fact a man in the subjective sense at a certain point in time. At the time person A states (132), he does in fact identify as a man.

Another possibility is that statement (133) implies or presupposes the following content in addition to its literal meaning.

(133b) *The speaker holds that transgender men's subjective sense of being men is inauthentic and heteronomous.*

Maybe person B is assuming that a transgender man's interpretation of internal stimuli associated with their gender, that is, experiences of bodily features and thoughts, feelings, and impressions of those experiences, can be subject to undue influence. Perhaps person B thinks person A has interpreted the internal stimuli as 'my own sense of my gender identity is that I self-identify as being a man' only because their head has been filled with lots of ideas from counsellors about how 'if you feel this, have such and such inkling, or experience your body a certain way, then it probably means you are transgender'. However, once again content (133b) fails to provide reasonable grounds to support the truth of (133). This is because content (133b) concedes the point that transgender men do in fact identify as men, even though it brands this self-identification as inauthentic or heteronomous. Even assuming that person A's internal thought processes were subject to undue influence from external sources, person A's subjective gender identity remains what it is.

A third possibility is that statement (133) implies or presupposes the following content in addition to its literal meaning.

(133c) *The speaker holds that transgender men's conscious sense of being men is belied by their subconscious acceptance that indeed they are not men but women.*

Maybe the speaker believes that deep down transgender men do not believe they are men. Perhaps the speaker thinks person A's conscious and subconscious beliefs are contradictory but that it is the subconscious beliefs that matter. However, as with the previous iterations, content (133c) fails to provide reasonable grounds to support the truth of (133) when taking into account the discursive exchange in which it figures. When person A states (132), they are not merely attesting to being a man in the subjective sense but they are also establishing a frame of reference for that sense. Because person A makes no mention of the subconscious level, the frame of reference is fixed at the conscious level. Person A is simply reporting what they consciously think about their own identity. So, when person B states (133), the relevant frame of reference remains the conscious level. Indeed, content (133c) concedes the point that transgender men's conscious sense is that of being men. Therefore, even if content (133c) is true and transgender men subconsciously accept they are not men, this does not show that person A is not a man in the subjective sense. All that is happening is that person B is seeking to subtly shift the frame of reference. But if the shift fails – such as if person A resists the shift (e.g. 'Yes I am a man in the subjective sense, and to be clear I am only talking about the conscious level') – then (133c) fails to provide reasonable grounds for the truth of (133).

We have argued that a truth defence is not effective for identity denials, just as it is not effective for hate speech in general, and that a truth defence may not even be possible for fundamental identity denials. However, what implications does all of this have for Facebook's community standard on hate speech, for example? Even though the community standard contains no reference to a truth defence, it is conceivable that Facebook's staff are labouring under an assumption that some speakers might have reasonable grounds for believing what they are saying is true. On this basis, Facebook's staff might distinguish the following two identity denials.

(90) Transwomen are not women.
(134) Jews are not a people who were victims of a genocide or Holocaust during World War II.

Facebook's staff might think that speakers could in theory have reasonable grounds on which to believe identity (90) is true, but no reasonable grounds on which to believe identity denial/elaborate Holocaust denial (134) is true. This potentially also explains why Facebook's community standard on hate speech includes a specific Tier 1 rule disallowing 'Holocaust denial',[88] whereas it contains no such prohibition on identity denials. However, why could a speaker of (90) have reasonable grounds on which to believe it is true but not a speaker of (134)? Maybe Facebook's staff are relying on a further distinction between statements about hard facts or actual people such as the events of World War II, and statements about abstract concepts such as *womanhood*. Then again, some speakers who make statements like (90) sincerely believe they are talking about hard facts and actual people, whereas some speakers who post content such as (134) might insist they are referring to an abstract concept as much as to historical events. So, it is not clear this distinction works in practice.

However, whatever the reason, if Facebook's staff are implicitly relying on a truth defence in order to distinguish between statements (90) and (134), this would miss a key point about hate speech. We believe most competent users of the term 'hate speech' subscribe to the reconcilabilist rule (R15), which entails that it can be appropriate to classify content as hate speech even if a speaker has reasonable grounds on which to believe it is true. In other words, falsity is not an essential feature of the ordinary concept *hate speech*. Similarly, we believe Facebook is right not to include a truth defence within its community standard. We also believe its staff should not implicitly rely on any such truth defence. In which case, it is still hard to see the justification for the community standard failing to classify identity denials as potential hate speech. And so, we recommend that that the policy is changed to include identity denials as a sui generis form of disallowed hate speech under Tier 2.

4.5 Identity Miscategorisations

A related, although slightly different, set of grey area cases of hate speech involve statements that knowingly and deliberately, or with reckless disregard, attribute a property, category, group membership, status, or identity to people that does not match or contradicts that which they take themselves to possess, where both the former and the latter are associated with protected characteristics. We shall call these identity miscategorisations. We use the prefix 'mis' in order to convey something similar to the prefix 'mis' in 'misrecognition', namely 'lacking due regard for the perspective of the target' or 'against the will of the target'.

We begin by emphasising that identity miscategorisations can relate to any protected characteristic and as such can include but are not limited to misracialising, misnationalising, misreligioning, missexualising, and misgendering. Consider the following examples.

(135) People with a drop of black blood are not white, they are black.
(136) People living in modern day Ukraine are not Ukrainian, they are Russian.
(137) Immigrants from Pakistan never really become British but remain Pakistanis until they die because that's where they were born.
(138) Igbo Jews are not in fact Jews racially speaking since they lack the genetic heritage of Jewish people, they are merely Africans that have adopted Jewish practices.
(139) Sufi Muslims are not Muslims at all, they are mystics and polytheists.
(140) So-called bisexuals are not really bisexual, they are just gay people wanting to fit in with social norms and to lessen the harsh view society has of them.
(141) I don't have a problem with men disposing of their genitals, but it does not make them women; they are still men, despite seeing themselves as women.
(142) So-called transgender people aren't really born in the wrong body, they are simply crossdressers who like the attention.
(143) Any cisgender woman who identifies as just a woman because she thinks there is no such thing as a cisgender woman is still a cisgender woman, as in, a member of a sub-category of women, whether she likes it or not.

In these examples, identity miscategorisations take a general form, in the sense that they are about or directly refer to an entire group or class of persons. However, identity miscategorisations can also take a targeted form, being directly addressed to or picking out particular individuals. Consider the following examples.

(144) Excuse me miss, you came here to protest about women's rights, but a man-hating lesbian is what you are.

(145) Listen to me pal, let me tell you what I think about all this 'trans' stuff you've been doing recently, whether you're tucked or untucked, whether you've had it removed or are still carrying timber, whether you want me to call you David, Natasha, or whatever, you are still a man if you ask me.

(146) Jane, I don't care what you say, you are a cisgender woman.

Now it is certainly conceivable for a speaker to cluelessly or accidentally miscategorise someone, especially when speech is addressed to a particular individual the speaker is meeting for the first time or to someone the speaker has known for some time but who has recently transitioned. A speaker might not intend to misgender the addressee, for example, it is simply that the speaker fails to notice gender presentation queues. In that scenario, the speaker does not actually know he or she is misgendering the addressee unless it is pointed out. In other situations, a speaker may be aware that the addressee self-identifies as a particular gender but inadvertently misgenders the addressee through a genuine slip of the tongue or accidental speech. In that situation no misgendering was intended even if it was a Freudian slip, for example. We believe most competent users of the ordinary term 'hate speech' would hesitate to apply the term in these sorts of cases.[89]

Therefore, for the purposes of our discussion, we shall define identity miscategorisations in terms of miscategorisations done knowingly and deliberately. Of course, this means that in order to know whether something qualifies as an identity miscategorisation it is necessary to understand the state of mind of the speaker as well as the target. Thus, a statement like (144) is only an identity miscategorisation in the relevant sense if in fact the speaker deliberately categorises the target as a lesbian whilst knowing the target categorises herself as a heterosexual feminist. Likewise, statement (145) is only an identity miscategorisation if the speaker deliberately categorises the target as a man whilst knowing the target categorises herself as a woman. And statement (146) is only an identity miscategorisation if the speaker deliberately categorises the target as a cisgender woman whilst knowing that the target categorises herself as just a woman. That said, a borderline case would be a speaker who demonstrates reckless disregard as to whether they are miscategorising people. We believe cases of reckless disregard should also be included within the class of identity miscategorisations.

It is also important to recognise that identity miscategorisations can take a wide variety of different linguistic forms. In the case of misgendering, for example, a speaker might employ gendered modes of address, pronouns, proper names, or titles that do not match the self-identified gender of the addressee. Consider the following examples.

(147) Dude, you're a dude.
(148) Listen to me for a second, lady.
(149) Caster Semenya is running tomorrow, should be an easy win for him.
(150) Of course she wants to be a man, who would choose to be a woman nowadays?
(151) Thank you, Mr. Garrison.
(152) Simon has an interesting new wardrobe.
(153) Good to see you again, Jane.

In addition, there may be contexts in which even the use or non-use of gender-neutral pronouns ('they', 'them') could rise to the level of misgendering. For example, if a speaker repeatedly and intentionally refuses to use 'she'/'her' to refer to a transgender women but insists instead on using 'they'/'them' against the wishes and contrary to the self-identified gender of the latter, this may be received as misgendering. Conversely, if a speaker deliberately fails to use 'they'/'them' to refer to a gender non-binary person but persists in using 'she'/'her' against the wishes and contrary to the self-identified gender of the latter, then once again this is likely to be received as misgendering.

It is also worth making the point that whilst identity miscategorisations and identity denials often go hand in hand, this is not always or necessarily the case. Consider the following examples.

(154) I've yet to meet a man in a dress, one of these transgender women, fellows, or whatever the hell you're supposed to call them, who doesn't make a goddam ridiculous sight.
(155) I pity these women who are so oppressed that they resort to identifying as transgender men.

These statements involve misgendering, but they do not directly and explicitly contain identity denials. In other words, (154) does not expressly deny that transwomen are women and (155) does not expressly deny that transmen are men. This is partly because they do not expressly rule out the possibility of people having more than one gender identity at the same time. That said, these sorts of statements could also convey non-literal content which does indeed contain identity denials, depending on the speaker, context, and receiving audience.

Along similar lines, it is important to note that misgendering does not necessarily involve the denial of people's identity as transgender. Consider the following statement.

(156) Transwomen are in fact men.

Statement (156) asserts that transwomen are in fact men but does not deny they are trans people. Nor does (156) directly and explicitly deny other elements of the lived experiences of transwomen – for example, transwomen's experiences of body dysmorphia and the mismatch between their relationship with their own bodies and their subjective gender identities and the attitudes and expectations of other people regarding their bodies and gender identities. Nevertheless, we still classify (156) as an identity miscategorisation even though it falls short of trans identity denial.

What about a statement that recognises the gender identity of transgender people but miscategorises them on grounds of sex? Consider the following statement.

(157) Although transwomen may be women in the sense of their gender identity, they remain men in the sense of their sex.

We propose that even statement (157) may count as an identity miscategorisation and potential hate speech depending on the circumstances. Suppose a proportion of transwomen have undergone comprehensive sex reassignment and body augmentation procedures and surgeries, possess a range of female secondary sex characteristics (e.g. enlarged breasts, vagina, clitoris, high pitch voice, rounded buttocks, upwards pointing nasal tip, slim jawline, increased estrogen and progesterone, decreased testosterone), and identify not merely as women but also as female. In such circumstances, a statement like (157) attributes the possession of the characteristic of being male to an entire group or class of people that does not match a characteristic that a proportion of those people take themselves to possess, namely being female. Insofar as this is done knowingly and deliberately, or with reckless disregard, we consider it to be a case of identity miscategorisation. Of course, sometimes a statement like (157) may also express, imply, presuppose, or infer the idea that sex is or should be a matter of essential features including chromosomes, gonads, hormones, and genitals, and that, therefore, persons who fail to pass any one of these tests cannot be considered female. From the perspective of (some) transgender people, however, this idea is not merely socially and scientifically arbitrary but exclusionary in the sense of being an identity denial (see Section 4.4).

4.5.1 *The Identity Miscategorisations Puzzle*

Identity miscategorisations are a puzzle for any society or specific organisations wishing to develop a coherent picture of the ordinary concept *hate speech* and in multiple ways. For one thing, like identity denials, it is an open question whether the general idea of hate speech as an attack against people can be plausibly applied to statements misclassifying people's identities. Because we addressed a similar conundrum at length in Section 4.4, we shall not seek to replicate it in this section. We take it as read that if there is a credible case for saying that identity denials are modes of attacking people, then so are identity miscategorisations.

Instead, we shall focus on a different aspect of the puzzle. The puzzle is that it may be difficult to understand why it would be appropriate to label misgendering as 'hate speech', for example, but then not apply the same label to other types of expressive slights. Compare these two statements.

(158) Listen to me fella, you aren't kidding anyone, you're a man.
(159) Are you a man or a woman?

If (158) is treated as hate speech, then surely it would be confusing to not also treat (159) as hate speech. Indeed, both (158) and (159) certainly look like they could be hurtful if addressed to a transgender person. On the other hand, treating both (158) and (159) would seem to make hate speech a broader category than it appeared. Call this the identity miscategorisations puzzle.

There are two main responses to the identity miscategorisations puzzle. The first is to insist that identity miscategorisations are not hate speech because on closer examination they are mere microaggressions and (according to the first response) mere microaggressions are not hate speech. We shall reject this response, however, on the grounds that in fact microaggressions are part of the hate speech conceptual family (see also Chapter 2). The second response (our proposed response) is to argue that, like identity denials, identity miscategorisations ought to be considered a sui generis form of hate speech, and that this approach is ultimately warranted because the latter also bear a striking resemblance to exemplars of hate speech across the dimensions of target, style, message, act, and effect. However, before running through these responses, we shall exemplify the puzzle by comparing Facebook's community standard on hate speech with the policies of other platforms.

4.5.2 *Identity Miscategorisations under Facebook's Community Standard on Hate Speech*

Whilst Facebook's community standard on hate speech does not include a specific rule disallowing misgendering, and Twitter's new hateful conduct policy (version April 2023) also does not, Twitter's old hateful conduct policy did.

> We prohibit targeting others with repeated slurs, tropes or other content that intends to dehumanize, degrade or reinforce negative or harmful stereotypes about a protected category. This includes targeted misgendering or deadnaming of transgender individuals.[90]

But it is striking that this old version of Twitter's hateful conduct policy disallows misgendering only when it takes a 'targeted' form. It makes no mention of misgendering of a general form. Likewise, TikTok's community guideline on hateful behaviour prohibits 'Intentionally targeting people who are transgender or gender non-conforming by referring to them using their former name or gender rather than their current name or expressed gender (deadnaming or misgendering).'[91] To see how these policies play out, consider once again the following statements.

(147) Dude, you're a dude.
(156) Transwomen are in fact men.

It is likely the aforementioned policies would treat (147) as disallowed hate speech but perhaps not (156).

TikTok's rationale for disallowing only targeted misgendering is not stated in the policy. At first glance, the limitation seems untenable given that TikTok's stated policy is to disallow 'any hateful behavior, hate speech, or promotion of hateful ideologies' (emphasis added), and it specifies 'anti-LGBTQIA+' as an example of a hateful ideology. It is arguable that misgendering of a general form such as (156) can be, and often is, also intended to do these sorts of things. Of course, there may be *some* people who identify as both transwomen and as biologically male and who may not find (156) hurtful. Even so, because (156) is an unqualified commentary on an entire group, it counts as misgendering the group insofar as this group predominantly includes people who do not identify as men.

However, the focus on targeted misgendering may reflect behind-the-scenes assumptions made by TikTok's policy teams. They might be assuming that targeted misgendering is more harmful including that it places in greater jeopardy the ability of transgender people to express themselves on TikTok; or that disallowing targeted misgendering is less disruptive to public discourse or in some way strikes a better balance between the free expression of all users or a more reasonable compromise between the right to free expression and the right to freedom from hate speech. Then again, none of these assumptions are self-evident and stand in need of justification.

There are two further loose ends. For one thing, TikTok's policy only refers to misgendering and deadnaming. It contains no reference to other forms of identity miscategorisation such as misracialising, misnationalising, misreligioning, and missexualising. We believe this omission is difficult to justify if one reflects not only on similarities between misgendering and these other forms of identity miscategorisation but also on similarities between identity miscategorisations in general and exemplars of hate speech. We shall return to this point in Section 4.5.4.

Second, speakers might in theory miscategorise a group of people identified by a protected characteristic by categorising them in terms of a further property, category, group membership, status, or identity that does not fit who or what they take themselves to be but which is not itself associated with a protected characteristic. Consider the following statement.

(160) So-called transgender women are in fact spirit animals that are put onto this earth to guide the rest of us on a path to enlightenment.

We surmise that TikTok is unlikely to deem (160) misgendering. For one thing, (160) attributes a characteristic (i.e. being a spirit animal) to transgender women that does not directly contradict who or what they take themselves to be in terms of gender. After all, statement (160) does not explicitly rule out the possibility that transgender women could be trans, women, and spirit animals at the same time, insofar as these are not mutually exclusive categories. Moreover, we believe (160) is not an identity miscategorisation because being a spirit animal is not a protected characteristic. Therefore, we recommend social media platforms define identity miscategorisations as speech that knowingly and deliberately, or with reckless disregard, attributes a property, category, group membership, status, or identity to a person or group that does not match or contradicts that which they take themselves to possess, where both the former and the latter are associated with protected characteristics.

However, this still leaves the other side of the puzzle introduced above. If social media platforms should, and in some cases already do, disallow identity miscategorisations, including but not limited to misgendering, and if identity miscategorisations are a sui generis form of hate speech, what does this imply about other expressive slights, including microaggressions, that may seem similar to identity miscategorisations? For example, should social media platforms ban users from sending both identity miscategorisations like (158) and microaggressions like (159) to transgender people?

Hitherto, the major social media platforms, including Facebook, TikTok, and Twitter, have not incorporated any specific prohibitions on 'microaggressions' within their hate speech policies, at least not within the public-facing versions. We believe the correct way to respond to the identity miscategorisations puzzle is to explore in more detail potential similarities between identity miscategorisations and microaggressions and between both of these forms of speech and exemplars of hate speech, including forms of hate speech that are already disallowed by the platforms. The purpose would be to determine whether the similarities are sufficient to warrant applying the label 'hate speech' to all of these forms. We shall try to make some progress on this important comparative project in Section 4.5.4, but before doing so we shall consider and reject the first main response to the identity miscategorisations puzzle.

4.5.3 *First Response: Identity Miscategorisations as Mere Microaggressions*

The first response to the identity miscategorisations puzzle is to insist that identity miscategorisations are not hate speech because, on closer examination, they are mere microaggressions and (according to the first response) mere microaggressions are not hate speech. Of course, microaggressions are themselves a notoriously diverse collection of expressive phenomena.[92] But the first response insists that identity miscategorisations are a natural fit for this diverse collection.

To explain, some microaggressions take the form of statements or questions addressed to individuals that treat them as exotic curiosities or freaks, or else that imply, presuppose, or infer they are somehow foreign or Other.

(161) I'd really like to sleep with you, I've never tried it with a black woman.
(162) I'm guessing you don't need to wear sunscreen in the summer, lucky you.
(163) Can I touch your hair, it's so curly.
(164) Where are you from? No, I mean where are you from originally?

(165) What's your name? … Err, can you repeat that again. … Sorry, one more time, I'm not getting it.
(166) Why did you choose to mutilate your own body?
(167) Do you still look like a man when you're naked?
(168) Do you have a vagina? Can you have actual sex with it?

Other microaggressions involve the denial, trivialisation, or sweeping under the carpet of historical experiences of bigotry and discrimination.

(169) Things are much better for you blacks nowadays, aren't they?
(170) You'll never experience the prejudice real women face every day.

Yet further examples of microaggressions ignore, express scepticism about, downplay, or ridicule the target's identity.

(171) Tell me, I'd really like to know, are you a man or a woman?
(172) You're a man, really?
(173) What's your real name, I mean the one you were born with?
(174) You're way too pretty to be a man, such a pity.
(175) So you're a nothing then, not male or female? How does that work?

According to the first response to the puzzle, targeted identity miscategorisations, including but not limited to misgendering, also belong to this broad family of microaggressions. Consider the following example.

(176) I'm sorry I can't refer to you as 'they', 'them', it's just not grammatically correct, you're a woman so I'm gonna have to use 'her'.

According to the first response, there are obvious similarities between (176) and statements such as (171), and certainly enough to make it credible to consider them both microaggressions.

In addition, the first response claims that because identity miscategorisations are mere microaggressions, they cannot be hate speech. One way to motivate the first response is to embrace the following rule of thumb about hate speech.

(R18) Hate speech is always explicit, crude, unsubtle, overt, and obvious.

If targeted identity miscategorisations like (176) are microaggressions, and if microaggressions take the form of implicit, covert, and subtle expressions, and if (R18) is correct, then it follows (according to the first response) that targeted identity miscategorisations cannot be hate speech.

However, we reject this response to the identity miscategorisations puzzle. Whilst we accept the premise that some identity miscategorisations can take the form of microaggressions, we refuse the conclusion that they cannot therefore qualify as hate speech. As mentioned in Chapter 2, microaggressions are strong candidates to be considered hate speech. That microaggressions are capable of stereotyping, demeaning, causing distress to, affronting the dignity of, treating as socially inferior, misrecognising, and creating a hostile and stressful environment for targeted people on the basis of protected characteristics, speaks to the presence of prototypical hate speech targets, styles, messages, acts, and effects. Linguistic intuitions would suggest microaggressions are part of the hate speech conceptual family (specifically the ordinary concept) and that targeted identity miscategorisations perhaps fall on the microaggressions side of the family.

Furthermore, there is credible evidence to suggest (R18) is false, at least as a rule of thumb about the ordinary concept *hate speech*. It is widely recognised in the literature that hate speech in the ordinary sense of the word can include implicit, covert, subtle, veiled, coded, implied, hinted, sanitised, or dog whistle varieties.[93] Indeed, Facebook's community standard explicitly recognises this feature of hate speech: 'Sometimes, based on local nuance, we consider certain words or phrases as frequently used proxies for PC groups.'[94] For these reasons, we endorse this alternative rule about the ordinary concept *hate speech*.

(R19) Hate can be explicit, crude, unsubtle, overt, and obvious, but it can also be implicit, subtle, veiled, tacit, hinted, implied, coded, covert, proxy, and unobvious.

Of course, the legal concept *hate speech* may differ from the ordinary concept in this particular respect. At least within some legal jurisdictions, as defined by some hate speech laws, illegal hate speech must be explicit and overt in nature.[95] We shall examine the differences between the ordinary and legal concepts in Chapter 5.

4.5.4 Second Response: Similarities between Identity Miscategorisations and Exemplars of Hate Speech

The second response (our proposed response) to the identity miscategorisations puzzle is to treat identity miscategorisations as a sui generis form of hate speech. It seeks to justify this not simply based on similarities with microaggressions but more fundamentally by showing that identity miscategorisations share sufficient similarities with a range of exemplars of hate speech based on the distinguishing qualities of target, style, message, act, and effect, and keeping in mind reasonable expectations about the social purposes served by the ordinary concept *hate speech*.

Beginning with target, we have described identity miscategorisations as speech that miscategorises people on the basis of their protected characteristics. In this way, identity miscategorisations typically have targets that overlap with targets of exemplars of hate speech. For example, statements misgendering trans people share their target with anti-trans slurs like 'tranny'. In relation to style, identity miscategorisations often explicitly take the form of generalisations about a group of people, a form of speech also found in stereotypes and group defamation, for instance. In terms of the message, identity miscategorisations portray their targets as something other than how the targets see themselves. This is a similar message not only to the identity attacks and identity denials discussed earlier in this chapter but also to other forms of hate speech such as stereotypes, caricatures, hate propaganda, group defamation, and microaggressions, for example (see also Chapter 2).

Another distinguishing quality relevant under the global resemblance test concerns what people do with words and the effect of those words. We shall now outline six prototypical hate speech acts and effects potentially performed or produced by identity miscategorisations as well as exemplars of hate speech. These acts and effect can be seen in various kinds of identity miscategorisations, including misracialising, misnationalising, misreligioning, missexualising, and misgendering.

First, like both slurs and identity denials, identity miscategorisations may *dehumanise* targeted persons such as by *disregarding their capacity for autonomous self-identification* or may *subordinate* them by *failing to treat them as equals* in collaborative processes of identity creation. This might happen if, for example, transgender people are spoken to as though they lack the capacity to shape their own gender identity or else lack the standing to participate as co-authors in the social creation of their identity through dialogue and negotiation. Importantly, this might be universally dehumanising and not something unique to transgender people. Indeed, recent experimental research into people's experiences of misgendering under simulated conditions showed that it was common even for cisgender people who have been misgendered to report 'that they felt a fundamental aspect of their identity had been misrepresented'.[96]

A second point of similarity is that miscategorisations can be used to *misrecognise* targeted people by *oversimplifying their identities.*[97] Consider the practice of referring to darker skinned people who identify as White with labels such as 'these black people' or to people who identity as Igbo Jews with phrases such as 'these Africans'. Like both slurs and identity denials, such practices misrecognise the lived experiences of people who feel themselves to be White or Jews and who are committed to the customs, traditions, and culture associated with the identities they take themselves to have. Identity miscategorisations essentialise the identity of the targeted individuals, making their complex, divergent but nonetheless real lived experiences somehow irrelevant. They make racial identity the master status.[98]

A third point of similarity is that identity miscategorisations can be used to *disparage*, *stigmatise*, *vilify*, *malign*, or *misrecognise* groups of people such as by *attacking their reputations* or *tarnishing their identities*. They share this in common with other forms of hate speech such as group defamation and negative stereotypes.[99] Consider the following elaborate miscategorisations which do not simply miscategorise the targets but simultaneously tarnish their identity by portraying them as deceptive, predatory, revolting, hideous, cowardly, disloyal, victims, deluded, mentally disturbed, abnormal, or difficult.

(177) The Igbo 'Jews' are not racially Jewish; they look like monochromatic minstrels with their black faces peering out from beneath their pure white Tallits.
(178) So-called bisexual men are no more than closet homosexuals – they are cowards who give the gay community a bad name.
(179) Transgender 'women' are not women, they are just men pretending to be women as a cunning new way to dominate the opposite sex.
(180) Men who self-identify as women are devious bastards who only profess to be women so they can manipulate and pressurise lesbians into having sex with them or else gain entry into women only spaces to prey on vulnerable women and young girls.
(181) Show me a 'transgender woman' and I will show you a goddam hideous looking man.
(182) So-called transgender women are just closet homosexuals – these men are scaredy-cats who make all gays look bad.
(183) The insane decision to amputate the male genitals does not in any way imply that the mutilated male ceases to be male; he was born male and will die male with or without the snip. The real question is what pathological self-delusion or mental disturbance drives men to such extremes.
(184) The idea of a woman choosing to turn her clitoris into a penis, well that's just disgusting to me.
(185) Transmen are butches who just take it one step too far – these women are betraying their lesbian sisters.
(186) Girls who get diagnosed with gender dysphoria and classified as transmen end up in a terrible position because they are influenced by online trans communities and groomed by unscrupulous medical clinics to transition at a vulnerable stage in their lives when they feel alienated and are desperate for self-acceptance and validation from others, but sadly later on in life these women always regret their 'decision'.
(187) These so-called genderqueer folk are so annoying; like everyone else they are either men or women, they are just being deliberately difficult.

Even though Facebook's community standard on hate speech, unlike TikTok's hateful behaviour policy, does not contain a specific rule on misgendering, arguably the above examples of elaborate misgendering would fall foul of Facebook's standard based on several of the specific forms of hate speech disallowed under Tier 2.[100]

A fourth point of similarity is that identity miscategorisations can be used to *mock*, *humiliate*, or *treat cruelly* targeted persons.[101] For example, elaborate forms of misgendering can *mock* targeted persons such as in the following comments made by Julie Bindel.

> Those who 'transition' seem to become stereotypical in their appearance – fuck-me shoes and birds-nest hair for the boys; beards, muscles and tattoos for the girls. Think about a world inhabited just by transsexuals. It would look like the set of Grease.[102]

Interestingly, whilst Facebook's community standard on hate speech does not disallow misgendering per se, the standard does include a specific Tier 1 rule against 'Mocking the concept, events or victims of hate crimes even if no real person is depicted in an image'.[103] Perhaps under a strict reading of this rule, the mocking must directly relate to the group of persons *as* victims of hate crime, in the sense of ridiculing them *for being* victims. Then again, arguably mocking any groups of people who are in general widely recognised as also being victims of hate crimes could constitute hate speech in some contexts.

In addition, it can be an act of *humiliation* to publicly misgender another person, especially in front of family, friends, and work colleagues, but even in front of strangers, if doing so has the intention and effect of making the targeted persons feel embarrassed, ashamed, or foolish. This may be true even of simple or basic misgendering. Indeed, it is perhaps worth noting here that Facebook's gaming community guidelines explicitly include a rule disallowing doxing. What is more, the degree of humiliation might be exacerbated when the speaker uses elaborate forms of misgendering in order to ridicule (cast the targeted persons as absurd or ridiculous) or degrade (rank the targeted persons as inferior to cisgender persons) the targeted persons in the eyes of others.

Furthermore, misgendering can amount to *cruelty* in contexts where the speaker knowingly inflicts emotional distress upon a vulnerable person in a way that violates a moral duty to treat the vulnerable with kindness, compassion, and recognition. Part of the cruelty may rest in the fact that in some contexts transgender people may be additionally vulnerable by virtue of being unable to hide their appearance from others and as a result are exposed to the risk of misgendering. In many instances trans people, like non-white people and people with visible disabilities, do not have the option of keeping their characteristics hidden. Their appearance is laid bare for others to assess (do they pass?), whether they like it or not. Akin to people who become captive audiences to hate speech which they cannot escape and do not freely choose to receive,[104] trans people cannot easily avoid being seen as trans nor avoid being vulnerable to acts of misgendering. *Some* trans people experience the dual captivity of feeling trapped in the wrong body and being locked into the social category of sex assigned at birth.[105]

A fifth point of similarity is that identity miscategorisations can be used to *harass*, *intimidate*, or even *incite hatred, discrimination, and violence* against targeted persons based on their protected characteristics, which are once again paradigmatic hate speech acts and effects. Misgendering other persons in public, for example, can be a form of harassment that violates a right not to discuss one's gender with other people. In such instances, the speaker creates a mismatch between the targeted individual's gender presentation and the speaker's accusation that the target has a different gender. This compels the targeted individual to deal with the incongruence, either by remaining silent and implicitly conceding the mismatch or by speaking back and closing the gap. Because the speaker has set an agenda for the conversation, the targeted individual is presented with a dilemma they did not consent to and would prefer not to have. Either they let the comment go and people may assume they are not the gender they are presenting themselves to be, or they challenge what has been said (e.g. 'I am a woman for your information'). Although they are not literally forced to engage in a conversation about their own gender, the speaker has put something out there and the targeted individual may feel compelled to tackle it so as to set the record straight and avoid further embarrassment or reputational damage, even though they do not want to have to do this. Misgendering creates an extra emotional burden for transgender people. They are compelled to choose between the potential humiliation that attends a tacit concession of not being what they present themselves to be, on the one hand, and the anxiety or fear that comes with correcting the speaker, such as having to wonder if the misgendering was intentional or merely accidental and having to calculate and worry about whether a correction will elicit a negative reaction and lead to further confrontation, on the other hand. This extra emotional burden is not carried by cisgender people who, generally speaking, do not have to worry about being misgendered, or have to worry about it much less (although there may be exceptions).

It might be objected that some transgender people place great value in, and obtain emotional comfort from, revealing their gender histories to other people. However, research suggests that, from the perspective of many transgender people, this value is contingent upon their exercising some agency and control in choosing the relationships in which to tell their stories.[106] Misgendering wrests this agency or control away from the targeted individuals by seizing the initiative and setting the agenda about how, when, where, and to whom they address their gender identity.

In fact, there may be parallels between misgendering as a form of harassment of trans people and the harassment of homosexuals and lesbians through outing.[107] It deserves mention that Facebook's community standard on bullying and harassment contains the following rule: 'Do not [. . .] Target private adults (who must self-report) or any private minors or involuntary minor public figures with: [. . .] Claims about romantic involvement, sexual orientation or gender identity.'[108] Whilst Facebook's standard does not explicitly mention misgendering, arguably both outing and misgendering qualify as 'claims about' gender identity. And so, in theory the Facebook standard could, and should, also prohibit bullying or harassment of trans people through targeted misgendering.[109] Indeed, when Facebook asks new users to fill out some of their personal details at the point of signing up to the platform, it allows them to specify their own gender identity using a free-form custom field, and to select their preferred pronouns. One effect of this policy is to ensure that Facebook itself does not misgender people.

Arguably, it could be possible to build a bridge between Facebook's community standard on bullying and harassment, on the one hand, and its standard on hate speech, on the other hand, by interpreting misgendering as not merely gender-based harassment but also hate speech, both in its targeted and general forms. Likewise, in the legal field, it may be possible to bring cases against speakers for misgendering others by applying certain forms of hate crime and hate speech offences, namely offences relating to causing annoyance, harassment, and hostile environment discrimination based on gender identity.[110]

In similar ways, elaborate forms of identity miscategorisations could be used to *threaten* or *intimidate* targeted individuals, or even to *promote or incite hatred, discrimination, and violence* against people based on protected characteristics. Consider the following words posted by Tracy Murphree on Facebook in 2016, during her successful campaign for sheriff in Denton County, Texas.

> If my little girl is in a public women's restroom and a man, regardless of how he may identify, goes into the bathroom, he will then identify as a John Doe until he wakes up in whatever hospital he may be taken to.[111]

The point is not limited to misgendering, consider these examples of elaborate misracialising and misreligioning.

(188) The next black person who enters this pool because he claims he is white, is gonna get my boot up his dirty black ass.

(189) Hazaras are not Muslim, they are pagans, Shia, they are infidels, we must wage jihad against them like we do all infidels.

Facebook's community standard on hate speech contains a general injunction against 'the use of harmful stereotypes', which Facebook defines as 'dehumanising comparisons that have historically been used to attack, intimidate or exclude specific groups, and that are often linked with offline violence'.[112] For its part, Twitter prohibits 'inciting fear or spreading fearful stereotypes about a protected category, including asserting that members of a protected category are more likely to take part in dangerous or illegal activities'.[113] Arguably, it would not be contrary to the spirit of these rules to apply them to elaborate identity miscategorisations such as (188) and (189) that are used to threaten or intimidate people, or with the intention or likely effect of promoting hatred, discrimination, or violence against people, identified by protected characteristics. Once again, there may be parallels here with the legal concept(s) *hate speech*, such as if laws banning public insults or incitement to hatred on grounds of gender identity are applied to cases of misgendering, for example.[114]

Finally, identity miscategorisations may share several types of harmful effects in common with exemplars of hate speech (see also Chapter 2). One harmful effect might be the unfair situation in which an important part of the lived experience and identity of a certain group of people is for all intents and purposes expunged from the communicative domain because others refuse to use words and categories to describe them that match how they understand or make intelligible who they are. This may be considered a form of *misrecognition* or *hermeneutical inequality*.[115] Another harmful effect may be the medium- and long-term psychological impact on individuals of being the victims of persistent or even daily identity miscategorisations over a prolonged period. This impact may include prototypical hate speech effects such as feeling unwanted or alienated, low self-esteem, and raised background levels of stress, anxiety, hypervigilance, fear, fatigue, low mood, or depression.[116]

4.5.5 *Defences against the Charge That Identity Miscategorisations Are Hate Speech*

Notwithstanding these points of similarity between identity miscategorisations and exemplars of hate speech, we shall now critically evaluate some potential bases on which people who make such statements might dispute accusations of hate speech. We shall argue that none of the proffered defences is credible.

For one thing, speakers might insist they are merely expressing home truths, as in, pointing out uncomfortable facts about other people which those people might not what to hear, especially from strangers, but which are facts nonetheless. People may prefer not to have home truths about their identity pointed out to them, but they do not have a right to demand that other people avoid speaking plain facts simply because those facts can be uncomfortable (according to the current defence).

Moreover, speakers might point out that talking about the nature and extension of properties, groups, categories, and identities is appropriate subject matter for social media posts; otherwise nobody could affirm their own identity, for example. To disallow identity miscategorisations but allow identity affirmations would be a double standard. Plus speakers could argue that it should not be the job of social media platforms to be arbiters of who gets to say what and about whom.

In addition, speakers might point to the fact that the term 'hate speech' even in its ordinary sense implies mens rea which they believe makes it inapt as a label for them. For example, they may propose social media platforms draw a distinction between being gender critical, on the one hand, and malicious misgendering, on the other hand. The speakers I have in mind view themselves as gender critical because (so they think) they have reasonable grounds to believe they are using correct gendered language, despite the language not matching people's self-identification, whereas they want social media platforms to reserve the label 'malicious misgendering' for shitposters who know the language they are using is incorrect but post it anyway just for the hell of it.[117]

Finally, speakers might make the argument that if the targets of home truths do not like what they are hearing, they can simply avoid social media. Nobody is forcing them to be receivers of online content, they can simply hit delete or log off.

However, we believe what such speakers are suggesting is a radical departure from the ordinary concept *hate speech* both as commonly understood by ordinary language users and as defined by some social media platforms. Firstly, we believe this understanding includes the reconcilabilist rule (R15), namely that labelling certain kinds of statements as 'hate speech' is reconcilable with also accepting that the hate speaker has reasonable grounds on which to believe such statements are true. This reconcilability is made possible by analysing what speakers say and do with identity miscategorisations that are similar to exemplars of hate speech across the distinguishing qualities of target, style, message, act, and effect.

Moreover, there is a morally relevant difference between people using social media platforms to make affirmations about their own identity and people using such platforms to pass judgment on (miscategorise) the identity of other people. The former is a matter of what we shall call personal identity expression, whereas the latter is an exemplification of external identity expression. Other things remaining equal, it is easier to make the case for platforms having a moral and social right to moderate external identity expression than personal identity expression.

Furthermore, it is misleading to suggest that ordinary people and social media platforms would label identity miscategorisations as 'hate speech' only because they are making a judgment about the epistemological incompetence of the speakers, such as that the speakers are not experts (*Who are you to say transwomen are not women?*), or are making a bald assumption that nobody has a right to say something about another person's identity (*People don't get to have a say in what sex or gender other people are*). If these judgments and assumptions were the only justifications being proffered, then the speaker might have reasonable grounds to object. However, there is a more legitimate justification for labelling identity miscategorisations as 'hate speech': namely, that the target, style, message, act, and effect of these statements are sufficiently similar overall to exemplars of hate speech to warrant applying that label, based on the global resemblance test.

Finally, it is simply a myth to think of the Internet as a place where ordinary people can freely avoid unwanted attacks.[118] Once content has been seen its effects cannot be wiped away simply by hitting the delete button. Moreover, given the integral part that social media plays in people's social, professional, civic, and romantic lives, it would be an unreasonable burden to expect people to log off.

4.6 Identity Appropriations

A final cluster of grey area cases of hate speech involves the conscious adoption of some of the appearance, mannerisms, behaviour, language, or culture of people who possess one property, status, or identity associated with a protected characteristic by members of another group who possess a different property, status, or identity, but at the same time without the latter claiming to actually possess the former property, status, or identity. We call these identity appropriations. Like identity attacks, identity denials, and identity miscategorisations, people fall prey to identity appropriations based on their protected characteristics, but what makes identity appropriations distinctive is that the wrong consists in the annexation of elements of people's identity.

Identity appropriations, as we define them, can take various forms but share two main features: first, the adoption of elements of another group's identity associated with a protected characteristic (but without the aim of permanently switching to that identity); second, an unintended attack on the people concerned. To be clear, the adoption of elements of another group's identity is a typically deliberate act in the sense it is not done accidentally, by mistake, or unconsciously. But words or behaviour that constitute identity appropriations in the sense we mean are never intended attacks, as in, they are done without the intention to attack and typically done without being fully aware that they can be experienced by victims as insults or as demeaning, insensitive, or disrespectful.

In these ways, identity appropriations are importantly different to identity attacks insofar as the latter are always intentional attacks on people, whether direct or indirect. So, for example, if someone transforms his appearance to become a caricature of a Black person with exaggerated or grotesque features and with intent to degrade and ridicule Black people as a group, then this goes beyond the category of identity appropriations as we understand it and falls back into the category of identity attacks discussed in Section 4.2.

We shall not seek to detail every form of identity appropriation but instead highlight some of the forms most germane to the subject matter of this book and most prominent in popular culture, social media, and news reporting at the present time. Perhaps the most notorious examples relate to appropriations of racial or ethnic identities, but other relevant appropriations relate to gender identity and sexual orientation identity. Consider the following examples.

(190) [Blackface: A White college student goes to a fancy dress party with make-up and clothing to look like Michael Jackson].

(191) [Blacktalk: A suburban White youth adopts language including slang words, styles of speech, and intonation associated with a particular form of Black hip hop culture].

(192) [Blackfishing: A White female celebrity or social influencer adopts a hair design, skin tone, clothing, and posture that mimics appearances associated with Black female identity and culture].

(193) [Playing Indian: A White hippie adopts elements of the clothing, adornments, speech, and rituals associated with Native American tribes or First Nations].

(194) [Womanface: A drag queen puts on make-up, wears clothing, and adopts a mode of gender presentation associated with certain ideas, norms, or conventions of being a woman or female identity].

(195) [Gayface: Two straight men make a conspicuous show of romantic affection between each other including sharing a lingering kiss on the mouth which is widely recognised as behaviour associated with being gay].

Adopting elements of the appearance, countenance, mannerisms, behaviour, language, or culture of people with a different identity is not the same as trying to become a member of another group or seeking to convince other people that one is in fact a member of another group. Consequently, most instances of identity appropriation are temporary, transparent, and not intended to be fully transformative. For example, a White suburban youth may dial up or dial down or even switch in and out of blacktalk depending on the situation and may grow out of this practice entirely as they progress into adulthood. Drag queens typically are not seeking to deceptively pass as women but to transparently emulate feminine presentation during their performances, although not all drag queens are hyperfeminine, of course. Straight men who make a conspicuous show of affection with each other are not looking to turn gay any more than a White person who dresses up as Michael Jackson is trying to acquire African descent. Young women who blackfish imitate the look of certain Black women without wishing to be Black women. Arguably, all of these people are in different ways merely seeking to *partake of* another identity. This is contrasted with people – think of Jessica Anne Krug or Rachel Dolezal – who *adopt* another identity in ways that are prolonged, deceptive, and transformative. They take on elements of another identity in subtle ways and continuously, such as changing the pronunciation of their own name, adjusting their skin tone, hair, mannerism, and language, with the intention of never being detected and ultimately gaining acceptance as and effectively becoming members of another group. These forms of identity transformation involve permanent change and misrepresentation.

Some behaviours almost always constitute identity appropriation, whereas others only become identity appropriations depending on the intention and context. Consider the following behaviour.

(196) [Digital blackface: A White person uses a black or brown face emoji when chatting online with a person of colour].

Whether such behaviour counts as identity appropriation depends on whether, in the context, the White person is using the black or brown face emoji to represent themselves or to represent their interlocutor. Compare these two online messages.

(197) I hope you have a great time at the concert tomorrow [brown smiling face emoji].

(198) I'm gonna head to the shops for some retail therapy [brown smiling face emoji].

Whatever the appropriateness or hate speechiness of these messages, arguably it would be more plausible to classify (198) as identity appropriation than (197).

In addition to this, it might not always be a straightforward matter to determine which identity someone putatively engaged in identity appropriation is in fact appropriating, if any. Consider once again the example of womanface specified in (194) above. Among ordinary people who would potentially recognise drag queens as engaged in 'identity appropriation', there is likely to be a set of assumptions that drag queens are cisgender gay men and that the identity being appropriated is female identity. But what about a transwoman drag queen or a cisgender female drag queen? Could either of these people be reasonably accused of unjust identity appropriation? If so, which identity? Female identity, trans identity, or even drag queen identity itself? More generally, could transvestites be guilty of appropriating the gender identity of others? If so, who? The opposite sex, transgender people, or none of the above? And what about cisgender female lesbians with masculine presentation? Are they guilty of identity appropriation of male identity in some relevant sense?

Notwithstanding these potential ambiguities, we believe the core examples (190)–(195) all exhibit the two main features which together distinguish identity appropriations: first, they involve one group of people's adoption of elements of another group's identity associated with protected characteristics; second, they are done without intent to attack the people concerned. That is not to say identity appropriations do not involve a failure to show proper respect, recognition, and consideration for other people, do not cause insult, and are not experienced as jarring, insensitive, disturbing, or degrading. Rather, it is to say identity appropriations, as we define the category, are not done with intent to attack others in these ways. Indeed, the appropriator may be oblivious to, or at least not fully aware of, other people's negative experience of the appropriation. Consistent with the central purpose of this chapter and the general aim of Part I of the book, the question we want to address in this section is whether such identity appropriations are appropriately labelled 'hate speech' in the ordinary sense of that term.

4.6.1 *The Identity Appropriations Riddle*

Identity appropriations are a riddle that must be decoded by any society or organisation seeking to conceptualise hate speech in the ordinary sense of the term. Like standard examples of hate speech, such behaviour targets people based on their protected characteristics but at the same time identity appropriations are unlike some exemplars of hate speech both in terms of a lack of intention to attack people and in terms of being embodied in behaviour rather than in speech per se. Call this the identity appropriations riddle.

As indicated in the previous paragraph, there are two aspects to this riddle. The first aspect can be expressed as follows. Does classifying words or behaviour as hate speech depend on the presence of an intention to attack people based on protected characteristics? On the one hand, if one answers this question in the affirmative, then one seems to be committed to the following rule of thumb.

(R20) Hate speech is an intentional attack against people in the sense that hate speakers are by definition aware that what they are doing is an attack, hate speech is experienced by victims as an attack, and is done with an intention to attack.

At first glance, this rule of thumb may appear plausible. It is surely relevant if a speaker does not intend to be disrespectful to other people or cause them to feel disrespected, for example. Identity appropriations as we understand them are not intended as attacks against people in that sense. Even so, moral culpability does not begin and end with intention. Failure to take proper care over one's words or behaviour and how these things land with other people can be morally culpable. And this might yet support applying the label 'hate speech' to identity appropriations.

On the other hand, if one answers the aforementioned question in the negative, then this means accepting the following alternative rule of thumb.

(R21) Hate speech can be an intentional or unintentional attack against people.

This rule has the virtue of recognising even unintentional attacks as hate speech. But by the same token, if a society or organisation jettisons (R20) and embraces (R21), maybe people would be right to worry that almost anything they say could be deemed hate speech by at least one other person, and that it would be difficult to predict when they might violate norms against hate speech, especially if ignorance is no longer a defence but itself morally culpable.

A second aspect of the identity appropriations riddle concerns the fact that this grey area of hate speech is typically embodied in behaviour as opposed to words per se, whereas many exemplars of hate speech take the form of words. It might be tempting to extrapolate from the latter the following rule of thumb.

(R22) Hate speech is a form of speech as opposed to behaviour.

At first sight, this rule may be appealing because it provides clarity and simplicity. However, on closer examination this rule provides these things at the cost of accurately capturing the concept at stake, which does appear to be broader than (R22) suggests.

Therefore, it might be more accurate to endorse this alternative rule of thumb.

(R23) Hate speech can be embodied in various styles including but not limited to words, signs, symbols, images, pictures, cartoons, memes, videos, flags, logos, uniforms, clothing, statues, monuments, gestures, and behaviours.

Then again, embracing (R23) could potentially set off an avalanche of cases falling under the label 'hate speech' including various types of microaggressions – consider a White hotel receptionist who carries on as though a Black guest is invisible or does not exist – that seem to be examples of behaviour rather than speech per se. Would this make the ordinary concept too large? Moreover, if identity appropriations are to be treated as hate speech, in harmony with (R23), what are the notable similarities between identity appropriations and exemplars of hate speech that make this classification credible?

As with the other grey areas discussed in this chapter, we believe there are two main ways of responding to the identity appropriations riddle. The first is to say that on closer examination, identity appropriations are not hate speech because they do not involve attacks against people of the relevant sort. One version of this response insists only intentional attacks can be appropriately classified as hate speech, and another version argues only speech can count as hate speech. The second response (our proposed response) is to maintain instead that identity appropriations can be hate speech precisely because the ordinary concept *hate speech* is a family resemblance concept that may include even unintentional attacks and things that seem to be more behaviour than speech. The key point is that identity appropriations are sufficiently similar to exemplars of hate speech taking into account the distinguishing qualities of target, style, message, act, and effect. Before comparing these different responses, however, we shall first illustrate the practical implications of the identity appropriations riddle once again using Facebook's community standard on hate speech as a case study.

4.6.2 *Identity Appropriations under Facebook's Community Standard on Hate Speech*

Facebook's community standard on hate speech includes a specific Tier 1 rule disallowing blackface.[119] This rule has also been the subject of a 2021 Facebook Oversight Board case, in which the Board confirmed its support for Facebook's application of the rule.[120] It is worth noting, however, that blackface is not mentioned by the public-facing hate speech policies of other major social media platforms including Twitter, YouTube, TikTok, Snap Inc., and WeChat. That said, this omission is not in itself determinative since, unlike Facebook, these other platforms do not release public-facing versions of their hate speech policies that are intended to describe in detail and mirror quite closely their authoritative internal policies. Furthermore, by classifying blackface as a form of hate speech Facebook is not out on a limb more broadly. For example, blackface is treated as a form of hate speech in at least some of the legal and philosophical literature on the legal concept,[121] and as a form of covert racist discourse in some of the linguistics literature.[122]

Nevertheless, there are unexplained and potentially inconsistent features of Facebook's specific rule disallowing blackface that underscore the nature and importance of the identity appropriations riddle. For one thing, the rule presents blackface as an instance of the more general Tier 1 category 'dehumanising speech or imagery'.[123] Yet neither Facebook's community standard nor Facebook's numerous public statements concerning the standard provide any explanation or justification as to why blackface is treated as an instance of Tier 1 dehumanising speech or imagery as opposed to an instance of other designated forms of hate speech or a unique form of hate speech in its own right. So, what is dehumanising about blackface?

Perhaps Facebook has in mind extreme forms of mimicry in which a White person wears make-up and clothes so as to present a grotesque facsimile of Black people, including synthetic-looking jet-black skin and inhumanly large bottom, lips, or penis, with the effect that the caricature presented of a Black person no longer appears human but cartoonish. Then again, does Facebook believe every form of blackface is prima facie dehumanisation? What about forms of blackface in which White people seek to closely resemble well-known Black figures, such as in the form of look-alikes and tribute acts, and so deliberately seek to avoid exaggerating Black characteristics? Surely these forms of identity appropriation are not dehumanising in the literal sense of making others appear non-human.

Perhaps Facebook is adopting instead an analytical position about dehumanising speech, namely it is simply stipulating that for a user to post a picture or video of blackface is a designated form of dehumanising speech under its policy. However, if Facebook is stipulating blackface to be an instance of dehumanising speech, this creates tension. For, as we have already pointed out, moderate forms of this behaviour do not present Black people as non-human and are quite unlike other forms of dehumanising speech specified in Facebook's standard, including comparing people to insects or animals, calling them filth, bacteria, a disease or faeces, labelling them as subhuman, referring to them as mere objects, or describing them as violent or sexual criminals.[124] So where does Facebook draw the line between what does and does not constitute dehumanising speech?

A related uncertainty hangs over other forms of identity appropriation besides blackface. For example, does Facebook's authoritative internal policy on hate speech cover caricatures of women in the form of womanface and caricatures of gay people in the form of gayface? Does Facebook's understanding of what a caricature is only cover wearing make-up and clothing so as to resemble a member of a different group associated with a protected characteristic, or can it also include taking on the stereotypical mannerisms or behaviour of other people as exemplified by drag queens or two straight men kissing each other on the mouth for comic effect? Moreover, does the policy extend beyond adopting the appearance of members of other groups so as to create caricatures to other forms of identity appropriation such as blackfishing in which features are not exaggerated to look grotesque but copied to make the appropriator look beautiful and attractive? Indeed, what about forms of womanface that purport to celebrate not caricature femininity? Without answers to these questions, Facebook's specific rule against blackface looks ad hoc rather than reflecting a coherent and fully thought-through policy on identity appropriations.

Reflecting these points, we recommend that Facebook should amend its community standard on hate speech (and the internal policy assuming they mirror each other) as follows: first, the standard should include and explicitly name not only blackface but other violating forms of identity appropriations; second, the standard should list identity appropriations as a sui generis form of hate speech, as opposed to simply one instance of dehumanising speech or imagery. Ultimately, however, the justification for this recommendation rests in identifying sufficient similarities between identity appropriations and exemplars of hate speech under the global resemblance test. But before attempting to make that case, we begin by explaining and rejecting the first response to the identity appropriations riddle.

4.6.3 *First Response: Identity Appropriations as Unintentional Attacks*

The first response insists that, on closer examination, identity appropriations are not hate speech because they do not fit a standard model of attacks against people. As mentioned above, there are different versions of this response. One version embraces rule (R20) and claims that only intentional attacks against people can be appropriately counted as hate speech. Since identity appropriations are at most only unintentional attacks, they cannot be hate speech (according to this response).

Of course, it would be scarcely credible to pretend that blackface, say, is never intended to attack people of colour. For example, the American history of blackface minstrels reached a nadir in Hollywood with D. W. Griffith's film *The Birth of a Nation* (1915), in which Black people are depicted as unintelligent, savage, animalistic, blood-thirsty murderers, and rapists. Today this film is almost universally regarded as racist ideological propaganda conveying an overt message of White supremacy and signalling a clear intention to attack Black people and the movement for racial equality in America.[125] However, the current response draws a distinction between overtly White supremacist blackface and more moderate or celebratory forms of blackface. If the latter are clearly not intended to attack Black people, then they do not fall under the category of identity appropriations as we have defined them. What is more, according to the first response, if moderate or celebratory forms of blackface are at most only unintentional attacks against people of colour, then they cannot be appropriately labelled 'hate speech'.

Likewise, womanface of the sort described in (194) above is usually intended as a celebration of femininity seasoned with each performer's own artistic flair and dramatic licence. Drag queens take inspiration from some aspects of female identity and culture but also demonstrate significant creativity to produce something substantively original, unique, and self-empowering – something which aims to neither plagiarise nor ridicule particular women. But even if womanface still involves an unintentional attack on women in general, then it still cannot qualify as hate speech absent an intention to attack, at least according to the first response.

However, this response suffers from two major defects. For one thing, it is a conceptual error to say the ordinary concept *hate speech* only applies to intentional attacks against people. After all, there are many exemplars of hate speech that could be plausibly classified as unintentional attacks against people but are hate speech nonetheless (see Chapter 2). Consider stereotypes and generalisations about Black, Jewish, or Muslim people that are made without the intention to incite hatred against Black people, Jews, or Muslims but nevertheless have that as a likely effect. For this reason, we reject (R20) and instead endorse (R21).

Furthermore, it is one thing to acknowledge that people who perform identity appropriations have various psychological motives or rationales for doing what they do; it is quite another to show that these motivations disqualify this performance from being hate speech. Consider once again example (190) involving the White college student who attends a fancy-dress party as Michael Jackson both to show his appreciation for the deceased pop legend and to express something of his own personality. Although perhaps a more sanitised form of blackface, it is an echo of a much older tradition of blackface minstrels which, according to some scholars, speaks to repressed White fears and desires towards black bodies, or what Eric Lott calls 'love and theft'.[126] In a similar vein, Brian Roberts describes blackface as a form of 'love-crime racism', as in, 'a type of racism characterized by a powerful white attraction to certain supposed black characteristics, a white desire for black style, dance, song, and modes of expression'.[127] More generally, Bell Hooks argues that, from a White perspective, '[t]he "real fun" [of identity appropriation] is to be had by bringing to the surface all those "nasty" unconscious fantasies and longings about contact with the Other embedded in the secret (not so secret) deep structure of white supremacy'.[128] Relatedly, it has been suggested these longings stem from sexually repressive aspects of White culture, meaning Whites feel ashamed about or disconnected from their own eroticism and so project it onto Black culture and identity.[129] Think of Jackson's signature moonwalk and crotch grab. Along similar lines, some scholars have suggested that because White culture is morally straightlaced, White people have historically taken vicarious pleasure from viewing the morally unrespectable antics of black minstrels who 'were free to fight, have sex, and eat anything they wanted'.[130] An alternative reading is that because White status and identity affords limited opportunities for poor or disadvantaged White people to express their own sense of 'loss, fear, sorrow, and remorse, feelings of being at risk, and anger and rage at being taken advantage of', blackface provides a chance to express this sorrow by performing the role of Black characters.[131] Insofar as blackface has served these different veneratory, erotic, and expressive functions over the decades, the first response claims this supports the assumption that blackface does not reflect an intention to attack and, therefore, identity appropriations cannot be deemed hate speech. However, even if the aforementioned motives do not include an intention to attack, these motives can be morally culpable in other ways, such as if they are exploitative. Furthermore, this response places too much emphasis on explaining the motives of people who perform or watch identity appropriations and pays insufficient attention to key similarities with exemplars of hate speech in terms of target, style, message, act, and effect (see Section 4.6.4).

We start from the baseline of our broader theoretical approach to the ordinary concept *hate speech* which includes the central insight that the word 'hate' in the term 'hate speech' is highly misleading. Not only are the semantics of the term 'hate speech' non-compositional but having an association with attitudes, perspectives, feelings, or emotions of hate or hatred is not a necessary condition of plausibly labelling things 'hate speech',[132] just as having an association with aggression is not a necessary condition of calling something a 'microaggression' and having an association with fear is not a necessary condition of calling behaviour 'homophobic'. Moreover, even if the performance of blackface is motivated by a supressed attraction, vicarious pleasure, or displaced sorrow, rather than being motivated by hatred per se, this behaviour can and does target people on the basis of the colour of their skin, convey prototypical hate speech messages, perform prototypical hate speech acts, and inflict prototypical hate speech effects on those targeted. If these similarities are sufficient for particular examples of blackface to pass the global resemblance test, then it is fitting to apply the label 'hate speech' to those examples. The same goes for other forms of identity appropriations. Suppose two straight friends engage in gayface not with any intention to attack homosexuals but as a form of virtue signalling. They want to express to the world just how enlightened, progressive, tolerant, and non-bigoted they are by openly and freely kissing each other on the mouths. That the performance is well intentioned could make it less morally culpable, but it does not mean it is blameless. After all, the signalling could distract the public from the very real injustices and disadvantages experienced by gay men. More importantly, the specific motivations and moral culpability of given instances of gayface is not determinative of its status as hate speech.

Following on from this last point, we do not mean to suggest that the deeper motivations of identity appropriators makes no difference whatsoever to the moral assessment of such behaviour. It could be that such motivations may constitute if not exculpating excuses or compelling justifications for what is otherwise moral wrongdoing then at least mitigating circumstances that lessen the degree of blameworthiness. Nevertheless, our view is that, from a moral, conceptual, and social point of view, as in, from the perspective of competent language users applying the ordinary concept *hate speech* in the light of the functions or purposes they reasonably expect the concept to play, such mitigations do not and should not make it inappropriate or unfitting to label identity appropriations as 'hate speech'.

That said, a defender of the first response might insist that it does and should make a morally relevant difference if a speaker does not intend to be disrespectful to other people or to cause them to feel disrespected, for example. Indeed, there is a generalisable sense in which identity appropriation is well-intentioned. As the old saying goes, imitation is the sincerest form of flattery. Moreover, when it comes to protected characteristics, it can be a minefield knowing what to say and do, when, and to whom. Moral and social norms and conventions around respectfulness can be hard to know and even harder to apply. Perhaps it is unreasonable to expect ordinary people who are not members of minority groups to always understand the rules and get them right in practice. And so, maybe it is unreasonable to hold people morally culpable for making honest mistakes (or so says the first response).

However, it is important to recognise that moral culpability does not begin and end with intention. There is such a thing as negligence after all. Failure to take proper care over one's words or behaviour and how these things land with other people can be morally culpable. Even if identity appropriations are not intentional attacks against other people, and even if they could be well intentioned in one sense, they typically involve ignorance, and some types of ignorance certainly can be morally culpable such as when it is reasonable to expect someone to take steps not to be ignorant, for example. Indeed, ignorance can also be a hallmark of hate speech.

Notwithstanding these points, another version of the first response to the identity appropriations riddle changes the point of emphasis to the style of identity appropriations. It embraces rule (R22) and opines that because identity appropriations tend to exhibit the style of behaviour rather than words per see, they cannot be hate speech. This argument displays virtues of clarity and simplicity. After all, it suggests the meaning of the ordinary phrase 'hate speech' is a function of the combined meanings of 'hate' and 'speech' (semantic compositionality), and places a particular emphasis on the concept *speech* which it interprets in a narrow way. It also provides a natural break on the potential over-expansion of the term 'hate speech' ensuring that its application does not extend beyond clear-cut examples of speech. In addition, it furnishes one way of trying to distinguish between the concepts of hate speech and hate crime.

However, on closer examination none of these reasons stack up. For one thing, there is good reason to believe the semantics of the ordinary term 'hate speech' are non-compositional.[133] Moreover, clearly there are exemplars of hate speech that do take the form of behaviour, such as a group of neo-Nazis marching through a Jewish neighbourhood whilst waiving swastika flags, wearing Nazi costumes, and performing the Nazi salute. Indeed, speaking and writing words is itself a type of behaviour, and when people use words, they often perform acts besides saying something, which is why there are such things as prototypical hate speech acts – for example, *prejudging*, *stereotyping*, *marginalising*, *subordinating*, *oppressing*, and *inciting*. For these reasons, (R23) seems a more accurate rule of thumb about hate speech. Furthermore, as we shall try to show in

Chapter 6, it does not take much reflection to see that the core distinction between at least the legal concepts of hate speech and hate crime is *not* the distinction between speech and behaviour.

4.6.4 Second Response: Similarities between Identity Appropriations and Exemplars of Hate Speech

The second response to the identity appropriations riddle (our proposed response) argues that such behaviour can be hate speech based on similarities between identity appropriations and exemplars of hate speech in terms of target, style, message, act, and effect. We shall now attempt to highlight several similarities.

One prosaic point of comparison between identity appropriations and exemplars of hate speech rests in the fact that both identify the relevant subjects or targets on the basis of their possession or perceived possession of protected characteristics. However, there is also a stylistic similarity in that, just as identity appropriators mimic or imitate their subjects, so prototypical hate speech caricatures such as pictures depicting Black people as monkeys, Jews as rats, or Muslims as pigs or terrorists, for example, also mimic their subjects, even though the mimicry involved in the latter examples is usually aimed at portraying the subjects in a bad light and therefore with an intention to attack the targets.

Of course, some forms of blackface are much closer to what we have called identity attacks (Section 4.2) than identity appropriations. When blackface is done to caricature Black people, for example, it can encode the same or similar sorts of stigmatising stereotypes about people of colour as are conveyed by other canonical forms of anti-black hate speech including racist slurs and hate propaganda. According to Tracey Owens Patton, for example, the blackface performances which have been a fixture of American popular culture since the 1800s 'reinforce negative stereotypes that are at the core of racism (visual and otherwise) against African Americans.'[134] In particular, Patton argues that blackface minstrels 'firmly entrenched Blacks, black entertainment, and black performers as buffoons in the white imagination.'[135] More than that, black minstrels explicitly portray an image of Black people as low types. As Brian Roberts explains, 'what made the minstrel show's humour and spark [...] was nothing if not an all-out celebration of the low and disreputable.'[136] 'They got drunk, sang, danced, and gambled away all their money'.[137]

However, even moderate or celebratory versions of blackface such as the White college student who attends a fancy-dress party as Michael Jackson described in (190) may express, imply, presuppose, or infer messages about Black people that are prototypical hate speech messages. For example, the idea conveyed by this form of blackface may be that Black people are typically singers and dancers or that Black people are only noticeable, valuable, or good when they are well-known entertainers (who make money for White-owned record companies and sponsors). These sorts of generalisations and value judgments about people simply based on the colour of their skin echo messages found in some exemplars of hate speech (see Chapter 2). Much the same might be true of blacktalk, which presents urban hip culture and thuggism as the epitome of Black identity and culture. It is telling that White people who engage in blackface and blacktalk rarely mimic Black doctors and supreme court justices, and it means these behaviours reinforce rather than challenge stereotypes about Black people. Likewise, blackfishing may end up conveying a message about Black women that is the same or very similar to other forms of anti-black hate speech, such as the paradoxical message that Blackness is attractive but Black women themselves are not good enough. As Wanna Thompson puts it: 'Black women are constantly bombarded with the promotion of European beauty standards in the media, so when our likeness is then embraced on women who have the privilege to fit traditional standards yet freely co-opt Blackness to their liking, it reaffirms the belief that people desire Blackness, just not on Black women.'[138]

Along similar lines, consider examples of gayface in which straight men discuss their 'bromance' and perform overt acts of physical affection towards each other, even kissing on the mouth. This is often done to show off or for humorous effect: not celebrating homosexual relationships but making fun of them. Or it can be done to prove the appropriators' own masculinity or heterosexuality (*Just look at how comfortable we are in our masculinity and heterosexuality that we can take on gay behaviours and not fear turning gay or being perceived as unmanly*). But either way, the message conveyed by this sort of behaviour is still that gay men are somehow ridiculous or that being gay is something Other, remarkable, or outside of the norm. Taken to the other extreme, gayface behaviour also conveys a message of misrepresentation that is similar to certain homophobic microaggressions: it sugar-coats or glosses over the dark side of homosexual experience. It presents a rose-tinted image of being gay as being all about men snogging men thereby de-emphasising or brushing under the carpet homosexuals' real experiences of hate crime, discrimination, and marginalisation.

As well as conveying prototypical hate speech messages, we propose that identity appropriations can also perform prototypical hate speech acts including *oppressing*, *stereotyping*, *misrecognising*, *subordinating*, *exploiting*, *marginalising*, and *treating cruelly* the people whose identities are appropriated. For example, identity appropriations can constitute acts of *theft* or *exploitation*, and in that sense share something in common with cultural appropriation in general, namely 'the appropriation of elements of a subordinated culture by a dominant culture without substantive reciprocity, permission, and/or compensation'.[139] In terms of blackfishing, for instance, we suggest that part of what is wrongful about a White person adopting a Black appearance in order to improve her own image or reputation and be on-trend, is not so much that she is passing as Black but that she is taking what is good about being Black and passing it off as White, thereby acquiring an unreciprocated benefit. When blackfishing occurs there is still a strong sense in which the White person remains White in the eyes of her audience. This means her White identity and culture retains its status as superior and does so by stealing what is desirable about Black identity and culture and effectively portraying it as being White. This allows the White person to achieve a reputational uplift or image enhancement which is gained off the back of the coolness of Black identity but without repaying the prestige associated with Whiteness back to Black people.

Relatedly, like forms of cultural appropriation, identity appropriation can involve an *oppressive violation* of 'the intimate practices' of the target culture or identity.[140] Part of what makes such appropriation wrongful is the way in which the 'boundary crossings' are unacknowledged by those making them and done without the permission of members of the groups subjected to them.[141] There are such things as moral rights of ownership in relation to identity and culture, even if they are not legally enforceable rights. For example, being members of certain forms of Black female culture and its associated intimacies of hair design, skin tone, fashion, and so on, may confer on such women a moral right to call out blackfishing and to determine what does and does not count as blackfishing in the first place as well as a right to expect that appropriators seek permission.

We maintain that both blackfishing and denials of engaging in blackfishing may also constitute an act of *misrecognition*, specifically a *failure to truly see the people they are appropriating from*. We do not mean by this a complete failure to acknowledge or recognise Black identity and culture. After all, those who perform blackfishing may insist that they are not intending to unacknowledge Black identity and culture. Quite the reverse, they are intending to celebrate it. Rather, what we mean is that people who engage in blackfishing and baulk at the suggestion that what they are doing is blackfishing typically fail to see the real lived experiences of the people whose identities they are appropriating and fail to understand why those experiences cannot be reproduced in White form. This sense of misrecognition is eloquently expressed in the following words spoken by Sabrina Williams, a 20-year-old African American woman from Florida, who in the early 1990s was asked about her views on cultural appropriation.

> When they don those clothes, to me it's like they're donning a costume, just like if they was to smear black paint on they face. They're degrading my culture. They're saying anyone can do this.[142]

We believe identity appropriations may also perform acts of *stereotyping, subordinating, epistemic injustice*, and *treating cruelly* the relevant subjects. For example, in the early incarnations of black minstrels in American popular culture, blackface revolved around exaggerated mimicry, where White actors played Black characters who were ridiculous.[143] Even if some of these performances were intended to be for comedic purposes only, not merely is such blackface disparaging but also contributes to the Othering of Black people and to the ranking of Black people as morally and socially inferior. It maintains racial hierarchies and White hegemony, reinforces ideas about White superiority, and normalises and legitimates acts of oppression and discrimination perpetrated against Black people.[144]

Over time blackface evolved in popular culture to include examples of well-intentioned or celebratory blackface, in which White people adopt the persona of Black figures supposedly to present positive images of them. Yet even this mode of blackface performs the prototypical hate speech act of *pigeonholing* and *Othering*. Thus, Lolita Buckner Inniss describes blackface as a form of 'ersatz carnival' insofar as it appears to celebrate nonconforming or Other identities but in fact simply ends up reproducing the insidious idea that they are lesser or transgressive.[145] As Patton argues, when ordinary people wear blackface at a Halloween party or other special event, they may feel as though the context of enjoyment and celebration 'relieves them of social responsibility', but in reality it only underscores the tin ear that White people have to 'the cultural undercurrent of racism that still exists'.[146] Indeed, blackface may be an instance of a general phenomenon of racist perception that Elizabeth Spelman calls 'boomerang perception'.[147] White people who engage in blackface appear superficially to be truly seeing Black people (*Look how similar we are to black people*) but in fact are still seeing only themselves (*Look how similar black people are to us*).

When White people adopt an appearance or way of talking associated with Black identity and culture, whilst simultaneously lacking situated knowledge of what it is really like to be Black, they are literally performing their own *prejudice* and *standpoint ignorance*.[148] They are also perpetrating acts of *epistemic injustice* against Black people. Suppose a young White suburban male adopts some of the slang of Black hip hop culture and does so with a presumption that because he has listened to a lot of hip hop music, he understands what the talk is about, what it means and what experiences it represents, and that his use of this talk is credible, authentic, and real. Arguably, this sort of blacktalk and the basic presumptions that underpin it involves the White youth ignoring, de-emphasising, or being oblivious to the fact that he lacks the epistemic tools or resources – for example, having an intimate understanding of police brutality and street hustle gained from living as an African American youth in an urban area – required to know what the talk really means and what it actually represents. The White youth may be guilty of what Gaile Pohlhaus Jr. calls 'willful hermeneutical ignorance', which she classifies as a form of epistemic injustice.[149]

Along similar lines, the White college student who attends a fancy-dress party as Michael Jackson might be well-intentioned but also unaware of how it could be seen as a slight, as conveying an unwanted message, or experienced as disturbing by Black students. This ignorance could rise to the level of an epistemic injustice if the White college student has not made a reasonable effort to reflect on or investigate whether dressing as Michael Jackson could have these negative effects, and if he has failed to make this effort precisely because he lacks enough moral concern for Black people to make a reasonable attempt at understanding or empathy. The same might be said of a White female celebrity or social influencer who engages in blackfishing without pausing to ask Black women how this may be experienced by them or even engaging in critical self-reflection about it. At first glance, this looks like a form of morally culpable ignorance (epistemic injustice) because it is ignorance borne of negligence, a failure to take reasonable steps not to be ignorant or unaware.

With regard to epistemic injustice, we believe identity appropriations may share this act-type in common not only with other grey area categories of hate speech discussed in Chapters 3 and 4 but also with some of the exemplars of hate speech discussed in Chapter 2. Consider the microaggression of using certain trigger words whilst at the same time ignoring, failing to understand, or refusing to acknowledge the history, significance, and conventional meaning of those words as slurs or stigmatising stereotypes. This epistemic injustice might be exemplified by using a racial slur but then expressing scepticism that the word really is a racial slur or trying to explain away its connotations. This may even be an instance of what Nora Berenstain calls 'epistemic exploitation': 'when privileged persons compel marginalized persons to produce an education or explanation about the nature of the oppression they face' this creates 'unrecognized, uncompensated, emotionally taxing, coerced epistemic labor [for the latter]'.[150] By analogy, maybe the White college student who dresses up as Michael Jackson is performing an act of epistemic exploitation by forcing Black students to take on the additional and uncompensated labour of educating him on why blackface is disrespectful and disturbing. Likewise, blackfishing might be epistemically exploitative insofar as the White female celebrity or social media influencer trades on the appearance of Black women whilst at the same time putting the onus on the latter to take on the work of patiently explaining why blackfishing can be so infuriating and jarring to them. This means not only do Black women not benefit from the publicity and social media income that accrues to White women from their engaging in blackfishing, but Black women also have the unpaid labour of calling it out and educating White women about it.

Ignorance and exploitation are not the only injustice associated with identity appropriation. Identity appropriations may also involve what we shall call discursive replacement. In the case of both blackface and playing Indian, for example, it is evident that when White people take on the appearance of Black people or the clothing and rituals of Native American people without having the epistemic credibility to really know what it is like to be Black or Native American, this is not merely an epistemic injustice, there is also a danger that the White appropriators will end up *taking the place* of Black people and Native American people in public discourse. This in turn may have the unjust consequence of further contributing to the misrepresentation of Black and Native American opinion and identity, and ultimately the *silencing* of these minority voices.[151]

Sticking with the question of whether identity appropriations sometimes perform acts of *oppression* or *subordination*, consider once again the behaviour of blacktalk and, in particular, the phenomenon of White people using the word 'nigga' to mimic how some groups of African Americans speak to each other. When African Americans use it, the aim is often to reclaim and resignify the meaning of the term 'nigger', to give it an empowering meaning. As such, these sorts of uses might trigger the following exception outlined in Facebook's community standard on hate speech: 'In other cases, speech that might otherwise violate our standards can be used self-referentially or in an empowering way.'[152] By contrast, when White people use the term 'nigga' in reference to themselves and Black people, the aim can be to sound black and to partake in a certain form of Black hip hop identity and culture.[153] Because of this, however, some blacktalk may end up being oppressive and subordinating. For one thing, in a study of the experiences of staff and students at predominantly White colleges in America, many people of colour reported that they felt uncomfortable and demeaned by having to endure racial slurs from White friends or colleagues who themselves believed they were using these terms affectionately.[154] Moreover, this sort of blacktalk may also end up conveying (expressing, implying, presupposing, or inferring) an image or representation of Black people that reinforces stigmatising stereotypes of Black people as criminals, edgy, urban, and hardened. As such, some blacktalk might fall into both the categories of indirect attacks and identity appropriations. Then again, as mentioned in Chapter 3, we do not claim that the various grey area categories we discuss in Part I are mutually exclusive.

Furthermore, for White people to use 'nigga' in this way might be bitterly ironic to the point of *cruelty* given the historical context. After all, the history of blackface in America is one in which sometimes White people would use black make-up and clothes to turn themselves into black ventriloquist dummies with words being supplied to them off stage by White people, including faux self-referential uses of the word 'nigger'.[155] When White people today use a similar form of blacktalk ('nigga'), it shows not merely an ignorance of Black experiences but also a callous indifference to how confronting or disturbing it might be for African Americans to feel that they are on the receiving end of history repeating itself.

So far, we have identified various notable similarities between identity appropriations and exemplars of hate speech. Together, they point in the direction of rejecting (R22) and instead embracing the following alternative rule of thumb.

(R23) Hate speech can be embodied in various styles including but not limited to words, signs, symbols, images, pictures, cartoons, memes, videos, flags, logos, uniforms, clothing, statues, monuments, gestures, and behaviours.

However, we now face another aspect of the identity appropriations riddle outlined in Section 4.6.1, namely that embracing (R23) could potentially set off an avalanche of cases counting as hate speech including, for example, microaggressions that seem to be examples of behaviour as opposed to speech. Consider the following example.

(199) [Snubbing: A White hotel receptionist ignores a Black guest by carrying on a telephone conversation or dealing with a White guest who arrived at reception after the Black guest whilst not acknowledging the Black guest's presence or responding to the Black guest's physical and verbal cues, as though the Black guest were not present, invisible, or did not exist].

To embrace (R23) could mean plunging a society or organisation into a much broader conceptual dilemma about whether to treat not only identity appropriations but also some or all forms of microaggressions as hate speech.

Our proposed response to this dilemma is to see the ordinary concept *hate speech* and *microaggressions* as discrete and independent, although partially overlapping, categories. In our view, the distinction between these two categories is not a distinction between words (hate speech) and behaviour (microaggressions). On the contrary, both categories can be instantiated by things that are complex amalgams of words and behaviour. Nevertheless, treating identity appropriations as hate speech does not necessarily mean treating all microaggressions as hate speech simply because both categories can be instantiated by words and behaviour.

In fact, identity appropriations are both similar and dissimilar to microaggressions in a number of ways. On the one hand, both identity appropriations and microaggressions can be verbal and/or behavioural, can be experienced by victims on a daily basis and so are not rare or extreme events, and tend to be experienced by victims as disturbing, demeaning, insensitive, or disrespectful. Yet microaggressions are generally understood to include intentional attacks as well as unintentional attacks,[156] whereas we have defined identity appropriations as always unintended attacks. In the final analysis, however, both identity appropriations and some microaggressions have enough in common with each other and with exemplars of hate speech to be plausibly categorised under the ordinary concept *hate speech*.

4.6.5 Defences against the Charge That Identity Appropriations Are Hate Speech

We shall end this discussion by looking at one further defence a person might make, or that others might make on behalf of someone, in the face of the charge that their identity appropriation amounted to hate speech. In particular, we shall critically examine the defence of socialisation. In the end we reject this defence on several grounds.

What if the White college student and the White celebrity have an excuse of upbringing for having not made an effort to reflect on how their behaviour might land with Black people? For example, maybe the White college student and the White celebrity were raised by their parents, schools, and broader White culture in such a way that they were never taught to check or reflect on how blackface and blackfishing might be experienced by Black people, and so it simply never occurred to them to do so. If society cannot reasonably expect people to avoid being ignorant of something if the reason for their failure to avoid ignorance stems from their socialisation, and if people cannot be morally culpable for ignorance if it is unreasonable to expect them to avoid being ignorant,[157] then it seems no epistemic injustice has been committed, and so it might be harder to make the case that the appropriation is hate speech (according to the socialisation defence).

However, we believe this defence fails on several grounds. First, the reason for the ignorance is not purely circumstantial or factual, it also has a moral tinge to it, and this makes a difference to the assessment of morally culpable ignorance, of the occurrence of epistemic injustice, and ultimately of the plausibility of applying the label 'hate speech', at least in terms of similarity of act. After all, what if the ultimate source of the failure to check or critically self-reflect associated with the above examples of blackface and blackfishing is 'moral ignorance'?[158] To be more specific, what if the White college student and the White celebrity failed to check or critically self-reflect due to their conscious or unconscious bigoted and prejudiced attitudes towards people who are non-white? What if they implicitly thought that it is not important to check or critically self-reflect because the feelings of Black people do not matter or do not need to be taken into consideration all because of the colour of their skin? Surely this cannot be a legitimate excuse for failing to take steps to avoid being ignorant about how one's expressive behaviour will impact the relevant people. Here the reason for failing to take steps (prejudiced attitudes) looks morally culpable. Even if the prejudiced attitudes reflect upbringing, society can reasonably expect better of individuals.

Second, the failure to take reasonable steps to avoid ignorance might also be associated with a kind of counter-factual moral culpability.[159] Suppose that even if, contrary to fact, the White college student and the White celebrity had stopped to check or critically self-reflect, they would still have performed the blackface and blackfishing regardless. This counterfactual might also be explained by their bigoted or prejudiced attitudes toward people who are non-white. Maybe they implicitly think the feelings and interests of Black people are morally unequal to those of White people, meaning that even if they had reflected on the fact that blackface and blackfishing can be experienced by Black people as insulting, disrespectful, and disturbing, they would have automatically weighed their own interests in having fun, engaging in self-expression, or enhancing their image as more important, and would have freely behaved in the same way without significant moral regret.

Finally, even if ignorance borne of socialisation could be morally exculpatory with respect to the acts of epistemic injustice, it does not follow from this that identity appropriations cannot be hate speech. Since hate speech is a family resemblance concept it can be associated with a variety of different types and tokens of distinguishing qualities. So, if a particular identity appropriation does not constitute an act of epistemic injustice, it might nevertheless constitute some other paradigmatic hate speech act, as in, an act associated with exemplars of hate speech.

PART II

The Legal Concept

5

Orienting the Ordinary and Legal Concepts of Hate Speech

5.1 Introduction

In Chapter 1 we provided a rough preliminary characterisation of the basic ontological difference between the ordinary and legal concepts of hate speech simply by saying that the ordinary concept is related to social norms, social rules, and social sanctions, such as social media platform content policies that disallow directly attacking people with racial slurs, for instance,[1] whereas the legal concept is intimately bound up with legal norms, laws, and legal sanctions, such as criminal laws that ban incitement to hatred, discrimination, or violence on grounds of race, for instance. However, the distinction between these two concepts is both more complicated and interesting than this simplified ontological characterisation suggests. For one thing, the simple characterisation does not say much about the myriad types of speech to which the two concepts refer and is silent on the differing social functions or purposes these concepts play, and so is at best capable of telling only part of the story about how they might overlap but also diverge. Furthermore, although social norms against hate speech could in theory exist independently of laws banning hate speech, it would be naive to assume the two concepts are unconnected in practice. Yet the simple characterisation says nothing about the relationship and interactions between the two concepts.

Therefore, the central aim of this chapter is to better orient the ordinary and legal concepts of hate speech. The chapter is structured as follows. Section 5.2 uncovers various ways in which the ordinary and legal concepts of hate speech come together, including in terms of the kinds of speech they both count as hate speech. In Section 5.3, however, we turn to consider the potential sources of divergence between the ordinary and legal concepts of hate speech including the differing social functions or purposes played by the two concepts. Section 5.4 addresses the nature of the relationship and interaction between the ordinary and legal concepts of hate speech. Is it one of independence or mutual influence, for example? Does the legal concept codify the ordinary concept? Does the ordinary concept justify or even ground the legal concept? We argue that the most plausible and widely applicable hypotheses about the nature of this relationship are those which posit interactions that are weaker, less concrete, and less controversial. Finally, in Section 5.5 we try to show why theoretical disagreements about the relationship between the ordinary and legal concepts of hate speech matter. In particular, we argue that shining a light on these deeper disagreements can help to explain both the source of some academic controversies about the legitimacy of hate speech laws and the source of some wider public debates about the rights and wrongs of social media platform content policies on hate speech.

5.2 On the Overlaps between the Ordinary and Legal Concepts of Hate Speech

Over and above distinguishing the ordinary and legal concepts of hate speech in terms of them being related to social norms and legal norms respectively, is it possible to distinguish these concepts in further, more substantive ways? We believe drawing substantive distinctions in this area is fraught with difficulty but that these difficulties are nevertheless worth confronting because they help to uncover some important sources of overlap between the ordinary and legal concepts of hate speech. In this section we critically examine several putative distinctions and highlight some of the relevant overlaps.

Types of hate speech: It may be tempting to assume there are decisive qualitative differences between the sorts of things deemed illegal or unlawful hate speech within given jurisdictions, on the one hand, and the sorts of things treated as impermissible or not allowed hate speech by social media platforms or by society in general. But in reality, there is significant overlap in the extensions of the ordinary and legal concepts of hate speech, in the sense that many types of hate speech fall under both concepts. Consider incitement to hatred, discrimination, and/or violence (what might be called incitement to harm). Explicit reference to this general type of hate speech (or parts thereof) can be found in definitions of 'hate speech' in the ordinary (nonlegal) sense of the term promulgated by some of the major social media platforms including Twitter,[2] TikTok,[3] Snap Inc.,[4] and YouTube.[5] Similarly, a large proportion of the hate speech laws currently found across the globe, including domestic and international law, are either laws banning incitement to hatred or laws banning incitement to hatred, discrimination, or violence.[6] Moreover, reference to this general type can also be found in conceptualisations of hate speech provided by numerous legal scholars who seek to interpret clusters of extant laws,[7] and in explicit definitions of the legal term 'hate speech' contained in at least some of those laws, both domestic and intentional.[8]

Of course, incitement to hatred, discrimination, and violence is itself a general form of hate speech, and there is more than one way of specifying or getting clear about which precise or exact instances of speech fall under this general form (the type-token distinction). Nevertheless, the key point here is that while there may be differences, there are also some obvious overlaps in the types of hate speech captured by the ordinary and legal concepts. To give another example, consider slurs, insults, derogatory terms, and epithets that target people based on protected characteristics. These are typically treated as a type of hate speech by the major social media platforms including Facebook,[9] for instance. At the same time, there are many legal jurisdictions in which criminal hate speech laws, civil and human rights laws, and/or tort laws are applied to cases involving racist slurs, for example.[10]

Harmfulness: Notwithstanding these points, it might be further suggested that the distinction between the ordinary and legal concepts of hate speech boils down to a distinction between lesser and greater harmfulness, meaning that illegal hate speech, for example, is simply hate speech which is or ought to be illegal because it falls on the more harmful end of the spectrum. However, this distinction is not necessarily borne out by the reality of social and legal norms against hate speech. For example, although Facebook offers a general definition of hate speech that does not in itself refer to the harmfulness of hate speech – 'We define hate speech as a direct attack against people [...] on the basis of what we call protected characteristics' – it does refer to 'threat of harm' in its specific rule on hate speech 'attacking concepts, institutions, ideas, practices or beliefs associated with protected characteristics'.[11] Conversely, although some judges in hate speech cases mention harmfulness to explain the purpose of these laws and/or as an aggravating factor justifying stiffer sentences, many types of hate speech laws do not specify concrete harms or harmfulness in general as an element of the offending behaviour (although there are exceptions such as laws banning incitement to hatred when it is likely to cause public disturbance[12] and tort laws applied to cases involving targeted hate speech that causes concrete harm to the plaintiff[13]).

Now it is evident that harm prevention plays an important justificatory role whether people are making the case for social sanctions against hate speech or else for legal sanctions against hate speech. After all, people who condemn hate speech in the ordinary sense of the term and call for social media platforms to remove it, for example, often do so because they, explicitly or implicitly, consider the speech to be harmful, just as people who argue certain forms of hate speech should be criminalised regularly justify this by highlighting the harms of such speech. Then again, it is unclear that the real-world rationales for the imposition of these different types of sanctions depend solely and decisively on degrees of harmfulness. In the case of laws banning incitement to hatred, for example, the reasons governments have for creating and extending such laws are certainly not exhausted by harm prevention.[14] Furthermore, when social media platforms do speak to the harmfulness of the online hate speech they disallow, they do not typically assume much less publicly argue that such hate speech is significantly less harmful than illegal hate speech or that the harmfulness is of an entirely different (lesser) order of magnitude. On the contrary, they often play up the degree of harmfulness. Consider Facebook's community standard on hate speech which opens with the following statement justifying the adoption of its standard: 'We believe that people use their voice and connect more freely when they don't feel attacked on the basis of who they are. That is why we don't allow hate speech on Facebook. It creates an environment of intimidation and exclusion, and in some cases may promote offline violence.'[15]

Wrongfulness: An alternative putative distinction rests on the assumption that hate speech in the ordinary sense of the term is significantly less wrongful than hate speech in the legal sense of the term, where this wrongfulness might be analysed in terms of the intent or mens rea of the hate speaker or as a matter of what is considered extreme and outrageous including hate speech that is unusual or out of the ordinary and/or beyond the pale or a gross violation of civility norms or democratic values. However, once again, it is doubtful that the ordinary and legal concepts of hate speech neatly occupy opposite ends of the wrongfulness spectrum. For example, Facebook's community standard on hate speech contains numerous specific rules disallowing forms of hate speech that could be reasonably considered extreme and outrageous in most if not all countries.[16] Conversely, not all hate speech laws specify intent or mens rea as an element of the offending behaviour, and many countries possess laws, both as written and as applied, that prohibit forms of hate speech that are not extreme and outrageous per se; or, at least, not significantly more extreme and outrageous than the sort of hate speech disallowed by social media platforms.[17]

Targets of hate speech: Some people might imagine that the ordinary concept *hate speech* relates to direct attacks on individuals or so-called targeted hate speech, whereas the legal concept concerns only generalised attacks against groups. However, the reality belies the distinction. Facebook's community standard on hate speech, for example, covers various forms of hate speech including targeted forms and forms that are generalised in nature and attack entire groups rather than targeting specific individuals.[18] Similarly, the broad category of unlawful hate speech can include generalised attacks against groups, such as incitement to hatred, whilst at the same time some tort law[19] as well as some civil and human rights law[20] is used as a means of legal redress by individuals that have been personally targeted with hate speech as contrasted with hate speech of a more generalised nature.

The wider point of overlap is this: both the ordinary and legal concepts of hate speech relate to speech that is either directly or indirectly group-based. Even hate speech that is targeted at or addressed to a specific individual typically carries a message that relates to some group, category, class, or set of people of which the target is a member or perceived to be a member. What is the basis of the group membership? Arguably, both the ordinary and legal concepts of hate speech relate to speech that ultimately categorises people on the basis of protected characteristics, meaning characteristics that either are or should be shielded by society (the ordinary concept) or protected by laws or legal remedies (the legal concept). Whilst not exact mirror images of each other, there is certainly substantial overlap between the sorts of protected characteristics associated with the ordinary and legal concepts of hate speech respectively. For example, there is significant overlap between the protected characteristics listed within Meta's (Facebook, Instagram) community standard on hate speech,[21] Twitter's hateful conduct policy,[22] TikTok's community guideline on hateful behaviour,[23] Snap Inc.'s community guideline on terrorism, hate groups and hate speech,[24] YouTube's hate speech policy,[25] and WeChat's objectionable content rule on hate speech,[26] on the one hand, and the protected characteristics recognised in a range of different hate speech laws found across Europe, Latin America, Canada, Australia, and parts of Africa,[27] on the other hand.

Formality: Finally, some people might assume that the ordinary concept *hate speech* only relates to social norms that are informal in nature, whereas the legal concept exclusively concerns legal norms that are formal in nature. But once again the truth is more complicated than this. For example, the social rules promulgated by universities and social media platforms tend to be far more formal than the social norms against hate speech that are broadly encapsulated in the ordinary concept *hate speech* across various fields of discourse including in the media, politics, the arts, popular culture, and public discourse in general, even though the former are not yet legal norms. Conversely, in the arena of international law, there are some international legal norms against hate speech that are far more informal than the legal rules against hate speech enshrined in hate speech laws at the domestic or national level (see also Chapter 7).[28] Therefore, sometimes there is overlap in formality between the ordinary and legal concepts.

In addition to the aforementioned substantive points of overlap, it is also worth noting at this stage further common understandings of hate speech visible in the definitions of hate speech proffered by philosophers and legal scholars respectively, some of which are more coherent and reliable than others. Over the past three decades several philosophers have sought to attribute core meanings to the general term 'hate speech',[29] but it is striking how, on the whole, albeit with some exceptions,[30] they have not strayed very far from the sorts of definitions already put forward by legal scholars.[31] It is quite possible, of course, that both the philosophers and legal scholars have been seeking to define only the legal concept. As Jeremy Waldron once said, 'There is such a thing as legal philosophy'.[32] But this straightforward explanation may not be correct. For one thing, it is noticeable that the philosophers have paid significantly less attention to extant laws, and in many cases no attention whatsoever. Moreover, some of the philosophical definitions plug into wider social understandings of what hate speech is that extend far beyond extant bodies of law and legal doctrine. Therefore, we keep an open mind about what, in reality, the philosophers have been doing all along: they may have been defining either the ordinary or legal concepts or both.[33]

At any rate, comparing the philosophical and legal literatures points to a further five specific points of overlap, which we shall now outline and critically assess, once again with the aim of demystifying the relationship between the ordinary and legal concepts of hate speech.

Speech act theory: When legal scholars working in the field of critical race theory coined the term 'hate speech' to describe words that *subordinate, wound, humiliate*, or *degrade* historically oppressed or victimised groups,[34] they were in one sense seeking to make an interpretive argument about the central purpose of an existing set of laws: namely, to curb the harmful things people *do* with hateful words as much as the hateful things they *say* with those words. At the same time, however, these critical race theorists foreshadowed the work of philosophers who would later utilise speech act theory in more systematic ways to characterise the ordinary or general concept *hate speech*.[35] This was partly because both critical race theorists and the philosophers they influenced were themselves inspired by the work of Catharine MacKinnon and Andrea Dworkin on the subordinating nature of pornography and the associated moral case for the legal prohibition of pornography.[36]

Legal doctrines: The legal scholar Kent Greenawalt analyses the term 'hate speech' by appealing to the legal doctrines of fighting words, hostile environment discrimination, and group libel.[37] Interestingly, similar characterisations can also be found in the work of the philosophers Susan Brison and Timothy C. Shiell.[38]

Targeted versus generalised: Several legal scholars have drawn distinctions between immediate, instant, face-to-face, targeted, and individualised forms of hate speech, on the one hand, and indirect, diffuse, generalised, and impersonal forms of hate speech, on the other hand.[39] These same distinctions are replicated by the philosopher Caleb Yong.[40]

The Myth of Hate: Numerous legal scholars have assumed that emotions, feelings, or attitudes of extreme dislike or hatred are part of the essential nature of hate speech and what distinguishes such speech from other kinds of speech, and they have also implied that the meaning of the term 'hate speech' is compositional, that is, a function of the literal meanings of the terms 'hate' and 'speech' combined.[41] Similar assumptions can be found in the work of some philosophers, notably Norman Fischer and Bhikhu Parekh.[42]

Definition: Legal scholars have tended to labour under the assumption that the term 'hate speech' is univocal and definable, in the sense that it has a single meaning, even if complex or disjunctive, and that this meaning can be defined.[43] Once again we note that some philosophers appear to labour under the same assumption.[44]

We find some of these points of common understanding between philosophers and legal scholars unproblematic. The first three speak to the subtle interplay or mutual influence between the ordinary and legal concepts of hate speech that we shall explore further in Section 5.4. Nevertheless, we also reject some of this received wisdom. For one thing, we reject the presumption that emotions, feelings, or attitudes of extreme dislike or hatred are part of the essential nature of hate speech, what we have previously dubbed the myth of hate.[45]

Furthermore, we reject the conventional wisdom that the term 'hate speech' is univocal or has a single meaning.[46] To expand on the second point, we believe the flaw in this conventional wisdom partly stems from a failure to attend to the distinction between the ordinary and legal concepts of hate speech. The fact that the term 'hate speech' can be, and often is, used to refer to two different concepts defies attempts to furnish it with a single meaning.

However, what about attempts to define the two concepts separately? Even though this is a more sophisticated project, we believe only the legal concept(s) *hate speech* admits of formal or analytical definition and that the ordinary concept *hate speech* is best understood as a family resemblances concept.[47] In other words, it is important to recognise the differences between two definitional projects. On the one hand, the aim to define the legal term 'hate speech' as it relates to particular bodies of law is not only common practice but also epistemically credible and instrumentally desirable. This might be done by defining the legal concept in terms of the putative hate speech laws of a particular jurisdiction, such as defining the legal concept *the stirring up hatred offences of England and Wales*, for example. Or it could be done by grouping laws into clusters based on shared similarities, and then defining each of the clusters – for example, the legal concept *incitement to hatred laws* may be instantiated in various different jurisdictions around the world.[48] Indeed, even the far more ambitious project of seeking to characterise a general legal concept *hate speech* that has the potential to describe a wide range of different bodies of law across jurisdictional boundaries might be worthwhile, even if ultimately unsuccessful in capturing both comprehensively and accurately the full gamut of relevant laws;[49] or successful only by means of defining a highly abstract and idealised catchall legal concept *hate speech* as a sort of ideal type.

We suggest that whether a given law can be plausibly counted as a hate speech law depends on not simply what type of words or behaviour are prohibited or regulated by it but also certain legal-technical qualities of the law as well the legislative purpose or function of the law. Building on these distinguishing features of hate speech laws, definitional clarity surrounding the legal concept(s) could be improved through the development of a formal definition: namely, providing necessary and/or sufficient conditions for the application of a particular legal concept *hate speech*. For example, in Chapter 6, we suggest a necessary condition for what we call the formal legal concept *hate speech*: specifically, that the formal legal concept only refers to laws which create discreet or bespoke crimes, offences, torts, or violations without corresponding or parallel basic or base versions of those crimes, offences, torts, or violations within the relevant jurisdictions (a legal-technical quality). In Chapters 7 and 8, by contrast, we shall focus on the sorts of words or behaviour typically prohibited by hate speech laws as well as the common legislative purposes or functions of such laws.

Arguably, in the case of the legal concept(s) *hate speech*, seeking definitional clarity and waging a war on ambiguity might serve to enhance not merely the publicity and public knowledge of the relevant legal rules or laws but also the degree of predictability or fair notice of liability to legal sanctions for using unlawful hate speech among members of the public who are subject to those rules and laws: public knowledge and predictability being important features of the rule of law.[50] Moreover, as Katharine Gelber points out, such clarity may also improve the quality of public debate both about what hate speech laws should or should not cover, and about why such laws might or might not be necessary and legitimate within a democratic society of equals in the first place.[51] In turn, better public debate about the legal concept(s) *hate speech* might help to reduce the risk of lawmakers and judges making bad laws, and could potentially increase the degree of compliance with good laws.

On the other hand, we believe that seeking to provide a singular, formal or analytical definition of the popular or general term 'hate speech' based on ordinary usage, what we call the ordinary concept *hate speech*, is both epistemically untenable and may be instrumentally undesirable. The fact that the ordinary concept can be used for myriad formal and informal purposes, purposes which in turn can vary across different social, cultural, and political contexts and can evolve over time, is precisely what makes the ordinary concept so useful but also hard to define. What is more, seeking to boil down the ordinary concept to a single meaning runs the risk of artificially restricting or otherwise misdirecting public debate about what hate speech is; debate about how best to tackle the problem; debate about which agents are best placed and/or most responsible for doing so; and, indeed, debate about whether it is even a 'problem to be tackled'. In trying to give an analytical definition of the ordinary concept *hate speech* academics may unconsciously fall back on features of the legal concept and as a result might end up not only reinventing the wheel (defining the legal concept) but also giving a false impression that the only way to tackle the problem of hate speech is through legal sanctions.

However, we do not mean to suggest that there is no value whatsoever in institutions and organisations providing limited or bounded definitions of hate speech in the ordinary sense of the term: which is to say, definitions of hate speech limited to application within the scope of particular institutions or organisations. For example, universities and social media platforms can, and do, define the sorts of hate speech which *they* do not allow. These definitions may have similar utility to legal definitions of hate speech, insofar as they provide both publicity of the relevant social rules and predictability of vulnerability to social sanctions for using disallowed hate speech among the cohort of people who are subject to those social rules.

Indeed, in some jurisdictions, such as England and Wales, governments are planning to introduce new internet laws which impose responsibilities on social media platforms to identify and remove 'content that is harmful' (even if legal) as well as some illegal content – responsibilities interpreted and enforced by the internet regulator.[52] Although the relevant bill does not explicitly name hate speech as falling within the general category of 'content that is harmful' (even if legal), it is conceivable that the internet regulator could over time interpret the relevant responsibilities to cover harmful hate speech (even if legal). In that event, it would be incumbent on social media platforms to, in effect, harmonise their own definitions of disallowed hate speech with the relevant internet laws, as interpreted and enforced by the internet regulator, in order to avoid legal sanctions and reputational damage. That said, England and Wales is an outlier in this emerging field of internet law: the vast majority of individual countries and international organisations which either have or are developing new internet laws impose only responsibilities on social media platforms to identify and remove illegal content including illegal hate speech.[53]

Importantly, however, the aforementioned limited definitions cannot serve, and are not intended to serve, as general definitions of the ordinary concept *hate speech*. That concept has a life of its own extending from universities and social media platforms, through to traditional media, and on to politics, popular culture, and public discourse across the board. Meta, for example, can certainly define the sort of hate speech disallowed on its platforms (Facebook, Instagram), but in doing so, it cannot, and arguably is not intending to (despite its influential role), define hate speech in the ordinary sense of the term for society in general. After all, we have argued there are forms of hate speech in the ordinary sense that Meta does allow (see Chapters 3 and 4). At most, Meta is merely defining the limited concept *hate speech disallowed on our platforms*, just as other tech companies define their own limited concepts.

Another main difference between the ordinary and legal concepts of hate speech is that the legal concept is more often associated with rigorous attempts to define the types of speech in question as narrowly as possible. For example, this might involve qualifying and restricting what may count as incitement to hatred, discrimination, and violence for the purposes of the legal definition.[54] The goal of producing ever narrower definitions of hate speech, or as narrow as can be feasible achieved whilst respecting other judicial goals (e.g. flexibility), would seem to be a virtue as applied to the legal concept(s), and may also be to some extent desirable as applied to the ordinary concept when defined in limited or bounded ways by specific institutions and organisations such as universities or social media platform. But we believe the aim of developing ever narrower definitions is a vice if pursued too zealously in relation to the ordinary concept in general terms, especially given its manifestations and roles in popular culture and public discourse.[55] We shall return to these roles in Section 5.3.

Now it might be objected at this stage that because the differences we have highlighted between the ordinary and legal concepts of hate speech in terms of definitional clarity and narrowness are conventional rather than analytical, in the sense that they simply reflect the customary practices or conventions of a certain type of society and its social and legal institutions as opposed to eternal and immutable truths about the core meanings or essences of these concepts, this means the differences are not set in stone. For example, it is conceivable that a society or, more specifically, the universities and major social media platforms of that society, might choose in the future to embrace the fundamental aim of achieving ever greater clarity and narrowness in the definition of hate speech in its ordinary meaning. Indeed, one of the chief aims of Part I of this book was to argue that Facebook can, and should, seek to clear up a range of ambiguities and inconsistencies within its definition of hate speech. Conversely, it is not beyond the realms of imagination (even if highly unlikely given the current disposition) that the legislature of a jurisdiction like England and Wales could change tack and move in the direction of creating broader rather than narrower definitions of the stirring up hatred offences or else that the court of appeal and ultimately the supreme court could make a series of legal decisions that, in effect, reinterpret current definitions of these offences to make them less narrow as applied than has previously been understood by magistrates' courts and crown courts.

However, it is one thing to hold, as we do, that the ordinary and legal concepts of hate speech are living and breathing concepts which evolve and change organically over time, not only in response to external factors but also through processes of mutual influence; it is quite another to expand the core of one's account of what distinguishes and unites these concepts to include potentially unlimited thought experiments and hypotheticals about what in theory could happen to these concepts in the longer term. We aim to distinguish the two concepts ontologically, as relating to social norms and legal norms respectively, in the here and now.

No doubt our study of these concepts will need to be updated going forward, but for the time being we maintain that there are clear differences in definitional clarity and narrowness between the ordinary and legal concepts, at least in most parts of the world.

Of course, an alternative, more radical response to the definitional challenges associated with the term 'hate speech' might be simply to campaign for a sea-change in language use: for example, to try to persuade ordinary people as well as social media platforms, the traditional media, and public and political figures to collectively cease using the term 'hate speech' in reference to the ordinary concept *hate speech*, reserving the term exclusively for the legal concept and legalistic meanings.[56] However, as we argued in Chapter 1, this radical suggestion underestimates the instrumental value of using a term that is already the subject of significant levels of public awareness and public knowledge and that already has a presence and a degree of traction in public discourse and public debate, despite the fact of its ambiguity. There is significant value in people being able to make the following sorts of coherent and potentially true statements invoking the ordinary concept *hate speech*.

(1) Did you see the cartoon last night where Cartman gave a hate speech on ginger kids? I get this was supposed to be ironic or satirical, but the bottom line is that if you air hate speech against people with ginger hair it's gonna be hurtful and may give the wrong message to young people.

(2) Misgendering is sufficiently similar to other things that social media platforms already deem to be hate speech that they really ought to take such speech more seriously and work harder to remove this content as they do other examples of hate speech like homophobic abuse and calls for gay people to undergo compulsory gay conversion therapy.

(3) Our government is too heavy-handed when it comes to hate speech. There is a lot of hate speech which is damaging but should nevertheless not be made illegal, and in fact should never even be considered as an appropriate object of legal restriction; it should be tackled instead with other remedies like better education and counterspeech.

Or consider a real-world example of official discourse about hate speech contained in the 2019 United Nations Strategy and Plan of Action on Hate Speech.

(4) Rather than prohibiting hate speech as such, international law prohibits incitement to discrimination, hostility and violence (referred to here as 'incitement'). [. . .] Hate speech that does not reach the threshold of incitement is not something that international law requires States to prohibit. It is important to underline that even when not prohibited, hate speech may be harmful.[57]

These sorts of statements are valuable contributions to public debate about hate speech and they are made possible (i.e. meaningful) by speakers invoking the ordinary concept *hate speech*. In some respects, it might be clearer if ordinary people used different phrases to label the ordinary and legal concepts of hate speech respectively. Gelber suggests that society and its institutions should stick with the term 'hate speech' for the legal concept but use some other term(s) for what we call the ordinary concept.[58] As evidenced by (4), the UN has proposed the reverse strategy: that we should stick with 'hate speech' for the ordinary concept but instead use 'incitement' for the legal concept. But the brute fact is that across the globe, people continue to use the term 'hate speech' and they switch back and forth between the ordinary and legal senses depending on the situation. In relation to its overall usage, the term *is* ambiguous in that sense. Campaigning for people to drop all nonlegal uses of the term 'hate speech' may risk throwing the baby out with the bathwater; by which we mean the valuable discourse typified by (1), (2), (3), and (4).

To clarify, we do not mean to suggest that one must accept the truth of these specific statements to see them as valuable instances of public discourse. True or false, we defend them as both meaningful and legitimate ways of people expressing their views about hate speech in the ordinary (nonlegal) sense of the word.

5.3 On the Divergent Orientations and Purposes of the Ordinary and Legal Concepts of Hate Speech

Notwithstanding areas of unavoidable and potentially beneficial overlap between the ordinary and legal concepts of hate speech, it is also important to understand how they diverge. Not only is it intrinsically important to get clear about the main differences between the two concepts, but it is also a necessary preliminary step towards a proper analysis of the complex relationship and interactions between them; which we seek to provide in Section 5.4. We believe some divergence can be traced to the different purposes that the ordinary and legal concepts serve,[59] and ultimately to different conceptual orientations; as we shall try to show now.

5.3.1 *The Ordinary Concept Hate Speech*

The ordinary concept *hate speech* serves myriad conceptual, moral, and social purposes, to be outlined in a moment. Before doing so, however, we need to make three general points about the distinctive orientation of these purposes from the outset, as contrasted with the orientation of the functions we believe are associated with the legal concept(s) *hate speech*.

First, typically the purposes served by the ordinary concept are oriented towards ordinary people and society in general being able to say and do things about the forms of speech referred to by the term 'hate speech' in its nonlegal sense, as distinct from whatever people working for legal institutions and quasi-governmental agencies might be saying and doing. Some of these purposes might be similar, but not always.

Second, the purposes associated with the ordinary concept tend to push in the direction of expansion, as in, towards greater inclusivity and variety in the sorts of expressive, communicative, and performative attacks labelled 'hate speech' in the general sense of the term. We believe this expansive conceptual coverage is not random but at the same time neither does it to submit to an analytical definition (a set of necessary and sufficient conditions). Instead, it exemplifies and depends on a complicated network or pattern of overlapping and criss-crossing similarities (family resemblance).[60] This is contrasted with the legal concept(s) *hate speech* which typically points towards a much narrower extension and may admit of forms of analytical definition in this sense.

Third, the purposes underlying the ordinary concept do not include among them, and do not typically require or depend on, what might be roughly called the purpose of conceptual refinement, as in, ever-greater clarity and precision in the definition of what counts as hate speech. On the contrary, the ordinary concept can perform most, if not all, of its myriad purposes with only a limited or minimal degree of refinement, certainly in comparison to the degree of refinement needed for the legal concept(s) *hate speech* to serve its functions. Indeed, some purposes are better served with a degree of constructive ambiguity.

Keeping these general orientations in mind, we shall now provide a sketch of some of the notable purposes that we believe may be served by the ordinary concept *hate speech* depending on the context and the people using the concept. Note, however, that we do not present this as an exhaustive list. Moreover, we do not suggest that the ordinary concept must play each of these purposes at the same time nor that these different purposes are always complementary; sometimes they may have conflicting implications.

Making sense: People often invoke the ordinary concept *hate speech* in an attempt to make sense of, understand, and categorise certain forms of speech; or even to demystify the speech. In particular, people may refer to 'hate speech' in the ordinary sense of the term in order to highlight similarities between a group of expressive, communicative, or performative attacks – for example, similarities around the characteristics of the people attacked, similarities around the messages of hostility, contempt, prejudice, bigotry, and subordination encoded by the attacks, or similarities in what speakers are doing with these attacks such as subordinating, oppressing, or marginalising people or else perpetuating such phenomena.

Alarm bell: People sometimes refer to 'hate speech' in the ordinary sense of the term in order to sound an alarm about a type of speech which they believe constitutes a wrong or that is harmful, deleterious, or corrosive in some way. For example, they might want to refer to speech that ranks people as inferior; speech that disproportionately harms already oppressed, disadvantaged, or victimised groups in society; speech that corrodes people's confidence in their security; speech that can be socially divisive; speech that can undermine people's sense that they are equal members of society in good standing; and so on.

Voice: People may talk about hate speech in the ordinary sense of the word as a way of giving expression or voice to their anger, resentment, or sense of grievance at being on the receiving end of what they consider to be unfair or unjust language.

Signalling: People might speak of 'hate speech' with its ordinary or general meaning for the purposes of signalling something about the speech in question and/or about the targets of the speech even though they are not themselves the targets. For example, they might wish to publicly express their personal disapproval of the speech in question. Alternatively, they may want to demonstrate their solidarity with or sympathy for the victims of such speech. As well as symbolising allyship, using the term 'hate speech' might also send the signal that the targets are equal members of society in good standing and as such have the moral right to expect not to be targeted with certain forms of speech. A social media platform in particular might also use the term 'hate speech' so as to signal that it treats users equitably and does not apply double standards in the decisions it takes about removing or reducing the distribution of content.

Dissent (counterspeaking, blocking, mobilising): People might also use the term 'hate speech' in its ordinary sense as an act of dissent. This might involve a conscious attempt to discredit, debunk, or delegitimise the speech in question – as an act of counterspeech. This might involve directly challenging or rejecting a hateful message that certain people are subhuman or not valued members of society, for instance. Note, counterspeech can be performed by victims and bystanders but also by people in official positions such as political figures.[61] The use of the term 'hate speech' in its ordinary sense can also be associated with attempts to deny that speakers have the licensed authority to use the relevant speech to perform acts of subordination, oppression, and marginalisation, as though saying 'not in my name', thereby potentially blocking the speaker's successful performance of those wrongful acts. Indeed, people may use the term 'hate speech' with its ordinary meaning as part of a process of mobilising public opinion against certain speech. These acts of dissent involve doing whatever is the opposite of accepting or reconciling oneself to the speech in question.

Moral norm: People might talk of 'hate speech' with its ordinary meaning in mind simply in order to convey the idea that the speech in question is morally objectionable, as in, violates some or other moral norm such as related to the wrongfulness or harmfulness of the speech in question.

Social norm: People may also refer to 'hate speech' in the ordinary sense to articulate or suggest that certain forms of speech are socially unacceptable. In doing so they might be invoking social obligations, including an obligation to refrain from certain forms of speech and a second-order obligation to enforce the first obligation through the social sanctioning of non-compliance. When it comes to the ordinary concept *hate speech*, social sanctions may include criticising, publicly shaming, stigmatising, or even shunning or refusing to be friends or deal with speakers who use the relevant speech. In the case of social sanctioning, the kind of agents enforcing the relevant social norms are typically ordinary citizens, civil society organisations, and businesses, rather than legal institutions and governmental agencies. That said, public figures including celebrities and politicians can also use their status to socially sanction hate speakers, even if not speaking in an official or governmental capacity.

Social rule: Groups of people and private organisations may refer to 'hate speech' in the ordinary sense of the term in order to formalise a social norm against certain types of speech, specifically by publicly articulating a social rule about speech that the group or organisation does not allow and declaring that rule-breakers will be sanctioned using the various tools and powers available to the group or organisation. Arguably, this is the sense of 'hate speech' implicitly invoked by universities in campus speech codes forbidding forms of discriminatory harassment. It is also explicitly used by social media platforms in their terms of service, community standards, and content policies on hate speech. They intend to set down social rules about the types of speech/speech conduct they will not allow and will sanction. This is typically grounded in a judgment that such content casts a pall over social connectivity and public discourse on their platforms, and that, from a commercial perspective, such content shows the platforms in a bad light. Interestingly, a commercial organisation might also have secondary rules about how the primary social rules are to be made.[62] For example, Facebook has an Oversight Board Charter which, amongst other things, establishes, first, that the decisions reached by the Oversight Board on particular cases of hate speech are binding and, second, that the Board can also make general policy recommendations which Facebook will consider when shaping the community standard (social rule) on hate speech promulgated by the platform.

Reflexive commentary: People may place the term 'hate speech' in quotations marks not merely to convey its ordinary meaning but also to comment on that meaning. This might be commentary in the shape of endorsement, as in, expressing approval of ideas or assumptions encoded in the ordinary meaning of the term (e.g. 'I would remind you the term "hate speech" as normally understood refers to morally problematic speech'). It may also be commentary in the form of criticism, such as expressing disapproval of such ideas or assumptions, or expressing concern over the implications of accepting these ideas or assumptions (e.g. 'The term "hate speech" is a weapon of liberal public opinion wielded against people with unpopular views'). And it can be used as commentary on what the ordinary meaning actually is or should be, such as to accept or challenge conventional wisdom about the content of the ordinary meaning (e.g. 'It is a mistake to assume that the term "hate speech" only applies to speech attacking oppressed groups').

Point of linguistic contact between groups: The ambiguity of the term 'hate speech' in its ordinary sense enables it to operate as kind of vernacular in which both speakers and targets of speech can debate what forms of speech cross lines of acceptability in different contexts. Even if they have in mind different ideas about what qualifies as hate speech, they can use this term as a point of linguistic contact to discuss similarities and dissimilarities between 'at issue' examples and paradigm examples. For example, the ordinary concept 'hate speech' is useful 'precisely because it can be diversified to encompass an array of things that are both like and unlike racist insults, and which are like and unlike each other.'[63]

5.3.2 *The Legal Concept(s) Hate Speech*

Like the ordinary concept, the legal concept(s) *hate speech* also serves different functions, some of which may be similar to the above-mentioned purposes, but some of which are also bespoke, and some reflecting the distinctive role played by legal concepts in general. However, typically the functions of the legal concept(s) *hate speech* are oriented differently to the purposes of the ordinary concept. The former purposes are typically oriented towards understanding and justifying bodies of law, legal norms, and legal sanctions. In other words, when legal professionals, legal scholars, policymakers, victims' groups, and other sorts of legally minded agents refer to 'hate speech' in the legal sense of the term, they mean to refer to speech that either does or should fall under certain legal jurisdictions, bodies of law, and patterns of legal enforcement (i.e. real or ideal law).

For this reason, almost all of the functions of the legal concept(s) *hate speech* point in the direction of a narrower set of speech/speech acts that can be rightly labelled 'hate speech' and create an impetus for maximising definitional clarity and precision. That said, even when it comes to legal uses of the term 'hate speech', the requirements of clarity and precision must be balanced against other jurisprudential considerations. For example, the legal concept *hate speech* and the laws with which it is associated must satisfy the twin demands of predictability and flexibility (i.e. being well defined enough for ordinary people to predict liability but also flexible enough for courts to adapt the law to new cases).

Consider, then, some of the functions that might be played by the legal concept(s) *hate speech*, some of which share similarities with purposes served by the ordinary concept, whilst others are more idiosyncratic, and some are familiar to legal concepts in general. As above, the list is intended to be more illustrative than comprehensive.

Legal norm: Legally minded agents may speak of hate speech in the legal sense simply in order to articulate a legal norm to the effect that the kind of speech in question is or should be illegal or unlawful. The legal norm is a sort of general legal standard of what is expected and is typically formally instantiated or manifested in hate speech laws, domestic and international, and/or informally articulated through recommendations, guidelines and other forms of soft law. Hate speech laws articulate precisely what is prohibited, whereas the legal norm against hate speech speaks to the idea of speech that ought not be used because it is illegal. When legal norms against hate speech are internalised within society, people may obey hate speech laws because of the norm. This in turn speaks to the broader notion of compellingness (see below).

Interpretation: Legal professionals and assorted other legally minded agents may talk about hate speech in the legal sense of the word in order to interpret bodies of law and legal practices. The jurisprudential literature on hate speech contains numerous competing, sometimes contradictory, definitions of hate speech, but there is a sense in which all these definitions seek, explicitly or implicitly, to interpret laws and the sorts of speech/speech acts that are or might be illegal under those laws.[64] In other words, legal concept(s) *hate speech* may encode understandings of what certain laws mean, what they have in common, what kind of laws they are, what sorts of things they prohibit, and on what basis. Moreover, agents may use the term 'hate speech' in reference to more specific legal concepts, such as the legal concept *incitement to hatred, discrimination, and violence*.[65] Furthermore, according to one prominent theory of legal interpretation due to Ronald Dworkin, there is also a constructive or justificatory dimension to legal interpretation.[66] This is about interpreting laws and legal practices in their best light, as in, showing or revealing how they can be the best examples of the kind of things they are. Moreover, the constructive legal interpretation of hate speech laws and legal practices may itself draw on social and moral norms about hate speech and ultimately on more general moral values in ethics, law, and politics. This in turn enables the interpretations to take on a reforming role, as in, to be used as guides for how existing laws should be reformed or new laws created. In one sense, this is about going beyond the description of actual hate speech laws to define an ideal type of hate speech law.

Warranting: Legally minded agents may refer to 'hate speech' in the legal sense of the term for the purpose of declaring that the speech in question is legally prohibitable or regulatable, meaning speech concerning which there is a pro tanto argument for legal prohibition or regulation and, therefore, speech which may be rightly subject to legal sanctions of various sorts.[67] There is usually also an assumption behind such uses that the justification or warrant will depend on the type of illegal hate speech involved, given legal norms around efficacy, the least restrictive alternative, proportionality, and so on.[68] Importantly, the warranting purpose behind using the legal concept(s) *hate speech* typically presupposes ideas about legitimate government interests in banning certain speech including those related to the wrongfulness or harmfulness of the speech. For example, one purpose in calling something 'hate speech' in the legal sense of the term is to suggest or presuppose that the speech warrants legal prohibition or regulation in virtue of its harmfulness, including the deleterious impact the speech has on victims, on peace and security, on social cohesion, on democratic values, for example.

High threshold of harmfulness: Related to the previous purpose, legally minded agents may refer to 'hate speech' in the legal sense of the term for the purpose of declaring that certain speech is legally prohibitable or regulatable because it constitutes especially serious or severe wrongful or harmful speech. Here the idea being explicitly or implicitly conveyed by the legal concept(s) *hate speech* is that the speech in question meets a high threshold of wrongfulness or harmfulness which the agent using the legal concept believes is required to warrant legal prohibition or regulation.[69]

Convergence and standardisation: Legally minded agents may in some instances refer to 'hate speech' in the legal sense with the specific intention of conveying a message about the way in which the logic of certain legal concept(s) *hate speech* point towards both convergence in what should count as illegal hate speech across different legal jurisdictions and standardisation in the sorts of laws, regulations, and legal sanctions used to combat hate speech. For example, agents might invoke an international legal concept of hate speech because they wish to refer to or articulate a soft social norm of the community of states or even a hard legal norm of international society. In the case of a soft social norm of the community of states, the norm may articulate an informal expectation, ambition, or direction of travel towards standardisation in the regulation of hate speech, such as standardisation in how states combat unlawful online hate speech through regulation of social media platforms.[70] In the case of a hard legal norm of international society, the norm might be codified in a document or instrument that sets out an agreed framework of ideal types of legally prohibitable hate speech and ideal types of national hate speech laws but with a margin of appreciation for domestic context and jurisprudential independence.[71] The relevant legal norm might oblige states not merely to enact relevant types of national hate speech laws but also to use their power and influence to persuade other states to do likewise.

Refinement: Legally minded agents may also talk of 'hate speech' in the legal sense of the term in order to underline the fact that when legal or governmental institutions seek to prohibit or regulate hate speech there is a need for the sort of 'definitional refinement'[72] that typically befits all legal remedies, measures, and sanctions. If law enforcement agencies and courts are going to apply and enforce the law, and if ordinary citizens are going to be able to predict their liability under the law, the law must be as precise and clear as feasible.

Signalling: Legally minded agents might use the phrase 'hate speech' in a legal sense for signalling purposes, although the signals tend to differ from the signals associated with the ordinary concept. For example, agents may wish to underscore or re-emphasise the official disapproval of certain forms of hate speech; disapproval that is embodied in legal norms, legal restrictions, and legal sanctions.[73] In addition to this, agents might also use the phrase 'hate speech' with its legal meaning in mind so as to express a kind of official or formal solidarity with victims of illegal hate speech in particular; to express in an official or formal way the idea that the targets are equal citizens in good standing and as such have a legal right not to be subject to illegal speech; or even as an act of remembrance for victims of atrocities which certain forms of illegal hate speech deny or glorify.[74]

Official dissent: Legally minded agents may refer to 'hate speech' in the legal sense of the term in order to perform acts of official dissent. For example, political figures may consciously use the phrase 'illegal hate speech' to describe speech they wish to counter (challenge or reject), and to do so partly on the grounds that the speech is prohibited by the laws of the land. This may be the ultimate form of official counterspeech, although not how the notion of official counterspeech is conventionally discussed in some of the literature, namely counterspeech as an alternative to legal prohibition as opposed to counterspeech premised on legal prohibition.[75] Likewise, legally minded agents might speak of 'hate speech' in the legal sense of the term in order to counter a specific message contained in some hate speech to the effect that certain groups do not, or should not, enjoy equal standing in the eyes of the law. The point of speaking about 'illegal hate speech' might be precisely to remind both hate speakers and their victims of the fact that the target group does, or should, enjoy an equal legal status of the sort that entitles them to legal protections against hate speech.[76] Furthermore, when agents talk about 'illegal hate speech', this might also be a way of them delegitimising the relevant speech in the eyes of the public,[77] and of denying the authority of hate speakers, thereby blocking their ability to use such speech to perform wrongful acts like subordination, oppression, and discrimination.[78]

Compellingness: Legally minded agents may attach a legal meaning to the term 'hate speech' so as to stress that there are some particularly compelling reasons to refrain from this sort of speech precisely because it is illegal. For example, they might assume that legal sanctions against unlawful hate speech are more restrictive, severe, intrusive, or coercive than any social sanctions imposed on people who use ordinary hate speech that is not unlawful. Or they might implicitly believe that legal norms are especially compelling or have a special compliance force not reducible to people making calculations weighing the potential benefits of using illegal speech against the expected costs of doing so given the existence of legal sanctions. Of course, in reality it might not be safe to assume that legal sanctions are more restrictive than social sanctions; it depends on the specific sanctions being compared.[79] Similarly, the abstract idea that legal norms have a special compliance force might be based on a myth either because the force simply does not exist or because it is not qualitatively different to and not stronger than the compliance force of social norms in general.[80] Nevertheless, the important point here is that people who speak of 'hate speech' in the legal sense of the term may well have such ideas in mind and, whether true or false, the presence of these ideas can be another distinguishing feature of the legal concept(s) *hate speech*.

Reflexive commentary: Akin to reflexive commentary associated with the ordinary or general term 'hate speech', legally minded agents might also place the term 'hate speech' in quotations marks or use the phrase 'so-called hate speech' in order to both refer to and comment on its legal meaning. This might be commentary in the form of either endorsement or criticism of the ideas encoded in the legal meaning; but it might also be legal commentary on what the legal meaning actually is, such as to accept or challenge conventional wisdom about the content of the legal meaning or to question how others have used or applied the legal concept *hate speech*.

It is worth noting that the legal concept *hate speech* may share some of the aforementioned social functions in common with other legal concepts, but it is distinguished from these other concepts partly because it does not serve exactly the same function-types and specific instances of function-types. Take the legal concept *genocide*. This concept might also be used to convey a high threshold of harmfulness, but here the threshold is even higher still. It might also be used for signalling and, of course, sometimes for reflexive commentary. For example, in international politics even the legal term 'genocide' is subject to dispute, with countries denying the existence of a genocide that the overwhelming majority of other countries have recognised and countries proclaiming the existence of a genocide that the vast majority of other countries do not recognise. In an unfortunate new trend in international human rights discourse known as 'accusation in the mirror'[81] or simply 'mirroring', states or non-state actors will make unfounded accusations of 'genocide', 'crimes against humanity', or 'war crimes' perpetrated by their real or perceived enemies in ways that mirror genocides or crimes which they in fact have perpetrated, are in the process of perpetrating, or are inciting, all the while also denying they are engaged in any such acts, including addressing the denials to those same enemies.[82] In response, other states are forced to place the term 'genocide' in quotation marks or to use the phrase 'so-called genocide'. However, few people, although with some partial exceptions,[83] seriously argue that the correct response to cynical abuse of terminology in this field is to simply abandon the legal concepts *genocide*, *incitement to genocide*, and *genocide denial*.

5.4 On the Relationship between the Ordinary and Legal Concepts of Hate Speech

Having demonstrated how the ordinary and legal concepts of hate speech overlap but also diverge, we turn next to the issue of how they relate to, or interact with, each other. What, more precisely, is the nature of the relationship between the ordinary and legal concepts of hate speech? This question relates not merely to the concepts but also to the things that fall under the extensions of these concepts including social norms, legal norms, public attitudes, bodies of law, social sanctions, and legal sanctions. How do these things relate to each other?

One preliminary observation is that whereas the ordinary concept typically exhibits super-inclusivity and wide variation in its extension as well as a high degree of flexibility and in some contexts even constructive ambiguity in the definition of the term 'hate speech', the legal concept tends more towards exclusivity and convergence in extension and errs on the side of maximising definitional precision and clarity. At first glance, these differences paint a picture of two concepts located at opposite ends of various spectrums. Then again, the gap between the concepts might be closer in some contexts than others, depending on the purposes to which the concepts are being put in those contexts. As discussed above, the need for a significant degree of clarity and precision is shared by some uses of the ordinary concept *hate speech*, such as when organisations like universities and social media platforms specify the class of not allowed hate speech (i.e. when the ordinary concept is used to articulate a social rule).

Nevertheless, even if the preliminary observation is true as a rule of thumb, it does not in itself tell us anything about the nature of the relationship between the ordinary and legal concepts of hate speech, as in, how they relate or interact with each other.

One possible answer to the relational question is negative: that the concepts exist and operate entirely independently of each other. For example, some people may be inclined to say that the legal concept(s) *hate speech* relates to laws and legal norms which are created ab initio or independently of the existence of any social norms against hate speech. However, at first glance this answer seems implausible. To give a concrete example, Delgado and Stefancic associate university speech codes that forbid forms of discriminatory harassment on campus across the United States with the ordinary concept *hate speech* rather than with the legal concept. Furthermore, according to their interpretation of the mindset of university administrators: 'They correctly note that the social norm against hate speech is now relatively well established, even if the legal version is not.'[84] Arguably, however, the existence of university speech codes forbidding forms of discriminatory harassment on campuses is at least partly connected to the existence of federal laws relating to hostile environment discrimination in the workplace, even if the connection is one of mutual influence or even analogical justification, rather than a case of one kind of norm creating another.[85]

In fact, there is an array of different ways in which the ordinary and legal concepts of hate speech might plausibly relate to, or interact with, each other, ranging from very close relationships to weaker or more tenuous relationships, as well as from concrete to more abstract relationships and from controversial to less controversial relationships. We list some of the possibilities below, starting with closest, most concrete, and most controversial relationships, although once again we do not claim to be providing an exhaustive list.

Creation: It is certainly conceivable that the legal concept(s) *hate speech* and, specifically, legal norms and statutes prohibiting hate speech, could spark the growth of a social norm linked to the ordinary concept; or in some circumstances could even give birth to the social norm. In other words, rather than the legal concept reinforcing an extant social norm forbidding hate speech, there might be contexts in which the legal concept itself kick-starts the evolution or spread of a social norm that had hitherto only existed in nascent form; or could even help to create a social norm where no such norm had previously existed at all. In other words, it is at least a possibility that the legal concept creates the ordinary concept.[86]

For this relationship to obtain within a given country, however, it would need to be the case that, prior to the legal concept *hate speech*, there was no ordinary concept to speak of, meaning in effect that the social norm forbidding hate speech grew out of people's internalisation of the legal norm. But it is not obvious which, if any, countries exemplify this sort of relationship. In the United States, for example, it is arguable that the work of critical race theorists played an important role in highlighting to the public how group libel laws had historically been used to tackle hate speech in various states; how tort law was already being used by victims of hate speech to seek redress, and could be developed even further; how cross burning statutes afforded a chance of legal protection, if only a slim chance; and how federal laws on hostile environment discrimination might serve to safeguard workers from racist abuse.[87] But it is not clear that this sort of legal activism itself created the social norm against hate speech that became prevalent across university campuses in the 1990s.

On the contrary, the social norm seemed to emerge despite the absence of a strong legal norm.[88]

To give another example, in England and Wales hate speech laws, and specifically, the stirring up hatred offences, have evolved in a piecemeal fashion over many decades. This is partly a story of protected characteristics expansion: from the relevant offences initially covering racial hatred only, to subsequently covering religious hatred, and then sexual orientation hatred. This expansion can be explained thusly: sometimes a change in the law came about because of the government's pressing interest in tackling street violence and public disturbances; sometimes in response to highly motivated, mobilised, and persuasive lobbying groups; and sometimes simply to provide parity of protection across groups.[89] There is no evidence to suggest, however, that the evolving legal norm itself created a social norm where none had previously existed; or even that it has amplified or rapidly increased the rate of growth of a social norm forbidding hate speech. Contrast this with how car seatbelt laws significantly contributed to the creation of a widespread social norm in favour of the use of seatbelts in England and Wales.

Enactment and enforcement: An alternative story (the exact reverse of the creation story) could be that the legal concept(s) *hate speech*, and in particular laws prohibiting hate speech, enact, as in, bring within the sphere of laws and legal proceedings, pre-existing social norms linked to the ordinary concept. Moreover, legal sanctions associated with the legal concept might also improve the enforcement of the social norms. To explain, social norms are susceptible to well-known collective action and free rider problems. For example, it may be in people's interests for others to refrain from hate speaking against them but in their interest to use hate speech themselves. Hence, there is a collective action problem in getting people to refrain from using hate speech. Perhaps social norms can be enough to minimise collective action problems in close-knit social groups with high levels of mutual concern. Yet hate speech often occurs in loose-knit societies which may be deeply divided along lines of race, ethnicity, religion, and politics. Issues of fairness also emerge when a social norm forbidding hate speech is capable of producing benefits to the public even with less than full compliance, and free riders benefit from the social norm without doing their fair share in supporting that norm through their own compliance. For both reasons, social norms need to be well enforced. Social norms against hate speech may be backed up by social sanctions including, criticising, publicly shaming, stigmatising, or even boycotting hate speakers. But these sanctions might not be powerful enough to resolve collective action and free rider problems. This is where legal sanctions come in. Legal sanctions could significantly increase the costs of noncompliance with the social norms, tipping the cost-benefit calculation in favour of making compliance the rational course of action.[90] In short, the legal concept(s) *hate speech* may provide enforcement solutions to problems of noncompliance that dog the ordinary concept and its social norms.

Codification: The legal concept(s) *hate speech* and the various legal norms and laws with which it is associated may also serve to codify, formalise, and render more precise the ordinary concept *hate speech* and the various moral and social norms with which it is connected. This potential relationship between the ordinary and legal concepts may obtain in the case of national legal norms and laws relating to hate speech, such as if these legal norms and laws are in one sense just more codified, formalised, and refined versions of social norms and social rules against hate speech found within the relevant domestic societies. But this relationship might also obtain in the case of international legal norms and legal instruments, meaning that these international legal norms and laws (soft and hard) serve to codify, formalise, or refine more informal social norms that exist at the level of international society.

Grounding: Yet another possibility is that moral and social norms forbidding hate speech linked to the ordinary concept may be among various grounds of legal norms and laws connected with the legal concept. According to the legal grounding hypothesis, the relationship is a matter of legal norms and laws holding (i.e. being true) partly in virtue of the relevant moral and social norms. For example, an international legal norm or legal instrument that says states have a legal obligation to criminalise certain forms of hate speech may hold partly in virtue of a moral norm that evaluates hate speech as morally objectionable and/or a social norm that says hate speech is socially unacceptable within the community of states. In other words, if it is true that states have a legal obligation to criminalise hate speech, this truth might depend not simply on the existence of international legal texts and decisions but also on normative grounds of law including moral and social norms against hate speech. Of course, this claim about the possible grounds of law not being exhausted by legal texts and decisions ('plain facts') and potentially also including normative facts itself depends on a wider theory of the nature of law.[91]

Justification: Alternatively, moral and social norms against hate speech linked to the ordinary concept might serve to justify the adoption and enforcement of legal norms and laws against hate speech linked to the legal concept. In the case of normative justification, the relationship is a matter of moral and social norms providing pro tanto reasons or arguments in favour of the legal norms and laws (i.e. showing them to be appropriate, reasonable, or rightful). Notice, however, that even where the ordinary concept *hate speech* justifies the adoption of a particular legal concept *hate speech*, the latter does not necessarily need to be couched in identical terms to the ordinary concept. For example, appeals to the popular or general idea of preventing harmful hate speech might, when taken into consideration alongside a range of other contextual and legal factors relevant to a particular jurisdiction, justify the adoption of laws banning the use of racial slurs to verbally attack people, based on protected characteristics.

Now it is important to mention at this point that these ways of specifying the connection between the ordinary and legal concepts of hate speech can be controversial and for different reasons. For one thing, there may be no clear-cut examples of countries that exemplify these putative relationships; meaning there is reasonable disagreement about whether specific countries constitute good case studies of the hypothesised relationships.

For another thing, some people may reject on principled grounds that a given relationship between the ordinary and legal concepts could ever obtain in any country. To give an example of such blanket rejection, one prominent criticism made against hate speech laws within the legal liberalism scholarship is that all moral and social norms forbidding hate speech are essentially civility norms or else norms based on external preferences, as in, preferences people have about what others should or should not say, and that as such they cannot serve to justify hate speech laws.[92] According to this criticism, it is false to claim (as forms of legal moralism appear to claim) that hate speech laws can be justified by what are in effect relativistic and external preference norms precisely because these norms are arbitrary and ignore, in deeply illiberal ways, the ethical independence of speakers to make their own judgments about what is right or wrong speech. This sort of claim (so the criticism goes) is on a par with the debunked legal moralism of Lord Devlin, who, in his book *The Enforcement of Morals*, sought to defend the legal enforcement of social norms against homosexuality on grounds of preventing the 'disintegration' of 'established morality' and ultimately of society itself.[93] Those who level this type of criticism against hate speech laws tend to argue instead that if any laws are to rightfully or legitimately restrict freedom of expression, then they must be designed to promote liberty and equality. Laws that are potentially compatible with legal liberalism might include time, place, manner restrictions, and perhaps even laws against hostile environment discriminatory in the workplace.

Nevertheless, this type of criticism of hate speech laws is itself controversial. Perhaps it would be an exaggeration to suggest that it is merely a strawman criticism. After all, there are scholars who do defend hate speech laws precisely on grounds of the enactment of civility norms.[94] But it is also an overgeneralisation to say that every legal concept *hate speech* and associated hate speech laws are ultimately justified by appeal to civility norms alone. This is a reductionist and uncharitable interpretation. Similarly, it is oversimplistic and perhaps even disingenuous to assume that the only available legal moralism about hate speech laws is one that seeks to defend such laws simply based on satisfying people's external preferences. In fact, there are many kinds of social norms forbidding hate speech besides civility norms. An alternative story could be that hate speech laws (all being well) enact social norms that are themselves based on ideas about it being unacceptable to use speech that society deems to be harmful to victims and corrosive of social harmony, for example. Furthermore, there are several varieties of legal moralism besides the crude, relativist, and overly moralistic versions associated with Devlin. Consider the more expansive versions of legal moralism (which move beyond external preferences) defended by thinkers like Michael Moore and R. A. Duff, for instance, which can include legal enforcement against private and public wrongs of different kinds.[95] In particular, it is possible to argue that hate speech laws, national and international, can be justified if they serve credible moral visions of an ideal society based on dignity for all, security of the person, the elimination of oppression and subordination, recognition of identity, social cohesion, democracy, and political legitimacy, for example.[96]

Putting aside these controversies, we shall now outline three further ways in which the ordinary and legal concepts of hate speech could plausibly relate to, or interact with, each other. Crucially, we believe these relationships are slightly weaker, less concrete, and arguably less controversial than those outlined above. We also believe it may be easier to apply these models to a range of specific countries. Whilst we do not have space here to provide detailed case studies, our objective is to promote this sort of research agenda.

Mutual influence: Just as the ordinary concept *hate speech* may inform, shape, and influence how legal scholars, legal professionals, and lawmakers develop the legal concept(s) *hate speech*, so the legal concept(s) *hate speech* can influence the evolution of the ordinary concept. One feature of this mutual influence might be a cross-pollination of ideas, principles, perspectives, areas of application, and relevant examples. This is not to suggest that the ordinary and legal concepts of hate speech are indistinguishable and lack separate lives of their own. Quite the reverse. When Matsuda coined the term 'hate speech' she referred to a set of examples of racist speech that she believed should be subject to a legal response and pointed to a diverse set of hate speech laws already found in the United States as well as in Europe and at the international level, and she did so without mentioning any social norms forbidding hate speech in the United States at the time.[97] The term 'hate speech' subsequently appeared in the media, popular culture, political debate, and public discourse, but took on its own nonlegal meaning, what we have dubbed the ordinary concept. The ordinary concept *hate speech* has also now been adopted by most of the major social media platforms including Meta (Facebook and Instagram), Twitter, TikTok, Snap Inc., YouTube, and WeChat; some of which not only have vast numbers of users in the United States but also in Europe and other parts of the world where hate speech laws are commonplace.[98] The upshot is that even if legal institutions ceased to enforce hate speech laws going forward, the ordinary concept *hate speech* would probably persist in some form or other.[99] Indeed, the very fact that various sorts of legal institutions as well as private organisations like social media platforms are capable of drawing distinctions between unlawful and lawful hate speech presupposes some sort of ordinary concept *hate speech*. Nevertheless, it would be equally wrong to suggest that the ordinary and legal concepts of hate speech are hermetically sealed and have no influence over each other. The ordinary concept mainly reflects how both private organisations and ordinary people use the term 'hate speech' but this is likely to be influenced in turn by how legal professionals, legal scholars, legal journalists, and lawmakers use this term. Likewise, it is highly probable that over time ordinary usage of the phrase 'hate speech' has impacted the sorts of cases that courts have interpreted as hate speech cases as well as the development of laws and legal texts on hate speech including to a limited extent within the United States but more so across Europe, Latin America, Canada, Australia, parts of Africa, and internationally.[100]

Entrenchment: The legal concept(s) *hate speech*, and allied legal norms and laws prohibiting hate speech, could help to entrench social norms forbidding hate speech such as by contributing to processes by which social norms become more enforced and even internalised. When lawmakers and judges go on the record to enact, enforce, or even simply to talk about hate speech laws, this might send a message about the state's commitment not just to the relevant legal norms and laws but also to social norms against hate speech. For elected representatives to denounce illegal hate speech may be interpreted by the public as a proxy for the denunciation of hate speech in general. The public may understand enough about political realities to know that hate speech laws often get watered down so end up having only limited applicability. But the effort to legislate may be taken by some sections of society to show that many legislators implicitly support wider social norms forbidding hate speech. This in turn might boost the public's own informal efforts at enforcing these social norms through various social sanctions. In other words, when members of the public see lawmakers and judges handing down legal sanctions against illegal hate speech, this may send a signal to them to persist with or even ramp up their social sanctions against ordinary hate speech including public shaming and boycotting hate speakers even if they are not guilty of using illegal hate speech. Over time, this implicit support from public officials combined with sustained informal enforcement of social norms forbidding hate speech could lead to the internalisation of these social norms meaning they may become second nature. When this happens, people affirm the social norms without thinking and comply with them because they are social norms rather than simply because they wish to avoid social sanctions.

Setting a standard: The ordinary concept *hate speech* may also provide a standard against which the legal concept(s) could be evaluated. When people believe that the ordinary concept sets an appropriate standard, this does not commit them to the implausible claim that the legal concept(s) should simply mirror the ordinary concept. They may also think it is right for the legal concept(s) to be sensitive to other legal and human rights norms as well as various political and practical realities, which together prevent full realisation of the ordinary concept and rightly so. After all, the ordinary and legal concepts serve different purposes. Nevertheless, people who believe that the ordinary concept *hate speech* should set a standard may still believe that it is fitting for this concept either to set the ultimate goal or telos of the legal concept(s) or to provide a baseline or measure for comparative evaluations of different legal concepts, along the lines of saying that one legal concept is different to or better than another legal concept by the standard of the ordinary concept. Either way, to say that the ordinary concept should set a standard is to say something about the right direction of travel in the evolution of the legal concept(s) and in the reform and enactment of associated legal norms and laws. For example, people may associate the ordinary concept *hate speech* with group defamation and might further claim that, in an ideal world, group defamation is what hate speech laws ought to be in the business of prohibiting.[101] Instead, people may identify hate speech in the ordinary sense of the term with language that demeans, degrades, or humiliates others on the basis of their race or similar group identities. On this basis, they might argue that this ordinary understanding of what hate speech involves should provide a model for causes of action under tort law.[102] Alternatively, people may conceptualise hate speech in the ordinary sense of the term as a matter of subordination or oppression (ranking people as inferior, enacting or legitimating discrimination, depriving people of rights and opportunities). Following on from this, they might argue for the reinterpretation or even the rewriting of hate speech laws to emphasise the prohibition of speech attacks that constitute acts of subordination or oppression. They might believe that courts or human rights tribunals can, and should, be tasked with making factual determinations of whether the speaker performed an act of subordination or oppression given the circumstances of the case.[103] These possibilities reflect the heterogeneous nature of the ordinary concept.

5.5 Why It Matters

We believe getting clear about how the ordinary and legal concepts of hate speech overlap but also diverge, and about how they relate to, or interact with, each other, is an indispensable tool in improving the quality of both scholarly normative argument and public debate more broadly about the right way to tackle the problem of hate speech.

For one thing, there may be arguments relating to interests, rights, and values that are better suited as arguments in favour of legal sanctions against hate speech in the legal sense of the term; and other interests, rights, and values that are more appropriate as arguments in favour of social sanctions against hate speech in the ordinary sense of the term. Therefore, it is important to get clear about which concept of hate speech is in play when people disagree about how to tackle the problem. Such clarification may help to prevent people from talking at cross purposes, such as if one person is offering a particular set of reasons to refrain from sanctioning hate speech and has in mind legal sanctions, but the other person is actually talking about hate speech in the ordinary sense of the term and is offering very different reasons in favour of social sanctions.

Furthermore, when critically evaluating hate speech laws, including the consideration of various moral, social, and legal norms that might tell either for or against such laws, it surely makes a difference how these laws and the legal concept(s) they embody relate to, or interact with, the ordinary concept *hate speech*. In other words, one source of theoretical disagreement, although not the only source of disagreement, between people who argue in favour of and people who argue against certain hate speech laws could be how they differently conceive of the fundamental relationship between the ordinary and legal concepts of hate speech.

Consider three concrete examples of how these sorts of disagreements can take shape. First, people might disagree about whether certain types of hate speech laws can be normatively justified or warranted all things considered,[104] and part of the disagreement could be about what the relevant normative principles are or about what ought to be the correct hierarchy, balancing act, or set of compromises among these principles. For instance, one person might believe that the only normative principles that really matter are those which relate to self-realisation, autonomy, democratic legitimacy, and the prevention of imminent harm, but a second person may insist that the key normative principles are not exhausted by such values and, moreover, that other relevant values include security, human and civic dignity, recognition of identity, the elimination of subordination and oppression, and political legitimacy. Nevertheless, the theoretical disagreement might also rest on the fact that these people have different beliefs about the fundamental relationship between the ordinary and legal concepts of hate speech. For example, the second person might believe that the main purpose of hate speech laws is to enact moral and social norms linked to the ordinary concept *hate speech*. Therefore, if the ordinary concept invokes a wide range of moral and social norms, then a wide range of such norms must also be important when evaluating hate speech laws. By contrast, the first person may reject this view about enactment, and for this reason only attributes to the normative justification of hate speech laws a much narrower set of normative considerations. Similarly, insofar as the first person recognises the goal of harm prevention, he or she might set a very high bar on harmfulness, as associated with the legal concept(s) *hate speech*. The second person, by contrast, might set the bar of harmfulness slightly lower, to reflect the ordinary concept and the idea that hate speech laws should enact the ordinary concept.

Turning to the second example, one person might believe that the ordinary and legal concepts of hate speech exist and operate entirely independently of each other and appropriately so. Partly because of this isolationist view, this person might hold that the only sorts of hate speech laws that can be justified are those capable of meeting a set of extremely demanding and stringent jurisprudential principles, such as laws serving pressing government interests, being narrowly tailored to and highly effective in meeting those interests, being the least restrictive alternative, and the strict avoidance of unintended consequences.[105] By contrast, another person might insist that the ordinary concept *hate speech* sets a telos for the evolution of the legal concept and/or a standard of evaluation for actual and possible hate speech laws. As a result, this person might end up measuring hate speech laws mainly against the standard set by the ordinary concept *hate speech* but also, as consequence, partly by a set of slightly less demanding and stringent jurisprudential principles, such as laws pursuing legitimate government interests, being rationally related to those interests, being proportionately restrictive, and the reasonable avoidance of unintended consequences.

In addition to disagreements about hate speech laws, there can also be reasonable disagreements about the ordinary concept *hate speech* including the sorts of moral norms, social norms, and social sanctions that should be linked to the concept. These disagreements are a familiar fixture of public discourse concerning the rights and wrongs of social media content codes on hate speech, including specific disagreements about what content should or should not be disallowed under these codes. However, here again we believe some of these disagreements can be traced in part to theoretical disagreements about the fundamental relationship between the ordinary and legal concepts of hate speech.

Consider a third example. Suppose senior managers responsible for content policy at a major social media platform implicitly believe that the ordinary and legal concepts of hate speech should exist and operate entirely independently of each other. Applying this isolationist logic, they conclude that the platform's content codes should omit any reference to hate speech which takes the form of incitement to hatred, discrimination, and violence; or, more broadly, incitement to harm. They think such hate speech lies within the natural territory of the legal concept(s) *hate speech* and that there is nothing to be gained by their platform's content codes straying into this territory. By contrast, suppose the content policy managers at other social media platforms believe instead that the ordinary and legal concepts of hate speech are mutually influencing and appropriately so. Because they take this philosophical view about the fundamental relationship between the ordinary and legal concepts, they are minded to include within their content codes references to incitement to hatred, discrimination, and violence; or incitement to harm. They see nothing wrong in such overlap because they recognise the ways in which the ordinary concept *hate speech* both shapes and is shaped by legal norms.

Although hypothetical, the divergent content policy decisions described in this example are borne out in relevant differences between actual policies promulgated by the major social media platforms. Compare Twitter's hateful conduct policy, TikTok's community guideline on hateful behaviour, Snap Inc.'s community guideline on hate speech, and YouTube's hate speech policy, all of which contain references to either incitement, incitement to harm, or incitement to hatred, discrimination, and violence (if one includes synonyms such as 'promote'), with Meta's community standard on hate speech which contains a reference to 'content that could incite imminent violence or intimidation'. Meta has not published its rationale for this. Therefore, it is unclear whether it reflects a departure from its deeper theoretical commitment to a hard separation between the ordinary and legal concepts of hate speech. Meta's deeper theoretical commitment to a hard separation is evidenced by its public statements about the division of labour between its content moderation and legal compliance teams and on the limited role of the Oversight Board.[106] Then again, this hard separation approach is also inconsistent with the inclusion within Meta's community standard on hate speech of the specific Tier 1 rule disallowing 'Holocaust denial'. This rule overlaps with hate speech laws banning Holocaust denial found in several countries (see Chapter 7). Interestingly, Meta's own publicly expressed rationale for introducing the specific rule disallowing Holocaust denial defends the policy as being part of a wider effort to combat anti-Semitism online and offline.[107] But it makes no mention of the obvious overlap with extant Holocaust denial legislation and the fact that removing Holocaust denial content in some countries would be a matter of not merely enforcing internal content policies but also of legal compliance.

No doubt there are other ways in which theoretical disagreements about the fundamental relationship between the ordinary and legal concepts of hate speech impact reasonable disagreements about hate speech laws and social rules forbidding hate speech. However, our goal here is not to map all the different permutations and disagreements. Instead, we have tried to motivate the importance of the deeper theoretical disagreements by illustrating some of the ways in which they can matter for both scholarly and public debate.

6

Between Hate Speech and Hate Crime

6.1 Introduction

Having in the previous chapter distinguished the legal concept *hate speech* from its ordinary (nonlegal) cousin, this chapter seeks to further distinguish between two somewhat similar but also substantially separate and distinct legal concepts, namely hate speech and hate crime. The central aim of the chapter is twofold: first, to provide limited formal characterisations of these two concepts that can be used to properly distinguish them and debunk some of the misleading statements, misnomers, and incorrect assumptions about these concepts that can be found not only in public discourse but also in some scholarly work and official texts on hate speech and hate crime; second, to apply these characterisations to a set of grey area laws which might appear at first glance to be ambiguous instances of hate speech law. The disambiguation of grey area laws represents another key frontier in our understanding of the legal concept *hate speech*. The main focus will be on England and Wales, but we shall also introduce laws and legal decisions from other jurisdictions, including at both the national and international levels, most notably the European Court of Human Rights (ECtHR), insofar as they make for illuminating and striking comparisons.

Our core thesis is that, in one sense, *hate speech* and *hate crime* are partially overlapping concepts, but that the overlap only exists between hate speech in the ordinary (nonlegal) sense of the term (i.e. the ordinary concept *hate speech*) and the legal concept *hate crime*. When it comes to the legal concepts of hate speech and hate crime, by contrast, we furnish each with mirror opposite formal characterisations such that they do not overlap and are mutually exclusive in that strict sense. These are intended to be idealised but also limited or minimalist characterisations, designed to give greater conceptual clarity when formally distinguishing the concepts, rather than furnishing full and substantive definitions of each concept. Sections 6.2 and 6.3 analyse the legal concepts of hate speech and hate crime respectively. We propose that the legal concept *hate speech*, formally speaking, only refers to laws which create bespoke crimes or other sorts of offences that do not have corresponding or parallel basic or base versions, whereas the legal concept *hate crime* only refers to laws which identify aggravated crimes that do have corresponding or parallel basic or base versions. Section 6.4 makes several key comparisons and contrasts between the concepts, beyond the merely formal analysis, while Section 6.5 develops an account of why the distinction between hate speech and hate crime matters legally speaking, both for victims and defendants. Finally, Section 6.6 discusses four potential grey areas of hate speech law, namely using threatening words or behaviour to stir up hatred; incitement to commit genocide; incitement to discrimination or violence; and torts and delicts involving racist abuse. Our purpose in this section is not only to shed light on but also to resolve the ambiguity, as well as to further illustrate and stress test our analyses.

6.2 The Legal Concept Hate Speech

Hate speech in the legal sense of the term may refer to words, symbols, images, or other expressive, communicative, or performative content or behaviour that targets people based on their possession or perceived possession of protected characteristics in ways that are either currently unlawful based on the criminal, civil, human rights, civil rights, or international laws in the relevant jurisdictions or concerning which there is a pro tanto case for them being made illegal. This pro tanto case can be made by legal professionals and legal scholars but also by normative philosophers, political scientists, and, of course, politicians, stakeholder organisations, non-governmental organisations, and the public at large.[1]

Efforts to legislate against hate speech long predate the first uses of the term itself in the late 1980s.[2] It is possible to trace the genealogy of laws restricting the use of hate speech from the most recent incarnations in the second half of the twentieth century such as incitement to hatred laws in Europe and Canada, federal laws relating to hostile environment discrimination in the United States, and anti-vilification laws in Australia; further back to group defamation laws during the late nineteenth and first half of the twentieth centuries in Europe, countries under British colonial rule, and in numerous states of the United States; still further back to the English common law offence of seditious libel; and perhaps all the way back to Roman laws on group defamation.[3] Today there may be as many as ten varieties of hate speech laws.[4]

Perhaps the most common or prevalent form of hate speech laws globally are criminal laws banning people from inciting or stirring up hatred against others on grounds of protected characteristics such as race, ethnicity, nationality, religion, sexual orientation, gender, disability, and so on.[5] By contrast, laws which prohibit provoking or fermenting enmity, hostility, or hatred between *any* sections of society in a manner which poses a threat to public order or public tranquillity, without limiting this to attacking, defaming, or inciting hatred on grounds of protected characteristics, are not strictly speaking hate speech laws but instead generalised public order laws.[6]

As discussed in Chapter 6, most legal scholars, legal professionals, and lawmakers believe that the scope and meaning of the legal concept *hate speech*, and of the various legal norms, laws, legal sanctions, and legal cases to which it refers, should be narrower and more clearly defined than the scope and meaning of the term 'hate speech' when used in its ordinary (nonlegal) sense. In this chapter we focus exclusively on the legal concept *hate speech*.

We propose a limited formal characterisation of the legal concept *hate speech* comprised of the following necessary condition: that the legal concept only refers to laws which create discrete or bespoke crimes, offences, torts, or violations without corresponding or parallel basic or base versions of those crimes, offences, torts, or violations within the relevant jurisdictions (a legal-technical quality).[7] To clarify, this is intended only as a limited characterisation and not as a complete definition. On its own, this formal characterisation is obviously too broad. Other necessary and sufficient conditions would be needed to fully articulate the concept, to capture all its substantive and distinguishing features. Our aim is more modest: to distinguish the legal concepts *hate speech* and *hate crime*. Therefore, we provide only enough of a characterisation, only part of a definition as it were, to serve that specific conceptual purpose.

Furthermore, the proposed necessary condition is not saying that the legal concept *hate speech* must only refer to existing laws. Rather, it is saying that insofar as the concept does refer to laws, these laws must create discrete or bespoke crimes, and so on. The legal concept can, and often does, refer to proposed laws or to laws that ought to be in place. Consider instances where an international human rights court, such as the ECtHR, promulgates a legal judgment that member states have a duty to prosecute hate speech; or, to be more precise, a duty to provide persons with avenues of legal redress against hate speech whether by properly and without discrimination applying existing laws or by writing new laws.[8] Moreover, the legal concept *hate speech* can also refer to things besides the hate speech laws themselves, including to general legal norms against hate speech (i.e. the general legal norm that declares hate speech to be illegal or unlawful within the jurisdiction as distinct from specific hate speech laws *qua* instantiations of the norm). Indeed, first and foremost the legal concept *hate speech* refers to instances of what are, or should be, unlawful speech (both specific and general kinds of instances), where the relevant laws and legal norms ground those instances.

The necessary condition reflects an important conceptual truth about the legal concept *hate speech*: that when the concept refers to laws which contain elements relating to protected characteristics, this is not simply a matter of adding something to extant laws. Rather, hate speech laws create new crimes, offences, torts, or violations relating to the use of given forms of speech. Among the various types of hate speech laws found in European countries, for example, there are laws banning group defamation based on protected characteristics, laws banning the stirring up of hatred on grounds of protected characteristics, laws banning incitement to hatred, discrimination, or violence on grounds of protected characteristics, laws banning Holocaust denial, and laws banning the dissemination of ideas based on racial superiority.[9] Various international hate speech laws or instruments create either legal obligations or nonbinding recommendations for states to adopt these types of hate speech laws,[10] including at the level of European international law.[11] These are appropriately labelled hate speech laws partly due to the absence of extant laws banning defamation of groups in general, incitement to hatred of groups in general, denial of any crimes committed against groups, and dissemination of ideas based on group superiority in general.

To give a concrete example, under public order law in England and Wales, it is a criminal offence to use threatening, abusive, or insulting words or behaviour with the intention or likelihood of stirring up hatred against people on grounds of their race,[12] and a criminal offence to use threatening words or behaviour with the intention of stirring up hatred against people on grounds of their religion or sexual orientation.[13] Most legal scholars, legal professionals, and legislators consider these offences to be clear-cut or even paradigmatic examples of hate speech law.[14] Likewise, we propose these laws satisfy our necessary condition for applying the legal concept *hate speech*. Since it is not in itself a criminal offence in England and Wales to use words or behaviour to stir up hatred against *any* other person or group, there is no corresponding or parallel basic or base criminal offence of stirring up hatred in general.

Note, however, that even though using words or behaviour to stir up hatred against people on grounds of protected characteristics may be referred to as 'hate speech' in the legal sense of the term, this does not mean that the same conduct can also be referred to as 'hate crime'. Consider the English case *R. v. Ali, Javed, and Ahmed.*[15] In July 2010 three devout but also socially conservative members of the Muslim faith distributed leaflets on the streets of Derby titled 'Turn or Burn', 'GAY – God Abhors You', 'Death Penalty?' as a protest to the Gay Pride Festival taking place that day. The defendants became the first people in England and Wales to be successfully prosecuted for criminal offences relating to intentionally stirring up hatred against other persons on grounds of sexual orientation. In his sentencing remarks Judge Burgess articulated the law's rationale as follows.

> For the vast majority of the time the vast majority of us get along together very well, and the greatest freedom that we all enjoy is to live in peace and without fear. The law has evolved and adapted to protect that freedom. In particular, laws have been passed to prevent written material being distributed which is intended to stir up hatred. This has proved necessary because a small minority of our broad community sometimes seeks to stir up hatred against their fellow citizens merely because those fellow citizens are perceived to be different in some way.[16]

However, Judge Burgess made no reference whatsoever in his sentencing remarks to this being a 'hate crime'. This underscores the fact that just because certain forms of hate speech are punishable by criminal law, for example, does not make them hate crimes properly called. We shall seek to analyse what hate crimes are in the next section.

Moving beyond the narrow jurisdiction of England and Wales to the case law of the ECtHR, when hate speech cases come before the ECtHR, it is typically because an applicant has been found guilty by national courts of hate speech offences under national hate speech laws and complains that the conviction violated their human right to freedom of expression enshrined in Art. 10(1) of the European Convention of Human Rights (ECHR). The ECtHR often considers whether the conviction and underlying hate speech law falls under one of the justifications for limiting free speech set out in Art. 10(2) (the 'necessary in a democratic society' test[17]). In doing so, the ECtHR gives a 'margin of appreciation' to national legislatures and courts in interpreting the ECHR including Art. 10(2): which is to say, it upholds the legal doctrine that as an international human rights court it should afford to states and national courts a degree of discretion, latitude, and diversity based on country context in how they interpret human rights obligations.[18]

The immediate or direct focus of the ECtHR case law on applicants who have been found guilty by national courts of being perpetrators of hate speech is striking given the victim-focused nature of the case law on hate crimes; to be discussed in the next section. In the majority of cases involving prosecutions under domestic hate speech laws, the ECtHR has decided against the applicant (relying on the margin of appreciation doctrine),[19] but in a minority of cases it has upheld the complaint, especially, although not always, when the words in question intermix both typical forms of hate speech and content of a clearly political and/or dissenting nature.[20] That said, in some cases the applicant's case has been rejected by the ECtHR in spite of the fact that the content and context of speech was political in nature.[21] Moreover, in a smaller subset of cases involving an admixture of hate speech and political content, the ECtHR has also ruled on whether the speech in question itself violated Art. 17 ('Prohibition of abuse of rights').[22] The key issue for consideration here is whether the applicant abused the right to freedom of expression: namely, by taking advantage of the right in order to justify, promote, or perform acts that, for example, would infringe the rights and freedoms protected in the ECHR. Incitement to hatred, discrimination, or violence is a case in point.[23]

Interestingly, in *Lilliendahl v Iceland*,[24] the ECtHR itself provided an overview and reflexive analysis of its own case law on hate speech. Here the ECtHR distinguished between, on the one hand, cases dealing with 'the gravest forms of "hate speech"', which the ECtHR associated with judgments concerning not only Art. 10 but also Art. 17, and, on the other hand, cases dealing with '[the] "less grave" forms of "hate speech"', which it connected with judgments purely about Art. 10.[25]

Importantly for the current chapter, included among the cases that the ECtHR mentions in relation to 'the gravest forms of "hate speech"' is *Norwood v. the United Kingdom*.[26] That earlier case was rejected as inadmissible by the ECtHR on the twin grounds that the original conviction was not a violation of Art. 10(1) and that the speech in question was itself a violation of the human rights of others under Art. 17. Norwood had been a regional organiser in the British National Party (BNP), a far-right political party in the UK. In 2001–2 he had displayed in the first-floor window of his flat a large BNP poster showing a photograph of the Twin Towers in flames accompanied by the slogan 'Islam out of Britain – Protect the British People' as well as the Islamic symbol of a crescent and star contained within a red prohibition sign. In *Lilliendahl v Iceland*, the ECtHR cites *Norwood* as a case involving 'inciting violence and hatred or destroying the rights and freedoms protected by the Convention'[27]

However, we would argue that, at least at the level of the relevant national jurisdiction (i.e. England and Wales), the case involving Norwood was not in fact a hate speech case in the strict legal sense (or formal sense) but instead an example of an expression-oriented hate crime. In *R. v. Norwood*,[28] Norwood was convicted of a public order offence aggravated by hostility, that is, a hate crime: specifically, the offence of displaying a sign which was threatening or abusive within the sight of persons likely to be caused harassment, alarm, or distress thereby, aggravated by religious hostility.[29] The conviction was later upheld in *Norwood v. DPP*.[30] We contend that although this case clearly involved hate speech in the ordinary (nonlegal) sense of the term, it was not a case of unlawful hate speech in the formal legal sense of the term we are proposing. This is because the relevant offence was an aggravated version of a corresponding or parallel basic or base offence under public order law in England and Wales.[31] This analysis of *Norwood* as a hate crime case foreshadows our more general account of what makes something a hate crime legally speaking, and it is to this account that we now turn.

6.3 The Legal Concept Hate Crime

The term 'hate crime', or sometimes 'bias-motivated crime', is typically used to refer to the committing of an act that is in itself a crime or other sort of offence but in circumstances where the perpetrator was motivated by, or demonstrated, hostility or prejudice towards aspects of the victim's identity or perceived identity that are protected characteristics, such as race, ethnicity, nationality, religion, sexual orientation, gender, disability, and so on, as recognised in existing statutes, for example. Typically, hate crimes are contrasted with crimes motivated by, or demonstrating, other sorts of emotions and attitudes (or non-bias motives) such as greed, insecurity, annoyance, revenge, political viewpoint, sexual desire, sadism, and so on.[32]

The idea of hate crime is often associated with 'acts of violence and intimidation, usually directed towards already stigmatized and marginalized groups',[33] but the corresponding or parallel basic or base offences involved in the carrying out of hate crimes are certainly not limited to violence and intimidation. Furthermore, to speak meaningfully and coherently of hate crime in the legal sense of the term can also cover instances where there is a pro tanto case for counting the conduct as a hate crime, even in the absence of actual hate crime laws in the relevant jurisdiction.[34] As with the legal concept *hate speech*, this case can be made by a variety of actors, including, but not limited to, legal professionals, politicians, victim groups, and social movements.[35]

Like hate speech laws, the history of hate crime legislation long predates the use of the terms 'hate crime' and 'bias-motivated crime'. In the United States, for example, current sentence-enhancement laws at both state and federal levels[36] can be traced back most recently to federal legislation of the mid-1990s which required the Sentencing Commission to increase legal sanctions or penalties for federal crimes motivated by, or committed on the basis of, the victim's actual or perceived race, colour, religion, national origin, ethnicity, or gender;[37] but further back to Title I of the Civil Rights Act of 1968 which created a range of separate aggravated offences;[38] still further back to the Civil Rights Act of 1871 (the so-called Ku Klux Klan Act), which granted authorities the power to suspend people's constitutional right not to be imprisoned without a trial, as part of efforts to combat the violence and intimidation of African Americans by the Ku Klux Klan during the Reconstruction Era;[39] and perhaps even as far back as legal responses to the mistreatment of slaves.[40]

We propose a limited formal characterisation of the legal concept hate crime based on the following necessary condition (the converse of the necessary condition for hate speech): in order to count as a hate crime in a formal legal sense of the term there must be a corresponding or parallel basic or base version of the relevant offence within the relevant jurisdiction which is upgraded to a hate crime in virtue of the existence of one or more elements of hostility, hatred, contempt, prejudice, bias, or bigotry.[41]

Once again, this is a limited characterisation in the sense that it is not a full analytical definition based on a complete set of necessary and sufficient conditions. Nor does it pretend to provide a full account of all the substantive and distinguishing features of the legal concept *hate crime*.[42] Rather, it identifies what we believe is a key conceptual difference between the legal concepts *hate speech* and *hate crime*, namely that in the case of hate crime there *is* a corresponding or parallel basic or base version of the crime, which is already a criminal or civil offence even without the added element of hostility or prejudice towards the victim based on their (perceived) protected characteristic(s), but this added element upgrades the crime to make it a hate crime. For example, assault, destruction of property, harassment, theft, and threats to kill are criminal offences in almost all countries that have systems of criminal law in place. But in countries with hate crime legislation – including generic penalty-enhancements for aggravated offences or separate aggravated offences with more severe penalty ranges – these criminal offences can be prosecuted and penalised as hate crimes. Non-crimes that are also motivated by, or demonstrate, prejudice or hostility, are typically captured by the different concept *hate incident*.[43]

In England and Wales, for example, hate crime legislation comes in two main forms. The first is *penalty enhancement*. Typically, this means, other things remaining equal, judges handing down sentences towards the top end of the relevant scale of sentences or tariff for the crime if the perpetrator was motivated by, or demonstrated, hostility towards aspects of the victim's identity or perceived identity that are protected characteristics.[44] Here hostility in the relevant legal sense need only be proven at the sentencing stage. The second form is *separate aggravated offences*. These are discrete aggravated offences with higher or more severe sentence ranges compared to the corresponding or parallel basic or base criminal offences.[45] Here hostility in the relevant legal sense must be proven at the offence stage as an element of the offending. Either way, however, there does align to both these forms of hate crime some basic or base offences that do not contain the aggravated feature of hostility. We shall provide two concrete examples in a moment.

By contrast, in England and Wales there is no corresponding or parallel basic or base criminal offence of stirring up hatred against other people in general, and so the offence of stirring up hatred on grounds of a protected characteristic (currently race, religion, or sexual orientation) can qualify as hate speech but cannot count as a hate crime on our proposed formal characterisations of these legal concepts.

In countries with hate crime statutes on the books, prosecutors must put evidence before the courts that a corresponding or parallel basic or base crime was, under the circumstances, motivated by, or demonstrated, hostility or prejudice (bias) and, therefore, can and should be prosecuted and/or penalised as a hate crime. This evidence can take various different forms including the following, which is intended as an illustrative rather than a definitive list.

(i) Statements, declarations, words, symbols, or gestures used by the perpetrator at the time of the offence, whether during, shortly before or shortly after, indicating hostility or prejudice towards individuals or groups with the same protected characteristic(s) as the victim, where such words might include but are not limited to forms of hate speech in the ordinary (nonlegal) sense.[46]

(ii) Previous declarations made by the perpetrator that suggest he or she harboured hostility or prejudice towards individuals or groups with the same protected characteristic(s) as the victim.

(iii) The perpetrator's membership of organisations or political parties that espouse hostility or prejudice towards individuals or groups with the same protected characteristic(s) as the victim.
(iv) The fact that the perpetrator singled out or selected the victim when other individuals could have been targeted who did not share the victim's protected characteristic(s).
(v) The fact that the perpetrator has previously singled out or selected similar victims when other individuals could have been targeted who did not share the victim's protected characteristic(s).

Interestingly, in a 2021 report the Law Commission of England and Wales recommended changes to how the motivation limb of the legal definition of hate crimes is currently interpreted within this jurisdiction. Specifically, it has recommended that biased-motivation should be defined in a broad way to include not only feelings or emotions of hostility but also attitudes of prejudice.[47] This recommendation reflects a wider understanding in the specialist literature that hate crime is not always motivated by affective mental states such as emotions or feelings of hostility or hatred, but can instead involve more attitudinal states like prejudice or bigotry.[48] Interestingly, this mirrors analyses of hate speech which decouple this concept from affective states such as hatred or anger viewed as essential elements of the concept.[49] 'Hate speech' came into the lexicon not long after 'hate crime', but it was clear right from the start that the term 'hate' was at best misleading and at worse a misnomer in both pieces of terminology. The people who coined these terms were never wedded to the simplistic notion that something is only hate speech or a hate crime if mental states of intense dislike or hatred are in play.[50]

It is also important to bear in mind that, independently of the fact that the perpetrator's words may be evidence of a motivation or demonstration of hostility or prejudice, some hate crimes involve corresponding or parallel basic or base offences that do not in themselves have a clear, obvious, and direct expressive dimension. Take the crime of theft, which in some cases might be motivated by racial hostility, but which does not in and of itself directly involve an expressive act. Of course, there may also be an indirect and implicit way in which all hate crimes 'say' something about the low or subordinated status of victims in the minds of perpetrators and even society in general.[51] But that reflects a different and more general point about hate crime. When we say that the criminal offence of theft is not in and of itself an expressive act, we mean to characterise theft as a type of conduct more typically carried out with action than speech.

However, other basic or base offences that can be aggravated by hostility (and, therefore, classed as hate crimes) do have an expressive dimension that would seem to be important parts of the offence, meaning they are carried out or performed using utterances or other forms of expressive, communicative, or symbolic words or behaviour. We offer two examples. First, in England and Wales it can be a criminal offence to paint graffiti onto any property belonging to another person (e.g. a house) if done without lawful excuse. This falls under the basic or base offence of criminal damage.[52] The act of spraying graffiti might be said to have an expressive dimension not found in the simple act of theft, for example. In addition to this, if the graffiti itself takes the form of a racially abusive word or symbol and targets the victims because of their race or perceived race (e.g. a swastika painted onto the door of a Jewish family), then there is scope for the criminal offence to become a hate crime – for example, for the sentence to be enhanced because it was racially aggravated,[53] or for it to be prosecuted as a separate aggravated offence associated with a higher sentence tariff.[54]

Second, in England and Wales it is a basic or base criminal offence under public order law to use threatening, abusive, or insulting words or behaviour, or disorderly behaviour, or to display any writing, sign or other visible representation, which is threatening, abusive, or insulting, with intent to cause *any* person harassment, alarm, or distress and thereby causing that or another person harassment, alarm, or distress.[55] This means that verbal abuse can be an element of the basic or base offence. However, where there is evidence that the basic offence was motivated by, or demonstrated, hostility towards the victim based on possession or perceived possession of certain protected characteristics, then there is scope for the offence to become a hate crime – that is, for the sentence to be enhanced because it was aggravated by hostility,[56] or for the offence to be prosecuted as a separate racially or religiously aggravated offence of intentional harassment, alarm, or distress with a more severe sentence range.[57] Relevant evidence of hostility might include the specific sort of verbal abuse that was an element of the basic offence in the circumstances. For example, if the verbal abuse that constituted the intentional harassment, alarm, or distress took the form of a racist slur like 'nigger', for example, then the conduct may be prosecuted as a hate crime.

In a nutshell, when conduct that is in itself already a criminal offence takes the form of, or is enacted or performed using, what would generally or ordinarily be referred to as 'hate speech' in the ordinary (nonlegal) sense, then this may be taken as evidence that the basic criminal offence was aggravated by hostility. Consider the English case *R. v. Stacey*.[58] In March 2012 Liam Stacey, a third-year undergraduate and user of the Twitter internet messaging service, had spent the afternoon watching sport and drinking beer. One of the games he watched was an English Premiership football match between Bolton Wanderers and Tottenham Hotspur in which a Black player, Fabrice Muamba, collapsed on the pitch with a life-threatening heart attack. Not long after the match Stacey posted this message on Twitter, 'LOL fuck Muamba he's dead.' Several people responded angrily to the message and attempted to censure Stacey. He responded with a string of further Tweets including, 'You are a silly cunt your mother's a wog and your dad is a rapist, bonjour you scruff northern cunt.' These responses elicited a range of more strident attacks against Stacey, such as 'You must be fucking barmy if you think a greasy little welsh sheep shagger could take on a fucking cockney you silly fat wanker'. Stacey replied in kind, 'I ain't your friend you wog cunt.' 'Go and pick some cotton.' In Court Stacey pleaded guilty to the criminal offence of racially aggravated intentional harassment, alarm, or distress – a hate crime. He was sentenced to fifty-six days imprisonment. District Judge John Charles made the following remarks at sentencing.

> It was racist abuse via a social networking site instigated as a result of a vile and abhorrent comment about a young footballer who was fighting for his life. At the moment not just the footballer's family, not just the footballing world but the whole world were literally praying for his life. Your comments aggravated this situation. I have no choice but to impose an immediate custodial sentence to reflect the public outrage at what you have done.[59]

It is important, however, not to confuse the nature of this case simply because it involved racist language. This was a hate crime case, not a hate speech case in the strict legal senses of these terms. This case did not involve the offence of stirring up racial hatred, for example.[60] The judge made no reference whatsoever in his sentencing remarks to this being a case of 'hate speech punishable by criminal law'. Rather, he made clear that this was a case of conduct that was in itself punishable by criminal law but aggravated by racial hostility. In other words, the fact that the abusive language used was racist (and hate speech in the ordinary sense of the term) was used as evidence for the criminal conduct being aggravated by racial hostility rather than as evidence that the language constituted criminal hate speech in the strict legal sense.

Putting this another way, clearly what Stacey said was hate speech in the ordinary (nonlegal) sense of that term, but the key point is that the conviction in this case was for the hate crime, not for hate speech per se. The case was prosecuted as an aggravated version of a corresponding or parallel basic or base public order offence, not as the distinct offence of stirring up hatred, even though the secondary effect of the prosecution was the legal sanctioning of words that would be considered hate speech in the ordinary sense. So, even though *Stacey* was a case that involved both hate speech in the ordinary sense and a hate crime, we propose that it was not formally a case involving a violation of bespoke hate speech laws in England and Wales. That said, the correct analysis may vary in other legal jurisdictions. For example, in jurisdictions where the use of racial slurs, insults, or epithets are illegal or unlawful without a corresponding or parallel basic or base offence, that is, in jurisdictions where this type of speech is treated as unlawful hate speech in its own right, then this type of speech could count as hate speech in both the ordinary and legal senses of the term.

Notwithstanding all of these points, to broaden out the discussion, we shall now also consider the concept of hate crime within the jurisprudence of the ECtHR. Hitherto, when hate crime cases come before the ECtHR, typically the focus has been twofold: first, on whether a state or individual has committed a hate crime that constitutes a violation of the victim's human rights such as articulated in Art. 2 ('Right to life'), Art. 3 ('Prohibition of torture'), and Art. 8 ('Right to respect for private and family life') of the ECHR; and, second, on whether the applicant is correct to complain that police, prosecutors, and/or courts at the national level have failed in their human rights responsibilities to properly recognise and then competently investigate, process, and judge the case as a possible hate crime in accordance with the procedural human rights associated with Art. 13 ('Right to an effective remedy') and Art. 14 ('Prohibition of discrimination') of the ECHR.[61] Here, arguably the immediate or direct focus is on victims of hate crime and their families.

Hitherto, applicants have rarely sought and successfully received relief from the ECtHR on the grounds that they were convicted of hate crimes by domestic courts in contravention of their own human rights, such as if the hate crime convictions violated procedural rights under Art. 6 ('Right to a fair trial'), for example, or, in the case of expression-oriented hate crimes, if the convictions violated the applicant's right to freedom of expression under Art. 10 of the ECHR. One exception is the above-mentioned ECtHR case *Norwood v. United Kingdom*, which we have argued was a hate crime case under domestic law (given our formal characterisation), even if it was implicitly classified as a hate speech case both by the applicant and the ECtHR. That (irregular) classification enabled the applicant to bring a legal challenge against his conviction for a hate crime by utilising legal doctrines and customs of the ECtHR normally associated with hate speech cases. Then again, the legal challenge was ultimately unsuccessful, with the ECtHR ruling that because the speech in question constituted a violation of Art. 17 it did not enjoy the protection of Art. 10.

6.4 Key Comparisons and Contrasts

Thus far we have argued that in one sense hate speech and hate crime are partially overlapping concepts, but that the overlap only exists between hate speech in the ordinary (nonlegal) sense of the term (i.e. the ordinary concept *hate speech*) and the legal concept *hate crime*. When it comes to the legal concepts *hate speech* and *hate crime*, by contrast, we furnish each with mirror opposite formal characterisations such that they do not overlap and are mutually exclusive in that strict sense.

To be clear, however, we do not mean to suggest that unlawful hate speech and hate crime cannot coincide in the same set of circumstances or legal case. On the contrary, it is not uncommon for victims to be the subject of both unlawful hate speech and hate crime during the same period, such as if they suffer a campaign of victimisation that includes, say, an arson attack aggravated by transphobic hostility and online homophobic insult or abuse. Nevertheless, even in complex cases involving multiple offences, it remains possible to separate the two kinds of offences.

Furthermore, the distinction is not intended to show, and nor does it show, that illegal hate speech is somehow less important or less serious than hate crime from a legal point of view; or vice versa. Rather, it is intended to separate the two legal concepts for the sake of analytical clarity but ultimately to improve the accuracy, specificity, and quality of both public debate and legal analysis when one or both legal concepts are invoked.

Partly drawing on the above analyses, we are now in a position to offer ten key comparisons and contrasts between the legal concepts *hate speech* and *hate crime*. We believe these comparisons and contrasts help to debunk some of the misleading statements, misnomers, and incorrect assumptions about these concepts that can be found not only in public discourse but also in some scholarly work and official texts on hate speech and hate crime.[62]

First, the distinction between hate speech and hate crime is not identical to and not reducible to the distinction between lawful and unlawful hate speech. When someone uses unlawful or illegal hate speech this does not necessarily mean they have also committed a hate crime. In other words, the legal term 'hate crime' is not conventionally used, and is not designed to serve, as a special label for illegal hate speech, that is to say, as a term to mark the distinction between lawful and unlawful hate speech.

The legal term 'hate crime' refers to a sub-category of criminal offences that, under the circumstances of being committed, were motivated by, or demonstrated, hostility or prejudice based on protected characteristics. By contrast, the term 'hate speech', when used in the legal sense, refers to a sub-category of hate speech that either is or should be unlawful under criminal, civil, or human rights laws within the relevant jurisdiction. When the term 'hate speech' is used in its ordinary (nonlegal) sense, it refers to all forms of hate speech. Therefore, whereas all hate crime involves criminal or civil offences, the term 'hate speech' in its ordinary sense can refer to instances of lawful hate speech, meaning speech that is not prohibited by hate speech laws and unlikely to be a cause of action in civil lawsuits or in human rights proceedings *qua* unlawful hate speech. But when used in its legal sense, the term 'hate speech' does refer to unlawful or illegal conduct, such as a crime, civil wrong, or human rights violation.

Second, the distinction between hate speech and hate crime is not identical to and not reducible to a distinction between expressive and non-expressive conduct. Just as hate speech has an expressive dimension, some hate crimes can have an expressive dimension. That said, whilst hate crimes can be carried out using speech or other forms of expressive conduct, not all hate crimes are performed with such conduct. Theft, assault, and damage to property, for example, can be hate crimes, even if they involve no speech or other forms of expressive conduct. On the other hand, all hate speech, whether lawful or unlawful, is enacted or performed using speech or other forms of expressive, communicative, or symbolic words or behaviour.

Third, when conduct that is in itself already a criminal offence takes the form of, or is performed using, what may be called hate speech in the ordinary (nonlegal) sense of the term, then this usage of hate speech may be presented to courts as evidence that in the circumstances the basic offence was aggravated by hostility or prejudice, and so the case can be prosecuted as a hate crime and can attract an enhanced or more severe penalty. However, this is not the only form of relevant evidence. Furthermore, what makes such cases hate crimes is the fact that they are aggravated by hostility. The presence of hate speech in the ordinary sense of the term does not make the conduct a hate crime; it merely serves as evidence that a crime may have been aggravated by hostility, and therefore, that it may be a hate crime.[63] Furthermore, whilst it is true that some hate crimes can be committed or enacted using hate speech in the ordinary sense of the term, not all uses of hate speech constitute hate crimes.

Fourth, in order to constitute hate speech in the legal sense of the term the laws in question must create discrete or bespoke crimes, offences, torts, or violations without corresponding or parallel basic or base versions of those crimes, offences, torts, or violations within the jurisdictions. Conversely, in order to constitute a hate crime there must be a corresponding or parallel basic or base version of the offence that is upgraded to a hate crime in virtue of the presence of the element of hostility, hatred, contempt, bias, prejudice, or bigotry in the particular circumstances of conduct. That said, there is nothing stopping countries from enacting both hate speech laws and hate crime laws. This means that theoretically there could be jurisdictions in which speakers who threaten or insult persons based on their race and for reasons of their race, for example, could be charged with hate speech offences (e.g. offences of using threatening or insulting words to incite racial hatred) and/or hate crime offences (e.g. racially aggravated versions of base or basic offences of threat or insult) in the event that both kinds of laws are in place and both kinds of laws are applicable to the same circumstances.

Fifth, hate crimes require a particular sort of disjunctive *mens rea*: namely, that the perpetrator was motivated by, *or* demonstrated, bias, prejudice, or hostility. By contrast, the illegal or unlawful use of hate speech typically relies on particular forms of expressive words or behaviour that target particular groups – for example, stirring up hatred against people based on protected characteristics. In the case of illegal hate speech, typically there is no need to prove, in addition, that the perpetrator was motivated by, or demonstrated, bias, prejudice, or hostility.

Interestingly, hate speech offences are typically not treated as basic offences that can be aggravated by hostility. This point is echoed in some notable international texts on hate speech. Consider General Policy Recommendation (GPR) No. 7 promulgated by the European Commission against Racism and Intolerance (ECRI), the Council of Europe's official human rights monitoring body.[64] It recommends states enact hate crime legislation according to which 'racist motivation constitutes an aggravating circumstance' for criminal offences, but it is careful to carve out an exception for illegal hate speech: 'The law should provide that, for all criminal offences not specified in paragraphs 18 and 19, racist motivation constitutes an aggravating circumstance.'[65] We believe it is no mere coincidence that many of the criminal laws recommended in paras. 18 and 19 happen to be hate speech laws. Although GPR no. 7 does not explain the purpose of the exception, one obvious explanation is that hate speech is not the same thing as hate crime.

This approach of separating hate crime and hate speech in the provisions of European instruments is echoed in the 2008 Council of the European Union Framework Decision on combating certain forms and expressions of racism and xenophobia by means of criminal law.[66] Art. 4 declares: 'For offences other than those referred to in Articles 1 and 2, Member States shall take the necessary measures to ensure that racist and xenophobic motivation is considered an aggravating circumstance, or, alternatively that such motivation may be taken into consideration by the courts in the determination of the penalties.' Like GPR No. 7, the Articles carved out of this hate crime provision relate to forms of hate speech, specifically incitement to hatred or violence and denial of genocide and other atrocity crimes.

Sixth, both hate speech and hate crime in the legal senses of these terms share the fact that they may or may not involve intention depending on the elements of the specific offences as defined in the relevant jurisdictions. For example, some hate speech laws require proof of intention, such as intention to stir up hatred[67] or intention to promote or propagate hatred,[68] but others require instead proof of either intention or likelihood of hatred being stirred up, for example.[69] Likewise, some hate crimes (such as crimes aggravated by hostility[70]), can involve or be connected with corresponding or parallel basic or base offences which themselves require intention, such as intention to cause harassment, alarm, or distress,[71] but others are connected with corresponding or parallel basic or base offences that require only likelihood, such as likely to cause harassment, alarm, or distress,[72] or with basic or base offences that require either intention or likelihood, such as intention or likelihood that the victim will believe that immediate unlawful violence will be used against him or another by any person.[73]

Seventh, both hate speech and hate crime in the legal senses of these terms also share the fact that they may or may not involve threats to public order or public security depending on the elements of the specific offences as defined in law. For example, some hate speech laws require that the speech in question simply stirs up hatred against one section of society based on protected characteristics,[74] but other hate speech laws require a further element, namely, that the relevant incitement to hatred (or similar) poses a threat to public order or public security.[75] Similarly, some hate crimes (such as crimes aggravated by hostility[76] or crimes aggravated by prejudice[77]) can be connected with corresponding or parallel basic or base offences which themselves do not require a threat to public order or public security,[78] but others can be connected with basic or base offences which do involve such threats.[79]

Eighth, when discussing hate speech and hate crime in the legal senses it is useful to draw a distinction between harm as elements of offences and harm as part of the wider justificatory case for creating those offences in the first place. For example, criminal offences relating to incitement to hatred typically do not require evidence that targets felt fearful or threatened, that hatred was in fact stirred up, or that certain acts of discrimination or violence ensued pursuant to the speech.[80] But these sorts of effects do figure prominently in the pro tanto case for banning incitement to hatred.[81] Similarly, hate crimes that involve corresponding or parallel basic or base offences such as assault do not typically require evidence that the psychological damage done to the victim was heightened by being aggravated offences, although courts may hear victim impact statements as they might for the basic or base offences. Yet evidence surrounding the special harmfulness of hate crime is an important part of the justificatory grounds for legislating against hate crime.[82]

That said, when the tort of intentional infliction of emotional distress is used as a civil remedy against extreme racial abuse, for example, then courts do require evidence of emotional trauma or psychological damage.[83] We shall discuss in the next section whether such tortuous wrongdoing can be coherently labelled 'hate speech'.

Ninth, there is an interesting difference in how hate speech and hate crime cases have emerged in the case law of the ECtHR. Typically, albeit there are some exceptions,[84] applicants in the former cases tend to be making complaints that their convictions under national hate speech laws violated their human right to freedom of expression,[85] whilst applicants in the latter cases, again with exceptions,[86] tend to be making complaints that national legal authorities have failed in their responsibilities to properly recognise, investigate, and process suspected hate crime cases.[87] Therefore, whereas the immediate focus of the vast majority of ECtHR hate speech case law is on applicants who have been found guilty by national courts of being perpetrators of hate speech, the direct focus of most ECtHR hate crime case law is on applicants who themselves or their family members have been victims of suspected hate crime. These trends may partly reflect the dispositions of actual and potential applicants as well as the results of national cases. But they may also reflect the receptiveness, decisions, and path dependency of the ECtHR itself, as a social and political actor as well as a legal institution. The Court appears to view the pressing issues of hate speech and hate crime differently: the former as, more often than not, an issue of balancing the right to freedom of expression (Art. 10) against other human rights including the right to respect for private and family life (Art. 8);[88] the latter as essentially an issue of upholding or securing the right of victims of hate crime to a proper legal process (Art. 13 and Art. 14).[89] Of course, it might also be argued that in both instances the court is implicitly and indirectly concerned with the rights of victims as well as the rights of those found guilty of offences or those who potentially could have been found guilty if, contrary to fact, the legal proceedings had been pursued.

Finally, the case law of the ECtHR is also striking in its opening up the possibility of divergence between how it and the relevant national courts understand the very same cases, whether as hate speech cases or as hate crime cases or both.[90] We believe that in the case of such divergence, the correct classification should be seen as, by default, a matter of how the offence is or should be classified under the relevant national or domestic laws. That said, it is of course possible and appropriate for the ECtHR to judge that a national court's classification of a case was itself mistaken or in error given the laws of that particular country, or that a national court's classification itself constitutes a gross violation of human rights, such as under Art. 13, for example, whilst also taking into account the margin of appreciation doctrine.

6.5 Why It Matters

We believe clarifying the distinction between the legal concepts *hate speech* and *hate crime* is not merely an important exercise of legal explanation and interpretation as an end in itself; whether something is classified as hate speech or hate crime also matters legally speaking for the relevant parties and it matters not only for victims but also for those convicted of offences. We proffer five reasons why the distinction matters.

First, in some jurisdictions there is differential coverage of protected characteristics between hate speech and hate crime. For example, currently in England and Wales the stirring up hatred offences cover only race, religion, and sexual orientation,[91] whereas sentence-enhancement hate crime legislation covers race, religion, disability, sexual orientation, and transgender identity.[92] As a victim who is disabled, gay, or transgender, therefore, it matters in terms of the prospects for a legal remedy whether the relevant words are classified by authorities as hate speech or hate crime.

Second, in some jurisdictions there is also a significant difference in maximum sentences associated with hate speech and hate crime respectively. Sticking with the example of England and Wales, a person guilty of an offence of stirring up hatred is liable on conviction on indictment to imprisonment for a term not exceeding seven years or a fine or both,[93] but a person guilty of a separate offence of racially or religiously aggravated intentional harassment, alarm, or distress is only liable on conviction on indictment to imprisonment for a term not exceeding two years or a fine or both.[94] As a speaker, therefore, it matters in terms of extent of liability whether one's words or behaviour are classified by authorities as hate speech or hate crime.

Third, turning to judicial practice within the ECtHR, hitherto there has been significantly greater emphasis placed on the duty of authorities to prosecute crimes (including but not limited to Art. 13) in relation to cases of hate crime than to cases of illegal hate speech. Whilst some legal scholars have argued quite persuasively that this pattern is morally and legally anomalous and that recent cases involving the duty to prosecute as applied to hate speech show that the ECtHR is beginning to move in the right direction,[95] so long as judicial practice remains unbalanced in this regard, then it matters whether a case comes before the ECtHR as a hate speech case or a hate crime case. From the victim's perspective, it clearly matters if, due to judicial practice, one's case is more likely to be heard by the ECtHR if national authorities failed to properly investigate and prosecute a hate crime as compared to illegal hate speech.

Fourth, based on its own reflective analysis, so far the ECtHR has only considered and accepted arguments concerning a violation of Art. 17 in cases involving 'the gravest forms of "hate speech"'.[96] Art. 17 has not been applied to cases involving hate crime. Indeed, the ECtHR's recently published *Guide on Article 17 of the European Convention on Human Rights* contains not a single occurrence of the term 'hate crime'.[97] It is arguable that the ECtHR should apply Art. 17 to cases involving hate crimes, since hate crimes may also be manifestly inconsistent with the purpose for which people are given the right to freedom of expression, for example. However, so long as the ECtHR does not do so, it matters from the perspective of legal argumentation, as in, the weapons in the arsenal of the court when dealing with abuse of rights, whether a case is classified as involving hate speech or hate crime.

Finally, hitherto individuals have rarely sought and successfully received relief from the ECtHR on the grounds that they were convicted of hate crimes by domestic courts in contravention of their own human rights. In particular, such individuals have rarely sought and successfully obtained decisions that their convictions for hate crimes were a violation of their Art. 10 right to freedom of expression. Not so with applicants challenging their convictions for illegal hate speech. So, it certainly matters to the speaker, in terms of their chances of being heard and agreed with by the ECtHR, whether they have been convicted of a hate crime or hate speech under national legislation. Of course, some applicants have attempted to buck the trend. In *Norwood v. United Kingdom*, for example, the applicant played on the ambiguity between hate speech and hate crime to bring his case to hearing by the ECtHR: even though his case involved a conviction for hate crime under national legislation, he relied on legal doctrines of the ECtHR normally associated with its hate speech cases, namely, Art. 10. Then again, the applicant's argument was ultimately rejected by the court.

To be clear, we are not saying that the practices and decisions of the ECtHR are just re cases potentially involving Art. 10 and the differential handling of hate speech and hate crime cases. In particular, we are not arguing that states should be able to bypass Art. 10 scrutiny simply by relying on the distinction between convictions for hate crime and hate speech respectively and, ultimately, on the legal-technical issue of whether there is or is not a basic or base offence. Rather, we are simply arguing that, at the level of legal doctrine and customary practice within the ECtHR, the distinction between hate speech and hate crime does matter because it has important implications for how and whether people convicted of these crimes can and do successfully bring cases by appealing to their rights under Art. 10.

6.6 Grey Areas of Hate Speech Law

In this section we apply the above analyses of the legal concepts *hate speech* and *hate crime* to four potential grey areas of hate speech law, namely: using threatening words or behaviour to stir up hatred; incitement to commit genocide; incitement to discrimination or violence; and torts and delicts involving racist abuse. Each of these areas of law shares in common the fact that they involve forms of speech or laws that do not, at least at first sight, seem to fit neatly into the legal categories of either hate speech or hate crime.

Our purpose in this section is twofold: first, to shed light on the status of certain forms of speech and legal restrictions that might seem ambiguous, and hopefully resolve the ambiguity; second, to further illustrate but also test our earlier analyses. In particular, we wish to stress test our proposed formal characterisation of the legal concept *hate speech* and, in particular, the necessary condition articulated above.

6.6.1 *The Use of Threatening Words or Behaviour with Intent to Stir Up Hatred on Grounds of Protected Characteristics*

Earlier we cited the examples of the stirring up hatred offences in England and Wales as paradigmatic examples of hate speech laws. However, the situation may be more complicated than it first appears. The potential ambiguity stems from the fact that the legal tests or elements of the offences differ depending on which protected characteristic is involved. In the case of offences of stirring up hatred on grounds of race, the legal tests or elements of the offences include, first, that there was either intent or likelihood of stirring up hatred, and second, that the person has used 'threatening, abusive or insulting' words or behaviour. By contrast, in the case of offences of stirring up hatred on grounds of religion and sexual orientation, the legal tests or elements of the offences include, first, that there was intent of stirring up hatred, and second, that the person has used 'threatening' words or behaviour.

At first sight, both kinds of offences look like hate speech law because both satisfy the necessary condition outlined above, namely, that the legal concept only refers to laws which create discrete or bespoke crimes, offences, torts, or violations without corresponding or parallel basic or base versions of those crimes, offences, torts, or violations within the relevant jurisdictions. However, on closer analysis, the narrow focus on 'threatening' words or behaviour within the offences relating to religion and sexual orientation puts into doubt the status of these offences as hate speech laws, as opposed to hate crime provisions.

The initial triggering point for doubt, although not itself the grounds for doubt, is the fact that there is a fundamental ambiguity in the scope of the threatening words or behaviour element of the stirring up hatred offences. Threatening against whom? To which group of people must the words or behaviour be threatening? There are two main possibilities, but under both possibilities the threatening words or behaviour element could potentially raise doubts over whether the offences really are about blocking hate speech.

One possibility is that the words or behaviour must be threatening against the audience in whom hatred is being stirred up. Consider the following threatening statements addressed not to Muslims but instead to an audience of non-Muslims.

(1) You'd better come to hate Muslims or else you'll have me to answer to.
(2) You'd better come to hate Muslims or else they will overrun this country and change it forever.

Notice that (1) is threatening because it is implying that the speaker will do something bad to the audience if they do not come to hate Muslims, whereas (2) is threatening in virtue of claiming that Muslims will do something bad to the audience if they do not come to hate Muslims.

It might not be immediately obvious why the state would wish to prohibit this sort of threatening language, but on reflection there are some compelling reasons. For one thing, the state might wish to directly protect the audience whose sense of personal security might be undermined by threatening words. Indeed, the audience's autonomy might also be put at risk by threatening words, as a form of coercion or undue influence on rational judgment-formation and decision-making.[98] The danger to the audience's sense of personal security and/or autonomy might be especially great when the speaker occupies a position of authority, such as a religious leader or a political figure.[99]

However, if what matters is whether the words or behaviour are threatening against the audience, then why focus on just the use of threatening words or behaviour to stir up hatred? Why not reframe the offences in terms of the use of threatening words or behaviour to express hatred? Indeed, why not rewrite the law so that the offences concern the use of threatening words or behaviour in general? Of course, from a practical perspective, rewriting the law in this manner could make the law redundant. This is because there are already public order offences in England and Wales that cover more general ways of using threatening words or behaviour besides stirring up hatred.[100] However, and this is our central point, these public order offences are either standard offences or can be charged as hate crimes if aggravated by hostility based on protected characteristics;[101] but they are not hate speech offences.

A second possibility is that the words or behaviour must be threatening against the group against whom hatred is being stirred up. Consider once again the English case *R. v. Ali, Javed, and Ahmed*. In his sentencing remarks, Judge Burgess focused on how the threatening words contained in the leaflets being handed out by the defendants in a public place had made gay people present at the time feel threatened.

> The leaflet depicted a mannequin swinging from a hangman's noose, under the caption of 'Death Penalty?' Next to that was the information that in 1533 Buggery was punished by hanging. On the other side was text which said among other things that the only debate among classical authorities about how to punish homosexuality was the method of carrying out the execution: burning, flinging from some high place or stoning. It said that the death sentence was the only way that the immoral crime (of

> homosexuality) can be erased from corrupting society. In the course of evidence we heard what effect, reading that leaflet had upon four homosexual men. All felt threatened.[102]

However, one immediate problem with the threatening words or behaviour element of the offences is that in many real-life instances of in-person stirring up hatred, the direct audience (i.e., the people directly receiving the words or spatio-temporarily present for the words) does not include members of the target group. Speech delivered by leaders of the British National Party (BNP) in England are a case in point. They typically hire out public houses or large halls for the purposes of hosting members of the Party, and where non-members are not invited and not allowed to attend.[103] Therefore, in one sense *R. v. Ali, Javed, and Ahmed* was an unusual or outlier case because the ultimate targets of the threatening words (homosexuals) happened to be members of the audience (the public). Often the stirring up of hatred is directly addressed to people who are not members of the target group. In which case, how can words be threatening if members of the target group are not around to feel threatened?

To help sharpen the point, consider two hypothetical examples of threatening speech addressed to audiences in person, where the speaker has absolutely no intention or expectation that Muslims would be in attendance.

(3) You think you can trust Muslims, think again, they are vile, backward, and dangerous people who deserve only our hatred, and when the good and reasonable people of this country are finally united in their hatred of this radical element in their midst, then Muslims had better watch out!

(4) Surely you can see that these Muslims don't belong here. Be honest, don't you think that they are like rats or cockroaches. And what would you do if you found pests or vermin in your house? That's right, you would call in pest control to exterminate them. I want us to do the same for Muslims.

Notice that (3) and (4) are threatening because they imply that the speaker, the audience, and society in general will do something bad to Muslims. Even so, if Muslims are not in attendance, then the immediate danger cannot be one of Muslims feeling directly threatened or intimidated by the words.

Notwithstanding these points, there is some evidence to suggest that courts in England and Wales typically apply a plain language or ordinary meaning standard to public order offences, including the stirring up hatred offences. According to this standard, unless the law or context otherwise requires, words in a statute must be given their ordinary meanings. The upshot is that in practice whether or not an utterance qualifies as 'threatening' depends on the legal test of whether a reasonable person would find it threatening and, importantly, the reasonable person test can be applied whether or not anyone who actually heard or read the words in fact found them to be threatening. In the case of the stirring up hatred offences, the test might take the form of asking whether a reasonable person would find the words or behaviour to be threatening against members of the target group.[104] This version of the test might be especially useful in circumstances where it is uncertain both who was in the audience and whether anyone actually felt threatened. Threatening words or behaviour conveyed via the Internet are obvious examples.

Arguably, there are at least two pressing dangers being addressed by the government in legislating against these sorts of statements. First, there is the threat to public order in the shape of disturbances of the peace, riots, or street violence indirectly caused by this sort of speech.[105] Second, there are the ways in which the stirring up feelings or attitudes of hatred, contempt, resentment, fear, and anxiety in audiences can contribute to a climate of hatred and in which there is an increased risk of acts of discrimination and violence against the targeted group.[106] There may well be other dangers, of course, but we shall not attempt to list them all here.[107]

However, even if the second possibility is correct, and the words or behaviour must be threatening against the group against whom hatred is being stirred up, then this element of the offence still remains ineffective, unmotivated, and potentially redundant. For one thing, adding the threatening words or behaviour element raises the threshold and creates a loophole, enabling criminals to avoid prosecution simply by assiduously avoiding using threatening words or behaviour.[108]

Furthermore, whilst threatening words and behaviour are commonly used to intimidate or spread fear in minority groups, it is more typical for hate groups in England, including far-right groups like the BNP, Britain First, or the English Defence League (EDL), to use a range of different forms of speech, whether offline or online, to stir up hatred against minority groups. This includes threatening words but also abusive or insulting words, negative stereotypes, hate propaganda, group defamation in the strict sense, Holocaust denial, and false rumours and disinformation.[109] Moreover, there is no evidence to suggest that threatening words are more likely than other words to succeed in stirring up hatred. Indeed, if the real goal is to block language that is the most effective at stirring up hatred, then why not cast the stirring up hatred offences in terms of the use of 'lies', 'propaganda', 'persuasive rhetoric', 'undue influence', 'indoctrination', 'radicalising' or 'grooming' to stir up hatred?

Perhaps the legislative purpose of the threatening words or behaviour element is to provide an additional, higher threshold for the sake of protecting free speech. But at least in the case of the offences of stirring up hatred on grounds of religion and sexual orientation, this is already protected in the relevant statutes with bespoke freedom of expression provisos.[110] Therefore, restricting the offences still further with the threatening words or behaviour element is redundant. Likewise, if in the future the stirring up hatred offences were expanded to cover other protected characteristics, then further freedom of expression provisos could be devised that make it unnecessary to have the high threshold.[111]

Alternatively, it could be that the real focus of the threatening words or behaviour element is to protect the targeted groups from being directly threatened or being made to feel threatened. Perhaps this feeds into wider concerns about a climate of fear in which minority groups live with a sense of physical insecurity,[112] and what effect this climate of fear might have in terms of people feeling safe to go out in public life and having the confidence, because not fearing physical attack, to contribute to public discourse and formation of democratic public opinion.[113]

However, if that is the real focus, then why include the stirring up hatred part of the offence? Why not rewrite the law so that the offences cover, for example, the use of threatening, intimidating, or menacing words or behaviour against people based on protected characteristics, with intent or likelihood of causing people to feel threatened, intimidated, or fearful? Once again, the answer is that if the laws were rewritten in this way, they could be redundant. This is because there are already sentencing provisions (hate crimes) in England and Wales that are capable of being applied to the use of threatening, intimidating, or menacing words or behaviour against people based on protected characteristics.[114] And these provisions concern hate crimes, not hate speech offences.

Putting these points together, the narrow focus on threatening words or behaviour within the stirring up hatred offences relating to religion and sexual orientation has the potential to put into doubt the status of these offences as hate speech laws, as opposed to hate crime provisions. Or, to be more precise, when the narrow focus on threatening words or behaviour is carried to its logical conclusion, it points in the direction of rewriting the relevant laws so as to create offences that look far more similar to hate crimes than to hate speech offences.

However, we believe these offences in the current versions are properly classified as hate speech offences. In other words, we advocate separating the issue of the classification of offences as either hate speech offences or hate crimes, on the one hand, from the issue of the evaluation of the offences as being badly drafted, on the other hand. It is possible that the inclusion of the threatening words or behaviour element makes the offences ineffective, unmotivated, illogical, incoherent, and even redundant. But simply being badly drafted does not turn hate speech offences into hate crimes. We believe the stirring up hatred offences in England and Wales remain bona fide hate speech offences partly because they create discrete or bespoke crimes without corresponding or parallel basic or base versions of those crimes.

Notably, in its 2021 report on extending and reforming the stirring up hatred offences, the Law Commission of England and Wales recommended both the inclusion of sex or gender and disability as protected characteristics and the standardisation of the legal tests or elements of the offences across the different protected characteristics.[115] Whilst not rendered explicit in the report, arguably the implied rationale for the reforms concerned issues of consistency, parity of protection, and impartiality (i.e., a lack of a valid reason to differentiate the legal tests or elements of the offences).[116] More specifically, the Report contains the following recommendation.

> We recommend that there be a single test applying to all forms of hatred. Under this test a person would be guilty of stirring up hatred if they used words or behaviour intended to stir up relevant hatred; or used threatening or abusive words or behaviour likely to stir up relevant hatred.[117]

We believe that this recommendation, if accepted by the government and ultimately by parliament, would go a long way to resolving the ambiguities we have highlighted, making the stirring up hatred offences even clearer instances of hate speech laws. There are no corresponding or parallel basic or base offences of using words or behaviour intended to stir up hatred against any group; or of using threatening or abusive words or behaviour likely to stir up hatred against any group. These would be bespoke laws.

6.6.2 *Incitement to Commit Genocide*

Is incitement to commit genocide a form of hate speech in the legal sense of the term? The answer to this question is more ambiguous than at first it might appear. Although there are at least some positive reasons to believe that it is hate speech, there are also other reasons to draw the negative conclusion. We begin by listing the positive reasons.

First, consider once again our proposed formal characterisation of the legal concept *hate speech* comprised of the following necessary condition: that the legal concept only refers to hate speech laws which create discrete or bespoke crimes, offences, torts, or violations without corresponding or parallel basic or base versions of those crimes, offences, torts, or violations within the relevant jurisdictions. We believe incitement to genocide satisfies this necessary condition. Incitement of genocide relates to 'direct and public incitement' to 'acts committed with intent to destroy, in whole or in part, a national, ethnic, racial or religious group, as such', as defined by the Genocide Convention 1948[118] and the Rome Statute of the International Criminal Court 1998.[119] There is no corresponding or parallel basic or base crime under international law of direct and public incitement to acts committed with intent to destroy, in whole or in part, *any* group as such.[120]

Of course, we have suggested a necessary condition for applying the legal concept *hate speech*, not a sufficient condition. Even if laws create discrete or bespoke crimes, this does not guarantee that they are hate speech laws or fall under the legal concept *hate speech*. A law could create an independent crime without a corresponding basic version of the crime but still fail to qualify as a hate speech law. Nevertheless, there are other reasons to classify incitement to genocide as hate speech in the legal sense of the term.

Second, incitement to genocide is both an expressive or communicative speech act and an act of incitement – qualities which it has in common with other forms of hate speech which are considered paradigmatic examples of illegal hate speech in many countries and recognised as such by international law, most notably, incitement to hatred, discrimination, and violence.[121] Of course, the fact that offences have an expressive or communicative dimension does not automatically mean they are hate speech offences. After all, as indicated earlier in the chapter, many hate crime offences have an expressive or communicative dimension. But it is another reason that adds to the credibility of classifying incitement to genocide as hate speech.

Third, just as incitement to hatred, discrimination, and violence are typically inchoate offences under national hate speech laws and recognised as such by international law, so incitement to genocide is an inchoate crime under international law, meaning the international crime of incitement to genocide can be considered to have been committed even if the substantive offence (genocide) which it is seeking to commission is not actually completed.[122]

Finally, incitement to genocide is conventionally regarded as hate speech in the literature. For example, in her seminal article 'Public Response to Racist Speech' Matsuda writes:

> The need to limit racist hate messages is implicit in basic human rights documents [...]. The United States is [...] a party to an international convention on genocide that forbids, inter alia, incitement to genocide.[123]

Likewise, international tribunals on genocide and legal scholars of those tribunals have recognised incitement to genocide as a particular form of hate speech or, more specifically, as 'the most egregious form of hate speech'.[124]

However, there are also some reasons that might tell against classifying incitement to genocide as hate speech. First, incitement to genocide is not listed as a form of hate speech in the defining international legal texts on hate speech including the International Convention on the Elimination of Racial Discrimination (ICERD)[125] and the International Covenant on Civil and Political Rights (ICCPR).[126] Nor is it listed in subsequent key texts relating to action plans for the realisation of the ICERD and ICCPR.[127] These international hate speech instruments instead focus on the following forms of hate speech: dissemination of ideas based on racial superiority or hatred; incitement to discrimination or violence against any race or group of persons of another colour or ethnic origin; advocacy of national, racial or religious hatred that constitutes incitement to discrimination, hostility, or violence.

Second, incitement to genocide instead appears in international laws surrounding the international crime of genocide. For example, in the Genocide Convention 1948 incitement to genocide is listed as a discrete crime alongside the crime of genocide itself. Fifty years later, the Rome Statute of the International Criminal Court 1998 specified incitement to genocide not as a separate crime from genocide itself but as part of the international crime of genocide, as in, one mode of participation in genocide for which individuals can be held criminally accountable.[128] Either way, in these documents incitement to genocide is either an international crime or a mode of criminal participation in an international crime under international law. Conversely, neither the Genocide Convention nor the Rome Statue mention or establish any sort of international crime of using the forms of hate speech listed in the ICERD and ICCPR.

More generally, even using these forms of hate speech is not, strictly speaking, an international crime under international hate speech instruments like ICERD and ICCPR. Rather, these instruments establish that states have obligations under international law to criminalise certain forms of hate speech at the national level. Likewise, international human rights committees and human rights courts have powers under international law (treaties, conventions) to consider if states have acted in ways (and this typically means the decisions reached by superior courts at the national level) that violate not only international norms and standards relating to hate speech but also the human right to freedom of expression in cases involving alleged hate speech under national hate speech laws.[129] These committees and courts rule on state violations of the relevant intentional norms and standards. Typically, they do not hand down verdicts on whether states or, for that matter, individual citizens, have themselves committed something approximating an international crime of using hate speech.

However, we believe the balance of evidence still suggests that incitement to genocide is rightly classified as hate speech in the legal sense of the term. From the mere fact that incitement to genocide is also recognised as an international crime whereas using other forms of hate speech is not in itself an international crime under international law, it does not automatically follow that incitement to genocide does not count as hate speech. The legal concepts *hate speech* and *international crimes* are not mutually exclusive. That something falls under one of these concepts does not preclude it from simultaneously falling under the other concept. Indeed, we believe it is true of incitement to genocide that it is both hate speech in the legal sense of the term and an international crime. Part of what makes it fall under both these legal concepts is the fact that its perpetrators can be subject to legal sanctions.

6.6.3 *Incitement to Discrimination or Violence on Grounds of Protected Characteristics*

However, what of incitement to violence or discrimination on grounds of protected characteristics? Is this hate speech in the legal sense of the term? Once again, it might seem obvious at first sight that it should qualify as hate speech, but there is room for ambiguity.

Starting with reasons to classify it as hate speech, the first good reason stems from the fact that incitement to discrimination or violence on grounds of certain protected characteristics is listed as a form of hate speech in the defining international legal texts on hate speech including the ICERD and ICCPR. In fact, virtually all other notable international hate speech instruments at both international and regional levels also count incitement to discrimination or violence on grounds of protected characteristics as hate speech.[130]

Second, among legal scholars, this sort of incitement to discrimination or violence is frequently cited as a paradigmatic example of hate speech in the legal sense of the term, meaning it figures in numerous definitions of the term 'hate speech' provided by legal scholars as descriptions or interpretations of a range of actual hate speech laws, domestic and international.[131] Matsuda, for example, points to the ICERD as one of the key international texts defining the legal concepts *hate propaganda* and *hate speech*.[132]

Nevertheless, there might still be room for ambiguity. Consider once again our proposal to define, in a limited way, the formal legal concept *hate speech* in terms of the following necessary condition: the formal legal concept only refers to laws which create discrete or bespoke crimes, offences, torts, or violations without corresponding or parallel basic or base versions of those crimes, offences, torts, or violations within the relevant jurisdictions. Under international hate speech instruments, when a state fails to prosecute incitement to discrimination or violence on grounds of protected characteristics, typically this is treated as a discrete violation without a corresponding or parallel basic or base version of the violation.[133] The relevant texts and decisions typically do not refer to, nor implicitly rely on, a generalised obligation on states to prosecute incitement to discrimination or violence against any groups regardless of protected characteristics, concerning which failures to meet the obligation might be deemed violations. So, this satisfies the necessary condition. But what about at the level of national hate speech laws? Take the case of Israel. Here, s. 144B of the penal code (as amended in 1986[134]) specifies an offence of incitement to racism: '(a) If a person publishes anything in order to incite to racism, then he is liable to five years imprisonment. (b) For the purposes of this section, it does not matter whether the publication did cause racism, and whether or not it is true.'[135] Moreover, s. 144A defines 'racism' to mean 'persecution, humiliation, degradation, a display of enmity, hostility or violence, or causing violence against a public or parts of the population, all because of their color, racial affiliation or national ethnic origin'.[136] At first glance, this offence may not satisfy the proposed necessary condition since there does appear to exist a corresponding or parallel basic or base version of the offence. After all, the penal code (as amended in 2002[137]) also contains s. 144D2(a) which specifies an offence of incitement to violence or terror: 'If a person publishes a call to commit an act of violence or terror, or praise, words of approval, encouragement, support or identification with an act of violence or terror (in this section: inciting publication) and if – because of the inciting publication's contents and the circumstances under which it was made public – there is a real possibility that it will result in acts of violence or terror, then he is liable to five years imprisonment.'[138] In other words, if ss. 144A and 144B create an offence of incitement to racism and, more specifically, incitement to racial violence, then s. 144D2(a) appears to provide the corresponding or parallel basic or base version of the offence, namely, incitement to violence or terror. Based on the proposed formal characterisation of hate speech, this would disqualify ss. 144A and 144B as being hate speech law.

However, on closer examination, the two offences contain important differences such that it is not credible to hold that s. 144D2(a) provides a basic version of the offence set out in ss. 144A and 144B. For example, the offence of incitement to racism, and more specifically, incitement to racist violence, does not include as an element of the offence that 'there is a real possibility that it will lead to a violent act', whereas the offence of incitement to violence or terror includes precisely that element. In this way, the offence of incitement to racist violence is a paradigmatic inchoate offence, whereas the offence of incitement to violence or terror adds a higher threshold. Moreover, the offence of incitement to racism is disjunctive in the sense that it covers various forms of racism including but not limited to violence, whereas the offence of incitement to violence or terror is disjunctive in relation to forms of violence or terror. This also makes the offences quite different, thereby making the latter not a basic version of the former. On the strength of such differences,[139] we conclude that the offence of incitement to racism does satisfy the proposed necessary condition after all and, therefore, could be labelled a hate speech offence under our formal characterisation of hate speech in the legal sense of the term.

Of course, Israel is only one country. Nevertheless, we believe its hate speech offences are not unusual or unique. Our working hypothesis is that other countries which also criminalise, in some form or other, incitement to hatred, discrimination, or violence on grounds of protected characteristics, similarly do not have on the books corresponding or parallel basic or base versions of the same offences that are almost identical save for not requiring the incitement to relate to protected characteristics.

Nevertheless, what about laws which prohibit inciting others to commit crimes, for example? Surely these sorts of criminal offences share similarities with laws prohibiting incitement to hatred, discrimination, or violence based on protected characteristics? However, on closer examination, such laws are highly unlikely to be identical to the relevant hate speech offences, based on distinctive nuances in the elements of the latter. Take the case of South Africa. Here, s. 16(2)(c) of the South African Bill of Rights makes clear that the right to freedom of expression does not extend to 'advocacy of hatred that is based on race, ethnicity, gender or religion, and that constitutes incitement to cause harm'. Similarly, s. 10(1)(b) of the Promotion of Equality and Prevention of Unfair Discrimination Act 2000 (PEPUDA) prohibits 'hate speech' in the form of words based on one or more protected characteristics 'that could be reasonably construed to demonstrate a clear intention to' 'be harmful or to incite harm'. (It should also be noted, however, that s. 10 of PEPUDA was declared unconstitutionally overbroad by the Constitutional Court in *Qwelane v South African Human Rights Commission and Another* [2021] ZACC 22.) But there is no corresponding or parallel basic or base offence in South Africa of using words with intent to be harmful or to incite harm generally, as in, to incite harm against any persons regardless of their characteristics. The common law offence of incitement to commit crime, for example, is far narrower than simply using words to be harmful or to incite harm.[140] Likewise, the offence of incitement to cause public violence, codified in s. 17 of the Riotous Assemblies Act No. 17 of 1956, is far more narrowly tailored than simply inciting harm: 'A person shall be deemed to have committed the common law offence of incitement to public violence if, in any place whatever, he has acted or conducted himself in such a manner, or has spoken or published such words, that it might reasonably be expected that the natural and probable consequences of his act, conduct, speech or publication would, under the circumstances, be the commission of public violence by members of the public generally or by persons in whose presence the act or conduct took place or to whom the speech or publication was addressed.'

Of course, South Africa is just one example. So, clearly there is a need for a comprehensive investigation looking at a range of countries that have both laws banning incitement to violence or discrimination on grounds of protected characteristics and general laws (common law or statues) prohibiting incitement. However, our working hypothesis is that the two sets of laws will always be sufficiently dissimilar to disqualify the latter as being corresponding or parallel basic or base offences related to the former. In countries where the hypothesis is confirmed, laws banning incitement to violence or discrimination on grounds of protected characteristics would meet our proposed test and could be considered hate speech laws in the strict sense. As with all idealised formal characterisations, however, there could exist outlier countries. But provided that the vast majority of countries confirm the working hypothesis, the proposed conceptualisation would retain its analytical power we believe.

6.6.4 *Torts and Delicts Used as Legal Remedies against the Use of Hate Speech*

The final grey area of hate speech in the legal sense of the term relates to countries in which certain torts or delicts can be, and sometimes are, used to provide civil redress to victims of hate speech. Two examples include the South African delict of injuria and the US tort of intentional infliction of emotional distress. There have been cases in both countries of plaintiffs successfully suing defendants for wrongdoing (torts, delicts) involving extreme verbal attacks containing racial slurs and other terms of racist abuse, for example.[141] Can such cases be labelled 'hate speech' cases?

Once again, we intend to answer this question by referring back to the proposed formal characterisation of hate speech, namely the necessary condition that the legal concept only refers to laws which create discrete or bespoke crimes, offences, torts, or violations without corresponding or parallel basic or base versions of those crimes, offences, torts, or violations. This we hope serves the twin purposes of evaluating if these really are ambiguous cases of hate speech and testing the credibility of the proposed formal characterisation.

At first glance, it might appear as though civil cases involving extreme racist abuse (or similar abuse based on other protected characteristics) do not satisfy the necessary condition owing to the existence of a corresponding or parallel basic or base version of the wrongdoing. In the United States, for example, s. 46(1) comment (d) of The Restatement of Torts (Second) states that the tort of intentional infliction of emotional distress 'does not extend to mere insults, indignities, threats, annoyances, petty oppressions, or other trivialities' but only to 'extreme and outrageous conduct'.[142] Similarly, in South Africa common law standards have been built up around the delict of injuria as it relates to cases of abusive speech. In *Brenner v. Botha*,[143] for example, Judge Boshoff held that '[i]n cases of verbal injury, otherwise than in cases of defamation, the words complained of must impair the plaintiff's dignity and must be insulting in the sense that they must amount to degrading, humiliating or ignominious treatment'.[144] This suggests that there are corresponding or parallel basic or base versions of the relevant wrongdoing which make no mention of protected characteristics. Therefore, based on our characterisation, it would seem as if cases where these torts or delicts are applied to extreme racist abuse are not hate speech cases. Potentially this is a counter-intuitive conclusion that puts a question mark over the characterisation.

However, we would argue that the situation is more complex than this. Essentially what is happening here is that courts are applying a common law tort (the tort of intentional infliction of emotional distress) or common law delict (injuria) to specific circumstances, and sometimes these circumstances involve extreme racist abuse (or similar). These torts or delicts are not in themselves hate speech laws strictly speaking; instead, they are civil remedies that can be used to redress the use of extreme racist abuse (or similar) based on a combination of court discretion and legal precedent.[145] Nevertheless, it is important to draw a distinction between, on the one hand, a tort or delict in its general form and, on the other hand, particular instantiations of a tort or delict, as in, specific tortuous or delictuous wrongdoings. When courts rule that specific uses of extreme racist abuse (or similar) qualify as specific tortuous or delictuous wrongdoings, the speech which has been judged to be wrongful can still qualify as hate speech in the legal sense of term even if the relevant tort or delict in its general form is not a hate speech law strictly speaking.

What, more exactly, qualifies the verbal attacks in question as hate speech in the legal sense of the term? First, the verbal attacks may involve racial slurs, epithets, insults, vilification, or other terms of racist abuse (or similar) which legal scholars conventionally recognise as hate speech.[146]

Second, the verbal attacks are made against people based on characteristics like race, which are generally regarded as protected in other parts of the legal system in the relevant country, including within hate speech law, civil rights law, and even the constitution itself.

Third, when the verbal attacks are interpreted by civil courts as rising to the level of extreme and outrageous conduct (tort of intentional infliction of emotional distress) or degrading, humiliating, or ignominious treatment (delict of injuria), then the speech is subject to forms of legal sanction, in particular, the defendant's liability to pay damages, potentially compensatory damages and punitive damages.

Fourth, the verbal attacks may involve speech that closely mirror forms of hate speech recognised as such by dedicated hate speech laws in the relevant country and/or by international hate speech instruments (conventions, declarations, reports, recommendations). In South Africa, for example, another part of PEPUDA, namely s. 10(1)(a), prohibits 'hate speech' in the form of words based on one or more protected characteristics 'that could be reasonably construed to demonstrate a clear intention to' 'be hurtful'. It is not difficult to see how racist abuse could be analogised to hurtful words. Turning to international hate speech instruments, whilst key texts on hate speech promulgated by the African Union and by the United Nations tend to focus on the element of incitement, other notable international texts have a wider understanding of hate speech as a legal concept. In the Americas, for example, the Inter-American Commission on Human Rights has recognised in its reports the problem of racist 'insults' and 'abuse' suffered by people of African descent in the Americas.[147] In the context of Europe, ECRI has recognised as hate speech the public use of 'insults' and 'vilification' (defined as 'abusive criticism') against people based on protected characteristics.[148] It has recommended that states criminalise such forms of hate speech.[149] It has also further recommended that states 'provide support for those targeted by hate speech both individually and collectively' *inter alia* by ensuring that 'they are aware of their rights to redress through administrative, civil and criminal proceedings'.[150]

Finally, shifting the focus to specific instantiations of the tort or delict, that is, specific tortuous or delictuous wrongdoings, makes it possible to see how they can satisfy our necessary condition and, therefore, could be counted as hate speech. The key point is that personal abuse or insults of a general nature which are not related to protected characteristics are unlikely to be recognised by civil courts as rising to the level of tortuous or delictuous wrongdoing because, in and of itself, the use of personal abuse or insults is unlikely to viewed by civil courts as extreme and outrageous conduct (US) or degrading, humiliating or ignominious treatment (South Africa). The upshot is that if personal abuse or insults of a general nature are not instantiations of the tort or delict, then they cannot be corresponding or parallel basic or base versions of those specific instantiations that do relate to racist abuse. This in turn means that the specific instantiations of the tort or delict that relate to extreme racist abuse (or similar) are discrete and bespoke hate speech wrongdoings and, therefore, satisfy the proposed necessary condition. Of course, drawing a wider conclusion relies on our ability to generalise from the cases of the United States and South Africa to other countries. But so long as the preponderance of countries show similar patterns of legal interpretation of the relevant torts and delicts, the proposed test will deliver intuitive results.

7

Denialist Speech

7.1 Introduction

In this chapter we address another grey area of the legal concept *hate speech*: Holocaust denial, genocide denial, and, more broadly, denial of atrocity crimes. Denialism provisions have a precarious position in the wider body of hate speech laws – politically, normatively, doctrinally, and conceptually. We seek to understand the nature and causes of that precarious position, both current and historic. And we ask this question: What is the right categorisation of denialist speech – an instance of existing types of illegal hate speech, a sui generis form of hate speech, or instead an entirely separate category of expressive phenomenon?

When mapping this hate speech frontier, we confront two major fault lines. One is the existence of markedly differing legal approaches to combating denialist speech at the domestic level, including whether it is tackled using existing hate speech laws or with bespoke denialism laws. The American political scientist Erik Bleich argues that denialism laws are 'a relatively recent development aimed at countering a specific form of hate speech' but also that such laws are 'not necessarily embedded in incitement to hatred provisions' and are 'only tangentially motivated by a desire to fight hate', and also that these laws 'have not been enacted or upheld equally across countries' and that the spread of these laws 'has been partial and subject to reversals'.[1] However, there is another way of looking at it: that the spread of denialism laws has not been limited to Western Europe, for example; that despite some reversals, the spread of these laws has not ceased; that there have been many successful prosecutions of deniers over a prolonged period of time despite the fact that denialism laws are 'not necessarily embedded in incitement to hatred provisions'; and that even though denialism laws have not always themselves incorporated incitement to hatred as elements of the offences, this does not in itself demonstrate that denialism laws are 'only tangentially motivated by a desire to fight hate'. Indeed, it seems more accurate to say that denialism laws have developed in a piecemeal yet nevertheless inexorable way, and exhibit significant variety, and this is all because such measures serve a plurality of different functions and purposes, including but not limited to preventing the stirring up of hatred.

A second major fault line is divergence between domestic and international law on denialist speech. The spike in the enactment of domestic laws banning Holocaust denial in Europe during the 1990s, for example, stands in marked contrast to the absence of provisions dedicated to combating the problem of Holocaust denial in the early landmark international laws dealing with incitement to genocide and hate speech in general, during the period from the end of World War II through to the late 1990s. The International Convention on the Elimination of all Forms of Racial Discrimination (ICERD),[2] for example, was a keystone international law against hate speech both because it is now widely recognised as such by judges and legal scholars alike and because it was given precisely this status by Mari Matsuda in her seminal article on the legal concept *hate speech*.[3] And yet the issue of denialism is not directly and explicitly addressed in either in the ICERD itself or in the travaux préparatoires, suggesting it was simply not on the radar. The situation has changed considerably since the late 1990s, of course, and denialism provisions are now a common fixture of international law. But this still begs the question of whether denialist speech can be aptly classified as hate speech in the legal sense of the term when some of the defining international instruments suggest otherwise.

Nevertheless, this chapter argues that denialist speech can, and should, be classified as a sui generis form of hate speech in the legal sense of the term. Our argument is grounded not only in the minimalist formal characterisation of the legal concept *hate speech* proposed in Chapter 6 but also in our interpretation of current national and international hate speech law. The rest of the chapter is structured as follows. Section 7.2 looks at the many faces of denialist speech, including forms of synchronous denialism that are often overlooked in these debates (something that may partly explain the absence of denialism provisions in the landmark international laws). Section 7.3 directly addresses the thorny problem of whether denialist speech is best seen as hate speech or an entirely sperate category of expressive phenomenon. In doing so we consult our minimalist formal characterisation, certain key decisions by human rights courts and human rights committees, and the scholarly literature. Section 7.4 explains why the issue of correct classification matters and points to several conceptual and practical legal consequences that raise the stakes. In Sections 7.5 and 7.6 we turn to examine in more detail the spread of denialism laws at the domestic level and try to uncover the many different functions or purposes served by such laws. We argue that getting clear about the plurality of purposes in fact strengthens rather than weakens the cause for classifying denialist speech as hate speech in the legal sense of the term. Finally, in Section 7.7 we tackle head on and attempt to neutralise two sceptical challenges to our main thesis. First, if denialist speech is rightly classifiable as hate speech, then why were denialism provisions absent from the early landmark international laws dealing with incitement to genocide and hate speech in general? And second, if denialist speech can be considered hate speech despite its absence from landmark international laws, then what about other things, such as defamation of religion, and what prevents our characterisation of hate speech in the legal sense from becoming absurdly capacious? We argue that the various reasons which explain the absence in no way preclude denialist speech from being classified as a sui generis form of hate speech, and, moreover, that the slippery slope envisaged in the second challenge fails to materialise since there are powerful reasons to say that defamation of religion is not part of the consensus international legal norm against hate speech.

7.2 The Many Faces of Denialist Speech, Old and New

Holocaust denial lulled during the 1950s, at a time when Nazi war crime trials were ceasing outside of Germany and international attention was focused on the Cold War.[4] However, Holocaust denial ramped up in the 1960s, persisted in the 1970s, rumbled on throughout the 1980s and 1990s, amid the *Historikerstreit* ('historians' dispute'[5]), accelerated during 2000s and 2010s, with the help of the global Internet, Web 1.0 and Web 2.0, and against the backdrop of the Israeli–Palestinian conflict, a surge in post-truth politics, a rise in conspiracy culture across the board, and the mainstreaming of right-wing extremist ideology, and reignited again in parallel with the *Historikerstreit 2.0* ('the Catechism debate'[6]) of 2021.[7]

However, it would be quite wrong to suggest that Holocaust denial originated in the 1960s. On the contrary, denialism existed synchronistically with the Holocaust itself. For example, in 1943, Heinrich Himmler gave a speech to SS Generals at Poznan in which he said: 'It should be discussed amongst us, and yet, nevertheless, *we will never speak about it in public.* […] I am talking about the "Jewish evacuation": the extermination of the Jewish people.'[8] To give another example, in 1944, in response to pressure from the Danish government, the Germans allowed the Red Cross to enter Theresienstadt concentration camp in what is now the

Czech Republic. They were shown happy, healthy residents who lived in comfortable barracks and enjoyed a wealth of amenities including gardens, a swimming pool, and cultural events. Theresienstadt was, according to the Germans, a spa town where elderly Jews could retire in safety. But it was an elaborate lie designed to undermine claims of a genocide. The camp had been substantially altered for the visit, adding facilities, improving buildings, and reducing overcrowding. The truth was that an estimated 33,000 people died at Theresienstadt and 70,000 were deported to death camps.[9] As a final example, between November 1945 and October 1946, the International Military Tribunal at Nuremberg tried 24 defendants for war crimes associated with the Holocaust, all of whom pleaded not guilty.[10] Mixed in with the 'superior orders defence' (the Nuremberg defence), were various denials or outright lies about what the defendants had seen and done.[11] For example, senior managers working for the German chemical and pharmaceutical company IG Farben who had visited the Monowitz concentration camp in German-occupied Poland (also known as Auschwitz III) testified that they had seen 'nothing out of the ordinary'; that 'the inmates were well-fed, well-clothed, and under no particularly tight discipline'; and that the site of the IG Farben factory 'had not been chosen in order to exploit Auschwitz's ready labour pool'.[12] In reality, 10,000 concentration camp prisoners lost their lives as a result of working for IG Farben,[13] not to mention the estimated 1.1 million people killed across the combined Auschwitz camp complex, including nearly 1 million Jews.[14]

These examples demonstrate that, whilst people might typically think of Holocaust denial as the questioning, trivialisation, distortion, or outright denial of historical events decades after the fact, denialist speech occurred both during and shortly after the Holocaust itself.[15] Indeed, the Himmler speech shows that denialism was as much a policy of the Nazis as the extermination of the Jewish people itself. Moreover, denialist speech helped make the continuation of that extermination possible. It is partly what enabled Allied leaders to justify not intervening sooner. Denialism was also used as propaganda tool aimed at encouraging Jews to allow themselves to be transported to their deaths in an orderly fashion.

Even though the Holocaust itself was a unique historical event, the synchronous denial of core international crimes has become a familiar mode of denialist speech. No sooner had the crime of genocide, crimes against humanity, war crimes, and the crime of aggression been established under the Rome Statute of the International Criminal Court (created in 1998 and in force from 2002) than it became standard operating practice within the field of military and state propaganda for perpetrators to deny their perpetration of atrocity crimes at the very moment of perpetration. Doing so is designed in part to make it harder for the international community to justify intervention.

Yet if denialist speech typically occurs not only after the event but can be synchronous with the perpetration of genocide and other core international crimes – and even perhaps an essential part of genocide itself, as Gregory H. Stanton has argued[16] – this begs the following important but hitherto unexplored questions. Given that denialist speech has existed for as long as the acts being denied have existed, why have denialism provisions only relatively recently been cemented in the structure of international laws against incitement to genocide and hate speech in general? Relevant international laws (hard and soft) from the 2000s through to the 2020s containing denialism provisions include the Council of the European Union Framework Decision on combating certain forms and expressions of racism and xenophobia by means of criminal law (Council Framework Decision),[17] the Council of Europe Additional Protocol to the Convention on Cybercrime concerning the criminalisation of acts of a racist and xenophobic nature committed through computer systems (Additional Protocol),[18] the Recommendation of the Committee of Ministers to member States on combating hate speech (Recommendation),[19] as well as several UN General Assembly resolutions and other international conclusions on Holocaust remembrance and denial.[20] Why were denialism provisions not part of the early landmark international laws dealing with incitement to genocide and hate speech? Relevant charters, conventions, and statutes dating from the end of World War II through to the end of the 1990s that omit denialism provisions include the Charter of the International Military Tribunal (Charter),[21] the Convention on the Prevention and Punishment of the Crime of Genocide (Genocide Convention),[22] the International Convention on the Elimination of All Forms of Racial Discrimination (ICERD),[23] the International Convention on Civil and Political Rights (ICCPR),[24] and the Rome Statute of the International Criminal Court (Rome Statute).[25] Finally, do the reasons that explain the omission of denialism provisions in these landmark international laws suggest that denialist speech should be treated, in a conceptual-legal sense, as a separate category of speech rather than a sui generis form of hate speech?

Before directly addressing these questions in Section 7.7, however, it is important firstly to recognise the many different forms Holocaust denial takes. The terms 'Holocaust denial', 'genocide denial', 'distortion', 'denialism', 'negationism', and 'revisionism' are sometimes used interchangeably but can also convey distinct ideas. For example, whereas 'negationism' and 'revisionism' can suggest the idea of rejecting or rewriting narratives about the past, 'denialism' might speak to the broader notion of 'being in denial' and so can also look to the present. Then again, the different connotations are not hard and fast and may differ depending on the speaker, receiver, and context. Moreover, there are competing accounts among scholars about what these terms ought to mean, as in, what interpretations of their meanings would best serve the point and purpose of using these terms in the first place. So, for example, some scholars define the term 'Holocaust denier' such that to qualify as a denier a person must be not simply in error but have an anti-Semitic agenda, namely denial of the Holocaust combined with an intention to convey the idea that Jews are evil and deceptive, with the ultimate goal of reinforcing and spreading the very anti-Semitism that produced the Holocaust.[26] This stipulative approach paves the way not merely for denialism to be semantically differentiated from serious, yet 'inaccurate',[27] historical research but also for denialism to be viewed as a form of hate speech in the legal sense of the term[28] and, moreover, as something for which there is a strong pro tanto case for prohibition.[29]

At any rate, what is relatively uncontroversial is that collectively these terms cover a wide portfolio of speech phenomena.[30] In fact, we suggest there are at least eight different kinds of Holocaust denial relevant to our discussion – most of which are replicatable to greater or lesser extents in denialism about other atrocity crimes besides the Holocaust.

(i) Bare/coldblooded/outright: The claim that the Holocaust simply did not happen and denial of key historical facts associated with it (such as relating to the gas chambers, the six million Jews murdered, the number of Jews either executed or gassed relative to the numbers of deaths from other causes such as disease or military action, the number of Jews sent to and conditions within the concentration camps, and Nazis' statistics on, and plans for, the Jewish population at different stages).[31]

(ii) Partial/revisionist: Acceptance that certain historical events occurred but combined with denial that the events in fact constituted a genocide as defined by international standards or some other authoritative standard (including the claim that the mass killings of Jews did not amount to intentional destruction of the Jewish people, or the claim that the mass killings of Jews was based not on their Jewishness as such but rather because many Jews played the role of usuries, a profession which marks people out as targets of anger and resentment); or acceptance that certain historical events occurred and that they constituted genocide but denial that a particular individual, state, or its people had anything to do with it.[32]

(iii) Elaborate/hotblooded/hardcore: The claim that not only did the Holocaust not happen but that the Jewish people have been actively involved in fabricating stories or spreading lies about the so-called Holocaust and, moreover, that Jews have an ulterior motive or malicious intent to lie about what really happened in World War II having to do with acquiring international support, public sympathy, wealth, power, and territory.[33]

(iv) Evaluative/apologist/glorificatory: The claim that the Holocaust did not happen combined with an articulation of personal identification with, sympathy for, or approval of the alleged perpetrators of it, including depicting alleged perpetrators as the real victims; the self-contradictory claim that the Jews did not suffer a genocide but also deserved their fate; and the counterfactual claim that the Holocaust did not happen but that if a genocide of the Jews did happen or were to happen in the future, that would be a good thing.

(v) Softcore/selective: The claim that there must be something rotten about Holocaust orthodoxy given that adherents to the orthodoxy are so fearful of other perspectives that they adopt memory laws to silence dissent; misrepresenting or exaggerating certain facts about the Holocaust in a way that provides source material or ammunition for hardcore deniers; deflecting ultimate guilt or responsibility for the Holocaust onto other states or actors besides the perpetrators themselves; minimising, trivialising, or normalising the nature, scale, or effects of the Holocaust on the Jewish people such as by claiming that the events of the Holocaust were entirely typical of massive state reconstruction or on a par with countless other historical events; dismissing the importance of the Holocaust by claiming that Jews should 'stop going on about it' just as current generations of Germans should cease apologising for it; belittling Jewish people who find Holocaust denial confronting or offensive by implying they are of limited intelligence or emotionally unstable.[34]

(vi) Synchronous/contemporaneous: Members of the Nazis regime denying that the Holocaust is happening whilst at the same time carrying it out (including denials of the mass killing of Jews, concentration camps, gas chambers, and the plan to exterminate the Jewish people).

(vii) Deflecting/denialism in the mirror: A state accusing other states of being engaged in core international crimes and in the denial of those crimes, whilst at the same time in fact being engaged in their own perpetration and denial of the same or similar crimes.

(viii) Complex/performative/atrocity-oriented: A state or non-state actor using the denial of genocide or other atrocity crimes as a tool to incite hatred, discrimination, violence, or genocide against an entire group or class of people, or in a manner capable of disturbing peace and security, or in order to cloak, normalise, justify, or excuse its ongoing or planned acts of genocide or other atrocities against an entire group or class of people.[35]

No doubt much more could be said and debated in relation to each of these different kinds of denialist speech, such as whether the kinds are mutually exclusive, how far each kind stretches, whether the list is exhaustive, and how relatable or generalisable these kinds are to examples other than Holocaust denial.[36] But rather than get lost in the weeds of these debates, we shall try to focus on the following core question. Is the legal term 'hate speech' rightly applicable to denialist speech and, if so, is it more applicable to some forms than others?[37] In the next section we search for what we believe are some initially plausible answers to that core question. Then, in Section 7.4, we explain why the question matters.

7.3 Classifying Denialist Speech as Hate Speech

Now in one sense it might seem quite straightforward to say that denialist speech is hate speech. After all, *if* the term 'hate speech' simply means *any* form of expression that attacks a group of persons who are historically victimised, oppressed, subordinated, or systematically disadvantaged, then Holocaust denial, for example, almost automatically falls under that definition.[38] However, this is an unsatisfactory definition of hate speech in the legal sense of the term, even though it might serve some of the aims associated with the ordinary concept (see Chapters 2–5). For the question 'Is Holocaust denial hate speech in the legal sense of the term?' to be meaningful and answers to it illuminating, it is crucial to begin with a characterisation of the latter which is much less vague and more narrowly framed.

Whilst in Chapter 5 we offered an ontological description of the legal concept *hate speech* as being bound up with legal norms, laws, and legal sanctions, in Chapter 6 we proposed a minimalist formal characterisation of that concept, according to which it only refers to legal norms or laws which support or create bespoke crimes or civil wrongs that do not have corresponding or parallel basic or base versions. Arguably, denialism laws satisfy that criterion: whilst criminal justice systems around the world include the special offence of perjury (lying under oath), there is no corresponding or parallel basic or base law prohibiting people from denying the fact of crimes in general.

This is a good start, but can we say something a bit more substantial? Now it might be tempting at this stage to assume that the legal concept *hate speech* only relates to hard laws (legally binding treaties, conventions, and protocols), prohibitionist laws (laws which prohibit or call for the prohibition of specified conduct), and criminal laws (laws that impose criminal sanctions on unlawful conduct). However, this assumption is not borne out by how the concept is in fact used and understood around the world, both in domestic and international law. Some legal norms against hate speech are instantiated through soft laws (resolutions, conclusions, recommendations, and standards), non-prohibitionist laws (laws that call on states to combat certain activities short of legally prohibiting them), and civil remedies (laws that provide means of redress and resolution between agents and which impose civil sanctions against the losing party). Once again, denialism laws do meet this threshold since, like hate speech laws, they can take various forms including hard and soft laws, prohibitionist and non-prohibitionist laws, and criminal and civil laws.

Instead, we believe it makes more sense to return to canonical texts on hate speech. Importantly, Holocaust denial was cited by Mari Matsuda as a paradigmatic type of hate speech in her landmark article on the legal concept.[39] Given the influence of that article on subsequent discourse, it is perhaps no surprise that Holocaust denial has remained associated with the legal concept as well as the ordinary concept ever since its publication.[40] Even focusing on the legal concept, however, the nature of this association is more complex than it may first appear. For one thing, it seems to be a fixed point of legal as well as ordinary meanings of the term 'hate speech' that it refers to speech targeting persons or groups or classes of persons based on protected characteristics such as (a non-exhaustive list) race, ethnicity, nationality, religion, and sexual orientation.[41] At first glance, this criterion is satisfied by Holocaust denial and genocide denial in general: such speech targets people based on protected characteristics at the very least in the indirect sense that the events being denied targeted people based on protected characteristics. For example, the International Holocaust Remembrance Alliance (IHRA), founded by the Swedish Prime Minister Göran Persson in 1998, defines the Holocaust as 'the Nazi programme to murder all European Jews during the Second World War'.[42] Similarly, Art. 2 of the Genocide Convention defines 'genocide' to mean specific acts 'committed with intent to destroy, in whole or in part, a national, ethnical, racial or religious group'. But what about denial of other atrocity crimes including crimes against humanity, war crimes, crimes against peace? Insofar as not all atrocity crimes stipulate that the victims must have been targeted based on protected characteristics,[43] this suggests that the relevant forms of denialist speech may not indirectly target people based on protected characteristics and, therefore, the status of such denialism as hate speech looks in doubt. However, much depends on the particular type of denialism law at issue. As we shall explain in Section 7.5, some denialism laws create qualified offences according to which denialist speech is an offence only if it is performed in the manner of specific acts (e.g. inciting hatred or threatening) and only if those acts directly target people based on named protected characteristics. Furthermore, it might be plausible to read denialism laws that establish unqualified offences of bare denial, including denying genocide and denying crimes against humanity, as essentially creating a new protected category, namely victims of atrocities. Interestingly, some social media platforms include within the list of protected characteristics they associate with the ordinary concept hate speech not only things like race, ethnicity, nationality, and veteran status but also status as victims of violence.[44]

A further complication stems from the fact that domestic and international laws on Holocaust and genocide denial rarely explicit refer to such phenomena as 'hate speech'. Of course, this may be partly explained by the fact that most domestic laws, and many international laws, that are routinely classified as hate speech laws by legal scholars likewise do not contain the term 'hate speech'. Indeed, when Matsuda and other critical race theorists started to use the term 'hate speech' (as a new addition to a lexicon that already included 'group defamation' and 'hate propaganda') it was to a large extent 'for the purposes of classifying and making generalisations about a particular group of laws'[45] – laws that did not contain the term. The neologism was intended to be explanatory rather than a carbon copy of those laws.

That said, if scholarly usage of the term 'hate speech' has in turn influenced the vocabulary of legal professionals and found its way into the language of several laws, case decisions, and international instruments on hate speech,[46] the degree of uptake of the term has tended to be lower within denialism law than hate speech law in general. Consider the UN General Assembly resolutions on Holocaust remembrance and denial. The Holocaust Remembrance Resolution of 1 November 2005 'Rejects any denial of the Holocaust as an historical event, either in full or part' yet omits to classify Holocaust denial as hate speech and fails to say anything that might imply such an association.[47] Even though the Holocaust Denial Resolution of 26 January 2007 does not explicitly state that Holocaust denial is a form of hate speech, it at least characterises the harms of denialism in such a way as to suggest overlap.[48] Likewise, the Holocaust Denial Resolution of 25 January 2022 does not say Holocaust denial is hate speech but does contain a general description of Holocaust denial as expressing anti-Semitism which strongly implies it could be.[49]

Communications of the UN Human Rights Committee, the monitoring body of the ICCPR, that touch on possible associations between the ideas of genocide denial and hate speech are similarly mixed. In *Faurisson v. France*,[50] for example, the Committee upheld a conviction for Holocaust denial but the decision contains not a single instance of the term 'hate speech'. This omission is probably best explained by the date of the case, 1993, only a few years since the coinage of the term by critical race theorists. Yet the ruling does contain usage of precursor terminology, specifically, 'incitement to racial hatred' and 'advocacy of national, racial or religious hatred that constitutes incitement to discrimination, hostility or violence', borrowing directly from the language of French domestic law[51] and Art. 20(2) of the ICCPR, a landmark international hate speech instrument. In 2011, however, the Committee overruled *Faurisson* via General Comment No. 34, finding that any restriction of genocide denial must comply with both Art. 19 and 20 of the ICCPR and that Art. 19 'does not permit general prohibition of expressions of an erroneous opinion or an incorrect interpretation of past events.'[52] The Comment contains not a single occurrence of the terms 'hate speech', 'incitement to hatred', or 'advocacy of national, racial or religious hatred'. At the time, Michael O'Flaherty, the author of the Comment, published a scholarly defence of the overruling of *Faurisson*, but the article similarly fails to clearly recognise or label denialist speech as 'hate speech'. Instead, it merely describes all criminal laws banning hate speech as part of a 'catastrophic' catalogue of 'threats' to freedom of expression and recommends 'non-criminal strategies to combat hate speech'.[53]

If O'Flaherty's article testifies to an ideological approach to the legal concepts *genocide denial* and *hate speech* bordering on the summarily dismissive, other international texts on the subject strike a more considered tone. For example, a combined UN and UNESCO report on Holocaust denial from 2022 states that '[n]ot all forms of Holocaust distortion constitute hate speech as defined by international standards' whilst at the same time implying that some forms of Holocaust distortion do reach this threshold.[54] Even so, it is noticeable that other recent UN resolutions on hate speech still omit to declare Holocaust denial a form of hate speech, despite listing various other recognised forms of hate speech.[55]

At the European level, however, there is a more stable practice of classifying genocide denial as racist or xenophobic content or, more generally, hate speech. For example, the Council Framework Decision and Additional Protocol to the Convention on Cybercrime are keystone European instruments on combatting racist and xenophobic content and both contain provisions calling on states to criminalise genocide denial.[56] (Indeed, these instruments build on the earlier but now obsolete Council of the European Union Joint Action concerning action to combat racism and xenophobia,[57] which also contains a denialism provision.[58]) Likewise, the Recommendation of the Committee of Ministers to member States on combating hate speech (2022) explicitly lists denial of atrocity crimes as a criminalisable form of 'hate speech'.[59] Similarly, the European Commission Against Racism and Intolerance (ECRI), the Council of Europe's human rights monitoring body, has promulgated a series of General Policy Recommendations (GPRs) touching on hate speech and genocide denial. Whilst not directly using the term 'hate speech', GPR No. 7 (2002, revised 2017) nevertheless recommends the criminalisation of various designated forms of hate speech, and in the very same paragraph recommends the identical approach for genocide denial as well.[60] Moreover, GPR No. 9 (2004, revised 2021) lists Holocaust denial as an example of 'hate speech'.[61] GPR No. 15 (2015) goes one step further in explicitly '[r]ecognising that hate speech may take the form of the public denial, trivialisation, justification or condonation of crimes of genocide, crimes against humanity or war crimes'.[62]

For its part, the European Court of Human Rights (ECtHR) has been using the term 'hate speech' in its legal judgments dealing with domestic hate speech laws for over twenty years[63] and this usage has found its way into some of its denialism case law. In *Behar and Gutman v. Bulgaria*,[64] for example, the ECtHR found that Bulgaria had violated the procedural rights of targets of Holocaust denial and other anti-Semitic content by failing to prosecute the speakers and, moreover, in its judgment the ECtHR explicitly uses the terms 'hate speech' and 'stir up hatred' to characterise Holocaust denial narratives and to support its decision.[65] In *Fatullayev v. Azerbaijan*,[66] by contrast, the ECtHR found in favour of a convicted genocide denier, but even here the ECtHR consciously assessed the case at least partly based on whether the circumstances rendered the words 'hate speech' as a recognised category of speech regulations deemed by the ECtHR as 'necessary in a democratic society' under its international legal norm against hate speech.[67] Likewise, in *Perinçek v. Switzerland*,[68] the ECtHR assessed the validity of a conviction for genocide denial by explicitly considering a range of relevant international and European hate speech instruments as well as the case law of the ECtHR dealing with domestic hate speech laws. That said, the ECtHR has not always handled denialism cases explicitly under a hate speech rubric. In other cases, the ECtHR has concluded that the convictions of Holocaust deniers were indeed valid under Arts. 10(2) and 17 of the European Convention on Human Rights (signed in 1950 and effective since 1953) but the decisions themselves contain no clear assertion that the denial was a form of 'hate speech' or constituted 'the stirring up of hatred' and omit assessment of landmark international and European hate speech instruments.[69]

To sum up all of the above, we see not merely terminological variations but profound conceptual-legal uncertainties about how to understand the connection between the legal concepts *genocide denial* and *hate speech.* Unsurprisingly, these variations and uncertainties are echoed in much of the academic literature on the subject. Some legal scholars simply assume that denialist speech is hate speech without pausing to offer a full characterisation of what hate speech actually is and without a proper explanation as to why denialist speech plausibly counts as hate speech. For example, Frederick Schauer's primary interest lies in investigating whether or not, based on the weighing up of the various expected epistemic and non-epistemic harms, there is an all things considered moral and legal case for banning given forms of hate speech, including Holocaust denial, whilst keeping in mind the fact that such denialism is not exceptional but simply an instance of a broader category of speech, public falsehoods. The basic idea or assumption that Holocaust denial is hate speech is something Schauer seems willing to grant without any real scrutiny for the sake of that wider investigation.[70]

By contrast, other scholars are more directly interested in providing illuminating and compelling characterisations of hate speech in the legal sense of the term. Based on these general characterisations, it would seem to follow that Holocaust denial is hate speech in their view. For example, Matsuda offers three identifying characteristics of hate speech: '1. The message is of racial inferiority; 2. The message is directed against a historically oppressed group; and 3. The message is persecutorial, hateful, and degrading.'[71] She goes on to discuss Holocaust denial with the clear implication that it possesses these characteristics.[72]

In addition to this, some scholars include within their general definitions of hate speech explicit reference to Holocaust denial as being something which 'fits into [the] category' of hate speech,[73] 'come[s] under the broad umbrella of hate speech offences',[74] 'is a form of hate speech',[75] or 'is a *sui generis* type of hate speech'[76] – all because of what hate speech is and what Holocaust denial is. Notice, however, that if one highlights empirical aspects of Holocaust denial that lift it into the category of hate speech, then one also needs to provide evidence of the relevant aspects. Cohen-Almagor, for example, claims that 'Holocaust denial is a form of hate speech because it wilfully promotes enmity against an identifiable group based on ethnicity and religion.'[77] Yet it is far from certain that all instances of Holocaust denial necessarily involve wilful promotion of enmity against an identifiable group. This generalisation stands in need of support from a sufficient number of robust social scientific studies of the phenomenon in question. Moreover, even if the generalisation holds true for a large majority of actual instances of Holocaust denial, that still leaves open the question of what to say and do, legally speaking, about the minority of instances where the generalisation fails.

Of course, one could seek instead to defend the statement 'Holocaust denial is a form of hate speech' on purely stipulative grounds: that is, by simply defining the meanings of the relevant terms in such a way as to make the statement true *a priori*. However, this stipulative approach has the undesirable consequence of turning an apparently informative statement like 'Holocaust denial is a form of hate speech' into an analytic statement such as 'bachelors are unmarried men' which, although true by virtue of the meanings of its terms, is empirically uninformative. Furthermore, the approach might blur important conceptual boundaries between the legal term 'Holocaust denial' and the broader legal term 'hate speech'. It is perhaps also worth noting here that similar problems emerge when looking at the relationship between the ordinary (as opposed to legal) meanings of the terms 'Holocaust denial' and 'hate speech'.[78]

Partly reflecting these issues, some scholars argue instead that instances of Holocaust denial *could potentially* be classified as hate speech in the legal sense of the term depending on whether the denial is being used to say or do things which themselves constitute illegal hate speech. In the words of Caroline Fournet and Clotilde Pégorier: 'Where denial is used not only to reduce survivors, witnesses and/or researchers to liars but also to rehabilitate and support former genocidal regimes, there appears to be reasonable ground to consider it as possibly falling within the category of hate speech, here understood as "incitement to hatred or discrimination against persons because they belong to a certain group".'[79]

Other scholars, by contrast, sound a note of caution about whether Holocaust denial could be treated as illegal hate speech given the relevant legal tests. Writing about racial vilification laws in Australia, for example, Dan Meagher observes that 'the relevant test under the [Racial Discrimination Act 1975] is to ask whether the impugned conduct is reasonably likely in all the circumstances to offend, insult, humiliate or intimidate a person or group on account of their race'.[80] Based on this, Meagher suggests it is 'possible that instances of history denial may not in all the circumstances offend this objective harm threshold for its racist message will elude all (including the "reasonable victim") but the relevantly specialised historian.'[81] Other scholars have expressed similar misgivings about the applicability of the public order offence of stirring up racial hatred, in place in England and Wales, to certain types of Holocaust denial. The offence only applies to words or behaviour that are 'threatening, abusive or insulting',[82] but, according to Geoffrey Bindman, 'Holocaust denial literature usually avoids this' and 'deliberately seeks credibility by using mild, pseudo-scientific language'.[83] Another key element of the offence is that the speaker 'intends thereby to stir up racial hatred' or 'having regard to all the circumstances racial hatred is likely to be stirred up thereby'. However, in the words of Jonathan Cooper and Adrian Marshall Williams, '[t]he more level-headed the recipient or the more apparently innocuous the literature, the more difficult it will be to show either of these'.[84]

We shall critically examine whether these misgivings are actually borne out in the relevant case law in Section 7.5. However, in the meantime, it seems safe to say there are at least dangers lurking behind classifying denialist speech as hate speech in a qualified way. On the one hand, if denialist speech only rises to the level of illegal hate speech when the circumstances in which it is expressed are such as to constitute by that expression some sort of illegal hate speech conduct, then potentially the threshold will very often not be reached. In that event, classifying denialist speech as illegal hate speech in a qualified way could prove too little: that it is only rarely illegal hate speech. On the other hand, the fact that certain forms of denialist speech can qualify as illegal hate speech under certain circumstances could yet make enacting bespoke denialism laws seem redundant. This is because classifying denialist speech as illegal hate speech even in a qualified way might prove too much: that because denialist speech can rise to the level of illegal hate speech in at least some circumstances, perhaps legislators and the public at large could end up assuming there is no pressing need to enact bespoke denialism laws. Of course, there still might be symbolic reasons to have in place not merely a general offence of stirring up racial hatred, for example, but also a separate offence of stirring up racial hatred by means of Holocaust or genocide denial. The offence might also attract a different (higher?) punishment. Even so, some people may find this consequence problematic because they believe that, as a general principle protecting the right to freedom of expression, it is illegitimate to punish speech for purely symbolic reasons.

Reflecting on all this, we submit denialist speech poses the following trilemma for legislators and judges. First, they could opt to classify denialist speech under the umbrella of already recognised forms of hate speech, such as racial vilification or incitement to hatred, discrimination, and violence. They could then punish deniers either by using existing hate speech laws or by creating separate denialism offences which also make racial vilification or incitement to hatred, discrimination, and violence, say, elements of the offences. But if they take this route, then they reach beyond the ordinary meaning of terms like 'Holocaust denial', gloss over reasonable disagreements about the true purpose of denialism laws, and could render such laws redundant given the applicability of existence of hate speech laws. Second, they could classify denialist speech as a sui generis form of hate speech and draft bespoke laws that utilise the ordinary meaning of terms like 'Holocaust denial' and/or create an unqualified offence of bare denialism. But if they did that, then they must not only identify compelling aims or purposes for such laws but also demonstrate how the laws serve those purposes. It might not be enough to rely on purposes associated with hate speech laws in general, such as the goal of preventing incitement to hatred, discrimination, or violence. After all, an unqualified offence of bare denialism could end up being applied in cases where the denial did not actually involve any such incitement, and the law would be overbroad in the sense of sweeping up more speech than the intended purpose of the law can justify. Third, they could classify denialist speech as a separate category of speech altogether, and not a form of illegal hate speech. But if they did that, then it could make it more difficult to justify making denialist speech a punishable offence. Call this the denialism trilemma.

Fortunately, we think there is a plausible way to escape this trilemma. The solution works by improving and bringing into better alignment understanding of both the classification of denialism laws (as hate speech) and the aims or purposes served by denialism laws. Our solution is to classify denialist speech as a sui generis form of hate speech in the legal sense of the term and to justify the enactment and enforcement of bespoke denialism laws on the basis that such laws serve a plurality of different aims and purposes. Potentially this means there can be a strong pro tanto reason to prohibit denialist speech but without falling prey to the redundancy problem and at the same time also minimising the danger of sweeping up more speech than the aims or purposes of denialism laws can justify. In Section 7.5 we offer a snapshot of current denialism laws around the world and in Section 7.6 spell out what we believe are the plurality of different aims and purposes being served by them. But before that, we first try to explain why it matters whether denialist speech is classified as hate speech or instead as an entirely separate category.

7.4 Why It Matters

We believe there are at least four significant reasons why getting the conceptual-legal classification of denialist speech right matters or makes a practical difference. First, as observed in Chapter 1, the failure or refusal to recognise certain kinds of expressive phenomena as hate speech can itself constitute a form of misrecognition of the identity of a group of people. To deny that Holocaust denial is hate speech, for example, might be to brush under the carpet the history and significance of denialism: the part it has played in the persecution of Jews along with hate propaganda and incitement to genocide, for example. Indeed, to downgrade Holocaust denial as merely words that Jews find offensive (and not hate speech) may signal ambivalence towards their fate or even a way of blaming the victim: the implicit suggestion that somehow the true source of 'the problem' with denialism lies in how the Jewish people react to the words rather than the meanings and intentions of deniers. Indeed, softcore denialism can include belittling Jewish people who find Holocaust denial confronting or offensive by implying they are of limited intelligence or emotionally unstable.

Second, classifying denialist speech as a form of hate speech in the legal sense of the term can make a difference insofar as it adds both gravity and stringency to legal norms against denialism. This classification says not simply that denialist speech is morally wrong but also that it is rightly subject to legal norms, laws, and legal sanctions. Of course, even if denialist speech were classified as an entirely separate category of speech to hate speech, this would not prevent governments from taking measures to combat it. Yet the normative case for governments and courts enacting and enforcing denialism laws is likely to be stronger if denialist speech can be classified as hate speech in the legal sense of the term. Call this the hate speech principle: Any governmental justification for prohibiting speech is stronger when the prohibition involves the restriction of hate speech as recognised by domestic and international legal standards than when no such limitations on hate speech are involved. The key point here is that most of the landmark international laws on hate speech are prohibitionist norms in the sense that they do not merely permit but actively obligate states to prohibit certain forms of hate speech.[85] In our view, it is no coincidence that the Council Framework Decision and the Additional Protocol to the Convention on Cybercrime treat denialism as racist and xenophobic content (hate speech) and are prohibitionist laws, whereas the three UN General Assembly resolutions on Holocaust remembrance and denial fail to treat Holocaust denial as hate speech and are non-prohibitionist laws. It is also worth noting here Principle 12.2 of the Camden Principles on Freedom of Expression and Equality promulgated by the international human rights organisation Article 19 back in April 2009: 'States should prohibit the condoning or denying of crimes of genocide, crimes against humanity and war crimes, but only where such statements constitute hate speech as defined by Principle 12.1.'[86] Thus, even for organisations whose primary mission is to protect freedom of expression, it makes a crucial difference whether denialist statements rise to the level of hate speech.

Third, classifying denialist speech as an entirely separate category of speech to hate speech could also have the effect of placing denialist speech into a broader camp of offensive or deeply confronting speech that includes blasphemy and defamation of religion, for example. Similar to the second reason, such a classification could make it harder to justify prohibiting denialist speech. This is because the normative case for prohibiting blasphemy and defamation of religion is much more uncertain and culturally dependent, and is not the subject of international consensus or even a tacit normative compromise, unlike hate speech. Putting this the other way around, one reason why the inclusion or non-inclusion of denialist speech under the legal concept *hate speech* matters is because it could have further implications for the conceptual-legal fate of other forms of speech like defamation or religion. If denialist speech is classified by the international community as a form of hate speech, this could make it harder for the community to resist the inclusion of defamation or religion under the same umbrella. We shall return to this contentious issue in international affairs at the end of the chapter.

Finally, the decision on whether or not to classify denialist speech as hate speech and, if so, as what type or form of hate speech, can have practical consequences for how, if at all, states choose to tackle denialist speech by means of particular legal prohibitions. For example, a state may take the view that because denialist speech can be interpreted as an instance of illegal hate speech, it can be tackled with extant hate speech laws rather than bespoke or stand-alone denialism laws. Indeed, insofar as international law obliges states to punish denialist speech, but some states might not have bespoke denialism laws in place, judges in domestic courts may have a secondary obligation to interpret the laws that do exist in a broad way such that they already conform to the relevant international norms against denialism.[87] Going a step beyond this, a state might take the principled view – one that could reflect its particular circumstances and domestic free speech norm – that denialist speech as such is not the sort of speech that warrants criminalisation. One way of expressing this principled view might be to say, as Michel Rosenfeld does, that it is 'easy' to justify banning '[o]bvious hate speech such as that involving crude racist insults or invectives' but 'not easy' to justify banning less obvious forms of hate speech 'such as Holocaust denials or other coded messages that do not explicitly convey insults, but are nonetheless designed to convey hatred or contempt'.[88] Another version of the principle, articulated by Peter Teachout, says that it is one thing to 'legitimately censor and punish speech that serves to incite racial suspicion and hatred under a law that makes that factor the central determining element'; quite another to 'censor and punish the exact same speech because the views expressed fail to conform to some state-established, orthodox version of history.'[89] Put in even more basic terms, a state might adopt a simple rule that says 'denialism should only be punished, if at all, where it falls within existing hate speech crimes'.[90] That said, it is also possible that a different state – reflecting its own circumstances and free speech norm – could elect instead to classify denialist speech as a sui generis form of hate speech and, based on this, it might choose to enact a bespoke denialism law. The law could create an unqualified offence of bare denialism, without the need to demonstrate that the denial was carried out in a manner likely to disturb public order or was threatening, abusive, or insulting, for example.[91] The take home message here is that the classification of denialist speech as hate speech of one type or another, or not at all, can make a real difference to what a state does to tackle denialist speech by means of legal interventions.

7.5 The Spread of Denialism Laws at the Domestic Level

Virtually every country in the world has some type of hate speech law in place, and many countries have one of the following specific types of criminal law: laws banning group defamation; laws banning incitement to hatred; laws banning incitement to hatred, discrimination, or violence; or laws banning either group defamation or incitement to hatred when it is capable of disturbing the public peace.[92] Not so with bespoke or standalone denialism laws, which, although not uncommon, are not a universal presence in domestic penal codes across Europe and remain extremely rare outside of that region.[93]

One reason, but not the only reason, for this disparity is that whilst virtually every country on the planet harbours at least some forms of hate speech, not every country is host to significant levels of genocide denial. Denial of the Herero and Namaqua genocide, the Armenian genocide, the Seyfo, the Holocaust, the Bangladesh genocide, the Rwandan genocide, the Bosnian genocide, and the Uyghur genocide, for example, is not equally distributed around the world. This in turn may also reflect the fact that genocides themselves are relatively infrequent events, typically affecting only a small part of the world's population at any given time. Of course, many recent state adopters of denialism laws bundle Holocaust and genocide denial together with denial of other core international crimes including crimes against humanity, war crimes, and crimes of aggression. But even if denialism is broadened out to include the denial of core international crimes, not every state sees substantial amounts of denialism. Denial of the Holodomor, the Nanjing Massacre, the Nakba, the Turkish invasion of Cyprus, the Ethiopian Red Terror, and the Russian invasion of Ukraine, for example, is also not evenly spread across the globe. This is once again partly because atrocity crimes are not quotidian events and, arguably, not part of universal human experience (at least in recent human history[94]). Furthermore, when denialism takes the form of publicly denying that a certain event constituted a core international crime, in order for this to be properly labelled 'denialist speech', it must be established that what is being denied, revised, or negated is or was a core international crime in the first place. Yet specific events are typically not officially established as being atrocity crimes by individual states acting in isolation but are subject to assessment by international bodies under agreed international legal norms. If alleged atrocity crimes are comparatively rare, then atrocity crimes that have been recognised by relevant international organisations, atrocity crimes committed by individuals for which evidence has been gathered, presented to, and guilty verdicts delivered by special tribunals or the International Criminal Court, and atrocity crimes for which states have been formally admonished by the international community are even rarer. So, if a specific crime is not yet agreed upon, then its denial may also be not yet agreed upon.

In this chapter, however, we also try to unpack some of the other possible reasons for the precarious position of denialism laws at both the domestic and international levels. Broadly speaking, that a state has used existing laws, including hate speech laws, to prosecute deniers, or has put in place bespoke denialism laws, and, indeed, the particular form of bespoke denialism laws, or has done neither of these things, reflects myriad factors: national experiences of atrocity crimes, whether as victim or perpetrator; social make-up and dominant political ideology including the particular balance of liberal and nationalist tendencies; legal culture and constitutional system; the influence of, and interactions between, civil society organisations, such as the relative influence of advocacy groups that work on behalf of groups that have been victims and civil rights organisations whose primary mission is to defend freedom of expression; and the degree to which the state is committed to complying with international anti-denialism norms articulated in relevant international treaties, agreements, and legal decisions, which in turn may depend on the extent to which the state has been actively involved in negotiations around the drafting of the relevant international laws, or instead merely subject to those laws.[95]

One especially important factor has to do with where the responsibility for specific atrocities rests. Many countries whose governments, military leaders, soldiers, and sometimes ordinary citizens have been alleged perpetrators of atrocity crimes do not have denialism laws in place, even though they do have hate speech regulations – most notably, Turkey,[96] Japan,[97] Pakistan,[98] China,[99] and Russia.[100] What unites several of these countries is, first, the fact that the relevant governments themselves continue to deny the existence of the alleged atrocity crimes and, second, the ways in which the boundaries between hate speech laws and counter-terrorism measures are sometimes blurred, whether in the laws as written, as applied, or both (what we have elsewhere dubbed the securitisation/terrorisation of hate speech law).[101] That said, Japan is an exception case both because its government has officially apologised for the Nanjing massacre, for instance, and because it has in place neither denialism laws nor criminal laws prohibiting hate speech, only regulations setting out governmental responsibilities 'to take measures to eliminate hate speech'.

In one sense, it stands to reason that states responsible for atrocity crimes should decline to enact denialism laws: the goal is to prevent reputational damage and preserve the sort of nationalistic propaganda upon which authoritarian rule often depends, including the powerful myth that genocides and crimes against humanity are the sorts of evils perpetrated solely by foreign powers. Indeed, in the case of Russia,[102] in 2014 the government added to the criminal code a new provision (the so-called Yarovaya Law) against 'wittingly spreading false information about the activities of the USSR during World War II' and (as amended in 2021) against 'public dissemination of knowingly false information about World War II veterans' – a so-called denazification law that has been exploited by the Putin regime to persecute people actively engaged in the acknowledgment, recognition, and collective admission of genocide, war crimes, and other atrocities perpetrated by the USSR.[103]

Turning from state responsibility for atrocity crimes to the site of those crimes, it is worth noting that whilst many countries in which historically documented atrocity crimes actually occurred now have denialism laws in place, many still do not. In 2016, for example, the Law Commission of Bangladesh drafted the Liberation War Denial Crimes Act, which is designed to prohibit certain forms of denialist speech including denial of core international crimes associated with the events of the Bangladesh Liberation War. But at the time of writing the draft Act has yet to be passed by the Bangladesh parliament amid continuing political disputes over whether it would enhance or undermine social unity and constitutional disagreements about whether it would violate the right to freedom of expression.

Indeed, in some exceptional instances, a country that was itself the scene of a genocide or other atrocity crimes may have denialism laws in place only as a result of intervention by external actors under special international governance arrangements, for example, and against the will of its own legislature. Bosnia and Herzegovina[104] is the archetype here. Without direct external intervention, it is unlikely a bespoke genocide denial law would have been passed in Bosnia and Herzegovina in 2021.[105]

Of course, there are several countries in which existing hate speech laws have been used on an ad hoc basis to prosecute specific instances of Holocaust denial. Take Austria, for example. Prior to its amendment in 1992, the National Socialism Prohibition Act 1947 did not contain a bespoke provision against Holocaust denial, but nevertheless its other provisions had been interpreted by some regional courts as having precisely that intention.[106] Likewise, in England and Wales, Part 3 of the Public Order Act 1986 has been used to prosecute people for stirring up of racial hatred against Jews in cases involving the publication of anti-Semitic material containing denials of the Holocaust.[107] Along similar lines, in 2014 the Commission to the European Parliament published a report on the implementation of the Council Framework Decision, and found that the Netherlands[108] and Finland,[109] as well as the UK, had 'submitted sentencing rulings for trivialisation, condoning and denial of the Holocaust, based on criminal-law provisions punishing respectively incitement, ethnic agitation or stirring up of hatred.'[110] Italy is another interesting case because, even though denialism is not a stand-alone crime, Art. 604-bis of the criminal code (as amended in 2018) provides that denialism is an aggravating circumstance attracting a longer prison sentence in relation to the offences of promoting ideas based on racial or ethnic superiority or hatred, and of incitement to discrimination or violence on racial, ethnic, national, or religious grounds. (In that sense it could be labelled a hate crime in the strict formal sense defended in Chapter 6.) Looking beyond Europe, courts in Australia have convicted people under racial vilification laws[111] in cases involving Holocaust denial,[112] just as courts in Brazil, for example, have convicted people under the country's anti-racism laws[113] also in cases centred around the publication of Holocaust revisionist material.[114]

In short, the absence of bespoke denialism laws has not prevented European countries, for example, from punishing Holocaust deniers, with some cases going back many decades, and well before the emergence of international instruments like the Council Framework Decision obliging states to enact such laws. That said, the model of using extant hate speech laws to punish Holocaust deniers has been rejected in some countries. In *Case of Constantinos Plevris*,[115] for example, the Supreme Court of Greece overturned a conviction for incitement to hatred in the case of a self-declared anti-Semite and Holocaust denier on the grounds that the relevant hate speech law[116] must be interpreted and applied 'strictly' so as not to infringe upon the right to freedom of expression enshrined in both the Greek Constitution and the European Convention. In the Court's assessment, *pace* the judgment of the Athens Court of Appeal, Plevris's book *Jews: The Whole Truth* did not constitute incitement to hatred as such, despite containing denialist and anti-Semitic ideas.

However, our main interest here is the connection between denialist speech and the legal concept *hate speech*. On the one hand, where standard hate speech laws are routinely used to prosecute and convict Holocaust or genocide deniers, it seems straightforward to make the argument that denialist speech (of a certain type) falls under the relevant domestic legal concept(s) *hate speech*. On the other hand, that might not be true of stand-alone denialism laws. It appears much less certain how to correctly classify these laws. Therefore, in this chapter we shall focus on stand-alone denialism laws, including both qualified and unqualified forms. We do so because here the status of denialist speech as hate speech in the legal sense of the term may be more precarious and, therefore, more interesting *qua* conceptual grey area.

In fact, several countries have enacted stand-alone laws prohibiting forms of denialist speech. Israel (1986)[117] was the first, followed by France (1990),[118] Austria (1992),[119] Germany (1994),[120] Belgium (1995),[121] Switzerland (1995),[122] and Luxembourg (1997),[123] among others. Throughout the 2000s, many of the former Soviet states introduced their own denialism laws which prohibit not only Holocaust denial but also denial of atrocity crimes committed by the USSR. Poland (1998)[124] led the way followed by the Czech Republic (2001),[125] the Slovak Republic (2001),[126]

Romania (2002),[127] Slovenia (2004),[128] Lithuania (2010),[129] and Hungary (2010),[130] for example. This partly reflected a broader desire of the former Soviet states to gain EU membership, thus necessitating these countries bringing their existing legal systems and bodies of law into line with European law including the Council Framework Decision. But it was also an opportunity for these states to acknowledge and highlight the horrors they had endured during Soviet occupation. More recently, Ukraine (2021)[131] passed a new anti-Semitism law which contains an unqualified provision prohibiting anti-Semitism in the form of Holocaust denial. Arguably, this can be seen not merely as part of a wider package of reforms developed by Ukraine to support its formal application to join the EU but also as a symbolic rejection of, and counter to, Putin's propaganda that Ukraine is governed by neo-Nazis. While denialism laws are primarily a European phenomenon, they do exist in other countries, including not only Israel but also Rwanda (2003)[132] and Cambodia (2013),[133] both of which were sites of genocide in the twentieth century.

When it comes to addressing the main conceptual dilemma of whether even stand-alone denialism laws can be considered hate speech laws, however, a key distinction is between unqualified and qualified denialism offences. Unqualified denialism offences are broad offences in the sense that they do not require denialist speech to be accompanied by further substantial qualifying conditions, or elements of the offence, such as involving incitement to hatred, discrimination, or violence, or being done in a manner capable of disturbing the public peace, for instance. The simple act of publicly denying the Holocaust, say, can be an offence. By contrast, qualified denialism offences tack on one or more further substantial qualifying conditions, rendering them more narrowly tailored and also creating a higher threshold for prosecution. Some of these qualified offences either mimic or reproduce the wording of Art. 1(2) of the Council Framework Decision: 'For the purpose of paragraph 1, Member States may choose to punish only conduct which is either carried out in a manner likely to disturb public order or which is threatening, abusive or insulting.'

Starting with qualified denialism offences, there is arguably a stronger case for saying that they count as hate speech laws when the relevant qualifying conditions themselves match or correspond to elements of prototypical hate speech laws. Although this will need to be assessed on a case-by-case basis, at least some generalisations can be safely made. First, there are countries in which denialism offences are qualified in the sense that the denials not only must be done in public but must also be done in a designated manner and against members of the groups victimised by the events being denied, based on protected characteristics. Countries with denialism offences falling into this category include: Greece[134] (only if the denial is done publicly and in a manner that is capable of inciting violence or hatred, or is of a threatening or insulting character, against members of the relevant group based on their protected characteristics); Serbia[135] (only if the denial is done publicly and in a manner that could lead to violence or incitement to hatred against members of the relevant group based on their protected characteristics); Portugal[136] (only if the denial is done publicly to defame or insult a person or group based on protected characteristics and with intent to incite or encourage discrimination against members of the relevant group); Malta[137] (only if the denial is done publicly and in a manner which is (a) likely to incite violence or hatred against members of the relevant group based on their protected characteristics; (b) likely to violate public order or to be threatening, abusive, or insulting); and Croatia[138] (only if the denial is done publicly and in a manner likely to incite violence or hatred against members of the relevant group based on their protected characteristics).

Second, there is another group of countries in which, although denialism offences contain qualifying conditions related to the manner of denial, the wording fails to clearly specify who must be victimised. Examples include Germany[139] (only if the denial is done publicly and in a manner capable of disturbing the public peace); and Lithuania[140] (only if the denial is done publicly and in a manner which disturbs public order or that is threatening, abusive, or insulting). These qualified denialism offences fall into a grey area because they lack a distinctive feature of prototypical hate speech laws: namely, hate speech laws make an explicit reference to certain acts (e.g. incitement to hatred, the use of threatening words or behaviour), being carried out directly against people based on their possession or perceived possession of protected characteristics. Perhaps the legislative intention behind these qualified denialism offences is that the relevant qualifying acts must be against certain groups. Even so, the lack of clarity makes them more ambiguous than the first group.

That leaves stand-alone denialism laws that create unqualified (or less qualified) denialism offences. Such laws can be found in several countries including, for instance, Israel,[141] France,[142] Austria,[143] Poland,[144] Belgium,[145] Switzerland,[146] Luxembourg,[147] Liechtenstein,[148] Slovenia,[149] Hungary,[150] Cyprus,[151] Rwanda,[152] and Cambodia.[153] These denialism laws prohibit certain forms of denialist speech simply as acts carried out in public, without further substantial qualifying conditions or elements of the offences. As an aside, it is worth noting here that countries which have created unqualified denialism offences (in our proposed sense) have tended to be the early adopters of denialism laws, who were motivated to adopt legislation without being influenced to do so by the Council Framework Decision – for example, Israel, France, Austria, Belgium, Switzerland, Luxembourg, and Poland. That said, some early adopters went on a journey from first creating unqualified denialism offences to later replacing them with qualified versions. In 1995, for example, Spain added to its penal code an updated version of the crime of genocide (itself dating back to 1971) which included a new unqualified offence of genocide denial. This made it a criminal offence to publicly justify or deny genocides recognised in international law irrespective of the manner of that justification or denial.[154] In 2007, however, the Constitutional Court ruled that the offence as written was invalid because overbroad.[155] Subsequently, the penal code was revised again in 2015 this time creating a qualified offence of genocide denial.[156] It is now a criminal offence to publicly deny, seriously trivialise or extol genocides or other atrocity crimes recognised in international law only if the denial is done against a group or persons belonging to a group, and for reasons of racism, anti-Semitism or for other reasons related to ideology, religion or beliefs, family circumstances, or the fact that the members belong to an ethnicity, race or nation, national origin, gender, sexual orientation or identity, or due to gender, illness or disability, if such conduct promotes or encourages a climate of violence, hostility, hatred or discrimination against such individuals.

Our main interest here is to ask whether unqualified denialism offences can be aptly classified as a sui generis kind of hate speech law, or else should be seen as an entirely separate category of legal norm. At first glance, it might seem as though such offences cannot be classified as hate speech laws. After all, unqualified denialism offences prohibit the relatively simple act of publicly denying the existence of certain genocides or other atrocity crimes, where it is the ideational content of what is said that marks out the speech for punishment. This is unlike hate speech laws that prohibit, for example, incitement to hatred, discrimination, or violence, where it is the act of turning an audience against members of a group identified by protected characteristics that matters.[157] However, and this point is crucial, laws banning incitement to hatred, discrimination, or violence do not exhaust the legal concept *hate speech*. Other hate speech laws provide for the punishment of speakers based on ideational content alone. In Italy, for example, Law No. 205 of 1993 (the so-called Mancino Law) contains a clause which provides for the punishment of people simply for propagating ideas based on racial or ethnic superiority or hatred.

Now it might be objected at this stage that publicly expressing ideas based on the ideology of racial hierarchy or hatred is qualitatively very different to publicly expressing the basic idea that certain historical events did not happen. The latter is a matter of rejecting things that are generally considered to be facts. Clearly, elaborate forms of Holocaust denial are ripe with anti-Semitic disparagements and prejudices, but at this stage we are speaking only of bare forms of denialist speech (assuming such forms do occur in reality). However, in response to this objection we would point to the fact there can be elaborate and bare forms of hate propaganda as well. Some instances of hate propaganda also take on the general style or form of rejecting certain things that are generally considered to be facts, most notably the moral fact that all races possess the same intrinsic moral worth or dignity and the moral fact that putative racial differences do not justify social hierarchies.

However, an objector might pursue a different line and insist that denialism laws have more in common with blasphemy laws than with hate speech laws. For one thing, there is a sense in which both denialism laws and blasphemy laws serve, in part, to defend the sensibilities of certain groups by banning material they find grossly offensive (or so the objector claims). Moreover, both denialism laws and blasphemy laws appear to restrict acts of denial or irreverence toward things considered sacred by a group of people. As Kahn puts it, 'the establishment of blanket Holocaust denial laws have given rise to charges that the laws create a modern-day blasphemy'.[158] Thus, writing in *The Spectator* in 2013, Ed West declared 'now that identity, whether of race, religion, class, sex or sexuality, is the new sacred, hate crime laws [*sic*] have become blasphemy laws in all but name' and '[o]ne of the first such laws [...] made Holocaust denial a crime'.[159] However, looking beyond mere appearances, arguably the real purpose behind Holocaust denial laws is not to protect people's sensibilities; it runs much deeper than that and is partly about protecting dignity. Similarly, part of the aim of Holocaust denial laws is not to conserve and protect the sacred in the strict sense of preserving something regarded with esteem and entitled to acknowledgment and due reverence. Rather, it is to defend simply *that which demands to be remembered*, something regarded with great sorrow and entitled to not only acknowledgment but also remembrance, commemoration, empathy, condolence, and respect. Arguably, denialism laws share this purpose in common with broader initiatives of Holocaust remembrance, reflected in the following words from the founding document of the IHRA: 'Together we must uphold the terrible truth of the Holocaust against those who deny it'.[160]

More generally, We believe classifying denialism laws as belonging to the broader category of hate speech laws is not untoward and certainly not untoward simply because the former come in a variety of types, including both qualified and unqualified offences. On the contrary, the variety of denialism laws reflects the variety of purposes served by such laws, which in turn mirrors the diversity of hate speech laws and hate speech law purposes.[161] In the next section we identify a range of purposes served by denialism laws, and show how this pluralistic picture strengthens rather than weakens our main thesis.

7.6 The Many Purposes of Denialism Laws

We believe the moral, social, and political purposes served by a given hate speech law, or type of hate speech law, can assist not only in normatively warranting the law, all things considered,[162] and in making the case for extending the law to cover further protected characteristics, say,[163] but also in the more fundamental conceptual-legal task of classifying it as a hate speech law in the first place. We submit that the same goes for denialism laws.

That said, sometimes the legislative purpose of a law is not explicitly stated or clearly specified in the law itself. So, for example, the legislative purpose of a Holocaust denial law could be to curb incitement to hatred, discrimination, or violence against Jews, but such incitement might not be specified as an element of the offence as written. (This purpose might be founded on an empirical finding that Holocaust denial tends on average to incite hatred against Jews, even if not every single instance of Holocaust denial does so.) As such, classifying a given denialism law as a hate speech law may become a matter of legal interpretation, combining interpretation of the meaning of the words written in the law with interpretation of the legislative purpose underpinning the law, a purpose which may be unwritten in the law but is nevertheless either articulated in parliamentary debates and government statements and guidance notes, for example, or else divinable as the spirit of the law itself independently of the express intentions of legislators.[164]

However, assuming that such purposes are explicitly stated or can be gleaned in some other way, what marks out or qualifies a given purpose as being a hate speech law type purpose? Putting this another way, what are typical hate speech law purposes against which denialism laws can be appropriately compared and analogised? At this point it is appropriate to return to Matsuda's landmark article. In it she cites not only American tort law[165] but also several other laws, both domestic and international, which either prohibit or call on states to prohibit hate speech in her sense of the term.[166] These laws include everything from the stirring up hatred offences in England and Wales; to Canadian laws banning the advocacy of genocide and publicly inciting hatred against an identifiable group where it is likely to lead to a breach of the peace; to racial vilification laws in Australia that make it unlawful for a person to publicly incite hatred towards, serious contempt for, or severe ridicule of, people on grounds of race; through to the ICERD which obligates states parties to declare unlawful all dissemination of ideas based on racial superiority or hatred as well as incitement to racial discrimination or violence.[167] Over time other studies have added yet more instances and types of hate speech law to Matsuda's original list.[168] Together this body of laws suggest a wide range of hate speech law purposes against which denialism laws can be compared and analogised. These purposes may include (a non-exhaustive list): protecting the dignity, reputation, and social standing of victimised groups; mitigating the psychological harms suffered by targets of hate speech; safeguarding people's sense of security; protecting public peace and security; upholding norms of recognition and intercultural respect and dialogue; and underpinning equal access to participation in public discourse and the formation of public opinion and thereby protecting democratic and political legitimacy.[169]

What, then, are the purposes served by denialism laws? What or who is protected by them? To make these questions slightly more manageable we shall focus on Holocaust denial laws, although we surmise that broader denialism laws may serve similar purposes. We propose that Holocaust denial laws are interpretable as serving the following purposes.

(i) To restrict the dissemination of falsehoods and protect a set of historical facts relating to the Jewish people.
(ii) To restrict the dissemination of falsehoods and so mitigate the distorting influence they might have on public discourse and thereby safeguard the holding of justified true beliefs or public knowledge about a set of historical facts relating to the Jewish people.
(iii) To defend that which demands to be remembered, commemorated, and respected.
(iv) To honour and preserve the dignity of Jews who were murdered in the Holocaust.
(v) To restrict material that is grossly offensive both from a Jewish perspective and from the standpoint of the community at large.
(vi) To send out a symbolic message that the state is making a clean break with a past racist regime.

(vii) To curb a form of speech that undermines intercultural dialogue and respect.
(viii) To restrict a form of speech that demonstrates cruelty towards or otherwise degrades or humiliates Jews as a group.
(ix) To restrict a form of speech that is designated or defined as a form of antisemitism.
(x) To curb the dissemination of ideas based on racial superiority or hatred towards Jews.
(xi) To block the spread of statements that contribute to the rehabilitation of Nazi ideology and the resurrection of a former genocidal regime.
(xii) To restrict a form of existential misrecognition of identity and in so doing support the persistence of Jewish identity over time.
(xiii) To restrict group defamation and protect the good name or reputation of Jews.
(xiv) To support the public assurance of the civic dignity or equal socio-legal status of Jewish citizens.
(xv) To restrict a form of speech that constitutes a denial of the right of existence of Jews.
(xvi) To restrict a form of speech that dehumanises Jews and rationalises, normalises, or paves the way for acts of discrimination and violence against members of this group, and thereby to protect the dignity, civil and political rights, and security of Jews.
(xvii) To restrict a form of speech that can be used to stir up hatred, discrimination, or violence against Jews and thereby protect the civil and political rights, and security of Jews.
(xviii) To restrict a form of speech that can create a climate that makes some Jews withdraw from public discourse and political life, and thereby to protect not only the democratic rights of Jews but also the democratic legitimacy of laws and even the political legitimacy of the state itself.
(xix) To restrict a form of speech that can cause social enmity or disharmony between sections of society and thereby to protect the public peace.
(xx) To curb a form of speech typically used by and circulated among extremist and violent neo-Nazi groups, whether as a ritual of membership, recruiting sergeant, or rallying call, and thereby to protect national security.

Having identified these purposes, the next step in the conceptual process is to compare them against the benchmark of typical hate speech law purposes briefly listed above.

7.6.1 Truth, Historical Research, and Academic Inquiry

If the central purpose of denialism laws were epistemic, namely, to protect a set of historical truths and knowledge thereof, then it could appear as though the state and the courts are adopting the role of arbiters of truth and custodians of knowledge. It is certainly the case that the ECtHR, for example, in its extensive case law dealing with denialism laws, has drawn a distinction between, on the one hand, denialist content questioning 'clearly established historical facts – such as the Holocaust – whose negation or revision would be removed from the protection of Article 10 by Article 17' and, on the other hand, content questioning events concerning which there is 'lack of either clarity or unanimity' and that are 'open to ongoing debate among historians' and which, therefore, 'should be able to take place freely' because it is 'an integral part of freedom of expression to seek historical truth'.[170]

At first glance, this might seem problematic for two reasons: first, banning speech on purely epistemic grounds appears troubling in itself given the high importance of giving both speakers and audiences alike the opportunity to discover truths and gain knowledge for themselves rather than having the state do it for them; and, second, it seems at odds with typical hate speech law purposes which appear not to be epistemic in nature. Starting with the first reason, Robert Kahn suggests that early prosecutions for Holocaust denial faltered when prosecutors struggled 'to show that Holocaust deniers also included direct anti-Semitic insults in their speeches' and that '[w]hen, in response, a number of countries adopted laws that banned Holocaust denial as such, alarms were raised about the creation of state-enforced official truths that would soon devour all areas of historical inquiry'.[171] No doubt some of the people raising alarms in Europe took inspiration from American First Amendment jurisprudence. The very idea of criminalising the expression of an opinion, even a denialist opinion, on account of its falsity is anathema to the domestic US free speech norm.[172] We shall say more about that norm in Section 7.7.

However, the domestic US free speech norm is not the only touchstone for assessing denialism laws. Take worries about 'the creation of state-enforced official truths'. Surely the state assumes precisely this role when it sets curricula for state schools, when publicly funded heritage organisations disseminate information to the public about historical people, places, and events, and when the state supports public memorials and national days of remembrance – all paid for out of compulsory taxation. Yet most people, in both America and Europe, seem to accept the basic principle that, even when compulsory taxes are used to fund public speech that some members of the public, such as denialists and revisionists, think is false, this mode of 'compelled speech' does not constitute an unjustifiable violation of the right to freedom of expression precisely because there is a legitimate state interest in taking a public stand on the side of truth and knowledge.[173] European free speech norms simply go one step further and say that even laws which actively prohibit forms of denialist speech and revisionism do not constitute an unjustifiable violation of the right to freedom expression and for exactly the same reason as just articulated: because there is a legitimate state interest in taking a public stand on the side of truth and knowledge.

In cases involving Holocaust deniers, some courts in Europe have pointed to the overwhelming consensus among historians about the relevant facts. In *Case of Doğu Perinçek*[174] from Switzerland in 2007, for example, the Lausanne District Police Court ('Tribunal') found the defendant guilty of denialist speech under the meaning of Art. 261-bis(4) of the Swiss criminal code. Perinçek, a Turkish national and political figure, had in 2005 given a series of public speeches in Switzerland where he denied that the mass killing of Armenians within the Ottoman Empire in 1915 constituted a genocide, and denounced genocide allegations as an 'international lie'. During the proceedings, Perinçek declared, 'I have not denied genocide because there was no genocide.'[175] For its part, the Tribunal heard evidence from six professional historians concerning the events of 1915. When Perinçek's counsel asked the Tribunal to gather yet further evidence, the judge demurred arguing that it was unnecessary to hear more evidence since the events had been analysed by 'hundreds of historians for decades', had been the 'object of innumerable publications', and had been fully addressed by the six historians whom the Tribunal regarded as 'competent' witnesses [trans.]. Since Art. 261-bis(4) does not explicitly name authoritative sources of decisions about what constitutes a genocide, it was up to the Tribunal to note that various Swiss governmental bodies and international organisations had recognised the Armenian genocide.[176] Perinçek, himself a former lecturer in public law, appealed the decision, accusing the judge of anti-Turkish animus, but the Criminal Court of Appeals of the Canton of Vaud reaffirmed his conviction.[177] The Federal Court upheld the conviction in 2007,[178] reasoning that 'the Appellant has failed to demonstrate how the police tribunal fell into arbitrariness merely by noting that there is a general consensus, especially among academic historians, on the classification of the events of 1915 as genocide' [trans.].[179] We shall discuss the subsequent judgment by the ECtHR finding in favour of Perinçek and against the Federal Court below, but for now we shall focus on the issue of truth and knowledge.

However, turning to the second problem, it deserves mention that, like all denialism laws, the Swiss denialism law specified in Art. 261-bis(4) does not provide for a truth defence against prosecution. As such, there was simply no legal avenue open to Perinçek under the Swiss denialism law, as written, for his counsel to mount a recognised legal defence to the effect that he could not have denied genocide because there was no genocide to be denied (as they might have attempted to prove in court). Arguably, this feature of denialism laws reflects the fact that legislators have already relied upon the overwhelming evidence for events surrounding the specific genocides and other core international crimes recognised by authoritative domestic and international courts and other bodies. Yet this marks a key difference between denialism laws and hate speech laws as a general category, namely that at least some hate speech laws, although not many, do contain truth defences, especially when it comes to group defamation laws and incitement to hatred laws. For example, the law of libel set out in Ch. 200, s. 510 of the Nevada Revised Statutes provides for libel of deceased persons and also libel of a 'community of persons'; it also explicitly provides for a truth defence.[180] Whether this particular provision is a hate speech law is a grey area since it does not specify that the community of persons must be identified by protected characteristics.[181] However, laws prohibiting incitement to hatred that contain a truth defence can be found in Canada,[182] India,[183] and Namibia.[184]

Nevertheless, we do not believe these apparent dissimilarities between denialism laws and certain sorts of hate speech laws are sufficient to demonstrate that denialism laws cannot be aptly classified as hate speech laws. For one thing, it would be wrong to assume the list of typical hate speech law purposes excludes epistemic purposes. On the contrary, arguably another important function served by some hate speech laws is to control speech that unfairly obstructs other people's acquisition of knowledge, such as through the circulation of misinformation that makes it harder for ordinary people who exist in echo chambers and deliberative conclaves to arrive at justified true beliefs about historical events or forms of undue influence in which public figures exploit their authority or standing to push their own prejudices and hatred under a veneer or cloak of historical debate.[185] Consider public figures who trade on the false assumption that they are *an authority* in the epistemic sense because they are *in authority* in the political sense or simply because they are celebrities or held *in esteem* by a certain community of people. Furthermore, the vast majority of hate speech laws do not provide for a truth defence, and so denialism laws and hate speech laws in general share this characteristic, if not in every single instance.

Yet it might be countered at this stage that we have missed the real danger posed by denialism laws: that what matters is not whether the defendant was speaking the truth but whether the style, mode, genre, or manner of speech was recognisable as academic-style research and historical inquiry in particular. On this view, the fact that certain content has the manner of historical inquiry can, and should, be highly relevant to determining whether it is rightly considered protected speech, just as it makes a difference if the manner of speech is artistic or satirical, for example. Following on from this, perhaps the real cause for alarm about states enacting denialism laws lies not so much in the creation of state-enforced official truths but rather in the fact that denialism laws prohibit instances of what is a protected style or genre of speech in general, namely, historical inquiry, and that, if such laws are not narrowly tailored enough, they could unintentionally sweep up or devour whole areas of historical inquiry associated with certain events or periods in history.

Indeed, one way this sweeping up might occur is if courts adopt very strict standards of what qualifies as bona fide historical inquiry. Sticking with the Swiss denialism law, there is some evidence that courts have done just that. Returning to *Case of Doğu Perinçek*, the Tribunal concluded that Perinçek's remarks had been borne of racist and nationalistic motives and did not fall within the scope of genuine historical debate. The Federal Court also sided with the Tribunal in this finding.[186] To give another example, in *Case of Jürgen Graf*[187] from 2000, the Supreme Court of Switzerland upheld the defendant's conviction for Holocaust denial under Art. 261-bis(4). The Court acknowledged the fact that the defendant was 'allegedly convinced of the correctness of his theses on the basis of his research work' but concluded nevertheless that the arguments he proffered in support of his denialist theses about the Holocaust were 'pseudo-scientific pseudo-argumentation' [trans.].[188] On one possible reading, the Court was essentially saying that the defendant's publications could not be plausibly classified as belonging to the style or genre of historical inquiry.

In reaching these sorts of decisions, courts might consciously or unconsciously adopt a general rule of thumb that says independent inquiry – such as work undertaken by individuals lacking postgraduate qualifications in the methods of historical research, who are institutionally unaffiliated, and who publish material outside of the normal peer-review system of academic scrutiny – is more likely to be bogus historical inquiry. More generally, if an individual is found not to have followed internationally accepted standards of evidence gathering and evaluation in historical research, including overreliance on untested sources and under-reliance on counter-evidence (evidentiary selectivity), then in the court's eyes this might call the work into doubt as genuine historical inquiry.[189] Then again, there may be grey area cases where a revisionist might plausibly claim to be a historian or else publishes works about which it is difficult to definitively say does not belong to the style or genre of historical inquiry. After all, not all bad historical inquiry is pseudohistorical inquiry. The deeper worry here, one that reflects aspects of the domestic US free speech norm, is that it is unwise or dangerous to put courts in the position of judging what qualifies as a proper historian or genuine historical inquiry because such judgments are vulnerable to the suppression of content which the court or society happens to disapprove of.

However, we would suggest that courts can, and should, draw a distinction between the style or genre of expression, on the one hand, and the purpose of expression, on the other hand. Material may take the style, form, manner, or mode of historical inquiry but nevertheless might have a purpose associated with hatred, bigotry, prejudice, and intolerance. Even where material does have historical inquiry as a purpose, courts should also ask whether that purpose is the sole or primary purpose, or instead a secondary purpose. If the purpose of the speech was not solely or primarily historical inquiry but instead was solely or primarily to perform a prototypical hate speech act, then the fact that the speech has the trappings of historical inquiry should not protect it. Arguably, making determinations not only about the style or genre of material but also about the underlying purpose of that material is not an unreasonable demand on courts out of keeping with other determinations they make, not least in cases involving other forms of illegal hate speech.[190]

In fact, there is some evidence to suggest that courts are already making precisely these sorts of determinations in denialism cases. For example, in *Case of Jürgen Graf* discussed above, the Supreme Court also said this about the argument proffered by the defendant for his theses: '[t]he "argument" [was] only a pretext'.[191] To give a third example from Switzerland, in *Case of Ali Mercan*[192] dating back to 2010, the Federal Court upheld a conviction for denial of the Armenian genocide under Art. 261-bis(4). Mercan was a member of the Workers' Party led by Perinçek and had called the Armenian genocide a 'historical and international lie' during a meeting held in Winterthur. The Court opined that 'if freedom of expression and academic freedom are invoked appropriately, that is with the aim of improving human knowledge, it is worthy of protection' [trans.].[193] It also accepted that 'a need for knowledge arises where events have not been conclusively explained' and where events 'are little in the consciousness of the general public', such as with the Armenian genocide in its view.[194] However, it also concluded that, whilst there is no objection to someone using freedom of expression to improve human knowledge, there is an objection if that freedom is 'abused for the purposes of discrimination or disparagement'.[195]

For its part, the ECtHR has in some cases likewise rejected applicants' claims that they were engaged in speech solely or primarily for the purpose of historical inquiry. In *Garaudy v. France* dating back to 2003,[196] for example, the ECtHR found that the Paris Court of Appeal had not violated Art. 10 of the European Convention by convicting the applicant under s. 24-bis of the Act of 29 July 1881 – France's bespoke denialism law. Roger Garaudy, an author and former politician, had claimed in his book *Les Mythes Fondateurs de la Politique Israélienne* that various myths had been exploited by Zionists in a conspiracy to dispossess the Palestinians of their homeland, including 'the myth of the six million' and 'the myth of justice at Nuremberg'. The ECtHR opined as follows:

> There can be no doubt that denying the reality of clearly established historical facts, such as the Holocaust, as the applicant does in his book, does not constitute historical research akin to a quest for the truth. The aim and the result of that approach are completely different, the real purpose being to rehabilitate the National-Socialist regime and, as a consequence, accuse the victims themselves of falsifying history. Denying crimes against humanity is therefore one of the most serious forms of racial defamation of Jews and of incitement to hatred of them.[197]

What this ruling suggests is an unwillingness of the ECtHR to exempt ersatz historical inquiry, as in, inquiry done with an ulterior motive of attacking the Jewish people.

A similar approach has been adopted by courts in jurisdictions where there are no stand-alone denialism laws, but nonetheless extant hate speech laws have been applied to denialism cases. For example, s. 18C of the Racial Discrimination Act 1975, Australia, makes it unlawful for a person to perform a public act that is 'reasonably likely, in all the circumstances, to offend, insult, humiliate or intimidate another person or a group of people', where 'the act is done because of the race, colour or national or ethnic origin of the other person or of some or all of the people in the group.' As written, the Act does not make denialist speech unlawful as such since in theory not every instance of denialist speech necessarily meets the threshold. In addition to this, s. 18D sets out the following multi-pronged exemption: 'Section 18C does not render unlawful anything said or done reasonably and in good faith: (a) in the performance, exhibition or distribution of an artistic work; or (b) in the course of any statement, publication, discussion or debate made or held for any genuine academic, artistic or scientific purpose or any other genuine purpose in the public interest; or (c) in making or publishing: (i) a fair and accurate report of any event or matter of public interest; or (ii) a fair comment on any event or matter of public interest if the comment is an expression of a genuine belief held by the person making the comment.' At first glance, this exemption sets a low bar for exemption in denialism cases. As Meagher puts it, '[t]he very nature and form of history denial lends itself to a defence that it was undertaken for at least one of these purposes.'[198] However, Meagher also points out that the qualifier 'reasonably and in good faith' does a lot of heavy lifting in terms of limiting the reach of the exemption. Good faith has to do with acting in a manner that is faithful not merely to the relevant exemption, such as an academic purpose, but also to the spirt of the norms (against racial vilification) and values (respect, tolerance, equality, and so on) upheld in the Act itself. Thus, 'if a historical work is motivated by spite, ill will or another improper purpose then the free speech/public interest protection otherwise available under Australian racial vilification law is lost.'[199] Thus, in some notable Holocaust denial cases, the Federal Court has disapplied the s. 18D exemption.[200] In the words of Justice Hely in *Jones v Scully*:[201]

> I do not accept that the respondent distributed the leaflet reasonably, or in good faith for a genuine academic purpose. Her affidavit does not establish that this is so, but rather it suggests that it is not. [...] At p 54 of her affidavit, an extract from an unidentified publication refers to the 'Holocaust extortion racket' and to 'Holocash' engaged in by 'Holocaust Swindlers'. This is amongst the materials on which the respondent relies as justifying her distribution of the leaflet. That confirms the impression gained from a reading of the leaflet itself, and from the whole of the evidence, that Mrs Scully is a person who holds strongly anti-Jewish views, and that this leaflet was distributed with the intention of vilifying Jews. In the context of the RDA, if that was the intention underlying the distribution of the leaflet, then reasonableness, good faith and genuineness of purpose would not be found.[202]

Of course, this approach still places a significant burden on courts to discover the primary intention underlying the dissemination of denialist material. If the threshold for proving hateful intention is placed too low, the law may sweep up an excessive amount of historical inquiry; if the threshold is too high, it could create a loophole that anti-Semites and Nazi-apologists, say, could exploit to evade punishment. However, the delicate judicial balancing act between overly high and overly low intention thresholds does not render denialism laws disanalogous to hate speech laws in general. In some jurisdictions, for example, intention is built into incitement to hatred laws as an element of the offending behaviour.[203] Here once again if the threshold is too low, then the law may sweep up an excessive amount of speech; if the threshold is too high, then the law becomes toothless.

7.6.2 Dignitary Affronts

A legislature might instead view the function of denialism laws being to restrict dignitary affronts of various types: everything from disparaging the memory of the dead; through to existential threats to identity; to denial of the fundamental human right to exist; to dehumanisation of both subject and speaker; and on to acts of cruelty. Arguably, justifying and applying denialism laws on the basis of preventing such dignitary affronts is a somewhat simpler or more straightforward task when compared to identifying proper historical inquiry or determining what was the true purpose or intention underlying such inquiry. Moreover, if this is a function of denialism laws, then it seems fitting to place them in the larger category of hate speech laws, since the latter can also serve to mitigate such affronts.[204]

As an aside, sometimes laws against violating the dignity of the dead have also been used to restrict denialist speech.[205] In *Case of Germar Rudolf* from Germany in 2007,[206] for example, the Regional Court of Mannheim held that the defendant's public denial of the Holocaust constituted a clear violation of s. 189 of the criminal code, which makes it a punishable offense to disparage the memory of a deceased person, and also a violation of the constitutionally protected right to human dignity under Art. 1 of the Basic Law of Germany. However, laws against violating the dignity of the dead are at best a grey area of hate speech law since they tend not to specify that the group whose memory is being violated are a group defined by protected characteristics such as race, ethnicity, nationality, religion, and so on, unless of course being deceased is itself treated as a protected characteristic.

Returning to the use of either existing hate speech laws or stand-alone denialism laws to punish deniers, in several cases the ECtHR has relied heavily on the idea that states are justified in restricting the expression of contempt towards, or affronts to the human dignity of, victims of genocide, including denying the identity of a community of people who partly define themselves in terms of their experiences as victims of certain genocide or other crimes.[207] There are different ways of unpacking the nature of this dignitary affront, philosophically. One is to say denialist speech disparages the memory of deceased persons by casting doubt on the truth and honesty of people who remember them. Another is to say denialist speech is an 'existential threat to identity'.[208] Holocaust denial, for example, may constitute an existential threat to the identity of deceased Jews *qua* victims of genocide; to the cultural identity of living Jews, by denying the memories that are partly constitutive of their identity as members of Jewish cultural communities; and to the persistence of Jewish cultural identity over time because it threatens the chain of cultural memory linking bearers of the Jewish cultural identity now to bearers of that same identity at a previous time by denying that the testimonies of Jews living now are true memories of the actual experiences of Jews in the past. Insofar as international trials establishing that certain acts or events constituted genocide or other core international crimes play a key role in formally preserving cultural memory of those events, it can be said that those trials serve as a tool of first resort against synchronous and asynchronous denialist speech. Denialism laws may in turn be viewed as a tool of last resort where revisionism persists even in the face of those trials.[209] Once again, the fact that denialism laws serve to protect certain groups against existential threats to their identity seems to be something they hold in common with hate speech laws in general.[210]

In addition to this, a common interpretation of the spirit of the Genocide Convention is that genocide is to be understood as a denial of the right of existence of entire human groups.[211] If genocide is a denial of the right of existence of entire human groups, then surely bare genocide denial is itself also a denial of the right of existence of entire human groups, not least because human existence is in one sense predicated on being acknowledged and remembered as having existed. Denialism may not be a denial of existence in the gravest sense of a deliberate attempt to murder out of existence an entire human group, but it is a denial in the grave sense of a deliberate attempt to wipe victims of genocide from public knowledge.[212] There have been high profile legal cases relating to the Rwandan genocide, for example, in which a public figure has engaged in public revisionism at the site of a genocide memorial, in violation of domestic laws against disseminating genocide ideology.[213] Moreover, some hardcore and evaluative forms of Holocaust denials may be interpreted as conveying an implied meaning or conversational implicature that Jews have no right to live or exist because they are liars or pose a threat to the rest of humanity. In this regard, denialist speech overlaps with certain kinds of unlawful hate speech, including unlawful hate propaganda of the sort that declares a certain group of people as lacking the right to exist, all because of their possession or perceived possession of protected characteristics.[214]

Furthermore, denialist speech might be interpreted as dehumanising groups whose members have been victims of genocide, and thereby rationalising, normalising, legitimising, or paving the way for further acts of discrimination, violence, and genocide against them.[215] In fact, Holocaust denial can involve direct and indirect forms of dehumanisation roughly corresponding with bare and elaborate forms of Holocaust denial identified in Section 7.2. In terms of direct dehumanisation, bare Holocaust denial might be viewed as dehumanising those murdered in the Holocaust insofar as existence (including either having existed or currently existing) is a core part of being fully human. Turning to indirect dehumanisation, elaborate Holocaust denial actively seeks to discredit people who are attempting to keep the memory of the Holocaust alive and this may be dehumanising in the sense that it tries to deny people the chance to be human where to be human is to have an identity and to tell stories, or have a message, about who or what one is and ones lived experience. Moreover, elaborate Holocaust denial presents members of the Jewish community as evil and subhuman. Implicit in Holocaust denial is the message that no subgroup that is truly human would fabricate such atrocities for its own gain in the way that Jews have done with the Holocaust, and that Jewish lies are evidence of the fact of their irredeemable wickedness, where irredeemable wickedness is a way of being less than fully human. If denialism laws serve to restrict dehumanising speech, then it is not difficult to make the case, as some scholars have done,[216] that denialism laws fit into the wider category of hate speech laws, since this seems to be a standard hate speech law purpose.

Indeed, the case for criminalising Holocaust denial may include not merely harm prevention (i.e. preventing the dignitary affront of dehumanisation) but also a paternalistic argument about dehumanisation of the speaker. For, arguably, Holocaust denial involves a double dehumanisation: Holocaust denial is a way of dehumanising its victims but also a way of dehumanising the speaker. Denial itself speaks to a lack of humanity, a deficit in the human facilities for epistemic or hermeneutical recognition, empathy, and compassion for other people's suffering and the ability to comprehend that all life is precious, and any loss of life matters objectively speaking. It is a shortfall in proper respect for the humanity invested not merely in others, whoever they may be, but also in oneself. Once again, there are parallels here with the legal concept *hate speech*. For example, several critical race scholars have defended hate speech laws precisely on the grounds that hate speakers not only harm others but also hurt themselves in ways that could justify legal intervention.[217]

Along similar lines, it might be argued that Holocaust denial involves an element of cruelty, degradation, and humiliation typical of other examples of hate speech. For one thing, to deny that the Holocaust happened may demonstrate cruel indifference towards human suffering and death, including both of those who died and those who survived but now face the anguish of confronting Holocaust denial in public discourse. Cruelty is certainly a feature often associated with hate speech, in both ordinary and legal senses of the term.[218] Indeed, at the doctrinal level, the idea that hate speech typically involves forms of cruel, degrading, or humiliating treatment can be used as a tool or device to put meat on the bones of abstract laws, including abstract torts. To that end, elsewhere we have proposed legal tests of cruelty, degradation, and humiliation as devices for interpreting abstract elements of the tort of intentional infliction of emotional distress and the delict of injuria in cases involving hate speech.[219] Such proposals might be extended further to cases where these torts or delicts are used as civil remedies against Holocaust deniers.[220]

Of course, in the case of the tort of intentional emotional distress, the evidentiary burden of proving emotional distress could potentially prevent the tort from serving as an effective means of legal redress. However, other torts or delicts, such as the delict of injuria or Richard Delgado's proposed tort of racial insult, do not require evidence of emotional distress.[221] Moreover, there might be a good argument for legislators or courts to create, whether by statute or precedent, a bespoke cause of action, such as a tort of genocide denial, or some other civil remedy, allowing victims of the Holocaust and their families to bring lawsuits against Holocaust deniers 'if people feel that they have been aggrieved to their very core', as the American legal scholar Arthur Berney puts it.[222] Importantly, using a civil remedy to address what is in essence a public wrong need not preclude that civil remedy from being classified under the legal concept *hate speech*. A great deal of hate speech law is criminal law, but not always or necessarily; a substantial body of hate speech laws involve civil remedies of one type or other.[223]

7.6.3 Injury to Reputation, Social Standing, and Public Assurance

Elaborate forms of Holocaust denial do not merely deny the Holocaust happened but also carry a further imputation that Jewish people have manufactured this 'hoax' (or 'Holohaux') for nefarious purposes.[224]

Arguably, such forms of Holocaust denial contain content which exemplifies or instantiates certain broader categories of illegal hate speech including but not limited to group defamation.[225] Group defamation *senso stricto* is about maligning, traducing, disparaging, casting aspersions, discrediting people on the basis of unfounded accusations, false rumours, or untrue statements, and in manner intended or capable of damaging or tarnishing the social reputation of people identified by protected characteristics, and bringing them into contempt in the eyes of the public. Consider once again the legal proceedings surrounding Roger Garaudy's book *Les Mythes Fondateurs de la Politique Israélienne.* Garaudy challenged his original conviction, but the Paris Court of Appeal demurred citing the fact that the 'explicit and avowed aim of the book' was the description of the Holocaust as a conspiracy. In the words of the Court, 'the book has a purpose that is indeed the one reflected in the charge: damaging the honour and reputation of that community' [trans.].[226] The ECtHR agreed with that broad assessment of the book concluding that the prosecution of Garaudy 'pursued at least two of the legitimate aims provided for in [Art. 10(2) of] the Convention: "the prevention of disorder and crime" and "the protection of the reputation and rights of others".'[227]

Of course, it is one thing to acknowledge in general terms the fact that Holocaust denial may rise to the level of group defamation; it is quite another to demonstrate this is true of a given bit of denialist content. After all, bare forms of Holocaust denial may deny the Holocaust happened whilst avoiding explicit articulation of further defamatory ideas such as that the Holocaust was a hoax created by Jews around the world to facilitate the creation of Israel. Indeed, the sobering experience of watching other deniers go through criminal and civil trials may provide an incentive to revisionists to strip back their words to the barest forms, least vulnerable to legal jeopardy, unless of course they are seeking the publicity that comes from a trial. That said, even bare Holocaust denial may convey (imply, presuppose, or infer) a connotation or implication which is elaborate in nature. This is certainly the view of the Jewish Policy Institute which suggests that 'there is an inherent antisemitism in Holocaust denial, although it may not necessarily be obvious or immediately apparent.' 'Its insidious antisemitism is evident in its clear implication that the Holocaust is an invention of Jews or their agents.'[228] If this is true, then the onus is on courts to make determinations of whether a given piece of negationist or revisionist literature only has a bare meaning or instead conveys an implied, covert, or dog-whistle style message that amounts to elaborate Holocaust denial, say. However, once again there is nothing out of the ordinary here: certainly nothing that would stop denialist speech from being classified as hate speech. After all, legal scholars have routinely pointed to the fact that hate speech in the legal sense of the term can take implicit, coded, covert, implied, or sanitised forms.[229]

That said, courts will not always read into denialist speech a deeper implied meaning. In *Williamson v. Germany*,[230] for example, the ECtHR took at face value the denialist words spoken by the British clergyman Bishop Richard Williamson during an interview for Swedish TV recoded in Germany, namely as examples of bare Holocaust denial (e.g. 'Germany has paid out billions and billions of Deutschmarks and now Euros because the Germans have a guilt complex about their having gassed six million Jews, but I don't think six million Jews were gassed').[231] Interestingly, Williamson's original conviction by German domestic courts had been in relation to Art. 130(3) of the criminal code, which prohibits publicly denying acts committed under Nazi rule in a manner capable of disturbing the public peace. The ECtHR was satisfied that Germany had in this case 'pursued the legitimate aim of preventing a disturbance of the public peace in Germany and thus the prevention of disorder and crime'.[232] But what is missing from the German denialism law, and from the ECtHR's judgment in this case, is reference to a mechanism that explains why or how bare denialism is capable of disturbing the public peace. We suggest the ways in which bare denialism often conveys, in an implicit or coded way, elaborate denialism is one such mechanism.

Now in *Williamson* the ECtHR judgment does mention the fact that '[The Regional Court] found that it had been clear to [the applicant] that his statements could attract interest around the world, but particularly so in Germany on account of the country's history, the interview taking place in Germany and the fact that the Pope at that time, Pope Benedict XVI, was German'.[233] But the ECtHR goes no further in explaining the mechanism by which such 'interest' might transform or ignite into a public disturbance. One possibility is that bare denialism could lead members of far-right organisations in Germany, along with members of anti-fascist groups, to take to the streets simply in the name of protecting historical truth. But put in those stark terms, the explanation seems overdone given the context. What would Germans care if a visiting British clergyman, being interviewed for a Swedish TV programme they will probably never see, denies the Holocaust? Indeed, the ECtHR's apparent tin ear to context in *Williamson* cuts against the grain of the contextualism it relied upon in *Perinçek*. In the latter case, the ECtHR put weight on the fact that the applicant was a Turkish national publicly denying the Armenian genocide whilst on a speaking tour of Switzerland, thus posing a limited threat. At any rate, that the German denialism law potentially overestimates the danger to public peace posed by bare Holocaust denial has long been a source of criticism. According to the American scholar Ronald Dworkin, for example, '[i]t is implausible that allowing fanatics to deny the Holocaust would substantially increase the risk of fascist violence in Germany' given the fact that neo-Nazis have already 'found hundreds of lies and distortions with which to inflame Germans who are angry, resentful and prejudiced'.[234] Why should bare Holocaust denial 'be picked out for special censorship and punished so severely?'[235] Our answer is this: bare Holocaust denial frequently conveys connotations or implications which constitute elaborate denialism and, more specifically, often implies the big lie that the Jews invented the story of the Holocaust for their own gain. This big lie may inflame Germans above other lies and distortions precisely because it goes to the very heart of post-war guilt and German identity. What could make Germans any angrier than to feel that they have been duped into apologising and paying a high price in terms of both financial reparations and reputational damage for something that never happened whilst Jews laugh all the way to the bank?[236]

As well as injuring the reputation of Jews, Holocaust denial may also undermine the confidence that Jews might otherwise feel that they are citizens in good standing, or what Jeremy Waldron calls the 'public assurance' of 'civic dignity'. This is people's publicly underwritten sense or confidence that they enjoy a high and equal socio-legal status within their political community.[237] A society is supposed to give its members, especially those who have suffered historical injustices or atrocity crimes, public assurance that they are citizens in good standing. Publicly disseminated Holocaust denial material might be just as corrosive of such assurance as other forms of hate speech, especially in Europe but potentially also in the United States, a place to which many Jews escaped before, during, and after the Holocaust.[238] As the Holocaust itself destroyed any last shred of confidence Jewish people might have felt that they had good standing in German society, so Holocaust denial may undermine the confidence of Jews about their standing today. It forces Jews to ask themselves the following unsettling questions. *If we really are members of this society in good standing, how come others are publicly denying the facts surrounding a past attempt to remove us from this society for good through a campaign of extermination?* And, *if we have a high and equal status, why are some people denying the facts of the*

Holocaust when doing so aims to rehabilitate the ideology that led to that genocide in the first place and lays the groundwork for a repeat of those dark days? By forcing Jewish people to ask themselves these questions, Holocaust denial undermines the public assurance of their civic dignity. In addition to this, for the state to sit back and allow public Holocaust denial to go unpunished might further undermine public assurance of the fact that Jews possess legal rights that are the trappings of a high and equal socio-legal status. Those trappings include not only the right to exist (the right not to be the victim of genocide) but also the right not to be the victim of group defamation. Waldron confines his analysis to justifying group defamation laws, but we suggest that very similar arguments can be made for denialism laws.[239]

The wider point here is that if all holocaust denial includes the claim, whether overt and explicit or covert and implicit, that Jews have invented the Holocaust as part of a conspiracy of acquisition and replacement, and if such a claim constitutes group defamation or incitement to hatred against Jews, and if such things are common forms of hate speech in the legal sense of the term (which they certainly are in at least some jurisdictions[240]), then it would seem to follow that Holocaust denial constitutes hate speech in that sense. Perhaps this also brings into play another horn of the denial trilemma. After all, if group defamation laws already exist in given jurisdictions, as arguably they do in Germany via s. 130(2)(1)(c) of the criminal code, and, moreover, if there is a reasonable prospect of convicting Holocaust deniers under such laws, then what is the pressing need for stand-alone denialism laws? Indeed, in some countries, like the United States, there may be a socio-legal consensus that bare Holocaust denial, when it really is nothing more, should not be criminalised because of the detrimental impact doing so may have on public discourse and the risk that censorship of specific viewpoints is afoot.[241] That said, arguably one rationale for picking out Holocaust denial for stand-alone prohibition, especially in a country like German but potentially in other countries as well, is symbolic. In the words of the ECtHR in *Perinçek v. Switzerland*, a dictum repeated in *Williamson v. Germany*: 'States which have experienced the Nazi horrors […] may be regarded as having a special moral responsibility to distance themselves from the mass atrocities that they have perpetrated or abetted, by, among other things, outlawing their denial.'[242] Crucially for our main thesis, the idea that it may be legitimate in certain contexts to create separate denialism offences for symbolic reasons is consistent with similar sorts of arguments made in defence of hate speech laws generally.[243]

7.6.4 *Mens Rea*

For denialist speech to appropriately fall under the legal concept *hate speech* it must be worthy of being subject to legal sanction. Some people may believe that in order for this to be the case, especially when it comes to criminal sanctions, denialist statements must be not merely false but also wrongful in the sense that they must involve some sort of mens rea. How so? One alternative is to say that denialist speech is not hate speech when it is simply a matter of people getting the facts wrong, especially when there is no evidence of an intention to get the facts wrong, as in, no evidence of an intention to say things that the speaker knows or reasonably believes to be false (malicious falsehood).[244] It is interesting to note here that worries about the possibility of some speakers lacking intent to get the facts wrong played a key role in the early free speech norms promulgated by social media platforms.[245]

However, there are plenty of ways for Holocaust denial to be wrongful and worthy of criminalisation that do not rely on evidence of an intention to get the facts wrong. For one thing, there can be such a thing as morally culpable ignorance which in some instances is a matter of epistemic irresponsibility or negligence, namely a failure to take reasonable steps not to be ignorant or unaware. Morally culpable ignorance may also reflect wilful ignorance: a deliberate attempt to remain uninformed such as by assiduously avoiding situations which are likely to result in one becoming better informed and exchanging one's false opinions for knowledge of the true facts even though these situations do not impose an unreasonable burden. These forms of mens rea may be associated with the 'epistemic vices'[246] of carelessness and dogmatism, or with what Miranda Fricker calls 'epistemic injustices',[247] a different conceptual framework which may facilitate a shift in the normative focus from the epistemic failings of the Holocaust denier, for example, to the epistemic wrong done to victims of the Holocaust whose personal testimonies are being negated.

However, when it comes to denialist speech, unlike other cases of false or inaccurate content, it might seem inadequate to understand the wrongdoing solely in terms of epistemic vices or injustices of a general nature such as a lack of respect for what other people know. What about the attitudes sitting behind the epistemic failings? Thus, another alternative is to say that the mens rea element consists not simply in epistemic failings as such but epistemic failings borne of unjust or discriminatory ideological commitments.[248] So, for example, it could be argued that, in order to warrant criminalisation, speech denying the Holocaust, must include the mens rea element of being motivated by racist, prejudiced, or discriminatory attitudes, or else feelings or sentiments of hatred or hostility, towards Jews and/or intent to disseminate ideas based on racial superiority or anti-Semitism. Certainly, this chimes with the widely held perspective that Holocaust denial only ever springs from an anti-Semitic motive. In the words of the American legal analyst Alan Dershowitz:

> Of course there are anti-Semitic implications in Holocaust denial. Holocaust denial is quintessentially anti-Semitic. It can have no other motive and no other intended effect.[249]

At first glance, it is unclear whether this is meant as an empirical generalisation about the actual motivation and intended effect of most or all Holocaust denial or else as some kind of analytic statement about the ordinary meanings of the terms involved, or even a positive contribution to a debate about what those meanings ought to be, namely the argument that it would be better for some reason if speech were only called 'Holocaust denial' if the motive and intended effect is anti-Semitism. If Dershowitz has the latter in mind, then society might need a different word to use as a label for speech which questions the Holocaust but does not have anti-Semitism as its motive and intended effect.

If, however, the claim is meant as an empirical generalisation, such as the idea that Holocaust denial is on average motivated by prejudice, bigotry, intolerance, hostility, contempt, or hatred towards the Jewish people (i.e., anti-Semitism), then it relies on, or must presuppose, some independent account of what counts as an anti-Semitic motive and intended effect. If would not be enough merely to assume that anti-Semitism is partly defined by, or constituted from, a belief that the Holocaust did not happen such that to engage in Holocaust denial is by definition to have anti-Semitic motivations, because then the explanation would be circular. Instead, an anti-Semitic motive might be evidenced by the fact that the speaker harbours other bigoted, prejudiced, discriminatory, contemptuous, or hateful attitudes or sentiments towards the Jewish people and associates with people who hold such ideological views. Indeed, it may be that phrases such as 'the myth of the six million' have a conventional meaning among members of certain subgroups, including online communities, as expressions of disapproval, mistrust, and antipathy towards the Jewish people, and avowals of solidarity or identification with the in-group. By using such phrases, a member of the group might both intend to express the viewpoint that Jews are devious liars and not to be trusted and intend for others to interpret his use of those phrases in accordance with that conventional meaning within the group. There might be an overlap here with certain theories about the conventional semantics of slurs (see also Chapter 2).

However, if the mens rea element of Holocaust denial is to be associated with motives of prejudice and hostility towards Jews, then notice how this would blur some of the conceptual boundaries between hate speech and hate crime. After all, the assessment of motives of prejudice and hostility are among the defining elements of hate crime law, whether one is talking about sentence enhancement hate crimes or discrete hate crimes (see Chapter 6). By contrast, for the vast majority of denialism laws, and indeed for the vast majority of hate speech laws, racist motive is not specified as an element of the offending behaviour in the law as written.[250] To take one example, Art. 261-bis(4) of the Swiss criminal code makes it an offence for a person to deny, trivialise, or justify genocide or other crimes against humanity, on the grounds of race, ethnic origin, religion, or sexual orientation. Whilst the law as written mentions 'grounds of race', meaning that the speech in question must in some sense be about people, or target people, in virtue of their race, the law does not explicitly state that there must be a racist 'motive'. As a consequence, Swiss courts have frequently seen fit to discuss, firstly, whether or not there is an implicit legislative intent behind Art. 261-bis(4) which necessitates interpreting the statute as though racist motive is a necessary element of the offence, and, secondly, whether the mass extermination of the Jews could ever be denied for other than racist or anti-Semitic motives.[251]

Notwithstanding these complexities, there is yet another way of looking at the mens rea of Holocaust denial, namely the intent to disseminate ideas based on racial superiority or hatred. For example, some legal scholars have taken the view that if hate speech or, more specifically, hate propaganda, in the legal sense of the term, is defined by international standards, including Art. 4(a) of the ICERD which calls on states to declare an offence punishable by law 'all dissemination of ideas based on racial superiority or hatred', for example, then Holocaust denial can be counted as 'a pernicious form of hate propaganda'.[252] The working assumption here seems to be that Holocaust denial *is itself* an idea necessarily based on racism or hatred towards Jews. But how so?

Perhaps the thought is that because Holocaust denial has no basis in fact and is fundamentally irrational in that sense, there can be no other reason for subscribing to Holocaust denial than racism or hatred towards Jews. But there is a difference between the psychological reasons that might drive a person to subscribe to denialism and denialism itself.

Typical reasons for ascribing to denialism might be anti-Semitic prejudice but this does not necessarily make denialism *as an idea* grounded in anti-Semitism. In what ways might denialism as an idea be grounded in racism or hatred? For example, is Holocaust denial grounded in anti-Semitism in the way that segregationism is grounded in anti-black racism? Arguably not. Segregationism is the advocacy of a system in which there is systematic separation of people into racial groups for the purposes of accommodation, education, work, recreation, and so on. It is clearly grounded in (false) theses about racial differences and natural hierarchy (i.e. racism). Holocaust denial, by contrast, at least in its bare forms, is simply the act of publicly denying the existence of the Holocaust. It is grounded in (false) theses about there being no gas chambers and no Nazi grand plan to exterminate the Jews. Taken in themselves, these theses are false but not racist, although certainly what attracts many people to such theses is their own racist prejudices.

However, we suggest that it is a very different story when it comes to hardcore, evaluative, and softcore forms of Holocaust denial. Consider statements which combine bare Holocaust denial with claims that Jewish people around the world fabricated the Holocaust to accumulate sympathy, power, and territory; with claims that if the Holocaust did happen, then it would be no bad thing; or with claims that Jews should stop being so sensitive about other people publicly expressing their Holocaust denial beliefs. Self-evidently, these forms of Holocaust denial *are* grounded in core tenets of anti-Semitic ideology. Hardcore Holocaust denial is based on (false) theses about the evil nature of the Jewish people; evaluative Holocaust denial is based on (false) theses about a hierarchy of fundamental moral worth of people; and softcore Holocaust denial is based on (false) theses about how Jews are unreasonably or unnaturally sensitive to the public dissemination of denials of the Holocaust, all because they are Jews.

Of course, at this stage it might be countered that another key mens rea element of Holocaust denial is intention to incite hatred against Jews, and that it is far from obvious whether this further element is present in all forms of Holocaust denial. However, we do not accept that this shows denialist speech cannot be hate speech; as we shall now explain.

7.6.5 *Intention or Likelihood of Inciting Hatred*

If the primary purpose of denialism laws were the restriction of speech that has the intention or likelihood of inciting hatred against members of the relevant groups, then the evidentiary hurdle is to show that denialist speech indeed has such intent or likely effect. But once again courts have reached different conclusions about this depending on the circumstances.

The case law and general comments of the UN Human Rights Committee are instructive here. In *Faurisson v. France*, the Committee was persuaded of the fact that denialist speech can sometimes constitute 'advocacy of national, racial or religious hatred that constitutes incitement to discrimination, hostility or violence', as provided under Art. 20(2) of the ICCPR. In the words of Prafullachandra Bhagwati in his concurring opinion:

> Since the statement made by the author, read in the context of its necessary consequence, was calculated or was at least of such a nature as to raise or strengthen anti-Semitic feelings and create or promote hatred, hostility or contempt against the Jewish community as dishonest fabricators of lies, the restriction imposed on such statement by the Gayssot Act was intended to serve the purpose of respect for the right and interest of the Jewish community to live free from fear of an atmosphere of antisemitism, hostility or contempt. The second element required for the applicability of article 19, paragraph 3, was therefore satisfied.

By 2011, however, the Committee had, via General Comment No. 34, overruled *Faurisson* on the grounds that denialist speech, as an instance of a more general kind of speech, namely, 'expressions of an erroneous opinion or an incorrect interpretation of past events', was in fact protected speech under Art. 19 of the ICCPR.[253] Yet it would be incorrect to interpret this Comment as a volte-face on the narrower question of whether denialist speech can sometimes constitute advocacy of national, racial, or religious hatred in the relevant manner. The Comment simply does not address that more thorny question.

However, it is not hard to find examples of the legal opinion that bare Holocaust denial does not necessarily constitute incitement to hatred, discrimination, or violence and cannot simply be assumed in all cases to contribute to a climate of hatred, discrimination, or violence. Consider *Case of Guenter Deckert* from Germany in 1994.[254] Here the Mannheim State Court ordered a re-trial of Deckert's first case after the far-right political activist had been convicted of offences under s. 130(1)(1) of the German criminal code, which prohibits inciting hatred, discrimination, or violence against people on account of their belonging to protected groups 'in a manner capable of disturbing the public peace'. During a public meeting, Deckert had translated to the audience the oration of an American Holocaust denier, Fred A. Leuchter. The retrial itself caused public uproar because, despite convicting Deckert of the offences, Judge Orlet also described facts related to the Holocaust as a mere 'thesis' and described

Deckert as 'no anti-Semite' but rather a 'responsible personality' who considered it 'desirable that research constantly rechecked even historical theses that are considered valid'.[255] Nevertheless, the chief reason the Mannheim State Court ordered the re-trial was that in its view the lower court had failed to gather enough evidence to demonstrate guilt under s. 130(1)(1) since it is at least conceivable that a historian could deny the Holocaust without in fact inciting hatred against the Jewish people.

Of course, one strategy is to drop the evidentiary burden built into incitement to hatred laws and simply prohibit denialist speech via standalone denialism offences. But this does not in itself settle the matter of whether all denialist speech incites hatred. This strategy also attracts the criticism that it sweeps up more speech that is warranted by the justification. In the words of the American political scientist Erik Bleich, an expert on comparative hate speech law in context, 'these laws are overly broad if they are not responding to the fundamental underlying problem of fighting incitement to racial hatred.'[256]

This same worry can also be seen in other leading Holocaust denial cases elsewhere in Europe. For example, in 2007 the Spanish Constitutional Court declared as unconstitutional the offence of genocide denial laid down in Art. 607(2) of the Spanish Criminal Code on the grounds that, to respect the constitutional and human right to freedom of expression, genocide denial could only be criminalised if it were intended to create or in fact created a social attitude of hostility towards genocide victims, whereas Art. 607(2) contained no such limiting requirement or qualification. In the Court's view:

> not even tendentially [...] can it be stated that all denial of conduct legally defined as a crime of genocide objectively pursues the creation of a social climate of hostility against those persons who belong to the same groups, and who in their day, were victims of a specific crime of genocide, the inexistence of which is claimed, nor can it be stated that any denial may per se be capable of achieving this. [trans.][257]

Similarly, in *Perinçek v. Switzerland* dating back to 2013, the ECtHR held that the applicant's 'rejection of the legal characterisation of the events of 1915 [as 'genocide'] was not in itself sufficient to amount to incitement of hatred towards the Armenian people.'[258] In reaching this judgment, the ECtHR placed an emphasis on the context of denialist speech.

> The next question is whether the statements could nevertheless be seen as a form of incitement to hatred or intolerance towards the Armenians on account of the applicant's position and the wider context in which they

> were made. In the cases concerning statements in relation to the Holocaust that have come before the former Commission and the Court, this has, for historical and contextual reasons, invariably been presumed [...]. However, the Court does not consider that the same can be done in this case, where the applicant spoke in Switzerland about events which had taken place on the territory of the Ottoman Empire about ninety years previously. While it cannot be excluded that statements relating to those events could likewise promote a racist and antidemocratic agenda, and do so through innuendo rather than directly, the context does not require this to be automatically presumed, and there is not enough evidence that this was so in the present case. The only element that could denote such an agenda was the applicant's self-professed affiliation with Talaat Pasha. However, the Swiss courts did not elaborate on this point, and there is no evidence that the applicant's membership of the so-called Talaat Pasha Committee was driven by a wish to vilify the Armenians and spread hatred for them rather than his desire to contest the idea that the events of 1915 and the following years had constituted genocide [...]. [trans.][259]

Clearly if genocide denial, say, cannot be simply presumed to have the intention and/or likely effect of inciting hatred against members of the relevant groups, then it must be proven on a case-by-case basis that a given bit of denialist speech had such an intention and/or likely effect given the context. There will be various impediments to meeting this threshold – some peculiar to individual countries but at least some more universal. Consider the challenge of explaining how speech could be plausibly said to 'stir up hatred' when the audience mainly consists of people who already share the opinions or worldview being expressed. Call this the preaching to the choir conundrum. When the main audience for, or consumers of, Holocaust denial tends to be other Holocaust deniers and anti-Semites who already share a similar viewpoint about the events of World War II and of Jews, as tends to be the case both offline and online, how could Holocaust denial have the intention and/or likely effect of stirring up hatred against the Jewish people? After all, it would be scarcely credible to maintain that this is a case of speakers bringing Jews into contempt in the eyes of the audience or else of creating feelings of intense animosity towards Jews ex nihilo where previously no adverse beliefs, attitudes, sentiments, or feelings were harboured.

However, there are various compelling answers to the preaching to the choir conundrum. First, although not true of all members of a receptive audience, there may be at least some individuals who do not have a strong pre-existing contempt for, or intense animosity towards, Jews, a deeply entrenched fear of, or clear-eyed perception of outgroup threat posed by, Jews, or a profound sense of grievance and associated desire for retribution against Jews. Rather, their receptiveness might be the result of a generalised receptiveness to conspiracy theories, a psychological need for social companionship, camaraderie, and a sense of belonging within a community, and a thirst for the consumption of popular culture (videos, memes, images, live streams) and merchandise (coffee mugs, T-shirts, posters). Even if their deeper values (e.g. a belief in social hierarchies) and worldview (e.g. mistrust of government, the media) may predispose them to being more receptive to denier ideology than to other alternatives, the greater and more immediate pay-off might be the comfort in feeling they have found 'their people', having their minds occupied, or simply being entertained, as opposed to finding an outlet for an existing heightened state of denialist, anti-Semitic arousal.[260] The arousal comes later, as a product of exposure to denialist speech.

Second, denialist speech might be intended, and have the effect, of stirring up hatred in various ways, even in the case of audience members who are already mistrustful of, or ill-disposed towards, the targeted group. It might turn weak feelings of mistrust or antipathy into strong feelings of hatred, as in, to whip people up into a frenzy or heightened state of anger, resentment, and odium (*I HATE THEM*!); enliven or awaken previously nascent or dormant attitudes or feelings of contempt or hatred towards the targeted group (*Only now do see how much I've always hated them)*; provide a grounding or new basis for existing negative sentiments towards the targeted group (*That's why I should hate them*); establish a cognitive focal point for non-cognitive feelings (*I knew there was a good reason why I hated them*); redirect existing feelings of hatred against a different, more generalised class of persons (e.g. non-WASPs, liars) in the direction of the targeted group by pointing out that members of the targeted group are not merely members of the wider, mistrusted class of persons but are the 'worst cases' or 'most despicable or dangerous members' of that class (*Since I hate liars, I ought to hate Jews*); or furnish a justification for feeling a certain way about Jews and acting on it (*Why shouldn't I give full rein to my hatred of them?*). For a person who is already mistrustful of, or ill-disposed towards, Jews, receiving content from a speaker who has a reputation as a trusted source of information, or simply receiving information from a very large number of likeminded 'patriots', to the effect that the Holocaust is a lie fabricated by Jews for nefarious purposes, could be enough to make them think that it is rational, normal, legitimate, or simply ok to feel negatively towards Jews and that there is no reason not to lose their inhibitions and set free their true feelings.

Overall, our key message here is that there is nothing in these explanations of how denialist speech can operate to stir up hatred even among members of a receptive audience that should preclude denialist speech from being considered hate speech in the legal sense of the term. After all, it can be pointed out that similar processes were at play when the Nazis used anti-Semitic hate propaganda to incite hatred against the Jews in Germany. As David Kretzmer puts it: 'For [the Nazi regime and ideology to thrive], it was essential that preexisting ideas, attitudes, and beliefs be socially prevalent, and that Hitler have the freedom to espouse publicly and disseminate his anti-Semitic propaganda which fed on those ideas, attitudes, and beliefs.'[261] Michel Rosenfeld makes a similar point about the function of cross burning in the American South. 'As Klan members are predisposed by their ideology to contemplate perpetrating violence motivated by racial hatred, the ritualistic convening involving cross burning seem particularly apt to whip up the emotions, to exacerbate the hatred, and dispel any lingering inhibitions to turn the shared hatred into violence.'[262]

Of course, it may be that, depending on the context, not all instances of denialist speech have the intention and/or likely effect of stirring up hatred against the targeted group. But, in our view, that does not make it inapt to classify denialist speech as hate speech in the legal sense of the term. Even if applying a denialism law to a particular case does not in fact mean punishing a speaker for stirring up of hatred, because in the circumstances of that case the denialism did not in fact rise to the level of stirring up hatred, that does not mean the denialism law cannot be considered a hate speech law. For one thing, the law may still serve as a deterrence to other deniers, including deniers in contexts in which there would be an intention and/or likely effect of stirring up hatred. Furthermore, just as hate speech laws can serve various functions at the same time, so denialism laws may also have multiple purposes simultaneously. We have already looked at several other purposes that are not to do with preventing the stirring up of hatred. Interestingly, other purposes relate to even more indirect harms than we have so far considered, where the evidential hurdle is even higher. It is to these we now turn; but once again we shall argue that denialism laws can be seen as hate speech laws.

7.6.6 Indirect Harms

For many legislatures and courts, the underlying purposes of denialism laws cannot be fully understood without also pointing to the indirect harms of denialist speech. Given the subject matter of this book, this insight has important conceptual-legal consequences. For, if the purposes of denialism laws include the prevention of indirect harms of the sort typically associated with hate speech in general, then it becomes even harder to say denialist speech does not fall under the legal concept *hate speech*. Moreover, this seems to be true not just of hardcore forms but also bare forms of denialist speech.

What, then, are the indirect harms associated with denialist speech and that might suggest an overlap with the indirect harms conventionally associated with hate speech in general? Below we provide an indicative list (non-exhaustive) of indirect harms associated with Holocaust denial once again on the assumption that many of these harms can be analogised to a greater or lesser extent to harms associated with denialist speech in general.

(i) Holocaust denial in its synchronous form can be a propaganda tool that diverts attention or spreads doubt and confusion about what is really happening and in a way that reduces the chances of intervention to stop it.
(ii) Holocaust denial can be a rhetorical strategy that helps to rehabilitate the political ideology and regime responsible for the Holocaust and in a way that clears the path for a return of the latter.
(iii) Holocaust denial is seen as important to neo-Nazis groups and anti-Fascist organisations alike and as such can be a catalyst for demonstrations and counter-demonstrations of the sort capable of disturbing the public peace.
(iv) Holocaust denial can be a recruiting sergeant for, rallying point among, extremist and violent neo-Nazi groups whose activities pose a threat to peace and security.
(v) Holocaust denial can undermine the social norm or expectation that *Stunde Null* would be and forever remain an absolute break with the past and a radical new beginning defined by the sweeping away of the old evils of anti-Semitism and people coming together to commit to and abide by the principle of never again.
(vi) Holocaust denial can serve to normalise and legitimate anti-Semitism in general.
(vii) Holocaust denial can contribute to a climate of anti-Semitism in which there is an increased risk of the repetition of similar events to those of the Nazi regime, including hatred, discrimination, violence, and atrocities committed against the Jewish people.
(viii) Holocaust denial can produce feelings of social exclusion, isolation, aloneness, intimidation, and fear among Jews, a sense that they belong to a group that is Other, not part of society, separate, alone, mistrusted, despised, unwanted, and at risk of violence.
(ix) Holocaust denial can produce feelings which cause some Jewish people to step back from public discourse and public life in general.
(x) Holocaust denial can cause some Jewish people to step back from public discourse and public life in general in a way that could undermine the democratic legitimacy of laws and even the political legitimacy of the state.

If these are some of the indirect harms of Holocaust denial – the prevention of which may be among the purposes served by denialism laws[263] – then it is not difficult to make the case that Holocaust denial, including bare Holocaust denial, is a form of hate speech in the legal sense of the term.[264] That is because these sorts of indirect harms also figure in conventional accounts of the indirect harms of hate speech the prevention of which is part of the legitimate function of hate speech laws in general.[265]

More difficult for legislators, public prosecutors, and courts is the task of assessing the degree to which these indirect harms exist in given contexts. But make such assessments is precisely what they have done and in a range of cases, especially involving Holocaust deniers. In *Garaudy v. France*, for example, the ECtHR held that the particular denialist speech in which the applicant was engaged 'calls into question the values on which the fight against racism and anti-Semitism is based and is likely to seriously disturb public order'.[266] Thus, the ECtHR concluded that the French domestic law – namely, s. 24-bis of the Act of 29 July 1881 – 'aims to secure the peaceful coexistence of the French population' and, therefore, that the proceedings against Garaudy pursued legitimate aims provided for in the European Convention under Art. 10(2) including 'the prevention of disorder or crime'.[267]

The case of Ernst Zündel, one of the most significant figures in the denialist movement during his lifetime, is similarly instructive. In 2003 the Canadian Citizenship and Immigration Minister issued a national security certificate for the detention and deportation of Zündel under the Canadian Immigration and Refugee Protection Act, which gives the Minister the right to deny access to Canadian territory to persons, including refugee claimants, who are 'security risks'. The Minister did not postulate any automatic connection between Holocaust denial as such and security risks, but instead relied upon the threat to Canada's national security from the particular circumstances surrounding Zündel's association with members of extremist and violent neo-Nazi groups. The validity of the certificate was upheld in 2004 by the Federal Court in *Zündel, Re*.[268] Based on a significant amount of public and private testimony, Justice Pierre Blais concluded that Zündel was directly involved with a number of individuals within 'the violent racist and extremist movement' including Zündel being in regular contact and even funding their activities. Zündel took his case to the UN Human Rights Committee in *Ernst Zündel v. Canada*.[269] He claimed, *inter alia*, a violation of Art. 19 of the ICCPR on the grounds that his detention and deportation were based solely on his public expression of unorthodox opinions about the fate of Jews during World War II and that his continued research and revision of errors in standard histories of the period were the types of activities that Art. 19 is designed to protect, and that the national security charges against him were politically motivated and arbitrary and so in violation of Art. 19.[270] The Committee, however, ruled this part of his complaint inadmissible on the grounds that Zündel 'failed to pursue this potential domestic remedy'.[271] Upon deportation to Germany, Zündel was immediately arrested by the authorities and charged with offences under ss. 130(1)(1) (incitement to hatred, discrimination, or violence) and 130(3) (Holocaust denial) of the German criminal code, for posting Holocaust denial material on his website *Zündelsite.org*. In *Case of Ernst Zündel*,[272] the Mannheim State Court convicted Zündel and handed down a prison sentence of five years. Both ss. 130(1)(1) and 130(3) require that the offending conduct be done 'in a manner capable of disturbing the public peace'. In his verdict Judge Meinerzhagen maintained that Zündel's conduct met the latter threshold not merely because of its ulterior motive ('Zündel aims to return to the fascist state') but because of the chosen means, namely the unlimited numbers of individuals who could access *Zundelsite.org* ('Therein especially lies the danger of that medium').

These cases speak to a clear overlap between the sorts of assessments of indirect harms involved in justifying and applying denialism laws and those involved in hate speech laws in general. Many jurists have also sought to draw parallels between these harms. The Canadian lawyer Martin Imbleau, for example, draws an analogy from the link between hate propaganda and core international crimes across to the link between denialist speech and such crimes. As he puts it, '[d]enial, like propaganda, may not be a clear and present danger, but it is a clear and future danger.'[273] Similarly, just as some legal scholars have described denialist speech as 'a precursor to the subordination, diminishment and ultimately the destruction of a people',[274] so others have characterised hate speech as 'a precursor to more violent types of hate crime, including assault and murder'.[275] Indeed, in the famous US Supreme Court case *R.A.V v. City of St. Paul* dating back to 1992,[276] involving the application of the City of St. Paul's Bias-Motivated Crime Ordinance to circumstances involving the burning of a cross on the property of an African American family, Justice Scalia asked Tom Foley, the lawyer defending the City of St. Paul, why the ordinance only covered cross burning that targeted the homes and businesses of African Americans and not people with disabilities, for instance. Foley replied that this was a matter of context: that cross burning had a particular historical significance to African Americans 'as a precursor to violence and hatred in this country'.[277] Although Foley's argument was ultimately rejected by Scalia, other justices were more sympathetic to this form of contextualism. For example, Justice Stevens held that the ordinance did in fact fall with the majority court's own exception that allowed content-based restrictions based on the 'secondary effects' of speech: 'Certainly a legislature [...] may determine that the risk of injury or breach of peace created by race-based threats is greater than that created by other threats.'[278]

To clarify, however, our purpose in this chapter, and the book, is not to mount a normative defence of various social and legal sanctions against hate speech. Rather, it is to explore the outer terrain of the ordinary and legal concepts of hate speech. Thus, we shall not attempt here to discuss the merits of the various principled and practical arguments for and against banning Holocaust denial.[279] Our central argument is instead that there is an overwhelming analogical as well as conceptual, doctrinal, and normative case for classifying genocide denial as a sui generis form of hate speech in the legal sense of the term and, moreover, that this case supports classifying as hate speech law both qualified denialism offences that prohibit *denialism plus* and unqualified denialism offences that prohibit bare denialist speech. Nevertheless, there is one final piece of the jigsaw puzzle that must be put into position before we can rest our argument. It has to do with the absence of denialism provisions in the landmark international laws dealing with incitement to genocide and hate speech in general. On the face of it, the absence of denialism provisions from these instruments seems to cast doubt on the plausibility of our central argument.

7.7 Denialism in International Law

The aim of this final section is to pose and answer the following sceptical questions. If denialist speech is or ought to be classifiable as hate speech in the legal sense of the term, and if certain early landmark international laws provide a key benchmark for such classification, then why were denialism provisions absent from those early texts? Do the most plausible explanations for this absence undermine our main thesis that denialist speech is aptly classified as a sui generis form of hate speech? Finally, if denialist speech can be counted as hate speech in the legal sense of the term despite the absence of denialism provisions from the landmark texts, then what about other forms of speech such as defamation of religion? The danger here is turning the legal concept into a porous idea that might contain anything. Operating as a broad umbrella concept might be a useful purpose of the ordinary concept *hate speech* (see also Chapter 5) but given the job of the legal concept in providing precision, publicity, and predictability, this result would seem to be catastrophic for the concept or, to be more exact, for our theory of the concept (*reductio ad absurdum*).

In what follows we begin by looking at the place of denialism provisions in recent international law. We then turn to highlight but also explain the absence of such provisions in the early landmark international laws on incitement to genocide and hate speech in general. We finish by addressing the potential for a slippery slope that ends with the inclusion of defamation of religion under the legal concept *hate speech*.

7.7.1 Denialism Provisions in Recent International Law

To understand the place of anti-denialism norms in international law it is important to note a broader distinction between two kinds of norms: prohibitionist and non-prohibitionist.[280] The first kind is exemplified in treaties which oblige states parties to prohibit denialist speech, whether as written or interpreted. The absence of denialism provisions in the text of the ICERD, for example, has not stopped the Committee on the Elimination of Racial Discrimination (CERD), which monitors compliance with the ICERD, from expanding its interpretation of the Convention to include a norm against certain forms of denialism. In 1997, for example, the Committee criticised Belgium's denial law for being too narrow by focusing only on the Holocaust and ignoring other genocides.[281] Indeed, in 2013 CERD promulgated its General Recommendation No. 35 which explicitly 'recommends that public denials or attempts to justify crimes of genocide and crimes against humanity, as defined by international law, should be declared as offences punishable by law, provided that they clearly constitute incitement to racial violence or hatred'.[282] The UN Special Rapporteur on contemporary forms of racism, xenophobia, and related intolerance has also emphasised the 'importance of criminalizing the approval, denial or belittlement of the Holocaust in national law, given that such denial could *potentially* promote racist ideologies and hence constitute hate speech under [Art. 4(a) of the ICERD].'[283]

The work of the CERD on hate speech in general, and denialist speech in particular, speaks to a sort of radical activism in support of victims and their perspectives,[284] and stands in marked contrast to the work of the UN

Human Rights Committee. Following its decision to overrule *Faurisson v. France*, the Committee has frequently expressed concern at the rise of denialism laws and stated that any laws that penalise the 'expression of opinions about historical facts' are incompatible with the ICCPR.[285] The primary concern here is with speakers and the right to freedom of expression. Indeed, unlike the CERD, the Committee often refers to denialism laws as 'memory laws'. Arguably, this is a loaded term which minimises and mischaracterises what is at stake: most ordinary genocide deniers are not people who were themselves directly involved in the events they are denying and so it is not their memories that are being regulated but those of the survivors and victims' families: the very same people whose memories the deniers are trivialising, minimising, or denying.

Prohibitionist norms against denialist speech are also exemplified by Art. 1(1)(c)/(d) of the Council Framework Decision, which came into force on 6 December 2008. This provision requires Member States to make denialist speech punishable under domestic law including denial of core international crimes as defined by the Rome Statute and denial of Nazi crimes as defined by the Charter of the International Military Tribunal. In 2014 the Report from the Commission to the European Parliament and the Council on the implementation found a mixed picture with many Member States relying on existing parts of domestic criminal codes and interpretative case law to comply with the requirements of the Council Framework Decision, rather than introducing specific new legislation.[286] From 1 December 2014, the EU was able to bring infringement proceedings against Member States. For example, the Commission sent 'letters of formal notice' to Belgium, Bulgaria, Finland, Poland, and Sweden in February 2021[287] and to Greece, the Netherlands, and Lithuania in June 2021.[288] Member States have two months to reply to the letters; after that the Commission may send a reasoned opinion. If that fails to persuade the Member States to act, the Commission may refer the matter to the European Court of Justice.

Council framework decisions cannot have the effect of determining domestic criminal liability, unless that effect derives from national legislation adopted for their implementation.[289] This partly explains why the aforementioned Council Framework Decision has brought only minor changes in domestic legislation. Because it does not impose stringent obligations on the Member States, their constitutions remain legally superior and so domestic obligations to respect freedom of expression are unaffected. The Greek legislature, for example, waited until 2014 before passing its denialism law.[290] Moreover, Greek denialism law departs in a crucial way from the Council Framework Decision: whereas the Decision identifies certain national and international courts as sources of authoritative classification of events as genocides or other atrocity crimes for the purposes of denialism laws, the Greek denialism law identifies its own parliament as the authoritative source of recognition. Thus, when the first prosecution under the denialism law was brought against the German historian Heinz A. Richter, the Court of First Instance in Rethymno acquitted Richter and held that the denialism law was unconstitutional, primarily on the grounds that, by identifying the Greek parliament as the source of authoritative recognition, the law had not only violated the principles of the rule of law (separation of powers) but also contravened European law (the Council Framework Decision).[291] Even though the Court's decision was not binding (because it was the decision of a Court of First Instance rather than the Special Highest Court of Greece), public prosecutors in Greece have failed to successfully bring new cases of denialism in the intervening years. This partly explains the EU decision to send a letter of formal notice to Greece in June 2021.[292]

Arguably, then, the true effect of the Council Framework Decision lies not in immediately triggering the enactment of new domestic denialism laws or altering existing criminal laws, or even requiring courts to make specific decisions in legal cases involving denialist speech. Rather, it requires but also legitimises a broad legislative and judicial reassessment and reinterpretation of the domestic legal offering in the light of the anti-denialism norm articulated in the Decision[293] (under the general European legal principle of conforming interpretation[294]). As a result, its effects have been more intangible and diffuse but arguably include gradually expanding the field of focus in Member States from solely Holocaust denial to denial of atrocity crimes in general. Thus, even though the Decision has had relatively little effect in Western Europe, with most states yet to adopt significant measures of execution, many former Soviet states have embraced it. Indeed, they have relied on its broader definition of denialist speech as impetus to criminalise both denial of Nazi crimes and crimes committed by their former communist regimes.

The prohibitionist norm against denialist speech has also been reaffirmed in other notable European laws. For example, building on the rubric of the Convention on Cybercrime (the so-called Budapest Convention),[295] the Additional Protocol concerning the criminalisation of acts of a racist and xenophobic nature committed through computer systems,[296] contains the following provision on denialist speech.

Article 6 – Denial, gross minimisation, approval or justification of genocide or crimes against humanity

(1) Each Party shall adopt such legislative measures as may be necessary to establish the following conduct as criminal offences under its domestic law, when committed intentionally and without right: distributing or otherwise making available, through a computer system to the public, material which denies, grossly minimises, approves or justifies acts constituting genocide or crimes against humanity, as defined by international law and recognised as such by final and binding decisions of the International Military Tribunal, established by the London Agreement of 8 August 1945, or of any other international court established by relevant international instruments and whose jurisdiction is recognised by that Party.

(2) A Party may either (a) require that the denial or the gross minimisation referred to in paragraph 1 of this article is committed with the intent to incite hatred, discrimination or violence against any individual or group of individuals, based on race, colour, descent or national or ethnic origin, as well as religion if used as a pretext for any of these factors, or otherwise (b) reserve the right not to apply, in whole or in part, paragraph 1 of this article.

As of July 2023, the Additional Protocol has been ratified by thirty-five countries including mainly members of the Council of Europe but also three non-member states: Morocco, Paraguay, and Senegal. Canada and South Africa have signed but not yet ratified. A further thirty non-member states have been automatically invited to accede to the Additional Protocol carried over from invitations to accede to the Convention on Cybercrime.[297] More importantly, several ratifying countries have entered either reservations or declarations relating to Art. 6(2)(a). For example, Greece made the following declaration upon ratification: 'the Hellenic Republic requires that the denial or the gross minimisation referred to in paragraph 1 of Article 6 is committed with the intent to incite hatred, discrimination or violence against any individual or group of individuals, based on race, colour, descent or national or ethnic origin, as well as religion if used as a pretext for any of these factors'.[298] Moreover, as provided by Art. 6(2)(b), a number of states have exercised their reserved right not to criminalise denialist speech, including all three of the aforementioned non-member states. Arguably, this fudge helps to preserve the spirit of the anti-denialism norm whilst at the same time allowing space for countries to not implement the norm based on their own context including history, social make-up, legal culture, and dominant ideologies.

It is important to note, however, that whereas the United States is a party to the Convention on Cybercrime Convention,[299] it has not signed the Additional Protocol. Arguably, this decision partly reflects the domestic

US free speech norm. Prohibiting denialist speech is simply not something the United States would seriously entertain given its First Amendment jurisprudence. Even though Art. 6(2)(b) explicitly gives states parities the right not to prohibit denialist speech, thus giving the United States a landing zone to be able to at least sign and ratify the Protocol, the United States has still not seen fit to do so. However, the United States has played a more prominent role in the emergence of non-prohibitionist international denialism laws, to which we now turn.

There have been three UN General Assembly resolutions on Holocaust remembrance and denial, all of which were adopted without a vote,[300] and all of which are both soft laws and non-prohibitionist laws. In January 2005, Member States of the UN convened a historic special session of the General Assembly to commemorate the sixtieth anniversary of the liberation of Auschwitz. Building on this momentum, Israel subsequently initiated the Holocaust Remembrance Resolution of 1 November 2005 which, amongst other things, 'Rejects any denial of the Holocaust as an historical event, either in full or part' and requests that the Secretary-General establishes outreach and educational programmes. Although the Resolution was initiated by Israel, it was supported by 114 states, including the United States.[301] In fact, the draft resolution was only included in the relevant session of the UN General Assembly after this was requested in a letter of 12 August 2005 by Australia, Canada, Israel, Russia, and the United States. The US involvement reflected not only its general role as a moral and political leader in international affairs but also the foreign policy goals of George W. Bush. After his first presidential term strained relations with European nations, in his second term he sought to recast his image abroad. For its part, Russia typically focuses on the crimes of Nazi Germany of which the Holocaust is one part and so remembrance of the war is part of a narrative about Russia's role in resisting fascism and oppression. Even though it has not been an instigator of Holocaust remembrance or moves to enshrine norms against Holocaust denial in international law, nevertheless in 2005 Russia was being wooed by America, who wanted Russia onside in what it saw as looming conflict with China. President Putin in return wanted Russia to assume an international presence as a befitting its status as a great power, and the seduction of Bush and the West was part of that strategy.[302]

Initiated by the United States, the Holocaust Denial Resolution of 26 January 2007 recalls the earlier resolution's rejection of Holocaust denial and reiterates the need for education. Whilst the United States has long supported Holocaust remembrance, it also used the resolution as an opportunity to make a wider point about the behaviour of Iran. In the words of the US representative, Mr Wolff, during a plenary session discussing the draft resolution:

> Just last month, the Iranian regime sponsored a conference questioning the historical fact of the atrocities of the Holocaust. Iranian President Ahmadinejad has also called for the State of Israel to be wiped off the map. That same regime is under Security Council sanctions right now to prevent it from developing nuclear weapons in direct violation of its obligations under the Treaty on the Non-Proliferation of Nuclear Weapons. The confluence of those three forces cannot be viewed abstractly or in isolation from each other. They create a cauldron of conflict that cannot be ignored. Some will cloak their hatred and hidden agenda by invoking the right to free speech and academic freedom. There is a categorical difference between free speech and speech which wilfully and maliciously ignores recognized historical facts in order to advance an ulterior agenda.[303]

The Iranian representative, Mr Gharibi, countered that in fact it was the United States that had 'mischievous intention' in presenting the draft resolution to the General Assembly.[304] He also defended the conference alluded to by Mr Wolff, saying that 'addressing historical events of horrific enormity with a view to avoiding their recurrence requires a commensurate degree of research, scrutiny and rigour' and that '[t]he seriousness and sincerity of that endeavour will indeed be undermined by rendering political judgments on such events and closing the door to any inquiry on their characteristics, scope and extent'.[305] Finally, Mr Gharibi argued that if the United States were really concerned about genocide, then 'the draft resolution would necessarily have referred to other cases of genocide perpetrated in various parts of the world in the past and at present, especially the crimes perpetrated in Hiroshima and Nagasaki, Palestine, Rwanda and the Balkans'.[306]

For his part, the Egyptian representative, Mr Abdelaziz, seized the chance to draw parallels between Holocaust denial and another grey area of hate speech, namely defamation of religion. He explained that in thinking about the draft resolution, 'we cannot help but be reminded of the question of a standard of morality in the exercise of the freedom of expression, which is related to other issues [...] [including] the controversy over the cartoons of the Prophet Mohammed, which has created tensions and divisions among peoples in many parts of the world.'[307] We shall return to that unresolved dispute below.

The third resolution was adopted fifteen years later. The Holocaust Denial Resolution of 25 January 2022 was initiated by Israel and Germany.

General Assembly resolutions can be adopted without a vote only if no state party declares clear intention to vote against. In getting the General Assembly to accept the resolution without a vote, Germany and Israel made reliance on the fact that Iran's voting rights had been temporarily suspended due to arrears in the payment of its financial contributions (or dues) to the UN – payments made technically challenging for Iran as a consequence of US sanctions on its international financial transactions. The 2022 resolution moves beyond the previous resolutions in four ways. First, it provides a more thorough definition of Holocaust denial; second, it states that Holocaust denial is a form of anti-Semitism; third, it refers to distortion as well as denial; and fourth, it explicitly acknowledges that freedom of expression may be subject to legal restrictions when 'necessary for respect of the rights or reputations of others, and for the protection of national security or of public order, or of public health or morals'. Even so, like its predecessors, the Resolution of 25 January 2022 does not directly call on states to prohibit denialist speech and, as such, is the lowest common denominator position and fails to reflect the view of states who go further. Instead, the resolution adopts a maximally contextualist approach, allowing each state to combat denialist speech in the manner necessary given its own history, social circumstances, and free speech norms. This also enables the UN to abstract from the conflict between US and European free speech norms on the question of whether criminalising denialist speech is a valid way to combat it.

Together these recent developments in the evolution of international anti-denialism norms raise the following important questions. Insofar as these norms have evolved to become a widely (although not universally) accepted piece of the architecture of the rules-based international system, why did this take so long? Why were denialism provisions not part of the earlier landmark international laws on incitement to genocide and hate speech in general? Do the reasons that explain this absence in turn suggest that denialist speech ought to be treated, in a conceptual-legal sense, as a separate category of speech rather than a sui generis form of hate speech? It is to these questions that we now finally turn.

7.7.2 The Absence of Denialism Provisions in the Early International Laws on Incitement to Genocide and Hate Speech

This subsection focuses on five landmark international laws. In relation to the regulation of incitement to genocide there is the Charter of the International Military Tribunal, the Genocide Convention, and the Rome

Statute. In relation to the regulation of hate speech in general, there is the ICERD and the ICCPR. Analysing these treaties and exploring their travaux préparatoires and wide historical contexts, it will become clear that the question of Holocaust and genocide denial was entirely absent from this field of international law spanning the period from the end of World War II through to the signing of the Rome Statute in 1998. This stands in marked contrast to the practices of several states in using existing criminal laws to prosecute Holocaust denial during this period and the decision by many European states to introduce stand-alone denialism laws in the 1990s.

Starting with the Charter of the International Military Tribunal of 1945, whilst the Charter does not list 'genocide'[308] or 'Holocaust'[309] as offences, it established crimes against humanity, war crimes, and crimes against peace. Of the 24 defendants who were charged with a combination of these crimes between November 1945 and October 1946, 19 were convicted.[310] While prosecutors frequently used Raphael Lemkin's concept of genocide during the trials, the judges did not adopt it in their verdicts.[311] However, the trials were significant for many reasons not least the fact that the Tribunal convicted some defendants of crimes based on conduct that was effectively incitement to genocide. The most prominent example of this was the *Case of Julius Streicher*,[312] a staunch Nazi and publisher of an anti-Semitic newspaper. He was not a member of government or the military, but the Tribunal deemed him culpable of infecting the German mind with the poison of anti-Semitism and convicted him of crimes against humanity for his role in stirring up hatred against Jews and the contribution this made to Jewish extermination.[313] However, there is no mention in the charter of the crime of genocide denial or even a procedural offence of perjury which in theory could have been applicable to defendants and witnesses found to have wilfully told untruths or made false representations under oath about facts relating to the Holocaust.

The Genocide Convention was being drafted and negotiated during the Nuremberg Trials and shares the same belief in the culpability of inciters. Many felt, and the USSR delegate argued, that it is 'impossible that hundreds of thousands of people should commit so many crimes unless they had been incited to do so' and that inciters are 'the ones really responsible for the atrocities committed' and ought to face justice.[314] By contrast, the United States was vocal in its opposition to creating an international crime of incitement to genocide, seeing it as a threat to free speech including by enabling repressive regimes to abuse domestic laws to stifle dissent. As US representative Maktos stated: 'protection against genocide should stop where freedom of speech began'.[315] Yet the United States found itself in the minority. Poland joined the USSR in insisting on the inclusion of incitement to genocide. Furthermore, many European states already had restrictions on incitement to genocide in place and did not share American fears for its abuse; quite the opposite, they feared (and had experienced) what the true abuse of free speech could create. Ultimately, the United States failed in its opposition,[316] and on 9 December 1948 the Genocide Convention made both genocide and incitement to commit genocide punishable offences. However, there is no mention of genocide denial in the travaux préparatoires and it is not included as an offence in the Convention.

During the 1960s we see a similar story in the drafting of the ICERD in which there is also no mention of genocide denial. We do see continued battles over free speech, but they have evolved. It was accepted that incitement to genocide was rightly considered a crime, but now the key source of division was whether states parties should have an obligation to make dissemination of ideas based on racial superiority or hatred a crime. Although it met with resistance,[317] the obligation was retained in the final version under Art. 4. However, in explaining its vote on the final version, the United States made clear that in its interpretation Art. 4 'did not impose on a state party the obligation to take any action impairing the right to freedom of speech'.[318] The Netherlands, Chile, the UK, Spain, France, Austria, and New Zealand all entered similar caveats in their explanations. The radical step of including in the ICERD state obligations to prohibit the dissemination of hate propaganda was rendered to a large extent toothless for those states that did not want to be bound by it. In fact, many states entered formal reservations or declarations to that effect upon signing the treaty.[319] Moreover, there is no mention of denialist speech in the ICERD treaty itself.

In the travaux préparatoires for the ICCPR, we see a similar story to the Genocide Convention and the ICERD: no mention of denial but ample concern for free speech.[320] The debate was roughly split along Cold War lines, with the USSR supporting greater restrictions and the United States vigorously resisting.[321] Annotations to the 1955 draft reveal a split between, on the one hand, those states who felt that Art. 19(3), which allowed speech restrictions for reasons of 'respect of the rights or reputations of others', 'national security', and 'public order', were sufficient to tackle the problem of hate speech, and, on the other hand, states who wanted a dedicated provision.[322] While the majority accepted the inclusion of Art. 20(2) which provides for the prohibition of 'Any advocacy of national, racial or religious hatred that constitutes incitement to discrimination, hostility or violence', once again the United States noted its interpretation that Art. 20(2) does not authorise or require legislation that would be incompatible with the First Amendment right to freedom of expression.[323]

Finally, both the travaux préparatoires for the Rome Statute and the Statute itself likewise contain a provision on incitement to genocide but no mention of genocide denial. The travaux préparatoires differ from the other main treaties, however, in that debate about free speech is minimal. The only mention is found in the Report of the Preparatory Committee on the Establishment of an International Criminal Court, which states simply: 'the opinion was expressed that the terms of incitement would have to be carefully worded so as to avoid any violations of the right to free speech'.[324] One might surmise that after fifty years of debate on how to balance the human right to freedom of expression with the protection of individuals and groups from genocide and incitement to genocide, a settled compromise had been reached. However, unlike the ICERD, for example, the Rome Statute does not have a monitoring body, and so whereas the CERD (the monitoring committee of the ICERD) has become a radical player in the international regulation of speech, there is no corresponding international body to reinterpret the Rome Statute as obliging states to prohibit denialist speech as something that could constitute incitement to genocide.

The absence of any mention of the issue of denialism in either the final texts or the travaux préparatoires for any of the five landmark international laws dealing with incitement to genocide and hate speech in general shows that, put simply, denialist speech was not on the radar. The idea that denial is a part of genocide came much later and is not widely shared. Stanton's identification of denial as the final stage of genocide did not appear until 1998. Nor did Stanton argue that denial of one genocide could be a precipitating factor in a subsequent genocide: he argues that while the process is not linear, 'logically the later stages must be preceded by the earlier stages'.[325] Denial is therefore seen by Stanton as something that happens after the fact and, moreover, that genocides are one-off events, rather than seeing the denial of a genocide as something that can occur synchronously with that genocide and also capable of contributing to the creation of another genocide for the exact same victimised group.

To clarify, our core message here is not that the period from the end of World War II through to 1998 was entirely inconsequential to the development of anti-denialist norms. On the contrary, the fact that incitement to genocide and hate speech in general was a sustained topic of debate throughout this period is significant because it shows that there was a global consensus (though not unanimity) that certain forms of speech can be legitimately punished. Arguably, once the idea that the right to freedom of expression is a limited right was accepted, a Rubicon was crossed and further speech restrictions became imaginable, including stand-alone denialism laws. In that sense it could be said that this period laid some of the normative groundwork for subsequent international laws that did contain denialism provisions. That said, all of this begs the question as to why these landmark international laws on incitement to genocide and hate speech in general did not themselves contain denialism provisions given that denialism itself occurred both prior to and during the relevant period. Furthermore, does the reason for the omission suggest that genocide denial is inaptly placed under the legal concept *hate speech* even today?

7.7.3 *Explanations for the Absence*

We shall now present several possible explanations for the absence of denialism provisions within the early landmark international laws dealing with incitement to genocide and hate speech in general. These can be grouped under three main headings: domestic context; the denialism blind spot; and contestation over the correct form of the free speech norm or, to be more precise, competition among alternative free speech norms.

7.7.3.1 Domestic Context

Contextual explanations emphasise that states have different histories and social needs and, therefore, face varying degrees of threat from, and have differing levels of responsibility for tackling, denialist speech. According to one version of this explanation, in a limited number of countries, due to their history and ethnic make-up, regulation of denialist speech was seen as necessary, but a much larger number of states did not see themselves in this way and so there was lacking the impetus for denialism provisions in international law. In Germany, for example, laws banning Holocaust denial were seen as necessary because descendants of victims and perpetrators continue to live in Germany, because Germany has a special responsibility to ensure the Holocaust is never forgotten and never repeated, and because German society remains susceptible to the horrors of anti-Semitism. Indeed, that Germany had a particular moral obligation to combat Holocaust denial can be seen as part of the 'ethical pact' at the heart of the post-war settlement in Europe.[326] In Kahn's words, '[a]nybody who denies the Holocaust undermines the sense of post-1945 Germany'.[327] From the perspective of other states, by contrast, denialism was viewed through the prism of a particular genocide, the Holocaust, and, therefore, tackling it was seen as primarily a necessity for, and the responsibility of, other states and Germany in particular. As such, there was no appetite for an international denialism law that binds all states equally.

In 2011, the American political scientist Erik Bleich opined that '[c]hallenging other genocides [besides the Holocaust] is neither a widespread nor a meaningful form of racism in most liberal democracies'.[328] Whether that generalisation still holds true today is, of course, another matter. Since then, there have been growing concerns about, and legal cases surrounding, denials of the Armenian genocide, for instance. And the war in Ukraine has put a renewed spotlight on the denial of international crimes committed by the USSR and, of course, by Russia more recently. Nevertheless, the wider point surely stands that during the period from the end of World War II through to 1998 most states looked upon denialism as essentially only a problem for countries that had been directly affected by the Holocaust.

A second contextual explanation is that different states see different events as genocide and there is, around the globe, significant variation on which genocides are accepted as such and considered serious enough to warrant prohibition. Early adopters of denialism laws were in Europe and focused solely on the Holocaust. In states with large Armenian populations, like France, amending denialism laws to cover denial of the Armenian genocide, for example, should be relatively straightforward in theory.[329] But attempts to add the Armenian genocide to the Holocaust denial laws in France have been unsuccessful.[330] It seems that from the perspective of some European states during the period from the end of World War II through to 1998, the experience of one genocide does not create the same obligations towards other genocides. Whilst these perspectives may not be universal, they may be prevalent enough to explain the absence of denialism provisions in the early landmark international laws on incitement to genocide and hate speech in general.

Whilst contextual explanations may shed light on the different negotiating positions of states going into the landmark international laws we are discussing, there is an obvious danger in states relying too heavily on their own circumstances. It is all too easy for states to see genocide as someone else's problem, and as a result it often takes time for a genocide to be recognised as such internationally, and even then, there is no guarantee that denials of its existence will be addressed in international law. For example, the genocide of native American or first nation peoples is one of the most complete ever seen and yet there is little sense in mainstream opinion in the United States that the government has a special responsibility not merely to memorialise it but also to prevent such a genocide from ever happening again by means of prohibiting denialist speech. Indeed, the United States has used its soft power as the global hegemon to limit the extent of speech restrictions in the landmark international laws. More generally, for states to rely on their own domestic context as a guide to when it is right to lend their support to international laws on genocide denial is highly partial and not in keeping with normative accommodation. Likewise, limiting the obligation to enact denialism laws to states that have directly experienced genocide and recognise themselves as such also undermines the preventive power of such laws. Genocides do not only happen where they have happened before, to the same group of people. A key purpose of denialism laws is preventing genocide and that includes novel and unforeseen genocides.

7.7.3.2 The Denialism Blind Spot

Three explanations fall under the heading of the denialism blind spot: the complacency explanation, the redundancy explanation, and the non-threat explanation. The complacency explanation represents states as seeing international laws on Holocaust denial as unnecessary because the allies prosecuted the perpetrators under the International Military Tribunal and subsequent trials.[331] Of course, it is another matter entirely whether the perception of states was borne out by the reality during the relevant period. Arguably, if states did believe at that time there was simply no need for international Holocaust denial laws, this assumption was belied by the fact that Holocaust denial ramped up in the 1960s, persisted in the 1970s, and rumbled on throughout the 1980s and 1990s amid the *Historikerstreit*. More importantly, however, the complacency explanation ignores the fact that during this period some states were already applying existing domestic laws to cases involving Holocaust denial, suggesting that they at least were not complacent.

The redundancy explanation claims that states did not adopt an international denialism law because they were working on the basis that Holocaust and genocide denial were already punishable under existing offences including disparaging the memory of deceased persons and incitement to racial hatred, discrimination, or violence. However, this fails to explain why mention of the issue of denialism was entirely absent from the discussions and negotiations surrounding the drafting of the five international laws we are looking at. If states took the view that denialism laws would be redundant given the sufficiency of existing laws, why was that view not expressed in the meetings? Indeed, the repeated and prolonged debate over incitement to genocide makes it clear that states were conscious of the different ways in which such incitement occurs. Yet there is no mention of denialist speech as one manner of inciting genocide. None of the instruments appear to have been drafted with the belief that genocide denial could constitute a potential threat.

Following on from this last point, the non-threat explanation says that states simply did not see the threat posed by denialist speech. Although they understood that hate propaganda and incitement to genocide were a danger because they were seen to contribute to the Holocaust, states failed to spot the danger from denialist speech as such. This in turn may reflect an assumption at the time that denialism typically takes the form of post hoc non-perpetrator negationism and revisionism. There was a failure among states to understand the prevalence of synchronous perpetrator denialism and the role it plays in enabling agents to carry out atrocity crimes. A related explanation points to an implicit assumption among states that denialist speech is not incitement to genocide: that denial and incitement to genocide are conceptually and legally separate. Only denial which crosses over into incitement to genocide is an offence. As such, denial is not threatening on its own, only when it becomes incitement. Looking at the negotiations for the landmark international laws, it is clear that the primary bone of contention was incitement to genocide and whether it should be an offence. Because denialist speech was not identified as a possible mode of incitement to genocide, it simply did not figure in the debate.

7.7.3.3 Normative Competition

The third and final set of explanations relies on the dynamics of norm competition. Put simply, the absence of denialism provisions in the early landmark international laws on incitement to genocide and hate speech in general is a function of the relative weakness of anti-denialism norms and the relative strength of competing free speech norms. Normative competition explanations are made more complicated, however, by a proliferation of different competitions: between anti-denialism and free speech norms, between the norms of different states and collections of states, and between domestic and international norms.

These different strands of competition can be illustrated by surveying the complex terrain of US free speech norms. The domestic vision of the US free speech norm sees free speech as not merely a constitutional essential but also central to American political identity in a way not replicated in the European context. As several scholars have argued, even groups who are often victimised by hate speech and, therefore, might be otherwise naturally in favour of hate speech regulations, such as ethnic, religious, and LGBTQI+ minorities, are more ambivalent about such regulations in the United States than in European countries. For, they also see the right to freedom of expression as an important tool for fighting discrimination.[332] Openly questioning key planks in the US Bill of Rights can be political suicide in America.

Not only is free speech a key marker of political identity but there is a clear narrative built into the domestic US free speech norm that freedom of expression is to be protected not necessarily at all costs and in all cases – after all, a relatively long list of speech is regulated in the United States because it is considered unprotected speech[333] – but certainly with a strong commitment to doctrinal discipline and a spirit of 'eternal vigilance'. When discussing free speech, the primary threat, domestically, is that posed by the natural inclination of governmental authorities to exploit speech restrictions for their own political ends – the threat that 'official suppression of ideas is afoot'.[334] Thus, the domestic US free speech norm is characterised by a principled commitment to the First Amendment 'strict scrutiny' standard of review consisting in a set of legal rules, principles, doctrines, and standards, including, amongst other things, content and viewpoint neutrality, narrow tailoring or the avoidance of overbreadth, serving a compelling government interest, the least restrictive alternative, and the imminent lawless action standard.

Of course, the domestic US free speech norm is not static but has evolved as the ideological make-up of US courts has shifted, partly in response to political and social changes. In 1952, for example, the Supreme Court upheld a catch-all group defamation law in Illinois.[335] But since then the Supreme Court has moved to an increasingly rigid application of the strict scrutiny standard of review and has, as a consequence, struck down as unconstitutional a range of regulations that governmental authorities had been using to restrict hate speech, including municipal ordinances limiting the activities of neo-Nazi demonstrators, cross burning statutes, and civil remedies,[336] for example. In addition, both state and federal courts have cut a swathe through campus speech codes in the United States.[337] Most recently, the Supreme Court has held that hate speech is protected speech.[338]

This shift is replicated in the US legal consensus on Holocaust denial laws. Among US judges and legal scholars, there are virtually no dissenting voices to the opinion that a Holocaust denial law could not survive First Amendment strict scrutiny review. (Of course, whether such a law ought to survive such review or whether such review is appropriate is another matter, especially considered from the perspective of the free speech norms of other countries, not to mention international free speech norms.) This is partly down to the rule that, other things being equal, laws restricting speech ought to be content and viewpoint neutral: it is not the role of government to regulate speech simply due to its message or perspective or to adopt the role of arbiter over what content is suitable or what viewpoint is favoured. This rule has evolved to become an important fixture of First Amendment jurisprudence.[339] A law prohibiting bare Holocaust denial, however, would seem to be entirely content and viewpoint discriminatory: it would be a prohibition of speech on a particular subject and a particular perspective on that subject. Such a law could not even claim to be, unlike many hate speech regulations, a hybrid law in the sense of prohibiting 'speech plus', as in, a combination of content plus action, such as the act of inciting hatred, the act of threatening, intimidating, or provoking a fight, or any act capable of disturbing the public peace. It also reflects the fact that a law prohibiting bare Holocaust denial effectively prohibits the dissemination of gratuitously false statements, a broad category of speech that, in *United States v. Alverez*,[340] the US Supreme Court has held to be not an unprotected category of speech under the First Amendment, for example.

Philosophically, it is likely that a doctrinal predisposition against Holocaust denial laws could be justified by appealing to a plurality of different underlying norms and deeper moral values.[341] Indeed, part of the potential strength of this normative justification rests in its capacity to be the subject of an overlapping consensus among multiple values. That said, the meaning of these values is itself contested, as in, subject to reasonable disagreement, and so it is also possible to make compelling arguments in favour of hate speech laws, including Holocaust denial laws, based on different or competing conceptions of the same or similar values.[342] There is no room to weigh in on, much less settle, this disagreement here, save for observing that such disagreement does exist among legal scholars and philosophers.

Additionally, there is what might be called the international US free speech norm, meaning the norm that the United States relies upon and seeks to defend on the international stage, especially in discussions over the nature and wording of international texts dealing with the right to freedom of expression and its proper limits. That there has evolved different domestic and international US free speech norms should not be considered inexplicable or extraordinary: after all, these norms to a large extent, although not entirely, emanate from different branches of government.[343] From a US foreign policy perspective, the primary threat to free speech, internationally, is that posed by totalitarian regimes who use censorship as a tool to suppress political opposition and to maintain their undemocratic grip on power – a tendency that must be strongly resisted according to the international US free speech norm for reasons of both domestic security and the goal of promoting democracy around the globe.

We suggest the international US free speech norm serves a dual purpose. First, it is partly designed to safeguard the domestic US free speech norm: to ensure that international texts do not create obligations that would be incompatible with the First Amendment under the strict scrutiny standard of review. In other words, the international US free speech norm operates as barrier against the importation of speech regulations found in other countries that would be deemed unconstitutional at home. To give one example, if legislatures in the United States sought to enact a law similar to that of the Yarovaya Law in Russia (a law prohibiting wittingly spreading false information about the activity of the USSR during World War II or about World War II veterans), it would almost certainly not survive First Amendment strict scrutiny review. Second, the international US free speech norm is designed to act as a magnet pulling on the trajectory of international free speech norms over time, and bringing them closer to the US orbit. The effects of this US influence can be seen in the evolution of the five landmark international laws we have discussed. In the immediate post-war period, America was implacably opposed to the inclusion of incitement to genocide as an international crime and vigorously but unsuccessfully opposed it in the negotiations for the Genocide Convention, the ICERD, and the ICCPR. By the time of the negotiations surrounding the drafting of the Rome Statute in the 1990s, America had come to accept the inclusion of incitement to genocide and this became settled practice internationally.

Turning to Europe, there are subtle differences in European free speech norms reflecting differences in social make-up, legal cultures, dominant ideologies, and historical experiences across the different parts of Europe, such as between different states inside Western Europe and more broadly between Western European states and formers Soviet states in Eastern Europe. These differences partly explain why Holocaust denial legislation has had a more chequered history in France as compared to Greece, for example, but also why many former Soviet states have been early adopters of denialism laws. Generally speaking, states emerging from under the yoke of the USSR have put a premium on civil and political rights including freedom of expression, but denialist speech is treated as a special case in these contexts given the importance that these countries also place on recognising and memorialising the crimes perpetrated against them by the Soviet regime. Then there are trans-European free speech norms associated with organisations like the Council of the European Union and the ECtHR. Nevertheless, taking European free speech norms in the round, it is relatively clear that, from the perspective of many of these norms, the main threats to free speech come from different sources compared to the threats identified by the domestic US free speech norm. In the former case, the principal threats are not only from unjustified governmental censorship as such but equally from racism, discrimination, the stirring up of hatred, incitement to genocide, and the looming threat of genocide itself – acts which undermine the free speech of all and pose a threat to democracy itself.

To be clear, we are not suggesting every adherent to European free speech norms is a 'militant democracy':[344] some European countries reject that approach because it implies sacrificing some fundamental civil and political rights for the sake of others and is associated with lower free speech protections. Greece's imposition of strict standards of judicial review on its denialism law, and Spain's journey from first adopting an unqualified Holocaust denial offence to replacing it with a qualified Holocaust denial offence are cases in point. Nevertheless, European countries tend on average to be more closely aligned with each other's free speech norms than with the domestic US free speech norm. The key marker of Western European identity revolves around the Holocaust and the moral obligation to remind the world of the potential consequences of discriminatory speech but also a recognition that Europe continues to be home to genocidal ideologies. In many Western European countries, banning holocaust denial is about making 'a strong, clear break with a past racist regime'.[345] The former Soviet states share the European experience of the Holocaust but add their own experience of Soviet atrocities. Both see the experience of genocide as part of their contemporary identity and therefore are more open to the idea that speech must be regulated for the protection of individuals and of society. European free speech norms typically centre on the context and not simply the content of speech.

All of this suggests a gap not merely between domestic and international US free speech norms but also between US and European free speech norms. We theorise the two things are related. Domestically, the Supreme

Court has applied strict scrutiny review to First Amendment cases in a manner that increasingly relies on rigid adherence to a specific set of rules and standards. This has turned the Supreme Court into an increasingly hostile environment (excuse the pun) for certain types of speech restrictions, most notably hate speech laws. However, while the US position on free speech was hardening domestically, largely at the hands of a Supreme Court known more for its isolationism than its judicial globalisation, its position on free speech internationally was becoming more contextualist. In relation to the international norm against incitement to genocide, the United States softened its stance and came to accept that the context of some countries was such that denialism provisions were necessary, even if not applicable to the United States itself. Concerning the international norm against genocide denial, the United States promoted a parallel, non-prohibitionist norm, as a sort of lowest common denominator norm that every state could accept. In general terms, taking a contextualist approach can be characterised by a context-sensitive reading of international texts relating to free speech and its limits; a reasonable assessment of the spirit as well as the letter of the international texts; recognition of how national experiences and histories can create a pressing social and democratic need for certain speech regulations in some countries; acknowledging precedents in other international legal cases and texts; and a greater degree of tolerance of the divergent free speech norms of other countries. Even so, there have been limits to the US shift towards greater contextualism internationally. As regards the grafted international norm against defamation of religion promoted by several majority Muslim countries, for example, the United States successfully resisted its inclusion in international resolutions by leveraging its own version of the international free speech norm.[346] Arguably, this reflected the enduring pull of the US domestic free speech norm.

From the perspective of outsiders looking in, it is noticeable how parts of the free speech lobby in America, especially conservative commentators and some of the legacy television channels on which they appear, are prone to glossing over the nuances of American First Amendment jurisprudence and to giving the false impression to their audiences that from a US perspective all speech should be free. Yet this belies the reality of the domestic US free speech norm, under which there are many categories of unprotected speech. Nevertheless, in the United States, genocide denial and defamation of religion are viewed differently to incitement to genocide, and partly because prohibiting the former would pose a much greater threat to freedom of expression than would prohibiting the latter.

Laws banning genocide denial and defamation of religion would be content and viewpoint discriminatory and would sweep up protected speech, whereas incitement to genocide is a form of *speech plus* that potentially could be analogised to other categories of unprotected speech under the First Amendment, not least incitement to imminent lawless action.[347] Moreover, international laws against incitement to genocide at least in theory could be interpreted domestically in a way that is compatible with domestic US free speech norms, such as if they were interpreted to require evidence of imminent danger to life.

Nevertheless, taken in the round, we maintain that the United States has modulated its international stance on free speech in response to the normative perspectives of other states, sometimes, although not always, becoming more aligned with European states. In order to broker a normative consensus, the United States has made at least some concessions in light of what some other states think and, importantly, in recognition of other country contexts. The United States wanted to play its part in the development of the relevant conventions and resolutions and was willing to engage in normative dialogue and learning, and in that way become a normative influencer but also influencee through processes of give and take.

Turning next to the gap between the United States and European free speech norms, at first glance the US free speech norms look sharply at odds with common European free speech norms, thus creating normative conflict at the international level. However, the real picture is far more complex. On the one hand, the domestic US free speech norm might not be as far removed from European free speech norms as first appears. The thesis of American judicial exceptionalism and isolationism says that American constitutional essentials and legal doctrines are exceptional and, furthermore, that its judges are inward-looking and pay little heed to the decision of courts in other countries or key international texts for that matter. It might be tempting, especially from a European perspective, to assume that exceptionalism and isolationism is not merely the best way but in fact the only way to describe the domestic US free speech norm, especially when it comes to the US judicial approach to hate speech laws. But there are a range of reasonable views on the thesis of American judicial exceptionalism and isolationism: from the strongly supportive through to the equivocal and on to the outright sceptical about the thesis.[348] It is certainly hard to ignore the fact that more speech restrictions have been deemed constitutionally valid by US courts than many American citizens and certainly people living outside of the United States might imagine. Moreover, whilst there is a consensus legal opinion about what the domestic US free speech norm says about hate speech laws (that hate speech is a protected category under the First Amendment), generally accepted opinion is not the same thing as universally agreed opinion. There are alternative interpretations, some of which do carve out a space for the legitimate punishment of hate speech, as exemplified in a number of legal opinions, including in some dissenting opinions of the Supreme Court, relating to group defamation, cross burning statutes, hostile working environment discrimination, and civil remedies.[349] To give one example, the American legal scholar Alexander Tsesis has pointed to some notable US cases that, either directly or indirectly, cast doubt on the twin dogmas that *Beauharnais vs. Illinois* is no longer good law and that hate speech is in fact a protected category under the First Amendment.[350] These more nuanced readings of First Amendment doctrine bring the domestic US free speech norm a tad closer to European free speech norms. Indeed, that there is a consensus legal opinion but also reasonable disagreement among a minority of legal minds about the constitutionality of hate speech laws and ultimately about the nature and purpose of First Amendment doctrine is hardly surprising given that judges and legal scholars alike all have their own implicit moral, ideological, and political standpoints.[351]

Then again, it is perhaps harder to doubt the thesis of American exceptionalism when it comes to laws banning bare Holocaust denial, one of the few areas of near perfect agreement among scholars about what type of laws cannot survive the First Amendment strict scrutiny standard of review. To borrow the words of Julia C. Suk: 'To the American legal mind, the punishment of Holocaust denial would not even constitute a hard case: such a prohibition would be a paradigmatic violation of the First Amendment's free-speech guarantee.'[352] Of course, there was a dissenting opinion in *Alverez*, a case having to do with the issue of people lying about having military medals (Justices Alito, joined by Justice Scalia and Justice Thomas). The dissent concerned the degree of protection the First Amendment affords to false statements that are both low value and harmful.

> Building on earlier efforts to protect the military awards system, Congress responded to this problem by crafting a narrow statute that presents no threat to the freedom of speech. The statute reaches only knowingly false statements about hard facts directly within a speaker's personal knowledge. These lies have no value in and of themselves, and proscribing them does not chill any valuable speech. By holding that the First Amendment nevertheless shields these lies, the Court breaks sharply from a long line of cases recognizing that the right to free speech does not protect false factual statements that inflict real harm and serve no legitimate interest.[353]

However, *Alverez* was not a case about denialist speech, and Suk is surely correct to surmise that the US Supreme Court would almost certainly strike down a stand-alone Holocaust denial law. Relevant grounds might include the law being content and viewpoint discriminatory, being overbroad and sweeping up high value speech (e.g. political speech, academic speech), and not being the least restrictive alternative in tackling the problem, insofar as a less restrictive alternative would be publicly funded education campaigns about the Holocaust, for example. If this counterfactual is correct, then it places the domestic US free speech norm quite a distance from many European free speech norms: under the latter, Holocaust denial laws are either not even a hard case but for the opposite reason (i.e. laws banning Holocaust denial are deemed 'necessary in a democratic society' and so permitted under Art. 10(2) of the European Convention) or at least a grey area case.

On the other hand, there are signs that at least some European free speech norms are moving closer to, not further away from, US free speech norms. For example, in a cluster of cases dealing with s. 332 of the Hungarian criminal code (formerly s. 269), the Hungarian Constitutional Court has imposed a high threshold interpretation of the meaning of 'incitement to hatred' under the code, with the judicial effect that prosecutors must now demonstrate a 'clear and present danger' of violence or active hatred.[354] For its part, arguably the ECtHR has implicitly adopted a stricter standard of Art. 10 scrutiny for certain forms of hate speech than others. Whereas in the majority of standard cases involving domestic hate speech laws, the ECtHR has decided against the applicant and supported the relevant convictions as 'necessary in a democratic society' (relying on the margin of appreciation doctrine),[355] in a growing number of more complex cases it has sided with the applicant and found a violation of Art. 10 when the statements in question intermix typical forms of hate speech with content of a clearly political and/or dissenting nature.[356] Indeed, in *Perinçek v. Switzerland* the ECtHR overturned a conviction for denial of the Armenian genocide partly on the grounds that in the particular context of speech, the denial did not amount to hate speech as understood in the case law of the ECtHR as well as by domestic courts.

Then again, such rulings do not, in themselves, demonstrate that overall European free speech norms are becoming more closely aligned to the domestic US free speech norm. For one thing, the example of the Hungarian Constitutional Court shows only that Hungary has in some respects moved closer to the United States (on the use of the clear and present danger test in hate speech cases). In other respects, the countries remain poles apart. After all, not only has Hungary retained and continued to enforce its stand-alone Holocaust denial law,[357] but provides for an unqualified offence of bare Holocaust denial, even though other European states have created qualified offences with a higher threshold for prosecution.

Furthermore, even if the ECtHR has implicitly adopted a stricter standard of Art. 10 scrutiny in cases involving an admixture of hate speech and political speech, it has still accepted that a state may be justified in punishing even political figures for engaging in gratuitous hate speech.[358] Moreover, hitherto the ECtHR has not adopted a keystone of the domestic US free speech norm, namely the rule disallowing content- and viewpoint-based restrictions. On the contrary, in *Perinçek* the ECtHR made no reliance on the doctrine of content and viewpoint neutrality. Instead, it focused on whether the context of the statements made by the applicant (namely, a Turkish national publicly denying the Armenian genocide during speeches delivered orally inside Switzerland) was sufficient to render the statements a form of incitement to hatred.[359] Furthermore, in several cases, the ECtHR has relied on the idea that denialist speech can be an affront to human dignity and sufficient by itself to validate the punishment of Holocaust deniers under Arts. 10(2) and 17 of the European Convention.[360] This alone marks a significant discrepancy between European and US free speech norms.

However, putting to one side the exact degree of misalignment between domestic and international US free speech norms and between US and European free speech norms, our key message is that an accommodation has been reached whereby states who favour the European vision have the latitude to apply international tools to that end. States like America can simply enter reservations and are not bound by the particular clauses to which they object. International negotiations can be concluded, and treaties signed, by agreeing to disagree. This partly explains why the debates around incitement to genocide were most fervent in the travaux for the Genocide Convention and lessened over time. The absence of Holocaust denial in the early landmark international laws is explainable by the relative strength of US free speech norms: over time the balance of normative persuasive force has shifted, with European free speech norms coming to the fore, and at the same time the international US free speech norm taking on a more contextualist quality. More recently, the United States has played a key part in the development of a parallel, non-prohibitionist international norm against denialism in the shape of several UN General Assembly resolutions on Holocaust remembrance and denial. Agreement on this norm has allowed the vast majority of states (although not all states) to signal their position that Holocaust denial is beyond the pale without compelling every state to adopt prohibition as the only or best measure to combat it. The same sort of compromise can also be seen in key elements of European law dealing with Holocaust denial, such as in Art. 6(2)(b) of the Additional Protocol discussed above, which explicitly gives states parties the right not to prohibit Holocaust denial.

7.7.4 *Where Does All This Leave Denialist Speech and the Legal Concept Hate Speech?*

Of the three sets of explanations offered to explain the absence of denialism provisions in the early landmark international laws on incitement to genocide and hate speech in general (domestic context, the denialism blind spot, and normative competition) we argue that the most powerful explanation is pluralistic, combining elements of each. Taking the domestic context into account can be a useful indicator but is by no means infallible. Clearly, states have differing associations with genocide: some states, like the United States, have perpetrated genocides but have failed to name them as 'genocide' in official apologies;[361] other states, such as Germany, Israel, and Palestine, see genocide awareness as fundamental to their identity; still other states, such as the USSR/Russia, typically portray genocide as a crime always done to them but never by them; yet more states appear to view genocide as something that happens elsewhere in the world. Yet these differences in domestic context alone cannot explain the absence of denialism provisions from the landmark international laws nor the failure of denialism to be even discussed or mentioned in the negotiations. There were surely enough countries with at least some association with core international crimes to merit denialism being on the agenda. The idea that the threat posed by denialist speech was simply a blind spot for the international community during the relevant period goes some way to plugging the explanatory gap. Changing perceptions of the threat posed by denialist speech also helps to explain why denialism provisions begin to emerge in international law after 1998. But the blind spot explanation is also inadequate as a sole explanation. For, it ignores the fact that during this period some states were already applying some existing domestic laws to cases involving Holocaust denial. The normative competition explanation adds the final layer needed to complete the picture. When looking at the travaux préparatoires, treaties, and compliance monitoring, it becomes clear that contestation between the United States and Western European free speech norms was a prevalent source of disagreement. This manifested itself in lengthy debate over whether there should be an obligation on the part of states parties to prohibit incitement to genocide. A truce emerged whereby the United States becomes a party to the relevant treaties and accepts the spirit of the norms, but does not accept that incitement to genocide should be illegal within the United States, and so enters reservations to parts of the treaties which say the opposite.

What does this pluralistic explanation suggest about the core question of how to correctly classify denialist speech? Does the explanation show that denialist speech is rightly understood as an instance of existing types of hate speech, as a sui generis form of hate speech, or as an entirely separate category of expressive phenomenon? Earlier in the chapter we argued that based on current domestic and international standards, it makes sense to classify denialist speech as a sui generis form of hate speech in the legal sense of the term. We believe the aforementioned pluralistic explanation is consistent with that general theory. For one thing, arguably the issue of denialism would have at least figured in the discussions and negotiations surrounding the early landmark international laws but for the circumstances of key states involved in those negotiations, especially the United States but also the USSR, and for the general lack of understanding of the threat posed by denialist speech. While these contingencies explain the absence, they do not show that denialist speech is inaptly included in the legal concept *hate speech*. What about the normative competition explanation? Even if the issue of denialism had been on the agenda, the normative competition explanation sheds light on the countervailing forces (free speech norms) that would have made it difficult for denialism provisions to make it from the agenda into the treaties themselves. But once again, these factors do not demonstrate that somehow it would be conceptually-legally wrongheaded to place denialist speech in the category of hate speech. If, contrary to fact, the issue of denialism had been on the international agenda during the period from the end of World War II through to 1998, the chances are it would have been subject to a similar process of normative compromise and accommodation that exemplified negotiations over incitement to genocide and other forms of hate speech during that period. These expressive phenomena hold a position within the landmark international laws – laws that embody or give meaning and precision to international legal norms – but at the same time states can diverge when it comes to the implementation of these norms in domestic law.

As discussed in Section 7.7.1, recent international law represents in effect an agreement to treat denialist speech as a form of hate speech in the legal sense of the term. This agreement may be a precarious legal compromise in some respects, but it is one that has survived because it is based on the contextualism baked into the relevant international laws (hard and soft). The compromise is twofold: first, to recognise as a legitimate state response to denialist speech both the use of existing laws, including extant hate speech laws, and the enactment of stand-alone denialism laws which effectively treat denialist speech as a sui generis form of hate speech, depending on domestic context; and second, to embrace both prohibitionist and non-prohibitionist norms against denialist speech, with the former embodied in European treaties, the jurisprudence of the ECtHR, and the activism of the CERD, and latter embodied in resolutions passed by the UN General Assembly.

Based on the broad utility of honouring the compromises often contained in international legal norms, we suggest that states should accept what we call the international legal norms principle: Any governmental justification for prohibiting speech at the national level is stronger when the prohibition involves the restriction of speech of the sort that is called for by relevant international legal norms, international treaties, and international court decisions than when the prohibition involves the restriction of speech not warranted in this way. International norms, treaties, and decisions relating to denialism are a case in point.

However, does this argument prove too much? Does it mean that anything could be considered hate speech simply provided it makes its way into a particular body of international law, regardless of the extent of domestic reservations and regardless of any qualities it might have that make it disanalogous to prototypical illegal hate speech? Surely this result would constitute a *reductio ad absurdum* of the story we are telling both about how to correctly classify denialist speech and how to characterise the legal concept *hate speech*. After all, normative competition is complicated by the existence of various competing free speech norms including not only US and European free speech norms but also non-Western free speech norms including religious norms such as those embraced by many majority Muslim countries. One effect of this competition has been heated international dispute about the correct classification of defamation of religion, as potentially another form of hate speech. Having uncorked the normative competition explanation, it cannot be put back in the bottle. Nevertheless, whilst we acknowledge this potential problem, we believe ultimately it does not represent a slippery slope that casts doubt over our theory that denialist speech is rightly classified as a sui generis form of hate speech.[362] We shall try to make good our defence in the next and final subsection of the chapter.

7.7.5 Unresolved Normative Dissonance

Despite in some respects softening its stance on free speech internationally, the United States remains a source of both normative accommodation and normative dissonance. Indeed, it is tempting to overstate both the extent of contextualism built into the international US free speech norm and the power of the United States in shaping international free speech norms more generally. For example, the softening of America's stance on the inclusion of incitement to genocide within international texts must be set against the fact that during the drafting of the ICERD and the ICCPR the United States fought doggedly to block Soviet proposals for a broader definition of hate speech including the inclusion of a legal norm against incitement to hatred as such.[363]

Furthermore, the United States has not been as powerful a norm entrepreneur regarding free speech over the past seventy-five years as some people might assume. After all, there are international norms against hate speech that are clearly inconsistent with US free speech norms,[364] but America has hitherto been unable to exert significant influence on the former. For example, the United States has been unable to block the activism of the CERD. Nor has it been able to stop European countries from advancing an alternative narrative on what laws are 'necessary in a democratic society' through the work of organisations and bodies like the Council of the European Union and the ECtHR. The fact that there are at least some legal minds in America who argue that the United States should take a leaf out of the book of European free speech norms and adopt greater contextualism at the domestic level, including when it comes to hate speech[365] and denialist speech,[366] might itself be testament to the pull of European norms. The primary, and inescapable, reason for this balance of normative power and associated divergence of free speech norms lies in the fact that the American position on free speech does mark it out as an outlier and one which does not regularly find support from other states. The Cold War conflict and clever manoeuvring by the USSR meant that the United States had to find common ground with a broad coalition of states who it wanted as allies against the Soviet Union, forcing it to recognise normative pluralism on the question of free speech.

In addition to this, as the case of international disputes over what to do about defamation of religion shows, sometimes attempts to resolve normative dissonances around free speech norms have failed at the international level partly because of the existence of divergent norms emanating from neither America nor Europe. During the 1990s and 2000s, for example, the United States used diplomacy and soft pressure to successfully prevent the grafted norm against defamation of religion from taking hold, leaving only the Western, more narrowly tailored, international norm against hate speech.[367] In this regard, the United States knowingly rejected the perspectives and concerns of leaders of majority Muslim countries (especially in relation to cartoons bringing the Prophet Muhammed into contempt), something the latter remain aggrieved about to this day. In 2021, for example, then prime minister of Pakistan, Imran Khan, made the following analogical argument for the enactment of defamation of religion laws: 'I also call on Western govts who have outlawed any negative comment on the holocaust to use the same standards to penalise those deliberately spreading their message of hate against Muslims by abusing our Prophet PBUH.'[368] This tweet is highly revealing for two reasons: first, it illustrates how political leaders in the Muslim world are willing to use Western social media channels to speak directly to an international public and to advocate for laws banning defamation of religion, which they continue to view as species of hate speech laws, contrary to the Western international free speech norm; second, it reveals how such leaders regard Holocaust denial laws as part of mainstream international legal norms against hate speech and, therefore, fitting anchor points for analogical arguments.

Efforts by the UN Secretariat, and in particular the Office of the High Commissioner for Human Rights, to resolve the normative dissonance created by competing free speech norms on the global stage have been ongoing since the late 1990s. In 2001, the UN launched its Durban World Conference on Racism. Through state involvement and expert panels, the UN produced the Rabat Plan of Action on the prohibition of advocacy of national, racial, or religious hatred that constitutes incitement to discrimination, hostility, or violence.[369] In some eyes, the Plan's effect has been underwhelming to the point of failure. At the first conference in 2001, the United States and Israel walked out over plans to condemn Zionism as racist in the final text. The Durban II Conference in 2009 was boycotted by the United States, Germany, Italy, Poland, the Netherlands, New Zealand, Australia, Canada, and Israel. The European nations that did attend walked out when Iranian president Ahmadinejad called Israel a 'cruel and repressive racist regime'.[370] In September 2021, the UN marked the twentieth anniversary of the original conference with Durban IV, but it was boycotted by thirty-eight states, including the United States, Canada, Israel, and most European states and the EU. We see a clear split between the West and the rest of the world, led by Iran. While it might seem that Israel has successfully mobilised her international allies, the boycott is about far more than Israel. It is a small part of much wider tensions over the competing values of the liberal West and the remainder of the globe. Israel's role in negotiating the international laws discussed in this chapter has been minimal, in part because of the distractions of Israel's difficult birth and in part because of the Arab world's persistent use of international fora to attack Israel. When favourable, even the United States has downplayed its ties to Israel. The upshot is that Israel, the country that could be expected to have most to say on the issue of Holocaust denial, has had no real normative sway on international anti-denialism norms. Despite being the first adopter of domestic denialism provisions, it has not persuaded the rest of the world to follow its lead. Indeed, majority Muslim countries typically do not have denialism provisions in place, and this may partly reflect a galvanising opposition to Israel in international affairs across the piece.

By contrast, a broader legal concept *hate speech* has been adopted, to some extent effectively, by Iran and other majority Muslim states, in disputes over intercultural religious tolerance and the limits of international free speech norms. For example, at the behest of a group of majority Muslim countries, including Egypt, Iran, and Turkey, for a period running from 1999 to 2010, the UN Commission on Human Rights (UNCHR), and its replacement the UN Human Rights Council (UNHRC), promulgated a slew of resolutions on defamation of religion that effectively sought to incorporate defamation of religion along with incitement to religious hatred under the broad umbrella of the powerful international norm against hate speech.[371] The United States, under President Obama, was instrumental in the ultimate demise of these resolutions which ceased in 2010.[372] Nevertheless, a clear fault line now exists between certain Western ideas about hate speech and non-Western, primarily Muslim ideas about hate speech: there is a belief held by many majority Muslim states, but not Western states, that the legal concept *hate speech* should encompass defamation of religion.[373]

To this end, Iran, like Turkey,[374] has penal code provisions that blur conventional boundaries between the legal concept *hate speech*, on the one hand, and other concepts such as blasphemy and outraging religious sensibilities, on the other hand. The blurring consists in treating acts such as defaming or insulting a religion as on a par with defaming or insulting a group of people identified by their religion. Since 2021, it is a criminally punishable offence in Iran to 'insult' Iranian ethnicities or divine religions or Islamic schools of thought recognised under the Constitution with the intent to cause violence or tensions in society or with the knowledge that such consequences will follow.[375]

But does this mean the legal concept *hate speech* does include defamation of religion? We believe that in answering this question it is important to draw a distinction, as we did in Chapter 5, between a general legal concept *hate speech* and more specific legal concepts *hate speech* which relate to particular jurisdictions. Thus, in a very limited sense it may be plausible to say that the Iranian and Turkish legal concepts *hate speech* do indeed incorporate defamation of religion. However, defamation of religion is not a criminal offence in most countries and in the vast majority of countries that do have hate speech laws in place and, more specifically, have laws banning incitement to religious hatred on the books,[376] these laws do not blur lines with defamation of religion, pace Iran and Turkey. Furthermore, what we shall call the consensus international legal norm against hate speech, including the current body of international laws dealing with this issue, does not incorporate rules against defamation of religion, despite briefly appearing in a slew of resolutions promulgated by one body of the UN system during the first decade of this century. This also means, we would argue, that our theory that genocide denial is a sui generis form of hate speech based on international standards does not constitute the first step on a slippery slope towards an absurdly capacious understanding of the legal concept *hate speech*.

8

Epilogue

8.1 Introduction

In this book we have explored several conceptual frontiers of hate speech, including grey area examples whose status as hate speech is marginal, uncertain, or subject to reasonable disagreement; differences between social media platform content policies on hate speech and hate speech laws; divergence between national and international hate speech laws; and sometimes fuzzy boundary lines where concepts of hate speech end and other concepts begin. In doing so we have combined conceptual analysis with doctrinal analysis, linguistic analysis, critical analysis, and diachronic analysis, reflecting the social, legal, moral, political, and historical nature of concepts of hate speech.

Now it is a popular misconception that conceptual analysis is a dry or purely academic enterprise in the sense of being of only theoretical interest and having no practical relevance or importance. The truth is otherwise. Conceptual analysis can aim for the improvement of the relevant concepts, to make them better serve the various functions or purposes a society can reasonably expect them to play. Indeed, conceptual analysis can also set forth a set of proposals about what those reasonable functions should be. The immediate aim is to establish coherence between meanings and purposes. But we believe this sort of analysis also has a loftier goal, namely to set out an agenda for societal change including not only influencing how people understand and use the concepts but also advocating concrete reforms to the various institutional and organisational rules in which the concepts spring to life.

The aim of this chapter is to pull together the various analyses and practical recommendations we have made concerning the two concepts of hate speech and to deal with potential objections and lingering worries. Section 8.2 focuses on the ordinary concept *hate speech* and confronts possible objections to our normative conceptualisation, including the core theory that hate speech in its ordinary sense is a family resemblance concept and that the best way to resolve grey area examples is by applying the global resemblance test, keeping in mind reasonable social purposes fulfilled by the concept. This section also summarises the many recommendations we made concerning how Meta (Facebook, Instagram) should amend and revise its community standard and authoritative internal policy on hate speech, and tries to allay residual doubts the company (and the reader) might have about these recommendations. Section 8.3 turns to consider the legal concept *hate speech* and deals with potential objections to our limited formal definition of the concept and our analyses of grey area laws including those that appear to fall between hate speech laws and hate crime provisions, and also denialism laws. In addition, we reiterate our guidance on how states can develop a coherent body of hate speech laws in the light of both national perspectives and international norms against hate speech, and offer some reasons why states should place special weight on the latter.

8.2 Understanding the Ordinary Concept

When presented with a putative example of hate speech in the ordinary sense of the term, competent language users have intuitions about whether it would be appropriate to call it 'hate speech'. Typically, these intuitions do not occur in isolation but are part of social practices. For most ordinary people these practices are governed at most by implicit conventions, for policy teams and moderators employed by organisations like universities, media companies, and social media platforms, these practices can be governed by formal and informal rules. In Part I of this book, we defended a normative conceptualisation that says these practices are at their best when they conform to what we called the global resemblance test, namely an overall assessment of whether the range, extent, degree, and salience of similarities between a grey area example and exemplars of hate speech across at least four out of five of the distinguishing qualities of target, styles, message, act, and effect justifies classifying the grey area example as hate speech on the basis that it resembles the exemplars as closely as the exemplars resemble each other, and in light of the social functions or purposes that a society and its major organisations can reasonably expect the ordinary concept to play. In this section we introduce and respond to possible objections to this normative conceptualisation, and also summarise the practical recommendations we made for reforming Facebook's community standard and authoritative internal policy on hate speech. We also address lingering worries Facebook might have about these recommendations.

8.2.1 Objections

One objection we might face is that, based on our normative conceptualisation, the ordinary concept *hate speech* seems amorphous and could come to mean almost anything. What if there is a significant shift in usage of the term 'hate speech' within a society partly driven by a change in content policies pursued by influential organisations like Facebook? What if the new applications represent a significant departure from exemplars of hate speech? After all, society is not a legal system and neither ordinary language users nor content policy teams are legal professionals bound by standards of deliberation and analogical reasoning involving precedents that have practical and theoretical authority. How would we know whether this is a normal stage in the evolution of the concept combining new applications alongside backward compatibility with previous applications or instead a paradigm shift and effectively the introduction of a new concept whilst coincidentally retaining the old terminology?

In one sense this objection raises the spectre of diachronic identity, a well-known philosophical problem in metaphysics concerning whether a changing thing can be one and the same thing before and after the change or becomes a different thing when the change is significantly great. To provide a concrete illustration relevant to the ordinary concept *hate speech*, in Chapter 3 we pointed out that Snap Inc. (formerly Snapchat) is alone among the major social media platforms in including 'weight' within its list of protected characteristics.[1] What if the other platforms follow suit? Would this constitute an evolution of one and the same ordinary concept *hate speech* or the introduction of a new concept whilst retaining the term 'hate speech'?

We believe the key to answering this question is to attend to the presence or absence of similarities between, say, fatist speech and racist speech, across the distinguishing qualities of target, style, message, act, and effect. If the new policy applies to examples of speech that satisfy the global resemblance test, then the policy is likely to signify only an evolution in the ordinary concept *hate speech* rather than the birth of a discrete new concept. By contrast, suppose all the major social media platforms changed their content policies on hate speech overnight to include musical preferences as a protected characteristic meaning content like 'I hate people who hate swing music' is removed as 'hate speech'. Insofar as this new application manifestly fails to satisfy the global resemblance test, it would suggest that the companies were misusing the label 'hate speech' and confusing the ordinary concept *hate speech* with some other concept, such as *intolerant speech*.

That said, the objector might insist that because our analysis relies on qualities that are themselves clusters of features, this could open the door to the ordinary concept being stretched beyond all recognition. For example, the message of some examples of hate speech is an expression of intense dislike or hatred. Arguably, a great deal of speech might share this feature in common with some exemplars of hate speech. If so, the ordinary concept *hate speech* could end up becoming an indefinitely extending concept (so the objector might argue). However, the expression of hatred is by no means the only or even the most common message conveyed by exemplars of hate speech (see Chapter 2). Moreover, to satisfy the global resemblance test, similarities must obtain in four out of five of the distinguishing qualities (clusters of features), and this is likely to prevent an indefinitely extending concept.

In a similar vein, even if social media platforms increased the scope of the ordinary concept *hate speech* by expanding the list of protected characteristics to include, for example, certain political beliefs or affiliations, the global resemblance test would still exert a constraining effect on what they can properly label 'hate speech'. For example, platforms would not be acting in a reasonable and conceptually coherent way if they applied the label *disallowed hate speech* to content flagged or reported by some users as being hate speech simply on the basis that those users hate or disapprove of the speech in question due to its political viewpoint. After all, if the term 'hate speech' simply meant whatever speech someone using the term happens to hate or disapprove of, then arguably the term would be useless in grown up debates about the reasonable limits of public discourse – the term would end up being so overused, subjective, and relativistic as to serve few social purposes and certainly no greater purpose than the phrases 'I hate that speech!' or 'I disapprove of that speech!'.[2] Therefore, even if Trump supporters happen to hate or disapprove of invectives against Trump, and call such invectives 'hate speech', for example, this does not mean they have used the term correctly. If the invectives lack global resemblance with prototypical examples of hate speech, then calling the invectives 'hate speech' should misfire.

A second potential objection is that there is a tension between, on the one hand, the claim we made in Chapter 3 that some styles of hate speech such as generalisations, stereotypes, archetypes, and caricatures depend on a representativeness bias (i.e. comparing new people with prototypes of people) and, on the other hand, our theory that the ordinary concept *hate speech* ideally involves competent language users and social media content policy teams, for instance, comparing possible grey area examples to exemplars of hate speech and assessing the overall similarity between the grey area examples and the exemplars. Is not our theory of hate speech in the ordinary sense of the term itself relying on a representativeness bias (i.e. comparing new examples with paradigmatic examples)?

We concede there is a possible tension here but draw two salient distinctions between the representativeness bias associated with styles of hate speech and the representativeness heuristic involved in understanding the ordinary concept *hate speech*. The first is that in the case of styles of hate speech, the object of the representativeness bias is people and it can lead to prototypical hate speech acts such as prejudgment and epistemic injustice, whereas in the case of the ordinary concept *hate speech* the object of the representativeness heuristic is examples of speech. The second distinction is that our normative conceptualisation of the ordinary concept *hate speech* contains elements that can serve to mitigate the representativeness heuristic. For one thing, we believe that applying the global resemblance test involves not merely searching for similarities but also recognising relevant dissimilarities, searching for possible anomalies and inconsistencies in the practices governing applications of the term 'hate speech', the consideration of potential exceptions, and identifying possible misuses and conceptual mistakes. The analysis includes being mindful of benchmark examples that share some similarities with the ordinary concept *hate speech* but which in fact belong to other concepts. Furthermore, we have argued that the concept is being used in the right way not merely when applications satisfy the global resemblance test but also when this overall assessment of similarities is itself sensitive to reflections about what best suits the social functions or purposes a society can reasonably expect the concept to serve. The notion of reasonable social functions or purposes is a normative constraint on the representativeness heuristic.

A third objection is that because our normative conceptualisation of the ordinary concept *hate speech* treats both reverse attacks and righteous attacks as falling within the extension of this concept, it overlooks folk ideas about hate speech being oppressive and unjustifiable and, furthermore, parts company with the work of Matsuda, who first coined the term 'hate speech' and who argued that reverse attacks and righteous attacks are not hate speech (see Chapter 3). This suggests (according to the objection) that we have not identified a single concept that happens to be family resemblance concept but rather uncovered multiple discrete, albeit partially overlapping, concepts. On this view, reverse attacks and righteous attacks might be instances of divisive speech but they are not hate speech.

However, we refuse this objection on two grounds. The first is that our normative conceptualisation of the ordinary concept *hate speech* does not completely detach the concept from the qualities of oppressiveness and unjustifiability. In fact, some reverse attacks can involve situationally reversed power dynamics or imbalances of power. Moreover, even if righteous attacks can be justifiable in one sense, they can still be unjustifiable all things considered. Of course, people who use hateful language are usually convinced they have a good reason for doing so. As Keith Bach puts it, '[w]hen a group is accorded a proprietary slur, its users deem the practice of using it justified by some imagined deficiency inherent in members of the group'.[3] Moreover, sometimes attacks can be righteous not merely in the subjective sense but also in the objective sense of being reasonable, in good faith, and proportionate. Nevertheless, even fully righteous attacks can be hate speech, and this is because justifiability does not begin and end with righteousness.

Our second ground is that if the distinguishing qualities that mark out exemplars of hate speech as being similar to each include target, style, message, act, and effect, then arguably reverse attacks and righteous attacks can resemble exemplars of hate speech in these qualities as closely as exemplars resemble each other (see Chapter 3). The crucial point is that the distinguishing qualities are themselves clusters of features (see Chapter 2). So even if reverse attacks and righteous attacks do not share exactly the same features with a given exemplar of hate speech, they may still exhibit other similar features. For example, reverse attacks might involve attacks on people identified by protected characteristics. And righteous attacks might stereotype, misrecognise, and prejudge members of the target group.

A final objection is that, even if one accepts the correctness of our normative conceptualisation of the ordinary concept *hate speech*, this does not make our approach important because in fact nothing hinges on it. Whether hate speech in the ordinary sense of the term is a family resemblance concept or is instead a concept with an essence makes no practical difference (so the objection runs).

Once again, we reject this objection on two grounds. For one thing, taking a different approach to understanding the ordinary concept *hate speech* (i.e. different to our approach) points in the direction of trying to give it a formal definition based on a complete set of necessary and sufficient conditions. We believe this would make the concept less useful. For example, understanding the ordinary concept as a family resemblance concept enables the term 'hate speech' to be used as a point of linguistic contact between different groups, as a sort of shared vernacular. Also, the family resemblance analysis provides not only breathing space for new applications of the term but also a heuristic device to assess the appropriateness of labelling given examples as 'hate speech'. In addition, depending on what a formal definition looks like, it could end up pushing the ordinary concept closer to the legal concept, such as if the formal definition invokes the necessary condition that the speech must be intended or likely to incite imminent violence. This could also make the ordinary concept less useful as a social norm, because applicable to far fewer cases of hate speech.

Furthermore, getting labelling right is not merely a dry conceptual exercise; the stakes are high for both individuals and society as a whole. In the case of the ordinary concept *hate speech*, the effects of getting labelling decisions wrong can include misapplying social sanctions, such as condemnation, naming and shaming, withholding of friendship and job opportunities, and last but by no means least having content removed or being subject to reduced circulation on social media platforms. The baneful consequences of mislabelling things as 'hate speech' that are not in fact hate speech are well documented and include a chilling effect on freedom of expression. But failing to label things as 'hate speech' which really are hate speech can also have dire consequences. It can be a form of identity misrecognition to be a member of a group targeted with derogatory words that society fails to acknowledge as hate speech. This failure may legitimate, embolden, and even authorise hate speakers. It can also be part of, or perpetuate, a wider pattern of oppression. To borrow an example from Chapter 3, at the level of everyday communicative interactions, people who call other people 'fatty' might be challenged about this language but may resist the accusation of 'hate speech' by saying things like 'Come off it, that's not hate speech; I only called *you* fatty'. However, by refusing to recognise the group-based and prejudiced nature of the word 'fatty', both the speaker and any social media platforms that allow this language are brushing under the carpet the history and significance of the word in the context of a fatist society. This could be experienced by the victim as a microaggression within the communicative interaction and as a form of identity misrecognition by the platform itself. It could also contribute to the wider environment of unjust norms surrounding body appearance and to systemic forms of social discrimination suffered by larger people. Similarly, there can be a failure by mainstream society (in which the male viewpoint is dominant) to recognise the gendered and slurring qualities of terms like 'bitch'. There is evidence to suggest men and women associate the term 'bitch' with different negative traits and that men are less likely than women to understand it as group-based and more likely to see it as merely a personal insult (see Chapter 3). The failure of both speakers and social media platforms to recognise the hate speechy qualities of such terms is yet another thing holding women down.

8.2.2 *Recommendations to Facebook*

Arguably, Facebook's community standard on hate speech is more complex, detailed, considered, coherent, responsive to feedback, evolving, transparent, reflective of its authoritative internal policy, and subject to independent oversight than any comparable public-facing hate speech code of any social media platform in existence globally. But it is also full of ambiguities, inconsistencies, and omissions. This matters intrinsically for the relevant users but also because Facebook plays a significant role in shaping what ordinary people think about the nature of hate speech and what they are likely to call 'hate speech' both inside and outside of the environment of the platform. The policy teams responsible for Facebook's community standard on hate speech are not astronomers studying a distant planetary object whose motion they have no chance of altering merely by plotting its course over time. An organisation with the reach and influence of Facebook does not merely respond to how the public understands the term 'hate speech' but also partly shapes the formation of that understanding. For these reasons, it is crucial Facebook does a good job.

Reflecting the normative conceptualisation of the ordinary concept *hate speech* we defended in Part I of this book, we argued along the way that Meta (Facebook, Instagram) should amend its community standard on hate speech as follows:

(i) The standard should, as far as possible, not merely describe or closely mirror the authoritative internal policy but replicate it as a carbon copy.[4]

(ii) The standard should make explicit that it is not defining unlawful hate speech but simply the hate speech disallowed by Meta.

(iii) The standard should make explicit that Meta does not disallow all hate speech as such but simply the speech Meta designates as hate speech (such as by adding the following statement to the preamble: 'We define hate speech as … but other definitions are available. This means that we only remove hate speech of the sort disallowed by Meta.').[5]

(iv) The standard should make explicit what it means by 'harm' and 'harmful' and the sorts of evidence that Meta relies on to make determination of the harmfulness of content.

(v) The standard should include at least one concrete example of a word that Meta treats as a designated slur in virtually all its markets and/or a series of words that it treats as designated slurs including at least one example for each market.[6] Designated slurs should include not merely 'nigger' but also 'bitch', for example.

(vi) The standard should make explicit that the rules disallowing hate speech are multidirectional in the sense that they apply equally to standard attacks and reverse attacks, and should contain at least one concrete example that is a reverse attack (e.g. 'Men are scum', 'white devil').

(vii) The standard should make explicit that the rules disallowing hate speech even apply to righteous attacks, and it should provide concrete examples (e.g. 'male chauvinist pig', 'TERF').

(viii) The standard should make explicit which specific designated slurs (e.g. 'nigger', 'retard', 'poof') are by default violating, whether used in referentially conventional or non-conventional ways.

We also argued that Meta should substantially revise both its authoritative internal policy and community standard on hate speech as follows:

(ix) The policy and standard should explicitly disallow incitement to harm and/or incitement to hatred, discrimination, and violence.

(x) The policy and standard should extend the list of Tier-insensitive primary protected characteristics to include certain forms of physical appearance (e.g. weight, deformity), certain types of sexual desires, preferences, or activities (or lack thereof) (e.g. asexuality), certain kinds of political or ideological beliefs and affiliations (e.g. being a communist in a virulently anti-communist society), certain sorts of social attitudes or commitments (e.g. being a critical feminist or an environmentalist in societies where this can make a person a target of violence and threats of violence), age, immigration status, and other comparable characteristics.

(xi) The policy and standard should extend the list of Tier-insensitive secondary ('quasi-') protected characteristics to include occupation, veteran status, hobbies, and other comparable characteristics.

(xii) The policy and standard should not designate as non-protected groups those described as having carried out violent crimes or sexual offences, if the groups are also partly identified by primary protected characteristics. For example, Meta should disallow the following: 'Black convicted rapists deserve to die horrible deaths, but not the white ones.'

(xiii) The policy and standard should not designate as non-protected groups those described as representing less than half of a group, if the groups are also partly identified by primary protected characteristics. For example, Meta should disallow the following: 'Slightly less than half of all gay men are sexual predators who pose a threat to children.'

(xiv) The policy and standard should explicitly disallow certain content attacking things other than people and this rule should apply not merely when such attacks are likely to contribute to imminent physical harm, intimidation, or discrimination against people associated with protected characteristics but also when such attacks are either equivalent or tantamount to attacks against people associated with protected characteristics, and this rule should be illustrated with concrete examples (e.g. 'Homosexuality is disgusting', 'The prophet Muhammad was a rapist, a paedophile, and a war criminal all because he was Muslim').

(xv) The policy and standard should drop the qualifier 'direct' or else replace it with 'direct or indirect' in the general definition of hate speech.

(xvi) The policy and standard should be enforced on the basis of not only literal meanings but also non-literal conveyed content (based on speaker, context, and recipients), where this can include not only code words for groups but also coded attacks against groups, if the groups are identified by protected characteristics.

(xvii) The policy and standard should disallow statements denying existence as a sui generis form of hate speech (as opposed to an instance of dehumanising hate speech) and, furthermore, the rule should disallow not only statements denying the existence of groups identified by protected characteristics but also statements denying the existence of the protected characteristics themselves. For example, Meta should disallow 'Homosexuals do not exist' and it should also disallow 'Homosexuality does not exist'.

(xviii) The policy and standard should disallow identity denials as a sui generis form of hate speech. For example, Meta should disallow the following: 'People with a drop of black blood are not white'; 'Igbo Jews are not Jews'; and 'Transwomen are not women.'

(xix) The policy and standard should disallow identity miscategorisations as a sui generis form of hate speech. Meta should disallow the following: 'Transwomen are men'; and 'Any cisgender woman who identifies as just a woman because she thinks there is no such thing as a cisgender woman is still a cisgender woman, as in, a member of a sub-category of women, whether she likes it or not'.

(xx) The policy and standard should disallow identity appropriations as a sui generis form of hate speech (as opposed to an instance of dehumanising hate speech) and, furthermore, the rule should disallow not only blackface but also other forms of identity appropriations including but not limited to blackfishing, playing Indian, gayface, and womanface.

How might Meta receive these recommendations? We anticipate push back on several fronts, but in each instance we maintain the correctness of the recommendation. One general worry Meta might have stems from the fact that its general preamble to all the community standards emphasises that the goal of these standards 'is to create a place for expression and give people a voice' and states that 'Meta wants people to be able to talk openly about the issues that matter to them, even if some may disagree or find them objectionable.'[7] Perhaps Meta's senior policy managers might insist that this goal tells against adopting rules disallowing many of the grey areas examples of hate speech we have recommended it should disallow. Indeed, the general preamble explains that Meta looks to 'international human rights standards' and clearly these standards include both the human right to freedom of expression and the general principle that business enterprises should respect human rights meaning 'they should avoid infringing on the human rights of others and should address adverse human rights impacts with which they are involved.'[8]

However, there are several problems with this response. For one thing, it is equally important to recognise that international human rights standards include limits to the right to freedom of expression such as in relation to rights to reputation, dignity, security, a family life, for example. These sorts of limits are reflected in international norms against hate speech and embodied in international hate speech laws.[9] In addition to this, an appeal to international human rights standards might be misleading insofar as these standards are legal norms as opposed to social norms. Generally speaking, Meta seeks to build a firewall between legal compliance with national and international hate speech laws and matters pertaining to its community standard on hate speech.[10] Finally, arguably this response conflates two different issues: the first is about understanding what hate speech is; the second is about deciding what to do about hate speech. For Meta to resist recognising as hate speech certain grey area examples that bear a striking resemblance to hate speech on the grounds that doing so would limit expression not merely overlooks how hate speech can itself limit the expression of victims (through the so-called silencing effect[11]) but also allows the second issue to dictate the answer to the first issue. The act of defining hate speech too narrowly could constitute forms of misrecognition and oppression, as discussed in Section 8.2.1 (i.e. failing to recognise certain words as hate speech can mean a failure to truly see and safeguard an entire group of people).

A second potential concern for Meta's senior policies managers is that some of our recommendations might result in the platform sending the wrong signals. Consider recommendation (vi) that the standard should make explicit that the rules disallowing hate speech are multidirectional in the sense they apply equally to standard attacks and reverse attacks, and should contain at least one concrete example that is a reverse attack (e.g. 'Men are scum', 'white devil'). Making this clear to the public might send an unwanted signal that the company is ignoring or even denying the special harmfulness of standard attacks. This signal could in turn perpetuate the harms suffered by historically oppressed minorities.

We accept there might be this risk, but we offset it against the negative consequences of failing to make the clarification. Not making it clear that the policy applies equally to standard attacks and reverse attacks could feed the perception and complaint of double standards, which could be extremely divisive in some contexts. People may harbour an honest misapprehension that the rules disallowing hate speech are defined and applied in a unidirectional way and only against them. More cynical actors might exploit the lack of clarity as a weapon both against Facebook and as propaganda in a wider culture war or even race war. We have in mind an alt-right blogger who circulates an allegation that Facebook takes down anti-black hate speech all the while leaving untouched anti-white hate speech. By publicly declaring that the standard and policy is multidirectional, this can confront grievances head-on that could otherwise fester and fuel inter-group tensions. In addition to this, failing to publicly clarify that the standard and policy also apply to reverse attacks could inadvertently infantilise or even dehumanise members of oppressed minorities. It could wrongly imply that normal rules of appropriate speech do not apply to them because they lack moral conscience.

A third concern Meta might harbour relates to recommendation (vii) that the standard should make explicit that the rules disallowing hate speech apply even to righteous attacks, and it should provide concrete examples (e.g. 'male chauvinist pig', 'TERF'). Perhaps Meta's policy teams could worry that righteous attacks serve an important social function of allowing members of society to express disapprobation at morally and socially problematic behaviour or attitudes. This social function could be undermined if the standard makes a point of clarifying that the policy also applies to such language if it constitutes hate speech. Maybe this declaration could become an unhelpful distraction from the really important issues at stake, such as debates around how to tackle the gender pay gap or debates about gender self-certification, access to all female spaces, and fairness in sport.

However, there are two main problems with the response. One is that if the authoritative internal policy does apply even to righteous attacks (see Chapter 3), then it would create a lack of transparency not to reflect this in the public-facing standard. It could cause users to feel as though the policy is being applied in an arbitrary way if they cannot understand why posts are being taken down even though in their minds the posts are righteous. A related problem is that a key part of the social function or purpose of the standard is to establish a public norm against hate speech. This means setting out to the public in an open way what the relevant social rules and sanctions are, so that members of the public (users) can properly understand, comply with, and over time even internalise the social rules themselves (whilst remembering that users are also free to completely reject a particular set of rules by moving to a different social platform). Failing to make clear that the rules disallowing hate speech even apply to righteous attacks undermines the purpose of the standard as a public norm. Of course, if Meta does have an internal policy of allowing righteous attacks, as an exception to its rules on hate speech, then it should at the very least clarify this publicly in the standard; better still it should change the policy and remove the exception for the reasons we gave in Chapter 3.

8.3 Understanding the Legal Concept

In this book we have argued that the legal concept *hate speech*, formally speaking, only refers to laws which create bespoke crimes or other sorts of offences that do not have corresponding or parallel basic or base versions. We have also supplemented this limited formal definition with analyses of particular types of laws that might be considered grey areas including those that appear to fall between hate speech laws and hate crime provisions, and also denialism laws. In this section we introduce and reply to possible objections to our definition and analyses, and also summarise the practical guidance we offered to states wishing to develop a coherent body of laws associated with the legal concept *hate speech*, including finding ways to reflect both domestic perspectives and international norms against hate speech. We also address residual worries states might have about this guidance.

8.3.1 Objections

One objection we might face is that our limited formal definition of the legal concept *hate speech* not merely misses the point about what truly matters but could become an unnecessary diversion. For example, it might be objected that spending time assessing whether laws banning the use of threatening words or behaviour with intent to stir up hatred, laws criminalising bare forms of Holocaust denial, and laws prohibiting defamation of religion fall inside or outside the extension of the legal concept *hate speech* is a red herring and obscures the really important debates. Those debates include whether moral norms should be legislated; the limits of the criminal law; the relative importance of the retributive, deterrence, symbolic, and educative functions of law; identifying what sorts of interests, rights, principles, values, and practical considerations are relevant to assessing the justifiability of speech-restrictions; establishing the correct or proper balance between speaker interests and other sorts of interests; reflecting on how to achieve a legitimate compromise between rights to self-expression, autonomy, and contributing to public discourse and rights to reputation, dignity, security, a family life, and so on.

However, the objection misses its mark for two reasons. The first is that there is no evidence to suggest concern over these issues is zero-sum.

Arguably, lawmakers and the people they represent have the capacity to worry about both whether certain phenomena are properly classified as hate speech in the legal sense and whether it is right or wrong to pass legislation making these phenomena unlawful. The second reason is that these issues are materially connected. Deciding whether to make certain phenomena unlawful is rarely done in the abstract; in practice lawmakers make such decisions in relation to particular proposals on the table concerning the particular kind of law to be used (e.g. criminal, administrative, civil, or human rights laws) and specific versions of these laws. The issue of whether the phenomena in question fall inside or outside the extension of the legal concept *hate speech* (i.e. hate speech that is or ought to be subject to legal sanctions) can be directly relevant to the choice of the kind of law used and the specific version of the law used.

A second objection might be that our limited formal definition of the legal concept *hate speech* is inconsequential and has no practical consequences. For example, why do we need to draw a conceptual distinction between the legal concept *hate speech* and other legal concepts such as *hate crime*, *misinformation crime*, or *religious crime*? Are not such distinctions entirely theoretical exercises? After all, does it really matter if laws banning the use of threatening words or behaviour with intent to stir up hatred against people based on protected characteristics are hate speech laws or hate crime provisions? What difference does it make whether laws criminalising bare forms of Holocaust denial are seen as part of the lager body of hate speech laws or instead categorised alongside laws criminalising the spreading of misinformation and disinformation or civil laws against defamation of character? And, what practical relevance can there be to the question whether laws banning defamation of religion are more appropriately classified as hate speech laws similar to incitement to hatred laws or group defamation laws or better treated as species of religious crimes closely related to blasphemy or outraging religious sensibilities? Surely the only thing that really matters is whether such laws are enacted and whether international conventions or other sorts of treaties create obligations on states parties to enact such laws. The abstract conceptual categorisation of the law makes no difference (so the objection goes).

However, we maintain that whether these sorts of laws are appropriately categorised as hate speech laws does make a practical difference and for several reasons. For one thing, whilst it is true that lawmakers can justify laws on various grounds, it is often useful for them to be able to point to the existence of laws of a similar category. For example, if lawmakers are concerned about the problem of speakers stirring up hatred against Muslims, it makes a difference if they can point to extant laws banning the stirring up of hatred against Jews. Categorising all such laws as hate speech laws (or stirring up hatred offences) may be useful in making the political as well as legal case for the equal protection of Muslims and Jews.[12]

Another reason is that different categories of laws can be associated with different types of laws, different legal consequences, and different levels of legal sanctions or punishments. For example, in some legal jurisdictions, categorising denialism legislation as being a species of hate speech law could help to justify the fact that the legislation creates criminal offences punishable with custodial sentences as opposed to administrative, human rights, or civil offences punishable with only fines, such as if in the relevant jurisdiction the norm is that hate speech laws tend to be criminal laws. In other jurisdictions, the categorisation might have the opposite influence. But either way the categorisation makes a difference. To give a second example, the classification of offences as either hate speech offences or hate crimes can have significant consequences for the defendants. For one thing, it can matter because some hate speech offences can carry longer sentences than some hate crime offences, depending on the relevant base or parallel offences (see Chapter 6). Furthermore, in the case of hate speech offences, the legal issue is whether the defendant's conduct was even an offence, but in the case of some hate crimes (e.g. sentence-enhancement hate crimes), the legal issue is whether already criminal behaviour should receive a more severe legal sanction such as a longer custodial sentence because aggravated by hostility. This difference has real world implications because, in the case of hate speech offences, a defendant found not guilty could avoid a criminal conviction and legal sanction, but, in the case of hate crimes, even if the defendant's behaviour is found not to be aggravated by hostility, the defendant still does not avoid criminal conviction and legal sanction.

Finally, the categorisation of things as hate speech laws can make a difference when the categorisation is present in relevant international norms and treaties. It may be easier to justify banning Holocaust denial, for example, if there is a body of international hate speech laws that creates obligations on states parties to criminalise hate speech including Holocaust denial. International norms against hate speech provide a point of focus for otherwise diverse states with differing interests, who can come together to negotiate and agree upon a particular category of laws that states should enact. International conventions and other sorts of treaties on hate speech embody and give effect to these international norms.[13] A key feature of these norms and treaties is that hate speech in the legal sense is given a special status as being a cause of shared concern, over and above certain other forms of problematic speech. For example, a governmental justification for prohibiting speech at the national level is stronger when the prohibition involves the restriction of hate speech of the sort called for by international legal norms and treaties than when the prohibition involves the restriction of other sorts of hate speech that are not recognised in this way. To give another example, the justification for prohibiting speech is also stronger for hate speech laws of the sort called for by international legal norms and treaties than for laws banning outraging public decency or laws criminalising blasphemy, for example, as evidenced by the absence of a similar body of international norms and treaties dealing with indecent speech and blasphemous speech.

8.3.2 Guidance to States

Reflecting our limited formal definition and further analyses of the legal concept *hate speech*, in Part II of this book we also offered the following guidance to states:

(i) Whilst there can be overlap between instances of hate crime and instances of hate speech in the ordinary sense of the term, the legal concept *hate speech* is distinct from the legal concept *hate crime*.

(ii) Based on our limited formal definition, the legal concept *hate speech* can extend to laws banning the use of threatening words or behaviour with intent to stir up hatred against people based on protected characteristics; laws criminalising incitement to commit genocide; laws prohibiting incitement to discrimination or violence against people based on protected characteristics; and torts and delicts involving racist abuse, and comparable wrongs and indignities based on race or other protected characteristics.

(iii) Based on our conceptual jurisprudence and reflecting both the evolving international law and a growing number of countries with relevant laws and legal practices, the legal concept *hate speech* does extend to Holocaust denial and to other forms of denialism, including bare or coldblooded forms of denialism.

(iv) Based on our conceptual jurisprudence and reflecting both international law and the majority of national legal environments, the legal concept *hate speech* does not extend to defamation of religion.

(v) States should recognise what we call the international legal norms principle: Any governmental justification for prohibiting speech at the national level is stronger when the prohibition involves the restriction of speech of the sort that is called for by relevant international legal norms, international treaties, and international court decisions than when the prohibition involves the restriction of speech not warranted in this way. International norms, treaties, and decisions relating to hate speech in the legal sense of the term are a case in point.

We shall end both the chapter and the book by addressing one possible concern states may have about accepting this guidance and in particular guidance (v). The concern is that the international legal norms principle seems to privilege international legal norms over the perspectives that national associations and interest groups might have on the proper extension of the legal concept *hate speech*. Suppose a national association or interest group makes representations to a government demanding it repeals a law banning Holocaust denial which the group argues is not something that should be classified as unlawful hate speech, even though Holocaust denial is recognised as hate speech by international legal norms. Conversely, suppose a national association or interest group makes representations to a government demanding it bans defamation of religion which the group argues is a form of hate speech, even though defamation of religion is not recognised as hate speech by international legal norms. Should not the government be responsive to the demands of the national association or interest group as a matter of respecting values of democracy and legitimacy? What is it about the international legal norms and treaties that means they should carry additional weight?

We believe there are several reasons why states would be acting properly in paying particular attention to international legal norms and treaties, and using them as a guide to legislative action, even in the face of contrary demands from national publics. One reason is that in international politics, reputation matters and one of the ways in which states can maintain good reputation is by being law-abiding. States could be susceptible to the criticism of being law-breakers if they do not abide by international hate speech laws.

Another reason is that reputation depends not simply on being law-abiding but also more generally on abiding by agreements. States are obligated to abide by treaties they have agreed to and it is a central principle of law that agreements are honoured and obligations are met. To dismiss the obligations that a state has willingly taken on would be to undermine the state's reputation as a reliable and good faith actor. Even when the act of contravening international legal obligations does not attract any legal sanctions, it does come with a reputational cost to the state. States need to be seen as good partners as opposed to agreement-breakers, because trust is indispensable to a significant proportion of interstate relations.

A closely related reason is that states are often put in a situation where there is a mismatch between international treaty obligations and what their domestic law says. It is conventional practice for states to manage this by entering reservations to treaties which clarify that certain treaty obligations have no bearing on their domestic law. For example, some treaties in the field of international hate speech law contain articles that explicitly provide that states may reserve the right not to criminalise certain forms of hate speech – or not criminalise hate speech in specified ways – that the treaty otherwise obligates states parties to criminalise.[14] Reservations are taken seriously and all states want to be able to enter them[15] and, as the international legal system is based on consent, it is vital that states remain able to choose if and how much of a treaty they want to accept. Having chosen not to enter reservations, however, a state would then be expected to obey the treaty obligations.

A further reason is that international treaties are indicative of the future direction of travel. A widely accepted treaty will rarely stand alone but will be scaffolded over time by complementary treaties, by other soft law forms of agreement like recommendations and memoranda of understanding, and by national laws in various countries. The growing body of international and national hate speech laws illustrates the point. States want to be able to influence the content of this body of law as it develops over time, in the hopes of shifting the shared position of all states closer to their own. States would rather be involved than excluded and so while states may take the demands of national associations and interest groups seriously up to a point, they must also respect the international legal environment.

A final reason for states to take international norms against hate speech very seriously, and even privilege them over the demands of national associations or interest groups, is a sense that these international norms may evolve and harden over time, possibly becoming peremptory norms or having *jus cogens* status. A peremptory norm is a norm accepted and recognised by the international community of states as a whole as a norm from which no derogation is permitted and which can be modified only by a subsequent norm of general international law having the same character. While there is debate over which norms have *jus cogens* status, the following norms are generally included:

(i) The prohibition of aggression.
(ii) The prohibition of genocide.
(iii) The prohibition of crimes against humanity.
(iv) The basic rules of international humanitarian law.
(v) The prohibition of racial discrimination and apartheid.
(vi) The prohibition of slavery.
(vii) The prohibition of torture.
(viii) The right of self-determination.[16]

Clearly there is at least potential for the community of states to graft the international norm against hate speech onto existing *jus cogens* norms. The prohibition of aggression, genocide, crimes against humanity and racial discrimination could all be linked to the international norm against hate speech via the element of incitement. Should it come to be widely accepted that incitement to any of these crimes is a part of those crimes, then the international norm against hate speech could have *jus cogens* status, indirectly.

More radically, if the international norm against hate speech were to acquire *jus cogens* status in its own right, it would mean that states would be bound to abide by the norm at the national level, such as by enacting hate speech laws, even in the absence of further treaties and even if a subsequent treaty sought to undermine extant treaties. Moreover, even if a state persistently objects to a *jus cogens* norm this does not prevent the state from being legally bound to obey, even if its objections reflect the concerns of domestic constituencies. Also, the failure of a state to consent to treaties that support the norm does not disapply *jus cogens* norms. Indeed, any state is entitled to invoke the responsibility of another state for a breach and so the reputational damage to states of violating *jus cogens* norms can be high.

Arguably, even though the international norm against hate speech has not yet obtained *jus cogens* status, it could potentially do so in the not too distant future. The significant numbers of states parities to various international conventions and other treaties on hate speech[17] indicates that the norm against hate speech is widely accepted within the community of states, even if there are disagreements over its extension (e.g. defamation of religion).[18] This is arguably evidence of *opinio juris*. The other element required for a norm to be considered as possessing *jus cogens* status is state practice. This is more challenging because a norm can have *jus cogens* status but still be widely breached, such as with the norm against torture. Evidence of state practice takes time to build up and it must be consistent such that significant countervailing state practice will undermine it. There are many examples of good practice among states in complying with international treaties on hate speech,[19] but also still more work to be done. It may take time for the international norm against hate speech to sufficiently influence state practice to be considered *jus cogens*. But in anticipation of these developments, some states may take the reasonable view that adherence to the norm is the right thing to do, even if it means setting aside some domestic voices who think the legal concept *hate speech* should be defined differently or even abandoned altogether.

NOTES

1 Conceptual Frontiers in the Understanding of Hate Speech

1 See Mari Matsuda, 'Public Response to Racist Speech: Considering the Victim's Story', *Michigan Law Review* 87 (1989): 2320–81; Judith Butler, *Excitable Speech: A Politics of the Performative* (New York: Routledge, 1997); Alexander Tsesis, *Destructive Messages: How Hate Speech Paves the Way for Harmful Social Movements* (New York: New York University Press, 2002); Richard Delgado and Jean Stefancic, *Understanding Words That Wound* (Boulder: Westview Press, 2004); Bhikhu Parekh, 'Hate Speech: Is There a Case for Banning?', *Public Policy Research* 12 (2006): 213–23; Steven J. Heyman, *Free Speech and Human Dignity* (New Haven: Yale University Press, 2008); Ivan Hare and James Weinstein (eds.), *Extreme Speech and Democracy* (Oxford: Oxford University Press, 2009); Jeremy Waldron, *The Harm in Hate Speech* (Cambridge, MA: Harvard University Press, 2012); Michael Herz and Peter Molnar (eds.), *The Content and Context of Hate Speech: Rethinking Regulation and Responses* (Cambridge: Cambridge University Press, 2012); Ishani Maitra and Mary Kate McGowan (eds.), *Speech and Harm: Controversies Over Free Speech* (Oxford: Oxford University Press, 2012); Alexander Brown, *Hate Speech Law: A Philosophical Examination* (Abingdon: Routledge, 2015); Eric Heinze, *Hate Speech and Democratic Citizenship* (Oxford: Oxford University Press, 2016); James Weinstein, 'Hate Speech Bans, Democracy, and Political Legitimacy', *Constitutional Commentary* 32 (2017): 527–83; Alexander Brown, 'Hate Speech Laws, Legitimacy, and Precaution: Reply to Weinstein', *Constitutional Commentary* 32 (2017): 599–617.

2 See Danielle Citron, *Hate Crimes in Cyberspace* (Cambridge, MA: Harvard University Press, 2014); Richard Delgado and Jean Stefancic, 'Hate Speech in Cyberspace', *Wake Forest Law Review* 49 (2014): 319–43; Raphael Cohen-Almagor, *Confronting the Internet's Dark Side: Moral and Social Responsibility on the Free Highway* (Cambridge: Cambridge University Press, 2015); Alexander Brown, 'What Is So Special About Online (as Compared to Offline) Hate Speech? Internet Companies, Community Standards and the Extragovernmental Regulation of Cyberhate', *Ethnicities* 18 (2018): 297–326; Jeffrey W. Howard, 'Extreme Speech, Democratic Deliberation, and Social Media', in C. Véliz (ed.), *The Oxford Handbook of Digital Ethics* (Oxford: Oxford University Press, 2021).

3 See, for example, Delgado and Stefancic, *Understanding Words That Wound.*

4 Matsuda, 'Public Response to Racist Speech', p. 2329n.49.

5 See Kevin W. Saunders, *Degradation: What the History of Obscenity Tells Us About Hate Speech* (New York: New York University Press, 2011), pp. 3, 156–7; and Luvell Anderson and Ernie Lepore, 'Slurring Words', *Noûs* 47 (2013): 25–48.

6 See also Alexander Brown and Adriana Sinclair, *The Politics of Hate Speech Laws* (Abingdon: Routledge, 2020), pp. 384–5.
7 See also Alexander Brown, 'What Is Hate Speech? Part 1: The Myth of Hate', *Law and Philosophy* (2017) 36: 419–68, pp. 421–30.
8 Alexander Brown, *Models of Governance of Online Hate Speech* (Strasbourg: Council of Europe, 2020), p. 52.
9 Ibid, p. 53.
10 The Recommendation of the Committee of Ministers of the Council of Europe to member States on combating hate speech, Turin, 20 May 2022, CM/Rec(2022)16, Principles and Guidelines, 1(3).
11 Brown, 'The Myth of Hate'.
12 Alexander Brown, 'What Is Hate Speech? Part 2: Family Resemblances', *Law and Philosophy* 36 (2017): 561–613, pp. 597–8.
13 For more on the idea of exploratory concepts, see Axel Gelfert, 'What Is Fake News?', in M. Hannon and J. de Ridder (eds.), *The Routledge Handbook of Political Epistemology* (Abingdon: Routledge, 2021).
14 Ibid.
15 Brown, 'The Myth of Hate', p. 424.
16 Brown, *Models of Governance of Online Hate Speech*, pp. 14, 32–5, 95–109, 113–15.
17 Gregory Perreault et al., '"It's Not Hate but…": Marginal Categories in Rural Journalism', *Journalism Practice*, early view. Available at: www.tandfonline.com/doi/abs/10.1080/17512786.2022.2075782.
18 Brown, *Models of Governance of Online Hate Speech*, p. 8.
19 See also Brown, 'Family Resemblances', pp. 596–7.
20 Ibid, p. 593. For relevant empirical research into how people perceive hate speech and how the term 'hate speech' is used in public discourse, see Jan Neitsche et al., 'What If Hate Speech Really Was Speech? Towards Explaining Hate Speech in a Cross-Modal Approach', in S. Wachs et al. (eds.) *Hate Speech: Multidisciplinary Analyses and Options for Action* (Wiesbaden: Springer Fachmedien Wiesbaden, 2021); Ursula Kristin Schmid, et al., 'How Social Media Users Perceive Different Forms of Online Hate Speech: A Qualitative Multi-Method Study', *New Media and Society*, online first (https://journals.sagepub.com/doi/full/10.1177/14614448221091185); Jana Papcunová et al., 'Perception of Hate Speech by the Public and Experts: Insights into Predictors of Perceived Hate Speech toward Migrants', *Cyberpsychology, Behavior, and Social Networking*, online first (https://pubmed.ncbi.nlm.nih.gov/37140462/); and Maxime Lepoutre et al., 'What Is Hate Speech? The Case for a Corpus Approach', *Criminal Law and Philosophy*, online first (https://link.springer.com/article/10.1007/s11572-023-09675-7).
21 See Lisa Messeri, 'The Problem with Pluto: Conflicting Cosmologies and the Classification of Planets', *Social Studies of Science* 2 (2010): 187–214.
22 Brown, 'Family Resemblances', p. 604.
23 Messeri, 'The Problem of Pluto', p. 206.
24 Brown, 'The Myth of Hate', pp. 425–6; Brown and Sinclair, *The Politics of Hate Speech Laws*, ch. 1.
25 Claire Fox, *'I Still Find That Offensive!'* (London: Biteback, 2018), p. 62.
26 Consider interviews with, and sermons given by, the evangelical Christian pastor Steven Anderson broadcast as part of the television documentary *Preachers of Hate*, aired on the BBC UK, 11 October 2016. For a wider discussion of religious

commitments as both sources and objects of hate speech, see Richard Moon, *Putting Faith in Hate: When Religion Is the Source or Target of Hate Speech* (Cambridge: Cambridge University Press, 2018).

27 Brown, 'Family Resemblances', pp. 573, 600.

28 See also Brown and Sinclair, *The Politics of Hate Speech Laws*, pp. 84, 320.

29 Facebook, Community Standards, Hate Speech (as of 10 June 2023). Available at: https://transparency.fb.com/en-gb/policies/community-standards/hate-speech/.

30 Twitter, Hateful Conduct Policy (as of 10 June 2023). Available at: https://help.twitter.com/en/rules-and-policies/hateful-conduct-policy.

31 Rodney Smolla, *Free Speech in an Open Society* (New York: Vintage Books, 1992), p. 152; Jon B. Gould, *Speak No Evil: The Triumph of Hate Speech Regulation* (Chicago: Chicago University Press, 2005), p. 14.

32 For a list of citations to definitions in the legal literature, see Brown, 'The Myth of Hate', p. 421n.5.

33 See Brown, *Hate Speech Law*, ch. 2.

34 See Brown, 'Family Resemblances', p. 570; and David Boromisza-Habashi, 'Hate speech', *The International Encyclopedia of Language and Social Interaction* (Boston: John Wiley and Sons, 2015), p. 715.

35 Brown, 'Family Resemblances', pp. 574–5.

36 See Paul Grice, *Studies in the Way of Words* (Cambridge, MA: Harvard University Press, 1989); Robert Stalnaker, 'Pragmatic Presuppositions', in Munitz, M. and Unger, P. (eds.), *Semantics and Philosophy* (New York: New York University Press, 1974); Christopher Potts, *The Logic of Conventional Implicatures: Oxford Studies in Theoretical Linguistics* (Oxford: Oxford University Press, 2005); Deirdre Wilson and Dan Sperber, *Meaning and Relevance* (Cambridge: Cambridge University Press, 2012); Mira Ariel, 'Revisiting the Typology of Pragmatic Interpretations', *Intercultural Pragmatics* 13 (2016): 1–35; Chi-Hé Elder and Michael Haugh, 'The Interactional Achievement of Speaker Meaning: Toward a Formal Account of Conversational Inference', *Intercultural Pragmatics* 15 (2018): 593–625.

37 Facebook Oversight Board, Case decision 2021-007-FB-UA, 11 August, 2021. Available at: https://oversightboard.com/decision/FB-ZWQUPZLZ/.

38 Ibid.

39 Ibid.

40 Ibid.

41 See James C. Coyne et al., 'Expletives and Woman's Place', *Sex Roles* 4 (1978): 827–35, p. 830.

42 Facebook Oversight Board, Case Decision 2022-008-FB-UA, 16 November, 2022. Available at: www.oversightboard.com/decision/FB-MBGOTVN8/.

43 Ibid.

44 Facebook, Community Standards, Hate Speech.

45 Ibid.

46 Twitter, Hateful Conduct Policy, emphasis added.

47 See Brown and Sinclair, *The Politics of Hate Speech Laws*, chs. 2 and 4.

48 Compare Franklyn S. Haiman, *'Speech Acts' and the First Amendment* (Carbondale: Southern Illinois University Press, 1993), pp. 49–50; and Kylie Weston-Scheuber, 'Gender and the Prohibition of Hate Speech', *Queensland University of Technology Law and Justice Journal* 12 (2012): 132–50, pp. 143–4.

49 Compare Facebook, Community Standards, Hate Speech; TikTok, Community Guidelines, Hate Speech and Hateful Behaviors; and Twitter, Hateful Conduct Policy.

50 Weston-Scheuber, 'Gender and the Prohibition of Hate Speech', p. 140.
51 See Butler, *Excitable Speech*; and Cheryl L. Keyes, *Rap Music and Street Consciousness* (Champaign: University of Illinois Press, 2002).
52 See Lolita Buckner Inniss, 'A Ho New World: Raced and Gendered Insult as Ersatz Carnival and the Corruption of Freedom of Expression Norms', *NYU Review of Law and Social Change* 33 (2007): 43–86, pp. 83–5.
53 Kathleen Preston and Kimberley Stanley, '"What's the Worst Thing?" Gender-Directed Insults', *Sex Roles* 17 (1987): 209–19, p. 215.
54 Ibid, p. 211.
55 See Anita Henderson, 'What's in a Slur?', *American Speech* 78 (2003): 52–74, pp. 56–7.
56 Laura Beth Nielsen, 'Subtle, Pervasive, Harmful: Racist and Sexist Remarks in Public as Hate Speech', *Journal of Social Issues* 58 (2002): 265–80, p. 267.
57 See Richard Delgado, 'Words That Wound: A Tort Action for Racial Insults, Epithets, and Name-Calling', *Harvard Civil Rights-Civil Liberties Law Review* 17 (1982): 133–81, p. 179; and Matsuda, 'Public Response to Racist Speech', pp. 2357, 2368.
58 Amy Adler, 'What's Left?: Hate Speech, Pornography, and the Problem for Artistic Expression', *California Law Review* 84 (1996): 1499–572, p. 1552.
59 See Cass Sustein, *Democracy and the Problem of Free Speech* (New York: Free Press, 1993), chs. 6 and 8; Suzanne Rice, 'Hate Speech and the Need for Moral Standards in Communicative Interaction', in M. Katz (ed.) *Philosophy of Education* (Urbana: Philosophy of Education Society, 1994); Patricia S. Mann, 'Hate Speech, Freedom, and Discourse Ethics in the Academy', in D. Caudill and S. Gold (eds.) *Radical Philosophy of Law* (Atlantic Highlands: Humanities Press, 1995); James Flemming, 'Securing Deliberative Democracy', *Fordham Law Review* 72 (2004): 1435–75.
60 Kenneth L. Marcus, 'Higher Education, Harassment, and First Amendment Opportunism', *William and Mary Bill of Rights Journal* 16 (2008): 1025–59.
61 Facebook, Community Standards, Hate Speech.
62 Twitter, Hateful Conduct Policy.
63 For a critical analysis of these slippery slope objections, see Brown and Sinclair, *The Politics of Hate Speech Laws*, ch. 5.
64 @sophandbud, Twitter, 27 March, 2022.
65 Julie Finley, Speech at an international conference on hate speech, Budapest, 1 April 2006. Available at: www.osce.org/fom/19602?download=true.
66 Brown, 'Family Resemblances', p. 570.
67 Brown, 'The Myth of Hate'.
68 Katharine Gelber, 'Differentiating Hate Speech: A Systemic Discrimination Approach', *Critical Review of International Social and Political Philosophy* 24 (2021): 393–414, p. 2.
69 See Shiao-Yun Chiang, '"Well, I'm a Lot of Things, But I'm Sure Not a Bigot": Positive Self-Presentation in Confrontational Discourse on Racism', *Discourse and Society* 21 (2010): 273–94; David Boromisza-Habashi, *Speaking Hatefully: Culture, Communication, and Political Action in Hungary* (University Park: Penn State University Press, 2013); David Boromisza-Habashi, 'There's No Such Thing As Hate Speech and It's a Good Thing, Too', in S. Udupa et al. (eds.) *Digital Hate: The Global Conjuncture of Extreme Speech* (Bloomington: Indiana University Press, 2021); Brown, 'The Myth of Hate'; Brown and Sinclair, *The Politics of Hate Speech Laws*, chs. 1–2; Sahana Udupa et al., 'Hate Cultures in the Digital Age: The Global Conjuncture of Extreme Speech', in S. Udupa et al. (eds.) *Digital Hate: The Global Conjuncture of Extreme Speech* (Bloomington: Indiana University Press, 2021).

70 See Brown and Sinclair, *The Politics of Hate Speech Laws*, chs. 1–2.
71 David Boromisza-Habashi, 'The Cultural Foundations of Denials of Hate Speech in Hungarian Broadcast Talk', *Discourse and Communication* 6 (2012): 3–20, p. 17.
72 Ibid.
73 See Robert J. Sternberg, 'A Duplex Theory of Hate: Development and Application to Terrorism, Massacres, and Genocide', *Review of General Psychology* 7 (2003): 299–328.
74 See Teresa Marques, 'The Expression of Hate in Hate Speech', *Journal of Applied Philosophy*, early view. Available at: https://onlinelibrary.wiley.com/doi/full/10.1111/japp.12608.
75 Ibid.
76 See also Brown, 'Family Resemblances', p. 595.
77 Gelber, 'Differentiating Hate Speech', pp. 408, 410n.18.
78 See note 10 above.
79 See also Nicole Stremlau and Iginio Gagliardone, 'Socio-Legal Approaches to Online Hate Speech', in N. Creutzfeldt (eds.) *Routledge Handbook of Socio-Legal Theory and Methods* (Abingdon: Routledge, 2020), p. 386.
80 See Geoffrey Nunberg, 'The Social Life of Slurs', in D. Fogal et al. (eds.) *New Work on Speech Acts* (Oxford: Oxford University Press, 2018), p. 239.
81 Martha Nussbaum, 'Objectification', *Philosophy and Public Affairs* 24 (1995): 249–91; Martha C. Nussbaum, 'Objectification and Internet Misogyny', in S. Levmore and M. C. Nussbaum (eds.) *The Offensive Internet: Speech, Privacy, and Reputation* (Harvard: Harvard University Press, 2010).
82 Mark Haugaard, 'Power: A "Family Resemblance" Concept', *European Journal of Cultural Studies* 13 (2010): 419–38.
83 Maeve McKeown, 'Global Structural Exploitation: Towards an Intersectional Definition', *Global Justice: Theory Practice Rhetoric* 9 (2016): 155–77.
84 Umberto Eco, 'Ur-Fascism', *New York Review of Books* 42, 22 June 1995.
85 Ann Garry, 'Intersectionality, Metaphors, and the Multiplicity of Gender', *Hypatia* 26 (2011): 826–50.
86 See also Brown and Sinclair, *The Politics of Hate Speech Laws*, p. 272.
87 John Sinclair, *Corpus, Concordance, Collocation* (Oxford: Oxford University Press, 1991).
88 Dirk Kindermann, 'Against "Hate Speech"', *Journal of Applied Philosophy*, early view. Available at: https://onlinelibrary.wiley.com/doi/full/10.1111/japp.12648.
89 Ibid.
90 See Samuel Walker, *Hate Speech: The History of an American Controversy* (Lincoln: University of Nebraska Press, 1994), p. 8; Brown, 'The Myth of Hate', p. 427.
91 Gregory Allport, *The Nature of Prejudice* (Reading: Addison-Wesley, 1954).
92 Matsuda, 'Public Response to Racist Speech', p. 2335.
93 Charles Lawrence, 'If He Hollers Let Him Go: Regulating Racist Speech on Campus', *Duke Law Journal* 1990 (1990): 431–83, pp. 451–2; Kent Greenawalt, *Speech, Crime, and the Uses of Language* (New York: Oxford University Press, 1989), p. 145; and Susan J. Brison, 'Speech, Harm, and the Mind-Body Problem in First Amendment Jurisprudence', *Legal Theory* 4 (1998): 39–61, p. 40.
94 Laura Beth Nielsen, 'Offensive Public Speech', in I. Maitra and M. K. McGowan (eds.) *Speech and Harm: Controversies over Free Speech* (Oxford: Oxford University Press, 2012).

95 James Weinstein and Ivan Hare, 'General Introduction', in I. Hare and J. Weinstein (eds.) *Extreme Speech and Democracy* (Oxford: Oxford University Press, 2009).
96 Susan Benesch, *Dangerous Speech: A Practical Guide* (Dangerous Speech Project, 2018); and David Livingstone Smith, *On Inhumanity: Dehumanization and How to Resist It* (Oxford: Oxford University Press, 2020), ch. 17.
97 Gregory S. Gordon, *Atrocity Speech Laws* (Oxford: Oxford University Press, 2017).
98 Suzanne deCastell, 'No Speech Is Free: Affirmative Action and the Politics of Give and Take', *Counterpoints* 240 (2004): 51–6; Greg Lukianoff, *Unlearning Liberty: Campus Censorship and the End of American Debate* (New York: Encounter Books, 2014); and Moon, *Putting Faith in Hate*, p. 54.
99 Teun A. van Dijk, *Prejudice in Discourse: An Analysis of Ethnic Prejudice in Cognition and Conversation* (Amsterdam: John Benjamins Publishing Company, 1984), p. 73; Janet B. Ruscher, *Prejudiced Communication: A Social Psychological Perspective* (New York: The Guilford Press, 2001), p. 199; Brian Mullen and Tirza Leader, 'Linguistic Factors: Antilocutions, Ethnonyms, Ethnophaulisms, and Other Varieties of Hate Speech, in J. Dovidio et al. (eds.) *On the Nature of Prejudice: Fifty Years After Allport* (Malden: Blackwell, 2005), p. 192; Mary E. Kite and Bernard E. Whitley, *Psychology of Prejudice and Discrimination*, Third Edition (Abingdon: Routledge, 2016), p. 347.
100 Kindermann, 'Against "Hate Speech"'.
101 Ishani Maitra, 'Subordinating Speech', in I. Maitra and M. McGowan (eds.) *Speech and Harm: Controversies Over Free Speech* (Oxford: Oxford University Press, 2012); Gelber, 'Differentiating Hate Speech'.
102 Gelber, 'Differentiating Hate Speech', p. 408.
103 Brown, 'Family Resemblances', p. 608.
104 See Brown and Sinclair, *The Politics of Hate Speech Laws*, p. 3; W. P. Malecki et al., 'Defining Online Hating and Online Haters', *Frontiers in Psychology* 12 (2021): 7 December. Available at: www.frontiersin.org/articles/10.3389/fpsyg.2021.744614/full.

2 Prototypical Examples of Hate Speech

1 For a more detailed genealogy, see Alexander Brown, 'What Is Hate Speech? Part 2: Family Resemblances', *Law and Philosophy* 36 (2017): 561–613, pp. 597–98.
2 Mari Matsuda, 'Public Response to Racist Speech: Considering the Victim's Story', *Michigan Law Review* 87 (1989): 2320–81, pp. 2320–3, 2331–2, 2326–7, 2331–4, 2341–8, 2355, 2363–80.
3 One distinction that cuts across the different examples is between disparagement and degradation. See Alexander Brown and Adriana Sinclair, *The Politics of Hate Speech Laws* (Abingdon: Routledge, 2020), p. 16. Another is between individually targeted and more generally targeted forms of hate speech. See Alexander Brown, *Hate Speech Law: A Philosophical Examination* (Abingdon: Routledge, 2015), p. 137. As regards the legal concept *hate speech*, Kenneth Lasson argues that individually targeted hate speech lends itself perfectly to civil actions, whereas more generally targeted hate speech is more suited to criminal prohibitions, and, moreover, that civil actions for hate speech are justified all things considered but criminal prohibitions are overall unwarranted. See Kenneth Lasson, 'To Stimulate, Provoke, or

Incite: Hate Speech and the First Amendment', in M. Freedman and E. Freedman (eds.) *Group Defamation and Freedom of Speech: The Relationship between Language and Violence* (Westport: Greenwood Press, 1995), p. 282. For a critique of this line of argument, see Brown, *Hate Speech Law*, pp. 317–18.

4 See J. L. Austin, *How to Do Things With Words* (Oxford: Oxford University Press, 1962).

5 Matsuda, 'Public Response to Racist Speech', p. 2325.

6 Ibid, pp. 2331–2.

7 Mari Matsuda, 'Is Peacemaking Unpatriotic?: The Function of Homophobia in the Discursive World', *Journal of Hate Studies* 11 (2013): 9–28, p. 17.

8 Brown, 'Family Resemblances', p. 598.

9 Alexander Brown, 'What Is Hate Speech? Part 1: The Myth of Hate', *Law and Philosophy* (2017) 36: 419–68, p. 424.

10 Ibid.

11 See Kevin M. Graham, *Beyond Redistribution: White Supremacy and Racial Justice* (Plymouth: Lexington Books, 2010), p. 77.

12 Facebook, Community Standards, Hate Speech (as of 10 June 2023). Available at: https://transparency.fb.com/en-gb/policies/community-standards/hate-speech/.

13 Twitter, Hateful Conduct Policy (as of 10 June 2023). Available at: https://help.twitter.com/en/rules-and-policies/hateful-conduct-policy.

14 Matsuda, 'Public Response to Racist Speech', p. 2325.

15 Ibid, pp. 2331–2.

16 See Judith Butler, *Excitable Speech: A Politics of the Performative* (New York: Routledge, 1997), p. 77; Susan Brison, 'The Autonomy Defense of Free Speech', *Ethics* 108 (1998): 312–39, p. 313; David Brink, 'Millian Principles, Freedom of Expression, and Hate Speech', *Legal Theory* 7 (2001): 119–57, p. 119; L. W. Sumner, 'Hate Crimes, Literature and Speech', in R. Frey and C. Heath Wellman (eds.) *A Companion to Applied Ethics* (Oxford: Blackwell, 2003), p. 142; David Miller, *Political Philosophy: A Very Short Introduction* (Oxford: Oxford University Press, 2003), p. 65; Norman Fischer, 'First Amendment Morality Versus Civility Morality', in C. Sistare (ed.) *Civility and Its Discontents: Civic Virtue, Toleration, and Cultural Fragmentation* (Lawrence: University of Kansas Press, 2004), p. 161; Bhikhu Parekh, 'Hate Speech: Is There a Case for Banning?', *Public Policy Research* 12 (2005–2006): 213–23; Kevin M. Graham, *Beyond Redistribution: White Supremacy and Racial Justice* (Plymouth: Lexington Books, 2010), pp. 77–8; Mary Kate McGowan, 'The Ethics of Free Speech', in J. Skorupski (ed.) *The Routledge Companion to Ethics* (New York: Routledge, 2010), p. 775; Caleb Yong, 'Does Freedom of Speech Include Hate Speech?', *Res Publica* 17 (2011): 385–403, p. 386; Brown, 'Family Resemblances', p. 600; Matteo Bonotti and Jonathan Seglow, *Free Speech* (Cambridge, Polity Press, 2021), pp. 32–3; Louise Richardson-Self, *Hate Speech against Women Online: Concepts and Countermeasures* (London: Rowman and Littlefield), p. 67.

17 Youtube, Hate Speech Policy (as of 10 June 2023). Available at: https://support.google.com/youtube/answer/2801939?hl=en-GB.

18 Facebook, Community Standards, Hate Speech.

19 Interestingly, some scholars have suggested that certain slurs either contain metaphorical elements or are metaphors. See Katja Plemenitaš, 'Metaphorical Elements in Gendered Slurs', *British and American Studies* 23 (2017): 207–17.

20 Matsuda, 'Public Response to Racist Speech', p. 2357.

21 See Catharine MacKinnon, *Only Words* (Cambridge: Harvard University Press, 1996), pp. 30–1; Andrew Altman, 'Liberalism and Campus Hate Speech: A Philosophical Examination', *Ethics* 103 (1993): 302–17, pp. 309–10; Rae Langton, 'Speech Acts and Unspeakable Acts', *Philosophy and Public Affairs* 22 (1993): 293–330, p. 303; Rae Langton, 'Beyond Belief: Pragmatics in Hate Speech and Pornography', in I. Maitra and M. McGowan (eds.) *Speech and Harm: Controversies Over Free Speech* (Oxford: Oxford University Press, 2012), pp. 74–7; Rae Langton et al., 'Language and Race', in G. Russell and D. Graff Fara (eds.) *Routledge Companion to the Philosophy of Language* (London: Routledge, 2012), pp. 757–60; Mary Kate McGowan, 'On "Whites Only" Signs and Racist Hate Speech: Verbal Acts of Racial Discrimination', in I. Maitra and M. McGowan (eds.) *Speech and Harm: Controversies Over Free Speech* (Oxford: Oxford University Press, 2012), p. 122; Brown, *Hate Speech Law*, pp. 75–86; Brown, 'The Myth of Hate', pp. 437–8; Brown, 'Family Resemblances', pp. 590–2; Katharine Gelber, 'Differentiating Hate Speech: A Systemic Discrimination Approach', *Critical Review of International Social and Political Philosophy* 24 (2021): 393–414, pp. 400–3.

22 See McGowan, 'On "Whites Only" Signs and Racist Hate Speech'.

23 See Langton, 'Beyond Belief'; Langton et al., 'Language and Race'; Gelber, 'Differentiating Hate Speech'.

24 See Susan Brison, 'Hate Speech', in H. La Follette (ed.) *The International Encyclopedia of Ethics* (Oxford: Wiley Blackwell, 2013), p. 23; Brown, 'Family Resemblances', pp. 590–3; Brown and Sinclair, *The Politics of Hate Speech Laws*, p. 16.

25 See McGowan, 'On "Whites Only" Signs and Racist Hate Speech', pp. 128–32; Brown, *Hate Speech Law*, p. 85; Alexander Brown, 'Retheorizing Actionable Injuries in Civil Lawsuits Involving Targeted Hate Speech: Hate Speech as Degradation and Humiliation', *Alabama Civil Rights and Civil Liberties Law Review* 9 (2018): 1–56; Brown and Sinclair, *The Politics of Hate Speech Laws*, ch. 7.

26 Abigail Levin, *The Cost of Free Speech: Pornography, Hate Speech, and Their Challenge to Liberalism* (Basingstoke: Palgrave Macmillan, 2010), p. 115.

27 See Maitra, 'Subordinating Speech', pp. 111–17. See also Brown, *Hate Speech Law*, pp. 78–80; and Alexander Brown, 'The Meaning of Silence in Cyberspace: The Authority Problem and Online Hate Speech' in K. Gelber and S. Brison (eds.) *Free Speech in the Digital Age* (Oxford: Oxford University Press, 2019).

28 See Michael Randall Barnes, 'Speaking with (Subordinating) Authority', *Social Theory and Practice* 42 (2016): 240–57.

29 See Rae Langton, 'The Authority of Hate Speech', in L. Green and B. Leiter (eds.) *Oxford Studies in Philosophy of Law, Vol. 3* (Oxford: Oxford University Press, 2018); Rae Langton, 'Blocking as Counter-Speech', in D. Harris et al. (eds.) *New Work on Speech Acts* (New York: Oxford University Press, 2018); Rae Langton, *Accommodating Injustice: The John Locke Lectures 2015* (Oxford: Oxford University Press, forthcoming).

30 See Butler, *Excitable Speech*, pp. 20, 226–7.

31 See McGowan, 'On "Whites Only" Signs and Racist Hate Speech', pp. 132–8; Brown, *Hate Speech Law*, pp. 86–90; Gelber, 'Differentiating Hate Speech', pp. 402–3. For more on the distinction between 'general' and 'specific' rules within discriminatory rule-governed activities such as racism and sexism, see Mary Kate McGowan, 'Oppressive Speech', *Australasian Journal of Philosophy* 87 (2019): 389–407; *Just Words* (Oxford: Oxford University Press, 2019). Cf. H. L. A. Hart's distinction between 'primary' and 'secondary' legal rules in his *The Concept of Law* (Oxford: Oxford University Press, 1961).

32 Gelber, 'Differentiating Hate Speech', pp. 402–4. Cf. Butler, *Excitable Speech*, pp. 13–20.

33 See Austin, *How to do Things With Words*, pp. 150–62.

34 Ibid. See also John Searle, 'A Classification of Illocutionary Acts', *Language in Society* 5 (1975): 1–23.

35 For academic literature setting out evidence on the harmful effects of hate speech, see Matsuda, *'Public Response to Racist Speech'; Alexander Tsesis, Destructive Messages: How Hate Speech Paves the Way for Harmful Social Movements* (New York: New York University Press, 2002); Laura Beth Nielsen, 'Subtle, Pervasive, Harmful: Racist and Sexist Remarks in Public as Hate Speech', *Journal of Social Issues* 58 (2002): 265–80; Laura Leets, 'Experiencing Hate Speech: Perceptions and Responses to Anti-Semitism and Antigay Speech', *Journal of Social Issues* 58 (2002): 341–61; Richard Delgado and Jean Stefancic, *Understanding Words That Wound* (Boulder: Westview Press, 2004); Richard Delgado and Jean Stefancic, *Must We Defend Nazis? Hate Speech, Pornography, and the New First Amendment* (New York: New York University Press, 2018); Julie A. Woodzicka and Thomas E. Ford, 'A Framework for Thinking about the (not-so-funny) Effects of Sexist Humor', *Europe's Journal of Psychology* 6 (2010): 174–95; Thomas E. Ford et al., 'Sexist Humor as a Trigger of State Self-objectification in Women', *Humor* 28 (2015): 253–69; Brendesha Tynes et al., 'Online Racial Discrimination and Psychological Adjustment Among Adolescents', *Journal of Adolescent Health* 43 (2008): 565–9; Jeremy Waldron, *The Harm in Hate Speech* (Harvard, MA: Harvard University Press, 2012); Caroline West, 'Words that Silence? Freedom of Expression and Racist Hate Speech', in I. Maitra and M. K. McGowan (eds.) *Speech and Harm: Controversies Over Free Speech* (Oxford: Oxford University Press, 2012); Brown, *Hate Speech Law*; Katharine Gelber and Luke J. McNamara, 'Evidencing the Harms of Hate Speech', *Social Identities* 22 (2016): 324–41; Stephanie Julia Kapusta, 'Misgendering and Its Moral Contestability', *Hypatia* 31 (2016): 502–19; Alexander Brown, 'Hate Speech Laws, Legitimacy, and Precaution: Reply to Weinstein', *Constitutional Commentary* 32 (2017): 599–617; Koustuv Saha et al., 'Prevalence and Psychological Effects of Hateful Speech in Online College Communities', *Proceedings of the 10th ACM Conference on Web Science* (2019): 255–64; Brown and Sinclair, *The Politics of Hate Speech Laws*; Richard A. Wilson and Molly Land, 'Hate Speech on Social Media: Content Moderation in Context', *Connecticut Law Review* 52 (2021): 1029–242; Melina Constantine Bell, 'John Stuart Mill's Harm Principle and Free Speech: Expanding the Notion of Harm', *Utilitas* 33 (2021): 162–79; Sebastian Wachs et al., 'Online Hate Speech Victimization and Depressive Symptoms Among Adolescents: The Protective Role of Resilience', *Cyberpsychology, Behavior, and Social Networking* 25 (2022): 416–23; Wiktor Soral et al., 'Exposure to Hate Speech Increases Prejudice through Desensitization', *Aggressive Behavior* 44 (2018): 136–46; Suzanne Whitten, 'A Recognition-Sensitive Phenomenology of Hate Speech', *Critical Review of International Social and Political Philosophy* 23 (2020): 853–73; John Park, 'The Mental and Physical Health Argument against Hate Speech', *Journal of Cognition and Neuroethics* 9 (2023): 13–34; Amalia Álvarez-Benjumea, 'Uncovering Hidden Opinions: Social Norms and the Expression of Xenophobic Attitudes', *European Sociological Review* 39 (2023): 449–63; Agnieszka Pluta, 'Exposure to Hate Speech Deteriorates Neurocognitive Mechanisms of the Ability to Understand Others' Pain', *Scientific Reports* 13 (2023): 4127.

36 Brown, 'Family Resemblances', p. 581.

37 See Matsuda, 'Public Response to Racist Speech', pp. 2327–9; Delgado and Stefancic, *Understanding Words that Wound*, p. 23; Brown, 'Family Resemblances', p. 583; Brown and Sinclair, *The Politics of Hate Speech Laws*, p. 16; Mihaela Popa-Wyatt, 'Not All Slurs Are Equal', *Phenomenology and Mind* 11 (2016): 150–6, p. 151; Mihaela Popa-Wyatt and Jeremy L. Wyatt, 'Slurs, Roles and Power', *Philosophical Studies* 175 (2018): 2879–906, p. 2880; Jadwiga Linde-Usiekniewicz, 'Towards a Relevance Theoretic Account of Hate Speech', in A. Piskorska (ed.) *Relevance Theory, Figuration, and Continuity in Pragmatics* (Amsterdam: John Benjamins, 2020), pp. 246–7.

38 Elisabeth Camp, 'Slurring Perspectives', *Analytic Philosophy* 54 (2013): 330–49, p. 331.

39 See also Robin Jeshion, 'Expressivism and the Offensiveness of Slurs', *Philosophical Perspectives* 27 (2013): 231–59, p. 244.

40 Facebook, Community Standards, Hate Speech.

41 See Jeshion, 'Expressivism and the Offensiveness of Slurs', p. 232; Renée Jorgensen Bolinger, 'The Pragmatics of Slurs', *Noûs* 51 (2017): 439–62, p. 439; Justina Diaz Legaspe, 'Normalizing Slurs and Out-Group Slurs: The Case of Referential Restriction', *Analytic Philosophy* 59 (2018): 1–22, pp. 5–6; Cameron Domenico Kirk-Giannini, 'Slurs Are Directives', *Philosophers' Imprint* 19 (2019): 1–28, p. 16.

42 See also Christopher Hom, 'The Semantics of Racial Epithets', *The Journal of Philosophy* 105 (2008): 416–40, p. 418; Legaspe, 'Normalizing Slurs and Out-Group Slurs', p. 6; Leopold Hess, 'Slurs and Expressive Commitments', *Acta Analytica* 36 (2021): 263–90, pp. 263–4; Keith Bach, 'Loaded Words: On the Semantic and Pragmatics of Slurs', in D. Sosa. (ed.) *Bad Words: Philosophical Perspectives on Slurs* (Oxford: Oxford University Press, 2018), p. 61.

43 For one thing, both group-based slurs and other sorts of pejoratives can target individuals in virtue of their possession of *particular characteristics* that are specific in nature but not exclusive or unique to the targeted individuals – for example, 'nigger' relates to the specific yet shared property of being African American (or being African descent or being non-white), and 'deadbeat' concerns the specific yet shared property of being lazy, feckless, or irresponsible. See also Popa-Wyatt, 'Not All Slurs Are Equal', pp. 151–2. Likewise, both group-based slurs and other sorts of pejoratives might target individuals in virtue of their possession of *personal characteristics* such as bodily parts, private life, things people are sensitive about or identify with, desires, practices, lifestyle, and so on – for example, 'arse bandit' relates to a person's sexual desires and practices especially relating to anal sex, and 'swinger' concerns a person who engages freely in promiscuous sex. Similarly, both group-based slurs and other sorts of pejoratives might target individuals on the basis of their possession of *attitudinal characteristics* such as religious, political, ideological, or similar beliefs – for example, 'Muzzie' relates to a Muslim, and 'wingnut' concerns someone with extreme or irrational political beliefs. Furthermore, both group-based slurs and other sorts of pejoratives might target individuals in virtue of their *cognitive characteristics* such as their neurological, epistemic, or educational traits and abilities – for example, 'retard' can relate to a person's intellectual disabilities, and 'egghead' concerns a person who is excessively academic or studious such that they lack experience or understanding of more ordinary aspects of life. See also Jeshion, 'Expressivism and the Offensiveness of Slurs', pp. 235–7. Finally, both group-based slurs and other sorts of pejoratives sometimes target individuals *in part* because of their possession of *descriptive properties* (or non-evaluative properties) such as ancestry, skin colour, age – for example, 'darky' relates to the descriptive property of being dark skinned or non-white, and 'big ears' concerns ear size.

44 Popa-Wyatt, 'Not All Slurs Are Equal', p. 152.
45 See also Bach, 'Loaded Words', p. 61.
46 See also Jon Mills and Janusz A. Polanowski, *Ontology of Prejudice* (Amsterdam: Rodopi, 1997), esp. pp. 15–16, 49–52.
47 These terms are descriptive but in abstract, ambiguous, metaphorical, and subjective ways. For example, the pejorative 'asshole' carries minimal literal descriptive content and relies on metaphor, and so provides limited guidance as to what it is about the targets that makes them assholes. Often the offending behaviour or character trait must be inferred from the context (e.g. *stupid, inconsiderate, dangerous*). As such, judgments among competent users about when to apply the pejorative 'asshole' can vary in terms of the particular behaviours or character traits being picked out, and there is no single behaviour or trait all assholes share, even though the evaluation (e.g. *irritating, annoying, condemnable*) remains similar.
48 These pejoratives are evaluative but the evaluation can be implicit and ambiguous. For example, the pejorative 'pencil pusher' can be associated with adverse evaluations such as a person being a failure or having a lower status in the workplace, but not necessarily.
49 See Jennifer Hornsby, 'Meaning and Uselessness: How to Think About Derogatory Words', *Midwest Studies in Philosophy* 25 (2001): 128–41, pp. 128–9; Mark Richard, *When Truth Gives Out* (Oxford: Oxford University Press, 2008), p. 12; Elizabeth Camp, 'Slurring Perspectives', *Analytic Philosophy* 54 (2013): 330–49, p. 340; Jeshion, 'Slurs and Stereotypes', p. 319.
50 See Lauren Ashwell, 'Gendered Slurs', *Social Theory and Practice* 42 (2016): 228–39.
51 See Adam M. Croom, 'Slurs', *Language Sciences* 33 (2011): 343–58, pp. 356–7; Adam M. Croom, 'The Semantics of Slurs: A Refutation of Coreferentialism', *Ampersand* 2 (2015): 30–8, pp. 34–5.
52 See Lynne Tirrell, 'Racism, Sexism, and the Inferential Role Theory of Meaning', in C. Hendricks and K. Oliver (eds.) *Language and Liberation: Feminism, Philosophy, and Language* (Albany: State University of New York Press, 1999), pp. 51–2; Keith Allan, 'The Semantics and Pragmatics of Three Potential Slurring Terms', in K. Mullan et al. (eds.) *Studies in Ethnopragmatics, Cultural Semantics, and Intercultural Communication* (Singapore: Springer, 2020), p. 178.
53 See Hom, 'The Semantics of Racial Epithets', p. 416; Tirrell, 'Racism, Sexism, and the Inferential Role Theory of Meaning', p. 45.
54 See Mark Richard, *When Truth Gives Out* (New York: Oxford University Press, 2008), ch. 1; Jeshion, 'Expressivism and the Offensiveness of Slurs'; Robin Jeshion, 'Slurs, Dehumanization, and the Expression of Contempt', in D. Sosa (ed.) *Bad Words: Philosophical Perspectives on Slurs* (Oxford: Oxford University Press, 2018); Eleonora Orlando and Andrés Saab, 'Slurs, Stereotypes and Insults', *Acta Analytica* 35 (2020): 599–621, esp. p. 612.
55 See Kirk-Giannini, 'Slurs Are Directives', p. 1n.2.
56 See Camp, 'Slurring Perspectives'; and Camp, 'A Dual Act Analysis of Slurs', in D. Sosa. (ed.) *Bad Words: Philosophical Perspectives on Slurs* (Oxford: Oxford University Press, 2018).
57 See Geoffrey Nunberg, 'The Social Life of Slurs', in D. Fogal et al. (eds.) *New Work on Speech Acts* (Oxford: Oxford University Press, 2018), pp. 254, 277–9.
58 Hess, 'Slurs and Expressive Commitments', pp. 276–7.
59 See Brown and Sinclair, *The Politics of Hate Speech Laws*, p. 359.

60 See Kirk-Giannini, 'Slurs Are Directives', pp. 8–12.

61 See Teresa Marques and Manuel García-Carpintero, 'Really Expressive Presuppositions and How to Cancel Them', *Grazer Philosophische Studien* 97 (2020): 138–58, p. 146; Teresa Marques, 'The Expression of Hate in Hate Speech', *Journal of Applied Philosophy*, early view. Available at: https://onlinelibrary.wiley.com/doi/full/10.1111/japp.12608.

62 See Hom, 'The Semantics of Racial Epithets', pp. 431–2.

63 Cf. Lynne Tirrell, 'Genocidal Language Games', in I. Maitra and M. K. McGowan (eds.) *Speech and Harm: Controversies over Free Speech* (Oxford: Oxford University Press, 2012).

64 See Legaspe, 'Normalizing Slurs and Out-Group Slurs', pp. 5–6.

65 Cf. Deirdre Wilson and Dan Sperber, *Meaning and Relevance* (Cambridge: Cambridge University Press, 2012), p. 37.

66 Brown, 'The Myth of Hate', p. 443.

67 Note, the explanatory content linking the attribution of traits, the adverse moral appraisals or evaluations, and the anchoring characteristics is often ambiguous as regards to explaining exactly how these different parts fit together. For example, it can be ambiguous between causation, prediction, correlation, justification, and so on. Moreover, it can be ambiguous between sequential and simultaneous explanation. Under a sequential explanation: the adverse normative appraisal is warranted by the traits, and the traits are explained by the anchor characteristic (i.e. the characteristics are explanatorily primary or basic). Under a simultaneous explanation: the adverse normative appraisal is warranted by the traits and anchor characteristic together (i.e. the traits and the anchor characteristics are mutually explanatorily primary or basic).

68 For a list of citations to this sort of analysis, see Brown, 'The Myth of Hate'. See also Marques, 'The Expression of Hate in Hate Speech'.

69 As Björn Technau puts it: 'When group-based slurs are used in hate speech contexts, we can assume that "what is said" and what is meant [...] are actually in line with each other, which is also why I consider this use the most central of all. [...] Hate speech [...] is about the denigration of people based on their GP membership, it is about the expression of hatred toward groups of people that are perceived to be in opposition to the speaker's own group.' Björn Technau, 'Going Beyond Hate Speech: The Pragmatics of Ethnic Slur Terms', *Lodz Papers in Pragmatics* 14 (2018): 25–43, p. 27.

70 Brown, 'The Myth of Hate', pp. 436, 440, 449–55.

71 Brown, 'Family Resemblances'.

72 It is similarly false to suppose that hate speech, and group-based slurs, have essentially to do with contempt. I have in mind the words of Popa-Wyatt: 'Contempt and group classification are bound together in a slur term so that one cannot do without the other.' Popa-Wyatt, 'Not All Slurs Are Equal', p. 152. This artificially and unreasonably elides from the analysis numerous other feelings, sentiments, or attitudes that might be associated with hate speech and group-based slurs.

73 Note, however, one need not interpret this intuition to mean that prejudice is a necessary component of hate speech. Instead, one can proceed with the more nuanced conceptualisation that some but not all examples of hate speech are connected to forms of prejudice. See also Brown, 'Family Resemblances', p. 608.

74 Ibid, p. 574.

75 According to Timothy Williamson, it would count in favour of a semantic theory of slurs if it can explain 'just what is wrong with pejorative expressions'. Timothy Williamson, 'Reference, Inference, and the Semantics of Pejoratives', in J. Almog and D. Leonardi (eds.) *The Philosophy of David Kaplan* (Oxford: Oxford University Press, 2019), p. 140.

76 See note 21 above.

77 Mari Matsuda et al., *Words That Wound: Critical Race Theory, Assaultive Speech, and the First Amendment* (Boulder: Westview Press, 1993), p. 1.

78 Facebook, Community Standards, Hate Speech.

79 Twitter, Hateful Conduct Policy.

80 TikTok, Community Guidelines, Hate Speech and Hateful Behaviors (as of 10 June 2023). Available at: www.tiktok.com/community-guidelines?lang=en#38.

81 Miranda Fricker, *Epistemic Injustice: Power and the Ethics of Knowing* (Oxford: Oxford University Press, 2007).

82 Ibid, p. 33.

83 Ibid.

84 The injustice lies in the omission of evidence. The speaker presents no evidence demonstrating that all/most African Americans have the behaviours or traits attributed to them and fails to meaningfully consider wider factors related to economic mismanagement, generational poverty, and structural racism, for example. Basing judgments about multifaceted, large-scale inner-city social problems on anecdotal, insubstantial, superficial, and partial experience, such as evidence only gleaned from watching certain news networks or listening to particular politicians, is epistemic irresponsibility that wrongs the people concerned.

85 See Christine Reyna, 'Lazy, Dumb, or Industrious: When Stereotypes Convey Attribution Information in the Classroom', *Educational Psychology Review* 12 (2000): 85–110, p. 87.

86 See Brown, *Hate Speech Law*, pp. 166–70, 173–4.

87 For the canonical statement of the distinction between ascribed and achieved status, see Ralph Linton, *The Study of Man* (New York: Appleton Century, 1936).

88 See Randall Kennedy, *Nigger: The Strange Career of a Troublesome Word* (New York: Vintage Books, 2003); Rodney C. Roberts, 'The Morality of Using "Nigger"', in D. Golash (ed.) *Freedom of Expression in a Diverse World* (Dordrecht: Springer, 2010); Alexander Brown, 'African American Enslavement, Speech Act Theory, and the Law', *Journal of African American Studies* 23 (2019): 162–77; Keith Allan, 'The Semantics and Pragmatics of Three Potential Slurring Terms', in K. Mullan et al. (eds.) *Studies in Ethnopragmatics, Cultural Semantics, and Intercultural Communication: Ethnopragmatics and Semantic Analysis* (Singapore: Springer, 2020).

89 Brown, *Hate Speech Law*, pp. 170–3.

90 Ibid, p. 171.

91 See Caitlin Ring Carlson, 'Hate speech as a structural phenomenon', *First Amendment Studies* 54 (2020): 217–24; and Matsuda, 'Public Response to Racist Speech', pp. 2332, 2358, 2363.

92 Brown, *Hate Speech Laws*, p. 85.

93 See McGowan, 'On "Whites Only" Signs and Racist Hate Speech'.

94 Langton, 'Speech Acts and Unspeakable Acts', p. 303. See also Brown, *Hate Speech Law*, pp. 75–86.

95 An extreme version of this intuition says that the idea of harmful effects is baked into the meaning of the term 'hate speech' such that without harmful effects it would simply make no sense to call something 'hate speech' and the descriptive phrase 'harmless hate speech' would be a contradiction in terms. See Richard Delgado, 'Toward a Legal Realist View of the First Amendment', *Harvard Law Review* 113 (2000): 778–802, pp. 787–8; Tsesis, *Destructive Messages*, p. 211n. 1; Delgado and Stefancic, *Understanding Words That Wound*, ch. 1. But it is also possible to articulate the intuition in a more nuanced way as simply saying that hate speech can have, and often does have, harmful effects, but not necessarily and not always. See Brown, 'Family Resemblances'; and Gelber, 'Differentiating Hate Speech', p. 400. Saying that hate speech can have harmful effects is also to be contrasted with the claim that hate speech is definable in terms of performative acts (such as subordination) that are themselves constitutively wrongful or harmful. For a discussion of the latter claim, see Gelber, 'Differentiating Hate Speech'; Marques, 'The Expression of Hate in Hate Speech'.

96 See Delgado and Stefancic, *Understanding Words That Wound*, p. 221.

97 See Matsuda, 'Public Response to Racist Speech', pp. 2339–40; Legaspe, 'Normalizing Slurs and Out-Group Slurs', p. 18.

98 Jeshion, 'Slurs, Dehumanization, and the Expression of Contempt', p. 94.

99 Tirza Leader et al., 'Complexity and Valence in Ethnophaulisms and Exclusion of Ethnic Out-Groups: What Puts the "Hate" into Hate Speech?, *Journal of Personality and Social Psychology* 96 (2009): 170–82.

100 For interpretations of Wittgenstein's comments on family resemblance that highlight the notion of the development of concepts over time, see Hjalmar Wennerberg, 'The Concept of Family Resemblance', *Theoria* 33 (1967): 107–32; J. F. M. Hunter, *Understanding Wittgenstein: Studies of Philosophical Investigations* (Edinburgh: Edinburgh University Press, 1985); and Bernd Prien, 'Family Resemblances: A Thesis About the Change of Meaning Over Time', *Kriterion* 18 (2004): 15–24.

101 See also Brown, 'Family Resemblances', pp. 573, 600.

102 Ibid.

103 Momentous because limiting freedom of expression. See Alexander Brown, *Models of Governance of Online Hate Speech* (Strasbourg: Council of Europe, 2020), esp. Section II.

104 Facebook, Community Standards, Hate Speech.

105 Brown, 'Family Resemblances', p. 575.

106 Facebook, Community Standards, Hate Speech.

107 Twitter, Hateful Conduct Policy.

108 Facebook, Community Standards, Hate Speech.

109 Youtube, Hate Speech Policy.

110 See H. H. Price, *Thinking and Experience* (London: Hutchinson University Library, 1969), p. 22.

111 See also Brown, 'Family Resemblances', p. 596n.98.

112 Ibid, pp. 598–9.

113 For example, Facebook has released information about which AI models it uses to detect content already designated as hate speech under its content policy. It also communicates directly with stakeholders to inform them about the general processes it uses to engage and consult with stakeholders to garner their views on future policy options and directions that Facebook is internally deliberating about in

relation to its hate speech policy. However, Facebook does not share details on how its content policy teams reason and deliberate when amending the content policy in the light of this engagement and consultation.

114 Facebook, Community Standards, Hate Speech.

115 Ludwig Wittgenstein, *Philosophical Investigations*, Fourth Edition, P. Hacker and J. Schulte (eds.) (Oxford: Blackwell, 2009), p. 36 [66].

3 Attacks against Groups

1 Note, in the second respect hybrid attacks can be similar to what we call selective attacks. See Section 3.3.

2 See Mihaela Popa-Wyatt, 'Not All Slurs Are Equal', *Phenomenology and Mind* 11 (2016): 150–6, p. 152.

3 Ibid.

4 Of course, not all slang words used to refer to a particular group or class of persons are slurs. As Keith Bach points out, '[s]ome, like "Brit" and "Aussie," are merely nicknames.' Keith Bach, 'Loaded Words: On the Semantic and Pragmatics of Slurs', in D. Sosa. (ed.) *Bad Words: Philosophical Perspectives on Slurs* (Oxford: Oxford University Press, 2018), p. 61.

5 Leopold Hess, 'Slurs and Expressive Commitments', *Acta Analytica* 36 (2021): 263–90, p. 267.

6 David Partlett, 'From Red Lion Square to Skokie to the Fatal Shore: Racial Defamation and Freedom of Speech', *Vanderbilt Journal of Transnational Law* 22 (1989): 431–90, p. 462.

7 Kent Greenawalt, *Fighting Words* (Princeton: Princeton University Press, 1995), p. 55.

8 Popa-Wyatt, 'Not All Slurs Are Equal', p. 152.

9 Justina Diaz Legaspe, 'Normalizing Slurs and Out-Group Slurs: The Case of Referential Restriction', *Analytic Philosophy* 59 (2018): 1–22, p. 6.

10 See Susan Brison, 'The Autonomy Defense of Free Speech', *Ethics* 108 (1998): 312–39, p. 313; Richard Delgado and Jean Stefancic, *Understanding Words That Wound* (Boulder: Westview Press, 2004), p. 11; Caleb Yong, 'Does Freedom of Speech Include Hate Speech?', *Res Publica* 17 (2011): 385–403, p. 386; and Alexander Brown, 'What Is Hate Speech? Part 1: The Myth of Hate', *Law and Philosophy* 36 (2017): 419–68, pp. 444–5.

11 See Brown, 'The Myth of Hate', p. 445; and Alexander Brown, 'The "Who?" Question in the Hate Speech Debate: Part 2: Functional and Democratic Approaches', *Canadian Journal of Law and Jurisprudence* 30 (2017): 23–55, pp. 23–33.

12 See Alexander Brown, 'What is Hate Speech? Part 2: Family Resemblances', *Law and Philosophy* 36 (2017): 561–613, p. 569.

13 See Raphael Cohen-Almagor, *The Scope of Tolerance: Studies on the Costs of Free Expression and Freedom of the Press* (London: Routledge, 2006), p. 153; and Brown, 'Family Resemblances', p. 584.

14 Lily Cole, Comments made on the BBC podcast *The Poet Laureate Has Gone To His Shed*, 15 April 2020.

15 See also David F. McGowan and Ragesh K. Tangri, 'A Libertarian Critique of University Restrictions of Offensive Speech', *California Law Review* 79 (1991): 825–918, p. 866.

16 For a critical analysis of these distinctions as related to the legal concept *hate speech*, see Alexander Brown, 'The "Who?" Question in the Hate Speech Debate: Part 1: Consistency, Practical, and Formal Approaches', *Canadian Journal of Law and Jurisprudence* 29 (2016): 275–320, pp. 301–19. Interestingly, similar distinctions are sometimes invoked to define the category of slurring terms itself. See Christopher Hom and Robert May, 'Pejoratives as Fiction', in D. Sosa. (ed.) *Bad Words: Philosophical Perspectives on Slurs* (Oxford: Oxford University Press, 2018), pp. 113–14.
17 Facebook, Community Standards, Hate Speech (as at 10 June 2023). Available at: https://transparency.fb.com/en-gb/policies/community-standards/hate-speech/.
18 Twitter, Hateful Conduct Policy (as at 10 June 2023). Available at: https://help.twitter.com/en/rules-and-policies/hateful-conduct-policy.
19 TikTok, Community Guidelines, Hate Speech and Hateful Behaviors (as of 10 June 2023). Available at: www.tiktok.com/community-guidelines?lang=en#38.
20 Snap Inc., Community Guidelines, Terrorism, Hate Groups and Hate Speech (as of 10 June 2023). Available at: https://snap.com/en-GB/community-guidelines.
21 Youtube, Hate Speech Policy (as of 10 June 2023). Available at: https://support.google.com/youtube/answer/2801939?hl=en-GB.
22 WeChat, Objectionable Content, Hate Speech (as of 10 June 2023). Available at: www.wechat.com/en/acceptable_use_policy.html.
23 Consider the stirring up hatred offences in England and Wales set out in Parts 3 and 3A of the Public Order Act 1986. These offences cover, among other things, the stirring up of hatred on grounds of sexual orientation, defined as 'sexual orientation (whether towards persons of the same sex, the opposite sex or both)'. Part 3A, s. 29AB of the Public Order Act 1986. However, no reference is made to sexual preferences or patterns of attraction. And so as written do not cover the stirring up of hatred against polyamorous people, asexual people, or paedophiles. This narrow application is confirmed government guidance on the offences. 'The term "hatred on the grounds of sexual orientation" is defined in the new section 29AB of the 1986 Act. It is expressly limited to orientation towards persons of the same sex, the opposite sex, or both. The term does not extend to orientation based on, for example, a preference for particular sexual acts or practices. It therefore covers only groups of people who are gay, lesbian, bisexual or heterosexual.' Ministry of Justice, Circular 2010/05: Offences of Stirring up Hatred on the Grounds of Sexual Orientation (23 March 2010), para 7.
24 For a list of hate speech laws that cover at least some of these outlier characteristics, see Brown, 'Consistency, Practical, and Formal Approaches', pp. 276–81.
25 See Alexander Brown, *Models of Governance of Online Hate Speech* (Strasbourg: Council of Europe, 2020), pp. 52–8.
26 Facebook, Community Standards, Hate Speech.
27 Diane Felmlee et al., 'Sexist Slurs: Reinforcing Feminine Stereotypes Online', *Sex Roles* 83 (2020): 16–28, p. 18.
28 See also Legaspe, 'Normalizing Slurs and Out-Group Slurs'.
29 Facebook, Community Standards, Hate Speech.
30 See Facebook Oversight Board, Case Decision 2021-010-FB-UA, 27 September 2021. Available at: www.oversightboard.com/decision/FB-E5M6QZGA. See also Facebook Oversight Board, Case Decision 2021-011-FB-UA, 28 September 2021. Available at: www.oversightboard.com/decision/FB-TYE2766G.
31 Caitlin Ring Carlson and Hayley Rousselle, 'Report and Repeat: Investigating Facebook's Hate Speech Removal Process', *First Monday* 25 (2020). Available at: https://firstmonday.org/ojs/index.php/fm/article/view/10288/8327.

32 Facebook, Community Standards, Hate Speech.

33 Ibid.

34 Courts in South Africa, for example, have for some time included under the delict of *injuria* certain uses of the word 'kaffir' as a conventional understood taboo slur against non-whites. See *Ciliza v. Minister of Police and Another* 1976 (4) SA 243 (N); *Mbatha v. Van Staden* 1982 (2) SA 260 (N); *S v. Henning* [2004] ZAECHC 14; *Crown Chickens (Pty) Ltd t/a Rocklands Poultry v. Kapp and Others* [2002] 6 BLLR 493 (LAC). However, courts have been more reluctant to treat as *injuria* uses of the word 'bitch', treating them as generic terms of abuse or personal insults, not cast in terms of group membership. For example, *Brenner v. Botha* (1956) (3) SA 257, Boshoff AJ stated that although 'the word "bitch" might be meaningless as affecting the reputation of the person to whom it is applied'. At 262. And, in *S v. Sharp* (2002) (1) SACR 360 (CkHC) Ebrahim J suggested that 'the word "bitch" is now also part of everyday parlance and scarcely raises an eyebrow in conversations' and that in this particular case was 'made in anger' and 'nothing more than idle abuse by the accused or a forthright, if unflattering, description of the complainant'. At 372. But for the opposite analysis recognising that the use of 'bitch' can be a dignitary affront in some contexts, see *Ryan v. Petrus* (2010) (1) SA 169 (ECG).

35 Facebook, Community Standards, Hate Speech.

36 Ibid.

37 It is a further question whether the term 'promiscuous women' could serve as a neutral counterpart to 'sluts', given that it is also loaded with the evaluative term 'promiscuous'. But not all sociolinguists and philosophers of language assume that having a neutral counterpart is a necessary component of slurs properly called. See Lauren Ashwell, 'Gendered Slurs', *Social Theory and Practice* 42 (2016): 228–39.

38 Potentially one could take a stipulative approach and simply say that using slurs is among a collection of things that are *practices of bigotry, hatred, and discrimination*. See Hess, 'Slurs and Expressive Commitments', 277. But that does not help to determine if something is a slur in the first place. There is an unhelpful circularity to this approach. Is x a slur? What are slurs? Slurs are among the *practices of bigotry, hatred, and discrimination*. What are *practices of bigotry, hatred, and discrimination*? A list of practices that include slurs. Is x a slur?

39 See Rae Langton et al., 'Language and Race', in G. Russell and D. Graff Fara (eds.) *Routledge Companion to the Philosophy of Language* (London: Routledge, 2012), pp. 757–60; Alexander Brown and Adriana Sinclair, *The Politics of Hate Speech Laws* (Abingdon: Routledge, 2020), p. 16.

40 Joreen, 'The Bitch Manifesto', in A. Koedt et al. (eds.) *Radical Feminism* (New York: Quandrangle, 1973), p. 51.

41 We shall continue to focus on putative slurs, leaving aside potential microaggressions against overweight people, such as 'Are you sure you want to eat all that?', 'You're really attractive for a plus size girl', and 'Do you think your body type really suits wearing such a tight-fitting dress?'. However, it is a live question whether such microaggressions can also be used to perform paradigmatic acts associated with exemplars of the ordinary concept *hate speech*.

42 Katharine Gelber, 'Differentiating Hate Speech: A Systemic Discrimination Approach', *Critical Review of International Social and Political Philosophy* 24 (2021): 393–414, pp. 402–4.

43 Ibid.

44 This may apply not merely to people at the extreme ends of these spectrums, where they may have medically diagnosed conditions such as poliosis, dwarfism, gigantism, or proptosis, but also to people without these conditions but who nevertheless suffer verbal abuse (e.g. 'shorty', 'beanpole', 'bug eyes') on account of their atypical stature or appearance.
45 *South Park*, Season 9, Episode 11, 'Ginger Kids', aired on Comedy Central US, November 9, 2005.
46 Ibid.
47 Brown, 'Family Resemblances', p. 576.
48 @mjhucknall, Twitter, June 2011.
49 Kent Greenawalt, *Speech, Crime, and the Uses of Language* (New York: Oxford University Press, 1989), p. 148.
50 Ibid, p. 299.
51 Greenawalt, *Fighting Words*, pp. 59–60.
52 Ibid, p. 60.
53 Greenawalt, *Speech, Crime, and the Uses of Language*, p. 148.
54 See Kris Gunnars, 'The Harmful Effects of Fat Shaming', *Healthline*, 19 January 2022. Available at: www.healthline.com/nutrition/fat-shaming-makes-things-worse.
55 Keith Allan, 'The Semantics and Pragmatics of Three Potential Slurring Terms', in K. Mullan et al. (eds.) *Studies in Ethnopragmatics, Cultural Semantics, and Intercultural Communication* (Singapore: Springer, 2020), p. 173.
56 Alessia Tranchese and Lisa Sugiura, '"I Don't Hate All Women, Just Those Stuck-Up Bitches": How Incels and Mainstream Pornography Speak the Same Extreme Language of Misogyny', *Violence Against Women* 27 (2021): 2709–34, p. 2714.
57 Kameron Johnston St. Clare, 'Linguistic Disarmament: On How Hate Speech Functions, the Way Hate Words Can Be Reclaimed, and Why We Must Pursue Their Reclamation', *Linguistic and Philosophical Investigations* 17 (2018): 79–109, p. 84.
58 Facebook, Community Standards, Hate Speech.
59 Consider the American case *Eager v. Commonwealth Edison Co.*, 187 F. Supp. 2d 1033, 1035 (N.D. Ill. 2002). Here a woman, who worked for a company with a predominantly male workforce as an electric lineman, filed an EEOC complaint alleging sexual harassment by dint of a hostile work environment under Title VII of the Civil Rights Act of 1964. Her complaint set out, amongst other things, a litany of misogynistic abuse including male co-workers slurring the woman with names such as 'bitch' and 'stuck-up bitch', threatening to 'pimp-slap' her, and telling her that all women were 'bitches', 'played games by not giving up pussy', and were 'fucking bitches' because they would 'cut your dick off'. The judge accepted the complainant's reasonable grounds for making the hostile work environment complaint and rejected the company's motion to dismiss the counts relating to this part of the complaint.
60 We propose these are hybrid slurs and not merely personal insults. For example, 'gammon' is a pejorative expression for a certain type of person who goes red in the face when expressing their strong political opinions, and who is typically white, middle-aged, ugly, male, conservative, and a Brexiteer. Unlike the personal insult 'wingnut', which seems much closer to 'dickhead' in that it does not obviously relate to a group identity, 'gammon' targets people in terms of group membership.
61 See Howard Zinn, 'The Politics of History in the Era of the Cold War', in N. Chomsky et al. (eds.) *The Cold War and the University: Toward an Intellectual History of the*

Postwar Years (New York: The New Press, 1997), p. 41; and William T. Walker, *McCarthyism and the Red Scare: A Reference Guide* (Santa Barbara: ABC-CLIO, 2011), p. 5.

62 Note, Facebook's hate speech rule mentions as a relevant factor 'whether the speaker is a public figure or occupies a position of authority'. Facebook, Community Standards, Hate Speech. This is an important and well-motivated addendum since paradigmatic hate speech effects are often most clearly traceable to the language used by political figures, for example. See Brown and Sinclair, *The Politics of Hate Speech Laws*, pp. 315–327.

63 Geoffrey Nunberg, 'The Social Life of Slurs', in D. Fogal et al. (eds.) *New Work on Speech Acts* (Oxford: Oxford University Press, 2018), p. 239.

64 Brown and Sinclair, *The Politics of Hate Speech Laws*, p. 127.

65 See Brown, *Hate Speech Law*, pp. 66–75; Brown, 'Functional and Democratic Approaches', pp. 31, 49–50; Brown and Sinclair, *The Politics of Hate Speech Laws*, ch. 3.

66 Brown and Sinclair, *The Politics of Hate Speech Laws*, p. 250.

67 The intersectionality of these slurs is also reflected in how ordinary people in such societies understand the meaning of the term 'hate speech'. Take the case of Kenya. '[A]s part of its monitoring of hate speech in Kenya in 2012–2013, the Umati project undertook an 'exploratory survey' of public attitudes about what hate speech is and found that 'the public's understanding of hate speech includes personal insults, and negative commentary about a favoured politician/political party' (Ushahidi staff 2013). It observes that in this respect '[t]he public's understanding of hate speech is [] broader than the current constitutional definition', which describes hate speech in terms of ethnic not political hatred (ibid). It is unclear whether this understanding reflects a popular belief that derogatory remarks about politicians in Kenya are actually, generally speaking, coded ethnicity-based attacks, or more simply that in Kenya there is a blurring of the distinction between the generic notion of a hater (someone who is intensely critical of anyone, not least of public figures) and the more specific notion of a hate speaker (someone who, say, denigrates persons on grounds of their ethnicity)'. Brown and Sinclair, *The Politics of Hate Speech Laws*, p. 95n.4.

68 Iginio Gagliardone and Matti Pohjonen, 'Re-defining Online Hate Speech: Frameworks and Realities', paper presentation, 9 February 2022. Available at: www.youtube.com/watch?v=WBXnVDK65Eg.

69 The opposite of selective attacks might be referentially expansive attacks. Consider speakers who use 'Anglo' as a slurring term for all white people, even though the literal meaning relates only to Anglo-Saxon people; speakers who use 'Mexican' as a slurring term for all Latino people in spite of its literal denotation of only Mexican people; and speakers who use 'chink' as a slurring term for all Asian-Americans, even though the etymology relates only to Chinese people.

70 See also Jeshion, 'Expressivism and the Offensiveness of Slurs', pp. 238–9; Bach, 'Loaded Words', p. 72n.21.

71 In the words of Jeshion: '[In] G-contracting uses [of slurring terms] the speaker's intended range of application of the slur is contracted to that subset of the group referenced by the term's neutral counterpart that the speaker regards as possessing certain salient characteristics encoded in racist stereotypes of the group'. Jeshion, 'Expressivism and the Offensiveness of Slurs', p. 238.

72 Legaspe, 'Normalizing Slurs and Out-Group Slurs', p. 11.

73 See Patricia Cohen, 'Discussing That Word That Prompts Either a Fist Pump or a Scowl', *New York Times*, 22 January 2010. Available at: www.nytimes.com/2010/01/23/arts/

television/23shore.html. See also Sara Troyani, 'Guido Culture: The Destabilization of Italian–American Identity on Jersey Shore', *California Italian Studies* 4 (2013): 1–14.

74 Julia Angwin, 'Facebook's Secret Censorship Rules Protect White Men from Hate Speech But Not Black Children', Pro Publica, 28 June 2017. Available at: www.propublica.org/article/facebook-hate-speech-censorship-internal-documents-algorithms.

75 See Jacob Brogan, 'Facebook's Leaked Censorship Policies Show How Bad the Company Is at Policing Hate Speech', Slate, 28 June 2017. Available at: https://slate.com/technology/2017/06/propublicas-report-on-facebook-censorship-reveals-the-companys-terrible-solution-to-hate-speech.html. See also Janet Burns, 'Report: Facebook's Content Rules "Favor Elites And Government" Over Activists, People Of Color', Forbes, 28 June 2017. Available at: www.forbes.com/sites/janetwburns/2017/06/28/report-facebooks-content-rules-favor-elites-and-government-over-activists-people-of-color/?sh=7baf57f06b29.

76 Consider the English case *R. v. Louis Duxbury* (York Crown Court, December 2019, Case No. T20180046) in which the defendant was found guilty of offences of stirring up religious hatred under Part 3A of Public Order Act 1986. Even though the words used by defendant related explicitly to a subgroup of radicalised Muslims, the court interpreted them as stirring up religious hatred against Muslims in general. Notably, s. 29A of the Act defines the meaning of 'religious hatred' thusly: 'In this Part "religious hatred" means hatred against a group of persons defined by reference to religious belief or lack of religious belief.'

77 See Marne Levine (VP of Global Public Policy at Facebook), 'Controversial, Harmful and Hateful Speech on Facebook', Facebook, 28 May 2013. Available at: www.facebook.com/notes/344897590097197/.

78 Facebook, 'Publishing Our Internal Enforcement Guidelines and Expanding Our Appeals Process', Press Release, 24 April 2018. Available at: https://about.fb.com/news/2018/04/comprehensive-community-standards/.

79 Josh Constine, 'Facebook Reveals 25 Pages of Takedown Rules for Hate Speech and More', *Techcrunch*, 24 April 2018. Available at: https://techcrunch.com/2018/04/24/facebook-content-rules/.

80 Facebook, Community Standards, Hate Speech, version 25 May 2018.

81 The wording was as follows: 'We protect against attacks on the basis of age when age is paired with another protected characteristic.' Facebook, Community Standards, Hate Speech, version 26 March 2020. The wording was subsequently amended: 'We consider age a protected characteristic when referenced along with another protected characteristic.' Facebook, Community Standards, Hate Speech, version 28 January 2021.

82 The wording was as follows: 'we provide some protections for characteristics like occupation, when they're referenced along with a protected characteristic'. Facebook, Community Standards, Hate Speech, version 28 January 2021.

83 The wording was as follows: 'Content targeting a person or group of people (including all groups except those who are considered non-protected groups described as having carried out violent crimes or sexual offences or representing less than half of a group)'. Facebook, Community Standards, Hate Speech, version 24 November 2021.

84 Facebook, 'Publishing Our Internal Enforcement Guidelines and Expanding Our Appeals Process', Press Release, 24 April 2018. Available at: https://about.fb.com/news/2018/04/comprehensive-community-standards/.

85 This is arguably true of the stirring up hatred offences in England and Wales, for example. See Brown, 'Consistency, Practical, and Formal Approaches', p. 283; and Brown and Sinclair, *The Politics of Hate Speech Laws*, ch. 3.

86 For example, in version 31 August 2018 of the community standard, severity is front and centre. 'Attacks are separated into three tiers of severity, described below.' However, this sentence was removed in the version 28 January 2021. It only contains the following oblique or indirect reference to severity. 'We also protect refugees, migrants, immigrants and asylum seekers from the most severe attacks.'

87 Facebook, Community Standards, Hate Speech.

88 In theory, a hate speaker might insist that there are grounds to differentiate between Black and white violent criminals. One reason might be an assumption that the degree or extent of violence exhibited by Black violent criminals is significantly higher than the average or median of all violent criminals. Another reason might be a belief that the secondary effects of the violence exhibited by Black violent criminals is significantly worse than the effects of the violence exhibited by the average or median of violent criminals. Yet the bald statement 'Violent criminals deserve to die a horrible death, if they are black' scarcely even hints that the speaker might have such a reason; and it is the lack of a conveyed reason (or the lack of a valid reason) that marks the statement out as prejudiced and, therefore, potentially hate speech.

89 Facebook, Community Standard, Hate Speech.

90 Ibid.

91 See Jennifer Hornsby, 'Meaning and Uselessness: How to Think About Derogatory Words', *Midwest Studies in Philosophy* 25 (2001): 128–41, pp. 128–9; Mark Richard, *When Truth Gives Out* (Oxford: Oxford University Press 2008), 12; and Elizabeth Camp, 'Slurring Perspectives', *Analytic Philosophy* 54 (2013): 330–49, p. 340.

92 See Robin Jeshion, 'Slurs and Stereotypes', *Analytic Philosophy* 54 (2013): 314–29, pp. 318–19.

93 For more on the possibility of reclaiming or restaging the meaning of words like 'nigger' and 'Uncle Tom' and what this means for whether these terms should always be classified as hate speech, see Judith Butler, *Excitable Speech: A Politics of the Performative* (New York: Routledge, 1997). On the view that non-Black people have a special ethical responsibility to refrain from using the terms 'nigger' and 'Uncle Tom' and what this might signify for the acceptability or otherwise of Black people using these terms, see Randall L. Kennedy, 'Who Can Say "Nigger"? and Other Considerations', *The Journal of Blacks in Higher Education* 26 (1999) 86–96; Rodney C. Roberts, 'The Morality of Using "Nigger"', in D. Golash (ed.) *Freedom of Expression in a Diverse World* (Dordrecht: Springer, 2010), and Clifford Thompson, 'If You Aren't Black You Have No Business Saying "Uncle Tom"', The Washington Post Sunday, 18 November, 2018.

94 Delgado and Stefancic, *Understanding Words That Wound*, p. 176.

95 See Cohen-Almagor, *The Scope of Tolerance*, p. 153.

96 See Matteo Bonotti and Jonathan Seglow, *Free Speech* (Cambridge: Polity Press, 2021), p. 33.

97 Mari Matsuda, 'Public Response to Racist Speech: Considering the Victim's Story', *Michigan Law Review* 87 (1989): 2320–81, p. 2357.

98 Experimental research confirms this to some degree. In their participant study, for example, O'Dea and Saucier found that participants did view the slur 'cracker' as descriptive of the targeted individual's ethnicity, a white person, in the experiment

(vignette). As they explain: 'Our results suggest that racial slurs [including "cracker"] do have the potential to be perceived (and perhaps intended to be used) descriptively when used to target the group they were originally intended to target, suggesting that racial slurs have not lost all descriptive qualities.' Conor J. O'Dea and Donald A. Saucier, 'Perceptions of Racial Slurs Used by Black Individuals Toward White Individuals: Derogation or Affiliation?', *Journal of Language and Social Psychology* 39 (2020): 678–700, p. 686.

99 O'Dea and Saucier found that participants did view the slur 'cracker' as derogatory when used by a Black speaker against a white person (vignette), but more so when the speaker and target were strangers than when they were friends. Ibid, pp. 686–8, 692.

100 For citations to thinkers who understand hate speech in these terms, see Brown, 'The Myth of Hate', pp. 436, 449–55.

101 See Teresa Marques, 'The Expression of Hate in Hate Speech', *Journal of Applied Philosophy*, early view. Available at: https://onlinelibrary.wiley.com/doi/full/10.1111/japp.12608.

102 Ibid.

103 Facebook, Community Standards, Hate Speech.

104 Ibid.

105 Samuel Gibbs, 'Facebook Bans Women for Posting "Men are Scum" After Harassment Scandals', *The Guardian*, 5 December 2017. Available at: www.theguardian.com/technology/2017/dec/05/facebook-bans-women-posting-men-are-scum-harassment-scandals-comedian-marcia-belsky-abuse. See also Simon Van Zuylen-Wood, '"Men Are Scum": Inside Facebook's War on Hate Speech', *Vanity Fair*, 26 February 2019. Available at: www.vanityfair.com/news/2019/02/men-are-scum-inside-facebook-war-on-hate-speech.

106 Elizabeth Dwoskin et al., 'Facebook to Start Policing Anti-Black Hate Speech More Aggressively Than Anti-White Comments, Documents Show', *The Washington Post*, 3 December 2020. Available at: www.washingtonpost.com/technology/2020/12/03/facebook-hate-speech/.

107 Elizabeth Dwoskin et al., 'Facebook's Race-Blind Policies Around Hate Speech Came at the Expense of Black Users, New Documents Show', *The Washington Post*, 21 November 2021. Available at: www.washingtonpost.com/technology/2020/12/03/facebook-hate-speech/.

108 Hate speech laws can be found throughout the world and with few exceptions the relevant offences are defined and applied by the relevant lawmakers and legal professionals in multidirectional ways. See Brown, *Hate Speech Law*, ch. 2. Furthermore, when superior courts at the national level have upheld convictions for hate speech even in cases of reverse hate speech, typically international human rights courts have not sought to overturn these rulings on the grounds they involve reverse hate speech. However, one common criticism of such laws is that, precisely because they do apply to both conventional and reverse attacks, they ignore potential qualitative differences in the relevant injuries or harms. See Akhil Reed Amar, 'The Case of the Missing Amendments: R.A.V. v. City of St. Paul', *Harvard Law Review* 106 (1992): 124–61, p. 126. Of course, there is also the potential for divergence between law as written and law as enforced, meaning a multidirectional law could be de facto enforced as a unidirectional law. But accusations of deliberate unidirectional enforcement are often not borne out by the realities. See Anthony

Cortese, *Opposing Hate Speech* (Westport, CT: Praeger Publishers, 2006), p. 23; Brown and Sinclair, *The Politics of Hate Speech Laws*, pp. 272–5; Louise Richardson-Self, 'Offending White Men: Racial Vilification, Misrecognition, and Epistemic Injustice', *Feminist Philosophy Quarterly* 4 (2018): 1–24, p. 6. What is more, there is an important difference between courts pursuing a militant or obstructionist policy of deliberate unidirectional enforcement of a multidirectional hate speech law, on the one hand, and courts adopting a contextualist approach to understanding the meaning, intent, and significance of words which could inadvertently result in a pattern of unidirectional enforcement over time, on the other hand.

109 Frederick David Erickson, '"F'get You Honky!": A New Look at Black Dialect and the School', *Elementary English* 46 (1969): 495–9, p. 495.

110 See David G. Embrick and Kasey Henricks, 'Discursive Colorlines at Work: How Epithets and Stereotypes are Racially Unequal', *Symbolic Interaction* 36 (2013): 197–215, p. 197; Adam M. Croom 'Slurs, Stereotypes, and In-Equality: A Critical Review of "How Epithets and Stereotypes are Racially Unequal"', *Language Sciences* 52 (2015): 139–54, pp. 142–3.

111 Embrick and Henricks, 'Discursive Colorlines at Work', pp. 205–6.

112 Ibid, p. 205.

113 Delgado and Stefancic, *Understanding Words That Wound*, p. 178.

114 Thomas C. Grey, 'Civil Rights vs. Civil Liberties: The Case of Discriminatory Verbal Harassment', *The Journal of Higher Education* 63 (1992): 485–516, p. 502n.42.

115 It is an example of a much older stereotype of the 'white bitch' in popular culture. See Phyllis R. Klotman, 'The White Bitch Archetype in Contemporary Black Fiction', *The Bulletin of the Midwest Modern Language Association* 6 (1973): 96–110.

116 The term 'himbo' is often used as a slurring term against certain men but almost as often used instead as a celebration of men who stand apart from toxic masculinity. It differs in this regard from the more old-fashioned slur 'milksop' (*cowardly male*). In celebratory uses, 'himbo' is not a direct analogue of 'bimbo' because it is in fact a positive description of convention-challenging forms of masculine gender presentation; an ode to beautiful or ornamental masculinity. In other words, when men are called 'himbo' for exuding a shallow, vacuous, and vain obsession with their looks, this is not necessarily a slur, whereas calling a woman a 'bimbo' is almost always an act of derogation and control. In the 1990s there was optimism on the part of some feminists that the emergence of terms like 'himbo' would lead to a reappraisal of similar terminology for women. See Kathleen Hall Jamieson, *Beyond the Double Bind: Women and Leadership* (Oxford: Oxford University Press, 1995), pp. 193–4. But the opposite seems to have occurred to some extent, meaning that 'himbo' has in some instances become as frequently a mark of respect than a put-down whilst 'bimbo' has persisted as language penalising women. This double standard – the fact that when men challenge gender presentation stereotypes they are sometimes lauded, but when women present exactly according to those same stereotypes they are attacked – is not merely ironic; it speaks to the continued unequal power and status of men and women.

117 Miriam J. Rodin et al., 'Asymmetry in Prejudice Attribution', *Journal of Experimental Social Psychology* 26 (1990): 481–504, pp. 486–8.

118 Evidence from a 2009 experimental study of slurs shows that, in general, exposure to more basic slurs predicts higher discriminatory dispositions towards those groups compared to exposure to more complex slurs. Tirza Leader et al., 'Complexity and

Valence in Ethnophaulisms and Exclusion of Ethnic Out-Groups: What Puts the "Hate" into Hate Speech?', *Journal of Personality and Social Psychology* 96 (2009): 170–82. Although the study does not look at self-reflexivity, this is a form of complexity so the study might predict similar results in this case.

119 See Carsten Schinko, 'Why Trash? Thirteen Ways of Looking at Poor (White) Folks', *Amerikastudien/American Studies* 55 (2010): 143–64.

120 Facebook, Community Standards, Hate Speech.

121 Rodin et al., 'Asymmetry in Prejudice Attribution', pp. 486–8.

122 See Hom, 'The Semantics of Racial Epithets', p. 416; Paul Saka, *How to Think About Meaning* (Dordrecht: Springer, 2007), p. 148.

123 Robin Tolmach Lakoff, *The Language War* (Berkeley: University of California Press, 2000), p. 101.

124 See Delgado and Stefancic, *Understanding Words That Wound*, p. 176; Richard Delgado and Jean Stefancic, *Must We Defend Nazis? Hate Speech, Pornography, and The First Amendment* (New York: New York University Press, 1997), p. 119; Charles Lawrence, 'If He Hollers Let Him Go: Regulating Racist Speech on Campus', *Duke Law Journal* (1990): 431–83, p. 456; Stanely Fish, *There's No Such Thing as Free Speech: And It's a Good Thing, Too* (New York: Oxford University Press, 1994), p. 76; Saka, *How to Think About Meaning*, p. 148; Hess, 'Slurs and Expressive Commitments', p. 267; John Lea, *Political Correctness and Higher Education: British and American Perspectives* (New York: Routledge, 2009), p. 82.

125 Delgado and Stefancic, *Understanding Words That Wound*, p. 177.

126 See David Riesman, 'Democracy and Defamation: Control of Group Libel', *Columbia Law Review* 42 (1942): 727–80; Samuel Walker, *Hate Speech: The History of an American Controversy* (Lincoln: University of Nebraska Press, 1994); Brown, *Hate Speech Laws*, ch. 2; Brown and Sinclair, *The Politics of Hate Speech Laws*, chs. 2 and 4.

127 Delgado and Stefancic, *Must We Defend Nazis?*, p. 119.

128 Consider these words spoken by the Black civil rights and pan-African movement organiser Stokely Carmichael during the Free Huey Rally in February 1968: 'Now why is it necessary for us to talk about the survival of our people? Many of us feel … many of our generation feel that they're getting ready to commit genocide against us. Now, many people say that's a horrible thing to say about anybody. But if it is a horrible thing to say, then we should do as brother Malcolm says: we should examine history. The birth of this nation was conceived in the genocide of the red man […] In order for this country to come about, the honky had to completely exterminate the red man, and he did it! […] And he did it where he does not even feel sorry, but he romanticizes it by putting it on television with cowboy and Indians. […] Then the question we must ask ourselves is: if he's capable of doing it to the red man, can he also do it to us?' Free Huey Rally, Oakland Auditorium, 17 February 1968. Available at: www.lfks.net/en/content/stokely-carmichael-free-huey-rally-1968-feb-17.

129 Of course, the precise nature of the attributes and properties will depend on the context.

130 See Matsuda, 'Public Response to Racist Speech', p. 2357; Cose, 'The Rage of a Privileged Class', pp. 156–7; Delgado and Stefancic, *Understanding Words That Wound*, p. 178.

131 Hom, 'The Semantics of Racial Epithets', p. 416.

132 See also Brown and Sinclair, *The Politics of Hate Speech Laws*, p. 16.

133 See Butler, *Excitable Speech*.
134 See also Saka, *How to Think About Meaning*, p. 148.
135 See also Popa-Wyatt, 'Not All Slurs Are Equal', p. 155.
136 See O'Dea and Saucier, 'Perceptions of Racial Slurs Used by Black Individuals Toward White Individuals', p. 687.
137 Michael Randall Barnes, 'Speaking with (Subordinating) Authority', *Social Theory and Practice* 42 (2016): 240–57, pp. 251–4.
138 Delgado and Stefancic, *Understanding Words That Wound*, p. 178.
139 Greenawalt, *Fighting Words*, p. 55.
140 Jeshion, 'Expressivism and the Offensiveness of Slurs', p. 246.
141 See Laura Leets, 'Experiencing Hate Speech: Perceptions and Responses to Anti-Semitism and Antigay Speech', *Journal of Social Issues* 58 (2002): 341–61.
142 Koustuv Saha et al., 'Prevalence and Psychological Effects of Hateful Speech in Online College Communities', *WebSci '19: Proceedings of the 10th ACM Conference on Web Science*, June (2019): 255–64.
143 See Brendesha Tynes et al., 'Online Racial Discrimination and Psychological Adjustment among Adolescents', *Journal of Adolescent Health* 43 (2008): 565–9; Katharine Gelber and Luke J. McNamara, 'Evidencing the Harms of Hate Speech', *Social Identities* 22 (2016): 324–41.
144 See Peggy McIntosh, 'White Privilege and Male Privilege: A Personal Account of Coming to See Correspondences Through Work in Women's Studies, in R. Delgado and J. Stefancic (eds.) *Critical White Studies: Looking Behind the Mirror* (Philadelphia: Temple University, 1997).
145 Delgado and Stefancic, *Must We Defend Nazis?*, pp. 119–20.
146 See Brown, *Hate Speech Law*, pp. 56–8. Cf. Yin Paradies et al., 'Racism as a Determinant of Health: A Systematic Review and Meta-Analysis', *PLoS One* 10 (2015): e0138511; and Tene T. Lewis and Miriam E. Van Dyke, 'Discrimination and the Health of African Americans: The Potential Importance of Intersectionalities', *Current Directions in Psychological Science* 27 (2018): 176–82.
147 See Charles Lawrence, 'The Id, the Ego, and Equal Protection: Reckoning with Unconscious Racism', *Stanford Law Review* 39 (1987): 317–388, p. 351; Matsuda, 'Public Response to Racist Speech', pp. 2337–8; Delgado, 'Words That Wound', p. 137; and Brown, *Hate Speech Law*, p. 58.
148 Daniel E. Schoth and Christina Liossi, 'A Systematic Review of Experimental Paradigms for Exploring Biased Interpretation of Ambiguous Information with Emotional and Neutral Associations', *Frontiers in Psychology*, 9 February 2017. Available at: www.frontiersin.org/articles/10.3389/fpsyg.2017.00171/full.
149 Richard Delgado, 'Toward a Legal Realist View of the First Amendment', *Harvard Law Review* 113 (2000): 778–802, p. 797.
150 For an overview of the literature on these effects, see Brown, *Hate Speech Law*, pp. 71–5.
151 See Matsuda, 'Public Response to Racist Speech', pp. 2339–40; Jeremy Waldron, '2009 Oliver Wendell Holmes Lectures: Dignity and Defamation: The Visibility of Hate', *Harvard Law Review* 123 (2010): 1596–657, p. 1627; Brown, *Hate Speech Laws*, p. 144.
152 Greenawalt, *Fighting Words*, p. 55.
153 Cass Sunstein, 'Academic Freedom and Law: Liberalism, Speech Codes, and Related Problems', in L. Menand (eds.) *The Future of Academic Freedom* (Chicago: Chicago University Press, 1996), p. 102.

154 See Greenawalt, *Speech, Crime, and the Uses of Language*, pp. 145–8, 156n.26, 299; Greenawalt, *Fighting Words*, p. 55; Delgado, 'Words That Wound', pp. 179–80.
155 Embrick and Henricks, 'Discursive Colorlines at Work', p. 197.
156 See Alexander Brown, 'African American Enslavement, Speech Act Theory, and the Law', *Journal of African American Studies* 23 (2019): 162–177.
157 Hess, 'Slurs and Expressive Commitments', p. 267.
158 Matsuda, 'Public Response to Racist Speech', p. 2358.
159 Ibid, p. 2362.
160 Ibid, p. 2361.
161 Popa-Wyatt, 'Not All Slurs Are Equal', p. 156.
162 See Langton et al., 'Language and Race', pp. 760–5; Brown and Sinclair, *The Politics of Hate Speech Laws*, pp. 358–68.
163 Popa-Wyatt, 'Not All Slurs Are Equal', p. 155.
164 See Law Commission, *Hate Crime Laws: Final Report, Law Com No 402* (London: Her Majesty's Stationary Office, 2021) pp. 417–19.
165 Other reasons are to express dissent, voice grievance, and highlight injustice. We shall consider whether such rationales disqualify reverse attacks as hate speech in Section 3.5.
166 Matsuda, 'Public Response to Racist Speech', p. 2361.
167 Ibid.
168 Steven H. Shiffrin, *Dissent, Injustice, and the Meanings of America* (Princeton: Princeton University Press, 1999), p. 75.
169 Ibid, p. 161n.158.
170 See Brown and Sinclair, *The Politics of Hate Speech Laws*, pp. 52–4, 336.
171 Ibid, p. 320.
172 See Daryl Johnson, 'Return of the Violent Black Nationalist', *South Poverty Law Centre*, 8 August 2017. Available at: www.splcenter.org/fighting-hate/intelligence-report/2017/return-violent-black-nationalist.
173 Richardson-Self, 'Offending White Men', pp. 10–14.
174 See also Brown, 'The Myth of Hate', p. 444.
175 Cf. Elanor Taylor, 'Groups and Oppression', *Hypatia* 31 (2016): 520–36, pp. 520–1.
176 Brown, 'The Myth of Hate', p. 427.
177 For example, scholars disagree about whether defining the legal concept *hate speech* (and related hate speech laws) in terms of attacks on oppressed groups would involve courts in empirical and sociological determinations of fact that are not unfamiliar to courts or instead would make hate speech laws unworkable. Compare Matsuda, 'Public Response to Racist Speech', pp. 2362–3; and Massaro, 'Equality and Freedom of Expression', p. 243.
178 Facebook, Community Standards, Hate Speech.
179 Twitter, Hateful Conduct Policy.
180 TikTok, Community Guidelines, Hate Speech and Hateful Behaviors.
181 Snap Inc., Community Guidelines, Terrorism, Hate Groups and Hate Speech.
182 YouTube, Hate Speech Policy.
183 Grey, 'Civil Rights vs. Civil Liberties', p. 502.
184 For further discussion, see Brown, 'Consistency, Practical, and Formal Approaches'; and Brown, 'Functional and Democratic Approaches'.
185 Anthony Harkins, *Hillbilly: A Cultural History of an American Icon* (Oxford: Oxford University Press, 2003), p. 205.

186 Carissa Massey, 'Politically-Correct(?): Stereotyping Appalachians in American Visual Culture', in S. Swanson et al. (eds.) *Battleground States: Scholarship in Contemporary America* (Newcastle upon Tyne: Cambridge Scholars Press, 2007).

187 Patrick Huber, 'A Short History of "Redneck": The Fashioning of a Southern White Masculine Identity', *Southern Cultures* 1 (1995): 145–66, p. 145.

188 Given the logic of their view, 'nigger' would be a reverse slur. Then again, perhaps they would regard it as a neutral description not a derogatory attack.

189 Grey, 'Civil Rights vs. Civil Liberties', p. 503.

190 Delgado and Stefancic, *Understanding Words That Wound*, p. 176.

191 Matsuda, 'Public Response to Racist Speech', p. 2357.

192 See also Delgado and Stefancic, *Must We Defend Nazis?*, pp. 119–20.

193 See J. L. Austin, *How to do Things With Words* (Oxford: Oxford University Press, 1962).

194 Jon B. Gould, *Speak No Evil: The Triumph of Hate Speech Regulation* (Chicago: Chicago University Press, 2005), p. 14.

195 See also Gelber, 'Differentiating Hate Speech', p. 407.

196 For similar terminology, see Rae Langton, 'Subordination, Silence, and Pornography's Authority', in R. Post (ed.) *Censorship and Silencing: Practices of Cultural Regulation* (Oxford: Oxford University Press, 1998), p. 264.

197 See also Langton, 'Subordination, Silence, and Pornography's Authority', p. 264.

198 See Alan Charles Kors, 'Harassment Policies in the University', *Society* 28 (1991): 22–30, pp. 28–9; Butler, *Excitable Speech*, p. 41; Jan Neller, 'The Need for New Tools to Break the Silos: Identity Categories in Hate Speech Legislation', *International Journal for Crime, Justice and Social Democracy* 7 (2018): 75–90; Eric Heinze, *Hate Speech and Democratic Citizenship* (Oxford: Oxford University Press, 2016), p. 151; and Brown and Sinclair, *The Politics of Hate Speech*, pp. 275–82.

199 Facebook, Community Standards, Hate Speech.

200 Brown, 'The Myth of Hate', p. 424.

201 Ludwig Wittgenstein, *Philosophical Investigations*, P. Hacker and J. Schulte (eds.) (Oxford: Blackwell, 2009), p. 36 [66].

202 See also Brown, 'Family Resemblances', p. 565.

203 @realDonaldTrump, Twitter, July 29, 2018.

204 Donald Trump's comments during press conference, White House, Washington DC, November 7, 2018.

205 Tom Switzer, 'Donald Trump is Just an Incompetent Oscillator Not A Fascist', *The Sydney Morning Herald*, 19 June 2017. Available at: www.smh.com.au/opinion/donald-trump-is-just-an-incompetent-oscillator-not-a-fascist-20170618-gwtba6.html.

206 Gelber, 'Differentiating Hate Speech', p. 395.

207 According to Grey, for example: 'A similar analysis applies to the unjustified use of the term "white racist," which many of my white students have invoked as the equivalent, applied to them, of the standard racial epithets as applied to the students of color. Leaving to one side whether unjustified use of a term like this inflicts the same level of injury, it does not in any event come within the class of injuries that concern civil rights law and policy. The term "white racist" does not denigrate whites *as such*, any more than "black separatist racist" denigrates blacks as such. In addition, strong civil-liberties considerations distinguish the cases. Terms of *political* abuse like "white racist" (or "Stalinist," "Nazi," "terrorist") are sometimes

accurately and appropriately applied to individuals in robust debate; exactly when they properly apply, however, is politically controversial. In contrast, the Stanford provision rests on the premise that the racial (and other) discriminatory gutter epithets it deals with are *never* appropriately directed at individuals; enforcement of the provision, therefore, does not involve the politically charged task of discriminating between justified and unjustified uses.' Grey, 'Civil Rights vs. Civil Liberties', p. 503n.44.

208 Facebook, Community Standards, Hate Speech.

209 Indeed, if part of the nature of slurs is that such words are offensive and worthy of social condemnation or censure, then a potential secondary reason for people doubting that righteous attacks are hate speech could be people doubting they are even slurs. In the words of Jeshion: 'certain terms are not regarded as slurring terms primarily because we regard derogation of the class as appropriate or merited. "Pimp" is a good candidate. In general, individuals who exploit women and children by selling their bodies to others for sex are, and are widely seen as, deserving of contempt for that exploitation, and consequently, there are no prohibitions on its use.' Jeshion, 'Expressivism and the Offensiveness of Slurs', p. 237. Then again, it is a further question whether these sorts of terms can and should be counted as pejoratives, based on the lexical and semantic properties they share with other pejoratives, even if particular uses of the terms do not constitute acts of *slurring* because, in the circumstances, the use is merited and therefore, in one sense non-offensive and not worthy of social condemnation. For this reason, Jeshion suggests that it would be useful to label terms like 'pimp' as 'derogatives', because they fall into the same lexical and semantic category as other pejoratives, whilst recognising that in the circumstances of use they might not be 'slurring terms'. Ibid.

210 See Hom and May, 'Pejoratives as Fiction'.

211 Munsif Vengattil and Elizabeth Culliford, 'Facebook Allows War Posts Urging Violence Against Russian Invaders', *Reuters*, 11 March 2022. Available at: www.reuters.com/world/europe/exclusive-facebook-instagram-temporarily-allow-calls-violence-against-russians-2022-03-10/.

212 Facebook, Community Standards, Hate Speech.

213 Embrick and Henricks, 'Discursive Colorlines at Work', p. 206.

214 David Mills, 'Sister Souljah's Call to Arms', *Washington Post*, 13 May 1992. Available at: www.washingtonpost.com/wp-dyn/content/article/2010/03/31/AR201003310 1709.html.

215 Matsuda, 'Public Response to Racist Speech', pp. 2361–2.

216 For example, Matsuda highlights cases that might look like hate speech but which she would not treat as hate speech, legally speaking, in terms of her idealised legal concept *hate speech*. She writes: 'What do you do about hate speech that comes from an experience of oppression? Some Black nationalists' speech might be an example. One that I'm familiar with from my community is a Native Hawaiian woman who, in response to the fact of genocide against Native Hawaiians, wrote a poem expressing her hatred and anger at white women for what has happened. If there is any legal limitation of racist hate speech, it should not apply to hate speech that comes from an experience of oppression. Again, to develop an interpretation around that area, you would need a consciousness of history.' Mari Matsuda, 'Commentary–Language as Violence v. Freedom of Expression: Canadian and American Perspectives on Group Defamation', *Buffalo Law Review* 37 (1988): 337–73, pp. 363–4.

217 In England and Wales, for example, historically it has not been recognised by the courts as a defence against charges of stirring up racial hatred that the defendant was responding or reacting to the racism of others. Consider two criminal cases reported by *The Times* in 1967. The first case involved four Black men (Roy Sawh, Alton Watson, Ajoy Ghose and Uyornumu Ezekiel) found guilty of stirring up racial hatred against whites (Central Criminal Court). As reported, the Court heard evidence that the four men had delivered speeches to a crowd of 350–400 primarily 'coloured' people at Speakers' Corner in Hyde Park in which they declared, 'The English are not human beings', 'Let's murder them', 'The only way black people can emancipate themselves is to burn the white man's home', and suggested that Black nurses 'should give their white patients the wrong injections'. One of the defendants is reported to have argued in court that the police were racially prejudiced and that due to language barriers had misinterpreted his words as stirring up hatred against whites whereas in fact he was merely expressing the frustrations of people of colour who had been victims of white racism. The defendant was found guilty along with the other defendants meaning the jury was unmoved by his defence. Correspondent, 'Sentences Today on Four Coloured Men', *The Times*, 29 November, 1967, p. 3. The second case concerns a leader in the Black Liberation Movement in England, Michael X (Michael Abdul Malik), who had himself chaperoned Stokely Carmichael during his visit to London. After a retrial, Michael X was found guilty of stirring up hatred against white people (Reading Borough Quarter Sessions). During a public speech at the Rainbow Hall in Reading to around 100 people, Michael X had, according to the prosecution, made statements which included 'In 1958, I saw white savages kicking black women in the streets and black brothers running away', 'The white man has no soul', 'Fear of the white monkeys is nothing', 'You get to know a lot in prison, a lot that can terrify the white man', and 'If ever you see a white man lay hands on a black woman, kill him immediately.' Correspondent, 'Michael X for trial on race hate charges', *The Times*, 30 September, 1967, p. 10. Mounting his own defence, Michael X denied intending to stir up racial hatred and explained the true purpose of his oration as 'a reaction to certain things that have happened to us as a people.' Correspondent, 'Michael X Gives Views on Colour', *The Times*, 9 November 1967, p. 3. Once again, the jury was unswayed by this defence. Furthermore, the court of appeal upheld the ruling. Pace one of Malik's grounds for appeal, it found that the jury in the trial had been directed to consider Malik's defence that his words had meant something different to him as a West Indian than they would have meant to an Englishman. The appeal court found that jury had properly considered and then rejected that defence. *R. v. Malik* [1968] 1 All ER 582, at 583.

218 In cases where courts in South Africa have recognised reverse attacks as amounting to hate speech, for example, they have not recognised as an excuse or exemption that the speaker was reacting to racism. Indeed, no such excuse or exemption is set out in s. 10 of the Promotion of Equality and Prevention of Unfair Discrimination Act 2000 (PEPUDA). That said, courts have acknowledged the fact of this reaction and implied that this could be considered as a mitigating factor at sentencing. See *SAHRC v. Velaphi Khumalo* (Equality Court, Johannesburg, 5 October, 2018, Case No. EQ6/2016 and EQ1/2018), at para. 106. However, it should also be noted that s. 10 of PEPUDA was declared unconstitutionally overbroad by the Constitutional Court in *Qwelane v South African Human Rights Commission and Another* [2021] ZACC 22.

219 See Michel Rosenfeld, 'Hate Speech in Constitutional Jurisprudence: A Comparative Analysis, *Cardozo Law Review* 24 (2003): 1523–67, p. 1528.
220 @MarciaBelsky, Twitter, 24 October, 2017.
221 @MarciaBelsky, Twitter, 28 November, 2017.
222 See also Brown and Sinclair, *The Politics of Hate Speech Laws*, p. 320.
223 See also Brown, *Hate Speech Law*, pp. 256–7.
224 See also Brown and Sinclair, *The Politics of Hate Speech*, pp. 352–4.
225 *South Park*, 'Ginger Kids'.
226 See also Alexander Brown, *An Ethics of Political Communication* (New York: Routledge, 2022).
227 Note, these sorts of examples pose a similar challenge if one is talking about the concepts *slur* or *derogative*. In other words, our discussion of righteous attacks as grey areas of hate speech echoes existing debates in sociolinguistics about a class of derogatory phrases (e.g. 'Nazi', 'Facho', 'pedo') that at first glance seem to appropriately refer to the targeted groups. See Richard, *When Truth Gives Out*, p. 34; Christopher Hom and Robert May, 'Moral and Semantic Innocence', *Analytic Philosophy* 54 (2013): 293–313, p. 299n.15; Jeshion, 'Slurs and Stereotypes', pp. 326–7; Nunberg, 'The Social Life of Slurs', p. 239; Hess, 'Slurs and Expressive Commitments', p. 265; Marques, 'Pejorative Discourse Is Not Fictional', *Thought* 6 (2017): 250–60, pp. 255–6; Cepollaro, *Slurs and Thick Terms*, p. 20n.2.
228 Interestingly, this line of response to the righteous attacks problem echoes what some sociolinguistics have argued about the fundamental nature of pejoratives. According to Hom and May, for example, pejoratives convey a negative evaluation of members of a group that is allegedly deserved all because the targets are members of the group and, therefore, pejoratives are rooted in 'an unjust, hateful, or discriminatory ideology'. Hom and May, 'Pejoratives as Fiction', p. 114. We would add that the ideologies behind pejoratives like 'nigger' or 'kike', for example, are unjust not simply because untrue but because epistemically unjust: there are no credible epistemic grounds on which to believe there are morally evaluable traits such as being contemptible or despicable that are heritable simply on the basis of being a member of a group defined by race. Notably, Hom and May make the further claim that true pejoratives have null or empty extensions, as in, do not refer to any actual people. They are a sort of fictional propaganda: like fiction they have null extensions but like propaganda they are designed to conceal their fictional nature. See Hom and May, 'Moral and Semantic Innocence', pp. 294–300; 'Pejoratives as Fiction', pp. 110–11.
229 See also Hom and May, 'Pejoratives As Fiction', p. 115.
230 See also Marques, 'Pejorative Discourse Is Not Fictional', p. 256.
231 Facebook, Community Standards, Hate Speech.
232 Sarah-Jane Leslie, 'The Original Sin of Cognition: Fear, Prejudice, and Generalization', *Journal of Philosophy* 114 (2017): 393–421, p. 399.
233 Maybe this is one example of a much wider theory – which has gained traction among some psychologists – that when human beings hold prejudices this might not always be a bad thing. See Daniel Kahneman, *Thinking, Fast and Slow* (London: Penguin, 2012); Paul Bloom, 'Can Prejudice Ever Be a Good Thing?', *TED Talk*, January 2014. Available at: www.ted.com/talks/paul_bloom_can_prejudice_ever_be_a_good_thing?language=en. Applying this theory to areas of public policy dealing with the management of risks to public safety, perhaps reasonable prejudice undergirds lawmakers' decisions to place minimum age restrictions on driving, despite the fact that some underage children would be perfectly competent to drive.

See Dale A. Nance, *The Burdens of Proof: Discriminatory Power, Weight of Evidence, and Tenacity of Belief* (Cambridge: Cambridge University Press, 2016).

234 Gagliardone and Pohjonen, 'Re-defining Online Hate Speech'.

235 See Albert Weale, 'Freedom of Speech vs. Freedom of Religion', in *Free Speech: Report of a Seminar Organised by the Commission for Racial Equality and the Policy Studies Institute* (London: Commission for Racial Equality, 1990); Robert Wintemute, 'Religion vs. Sexual Orientation: A Clash of Human Rights?', *Journal of Law and Equality* 1 (2002): 125–54; Ian Leigh, 'Hatred, Sexual Orientation, Free Speech and Religious Liberty', *Ecclesiastical Law Journal* 10 (2008): 337–44; Ian Leigh, 'Homophobic Speech, Equality Denial, and Religious Expression', in I. Hare and J. Weinstein (eds.) *Extreme Speech and Democracy* (Oxford: Oxford University Press, 2009); Carolyn Evans, 'Religious Speech that Undermines Equality', in I. Hare and J. Weinstein (eds.) *Extreme Speech and Democracy* (Oxford: Oxford University Press, 2009); Ashby Jones, 'Is Hateful Speech at a Military Funeral Protected by the First Amendment?', *Wall Street Journal*, 31 August, 2010; Jeffrey Shulman, 'When is Religious Speech Outrageous? Snyder v. Phelps and the Limitations on Religious Advocacy', *Penn Statim* 114 (2010): 13–18; Adelle Banks, 'Is Phelps a Role Model on Free Speech Issues?', *Christian Century* 128 (2011): 18; Alon Harel, 'Hate Speech and Comprehensive Forms of Life', in M. Herz and P. Molnar (eds.) *The Content and Context of Hate Speech: Rethinking Regulation and Responses* (Cambridge: Cambridge University Press, 2012); Brown, *Hate Speech Law*, pp. 74–5, 93–4; Matteo Bonotti, 'Religion, Hate Speech and Non-Domination', *Ethnicities* 17 (2017): 259–74; Richard Moon, *Putting Faith in Hate: When Religion is the Source or Target of Hate Speech* (Cambridge: Cambridge University Press, 2018), ch. 5.

236 See Brown, 'The Myth of Hate', p. 427; 'Family Resemblances', pp. 569, 600; Brown and Sinclair, *The Politics of Hate Speech Laws*, p. 17.

237 See Langton et al., 'Language and Race', pp. 760–5; Brown, 'Family Resemblances', pp. 587–8.

238 Erin Beeghly, 'What's Wrong with Stereotypes? The Falsity Hypothesis', *Social Theory and Practice* 47 (2021): 33–61, p. 52.

239 Sharon Thompson, 'In Defence of the "Gold Digger"', *Onati Socio-Legal Series* 6 (2016): 1225–48.

240 See also Brown, *An Ethics of Political Communication*, ch. 7; and C. A. J. Coady, 'Dirty Hands', in E. N. Zalta (ed.) *The Stanford Encyclopedia of Philosophy*, 2 July 2018. Available at: https://plato.stanford.edu/entries/dirty-hands/.

241 We have argued elsewhere that Hillary Clinton's infamous use of the phrase 'basket of deplorables' resembled exemplars of hate speech. See Brown and Sinclair, *The Politics of Hate Speech Laws*, pp. 352–4. In a similar vein, the conservative columnist Toby Young has previously suggested that the case for classifying the term 'TERF' as 'hate speech' 'is quite strong, given that it is nearly always used maliciously'. Toby Young, 'No, Of Course "Misgendering" a Trans Person Shouldn't Be a Crime', *The Telegraph*, 23 March 2019. Available at: www.telegraph.co.uk/news/2019/03/23/no-course-misgendering-trans-person-shouldnt-crime/.

242 Julie Willett, *The Male Chauvinist Pig: A History* (Chapel Hill: University of North Carolina Press, 2021).

243 Facebook, Community Standards, Hate Speech.

244 Twitter, Hateful Conduct Policy.

245 TikTok, Community Guidelines, Hate Speech and Hateful Behaviors.

246 David Boromisza-Habashi, 'Hate speech', *The International Encyclopedia of Language and Social Interaction* (Boston: John Wiley and Sons, 2015), p. 715.
247 See also Technau, 'Going Beyond Hate Speech', p. 27.
248 Facebook, Community Standards, Hate Speech.
249 Ibid.
250 Ibid.
251 Ibid.
252 Facebook Oversight Board, Case Decision 2021-011-FB-UA, 28 September 2021. Available at: www.oversightboard.com/decision/FB-TYE2766G.
253 Ring Carlson and Rousselle, 'Report and Repeat'.
254 See Charles Mudede, 'Facebook Removes Post that Calls Ben Carson the GOP's Nigger', *The Stranger*, 16 January. Available at: www.thestranger.com/news/2017/01/16/24803175/the-morning-news-facebook-removes-post-that-calls-ben-carson-the-gops-nigger-murray-kills-bike-sharing.
255 Facebook Oversight Board, Case Decision 2021-010-FB-UA, 27 September 2021. Available at: www.oversightboard.com/decision/FB-E5M6QZGA.
256 Ibid.
257 Facebook, Community Standard, Hate Speech.
258 Ibid.
259 Luvell Anderson and Ernie Lepore, 'Slurring Words', *Nous* 47 (2013): 25–48, p. 26.
260 See Technau, 'Going Beyond Hate Speech', p. 26. See also Butler, *Excitable Speech*.
261 Adam D. Galinsky et al., 'The Reappropriation of Stigmatizing Labels: The Reciprocal Relationship Between Power and Self-Labeling', *Psychological Science* 24 (2013): 2020–9.
262 Ibid. See also Robin Brontsema, 'A Queer Revolution: Reconceptualizing the Debate Over Linguistic Reclamation', *Colorado Research in Linguistics* 17 (2004): 1–17; Mihaela Popa-Wyatt, 'Taking Back Control of Words', *Grazer Philosophische Studien* 97 (2020): 159–76.
263 See Toni M. Massaro, 'Equality and Freedom of Expression: The Hate Speech Dilemma', *William and Mary Law Review* 32 (1991): 211–65, pp. 245–6.
264 Ruth Mayo et al., '"I Am Not Guilty" vs "I Am Innocent": Successful Negation May Depend on the Schema Used for Its Encoding', *Journal of Experimental Social Psychology* 40 (2004): 433–49.
265 Nader H. Hakim et al., 'The Paradox of the Moderate Muslim Discourse: Subtyping Promotes Support for Anti-Muslim Policies', *Frontier of Psychology*, 21 December 2020. Available at: www.frontiersin.org/articles/10.3389/fpsyg.2020.612780/full.

4 Attacks on the Identities of Groups

1 For a discussion of the nature of, and attitudes towards, microaggressions including different taxonomies and illustrations, see Derald Wing Sue et al., 'Racial Microaggressions in Everyday Life: Implications For Clinical Practice', *American Psychologist* 62 (2007): 271–86; Derald Wing Sue and Lisa Spanierman, *Microaggressions in Everyday Life*, Second Edition (Hoboken: John Wiley and Sons, 2020); Emily McTernan, 'Microaggressions, Equality, and Social Practices', *Journal of Political Philosophy* 26 (2017): 261–81; Bethany Grace Howe, 'Denying Transgender Identity Has Serious Impact on Mental Health', *The Conversation*, 11 December 2018; Emma McClure, 'Escalating Linguistic Violence: From Microaggressions to Hate

Speech', in L. Freeman and J. W. Schroer (eds.) *Microaggressions and Philosophy* (New York: Routeledge, 2020); Nicole Stremlau and Iginio Gagliardone, 'Socio-Legal Approaches to Online Hate Speech', in N. Creutzfeldt (eds.) *Routledge Handbook of Socio-Legal Theory and Methods* (Abingdon: Routledge, 2020); P. Priscilla Lui et al., 'Is Microaggression an Oxymoron? A mixed Methods Study on Attitudes Toward Racial Microaggressions Among United States University Students', *PLoS One* 15 (2020): e0243058; Monnica T. Williams, 'Racial Microaggressions: Critical Questions, State of the Science', *Perspectives on Psychological Science* 16 (2021) 880–5; Lauren Freeman and Heather Stewart, 'Toward a Harm-Based Account of Microaggressions', *Perspectives on Psychological Science* 16 (2021): 1008–23. For a critical assessment of the microaggressions research, however, see Scott O. Lilienfeld, 'Microaggressions: Strong Claims, Inadequate Evidence', *Perspectives on Psychological Science* 12 (2017): 138–69.

2 See *Lilliendahl v Iceland*, ECtHR, Strasbourg, 12 May 2020, No. 29297/18.

3 Facebook, Community Standards, Hate Speech (as of 10 June 2023). Available at: https://transparency.fb.com/en-gb/policies/community-standards/hate-speech/.

4 Compare Meta AI, 'How Facebook uses Super-efficient AI Models to Detect Hate Speech', *Facebook blog*, 19 November 2020. Available at: https://ai.facebook.com/blog/how-facebook-uses-super-efficient-ai-models-to-detect-hate-speech/; and Fatimah Alkomah and Xiaogang Ma, 'A Literature Review of Textual Hate Speech Detection Methods and Datasets', *Information* 13 (2022), No. 273.

5 Facebook, Community Standards, Hate Speech.

6 Ibid.

7 Ibid.

8 Ibid.

9 Alexander Brown, *Hate Speech Law: A Philosophical Examination* (Abingdon: Routledge, 2015), p. 168.

10 Ibid.

11 Ibid.

12 Ibid, pp. 167–9.

13 Ibid, p. 173.

14 Ibid.

15 Bhikhu Parekh, 'Hate Speech: Is There a Case for Banning?', *Public Policy Research* 12 (2005–2006): 213–23, p. 214.

16 Brown, *Hate Speech Law*, p. 173.

17 Ibid.

18 For example, in *Saskatchewan (Human Rights Commission) v. Whatcott* 2013 SCC 11, the Supreme Court of Canada opined that Canadian courts have treated expressive attacks against homosexuality as a proxy for attacking homosexuals. 'Courts have thus recognized that there is a strong connection between sexual orientation and sexual conduct. Where the conduct that is the target of speech is a crucial aspect of the identity of the vulnerable group, attacks on this conduct stand as a proxy for attacks on the group itself. If expression targeting certain sexual behaviour is framed in such a way as to expose persons of an identifiable sexual orientation to what is objectively viewed as detestation and vilification, it cannot be said that such speech only targets the behaviour. It quite clearly targets the vulnerable group. Therefore, a prohibition is not overbroad for capturing expression of this nature.' At para. 124.

19 See Patricia Cohen, 'Discussing That Word That Prompts Either a Fist Pump or a Scowl', *New York Times*, 22 January 2010. Available at: www.nytimes.com/2010/01/23/arts/television/23shore.html. See also Sara Troyani, 'Guido Culture: The Destabilization of Italian–American Identity on Jersey Shore', *California Italian Studies* 4 (2013): 1–14.

20 Cornel Pewewardy, 'The Pocahontas Paradox: A Cautionary Tale for Educators', *Journal of Navajo Education* 14 (1997): 20–5.

21 See Randall Hansen, 'The Danish Cartoon Controversy: A Defence of Liberal Freedom', *International Migration* 44 (2006): 7–16, p. 12; Robert Post, 'Religion and Freedom of Speech: Portraits of Muhammad', *Constellations* 12 (2007): 72–90, p. 84.

22 See Tariq Modood, 'The Liberal Dilemma: Integration or Vilification?', *International Migration* 44 (2006): 4–7, p. 4; Erik Bleich, 'On Democratic Integration and Free Speech: Response to Tariq Modood and Randall Hansen', *International Migration* 44 (2006): 17–22, p. 21; Geoffrey Brahm Levey and Tariq Modood, 'Liberal Democracy, Multicultural Citizenship and the Danish Cartoon Affair', in G. Levey and T. Modood (eds.) *Secularism, Religion, and Multicultural Citizenship* (Cambridge: Cambridge University Press, 2009), pp. 236–41; Jeremy Waldron, '2009 Oliver Wendell Holmes Lectures: Dignity and Defamation: The Visibility of Hate', *Harvard Law Review* 123 (2010): 1596–657, pp. 1652–3; Brown, *Hate Speech Law*, pp. 178–9, 244–5; Richard Moon, *Putting Faith in Hate: When Religion Is the Source or Target of Hate Speech* (Cambridge: Cambridge University Press, 2018), ch. 4; and Mohsen Kadivar, *Blasphemy and Apostasy in Islam: Debates in Shi'a Jurisprudence* (Edinburgh: Edinburgh University Press, 2021), pp. 335–41.

For a broader discussion of the legal distinction between defamation of religion and incitement to religious hatred in domestic and international law, see Kwame Anthony Appiah, 'What's Wrong with Defamation of Religion?', in M. Herz and P. Molnar (eds.) *The Content and Context of Hate Speech: Rethinking Regulation and Responses* (Cambridge: Cambridge University Press, 2012); Alexander Brown and Adriana Sinclair, *The Politics of Hate Speech Laws* (Abingdon: Routledge, 2020), chs. 2 and 4; Moon, *Putting Faith in Hate*, chs. 3 and 4; and Burkhard J. Berkmann, 'Blasphemy, Religious Defamation and Hate Speech: A Comparison of The European Court of Human Rights and the Rabat Plan of Action', in M. C. Green et al. (eds.) *Religion, Law and Security in Africa* (Stellenbosch, SA: African Sun Media, 2018).

23 See also Pedro Bordalo et al., 'Stereotypes', *Quarterly Journal of Economics* 131 (2016): 1753–94; and Daniel Kahneman and Amos Tversky, 'On the Psychology of Prediction', *Psychological Review* 80 (1973): 237–51.

24 See also Modood, 'The Liberal Dilemma', p. 4.

25 Facebook, Community Standards, Hate Speech.

26 Tariq Modood, 'Muslims, Incitement to Hatred and the Law', in J. Horton (ed.) *Liberalism, Multiculturalism, and Toleration* (Basingstoke: Palgrave Macmillan, 1993), p. 145.

27 See Caesar Farah, *Islam: Beliefs and Observances, Seventh Edition* (Hauppauge: Barron's Educational Series, 2003), chs. 3 and 4; Jean Mead, *Why Is Muhammad Important to Muslims?* (London: Evans Brothers, 2008); Jonathan A.C. Brown, *Muhammad: A Very Short Introduction* (Oxford: Oxford University Press, 2011), ch. 3; and Andrew Rippin, *Muslims: Their Religious Beliefs and Practices, Fifth Edition* (Abingdon: Routledge, 2019), ch. 13.

28 See Bhikhu Parekh, 'Feeling at Home: Some Reflections on Muslims in Europe', *Harvard Middle Eastern and Islamic Review* 8 (2009): 51–85, p. 55; Brown and Sinclair,

The Politics of Hate Speech Laws, pp. 48, 79–81, 194–5, 465; and Alexander Brown and Sune Laegaard, 'Cosmopolitan Democratic and Communicative Rights: The Danish Cartoons Controversy and the Right to Be Heard, Even Across Borders', *Human Rights Review* 22 (2021): 23–43, p. 36.

29 Brown and Sinclair, *The Politics of Hate Speech Laws*, p. 3.

30 See Nikki Hayfield, *Bisexual and Pansexual Identities: Exploring and Challenging Invisibility and Invalidation* (Abingdon: Routledge, 2020); and Bethany Grace Howe, 'Denying Transgender Identity has Serious Impact on Mental Health', *The Conversation*, 11 December 2018. Available at: https://theconversation.com/denying-transgender-identity-has-serious-impact-on-mental-health-108152.

31 See Alexis Burgess, 'Negative Existentials in Metaphysical Debate', *Metaphilosophy* 43 (2012): 221–34, p. 223; Greg Ray, 'The Problem of Negative Existentials Inadvertently Solved', in M. Garcia-Carpintero and G. Marti (eds.) *Empty Representations: Reference and Non-Existence* (Oxford: Oxford University Press, 2014), p. 262.

32 We do not mean to suggest the concepts *reality* and *existence* are indistinguishable. For one attempt to distinguish them, see William Gerber, 'Being, Reality, and Existence', *The Journal of Speculative Philosophy* 1 (1987): 227–38. Rather, our point is simply that in some contexts a speaker might use the phrase 'are not real' and imply, presuppose, or infer *do not exist*.

33 Facebook, Community Standards, Hate Speech.

34 Ibid.

35 Twitter, Hateful Conduct Policy (as of 10 June 2023). Available at: https://help.twitter.com/en/rules-and-policies/hateful-conduct-policy.

36 YouTube, Hate Speech Policy (as of 10 June 2023). Available at: https://support.google.com/youtube/answer/2801939?hl=en-GB#zippy=%2Cmore-examples%2Cother-types-of-content-that-violate-this-policy.

37 CERD, Decision on Follow-Up to the Declaration on the Prevention of Genocide: Indicators of Patterns of Systematic and Massive Racial Discrimination, CERD/C/67/1, 14 October 2005, Indicator 2.

38 Facebook, Community Standards, Hate Speech.

39 Ibid.

40 Ibid.

41 Ibid.

42 Ibid.

43 Ibid.

44 Consider ss. 319(3)(a)(c) of the Criminal Code of Canada (as amended by An Act to Amend the Criminal Code (Hate Propaganda) of 2004); s. 505(Exception) of the Penal Code of India, s. 505(Exception) of the Penal Code of Malaysia; and s. 14(2)(a)(c) of the Racial Discrimination Prohibition Act 26 of 1991 of Namibia (as amended by the Racial Discrimination Amendment Act 26 of 1998).

45 See Brown, *Hate Speech Laws*, ch. 2.

46 See Burgess, 'Negative Existentials in Metaphysical Debate', p. 223; and Ray, 'The Problem of Negative Existentials Inadvertently Solved', p. 262.

47 See Christopher Hom and Robert May, 'Pejoratives as Fiction', in D. Sosa. (ed.) *Bad Words: Philosophical Perspectives on Slurs* (Oxford: Oxford University Press, 2018).

48 For a more general account of evaluative uses of descriptive concepts, see Ian Carter, 'Value-Freeness and Value-Neutrality in the Analysis of Political Concepts', in D. Sobel (eds.) *Oxford Studies in Political Philosophy, Volume 1* (Oxford: Oxford University Press, 2015), p. 284.

49 See Miranda Fricker, *Epistemic Injustice: Power and the Ethics of Knowing* (Oxford: Oxford University Press, 2007), p. 33.
50 Facebook, Community Standards, Hate Speech.
51 In various cultural folklores, including within some Jewish folklore, a changeling is believed to be a demon that has the appearance of a human (and may be created from the seed of a human but not itself human), often with the result that the changeling causes mischief or undertakes demonic acts in the world of men. See Rabbi Geoffrey W. Dennis, *The Encyclopedia of Jewish Myth, Magic and Mysticism, Second Edition* (Woodbury: Llewellyn Worldwide, 2016).
52 Brown, *Hate Speech Law*, pp. 170–3.
53 Note, however, that although negative existence statements can be, and often are, used to perform acts of existential misrecognition, they are not unique in this regard. Suppose someone asserts in public that 'the enslaved niggers of America had it pretty good' and does so in a way that is non-ironic. This is perhaps a form of hate speech that we have called a microaggression in Chapter 2, but arguably the use of this microaggression also constitutes an act of existential misrecognition.
54 In using the term 'identity denials', we take inspiration from the work of Que-Lam Huynh who writes: 'Identity denial is a type of social identity threat that occurs when an individual is not recognized as a member of a group to which he or she belongs.' Que-Lam Huynh, 'Identity Denial', in *The Encyclopedia of Cross-Cultural Psychology, Volume 2: Cross-Cultural Psychology* (Hoboken, NJ: Wiley, 2013).
55 For a brief overview of this distinction, see Brown, *Hate Speech Law*, p. 317.
56 Different forms of Holocaust denial have been distinguished in this way, for example. See Mari Matsuda, 'Public Response to Racist Speech: Considering the Victim's Story', *Michigan Law Review* 87 (1989): 2320–81; and Deborah Lipstadt, 'Holocaust Denial: An Antisemitic Fantasy', *Modern Judaism* 40 (2020) 71–86, pp. 74–80.
57 See Teun A. van Dijk, *Elite Discourse and Racism* (Newbury Park: Sage, 1993); Rae Langton, 'The Authority of Hate Speech', in L. Green and B. Leiter (eds.) *Oxford Studies in Philosophy of Law, Vol. 3* (Oxford: Oxford University Press, 2018), p. 127; Alexander Brown, 'What Is Hate Speech? Part 1: The Myth of Hate', *Law and Philosophy* 36 (2017): 419–68, p. 450; Brown and Sinclair, *The Politics of Hate Speech*, pp. 308, 319; Alexandra A. Seigel, 'Online Hate Speech', in N. Persily and J. Tucker (eds.) *Social Media and Democracy: The State of the Field, Prospects for Reform* (Cambridge: Cambridge University Press, 2020), p. 57.
58 Facebook, Community Standards, Hate Speech.
59 Consider Principle 3 of the Yogyakarta Principles, March 2007: 'Each person's self-defined sexual orientation and gender identity is integral to their personality and is one of the most basic aspects of self-determination, dignity and freedom.' Available at: https://yogyakartaprinciples.org. See also Simona Giordano, *Children with Gender Identity Disorder: A Clinical, Ethical, and Legal Analysis* (Abingdon: Routledge, 2013), p. 48.
60 Consider Stonewall's definition of the term 'transphobia' included in its online 'List of LGBTQ+ terms': 'The fear or dislike of someone based on the fact they are trans, including denying their gender identity or refusing to accept it. Transphobia may be targeted at people who are, or who are perceived to be, trans.' Stonewall, List of LGBTQ+ terms. Available at: www.stonewall.org.uk/help-advice/faqs-and-glossary/list-lgbtq-terms.
61 Facebook, Community Standards, Hate Speech.
62 Brown, *Hate Speech Law*, pp. 173–4.

63 It is an open question whether these different markers of sex or gender identity reference a single pluralistic concept of gender or instead speak to multiple discrete concepts of gender. See also Katharine Jenkins, 'Amelioration and Inclusion: Gender Identity and the Concept of Woman', *Ethics* 126 (2016): 394–421; and Katharine Jenkins, 'How to be a Pluralist About Gender', in R. Halwani et al. (eds.) *The Philosophy of Sex: Contemporary Readings*, Eighth Edition (Lanham: Rowman & Littlefield, 2022).

64 Everett C. Hughes, Presidential address given at the annual meeting of the American Sociological Association, 1963. Cited by Ashley Crossman, 'What Is a Master Status?', ThoughtCo, 6 October 2019. Available at: www.thoughtco.com/master-status-3026399.

65 Brown, *Hate Speech Law*, pp. 167–9.

66 Interestingly, a recent study of transgender people's thoughts and feeling towards identity reveals they place an importance on their 'personal agency in achieving internal and external identity accord'. See Carole J. Hetzel and K. Mann, 'The Social Psychological Dynamics of Transgender and Gender Nonconforming Identity Formation, Negotiation, and Affirmation', *Journal of Social and Personal Relationships* 38 (2021): 2566–86. Similarly, there are sets of internationally recognised principles associated with the human right to gender identity which assume autonomous self-identification in this strong sense. Consider once again Principle 3 of the Yogyakarta Principles. Whilst these principles relate to legal recognition of gender identity and the right not to have to undergo medical treatments in order to have one's gender legally recognised, for example, there are similarities with the sort of misrecognition and dehumanisation involved in negative being statements. To use speech to withhold social recognition of gender identity and the capacity for gender self-identification is anathema to these principles.

67 Of course, some feminists who are social constructivists about gender maintain that their theories are compatible with viewing transwomen as women – if they function as women in a society and are subject to systematic subordination as women, for example. See Sally Haslanger, *Resisting Reality* (Oxford: Oxford University Press, 2012), p. 237n.17. However, even here it is unclear that the social constructivist theory Haslanger propounds in practice has the inclusive entailments and implications she assumes. Take transwomen who present as women but whose presentation is rejected by society, such that they are treated as men. They may be subordinated, but they are not being subordinated as women, and so in fact they cannot be women based on Haslanger's social constructivist theory of gender. See Jenkins, 'Amelioration and Inclusion', pp. 398–402.

68 See William B. Swann, 'Identity Negotiation: Where Two Roads Meet', *Journal of Personality and Social Psychology* 53 (1987): 1038–51; William B. Swann, and Robin J. Ely, 'A Battle of Wills: Self-Verification Versus Behavioral Confirmation', *Journal of Personality and Social Psychology* 46 (1984): 1287–302.

69 It is worth noting that in the offline world, silence is often interpreted to signify bystanders licensing the speaker to perform certain speech actions, but such an interpretation may be far more problematic in the online world, where silence may mean various things. Compare Alexander Brown, 'The Meaning of Silence in Cyberspace: The Authority Problem and Online Hate Speech' in K. Gelber and S. Brison (eds.) *Free Speech in the Digital Age* (Oxford: Oxford University Press, 2019); and Ishani Maitra, 'Subordinating Speech', in I. Maitra and M. McGowan (eds.) *Speech and Harm: Controversies Over Free Speech* (Oxford: Oxford University Press, 2012).

70 See Langton, 'The Authority of Hate Speech'.
71 See Matsuda, 'Public Response to Racist Speech', pp. 2332, 2358, 2363; Langton, 'Speech Acts and Unspeakable Acts', pp. 300–3; Langton et al., 'Language and Race', pp. 750–8; Brown, *Hate Speech Law*, pp. 75–86; Katharine Gelber, 'Differentiating Hate Speech: A Systemic Discrimination Approach', *Critical Review of International Social and Political Philosophy* 24 (2021): 393–414, p. 403.
72 Facebook, Community Standards, Hate Speech.
73 See also Legaspe, 'Normalizing Slurs and Out-Group Slurs', p. 11.
74 Kevin M. Graham, 'Racism and the Limits of Distributive Justice', *Public Affairs Quarterly* 15 (2001): 271–89, p. 278.
75 See Matsuda, 'Public Response to Racist Speech', p. 2348; Langton, 'Speech Acts and Unspeakable Acts', p. 303; Langton et al., 'Language and Race', p. 758; Tsesis, *Destructive Messages*, p. 211n.1; Cohen-Almagor, *The Scope of Tolerance*, p. 11; Kylie Weston-Scheuber, 'Gender and the Prohibition of Hate Speech', *Queensland University of Technology Law and Justice Journal* 12 (2012): 132–50, pp. 139–40; Alexander Brown, 'What Is Hate Speech? Part 2: Family Resemblances', *Law and Philosophy* 36 (2017): 561–613, p. 588; Brown and Sinclair, *The Politics of Hate Speech Laws*, ch. 4.
76 See Katharine Jenkins, 'Ontic Injustice', *Journal of the American Philosophical Association* 6 (2020): 188–205.
77 Ibid.
78 Of course, there is a reasonable disagreement as to whether constraints on transwomen from entering women only spaces such as changing rooms and refuges, for example, are indeed wrongful in the sense of being unjustifiable and on a par with 'Whites only' signs. There may also be reasonable disagreement about whether bans on transmen from joining men only clubs and support groups amount to unfair discrimination. However, taking identity denials as a general category of speech, we believe at least in principle it is possible to see how identity denials could enact or facilitate unfair discrimination against certain groups of people under certain circumstances.
79 See Talia Mae Bettcher, 'Evil Deceivers and Make-Believers: On Transphobic Violence and the Politics of Illusion', *Hypatia* 22 (2007): 43–65; and Lola Olufemi, *Feminism Interrupted: Disrupting Power* (London: Pluto Press, 2020), ch. 4.
80 For a defence of the related view that speech cannot be, or should not be, counted as unlawful hate speech (i.e. falling under the legal concept *hate speech*) if the speech is public discourse as evidenced by it occurring in the context of the public sphere, or as evidenced by its content as a subject of public concern, see Robert Post, 'Racist Speech, Democracy, and the First Amendment', *William and Mary Law Review* 32 (1991): 267–327; Robert Post, 'Reconciling Theory and Doctrine in First Amendment Jurisprudence', in L. Bollinger and G. Stone (eds.) *Eternally Vigilant: Free Speech in the Modern Era* (Chicago: University of Chicago Press, 2002); Robert Post, 'Hate Speech', in I. Hare and J. Weinstein (eds.) *Extreme Speech and Democracy* (Oxford: Oxford University Press, 2009); Robert Post, 'Participatory Democracy and Free Speech', *Virginia Law Review* 97 (2011): 477–89; Robert Post, 'Interview', in M. Herz and P. Molnar (eds.) *The Content and Context of Hate Speech: Rethinking Regulation and Responses* (Cambridge: Cambridge University Press, 2012); Robert Post, 'The Legality and Politics of Hatred', in T. Brudholm and B. Schepelern Johansen (eds.) *Hate, Politics, Law: Critical Perspectives On Combating Hate* (Oxford: Oxford University Press 2018); and James Weinstein, 'A Constitutional Roadmap to the Regulation of

Campus Hate Speech', *Wayne Law Review* 38 (1992): 163–247; James Weinstein, '*Hate Speech, Pornography and Radical Attacks on Free Speech Doctrine* (Boulder: Westview Press, 1999); James Weinstein, 'Hate Speech, Viewpoint Neutrality, and the American Concept of Democracy', in T. Hensley (ed.) *The Boundaries of Freedom of Expression and Order in a Democratic Society* (Kent: Kent State University Press, 2001); James Weinstein, 'Extreme Speech, Public Order, and Democracy: Lessons From the Masses', in I. Hare and J. Weinstein (eds.) *Extreme Speech and Democracy* (Oxford: Oxford University Press, 2009); James Weinstein, 'Participatory Democracy as the Central Value of American Free Speech Doctrine', *Virginia Law Review* 97 (2011): 491–514; James Weinstein, 'Hate Speech Bans, Democracy, and Political Legitimacy', *Constitutional Commentary* 32 (2017): 527–83.

81 For an analogous discussion of how hate speech laws, for example, can be narrowly tailored to capture these features of paradigmatic hate speech, see Alexander Brown, 'Hate Speech Laws, Legitimacy, and Precaution: Reply to Weinstein', *Constitutional Commentary* 32 (2017): 599–617, pp. 606–9.

82 Cited in Nick Dufy, 'Germaine Greer: Lopping Off Your D**k and Wearing a Dress Doesn't Make you a F***ing Woman', *Pink News*, 26 October 2015. Available at: www.pinknews.co.uk/2015/10/26/germaine-greer-lopping-off-your-dk-and-wearing-a-dress-doesnt-make-you-a-fing-woman/.

83 See also Brown and Sinclair, *The Politics of Hate Speech Laws*, pp. 379–80.

84 We have in mind a speaker who is engaged in what Sally Haslanger calls an 'ameliorative' project, one 'that seeks to identify what legitimate purposes we might have (if any) in categorizing people on the basis of race or gender, and to develop concepts that would help us achieve these ends'. Sally Haslanger, 'What Are We Talking About? The Semantics and Politics of Social Kinds', *Hypatia*, 20, 10–26', p. 11.

85 Facebook, Community Standards, Hate Speech.

86 See Kathleen Stock, *Material Girls: Why Reality Matters for Feminism* (London, Fleet, 2021), pp. 112–19.

87 Ibid, p. 125.

88 Facebook, Community Standards, Hate Speech.

89 See also Dennis Baron, *What's Your Pronoun?: Beyond He and She* (New York: Liveright Publishing, 2020).

90 Twitter, Hateful Conduct Policy (version March 2023).

91 TikTok, Community Guidelines, Hate Speech and Hateful Behaviors (as of 10 June 2023). Available at: www.tiktok.com/community-guidelines?lang=en#38.

92 For a discussion of the nature of microaggressions including illustrations, see the list of citations in note 1 above.

93 See note 57 above.

94 Facebook, Community Standards, Hate Speech.

95 See Brown, *Hate Speech Law*, ch. 2; and Brown and Sinclair, *The Politics of Hate Speech*, p. 161.

96 See Jessica MacNamara et al., 'Experiencing Misgendered Pronouns: A Classroom Activity to Encourage Empathy', *Teaching Sociology* 45 (2017): 269–78, p. 273.

97 This general type of prototypical hate speech act can be associated with both the ordinary and legal concepts of hate speech. See Monica Mookherjee, 'Permitting Dishonour: Culture, Gender, and Freedom of Expression', in G. Newey (ed.) *Freedom of Expression: Counting the Costs* (Cambridge: Cambridge Scholars Press, 2007), p. 117; and Brown, *Hate Speech Law*, pp. 173–4.

98 See note 64 above.

99 See Brown, *Hate Speech Law*, pp. 169–70; Brown, 'Family Resemblances', p. 600; Caitlin Ring Carlson, *Hate Speech* (Cambridge: The MIT Press, 2021), p. 4; and Shon Faye, *The Transgender Issue: An Argument for Justice* (London: Allen Lane, 2021).

100 Facebook, Community Standards, Hate Speech.

101 This cluster of general prototypical hate speech acts frequently figures in characterisations of both the ordinary concept and the legal concept. See Matsuda, 'Public Response to Racist Speech', p. 2368; Matsuda et al., *Words That Wound*, p. 1; Lawrence, 'If He Hollers Let Him Go', p. 475; Anthony Cortese, *Opposing Hate Speech* (Westport, CT: Praeger Publishers, 2006), pp. 9, 143; Parekh, 'Hate Speech', p. 217; Delgado and Stefancic, *Understanding Words That Wound*, p. 63; Brown, *Hate Speech Law*, pp. 130–2; Brown, 'Family Resemblances', p. 600; Brown, 'Retheorizing Actionable Injuries', pp. 37–9.

102 This is a non-hypothetical example. See Julie Bindel, 'Beware Gender Benders', *The Guardian*, 31 January 2004. Available at: www.theguardian.com/world/2004/jan/31/gender.weekend7.

103 Facebook, Community Standards, Hate Speech.

104 See Alexander Brown, 'Averting Your Eyes in the Information Age: Online Hate Speech and the Captive Audience Doctrine', *Charleston Law Review* 12 (2017): 1–54.

105 Of course, not all trans people experience being trans as 'being trapped in the wrong body' and, for those trans people who do not, media discourse about trans people that privileges this metaphor can itself be essentialising and restricting. See Bernadette Barker-Plummer, 'Fixing Gwen', *Feminist Media Studies* 13 (2013): 710–24.

106 Hetzel and Mann, 'The Social Psychological Dynamics of Transgender and Gender Nonconforming Identity Formation, Negotiation, and Affirmation'.

107 For a discussion of how outing deprives people of dignity, privacy, and autonomy and how it might be tackled through tort law, see Katheleen Guzman, 'About Outing: Public Discourse, Private Lives', *Washington University Law Quarterly* 73 (1995): 1531–600.

108 Facebook, Community Standards, Bullying and Harassment. Available at: https://transparency.fb.com/en-gb/policies/community-standards/bullying-harassment/.

109 This is echoed by some national human rights commissions. For example, the Ontario Human Rights Commission has promulgated a list of forms of gendered harassment that includes both refusing to refer to a person by their self-identified name and proper personal pronoun and outing or threatening to out someone as trans. Ontario Human Rights Commission, Policy on Preventing Discrimination Because of Gender Identity and Gender Expression, 31 January 2014, p. 18. Available at: www.ohrc.on.ca/en/policy-preventing-discrimination-because-gender-identity-and-gender-expression.

110 In some jurisdictions, cases have brought against speakers for misgendering but with mixed success. Consider two illustrations. First, under public order law in England and Wales, targeted misgendering could rise to the level of criminality in circumstances where it is used to cause harassment, alarm, or distress (ss. 4 and 4A of the Public Order Act 1986), to cause distress or anxiety (s. 1 of the Malicious Communications Act 1988), or to cause annoyance, inconvenience or needless anxiety (s. 127(2) of the Communications Act 2003), where sentences could also be increased if judges deem the offences to have been aggravated by hostility on grounds of transgender identity (s. 146 of the Criminal Justice Act 2003, as amended by s. 65

of the Legal Aid, Sentencing and Punishment of Offenders Act 2012). For example, in *R. v. Kate Scottow* (St. Albans Magistrates Court, 7 February 2020) a defendant was found guilty of one offence of improper use of a public communications network contrary to s. 127(2)(c) of the Communications Act 2003, which provides that an offence is committed if a person 'persistently makes use of a public electronic network' and 'for the purpose of causing annoyance, inconvenience or needless anxiety to another'. The conviction related to a series of tweets sent by the defendant about a transgender woman, including 'he is a very sick individual I've evidence of that'. However, this conviction was overturned on appeal, partly on the grounds that in the opinion of the appellate judges, the actions of the defendant had not been 'persistent' and insufficient evidence had been presented to show the messages had been sent 'for the purpose of causing annoyance, inconvenience or needless anxiety to another' within the meaning of s. 127(2)(c). *Scottow v. CPS* [2020] EWHC 3421 (Admin).

A second example relates to human rights law in British Columbia, Canada. In *Nelson v. Goodberry Restaurant Group Ltd. dba Buono Osteria and Others* (2021 BCHRT 137), the British Columbia Human Rights Tribunal found an employer guilty of both hostile environment discrimination and discriminatory dismissal, both on grounds of gender identity. The decision related to the failure by the employer to deal appropriately with conflict and injury to dignity, feelings, and self-respect caused by co-workers who persistently referred to a self-identifying non-binary employee with the wrong pronouns ('she', 'her') and unwanted, gendered nicknames ('sweetie', 'honey'). The Tribunal stated (at para. 82): 'Like a name, pronouns are a fundamental part of a person's identity. They are a primary way that people identify each other. Using correct pronouns communicates that we see and respect a person for who they are. Especially for trans, non-binary, or other non-cisgender people, using the correct pronouns validates and affirms they are a person equally deserving of respect and dignity. As Jessie Nelson explained in this hearing, their pronouns are "fundamental to me feeling like I exist". When people use the right pronouns, they can feel safe and enjoy the moment. When people do not use the right pronouns, that safety is undermined and they are forced to repeat to the world: I exist.'

111 Tracy Murphree, Facebook, 22 April 2016.

112 Facebook, Community Standards, Hate Speech.

113 Twitter, Hateful Conduct Policy.

114 In Norway, for example, Art. 185 of the penal code makes it a criminal offence for any person with intent or gross negligence to publicly make a discriminatory or hateful statement against persons on grounds of protected characteristics including, amongst other things, 'gender identity or gender expression', where 'discriminatory or hateful statement' means threatening or insulting a person or promoting hatred, persecution or contempt for another person based on his or her possession of a protected characteristic. In September 2022, the Norwegian Supreme Court upheld a conviction by the lower courts under Art. 185 in relation to the defendant having posted a series of transphobic comments on Facebook. These comments included the following (misgendering): 'Do you really think that a single person thinks you are a woman and you are not an old man with strange fantasies'; and '"B" does not exist. It is a sick fantasy in C's mind.' *A. v. The Public Prosecution Authority*, Supreme Court, Oslo, 30 September 2022, No. 22-085322STR-HRET.

115 See Stephanie Julia Kapusta, 'Misgendering and Its Moral Contestability', *Hypatia* 31 (2016): 502–19, p. 504.

116 Ibid.
117 See also Young, 'No, Of Course "Misgendering" a Trans Person Shouldn't Be a Crime'.
118 See Brown, 'Averting Your Eyes in the Information Age'.
119 Facebook, Community Standards, Hate Speech.
120 Facebook Oversight Board, Case decision 2021-002-FB-UA, 13 April 2021. Available at: https://oversightboard.com/decision/FB-S6NRTDAJ/.
121 David O. Brink, 'Millian principles, freedom of expression and hate speech', *Legal Theory* 7 (2001): 119–57, p. 132; Caleb Yong, 'Does Freedom of Speech Include Hate Speech?', *Res Publica* 17 (2011): 385–403, p. 396.
122 Nassira Nicola, 'Black Face, White Voice: Rush Limbaugh and the "Message" of Race', *Journal of Language and Politics* 9 (2010): 281–309.
123 Facebook, Community Standards, Hate Speech.
124 Ibid.
125 See John Strausbaugh, *Black Like You: Blackface, Whiteface, Insult and Imitation in American Popular Culture* (New York: Penguin, 2006), ch. 6; and Eric M. Armstrong, 'Revered and Reviled: D.W. Griffith's "The Birth of a Nation"', *The Moving Arts Film Journal*, 26 February 2010.
126 Eric Lott, 'Love and Theft: The Racial Unconscious of Blackface Minstrelsy', *Representations* 39 (1992): 23–50.
127 Roberts, *Blackface Nation*, p. 20.
128 Bell Hooks, *Black Looks: Race and Representation* (Boston: South End Press. 1992), pp. 21–2.
129 Ibid, p. 27.
130 Roberts, *Blackface Nation*, p. 20.
131 Thandeka, 'Whites: Made in America: Advancing American Philosophers' Discourse on Race', *The Pluralist* 13 (2018): 26–50, p. 38.
132 See Brown, 'The Myth of Hate'.
133 Brown, 'The Myth of Hate', p. 445; and Brown, 'Family Resemblances'.
134 Tracey Owens Patton, 'Jim Crow on Fraternity Row: A study of the Phenomenon of Blackface in the White Southern Fraternal Order', *Visual Communication Quarterly*, 15 (2008): 150–68, p. 152.
135 Ibid, p. 150.
136 Brian Roberts, *Blackface Nation: Race, Reform, and Identity in American Popular Music, 1812–1925* (Chicago: University of Chicago Press, 2017), p. 20.
137 Ibid.
138 Wanna Thompson, 'How White Women On Instagram Are Profiting Off Black Women', *Paper Magazine*, 14 November 2018. Available at: www.papermag.com/white-women-blackfishing-instagram-2619714094.html?rebelltitem=6#rebelltitem6.
139 Richard A. Rogers, 'From Cultural Exchange to Transculturation: A Review and Reconceptualization of Cultural Appropriation', *Communication Theory* 16 (2006): 474–503, p. 477.
140 C. Thi Nguyen and Matthew Strohl, 'Cultural Appropriation and the Intimacy of Groups', *Philosophical Studies* 176 (2019): 981–1002.
141 Ibid.
142 William Upski Wimsatt, *Bomb the Suburbs* (Brooklyn: Soft Skull Press, 1994), p. 22.
143 See Strausbaugh, *Black Like You*.

144 Patton, 'Jim Crow on Fraternity Row', p. 164; Roberts, *Blackface Nation*, p. 21.

145 Lolita Buckner Inniss, 'A Ho New World: Raced and Gendered Insult as Ersatz Carnival and the Corruption of Freedom of Expression Norms', *NYU Review of Law and Social Change* 33 (2007): 43–86, pp. 78–80.

146 Patton, 'Jim Crow on Fraternity Row', p. 155.

147 Elizabeth Spelman, *Inessential Woman* (Boston: Beacon, 1988), p. 12.

148 We are assuming for the sake of argument that people of colour have privileged access to knowledge of their own experiences, identity, and culture, meaning that the latter cannot be directly and fully apprehended or understood by white people. For a general discussion of standpoint epistemology as it relates to an agent's social identity, see Briana Toole, 'From Standpoint Epistemology to Epistemic Oppression', *Hypatia* 34 (2019): 598–618; and Alexia Leclerc, 'Impartiality as an Epistemic Privilege', *Ithaque* 28 (2021): 1–17.

149 Gaile Pohlhaus Jr. 'Relational Knowing and Epistemic Injustice: Toward a Theory of Willful Hermeneutical Ignorance', *Hypatia* 27 (2012): 715–34.

150 Nora Berenstain, 'Epistemic Exploitation', *Ergo* 3 (2016): 569–90, p. 570.

151 See Philip J. Deloria, *Playing Indian* (New Haven: Yale University Press, 1999). This is one instance of a wider pattern of oppression that some scholars associate with cultural appropriation and epistemic violence in general. See Erich Matthes, 'Cultural Appropriation Without Cultural Essentialism?', *Social Theory and Practice* 42 (2016): 343–66; and Kristie Dotson, 'Tracking Epistemic Violence, Tracking Practices of Silencing', *Hypatia* 26 (2011): 236–57.

Note, however, that such scholars tend to be sceptical about whether there could be such a thing as reverse oppressive cultural appropriation, for example. See Erich Hatala Matthes, 'Cultural Appropriation and Oppression', *Philosophical Studies* 176 (2019): 1003–13. As discussed in Chapter 3, we believe there may be microenvironments in which oppressive acts occur even though the normal racial hierarchies are reversed.

152 Facebook, Community Standards, Hate Speech.

153 Bakari Kitwana, *Why White Kids Love Hip Hop: Wankstas, Wiggers, Wannabes, and the New Reality of Race in America* (New York: Basic Civitas, 2006).

154 Stacy Anne Harwood et al., 'Racial Microaggressions in the Residence Halls: Experiences of Students of Color at a Predominantly White University', *Journal of Diversity in Higher Education* 5 (2012): 159–73.

155 Elizabeth Stordeur Pryor, 'The Etymology of Nigger: Resistance, Language, and the Politics of Freedom in the Antebellum North', *Journal of the Early Republic* 36 (2016): 203–45.

156 See note 1 above.

157 See Gideon Rosen, 'Culpability and Ignorance', *Proceedings of the Aristotelian Society* 103 (2003): 61–84; Gideon Rosen, 'Skepticism about Moral Responsibility', *Philosophical Perspectives* 18 (2004): 295–313; and Neil Levy, 'Culpable Ignorance and Moral Responsibility: A Reply to FitzPatrick', *Ethics* 119 (2009): 729–41.

158 See also Elizabeth Harman, 'Does Moral Ignorance Exculpate?', *Ratio* 24 (2011): 443–68; Angela Smith, 'Responsibility for Attitudes: Activity and Passivity in Mental Life', *Ethics* 115 (2005): 236–71; Matthew Talbert, 'Unwitting Wrongdoers and the Role of Moral Disagreement in Blame', in D. Shoemaker (ed.) *Oxford Studies in Agency and Responsibility: Volume 1* (Oxford: Oxford University Press, 2013).

159 See also Kevin Timpe, 'Tracing and the Epistemic Condition on Moral Responsibility', *The Modern Schoolman* 88 (2011): 5–28.

5 Orienting the Ordinary and Legal Concepts of Hate Speech

1 To clarify, we do not mean to suggest that the definitions of hate speech promulgated by universities and social media platforms are identical to, or synonymous with, the ordinary concept *hate speech*. For all the reasons explained in Chapters 2–4, hate speech in the ordinary (nonlegal) sense of the word is almost certainly broader than even the total set of forms of hate speech currently forbidden by these platforms. Nevertheless, we believe that platform definitions do provide a reasonable proxy for the ordinary concept simply for the purposes of broadly distinguishing the ordinary and legal concepts of hate speech.

2 Twitter, Hateful Conduct Policy (as of 10 June 2023). Available at: https://help.twitter .com/en/rules-and-policies/hateful-conduct-policy.

3 TikTok, Community Guideline on Hate Speech and Hateful Behaviors (as of 10 June 2023). Available at: www.tiktok.com/community-guidelines?lang=en#38.

4 Snap Inc., Community Guidelines, Terrorism, Hate Groups and Hate Speech (as of 10 June 2023). Available at: https://snap.com/en-GB/community-guidelines.

5 YouTube, Hate Speech Policy (as of 10 June 2023). Available at: https://support .google.com/youtube/answer/2801939?hl=en-GB.

6 See Alexander Brown, *Hate Speech Law* (Abingdon: Routledge, 2015), pp. 26–7; Alexander Brown and Adriana Sinclair, *The Politics of Hate Speech Laws* (Abingdon: Routledge, 2020), pp. 134–6.

7 See Mari Matsuda, 'Public Response to Racist Speech: Considering the Victim's Story', *Michigan Law Review* 87 (1989): 2320–81, pp. 2341–6; Frederick Schauer, 'Uncoupling Free Speech', *Columbia Law Review* 92 (1992): 1321–57, p. 1349; Alexander Tsesis, *Destructive Messages: How Hate Speech Paves the Way for Harmful Social Movements* (New York: New York University Press, 2002), p. 211n.1; Raphael Cohen-Almagor, *The Scope of Tolerance: Studies on the Costs of Free Expression and Freedom of the Press* (London: Routledge, 2006), p. 11; Raphael Cohen-Almagor, 'Holocaust Denial Is a Form of Hate Speech', *Amsterdam Law Forum* 2 (2009): 33–42, p. 35; and Kylie Weston-Scheuber, 'Gender and the Prohibition of Hate Speech', *Queensland University of Technology Law and Justice Journal* 12 (2012): 132–50, pp. 139–40; Sarah Sorial, 'Hate Speech and Distorted Communication: Rethinking the Limits of Incitement', *Law and Philosophy* 34 (2015): 299–324, p. 300.

8 At the level of domestic law, consider s. 10 of the Promotion of Equality and Prevention of Unfair Discrimination Act 2000 (South Africa), albeit this law has recently been deemed to be unconstitutional. In terms of international instruments, consider the Appendix to the Committee of Ministers of the Council of Europe Recommendation No. R (97) 20, 30 October 1997; and the UN General Assembly Resolution on Promoting Interreligious and Intercultural Dialogue and Tolerance in Countering Hate Speech, 25 July 2019 (A/RES/73/328).

9 Facebook, Community Standards, Hate Speech (as of 10 June 2023). Available at: https://transparency.fb.com/en-gb/policies/community-standards/hate-speech/.

10 See Brown, *Hate Speech Law*, pp. 23–4; and Alexander Brown, 'Retheorizing Actionable Injuries in Civil Lawsuits Involving Targeted Hate Speech: Hate Speech as Degradation and Humiliation', *Alabama Civil Rights and Civil Liberties Law Review* 9 (2018): 1–56.

11 Facebook, Community Standards, Hate Speech.

12 See Brown, *Hate Speech Law*, pp. 28–9.

13 See note 10 above.

14 See Brown and Sinclair, *The Politics of Hate Speech Laws*, ch.
15 Facebook, Community Standards, Hate Speech.
16 Ibid.
17 See Brown, *Hate Speech Law*, ch. 2; and Brown and Sinclair, *The Politics of Hate Speech Laws*, ch. 2.
18 Facebook, Community Standards, Hate Speech.
19 See note 10 above.
20 See Brown, *Hate Speech Law*, pp. 33–5; Katharine Gelber and Luke McNamara, 'Anti-Vilification Laws and Public Racism in Australia: Mapping the Gaps Between the Harms Occasioned and the Remedies Provided', *University of New South Wales Law Journal* 39 (2016): 488–511; Brown and Sinclair, *The Politics of Hate Speech Laws*, pp. 54–60.
21 Facebook, Community Standards, Hate Speech.
22 Twitter, Hateful Conduct Policy.
23 TikTok, Community Guidelines, Hate Speech and Hateful Behaviors.
24 Snap Inc., Community Guidelines, Terrorism, Hate Groups and Hate Speech.
25 YouTube, Hate Speech Policy.
26 WeChat, Objectionable Content, Hate Speech (as of 10 June 2023). Available at: www.wechat.com/en/acceptable_use_policy.html.
27 See Alexander Brown, 'The "Who?" Question in the Hate Speech Debate: Part 1: Consistency, Practical, and Formal Approaches', *Canadian Journal of Law and Jurisprudence* 29 (2016): 275–320, pp. 276–81.
28 See also Brown and Sinclair, *The Politics of Hate Speech Laws*, ch. 4.
29 See Andrew Altman, 'Liberalism and Campus Hate Speech: A Philosophical Examination', *Ethics* 103 (1993): 302–17, pp. 309–10; Judith Butler, *Excitable Speech: A Politics of the Performative* (New York: Routledge, 1997), p. 77; Susan Brison, 'The Autonomy Defense of Free Speech', *Ethics* 108 (1998): 312–39, p. 313; Susan Brison, 'Hate Speech', in H. La Follette (ed.) *The International Encyclopedia of Ethics* (Oxford: Wiley-Blackwell, 2013), p. 2332; David Brink, 'Millian Principles, Freedom of Expression, and Hate Speech', *Legal Theory* 7 (2001): 119–57, p. 119; L. W. Sumner, 'Hate Crimes, Literature and Speech', in R. Frey and C. Heath Wellman (eds.) *A Companion to Applied Ethics* (Oxford: Blackwell, 2003), p. 142; David Miller, *Political Philosophy: A Very Short Introduction* (Oxford: Oxford University Press, 2003), p. 65; Norman Fischer, 'First Amendment Morality Versus Civility Morality', in C. Sistare (ed.) *Civility and Its Discontents: Civic Virtue, Toleration, and Cultural Fragmentation* (Lawrence: University of Kansas Press, 2004), p. 161; Bhikhu Parekh, 'Hate Speech: Is There a Case for Banning?', *Public Policy Research* 12 (2005–2006): 213–23, p. 214; Jeremy Waldron, 'Dignity and Defamation: The Visibility of Hate', *Harvard Law Review* 123 (2010): 1596–657, pp. 1600–1; Kevin M. Graham, *Beyond Redistribution: White Supremacy and Racial Justice* (Plymouth: Lexington Books, 2010), pp. 77–8; Mary Kate McGowan, 'The Ethics of Free Speech', in J. Skorupski (ed.) *The Routledge Companion to Ethics* (New York: Routledge, 2010), p. 775; Caleb Yong, 'Does Freedom of Speech Include Hate Speech?', *Res Publica* 17 (2011): 385–403, p. 386; Rae Langton, 'Beyond Belief: Pragmatics in Hate Speech and Pornography', in I. Maitra and M. McGowan (eds.) *Speech and Harm: Controversies Over Free Speech* (Oxford: Oxford University Press, 2012), pp. 74–7; Rae Langton et al., 'Language and Race', in G. Russell and D. Graff Fara (eds.) *Routledge Companion to the Philosophy of Language* (London: Routledge, 2012), pp. 757–60; Matteo Bonotti and Jonathan Seglow, *Free Speech* (Cambridge, Polity Press, 2021), pp. 32–3.

30 See Louise Richardson-Self, *Hate Speech against Women Online: Concepts and Countermeasures* (London: Rowman and Littlefield), p. 67.

31 See Matsuda, 'Public Response to Racist Speech', p. 2357; Suzanna Sherry, 'Speaking of Virtue: A Republican Approach to University Regulation of Hate Speech', *Minnesota Law Review* 75 (1991): 933–44, p. 933; Sandra Coliver, 'Hate Speech Laws: Do They Work?', in S. Coliver (ed.) *Striking a Balance: Hate Speech, Freedom of Expression and Non-Discrimination* (London: Article 19 International Centre Against Censorship/Human Rights Centre, University of Essex, 1992), p. 363; Frederick Schauer, 'Uncoupling Free Speech', *Columbia Law Review* 92 (1992): 1321–57, p. 1349; Rodney Smolla, *Free Speech in an Open Society* (New York: Vintage Books, 1992), p. 152; Charles Lawrence et al., 'Introduction', in M. Matsuda et al. (eds.) *Words That Wound: Critical Race Theory, Assaultive Speech, and the First Amendment* (Boulder: Westview Press, 1993), p. 1; Ira Glasser, 'Introduction', in H. Gates et al. (eds.) *Speaking of Race, Speaking of Sex: Hate Speech, Civil Rights, and Civil Liberties* (New York: New York University Press, 1994), p. 1; Laura Lederer and Richard Delgado, 'Introduction', in L. Lederer and R. Delgado (eds.) *The Price We Pay: The Case Against Racist Speech, Hate Propaganda, and Pornography* (New York: Hill and Wang, 1995), pp. 4–5; Kathleen Sullivan and Gerald Gunther, *Constitutional Law* (New York: Foundation Press, 1995), p. 1131; Larry Alexander, 'Banning Hate: Speech and the Sticks and Stones Defense', *Constitutional Commentary* 13 (1996): 71–100, p. 71; Bryan A. Garner, *Black's Law Dictionary, Seventh Edition* (St. Paul, MN: West Group, 1999), pp. 1407–8; John. T. Nockleby, 'Hate Speech', in L. Levy and K. Karst (eds.) *Encyclopedia of the American Constitution, Volume 3, Second Edition* (Detroit, MI: Macmillan, 2000), p. 1277; Tarlach McGonagle, 'Wresting Racial Equality From Tolerance of Hate Speech', *Dublin University Law Journal* 23 (2001): 21–54, p. 23; Kevin Boyle, 'Hate Speech – The United States Versus the Rest of the World?', *Maine Law Review* 53 (2001): 487–502, p. 489; J. Angelo Corlett and Robert Francescotti, 'Foundations of a Theory of Hate Speech', *The Wayne Law Review* 48 (2002): 1071–100, p. 1083; Tsesis, *Destructive Messages*, p. 211n.1; Jon B. Gould, *Speak No Evil: The Triumph of Hate Speech Regulation* (Chicago: Chicago University Press, 2005), p. 14; Cohen-Almagor, *The Scope of Tolerance*, p. 153; Cohen-Almagor, 'Holocaust Denial Is a Form of Hate Speech', p. 35; Raphael Cohen-Almagor, 'Fighting Hate and Bigotry on the Internet', *Policy and Internet* 3 (2011): 1–26, pp. 1–2; James Weinstein and Ivan Hare, 'General Introduction: Free Speech, Democracy, and the Suppression of Extreme Speech Past and Present', in I. Hare and J. Weinstein (eds.) *Extreme Speech and Democracy* (Oxford: Oxford University Press, 2009), p. 4; Kathleen Mahoney, 'Hate Speech, Equality, and the State of Canadian Law', *Wake Forest Law Review* 44 (2009): 321–51, pp. 325–6; Robert Post, 'Hate Speech', in I. Hare and J. Weinstein (eds.) *Extreme Speech and Democracy* (Oxford: Oxford University Press, 2009), p. 127; Steven P. Lee, 'Hate Speech in the Marketplace of Ideas', in D. Golash (ed.) *Freedom of Expression in a Diverse World* (Dordrecht: Springer, 2010), p. 22; Douglas M. Fraleigh and Joseph S. Tuman, *Freedom of Expression in the Marketplace of Ideas* (Thousand Oaks, CA: Sage, 2011), p. 139; Susan Benesch, *Dangerous Speech: A Proposal to Prevent Group Violence* (New York: World Policy Institute Paper, 2012), p. 1; Eduardo Bertoni and Julio Rivera, 'The American Convention on Human Rights: Regulations on Hate Speech and Other Similar Expressions', in M. Herz and P. Molnar (eds.) *The Content and Context of Hate Speech: Rethinking Regulation and Responses* (Cambridge: Cambridge University Press, 2012), p. 499; Jeremy Waldron, *The Harm in Hate Speech* (Harvard: Harvard University Press, 2012), pp. 8–9; Uladzislau Belavusau, 'Hate Speech', *Max*

Planck Encyclopedia of Comparative Constitutional Law (Oxford: Oxford University Press, 2017); Weston-Scheuber, 'Gender and the Prohibition of Hate Speech', pp. 139–40; Chris Demaske, *Free Speech and Hate Speech in the United States: The Limits of Toleration* (New York: Routledge, 2020), ch. 2; Jennifer Schweppe, 'What Is a Hate Crime?', *Cogent Social Sciences* 7 (2021): 1–14, p. 8.

32 Jeremy Waldron, *Dignity, Rank, and Rights: The Berkeley Tanner Lectures* (New York: Oxford University Press, 2012), p. 15.

33 For the original source of the distinction between the ordinary and legal concepts of hate speech, see Alexander Brown, 'What Is Hate Speech? Part 1: The Myth of Hate', *Law and Philosophy* 36 (2017): 419–68.

34 See Matsuda, 'Public Response to Racist Speech', pp. 2358, 2363; Richard Delgado, 'Campus Antiracism Rules: Constitutional Narratives in Collision', *Northwestern University Law Review* 85 (1991): 343–87, pp. 383–4; Charles Lawrence, 'Cross Burning and the Sound of Silence: Anti-Subordination Theory and the First Amendment', *Villanova Law Review* 37 (1992): 787–804, p. 792; Lawrence et al., 'Introduction', p. 1.

35 See Altman, 'Liberalism and Campus Hate Speech', pp. 309–10; Langton, 'Beyond Belief', pp. 74–7; Langton et al., 'Language and Race', pp. 757–60; Ishani Maitra, 'Subordinating Speech', in I. Maitra and M. McGowan (eds.) *Speech and Harm: Controversies Over Free Speech* (Oxford: Oxford University Press, 2012), pp. 96–118; Mary Kate McGowan, 'On "Whites Only" Signs and Racist Hate Speech: Verbal Acts of Racial Discrimination', in I. Maitra and M. McGowan (eds.) *Speech and Harm: Controversies Over Free Speech* (Oxford: Oxford University Press, 2012), p. 122; Brown, *Hate Speech Law*, pp. 75–86. These ideas have also influenced definitions of hate speech advanced by political scientists. See Katharine Gelber, 'Differentiating Hate Speech: A Systemic Discrimination Approach', *Critical Review of International Social and Political Philosophy* 24 (2021): 393–414, p. 398.

36 See Catharine MacKinnon, *Feminism Unmodified* (Cambridge: Cambridge University Press, 1987); Catharine MacKinnon, *Only Words* (Cambridge: Harvard University Press, 1993); Catharine MacKinnon and Andrea Dworkin (eds.) *In Harm's Way: The Pornography Civil Rights Hearings* (Cambridge: Harvard University Press, 1997). This influence is explicitly recognised by the relevant critical race theorists and philosophers alike. See Matsuda, 'Public Response to Racist Speech', pp. 2331–2; Langton, 'Beyond Belief', p. 80.

37 Kent Greenawalt, *Fighting Words: Individuals, Communities and Liberties of Speech* (Princeton: Princeton University Press, 1995), chs. 4 and 5.

38 Brison, 'The Autonomy Defense of Free Speech', p. 314; Timothy C. Shiell, *Campus Hate Speech on Trial, Second Edition* (Lawrence: University of Kansas Press, 2009), p. 162.

39 See Alan E. Brownstein, 'Hate Speech and Harassment: The Constitutionality of Campus Codes That Prohibit Racial Insults', *William and Mary Bill of Rights Journal* 3 (1994): 179–217, p. 179; Greenawalt, *Fighting Words*, p. 63; Nicholas Wolfson, *Hate Speech, Sex Speech, Free Speech* (Westport, CT: Praeger Publishers, 1997), p. 60; Steven H. Shiffrin, *Dissent, Injustice, and the Meanings of America* (Princeton, NJ: Princeton University Press, 1999), pp. 76–7; Thomas Peard, 'Regulating Racist Speech on Campus', in C. Sistare (ed.) *Civility and Its Discontents: Civic Virtue, Toleration, and Cultural Fragmentation* (Lawrence: University of Kansas Press, 2004), p. 142; Richard Delgado and Jean Stefancic, 'Four Observations About Hate Speech', *Wake Forest Law Review* 44 (2009): 353–70, pp. 362–3; Eric Heinze, *Hate Speech and Democratic Citizenship* (Oxford: Oxford University Press, 2016), p. 282.

40 Yong, 'Does Freedom of Speech Include Hate Speech?', pp. 394–6.
41 See Glasser, 'Introduction', p. 1; Garner, Black's Law Dictionary, pp. 1407–8; Nadine Strossen, 'Incitement to Hatred: Should There Be a Limit?', *Southern Illinois University Law Journal* 25 (2001): 243–79, p. 244; Corlett and Francescotti, 'Foundations of a Theory of Hate Speech', p. 1083; Post, 'Hate Speech', pp. 123–5; Weinstein and Hare, 'General Introduction', p. 4; Iginio Gagliardone et al., *Mapping and Analysing Hate Speech Online: Opportunities and Challenges for Ethiopia* (Oxford: University of Oxford Programme in Comparative Media and Law Policy, 2014), p. 9.
42 Fischer, 'First Amendment Morality Versus Civility Morality', pp. 161–2; Parekh, 'Hate Speech', p. 214.
43 See Cohen-Almagor, The Scope of Tolerance, p. 153; Cohen-Almagor, 'Holocaust Denial Is a Form of Hate Speech', p. 35; Cohen-Almagor, 'Fighting Hate and Bigotry on the Internet', pp. 1–2.
44 See Altman, 'Liberalism and Campus Hate Speech', pp. 309–10; Brison, 'The Autonomy Defense of Free Speech', p. 313; Brison, 'Hate Speech', p. 2332; Brink, 'Millian Principles, Freedom of Expression, and Hate Speech', p. 119.
45 Brown, 'The Myth of Hate'. See also Waldron, 'Dignity and Defamation', p. 1601; Gelber, 'Differentiating Hate Speech', p. 408.
46 Alexander Brown, 'What Is Hate Speech? Part 2: Family Resemblances', *Law and Philosophy* 36 (2017): 561–613.
47 Ibid.
48 See also Brown, *Hate Speech Law*, pp. 26–8.
49 It may be that ultimately there is no single legal definition capable of accurately capturing literally every national law that seems to be a candidate for hate speech law given the sheer variety of relevant jurisdictions, bodies of law, and patterns of enforcement. See Brown, *Hate Speech Law*, ch. 2. In stronger terms: 'The many significant differences among the hate speech laws found around the world make it obvious that there is no such thing as a "universal standard" for prosecuting hate speech.' Abraham H. Foxman and Christopher Wolf, *Viral Hate: Containing Its Spread on the Internet* (New York: Palgrave Macmillan, 2013), p. 74. Likewise, international legal texts also differ markedly in how they characterise hate speech, such that it may also be difficult to provide a single definition of the international legal concept *hate speech*. See Brown and Sinclair, *The Politics of Hate Speech Laws*, ch. 4.
50 See Trevor Allan, *Constitutional Justice: A Liberal Theory of the Rule of Law* (Oxford: Oxford University Press, 2001); Brian Tamanaha, *On the Rule of Law* (Cambridge: Cambridge University Press, 2004); Tom Bingham, *The Rule of Law* (London: Allen Lane, 2010); and Jeremy Waldron, 'The Rule of Law', *Stanford Encyclopedia of Philosophy*, 22 June 2016. Available at: https://plato.stanford.edu/entries/rule-of-law/.
51 See Gelber, 'Differentiating Hate Speech', pp. 396–7.
52 See the Online Safety Bill 2022.
53 See Alexander Brown, *Models of Governance of Online Hate Speech* (Strasbourg: Council of Europe, 2020).
54 Consider Part 3A of the Public Order Act 1986 (England and Wales) which limits incitement to hatred in the legal sense to only threatening words or behaviour used with intent to stir up hatred on grounds of religion or sexual orientation.
55 See also Brown, 'The Myth of Hate', pp. 580–1.
56 Gelber, 'Differentiating Hate Speech', p. 409.

57 United Nations, *UN Strategy and Plan of Action on Hate Speech*, May 2019. Available at: www.un.org/en/genocideprevention/documents/advising-and-mobilizing/Action_plan_on_hate_speech_EN.pdf.
58 Gelber, 'Differentiating Hate Speech', p. 408. 410n.18.
59 For a defence of using the social purposes of the concept of hate speech as source material for conceptual analysis, see Robert Post, 'Interview', in M. Herz and P. Molnar (eds.) *The Content and Context of Hate Speech: Rethinking Regulation and Responses* (Cambridge: Cambridge University Press, 2012), p. 31; and Brown, 'Family Resemblance', pp. 567–73. For a general defence of this approach to conceptual analysis, see Frank Jackson, *From Metaphysics to Ethics: A Defence of Conceptual Analysis* (Oxford: Oxford University Press, 1998), p. 45; Alexis Burgess and David Plunkett, 'Conceptual Ethics I', *Philosophy Compass* 8 (2013): 1091–101; Amie L. Thomasson, 'A Pragmatic Method for Normative Conceptual Work', in A. Burgess et al. (eds.) *Conceptual Engineering and Conceptual Ethics* (Oxford: Oxford University Press).
60 See Brown, 'Family Resemblance', pp. 593–604.
61 For the conventional view of official counterspeech, see Katharine Gelber, '"Speaking Back": The Likely Fate of Hate Speech Policy in the United States and Australia', in I. Maitra and M. McGowan (eds.) *Speech and Harm: Controversies over Free Speech* (Oxford: Oxford University Press, 2012).
62 Robert D. Cooter, 'Three Effects of Social Norms on Law: Expression, Deterrence, and Internalization', *Oregon Law Review* 79 (2000): 1–22, p. 5.
63 Brown, 'Family Resemblances', p. 604.
64 For a list of references to this body of definitions, see note x above.
65 This concept could be used to highlight and interpret similarities between international legal texts, national legislative acts or statutes, case decisions, and patterns of enforcement which all appear to relate to acts of inciting hatred, discrimination, or violence. See, for examples, Brown, *Hate Speech Law*, pp. 26–8.
66 Ronald Dworkin, *Law's Empire* (Cambridge: Harvard University Press, 1986), ch. 2; Ronald Dworkin, *Justice for Hedgehogs* (Cambridge: Harvard University Press, 2011), chs. 7–8.
67 See also Brown, 'Family Resemblances', pp. 578–81.
68 See Brown, *Hate Speech Law*, ch. 9.
69 See Matsuda, 'Public Response to Racist Speech'; Richard Delgado and Jean Stefancic, *Understanding Words That Wound* (Boulder: Westview Press, 2004); Tsesis, *Destructive Messages*; Parekh, 'Hate Speech'; Steven J. Heyman, *Free Speech and Human Dignity* (New Haven: Yale University Press, 2008); McGowan, 'On "Whites Only" Signs and Racist Hate Speech'; Brown, *Hate Speech Law*; Alexander Brown, 'Hate Speech Laws, Legitimacy, and Precaution: Reply to Weinstein', *Constitutional Commentary* 32 (2017): 599–617; Brown and Sinclair, *The Politics of Hate Speech Laws* (Abingdon: Routledge, 2020); Gelber, 'Differentiating Hate Speech'.
70 See Brown, *Models of Governance of Online Hate Speech*, pp. 14–16.
71 See Brown and Sinclair, *The Politics of Hate Speech Laws*, ch. 4.
72 Tarlach McGonagle, 'A Survey and Critical Analysis of Council of Europe Strategies for Countering "Hate Speech"', in M. Herz and P. Molnar (eds.) *The Content and Context of Hate Speech: Rethinking Regulation and Responses* (Cambridge: Cambridge University Press, 2012), p. 457.
73 David Partlett, 'From Red Lion Square to Skokie to the Fatal Shore: Racial Defamation and Freedom of Speech', *Vanderbilt Journal of Transnational Law* 22 (1989): 431–90, p. 469.

74 See also David Kretzmer, 'Freedom of Speech and Racism', *Cardozo Law Review* 8 (1987): 445–514, p. 456; Julie C. Suk, 'Denying Experience: Holocaust Denial and the Free-Speech Theory of the State', in M. Herz and P. Molnar (eds.) *The Content and Context of Hate Speech: Rethinking Regulation and Responses* (Cambridge: Cambridge University Press, 2012), p. 154.

75 For the conventional view of official counterspeech, see Gelber, '"Speaking Back"'.

76 See Matsuda, 'Public Response to Racist Speech', p. 2322; Waldron, 'Dignity and Defamation', pp. 1622–3, 1632; and Brown, *Hate Speech Law*, pp. 148–9.

77 Anna Elisabetta Galeotti, *Toleration as Recognition* (Cambridge: Cambridge University Press, 2002), p. 156.

78 Abigail Levin, *The Cost of Free Speech: Pornography, Hate Speech, and their Challenge to Liberalism* (Basingstoke: Palgrave Macmillan, 2010), p. 115.

79 See Brown, *Hate Speech Laws*, pp. 254–6.

80 See Adriana Sinclair, 'Legal Norms are Not Distinctive: Assessing the Claim of Distinctive Legal Normativity in International Law' (unpublished paper).

81 See Susan Benesch, 'Vile Crime or Inalienable Right: Defining Incitement to Genocide', *Virginia Journal of International Law* 48 (2008): 485–528, pp. 504–6.

82 The underlying purpose of mirroring is to make the accusers own acts appear not merely excusable or normalised but necessary in the face of a threat. Consider how the political leadership in Iran has described Israel as a 'disgraceful blot' ('tumor') that should be 'wiped off the face of the earth' whilst at the same time claiming that Israel is engaged in a genocide against the Palestinian people, which, according to Iran, Israel justifies on the basis of lies and fabrications about its own Holocaust: where Iran is using the accusation of Palestinian genocide as an implicit justification for its incitement to genocide of the Jewish people in Israel. Or consider how some Afrikaner organisations in South Africa have simultaneously declared that the present government of South Africa is allowing, or even presiding over, a 'white genocide', as in, a campaign to exterminate Afrikaners, whilst at the same time denying that the apartheid system was in fact a crime against humanity, in contradiction to several international resolutions and conventions affirming the opposite. Or consider how the Russian Minister of Foreign Affairs Sergey Lavrov has, by turns, accused Ukraine of 'genocide' and 'war crimes' against Russians in Ukraine, accused the West of denialism ('turning a blind eye') in relation to Ukraine's alleged war crimes in eastern and southern regions of Ukraine, accused the West of attempting a 'genocide by sanctions' against the Russian people, all the while itself denying that the actions of the Russian military in Ukraine constitute a genocide or war crimes against Ukrainians. For its part, Ukraine has filed court cases claiming it was not guilty of genocide and, therefore, that Russia had no grounds for its invasion of Ukraine.

83 There are historians who argue that part of the problem with the genocide discourse of contemporary international law is that it can detract from systematic violence against civilians perpetrated by governments of all types. See A. Dirk Moses, *The Problems of Genocide: Permanent Security and the Language of Transgression* (Cambridge: Cambridge University Press, 2021).

84 Richard Delgado and Jean Stefancic, *Must We Defend Nazis? Why the First Amendment Should Not Protect Hate Speech and White Supremacy* (New York: New York University Press, 2018), p. 32.

85 See also Ellen E. Lange, 'Racist Speech on Campus: A Title VII Solution to a First Amendment Problem', *Southern California Law Review* 64 (1990): 105–34; Phil Cox, 'The Disputation of Hate: Speech Codes, Pluralism, and Academic Freedoms', *Social*

Theory and Practice 21 (1995): 113–44; Brown, *Hate Speech Law*, p. 192; Alexander Tsesis, 'Campus Speech and Harassment', *Minnesota Law Review* 101 (2017): 1863–917.

86 Cf. Jack Greenberg, *Crusaders in the Court: How a Dedicated Band of Lawyers Fought for the Civil Rights Revolution* (New York: Basic Books, 1994).

87 See Matsuda, 'Public Response to Racist Speech'; Lawrence, 'Cross Burning and the Sound of Silence'; and Richard Delgado, 'Words That Wound: A Tort Action for Racial Insults, Epithets, and Name-Calling', *Harvard Civil Rights-Civil Liberties Law Review* 17 (1982): 133–81.

88 Delgado and Stefancic, *Must We Defend Nazis?*, p. 32.

89 See Brown and Sinclair, *The Politics of Hate Speech Laws*, ch. 3.

90 See also Cooter, 'Three Effects of Social Norms on Law', pp. 15–17.

91 See Dworkin, *Law's Empire*, ch. 1.

92 See Robert Post, 'Racist Speech, Democracy, and the First Amendment', *William and Mary Law Review* 32 (1991): 267–327, p. 286; Robert Post, 'Hate Speech', in I. Hare and J. Weinstein (eds.) *Extreme Speech and Democracy* (Oxford: Oxford University Press, 2009), pp. 135–6; Philip Pecorin, 'Hate Speech: A Defense', *The City University of New York UFS Blog*, 10 April 2018. See also Ronald Dworkin, *Freedom's Law: The Moral Reading of the American Constitution* (Cambridge: Harvard University Press, 1996), pp. 200–1; Ronald Dworkin, 'Foreword', in I. Hare and J. Weinstein (eds.) *Extreme Speech and Democracy* (Oxford: Oxford University Press, 2009); Ronald Dworkin, *Justice for Hedgehogs* (Cambridge: Harvard University Press, 2011), pp. 372–3; Ronald Dworkin, 'Reply to Jeremy Waldron', in M. Herz and P. Molnar (eds.) *The Content and Context of Hate Speech: Rethinking Regulation and Responses* (Cambridge: Cambridge University Press, 2012), pp. 342–3.

93 Lord Patrick Devlin, *The Enforcement of Morals* (Oxford: Oxford University Press, 1965), pp. 13–14.

94 See Rhonda Hartman, 'Revitalizing Group Defamation as a Remedy for Hate Speech on Campus', *Oregon Law Review* 71 (1992): 855–900, p. 859; Thomas David Jones, *Human Rights: Group Defamation, Freedom of Expression and the Law of Nations* (The Hague: Kluwer Law International, 1998), pp. 88–9; Parekh, 'Hate Speech', pp. 217–18, 223.

95 Michael S. Moore, *Placing Blame: A General Theory of the Criminal Law* (Oxford: Oxford University Press, 1997); Michael S. Moore, 'Liberty's Constraints on What Should Be Criminalized', in R. A. Duff (eds.) *Criminalization: The Political Morality of the Criminal Law* (Oxford: Oxford University Press, 2014); Michael S. Moore, 'Legal Moralism Revisited', *San Diego Law Review* 54 (2017): 441–63; and R. A. Duff, 'Legal Moralism and Public Wrongs', in K. Kessler Ferzan and S. J. Morse (eds.) *Legal, Moral, and Metaphysical Truths: The Philosophy of Michael S. Moore* (Oxford: Oxford University Press, 2016).

96 See also Brown and Sinclair, *The Politics of Hate Speech Laws*, p. 290.

97 In fact, the sole reference to social norms in Matsuda's seminal article is her suggestion that courts should rely on the 'linguistic and cultural norms' of historically oppressed groups when determining whether certain intra-victim-group language is in fact persecutorial, hateful, and degrading and, therefore, should be subject to a legal response. Matsuda, 'Public Response to Racist Speech', p. 2364.

98 One obvious exception is Sina Weibo which has no equivalent community guideline explicitly forbidding hate speech.

99 Arguably, it would persist for the same reason it developed a life of its own in the first place: namely, that ordinary people find it useful to have the word 'hate speech' in their lexicon and useful in one or more of the various ways outlined in Section 5.3.1 above.
100 See Brown, 'The Myth of Hate', pp. 434–5; and Brown and Sinclair, *The Politics of Hate Speech Laws*, chs. 2 and 4.
101 See Hartman, 'Revitalizing Group Defamation as a Remedy for Hate Speech on Campus'; and Waldron, 'Dignity and Defamation'.
102 See Delgado, 'Words That Wound'; and Brown, 'Retheorizing Actionable Injuries in Civil Lawsuits Involving Targeted Hate Speech'.
103 See McGowan, 'On "Whites Only" Signs and Racist Hate Speech', pp. 142–5; and Gelber, 'Differentiating Hate Speech', p. 409.
104 For more on what this sort of all things considered justification or warranting might entail, see Brown, *Hate Speech Law*, chs. 1 and 10.
105 Ibid, ch. 9.
106 See Brown, *Models of Governance of Online Hate Speech*, pp. 52–8.
107 Monika Bickert, Vice President of Content Policy, Facebook, 'Removing Holocaust Denial Content', 12 October 2020. Available at: https://about.fb.com/news/2020/10/removing-holocaust-denial-content/.

6 Between Hate Speech and Hate Crime

1 See Alexander Brown and Adriana Sinclair, *The Politics of Hate Speech Laws* (Abingdon: Routledge, 2020).
2 Alexander Brown, 'What Is Hate Speech? Part 2: Family Resemblances', *Law and Philosophy* 36 (2017): 561–613, pp. 597–8.
3 See David Riesman, 'Democracy and Defamation: Control of Group Libel', *Columbia Law Review* 42 (1942): 727–80; Samuel Walker, *Hate Speech: The History of an American Controversy* (Lincoln: University of Nebraska Press, 1994); Alexander Brown, *Hate Speech Law* (Abingdon: Routledge, 2015), ch. 2; Brown and Sinclair, *The Politics of Hate Speech Laws*, chs. 2 and 4.
4 See Brown, *Hate Speech Law*, ch. 2.
5 See Brown, *Hate Speech Law*, pp. 26–8.
6 See s. 153 of the penal code (India), not to be confused with s. 153A; see also Art. 286 of the penal code (Venezuela) (enacted by Law No. 5494 of 20 Oct. 2000).
7 See also Organization for Security and Co-operation in Europe (OSCE), *Hate Crime Laws: A Practical Guide*, 9 March 2009, pp. 25–6. Available at: www.osce.org/odihr/36426.
8 See *Beizaras and Levickas v. Lithuania*, ECtHR, Strasbourg, 14 January 2020, No. 41288/15; *Association Accept and Others v. Romania*, ECtHR, Strasbourg, 1 June 2021, No. 19237/16; *Behar and Gutman v. Bulgaria*, ECtHR, Strasbourg, 16 February 2021, No. 29335/13; and *Budinova and Chaprazov v. Bulgaria*, ECtHR, Strasbourg, 16 February 2021, No. 12567/13. See also Stephanos Stavros, 'Association Accept and Others v. Romania: The European Court of Human Rights Takes a Fresh Look at Homophobic Speech and Biased Criminal-Law Enforcement', Oxford Human Rights Hub, 8 July 2021; Stephanos Stavros, 'Criminal Law Responses to Hate Speech: Towards a Systematic Approach in Strasbourg?', in L. Lavrysen

and N. Mavronicola (eds.) *Coercive Human Rights: Positive Duties to Mobilise the Criminal Law under the ECHR* (Oxford: Hart Publishing, 2020), p. 127; and Stephanos Stavros, 'A Duty to Prosecute Hate Speech under the ECHR?', *Oxford Human Rights Hub*, 9 April 2015.

9 See Brown, *Hate Speech Law*, ch. 2.

10 Brown and Sinclair, *The Politics of Hate Speech Laws*, pp. 134–8.

11 Ibid, p. 136.

12 Part 3 of the Public Order Act 1986.

13 Part 3A of the Public Order Act 1986.

14 Geoffrey Bindman, 'Outlawing Hate Speech', *Law Society's Gazette* 89 (1992): 17–23; Ivan Hare 'Blasphemy and Incitement to Religious Hatred: Free Speech Dogma and Doctrine', in I. Hare and J. Weinstein (eds.) *Extreme Speech and Democracy* (Oxford: Oxford University Press, 2009); David Williams, 'Hate Speech in the United Kingdom: An Historical Overview', in I. Hare and J. Weinstein (eds.) *Extreme Speech and Democracy* (Oxford: Oxford University Press, 2009); Kay Goodall, 'Challenging Hate Speech: Incitement to Hatred on Grounds of Sexual Orientation in England, Wales and Northern Ireland', *International Journal of Human Rights* 13 (2009): 211–32; Brown and Sinclair, *The Politics of Hate Speech Laws*, ch. 3; Alexander Brown, 'Hate Speech Laws, Legitimacy, and Precaution: Reply to Weinstein', *Constitutional Commentary* 32 (2017): 599–617.

15 *R. v. Ali, Javed, and Ahmed*, Derby Crown Court, 10 February 2012, No. T20110109.

16 Transcript obtained directly from Judge Burgess.

17 'The exercise of these freedoms, since it carries with it duties and responsibilities, may be subject to such formalities, conditions, restrictions or penalties as are prescribed by law and are necessary in a democratic society, in the interests of national security, territorial integrity or public safety, for the prevention of disorder or crime, for the protection of health or morals, for the protection of the reputation or rights of others, for preventing the disclosure of information received in confidence, or for maintaining the authority and impartiality of the judiciary.'

18 Andrew Legg, *The Margin of Appreciation in International Human Rights Law: Deference and Proportionality* (Oxford: Oxford University Press, 2012).

19 See *Glimmerveen and Hagenbeek v. the Netherlands*, ECtHR, Strasbourg, 11 October 1979, Nos. 8348/78 and 8406/78; *Jersild v. Denmark*, ECtHR, Strasbourg, 23 September, 1994, No. 15890/89; *Garaudy v. France*, ECtHR, Strasbourg, 7 July 2003, No. 65831/01; *Soulas and others v. France*, ECtHR, Strasbourg, 10 July 2008, No. 15948/03; *Balsyte-Lideikiene v. Lithuania*, ECtHR, Strasbourg, 4 November 2008, No. 72596/01; *Féret v. Belgium*, ECtHR, Strasbourg, 16 July 2009, No. 15615/07; *Willem v. France*, ECtHR, Strasbourg, 16 July 2009, No. 10883/05; *Aksu v. Turkey*, ECtHR, Strasbourg, 15 March 2012, Nos. 4149/04 and 41029/04; *Vejdeland and Others v. Sweden*, ECtHR, Strasbourg, 9 February 2012, No. 1813/07; *Atamanchuk v Russia*, ECtHR, Strasbourg, 11 February 2020, No. 4493/11; *Sanchez v. France*, ECtHR, Strasbourg, 2 September 2021, No. 45581/15.

20 See *Erbakan v. Turkey*, ECtHR, Strasbourg, 6 July 2006, No. 59405/00; *Perinçek v. Switzerland*, ECtHR, Strasbourg, 17 December 2013, No. 27510/08; and *Stomakhin v. Russia*, ECtHR, Strasbourg, 9 May 2018, No. 52273/07.

21 See *Sanchez v. France*; *Pastörs v. Germany*; and *Atamanchuk v Russia*.

22 See *Garaudy v. France*; *Marais v. France*, ECtHR, Strasbourg, 24 June 1996, No. 31159/96; *Pavel Ivanov v. Russia*, ECtHR, Strasbourg, 20 February 2007, No. 35222/04 (Decision on admissibility); *Perinçek v. Switzerland*; *Belkacem v. Belgium*, ECtHR, Strasbourg, 27 June 2017, No. 34367/14; and *Pastörs v. Germany*, ECtHR, Strasbourg, 3 January 2020, No. 55225/14.

23 See ECtHR, *Guide on Article 17 of the European Convention on Human Rights: Prohibition of Abuse of Rights*, 31 August 2022. Available at: www.echr.coe.int/Documents/Guide_Art_17_ENG.pdf.

24 *Lilliendahl v Iceland*, ECtHR, Strasbourg, 12 May 2020, No. 29297/18.

25 Ibid, at paras. 34–5.

26 *Norwood v. the United Kingdom*, ECtHR, Strasbourg, 16 November 2004, No. 23131/03.

27 *Lilliendahl v Iceland*, at para. 26.

28 *R. v. Norwood*, Oswestry Magistrates Court, 13 December 2002.

29 See ss. 28 and 31 of the Crime and Disorder Act 1998 (England and Wales), and in relation to s. 5 of the Public Order Act 1986.

30 *Norwood v. DPP* [2003] EWHC 1564 (Admin.)

31 See s. 5 of the Public Order Act 1986.

32 See Jacobs and Potter, *Hate Crimes*, p. 80; Gavin F. Quill, 'Motivation, Causation and Hate Crimes Sentence Enhancement: A Cautious Approach to Mind Reading and Incarceration', *Drake Law Review* 59 (2010): 181–216, p. 207n.158.

33 Barbara Perry, *In the Name of Hate: Understanding Hate Crimes* (New York: Routledge, 2001), p. 10.

34 See also Jennifer Schweppe, 'What Is a Hate Crime?', *Cogent Social Sciences* 7 (2021): 1–14, p. 11.

35 See James R. Jacobs and Kimberly Potter, *Hate Crimes: Criminal Law and Identity Politics* (Oxford: Oxford University Press, 1998); Paul Iganski and Abe Sweiry, 'Hate Crime', in A. Treviño (ed.) *The Cambridge Handbook of Social Problems* (Cambridge: Cambridge University Press, 2018).

36 Jacobs and Potter, *Hate Crimes*, ch. 3; Sarah A. Soule and Jennifer Earl, 'The Enactment of State-Level Hate Crime Law in the United States: Intrastate and Interstate Factors', *Sociological Perspectives* 44 (2001): 281–305.

37 See the Violent Crime Control and Law Enforcement Act of 1994 (US).

38 See Ely Aaronson, *From Slave Abuse to Hate Crime: The Criminalization of Racial Violence in American History* (Cambridge: Cambridge University Press, 2014), chs. 4 and 5.

39 Frederick M. Lawrence, *Punishing Hate: Biased Crimes Under American Law* (Cambridge: Harvard University Press, 1999), ch. 6; Aaronson, *From Slave Abuse to Hate Crime*, ch. 3.

40 Aaronson, *From Slave Abuse to Hate Crime*, ch. 2.

41 See also OSCE, *Hate Crime Laws*, p. 16.

42 For such an attempt, see Schweppe, 'What Is a Hate Crime?', pp. 11–12.

43 Ibid, p. 7.

44 See s. 66 of the Sentencing Act 2020 (England and Wales).

45 See ss. 28–32 of the Crime and Disorder Act 1998 (England and Wales).

46 See also OSCE, *Hate Crime Laws*, p. 26.

47 See Law Commission, *Hate Crime Laws: Final Report*, Law Com No. 402 (London: Her Majesty's Stationary Office, 2021), Recommendation 20, p. 541.

48 Paul Iganski and Jack Levin, *Hate Crime: A Global Perspective* (Abingdon: Routledge, 2015), ch. 7.

49 See Jeremy Waldron, 'Dignity and Defamation: The Visibility of Hate', *Harvard Law Review* 123 (2010): 1596–657, p. 1601; Alexander Brown, 'What Is Hate Speech? Part 1: The Myth of Hate', *Law and Philosophy* 36 (2017): 419–68; Katharine Gelber, 'Differentiating Hate Speech: A Systemic Discrimination Approach', *Critical Review of International Social and Political Philosophy* 24 (2021): 393–414, p. 408.

50 See Brown, 'The Myth of Hate'; and Nathan Hall, *Hate Crime, Second Edition* (Abingdon: Routledge, 2013), p. 9.

51 See also Neil Chakraborti, 'Framing the Boundaries of Hate Crime', in N. Hall (ed.) *The Routledge International Handbook on Hate Crime* (London and New York: Routledge, 2015), pp. 15–16.

52 See s. 1 of the Criminal Damage Act 1971.

53 See s. 66 of the Sentencing Act 2020.

54 See s. 31 of the Crime and Disorder Act 1998.

55 See s. 4A of the Public Order Act 1986.

56 See s. 66 of the Sentencing Act 2020.

57 See s. 31 of the Crime and Disorder Act 1998.

58 *R. v. Stacey*, Swansea Crown Court, 30 March 2012, No. A20120033.

59 Judge's sentencing remarks available on lawpages.com. Available at: www.thelawpages.com/court-cases/LS-8057-1.law.

60 See Part III of the Public Order Act 1986.

61 See *Šečić v. Croatia*, ECtHR, Strasbourg, 31 May 2007, No. 40116/02; *Angelova and Iliev v. Bulgaria*, ECtHR, Strasbourg, 26 July 2007, No. 55523/00; *M.C. and A.C. v. Romania*, ECtHR, Strasbourg, 12 July 2016, No. 12060/12; *R. B. v. Hungary*, ECtHR, Strasbourg, 12 April 2016, No. 64602/12; *Škorjanec v. Croatia*, ECtHR, Strasbourg, 28 March 2017, No. 25536/14.

62 Consider three illustrations of erroneous, or at best misleading, statements about the relationship between hate speech and hate crime. First: 'hate speech is a hate crime'. Richard Delgado and Jean Stefancic, 'Hate Speech Is a Hate Crime', in R. Espejo (ed.) *What Is a Hate Crime?* (San Diego: Greenhaven Press, 2002). Second: 'Hate speech is, as has been seen, concerned with various forms of expression directed against a person or group of persons on the ground of the personal characteristics or status of the person or group of persons and action against it does not necessarily entail the imposition of criminal sanctions. However, when hate speech takes the form of conduct that is in itself a criminal offence – such as conduct that is abusive, harassing or insulting – it may also be referred to as hate crime.' ECRI, GPR No. 15 On Combating Hate Speech, Explanatory Memorandum, para. 21 (p. 19). Available at: https://rm.coe.int/ecri-general-policy-recommendation-no-15-on-combating-hate-speech/16808b5b01. Third: 'Hate crime/hate speech is any criminal offence where the balance of evidence suggests that the victim has been targeted because of their race/ethnicity, religion/belief, nationality, gender/gender identity, disability, age, sexual orientation or any other actual or perceived (immutable) difference. [...] Hate speech can be seen as a particularly serious form of hate crime.' Red Network, Thesaurus, 'Hate Crime and Hate Speech'. Available at: www.red-network.eu/?i=red-network.en.thesaurus.

63 See also Abraham H. Foxman and Christopher Wolf, *Viral Hate: Containing Its Spread on the Internet* (New York: Palgrave Macmillan, 2013), p. 69; Schweppe, 'What Is a Hate Crime?', p. 8.

64 ECRI, GPR No. 7 on National Legislation to Combat Racism and Racial Discrimination, adopted 13 December 2002 and revised 7 December 2017. Available at: www.coe.int/en/web/european-commission-against-racism-and-intolerance/recommendation-no.7.
65 Ibid, at para. 21.
66 Council of the European Union, 28 November 2008, 2008/913/JHA.
67 See Part 3A of the Public Order Act 1986.
68 See s. 10(1)(c) of the Promotion of Equality and Prevention of Unfair Discrimination Act 2000 (South Africa).
69 See Part 3 of the Public Order Act 1986.
70 See s. 66 of the Sentencing Act 2020 (England and Wales).
71 See s. 4A of the Public Order Act 1986.
72 See s. 5 of the Public Order Act 1986.
73 See s. 4 of the Public Order Act 1986.
74 See Parts 3 and 3A of the Public Order Act 1986 (England and Wales); and s. 4 of the Hate Crime and Public Order (Scotland) Act 2021 (Scotland). See also Brown, *Hate Speech Law*, pp. 26–8.
75 See s. 216(1) of the penal code (Turkey); s. 319(1) of the criminal code (Canada); s. 130(1)(1) of the criminal code (Germany). See also Brown, *Hate Speech Law*, pp. 28–9.
76 See s. 66 of the Sentencing Act 2020 (England and Wales).
77 See s. 1 of the Hate Crime and Public Order (Scotland) Act 2021 (Scotland).
78 Consider the statutory Scottish offence of threatening or abusive behaviour, under s. 38 of the Criminal Justice and Licensing (Scotland) Act 2010 (Scotland).
79 Consider the Scottish common law offence of breach the peace. According to the leading case on breach of the peace, the relevant conduct must be 'severe enough to cause alarm to ordinary people and threaten serious disturbance to the community.' *Smith v Donnelly* (2001 SCCR 800).
80 See Brown, *Hate Speech Law*, pp. 26–8.
81 See Mari Matsuda, 'Public Response to Racist Speech: Considering the Victim's Story', *Michigan Law Review* 87 (1989): 2320–81; Brown, *Hate Speech Law*.
82 See Paul Iganski and Spiridoula Lagou, 'Hate Crimes Hurt Some More Than Others: Implications for the Just Sentencing of Offenders', *Journal of Interpersonal Violence* 30 (2015): 1696–718.
83 See Matsuda, 'Public Response to Racist Speech'; Alexander Brown, 'Retheorizing Actionable Injuries in Civil Lawsuits Involving Targeted Hate Speech: Hate Speech as Degradation and Humiliation', *Alabama Civil Rights and Civil Liberties Law Review* 9 (2018): 1–56, pp. 6–11.
84 For atypical cases involving a failure to properly investigate and bring prosecutions for incidents involving alleged unlawful hate speech (as well as hate crimes), see note 8 above.
85 See *Jersild v. Denmark*, *Garaudy v. France*; *Soulas and others v. France*; *Balsyte-Lideikiene v. Lithuania*; *Féret v. Belgium*; *Willem v. France*; *Aksu v. Turkey*; *Erbakan v. Turkey*; *Perinçek v. Switzerland*; *Stomakhin v. Russia*; *Vejdeland and Others v. Sweden*; *Atamanchuk v Russia*; *Sanchez v. France*.
86 For an atypical case involving a complaint against a successful prosecution for a hate crime, see *Norwood v. United Kingdom*.
87 See *Šečić v. Croatia*; *Angelova and Iliev v. Bulgaria*; *M.C. and A.C. v. Romania*; *R. B. v. Hungary*; *Škorjanec v. Croatia*.

88 See *Aksu v. Turkey*, at para. 62; *Perinçek v. Switzerland*, at paras. 198–9; *Lilliendahl v Iceland*, at paras. 31, 47; and *Šimunić v. Croatia*, ECtHR, Strasbourg, 22 January 2019, No. 20373/17, at para 45.

89 The balancing metaphor, as in, 'balance of rights' or 'balance of interests', does not explicitly figure in the ECtHR's reasoning in hate crime cases, including, for example, *Šečić v. Croatia, Angelova and Iliev v. Bulgaria, M.C. and A.C. v. Romania, R. B. v. Hungary*, and *Škorjanec v. Croatia.*

90 See *Lilliendahl v Iceland*, at para. 26.

91 See Parts 3 and 3A of the Public Order Act 1986.

92 See s. 66 of the Sentencing Act 2020.

93 See ss. 27 and 29L of the Public Order Act 1986.

94 See s. 31 of the Crime and Disorder Act 1998.

95 See note 8 above.

96 *Lilliendahl v Iceland*, at paras. 34–5.

97 See note 23 above.

98 See Brown, *Hate Speech Law*, pp. 60–6.

99 See Brown and Sinclair, *The Politics of Hate Speech Laws*, pp. 342–5. Consider *R. v. El-Faisal* (Central Criminal Court, March 2003, Case No. T20027343). In this case police investigating possible al-Qaeda links in the UK found tape recordings of speeches given by the Jamaican-born Muslim cleric Abdullah el-Faisal labelled 'No peace with the Jews' and 'Jewish Traits.' He was convicted inter alia of two counts of distributing threatening recordings with intent to stir up racial hatred – the first Muslim cleric to be convicted of such offenses in the UK. In his sentencing remarks (7 March) Judge Beaumont touched upon el-Faisal's special responsibilities. 'In my judgment, your offending was aggravated by the fact that as a cleric you were sent to this country to preach and minister to the Muslim community in London, and so had a responsibility to the young and impressionable within that community at times of conflict abroad and understandable tensions in the communities here over the period which is spanned by the indictment.' Transcript obtained from Smith Bernal Reporting Ltd. Interestingly in January 2020 the Sentencing Council of England updated its sentencing guidelines for the stirring up hatred offences including specifying within the category of 'high culpability' circumstances in which the offender 'uses position of trust, authority or influence to stir up hatred'. Available at: www.sentencingcouncil.org.uk/offences/magistrates-court/item/racial-hatred-offences-hatred-against-persons-on-religious-grounds-or-grounds-of-sexual-orientation/.

100 Consider ss. 4, 4a, and 5 of the Public Order Act 1986.

101 See s. 66 of the Sentencing Act 2020.

102 Transcript obtained directly from Judge Burgess.

103 Alexander Brown, 'The Racial and Religious Hatred Act 2006: A Millian Response', *Critical Review of International Social and Political Philosophy* 11 (2008): 1–24, p. 8.

104 By way of evidence for this, consider *R. v. Bamber* (Preston Crown Court, June 2010, Case No. No. T20091255). In this case an activist from the British National Party (BNP), Anthony Bamber, faced charges of incitement to religious hatred against Muslims, for having distributed leaflets blaming a Muslim 'invasion' for introducing various ills into society including bringing heroin into 'our' land. The jury found him not guilty. Summing up the case prior to the jury retiring to reach a verdict, Judge Badley proffered the following reasonable person test for the meaning

of 'threatening'. 'What it doesn't mean, is it is not abusive or upsetting. It doesn't prohibit public discussion, criticism, antipathy, dislike, ridicule, insult or abuse of particular religions or their followers; that is, free speech is not stopped. The word 'threatening' should have its ordinary meaning. You should ask what would be the impact of the material on a reasonable member of the public. An objective test – would a reasonable member of the public consider them threatening?' This followed a precedent established by the House of Lords in relation to other public order offences, namely, a presumption in favour of interpreting words in statutes as conveying ordinary meanings. See *Brutus v. Cozens* [1972] 2 All ER 1297 (involving a prosecution for the use of insulting words or behaviour with intent to provoke a breach of the peace or whereby a breach of the peace is likely to be occasioned under s. 5 of the Public Order Act 1936). Therefore, on this approach, it is a matter of courts to decide the question of fact as to whether, given the ordinary meaning of the word 'threatening', certain words or behaviour would be deemed threatening by a reasonable member of the public. Common threatening words might include, for example, 'watch it', 'or else', 'if they aren't careful', 'just wait until', 'they will be in trouble if they don't stop', 'don't even think about doing that'.

105 Brown and Sinclair, *The Politics of Hate Speech Laws*, ch. 3.

106 See Brown, *Hate Speech Laws*, pp. 66–71; Brown and Sinclair, *The Politics of Hate Speech Laws*, ch. 7.

107 See also Brown, *Hate Speech Laws*, chs. 3–7.

108 See Ivan Hare, 'Crosses, Crescents and Sacred Cows: Criminalising Incitement to Religious Hatred', *Public Law* (2006): 521–37, pp. 528–9; Law Commission, *Hate Crime Laws*, pp. 395–6.

109 See Brown, 'The Racial and Religious Hatred Act 2006', p. 5; Brown, *Hate Speech Laws*, pp. 26–7; Brown and Sinclair, *The Politics of Hate Speech Laws*, pp. 76–7; Commission for Countering Extremism, *COVID-19 How Hateful Extremists are Exploiting the Pandemic* (July 2020); Commission for Countering Extremism, *Operating With Impunity – Hateful Extremism: The Need for a Legal Framework* (February 2021).

110 See ss. 29J and 29JA of the Public Order Act 1986. See also Alexander Brown, 'The "Who?" Question in the Hate Speech Debate: Part 2: Functional and Democratic Approaches', *Canadian Journal of Law and Jurisprudence* 30 (2017): 23–55, pp. 34–43.

111 Ibid, p. 36. See also Alexander Brown, 'New Evidence Shows Public Supports Banning Hate Speech Against People with Disabilities', *The Conversation*, 1 March 2017. Available at: https://theconversation.com/newevidence-shows-public-supports-banning-hate-speech-against-people-with-disabilities-7380.

112 See also Brown, *Hate Speech Law*, pp. 71–5.

113 Ibid, p. 198. See also Brown, 'Hate Speech Laws, Legitimacy, and Precaution'.

114 Consider the hate crime provisions set out in s. 66 of the Sentencing Act 2020 which give courts the power to hand down sentences at the higher end of the relevant spectrums when the offending was aggravated by hostility based on protected characteristics. These provisions are applicable to a range of offences relating to the use of threatening, intimidating, or menacing words or behaviour, including but not limited to ss. 4, 4A, 5 of the Public Order Act 1986, as well as the offences described in s. 1 of the Malicious Communications Act 1988 and s. 127 of the Communications Act 2003.

115 Law Commission, *Hate Crime Laws*, Recommendations 21, 22 and 23, p. 541.

116 Ibid, pp. 396–8. See also Alexander Brown, 'The "Who?" Question in the Hate Speech Debate: Part 1: Consistency, Practical, and Formal Approaches', *Canadian Journal of Law and Jurisprudence* 29 (2016): 275–320.

117 Law Commission, *Hate Crime Laws*, Recommendation 21, p. 541.

118 See Articles II and III(c) of the Convention on the Prevention and Punishment of the Crime of Genocide, 9 December 1948, General Assembly Resolution A/RES/3/260, effective 12 January 1951.

119 Articles 6 and 25(3)(e) of the Rome Statute of the International Criminal Court, Rome, 17 July 1998, United Nations, Treaty Series, vol. 2187, No. 38544, effective 1 July 2002.

120 Of course, there are arguments within genocide studies as to whether extending the list of national, ethnic, racial or religious groups by adding further specific groups, such as defined by sexual orientation, gender, or disability, for instance, might be within the spirit if not the letter of extant international conventions on genocide. See Stuart Stein, 'Geno- and Other Cides: A Cautionary Note on Knowledge Accumulation', *Journal of Genocide Research* 4 (2002): 39–63; Sonali B. Shah, 'The Oversight of the Last Great International Institution of the Twentieth Century: The International Criminal Courts Definition of Genocide', *Emory International law Review* 16 (2002): 351–89; Matthew Waites, 'Genocide and Global Queer Politics', *Journal of Genocide Research* 20 (2017): 44–67. However, even if the conventions were amended or simply reinterpreted to cover groups defined by sexual orientation, gender, and disability, this would still not make it the case that there exists in international law a corresponding or parallel basic or base crime of inciting the destruction of any group.

121 See Brown, *Hate Speech Law*, ch. 2; Brown and Sinclair, *The Politics of Hate Speech Laws*, ch. 4.

122 Wibke K. Timmermann, *Incitement in International Law* (Abingdon: Routledge, 2014), pp. 200–1.

123 Matsuda, 'Public Response to Racist Speech', p. 2346.

124 See Audrey Fino, 'Defining Hate Speech: A Seemingly Elusive Task', *Journal of International Criminal Justice* 18 (2020): 31–57, p. 31. See also *Nahimana, Barayagwiza, Ngeze v. Prosecutor*, International Criminal Tribunal for Rwanda Appeals Chamber, 28 November 2007, Case No. ICTR-99-52-A, at para. 692.

125 Art. 4 of the International Convention on the Elimination of Racial Discrimination (ICERD), New York, December 21 1965.

126 Art. 20(2) of the International Covenant on Civil and Political Rights (ICCPR), New York, December 19 1966.

127 Consider the Office for the High Commissioner on Human Rights CCPR General Comment No. 11 on Prohibition of Propaganda for War and Inciting National, Racial or Religious Hatred (Article 20), 29 July 1983, CCPR/C/GC/11; and the Office for the High Commissioner on Human Rights Rabat Plan of Action, 11 January 2013, A/HRC/22/17/Add.4. For related international texts on hate speech, including at regional levels, see Brown and Sinclair, *The Politics of Hate Speech Laws*, pp. 134–6.

128 Thomas E. Davies, 'How the Rome Statute Weakens the International Prohibition on Incitement to Genocide', *Harvard Human Rights Journal* 22 (2009): 245–70, p. 245.

129 For a list of such cases at international and regional levels, see Brown and Sinclair, *The Politics of Hate Speech Laws*, pp. 134–6.

130 Ibid.

131 See Frederick Schauer, 'Uncoupling Free Speech', *Columbia Law Review* 92 (1992): 1321–57, p. 1349; Alexander Tsesis, *Destructive Messages: How Hate Speech Paves the Way for Harmful Social Movements* (New York: New York University Press, 2002), p. 211n.1; Raphael Cohen-Almagor, *The Scope of Tolerance: Studies on the Costs of Free Expression and Freedom of the Press* (London: Routledge, 2006), p. 11; Raphael Cohen-Almagor, 'Holocaust Denial Is a Form of Hate Speech', *Amsterdam Law Forum* 2 (2009): 33–42, p. 35; and Kylie Weston-Scheuber, 'Gender and the Prohibition of Hate Speech', *Queensland University of Technology Law and Justice Journal* 12 (2012): 132–50, pp. 139–40.

132 Matsuda, 'Public Response to Racist Speech', pp. 2341–6.

133 See Brown and Sinclair, *The Politics of Hate Speech Laws*, ch. 4.

134 Penal Law (Amendment No. 20), 1986.

135 *Penal Law 5737–1977, Eighth Edition* (Haifa: A. Greenfield-A.G. Publications, 2013).

136 Ibid.

137 Penal Law (Incitement to Violence or Terror) (Amendment No. 66), 2002.

138 *Penal Law 5737–1977, Eighth Edition.*

139 For the Supreme Court of Israel's similar analysis on the differences between these offences, See the judgment in *Mahajna v. State*, 18 April 2016, Case No. HCJ 7669/15.

140 See *S. v Nkosiyana* 1966 4 SA 655 (A) 658 (South Africa).

141 See Brown, *Hate Speech Law*, pp. 31–3; Brown, 'Retheorizing Actionable Injuries in Civil Lawsuits Involving Targeted Hate Speech', pp. 9–10, 13.

142 *Restatement (Second) of Torts* (American Law Institute, 1979).

143 *Brenner v. Botha* 1956 (3) SA 257 (T) (South Africa).

144 Ibid, at 261–2.

145 See also Brown, *Hate Speech Law*, pp. 5, 31–3; Brown, 'Retheorizing Actionable Injuries in Civil Lawsuits Involving Targeted Hate Speech'.

146 See Matsuda, 'Public Response to Racist Speech', p. 2332; Richard Delgado, 'Toward a Legal Realist View of the First Amendment', *Harvard Law Review* 113 (2000): 778–802, p. 786; Richard Delgado and Jean Stefancic, *Understanding Words That Wound* (Boulder: Westview Press, 2004), p. 1; Steven J. Heyman, *Free Speech and Human Dignity* (New Haven: Yale University Press, 2008), p. 165; Douglas M. Fraleigh and Joseph S. Tuman, *Freedom of Expression in the Marketplace of Ideas* (Thousand Oaks, CA: Sage, 2011), p. 139; Brown, 'Retheorizing Actionable Injuries in Civil Lawsuits Involving Targeted Hate Speech'; Richard Delgado and Jean Stefancic, 'Retheorizing Actions for Targeted Hate Speech: A Comment on Professor Brown', *Alabama Civil Rights and Civil Liberties Law Review* 9 (2018): 169–84; Steven J. Heyman, 'When Is Hate Speech Wrongful? A Comment on Alexander Brown's Hate Speech as Degradation and Humiliation', *Alabama Civil Rights and Civil Liberties Law Review* 9 (2018): 185–96.

147 Inter-American Commission on Human Rights, *The Situation of People of African Descent in the Americas*, 5 December 2011, Oea/Ser.L/V/Ii., Doc. 62, paras. 118, 142. Available at: www.oas.org/en/iachr/afro-descendants/docs/pdf/AFROS_2011_ENG.pdf.

148 See ECRI, GPR No. 15, 8 December 2015, Preamble, p. 3, and Explanatory Memorandum, p. 16. Available at: www.coe.int/en/web/european-commission-against-racism-and-intolerance/recommendation-no.15.

149 See ECRI, GPR No. 7, at para. 18(b).

150 Ibid, Recommendation 5, p. 7.

7 Denialist Speech

1 Erik Bleich, 'From Race to Hate: A Historical Perspective', in T. Brudholm and B. Schepelern Johansen (eds.) *Hate, Politics, Law: Critical Perspectives on Combating Hate* (Oxford: Oxford University Press, 2018), p. 29.

2 UN General Assembly, New York, 21 December 1965.

3 Mari Matsuda, 'Public Response to Racist Speech: Considering the Victim's Story', *Michigan Law Review* 87 (1989): 2320–81, p. 2341.

4 See The United States Holocaust Memorial Museum, 'Postwar Trials'. Available at: https://encyclopedia.ushmm.org/content/en/article/war-crimes-trials.

5 During this period some historians sought to compare the atrocities perpetrated by the Nazi regime to the crimes of the communist regime in the USSR.

6 During this period some historians also sought to compare the atrocities perpetrated by the Nazi regime to the violence of colonialism, for example.

7 See Lucy S. Dawidowicz, *The Holocaust and the Historians* (Cambridge: Harvard University Press, 1983); Deborah Lipstadt, *Denying the Holocaust: The Growing Assault on Truth and Memory* (New York: Free Press, 1993); Florin Lobont, 'Antisemitism and Holocaust Denial in Post-Communist Eastern Europe', in D. Stone (ed.) *The Historiography of the Holocaust* (Basingstoke: Palgrave Macmillan, 2004); Gavriel D. Rosenfeld, *Hi Hitler! How the Nazi Past Is Being Normalized in Contemporary Culture* (Cambridge: Cambridge University Press, 2015); Paul Behrens et al. (eds.) *Holocaust and Genocide Denial: A Contextual Perspective* (Abingdon: Routledge, 2017), Parts I and II; Deborah Lipstadt, *Antisemitism: Here and Now* (London: Scribe Publications, 2019); and Philip Spencer, 'Thinking about the Holocaust, Genocide and Antisemitism Today: On the Limitations of a New, Anti-Imperialist Revisionism', *Society* 59 (2022): 12–15. For a set of key dates in the spread of Holocaust denial, see The United States Holocaust Memorial Museum, 'Holocaust Denial: Key Dates'. Available at: https://encyclopedia.ushmm.org/content/en/article/holocaust-denial-key-dates.

8 Heinrich Himmler's speech, Poznan, German occupied Poland, 4 October 1943, English translation, emphasis added. Available at: https://web.archive.org/web/20120212053624/http://www.holocaust-history.org/himmler-poznan/speech-text.shtml.

9 See The United States Holocaust Memorial Museum, 'Theresienstadt: A Documentary Film, 1944'. Available at: https://perspectives.ushmm.org/item/theresienstadt-a-documentary-film-1944.

10 Annette Weinke, *Die Nürnberger Prozesse [The Nuremberg Trials]* (Munich: C.H.Beck, 2006), p. 40.

11 Kim Christian Priemel, *The Betrayal: The Nuremberg Trials and German Divergence* (Oxford: Oxford University Press, 2016), p. 225.

12 Ibid, p. 227.

13 Auschwitz-Birkenau Memorial and Museum, 'Living Conditions and Number of Victims'. Available at: www.auschwitz.org/en/history/auschwitz-iii/living-conditions-and-number-of-victims/.

14 See The United States Holocaust Memorial Museum, 'Auschwitz'. Available at: https://encyclopedia.ushmm.org/content/en/article/auschwitz.

15 See also A. Dirk Moses, *The Problems of Genocide: Permanent Security and the Language of Transgression* (Cambridge: Cambridge University Press, 2021), ch. 5.

16 Gregory H. Stanton, 'The Ten Stages of Genocide', Holocaust Memorial Day Trust. Available at: www.hmd.org.uk/learn-about-the-holocaust-and-genocides/what-is-genocide/the-ten-stages-of-genocide/.

17 Council of the European Union, 28 November 2008, 2008/913/JHA.

18 Council of Europe, Strasbourg, 28 January 2003, European Treaty Series No. 189.

19 Committee of Ministers of the Council of Europe, Turin, 20 May 2022, CM/Rec(2022)16.

20 See UN General Assembly Resolution on Holocaust Remembrance, New York, 1 November 2005, A/RES/60/7; UN General Assembly Resolution on Holocaust Denial, New York, 26 January 2007, A/RES/61/255; UN General Assembly Resolution on Holocaust Denial, New York, 20 January 2022, A/RES/76/250; Council of the European Union Conclusions on combating racism and antisemitism, Brussels, 2 March 2022, 6406/1/22.

21 London, 8 August 1945.

22 UN General Assembly, Paris, 9 December 1948.

23 UN General Assembly, New York, 21 December 1965.

24 UN General Assembly, New York, 16 December 1966.

25 Rome, 17 July 1998.

26 See Deborah Lipstadt, 'Holocaust Denial: An Antisemitic Fantasy', *Modern Judaism* 40 (2020): 71–86, p. 75; and Matteo Bonotti and Jonathan Seglow, *Free Speech* (Cambridge: Polity Press, 2021), pp. 56, 59.

27 Bonotti and Seglow, *Free Speech*, p. 56.

28 Ibid, pp. 59–60.

29 Ibid, pp. 61–71.

30 This variety is also recognised in the International Holocaust Remembrance Alliance (IHRA) working definition of Holocaust denial and distortion. Available at: www.holocaustremembrance.com/resources/working-definitions-charters/working-definition-holocaust-denial-and-distortion.

31 See Mari Matsuda, 'Public Response to Racist Speech: Considering the Victim's Story', *Michigan Law Review* 87 (1989): 2320–81, pp. 2366–7; Robert A. Kahn, 'Holocaust Denial and Hate Speech', in L. Hennebel and T. Hochmann (eds.) *Genocide Denials and the Law* (Oxford: Oxford University Press, 2011); Alan Haworth, *Free Speech: All that Matters* (London: John Murray Learning, 2015), pp. 45–8; Lipstadt, *Antisemitism*, ch. 5.

32 Simon Geissbühler, 'Staring at the Past with Eyes Wide Shut: Holocaust Revisionism and Negationism in Romania', *Israel Journal of Foreign Affaires* 6 (2012): 127–35.

33 Kahn, 'Holocaust Denial and Hate Speech'; Lipstadt, *Antisemitism*, ch. 5.

34 See Michael Shafir, *Between Denial and "Comparative Trivialization": Holocaust Negationism in Post-Communist East Central Europe* (Jerusalem: Vidal Sassoon International Center for the Study of Antisemitism, 2002); Lipstadt, *Antisemitism*, ch. 5; and Lipstadt, 'Holocaust Denial', pp. 76–83.

35 See also Gregory S. Gordon, *Atrocity Speech Laws* (Oxford: Oxford University Press, 2017).

36 For one thing, it is relatively clear that these forms are not mutually exclusive. It is arguable that Russian propaganda surrounding the annexation of Crimea in 2014 and the invasion of Ukraine in 2022, for example, exemplifies a combination of these different forms of hate speech. There is evidence of denialism in the mirror but also atrocity-oriented denial: the aim being not merely to gaslight the enemy and sow confusion and disunity among the enemy's allies but also to represent the state's own actions as both normal and necessary in the face of a threat, as a form of domestic propaganda justifying Russia's atrocities against the Ukrainian people.

However, it is an open question how widely the category of softcore Holocaust denial should extend. For example, is any insensitive mention of the Holocaust or terminology relating to the Holocaust a form of softcore denial even if it is not used to express bare denials? Much depends on whether the mention has the purpose or effect of diminishing or trivialising the Holocaust. It surely also matters whether the usage carries an implicit or veiled threat of something like the Holocaust as an appropriate response to a different protected group. By way of illustration, in a speech to the Australian parliament in 2018, the cross-bench senator Fraser Anning used the expression 'final solution to the immigration problem' in the course of advocating for 'a plebiscite to allow the Australian people to decide whether they want wholesale non-English speaking immigrants from the third world, and particularly whether they want any Muslims'. Katharine Murphy and Amy Remeikis, 'Australian Senator Calls for "Final Solution to Immigration Problem"', *The Guardian*, 14 August 2018. Available at: www.theguardian.com/australia-news/2018/aug/14/australian-senator-calls-for-final-solution-to-immigration-problem. Arguably in the process he, first, violated the memory and dignity of Jews involved in the Holocaust, and, second, implicitly threatened or intimidated, directly, all potential Muslim and non-English speaking considering seeking entry into Australia, and, indirectly, all Muslim and non-English speaking migrants currently living in Australia and potentially all Australian citizens who are Muslims or have ancestry from developing nations across Africa, Asia, and Latin America. If a group of citizens hear their own country's politicians using the term 'final solution' in calling for an end to immigration involving people they perceive to be like them, surely it would be not irrational for them to fear that this would be just the first step in a series of policies that would ultimately target them as a well, especially if they already face discrimination. Of course, conservative political commentators might say that people have no cause to be concerned because, they claim, Anning was probably just using the occasion of his maiden address to use rhetoric that would be likely to raise his profile and 'make a name for himself'. They might add that he was not speaking for the government nor indeed for parliament. But what matters is whether his words could be received by ordinary people as indirectly threatening or intimidating. From their perspective the mere fact that he is an elected representative lends a menacing edge to his words. As a member of parliament he is only step removed from holding political power. At the very least, how could his Muslim and non-English speaking constituents feel comfortable that Anning is representing their identities having heard him apply the term 'final solution' to people like them? For an analysis of the nature and effect of hyper-political hate speech (i.e. hate speech by politicians), and how to legitimately regulate it, see Alexander Brown and Adriana Sinclair, *The Politics of Hate Speech Laws* (Abingdon: Routledge, 2020), Part III.

37 See also Kahn, 'Holocaust Denial and Hate Speech'.

38 For this definition of the term 'hate speech', See Jon B. Gould, *Speak No Evil: The Triumph of Hate Speech Regulation* (Chicago: University of Chicago Press, 2005), p. 14.

39 Matsuda, 'Public Response to Racist Speech', pp. 2366–7.

40 Speaking in relation to the ordinary concept, the political theorist Bhikhu Parekh writes: 'Hate speech has three essential features. First, it singles out an individual or a group of individuals on the basis of certain characteristics. [. . .] Secondly, hate speech stigmatises its target by ascribing to it a set of constitutive qualities that are widely viewed as highly undesirable. [. . .] Thirdly, the target group is placed outside the pale of normal social relationships. [. . .] Holocaust denial, for example, is not by itself a case of hate speech. Although untrue, it is an opinion like any other, and should be tolerated in a free society in the same way that we put up with believers in witchcraft and a flat earth. However, it could also be a coded way of saying that the Jews cannot be trusted, will resort to any means to get their way, represent a hostile presence, that no shared life is possible with them, and so on. It then has all the three features of hate speech.' Bhikhu Parekh, 'Hate Speech: Is There a Case for Banning?', *Public Policy Research* 12 (2005–2006): 213–23, pp. 214–15. Parekh's analysis depicts Holocaust denial as potential hate speech. Some key institutions associated with the defence of Jewish rights, however, have publicly expressed the view that Holocaust denial is by nature a form of hate speech in the ordinary sense of the term. Consider the words of the Auschwitz Memorial: 'Holocaust denial is a lie fueled by antisemitic hatred. It hurts people and disrespects the memory of the victims. The fact that after so many years, @Facebook has changed its hate speech policy and will ban Holocaust denial & distortion is a step in the right direction.' @AuschwitzMuseum, Twitter, 13 October 2020. Or consider this contribution from the CEO of the Anti-Defamation League (ADL): '#Holocaust denial is hate speech plain and simple.' @JGreenblattADL, Twitter, 1 July 2020. These perspectives are echoed elsewhere on social media especially among liberal commentators. Consider the following tweet from the Democratic governor of New Jersey Phil Murphy: 'Holocaust denial is hate speech – plain and simple'. @GovMurphy, Twitter, 14 August 2020.

Interestingly, many campus speech codes in universities across America disallow forms of 'discriminatory harassment', and at least some scholars have argued for application of such codes to all forms of hate speech including Holocaust denial. In the words of Alexander Tsesis: 'Academic freedom is not a license for harassment. Neither does the hate speech further the pursuit for truth: calling Jews vermin, claiming it is they who were responsible for the 9/11 attacks, or purporting that the Holocaust is a myth have nothing to do with a university's mission to pursue truth. These derogatory statements are meant to exclude and stamp them with labels of outsiders and charlatans. Derisive speech becomes academically punishable when it is meant to defame, intimidate, threaten, terrify, or instigate violence.' Alexander Tsesis, 'Campus Antisemitic Speech and the First Amendment', in C. Asher Small (ed.) *Global Antisemitism: A Crisis of Modernity* (Leiden: Martinus Nijhoff, 2013), p. 157. Even those academics who reject campus speech codes as 'pernicious', 'absurd', and 'unconstitutional', have sometimes defended the practice of no-platforming Holocaust deniers *qua* peddlers of hatred. Consider the words of Kenneth Lasson: 'Holocaust denial should be recognized not as an attempt at free inquiry, but as an exercise in distortion. Universities should be regarded as places with the moral responsibility of training students to think critically, not of providing platforms for bigots whose sole purpose is to stir up hatred. Allowing them to discard the documented facts of history can hardly be understood as the honest scholar's quest for truth. [...] When perpetrated in an academic environment, Holocaust denial is a particularly pernicious form of hate speech. On American campuses, regardless of whether a student organization is privately or publicly funded, rejection of its right to sponsor a Holocaust-denial speaker need not be viewed as suppression of free speech. Nor has freedom of the press been infringed when an advertisement denying the Holocaust is spurned by a student newspaper.' Kenneth Lasson, 'Holocaust Denial and the First Amendment: The Quest for Truth in a Free Society', *George Mason Law Review* 6 (1997): 35–86, p. 85–6.

Furthermore, at least some major social media platforms promulgate public facing content policies that explicitly disallow Holocaust denial. TikTok's policy on Hate Speech and Hateful Behaviors, for example, disallows 'Denying well-documented historical events that harmed groups based on a protected attribute, such as denial of the Holocaust or the genocide against the Tutsi in Rwanda.' TikTok, Community Guidelines, Hate Speech and Hateful Behaviors (as of 10 June 2023). Available at: www.tiktok.com/community-guidelines?lang=en#38. Similarly, since 2020 Facebook's community standard on hate speech has included a Tier 1 rule disallowing 'Holocaust denial'. Facebook, Community Standards, Hate Speech (as of 10 June 2023). Available at: https://transparency.fb.com/es-la/policies/community-standards/hate-speech/.

Moreover, whilst the public facing content policies of some major social media platforms, notably YouTube, Snap Inc, WeChat, make no reference to disallowing Holocaust denial, this is not the final word on their internal enforcement policies. For example, in 2019 YouTube publicly clarified through the media that with immediate effect it would be applying its hate speech policy in such a way as to disallow certain Holocaust denial content in the form of denying that factual events ever happened. Paresh Dave, 'YouTube Reversal Bans Holocaust Hoaxers, Stops Pay for Borderline Creators', Reuters, 5 June 2019. Available at: www.reuters.com/article/us-alphabet-youtube-hatespeech-idUSKCN1T623X. To take another example, Twitter does not treat Holocaust denial in itself as hate speech but does disallow content relating to the Holocaust, including media depictions of victims of the Holocaust, when sent with intent to harass. 'We prohibit targeting individuals or groups with content that references forms of violence or violent events where a protected category was the primary target or victims, where the intent is to harass. This includes, but is not limited to media or text that refers to or depicts: [...] genocides, (e.g., the Holocaust); lynchings.' Twitter, Hateful Conduct Policy (as of 10 June 2023). Available at: https://help.twitter.com/en/rules-and-policies/hateful-conduct-policy.

41 See Human Rights Watch, *'Hate Speech' and Freedom of Expression: A Human Rights Watch Policy Paper* (New York: Fund for Free Expression, 1992), p. 1; Susan Brison, 'The Autonomy Defense of Free Speech', *Ethics* 108 (1998): 312–39, p. 313; Alexander Tsesis, *Destructive Messages: How Hate Speech Paves the Way for Harmful Social Movements* (New York: New York University Press, 2002), p. 211n.1; Richard Delgado and Jean Stefancic, *Understanding Words That Wound* (Boulder: Westview Press, 2004), p. 11; Caleb Yong, 'Does Freedom of Speech Include Hate Speech?', *Res Publica* 17 (2011): 385–403, p. 386; Eduardo Bertoni and Julio Rivera, 'The American Convention on Human Rights: Regulations on Hate Speech and Other Similar Expressions', in

M. Herz and P. Molnar (eds.) *The Content and Context of Hate Speech: Rethinking Regulation and Responses* (Cambridge: Cambridge University Press, 2012), p. 499; Sarah Sorial, 'Hate Speech and Distorted Communication: Rethinking the Limits of Incitement', *Law and Philosophy* 34 (2015): 299–324, p. 299; Alexander Brown, 'What Is Hate Speech? Part 1: The Myth of Hate', *Law and Philosophy* 36 (2017): 419–68, pp. 436–7; and See Alexander Brown, 'The "Who?" Question in the Hate Speech Debate: Part 1: Consistency, Practical, and Formal Approaches', *Canadian Journal of Law and Jurisprudence* 29 (2016): 275–320, pp. 276–81.

42 IHRA, 'The Holocaust and Other Genocides'. Available at: www.holocaustremembrance.com/resources/educational-materials/holocaust-and-other-genocides.

43 To clarify, there are, of course, some crimes against humanity the definitions of which do refer to protected characteristics, such as the crime of persecution and the crime of Apartheid. See Arts. 7(1)(h)/(j) and 7(2)(h) of the Rome Statute.

44 Consider YouTube which lists 'victims of a major violent event and their kin' as a protected characteristic under its hate speech policy. Available at: https://support.google.com/youtube/answer/2801939?hl=en-GB.

45 Brown, 'The Myth of Hate', p. 434.

46 Ibid, pp. 434–5. See also Brown and Sinclair, *The Politics of Hate Speech Laws*, ch. 4.

47 New York, 1 November 2005, A/RES/60/7.

48 'Recalling also that, for this reason, resolution 60/7 rejects efforts to deny the Holocaust which, by ignoring the historical fact of those terrible events, increase the risk they will be repeated'. New York, 26 January 2007, A/RES/61/255.

49 'Bearing in mind that Holocaust denial in its various forms is an expression of antisemitism'. New York, 25 January 2022, A/RES/76/250.

50 UN Human Rights Committee, Communication No. 550/1993, 8 November 1996.

51 Art. 24 of the Press Law of 29 July 1881 (as amended the Law of 1 July 1972, the Law of 30 December 2004, and the Law of 6 August 2012).

52 UN Human Rights Committee, General Comment No. 34 on Article 19: Freedoms of Opinion and Expression, 12 September 2011, para. 49.

53 Michael O'Flaherty, 'Freedom of Expression: Article 19 of the International Covenant on Civil and Political Rights and the Human Rights Committee's General Comment No. 34', *Human Rights Law Review* 12 (2012): 627–54, pp. 632–3.

54 United Nations and UNESCO, *History Under Attack Holocaust Denial and Distortion on Social Media* (Paris: UNESCO, 2022), p. 27n.40.

55 See UN General Assembly Resolution on Promoting Interreligious and Intercultural Dialogue and Tolerance in Countering Hate Speech, New York, 25 July 2019, A/RES/73/328.

56 See Art. 1(1)(c)/(d) of the Council Framework Decision and Art. 6 of the Additional Protocol to the Convention on Cybercrime.

57 Brussels, 15 July 1996, 96/443/JHA.

58 Ibid, Title I(A)(c).

59 Recommendation of the Committee of Ministers to member States on combating hate speech, Principles and guidelines, 11(e).

60 ECRI General Policy Recommendation No. 7 on National Legislation to Combat Racism and Racial Discrimination, 13 December 2002, revised 7 December 2017, para. 18.

61 ECRI General Policy Recommendation No. 9 on Preventing and Combating Antisemitism, 25 June 2004, revised 1 July 2021, Preamble and para. 2.

62 ECRI General Policy Recommendation No. 15 on Combating Hate Speech, 8 December 2015, Preamble.

63 See *Surek v. Turkey*, ECtHR, Strasbourg, 8 July 1999, No. 26682/95; *Gündüz v. Turkey*, ECtHR, Strasbourg, 14 June 2004, No. 35071/97; and *Lilliendahl v Iceland*, ECtHR, Strasbourg, 12 May 2020, No. 29297/18.

64 ECtHR, Strasbourg, 16 February 2021, No. 29335/13.

65 Ibid, at paras. 51, 53, 101, 104.

66 ECtHR, Strasbourg, 22 April 2010, No. 40984/07.

67 Ibid, para. 126.

68 ECtHR, Strasbourg, 17 December 2013, No. 27510/08.

69 See *Witzsch v. Germany*, ECtHR, Strasbourg, 13 December 2005, No. 7485/03; and *Pastörs v. Germany*, ECtHR, Strasbourg, 3 January 2020, No. 55225/14.

70 See Frederick Schauer, 'Social Epistemology, Holocaust Denial, and the Post-Millian Calculus', in M. Herz and P. Molnar (eds.) *The Content and Context of Hate Speech: Rethinking Regulation and Responses* (Cambridge: Cambridge University Press, 2012), pp. 141–3.

71 Matsuda, 'Public Response to Racist Speech', p. 2357.

72 Ibid, pp. 2366–7.

73 Kathleen E. Mahoney, 'Hate Speech, Equality, and the State of Canadian Law', *Wake Forest Law Review* 44 (2009): 321–51, p. 325.

74 Jennifer Schweppe, 'What Is a Hate Crime?', *Cogent Social Sciences* 7 (2021): 1–14, p. 9.

75 Raphael Cohen-Almagor, 'Holocaust Denial Is a Form of Hate Speech', *Amsterdam Law Forum* 2 (2009): 33–42, p. 35.

76 Tarlach McGonagle, 'Wresting Racial Equality From Tolerance of Hate Speech', *Dublin University Law Journal* 23 (2001) 21–54, pp. 23, 40.

77 Cohen-Almagor, 'Holocaust Denial Is a Form of Hate Speech', p. 35.

78 For example, Facebook's general definition of hate speech runs as follows: 'We define hate speech as a direct attack against people – rather than concepts or institutions – on the basis of what we call protected characteristics'. Facebook, Community Standards, Hate Speech. Yet the standard also contains a specific Tier 1 rule disallowing 'Holocaust denial'. Ibid. If Holocaust denial cannot be plausibly interpreted as 'a direct attack against people', then the specific rule against Holocaust denial looks like an exception to Facebook's general definition of hate speech. Indeed, this may not be all that surprising given that this specific rule was introduced by Facebook a long time after the community standard on hate speech was first published. That said, Facebook's standard also carves out an exception that disallows 'Content attacking concepts, institutions, ideas, practices or beliefs associated with protected characteristics, which are likely to contribute to imminent physical harm, intimidation or discrimination against the people associated with that protected characteristic.' Ibid. So maybe the inclusion of the specific rule against Holocaust denial reflects a presumption or generalisation at Facebook that Holocaust denial is by nature a form of content that falls under the aforementioned exception. Furthermore, in an interview with Fox News in May 2020 Mark Zuckerberg famously said this about the appropriate role of social media platforms including Facebook. 'I just believe strongly that Facebook shouldn't be the arbiter of truth of everything that people say online.' Yael Halon, 'Zuckerberg Knocks Twitter for Fact-Checking Trump, Says Private Companies Shouldn't be "the Arbiter of Truth"', *Fox News*, 27 May 2020. Available at: www.foxnews.com/media/facebook-mark-zuckerberg-twitter-fact-checking-trump. This also suggests that Facebook disallows Holocaust denial not so much on the grounds that this involves

denying what is true but on the grounds of the contribution of such denials to imminent harm. Indeed, it is notable that Facebook's community standard on hate speech includes no reference to a truth defence, as in, no exception for statements that are true or that the user has reasonable grounds to be believe are true. Facebook, Community Standards, Hate Speech. However, the rationale that Facebook publicly circulated in October 2020 for introducing the specific Tier 1 rule against Holocaust denial makes no mention of 'harm', 'imminent harm', or 'incitement to hatred, discrimination, or violence'. Monika Bickert, Vice President of Content Policy, Facebook, 'Removing Holocaust Denial Content', 12 October 2020. Available at: https://about.fb.com/news/2020/10/removing-holocaust-denial-content/. The proffered rationale instead speaks to 'our effort to fight hate on our services', 'Our decision is supported by the well-documented rise in anti-Semitism globally', and 'the alarming level of ignorance about the Holocaust, especially among young people'.

79 Caroline Fournet and Clotilde Pégorier, 'Combating Genocide Denial Via Law: État des Lieux of Anti-Denial Legislation', in P. Behrens et al. (eds.) *Holocaust and Genocide Denial: A Contextual Perspective* (Abingdon: Routledge, 2017), p. 212.

80 Dan Meagher, 'Regulating History: Australian Racial Vilification Law and History Denial', *The University of Queensland Law Journal* 29 (2005): 499–532, p. 516.

81 Ibid.

82 See Part III of the Public Order Act 1986.

83 Geoffrey Bindman, 'Outlawing Holocaust Denial', *New Law Journal* 147 (1997): 466–8, p. 466.

84 Jonathan Cooper and Adrian Marshall Williams, 'Hate Speech, Holocaust Denial and International Human Rights Law', *European Human Rights Law Review* 6 (1999): 593–613, p. 596.

85 For a broader discussion of international hate speech laws, see Stephanie Farrior, 'Molding the Matrix: The Historical and Theoretical Foundations of International Law concerning Hate Speech', *Berkeley Journal of International Law* 14 (1996): 1–98; Wibke Kristin Timmermann, 'The Relationship between Hate Propaganda and Incitement to Genocide: A New Trend in International Law Towards Criminalization of Hate Propaganda?', *Leiden Journal of International Law* 18 (2005): 257–82; Mariana Mello, 'Hagan v. Australia: A Sign of the Emerging Notion of Hate Speech in Customary International Law', *Loyola of Los Angeles International and Comparative Law Review* 28 (2006): 365–78; Perry Keller, *European and International Media Law: Liberal Democracy, Trade, and the New Media* (Oxford: Oxford University Press, 2011), ch. 13; Toby Mendel, 'Does International Law Provide for Consistent Rules on Hate Speech?', in M. Herz and P. Molnar (eds.) *The Content and Context of Hate Speech: Rethinking Regulation and Responses* (Cambridge: Cambridge University Press, 2012); Natalie Alkiviadou, 'The Legal Regulation of Hate Speech: The International and European Frameworks', *Croatian Political Science Review* 55 (2018): 203–29; Philippa Hall, 'Dialogues and Diversity in Korea, Japan, and France: The Contribution of International Law to Hate Speech Legislation in National and Transnational Contexts', in M. Kang et al. (eds.) *Hate Speech in Asia and Europe: Beyond Hate and Fear* (Abingdon, Routledge, 2019); Brown and Sinclair, *The Politics of Hate Speech Laws*, ch. 4; Natalie Alkiviadou, 'The Legal Regulation of Hate Speech: The United Nations Framework as the Common Denominator for Europe and Asia', *European-Asian Journal of Law and Governance* 10 (2020): 22–41; Mona Elbahtimy, *The Right to Protection from Incitement to Hatred: An Unsettled Right* (Cambridge: Cambridge University Press, 2021).

86 Available at: www.article19.org/data/files/pdfs/standards/the-camden-principles-on-freedom-of-expression-and-equality.pdf.

87 Consider once again the Council Framework Decision discussed in the previous section. As Paulo Lobba explains: '[I]t should be recalled that judges are under an obligation to construe domestic criminal law in accordance with the 'wording and purpose' of any EU framework decision – the so-called 'principle of conforming interpretation'. In systems where incitement to hatred is punishable and yet denialist speech is not specifically criminalised, such a rule of interpretation may offer support to a court's finding that hate speech may also encompass statements denying, condoning or trivialising the Holocaust or other international crimes.' Paulo Lobba, 'From Introduction to Implementation: First Steps of the EU Framework Decision 2008/931/JHA against Racism and Xenophobia', in P. Behrens et al. (eds.) *Holocaust and Genocide Denial: A Contextual Perspective* (Abingdon: Routledge, 2017), p. 199.

88 Michel Rosenfeld, 'Hate Speech in Constitutional Jurisprudence: A Comparative Analysis', in M. Herz and P. Molnar (eds.) *The Content and Context of Hate Speech: Rethinking Regulation and Responses* (Cambridge: Cambridge University Press, 2012), p. 246.

89 Peter R. Teachout, 'Making "Holocaust Denial" a Crime: Reflections on European Anti-Negationist Laws from the Perspective of US Constitutional Experience', *Vermont Law Review* 30 (2006): 655–92, pp. 670–1.

90 Lobba, 'From Introduction to Implementation', p. 190.

91 Cf. Art. 1(2) of the Council Framework Decision.

92 See Brown, *Hate Speech Law*, ch. 2.

93 Ibid. See also Robert Kahn, *Holocaust Denial and the Law: A Comparative Study* (New York: Palgrave Macmillan, 2004).

94 See Steven Pinker, *The Better Angels of Our Nature: A history of Violence and Humanity* (London: Penguin, 2011).

95 See also Bleich, 'From Race to Hate'; Kosopov, *Memory Laws, Memory Wars; Guenter Lewy, Outlawing Genocide Denial: The Dilemmas of Official Historical Truth* (Salt Lake City: University of Utah Press, 2014); and Paul Behrens et al. (eds.) *Holocaust and Genocide Denial: A Contextual Perspective* (Abingdon: Routledge, 2017). Cf. Samuel Walker, *In Defense of American Liberties: A History of the ACLU* (New York: Oxford University Press, 1990); and Brown and Sinclair, *The Politics of Hate Speech Laws*, ch. 2.

96 Art. 216 of the Penal Code (formerly Art. 312).

97 Hate Speech Act of 2016.

98 Art. 153A of the Penal Code.

99 Arts. 249 and 250 of the Criminal Law.

100 Art. 282(1) of the Criminal Code (only partially decriminalising in 2019).

101 In the case of China, consider the blurring of the lines in the wording of Art. 4 of the Counterterrorism Law of the People's Republic of China (Order No. 36 of the President, 2015): 'The state shall combat all forms of extremism, such as the incitement to hatred and discrimination and agitation for violence by distorting religious doctrine or other methods, so as to eliminate the ideological basis of terrorism' [trans.]. Available at: http://en.pkulaw.cn/index.aspx. In Russia, defendants have been convicted simultaneously of crimes under a combination of Art. 280 (public appeals for extremist activities) and Art. 282(1) (incitement to hatred). This has made the task of the ECtHR more complicated, when applicants have brought cases

before it, requiring the ECtHR to untangle the different threads of speech prosecuted under the different provisions. See *Stomakhin v. Russia*, ECtHR, Strasbourg, 9 May 2018, No. 52273/07.

We also note, however, that the rhetorical securitisation/terrorisation of some official discourse around hate speech laws is not exclusive to non-Western countries. See also Brown and Sinclair, The Politics of Hate Speech Laws, ch. 2; and Katharine Gelber, 'Terrorist-Extremist Speech and Hate Speech: Understanding the Similarities and Differences', *Ethical Theory and Moral Practice* 22 (2019): 607–22. At times, the ECtHR has also blurred the lines in an unhelpful way between terrorist propaganda and hate speech. In *Faruk Temel v. Turkey*, for example, the applicant challenged his conviction under Turkish law for making propaganda for a terrorist organisation in contravention of Art. 169 of the penal code, claiming that it was a violation of his human right to freedom of expression under Art. 10(1). However, the ECtHR supplemented its assessment of the case with an ad hoc opinion on the separate issue of whether the speech in question constituted 'hate speech', which is among the various categories of speech the regulation of which has been previously recognised by the ECtHR as 'necessary in a democratic society' under Art. 10(2). *Faruk Temel v. Turkey*, ECtHR, Strasbourg, 1 May 2011, No. 16853/05, para. 62.

102 Art. 354.1 of the Criminal Code.

103 See Nikolay Kosopov, *Memory Laws, Memory Wars: The Politics of Memory in Europe and Russia* (Cambridge: Cambridge University Press, 2017); and Jacob Mchangama, 'First They Came for the Holocaust Deniers, and I Did Not Speak Out', *Foreign Policy*, 2 October 2016. Available at: https://foreignpolicy.com/2016/10/02/first-they-came-for-the-holocaust-deniers-and-i-did-not-speak-out/.

104 Art. 145a(3) of the Criminal Code (as amended by the Law on Amendment to the Criminal Code of Bosnia and Herzegovina 2021 and passed by the High Representative of Bosnia and Herzegovina, Valentin Inzko, using the Bonn powers).

105 For further discussion of why this is the case, see Lea David, 'Policing Memory in Bosnia: Ontological Security and International Administration of Memorialization Policies', *International Journal of Politics Culture and Society* 32 (2019): 211–25.

106 Brigitte Bailer-Galanda, '"Revisionism" in Germany and Austria: The Evolution of a Doctrine', in H. Kurthen et al. (eds.) *Antisemitism and Xenophobia in Germany After Unification* (Oxford: Oxford University Press, 1997). p. 188.

107 See *R. v. Birdwood* (1995) No. 94/2421/X2 (EWCA, 11 Apr.), 6 Archbold News 2.

108 Arts. 137c, 137d, and 137e of the Penal Code.

109 ss. 10 and 10(a) of the Criminal Code.

110 Report from the Commission to the European Parliament and the Council on the Implementation of Council Framework Decision 2008/913/JHA, COM(2014)27, 27 January 2014. Available at: https://eur-lex.europa.eu.

111 s. 18C(1) of the Racial Discrimination Act 1975.

112 See *Jones v. Scully* (2002) 120 FCR 243; *Jones v. Toben* [2002] FCA 1150; *Toben v. Jones* (2003) 199 ALR 1.

113 The Racism Law (No. 7.716/89).

114 See Luiz Nazario, 'The Case of the Brazilian Revisionist S.E. Castan', in E. Webman (ed.) *The Global Impact of the Protocols of the Elders of Zion* (Abingdon: Routledge, 2011).

115 15 April 2010, No. 3/2010.

116 Law 927/1979 (as amended by laws 1419/1984 and 2910/2001).

117 Denial of Holocaust (Prohibition) Law (No. 5746–1986).
118 Art. 24-bis of Law on the Freedom of the Press of 1881 (as amended by the Gayssot Act of 1990, No. 90–615).
119 s. 3h of the National Socialism Prohibition Act 1947 (as amended in 1992).
120 Art. 130(3) of the Criminal Code.
121 The Holocaust Denial Law of 23 March 1995.
122 Art. 261-bis of the Criminal Code (as amended by Art. 1 of the Federal Act of 18 June 1993 and entered into force on 1 January 1995 following referendum FF 1993 II 868–9).
123 Art. 457(3) of the Criminal Code.
124 Art. 55 of the Act of 18 December 1998 on the Institute of National Remembrance Commission for the Prosecution of Crimes against the Polish Nation.
125 Art. 261 of the Criminal Code (as amended in 2001), replaced with Art. 405 of the Criminal Code (as amended in 2010).
126 Art. 261 of the Criminal Code (as amended in 2001), replaced by Art. 424a(1)(b) of the Criminal Code (as amended in 2005), in turn replaced by Art. 422d of the Criminal Code (as amended in 2011), and also Art. 130(7)(d) of the Criminal Code.
127 Art. 6 of Emergency Ordinance No. 31/2002 of 13 March 2002 (approved with amendments and additions by Law No. 107/2006 of 27 April 2006, and amended and supplemented by Law No. 217 of 23 July 2015).
128 Art. 300(1) of the Criminal Code (as amended in 2004), replaced with Art. 297(2) of the Criminal Code (as amended in 2008).
129 Art. 170–2 of the Criminal Code.
130 Art. 333 of the Penal Code.
131 Law No. 5109 On Prevention and Counteraction to Antisemitism in Ukraine.
132 Art. 4 of Law No. 33bis/2003 of 2003 Repressing the Crime of Genocide, Crimes Against Humanity and War Crimes.
133 Law on the Denial of Crimes Committed During Democratic Kampuchea of 7 June 2013.
134 Art. 2 of Law 927/1979 (as amended by Law 4285/2014).
135 Art. 387(5) of the Criminal Code.
136 Art. 240(2)(b) of the Criminal Code.
137 Art. 82B of the Criminal Code.
138 Art. 325(2) of the Criminal Code.
139 Art. 130(3) of the Criminal Code.
140 Art. 170–2 of the Criminal Code.
141 Denial of Holocaust (Prohibition) Law (No. 5746–1986).
142 Art. 24-bis of Law on the Freedom of the Press of 1881 (as amended by the Gayssot Act of 1990, No. 90–615).
143 Art. 3h of the National Socialism Prohibition Act 1947 (as amended in 1992).
144 Art. 55 of the Act of 18 December 1998 on the Institute of National Remembrance Commission for the Prosecution of Crimes against the Polish Nation.
145 The Holocaust Denial Law of 23 March 1995.
146 Art. 261 of the Criminal Code.
147 Art. 457(3) of the Criminal Code.
148 Art. 283(1)(5) of the Criminal Code.
149 Art. 300(1) of the Criminal Code (as amended in 2004), replaced with Art. 297(2) of the Criminal Code (as amended in 2008).

150 Art. 333 of the Penal Code.
151 Art. 3 of Law No. 134(I)/2011 of 2011 on Combating Certain Forms and Expressions of Racism and Xenophobia through Criminal, as amended by Law No. 45(I)/2015.
152 Art. 4 of Law No. 33bis/2003 of 2003 Repressing the Crime of Genocide, Crimes Against Humanity and War Crimes.
153 Law on the Denial of Crimes Committed During Democratic Kampuchea of 7 June 2013.
154 Art. 607.2 of the Criminal Code (as amended in 1995 and subsequently repealed).
155 The Spanish Constitutional Court Judgment No. 235/2007 of 7 November 2007 (BOE-T-2007-21161).
156 Art. 510(1)(c) of the Criminal Code.
157 See Brown, *Hate Speech Law*, ch. 2.
158 Kahn, 'Holocaust Denial and Hate Speech', p. 107.
159 Ed West, 'Bob Dylan Falls Foul of Europe's Neo-Blasphemy Laws', *The Spectator*, 4 December 2013. Available at: www.spectator.co.uk/article/bob-dylan-falls-foul-of-europe-s-neo-blasphemy-laws.
160 The Declaration of the Stockholm International Forum on the Holocaust, January 2000. Available at: www.holocaustremembrance.com/about-us/stockholm-declaration.
161 See *Hate Speech Law*, chs. 2–9.
162 Ibid, pp. 239–42.
163 See Alexander Brown, 'The "Who?" Question in the Hate Speech Debate: Part 2: Functional and Democratic Approaches', *Canadian Journal of Law and Jurisprudence* 30 (2017): 23–55, pp. 23–43.
164 For competing views of the nature of legal interpretation in general, see Antonin Scalia, *A Matter of Interpretation: Federal Courts and the Law* (Princeton: Princeton University Press, 1997); John F. Manning, 'The New Purposivism', *Supreme Court Review* 2011 (2011): 113–82; Larry Alexander and Saikrishna Prakash, '"Is that English You're Speaking?" Some Arguments for the Primacy of Intent in Interpretation', *San Diego Law Review* 41 (2004): 967–96; Henry M. Hart and Albert M. Sacks, *The Legal Process: Basic Problems in the Making and Application of Law* (Westbury: Foundation Press, 1994).
165 Matsuda, 'Public Response to Racist Speech', p. 2360.
166 Ibid, pp. 2341–8.
167 Ibid.
168 See Brown, *Hate Speech Law*, ch. 2; and Brown and Sinclair, *The Politic of Hate Speech Laws*, ch. 4.
169 For further discussion, see Brown, *Hate Speech Laws*. For a succinct list of further readings, see Brown and Sinclair, *The Politics of Hate Speech Laws*, p. 18.
170 See *Lehideux and Isorni v. France*, ECtHR, Strasbourg, 23 September 1998, No. 24662/94, para. 47; and *Fatullayev v. Azerbaijan*, ECtHR, Strasbourg, 22 April 2010, No. 40984/07, para. 87.
171 Kahn, 'Holocaust Denial and Hate Speech', p. 107.
172 See also Schauer, 'Social Epistemology, Holocaust Denial, and the Post-Millian Calculus', p. 130.
173 In the US, however, a line is drawn between compulsory taxation used to fund government speech in general and state laws compelling certain public sector workers

to pay union fees, where those fees are used to fund union speech, including collective bargaining speech, that some workers disagree with. See *Janus v. AFSCME*, 585 U.S. ___ (2018).

174 9 March 2007, unpublished transcript obtained and translated by the authors.

175 Staff reporter, 'Turk Guilty Over Genocide Remarks', BBC News, 9 March 2007. Available at: http://news.bbc.co.uk/1/hi/world/europe/6434041.stm.

176 For example, in 2003 the Swiss National Council had passed a *Postulat* acknowledging the events of 1915 as a genocide. National Council Motion No. 02.3069, Bern, 16 December 2003.

177 13 June 2007, No. PE05.025301.

178 12 December 2007, No. 6B_398/2007.

179 Ibid, para. 4.6.

180 Available at: www.leg.state.nv.us/nrs/nrs-200.html.

181 Then again, it also does not rule out being applied to cases of libel against a community of persons identified by protected characteristics.

182 ss. 319(2) and 319(3)(a)(c) of the Criminal Code (as amended by An Act to Amend the Criminal Code (Hate Propaganda) of 2004).

183 s. 505 (Exception) of the Penal Code.

184 ss. 11(1)(b) and 14(2)(a)(c) of the Racial Discrimination Prohibition Act 26 of 1991, as amended by the Racial Discrimination Amendment Act 26 of 1998.

185 See Brown, *Hate Speech Law*, pp. 118–20; and Brown and Sinclair, *The Politics of Hate Speech Laws*, p. 313.

186 12 December 2007, No. 6B_398/2007, para. 5.2.

187 22 March 2000, No. 6S.719/1999.

188 Ibid, s. 2(e)(bb).

189 *Irving v. Penguin Books Limited*, Deborah E. Lipstat [2000] EWHC QB 115.

190 See Brown, *Hate Speech Laws*, ch. 2.

191 *Case of Jürgen Graf*, s. 2(e)(bb).

192 16 September 2010, 6B_297/2010.

193 Ibid, s. 1.

194 Ibid.

195 Ibid.

196 ECtHR, Strasbourg, 7 July 2003, No. 65831/01.

197 Ibid.

198 Meagher, 'Regulating History', p. 517.

199 Ibid, p. 519.

200 See *Jones v. Scully* [2002] FCA 1080; *Jones v Toben* [2002] FCA 1150; and *Toben v Jones* [2003] FCAFC 137.

201 Ibid.

202 Ibid, para. 186.

203 Consider Part 3A of the Public Order Act 1986 (England and Wales).

204 See Brown, *Hate Speech Law*, pp. 91–6.

205 See Edward J. Eberle, *Dignity and Liberty: Constitutional Visions in Germany and the United States* (Westport, CT: Praeger Publishers, 2002), pp. 117–18; Brown, *Hate Speech Law*, pp. 96–8.

206 15 March 2007, 2 KLs 503 17319/01.

207 See *Witzsch v. Germany*, at 8; *Pastörs v. Germany*, para. 48; and *Behar and Gutman v. Bulgaria*, para. 67. Cf. *Fatullayev v. Azerbaijan*, para. 98; and *Perinçek v. Switzerland*, para. 156.

208 Brown, *Hate Speech Law*, pp. 170–2.
209 See also Caroline Fournet, *The Crime of Destruction and the Law of Genocide: Their Impact on Collective Memory* (Abingdon: Routledge, 2016).
210 See Brown, *Hate Speech Laws*, ch. 6.
211 Consider the words of the International Court of Justice (ICJ): 'The origins of the Convention show that it was the intention of the United Nations to condemn and punish genocide as "a crime under international law" involving a denial of the right of existence of entire human groups, a denial which shocks the conscience of mankind and results in great losses to humanity, and which is contrary to moral law and the spirit and aims of the United Nations.' ICJ, *Reservations to the Convention on the Prevention and Punishment of the Crime of Genocide*, Advisory Opinion of 28 May 1951.
212 See also Brown, *Hate Speech Law*, pp. 170–2.
213 See Case of Victoire Ingabire, Supreme Court of Rwanda, 13 December 2013. But see also African Court on Human and Peoples' Rights, 7 December 2018, No. 003/2014.
214 Statements to the effect that the Jewish people have no right of existence are seen by many people as core instances of anti-Semitic hate propaganda of the sort for which there is a pro tanto case for legal sanction. See Jonathan Sacks, 'Commentary: Are Jews safe in Europe?', *Philadelphia Inquirer*, 6 October 2016. Available at: www.inquirer.com. Moreover, we have also seen in Chapter 4 how statements proclaiming that a group of people do not exist or that they should not exist or denying they have a right to exist may be hate speech in the ordinary sense of the term.
215 See also Kathleen E. Mahoney, 'Hate Speech: Affirmation or Contradiction of Freedom of Expression', *University of Illinois Law Review* (1996): 789–808, pp. 792, 803.
216 See Raphael Cohen-Almagor, 'Facebook and Holocaust Denial', *Justice* 57 (2016): 10–16, pp. 12–13.
217 See Matsuda, 'Public Response to Racist Speech', p. 2340n.101; Richard Delgado and Jean Stefancic, *Understanding Words That Wound* (Boulder: Westview Press, 2004), pp. 16–18; Richard Delgado and Jean Stefancic, 'Four Observations about Hate Speech', *Wake Forest Law Review* 44 (2009): 353–70, p. 365.
218 See Matsuda, 'Public Response to Racist Speech', p. 2368; Richard Delgado, 'Campus Antiracism Rules: Constitutional Narratives in Collision', *Northwestern University Law Review* 85 (1991): 343–87, p. 380n.319; Anthony Cortese, *Opposing Hate Speech* (Westport, CT: Praeger Publishers, 2006), p. 143.
219 See Brown, *Hate Speech Law*, pp. 130–2; and Alexander Brown, 'Retheorizing Actionable Injuries in Civil Lawsuits Involving Targeted Hate Speech: Hate Speech as Degradation and Humiliation', *Alabama Civil Rights and Civil Liberties Law Review* 9 (2018): 1–56.
220 See Geri J. Yonover, 'Anti-Semitism and Holocaust Denial in the Academy: A Tort Remedy', *Dickinson Law Review* 101 (1996): 71–94, esp. 83–94.
221 See Brown, 'Retheorizing Actionable Injuries in Civil Lawsuits Involving Targeted Hate Speech'. See also Richard Delgado, 'Words That Wound: A Tort Action for Racial Insults, Epithets, and Name-Calling', *Harvard Civil Rights-Civil Liberties Law Review* 17 (1982): 133–81; Richard Delgado, 'Professor Delgado Replies', *Harvard Civil Rights-Civil Liberties Law Review* 18 (1983): 593–7; and Richard Delgado and Jean Stefancic, 'Retheorizing Actions for Targeted Hate Speech: A Comment on Professor Brown', *Alabama Civil Rights and Civil Liberties Law Review* 9 (2018): 169–84.
222 Arthur Berney, 'Comments' in Gerald Tishler, 'Debate: Freedom of Speech and Holocaust Denial', *Cardozo Law Review* 8 (1987): 559–94, p. 576.

223 See Brown, *Hate Speech Law*, ch. 2; Katharine Gelber and Luke McNamara, 'Private Litigation to Address a Public Wrong: A Study of Australia's Regulatory Response to "Hate Speech"', *Civil Justice Quarterly* 33 (2014): 307–34; Joanna Botha and Avinash Govindjee, 'The Regulation of Racially Derogatory Speech in the Promotion of Equality and Prevention of Unfair Discrimination Act 4 of 2000', *South African Journal on Human Rights* 32 (2016): 293–320.

224 See Matsuda, 'Public Response to Racist Speech', pp. 2366–7; Lipstadt, *Antisemitism*, ch. 5; Cohen-Almagor, 'Holocaust Denial Is a Form of Hate Speech'; Cohen-Almagor, 'Holocaust Denial and Facebook'.

225 See Brown, *Hate Speech Law*, pp. 19–21.

226 16 December 1998.

227 *Garaudy v. France*, s. 'The Law'.

228 Jewish Policy Institute, *Combating Holocaust Denial Through Law in the United Kingdom* (London: Institute for Jewish Policy Research, 2000), p. 4.

229 See Matsuda, 'Public Response to Racist Speech', p. 2332; Delgado and Stefancic, *Understanding Words That Wound*, p. 11.

230 ECtHR, Strasbourg, 8 January 2019, No. 64496/17.

231 Ibid, para. 26.

232 Ibid, para. 24.

233 Ibid, para. 27.

234 Ronald Dworkin, 'Should Wrong Opinions be Banned?', *The Independent*, 27 May 1995. Available at: www.independent.co.uk/voices/should-wrong-opinions-be-banned-1621519.html.

235 Ibid.

236 Of course, there is bitter irony in this big lie – a sort of big lie in the mirror. First, Hitler accused Jews of using the propaganda technique of 'the big lie' ('*große Lüge*') in relation to the causes of World War I, whilst he himself later used the very same technique against Jews during World War II to claim that they had started the war and were conspiring to destroy Germany and its gentile population, suggesting that any actions taken against the Jews were in self-defence. Moreover, both the Nazis themselves and subsequent deniers promulgated another big lie, namely that the Nazis did not have or carry out any plan to exterminate the Jewish people. Finally, comes the big lie that the Jews themselves invented the story of the Holocaust.

237 Jeremy Waldron, *The Harm in Hate Speech* (Harvard: Harvard University Press, 2012), ch. 4.

238 Ibid, pp. 81, 102.

239 See also Brown, *Hate Speech Law*, pp. 146–7.

240 Ibid, ch. 2.

241 Indeed, in those countries the general view might be that bare Holocaust denial is more appropriately associated with the ordinary concept *hate speech* and with social norms and social sanctions, such as through campus codes promulgated by universities and content codes drafted and policed by social media platforms. It is perhaps no surprise that the main thrust of Jonathan Greenblatt's (the CEO of the Anti-Defamation League) commentaries on Holocaust denial have been to advocate a change in Facebook's community standard on hate speech (a change which later happened) rather than to argue for the restitution of criminal group defamation laws in America. Jonathan Greenblatt, 'Holocaust Denial Is a Form of Hate', *New York Daily News*, 29 July 2018. Available at: www.nydailynews.com.

242 *Perinçek v. Switzerland*, Para. 243. See also *Williamson v. France*, para. 27.
243 For a broader discussion of the legitimacy of prohibiting hate speech for symbolic purposes, see Brown, *Hate Speech Law*, pp. 240–2.
244 See Cohen-Almagor, 'Holocaust Denial is a Form of Hate Speech', p. 35.
245 For example, prior to Facebook changing its community standard on hate speech to disallow Holocaust denial in 2020, Mark Zuckerberg had previously sought to justify the old content policy of permitting denialist speech on the grounds that it was difficult to determine intent in the form of wilful ignorance. In July 2018 Zuckerberg said the following: 'I find [Holocaust denial] deeply offensive. But at the end of the day, I don't believe that our platform should take that down because I think there are things that different people get wrong. I don't think that they're intentionally getting it wrong […] It's hard to impugn intent and to understand the intent. I just think, as abhorrent as some of those examples are, I think the reality is also that I get things wrong when I speak publicly. I'm sure you do. I'm sure a lot of leaders and public figures we respect do too, and I just don't think that it is the right thing to say, "We're going to take someone off the platform if they get things wrong, even multiple times".' Kara Swisher, 'Full transcript: Facebook CEO Mark Zuckerberg on Recode Decode', *Vox*, 18 July 2018. Available at: www.vox.com/2018/7/18/17575158/mark-zuckerberg-facebook-interview-full-transcript-kara-swisher.

Zuckerberg faced a public backlash for his justification of Facebook's permissive policy since he appeared to be defending Holocaust deniers. People believe that denialism is more than merely speakers getting the facts wrong. Indeed, if Holocaust denial were just speakers getting the facts wrong, why would it be offensive? This backlash prompted Zuckerberg to walk back his earlier remarks: 'I personally find Holocaust denial deeply offensive, and I absolutely didn't intend to defend the intent of people who deny that.' Kara Swisher, 'Mark Zuckerberg Clarifies', *Vox*, 18 July 2018. Available at: www.vox.com/2018/7/18/17588116/mark-zuckerberg-clarifies-holocaust-denial-offensive. When Facebook finally moved to ban Holocaust denial on the platform in October 2020, Zuckerberg explained: 'I've struggled with the tension between standing for free expression and the harm caused by minimizing or denying the horror of the Holocaust. My own thinking has evolved as I've seen data showing an increase in anti-Semitic violence, as have our wider policies on hate speech.' Elizabeth Culliford, 'Facebook to Ban Content that Denies or Distorts the Holocaust', *Reuters*, 12 October 2020. Available at: www.reuters.com/article/facebook-policy-holocaust-int-idUSKBN26X1WT. It is striking how this justification of the ban on Holocaust denial focuses entirely on the harmful effects of Holocaust denial, as opposed to the issue of intent to get the facts wrong or whether denialist speech falls under the wide protection normally afforded by Facebook to lies or content that is inaccurate. The shift from treating denialist speech as a species of inaccurate content to treating it as harmful content is also seen in the official justification for the policy change published by Meta, which defends the ban on Holocaust denial as part of a wider effort to combat anti-Semitism online and offline. Monika Bickert, Vice President of Content Policy, Facebook, 'Removing Holocaust Denial Content', 12 October 2020. Available at: https://about.fb.com/news/2020/10/removing-holocaust-denial-content/.
246 Quassim Cassam, 'Vice Epistemology', *The Monist* 99 (2016): 159–80.
247 See Miranda Fricker, *Epistemic Injustice: Power and the Ethics of Knowing* (Oxford: Oxford University Press, 2007), p. 33.

248 Imge Oranlı, 'Epistemic Injustice from Afar: Rethinking the Denial of Armenian Genocide', *Social Epistemology* 35 (2021): 120–32.

249 Comments by Alan Dershowitz in Jamie Glazov, 'Symposium: Criminalizing Holocaust Denial', Front Page Magazine, 27 July 2007.

250 Note, motive is not the same as intention. Even if a hate speech law stipulates intention to stir up racial hatred as an element of the offence – see Part 3 of the Public Order Act 1986 (England and Wales), for example – this is not the same as stipulating a racist motive or reason for engaging in the intentional act. A person might perform the intentional act merely to curry favour or to sow division for personal gain without having a racist motive.

251 See Lewy, *Outlawing Genocide Denial*, ch. 4.

252 Tasmin Solomon, 'Problems in Drafting Legislation Against Racist Activities', *Australian Journal of Human Rights* 1 (1994): 265–84, p. 269.

253 UN Human Rights Committee, General Comment No. 35, para. 49.

254 15 March 1994, 1 StR 179/93.

255 See Peter Wyden, *The Hitler Virus: The Insidious Legacy of Adolf Hitler* (New York: Arcade Publishing, 1998), ch. 3.

256 Bleich, *The Freedom to Be Racist?*, p. 60.

257 Judgment No. 235/2007 of 7 November 2007 (BOE-T-2007-21161). Unofficial English translation. Available at: www.tribunalconstitucional.es/Resoluciones Traducidas/235-2007,%20of%20November%207.pdf.

258 *Perinçek v. Switzerland*, para. 52.

259 Ibid, para. 234.

260 See also Brown, 'The Myth of Hate', pp. 440–1; and Marc Fisher, 'From Memes to Race War: How Extremists use Popular Culture to Lure Recruits', *Washington Post*, 30 April 2021. Available at: www.washingtonpost.com/nation/2021/04/30/extremists-recruiting-culture-community/.

261 David Kretzmer, 'Freedom of Speech and Racism', *Cardozo Law Review* 8 (1987): 445–513, p. 464.

262 Rosenfeld, 'Hate Speech in Constitutional Jurisprudence', p. 259.

263 See also Lewy, *Outlawing Genocide Denial*, p. 156; and Tsesis, 'Genocide Censorship vs. Genocide Denial Laws', p. 115; and Lawrence Douglas, *The Memory of Judgment: Making Law and History in the Trials of the Holocaust* (New Haven: Yale University Press, 2001), p. 55.

264 See Kahn, 'Holocaust Denial and Hate Speech', pp. 106–7.

265 For an overview of these accounts, see Brown, *Hate Speech Law*, chs. 3 and 7; and Brown, 'Hate Speech Laws, Legitimacy, and Precaution'.

266 *Garaudy v. France*, s. The Law.

267 Ibid.

268 (2004) 244 FTR 292 (FC), 21 January 2004.

269 UN Human Rights Commission, Communication No. 1341/2005, 4 April 2007.

270 Ibid, para. 3.5.

271 Ibid, para. 4.9.

272 15 February 2007, 6 KLs 503 4/96.

273 Martin Imbleau, 'Denial of the Holocaust, Genocide, and Crimes against Humanity: A Comparative Overview of Ad Hoc Statutes', in L. Hennebel and T. Hochmann (eds.) *Genocide Denials and the Law* (New York: Oxford University Press, 2011), pp. 276.

274 Berney, 'Comments', p. 572.

275 Cheryl Redhorse Bennett, *Our Fight Has Just Begun: Hate Crimes and Justice in Native America* (Tucson: University of Arizona Press, 2022), p. 28.

276 (1992) 505 US 377.

277 Cited in Susan Dudley Gold, *Protecting Hate Speech: R.A.V. v. St. Paul* (New York: Cavendish Square Publishing, 2014), p. 64.

278 *R.A.V v. City of St. Paul*, at 424–5.

279 For example, some people will argue that banning Holocaust denial risks turning deniers into martyrs and giving them a public platform. They may even suggest that high profile trials involving Holocaust deniers could have at least similar sorts of indirect harms to denial itself, such as being capable of disturbing the public peace. However, another way of looking at this is to say that trials provide opportunities to show deniers for what they really are. They are also a valuable opportunity to give victims their day in court and to provide public assurances that they belong to groups who are in good standing. Indeed, nobody seriously believes public figures should be exempt from criminal trials for other sorts of crimes in case they use the proceedings for their own publicity. Indeed, there is a more obvious way to deal with the problem of defendant's turning courts into a three-ring circus besides decriminalising denialist speech or ordering such trials to take place behind closed doors or else removing denialism laws from criminal statutes and dealing with the problem through civil remedies involving private dispute resolution mechanism. That is for judges to take control of courtrooms and not allow defendant's to use proceedings as a soapbox. For further discussion of these issues, see Brown, *Hate Speech Law*, pp. 249–50; Brown and Sinclair, *The Politics of Hate Speech Laws*, pp. 478–9.

280 In using the term 'prohibitionist norms' we take some inspiration from Ethan A. Nadelmann, 'Global Prohibition Regimes: The Evolution of Norms in International Society', *International Organization* 44 (1990): 479–526.

281 CERD, A/52/18 (1997) 31, para. 217.

282 CERD/C/GC/35, para. 13.

283 Special Rapporteur on contemporary forms of racism, racial discrimination, xenophobia and related intolerance report on implementation of GA resolution 68/150, para. 39. Emphasis added. The paragraph reads: 'Shall declare an offence punishable by law all dissemination of ideas based on racial superiority or hatred, incitement to racial discrimination, as well as all acts of violence or incitement to such acts against any race or group of persons of another colour or ethnic origin'.

284 See also Brown and Sinclair, *The Politics of Hate Speech Laws*, pp. 139–63.

285 UN Human Rights Committee, General Comment No. 34, para. 51.

286 Report from the Commission to the European Parliament and the Council on the implementation of Council Framework Decision 2008/913/JHA on combating certain forms and expressions of racism and xenophobia by means of criminal law, Brussels, 27 January 2014, COM(2014) 27 final. Available at https://eur-lex.europa.eu/legal-content/EN/TXT/?uri=CELEX%3A52014DC0027.

287 Available at: https://ec.europa.eu/commission/presscorner/detail/en/inf_21_441.

288 Available at: https://ec.europa.eu/newsroom/just/items/713873/en.

289 Case of Maria Pupino, Court of Justice of the European Union, 16 June 2005, Case No. C-105/03, paras 44–5.

290 Art. 2 of Law 927/1979 (as amended by Law 4285/2014).

291 Decision No. 2383/2015, 10 February 2016.

292 Available at: https://ec.europa.eu/newsroom/just/items/713873/en.
293 Lobba, 'From Introduction to Implementation', pp. 199–200.
294 See Martin Brenncke, *Judicial Law-Making in English and German Courts: Techniques and Limits of Statutory Interpretation* (Cambridge: Cambridge University Press, 2018), ch. 4.
295 Council of Europe, Budapest, 23 November 2001, European Treaty Series No. 185.
296 Council of Europe, Strasbourg, 28 January 2003, European Treaty Series No. 189.
297 Available at: www.coe.int/en/web/conventions/full-list?module=signatures-by-treaty&treatynum=189.
298 Available at: www.coe.int/en/web/conventions/full-list?module=declarations-by-treaty&numSte=189&codeNature=1&codePays=GRE.
299 Available at: www.coe.int/en/web/conventions/full-list?module=signatures-by-treaty&treatynum=185.
300 Adoption of resolutions without a vote is the norm within the UN General Assembly with only contentious issues put to a vote. A simple majority would apply on the particular issue of Holocaust remembrance and denial, and so any draft resolution which was supported by the majority of states would certainly pass.
301 A/60/L.12, Add1.
302 See Peter Baker, 'The Seduction of George W. Bush', *Foreign Policy*, 6 November 2013. Available at: https://foreignpolicy.com/2013/11/06/the-seduction-of-george-w-bush/.
303 A/61/PV.85.
304 Ibid.
305 Ibid.
306 Ibid.
307 Ibid.
308 The concept of genocide was created by Raphael Lemkin in 1944. See Raphael Lemkin, *Axis Rule in Occupied Europe* (Washington: Carnegie Endowment for International Peace, 1944).
309 The concept of the Holocaust was only used to describe the genocide of the Jews by the Nazis in the 1960s. There were two reasons for this. First, the first English language translation of the Israeli Declaration of Independence was published and it refers to the 'Nazi holocaust' and second, the high-profile Eichmann trial which brought international attention back to the war and the Holocaust.
310 Weinke, *The Nuremberg Trials*.
311 The United States Holocaust Memorial Museum, 'International Military Tribunal at Nuremberg'. Available at: https://encyclopedia.ushmm.org/content/en/article/international-military-tribunal-at-nuremberg.
312 International Military Tribunal, Nuremberg, 1 October 1946.
313 Ibid, Judgment of Julius Streicher. Available at: https://crimeofaggression.info/documents/6/1946_Nuremberg_Judgment.pdf.
314 UN General Assembly, 84th Meeting, 26 October 1948, A/C.6/SR.84, p. 219.
315 Maktos quoted in Hirad Abtahi and Philippa Webb, *The Genocide Convention: Travaux Préparatoires* (Leiden: Nijhof, 2008), p. 1542. See also Jeroen Temperman, *Religious Hatred and International Law: The Prohibition of Incitement to Violence or Discrimination* (Cambridge: Cambridge University Press, 2016), pp. 31–63.
316 The US lost by 26 votes to 6, with 10 abstentions.

317 See the attempt by Argentina, Colombia, Ecuador, Panama, and Peru to remove 'dissemination of ideas' from the wording, leaving only incitement behind. See A/L.480, quoted in Patrick Thornberry, *The International Convention on the Elimination of All Forms of Racial Discrimination* (Oxford: Oxford University Press, 2016), p. 277.

318 A/C.3/SR.1318, para. 59.

319 Thornberry notes that most reserving states 'make reference to the principles of freedom of expression [...] and repeatedly refer to the Universal Declaration of Human Rights, Articles 19 and 20 [freedom of opinion and expression, and freedom of association]', Thornberry, *The International Convention on the Elimination of all Forms of Racial Discrimination*, p. 279.

320 Office of the United Nations High Commissioner for Human Rights, Travaux Préparatoires of article 20 of the International Covenant on Civil and Political Rights. Available at: www.ohchr.org/en/freedom-of-expression/travaux-preparatoires-article-20-international-covenant-civil-and-political-rights.

321 See Temperman, Religious Hatred and International Law, pp. 31–63.

322 Clotilde Pégorier, 'Speech and Harm: Genocide Denial, Hate Speech and Freedom of Expression', *International Criminal Law Review* 18 (2018): 97–126, p. 112.

323 Ibid, p. 113.

324 *Report of the Preparatory Committee on the Establishment of an International Criminal Court, Proceedings of the Preparatory Committee during March-April and August 1996, Fifty-first Session Supplement No. 22* (A/51/22), F. 2. (i) 203 (New York: UN General Assembly Official Records, 1996).

325 Stanton, 'The Eight Stages of Genocide', Working Paper (GS 01) of the Yale Program in Genocide Studies, 1998. Available at: www.genocide-watch.com/images/8StagesBriefingpaper.pdf. Stanton subsequently expanded the list to ten stages.

326 Lobba, 'From Introduction to Implementation', pp. 201–2.

327 Robert Kahn quoted in Dan Glaun, 'Germany's Laws on Hate Speech, Nazi Propaganda & Holocaust Denial: An Explainer', *Frontline*, 1 July 2021. Available at: www.pbs.org/wgbh/frontline/article/germanys-laws-antisemitic-hate-speech-nazi-propaganda-holocaust-denial.

328 Erik Bleich, *The Freedom to Be Racist? How the United States and Europe Struggle to Preserve Freedom and Combat Racism* (Oxford: Oxford University Press, 2011), p. 60.

329 The Armenian population in France is approximately 650,000, the largest in Europe. Office of the High Commissioner for Diaspora Affairs, 'France'. Available at: http://diaspora.gov.am/en/pages/37/france.

330 In 2012 the Constitutional Council of France ruled that extending the Gayssot act to include the Armenian genocide would be unconstitutional and violate freedom of speech. Constitutional Council of France, Decision No. 2012–647 DC of 28 February 2012, Law on the Punishment of Denials of the Existence of Genocides Recognised by Law. Available at: www.conseil-constitutionnel.fr/en/decision/2012/2012647DC.htm.

331 Subsequent trials at Nuremberg tried 183 people under the Charter. The United States Holocaust Memorial Museum, 'International Military Tribunal at Nuremberg'. Available at: https://encyclopedia.ushmm.org/content/en/article/international-military-tribunal-at-nuremberg.

332 See Walker, In Defense of American Liberties, ch. 10; and Martha T. Zingo, *Sex/Gender Outsiders, Hate Speech and Freedom of Expression: Can They Say That About Me?* (Westport, CT: Praeger Publishers, 1998).

333 Stanley Fish, *There's No Such Thing as Free Speech: And It's a Good Thing, Too* (New York: Oxford University Press, 1994); Victoria L. Killion, *The First Amendment: Categories of Speech*, Report No. IF11072 (Washington, DC: Congressional Report Service, 2019).

334 *R.A.V. v. City of St. Paul*, 505 U.S. 377 (1992), at 390.

335 Beauharnais vs. Illinois 343 U.S. 250 (1952).

336 See, respectively, *Smith v. Collin*, 439 US 916 (1978); *R.A.V. v. City of St. Paul* 505 US 377 (1992); *Virginia v. Black*, 538 US 343 (2003); and *Snyder v. Phelps*, 562 US (2011).

337 See *Doe v. University of Michigan*, 721 F. Supp. 852 (US District Court, East. Dist. Mich., 1989); *UWM Post v. Board of Regents of the University of Wisconsin*, 774 F. Supp. 1163 (US District Court, East. Dist. Wisc., 1991); *Dambrot v. Central Michigan University*, 55 F.3d 1177 (US Court of Appeals, 6th Cir., 1995); and *Corry v. Stanford*, No. 740309 (Cal. Super. Court, 27 February 1995).

338 *Matal v. Tam*, 582 U.S. ___ (2017).

339 In the words of Justice Sandra Day O'Connor in *City of Ladue v. Gilleo*, 512 U.S. 43 (1994), 'no better alternative has yet come to light'.

340 567 U.S. 709 (2012).

341 Relevant underlying moral values might include: norms of self-expression and autonomy; epistemic norms related to knowledge, or what Mill called 'the clearer perception and livelier impression of truth, produced by its collision with error'; norms on how to balance epistemic and non-epistemic harms; norms of dissent; and norms relating to the legitimacy of the state: that no 'downstream' regulations in other areas of public policy could be legitimate that 'cut off racists and Holocaust deniers from the opportunity to influence democratic will formation'. See Dworkin, 'Should Wrong Opinions be Banned?'; Kenneth Lasson, 'Holocaust Denial and the First Amendment: The Quest for Truth in a Free Society', *George Mason University Law Review* 6 (1997): 35–86; Steven H. Shiffrin, *Dissent, Injustice, and the Meanings of America* (Princeton: Princeton University Press, 1999); Stanley Fish, 'Holocaust Denial and Academic Freedom', *Valparaiso University Law Review* 35 (2001): 499–524; Catriona McKinnon, 'Should We Tolerate Holocaust Denial?', *Res Publica* 13 (2007): 9–28; Ronald Dworkin, 'Forward', in I. Hare and J. Weinstein (eds.) *Extreme Speech and Democracy* (Oxford: Oxford University Press, 2009); Edwin C. Baker, 'Autonomy and Hate Speech', in I. Hare and J. Weinstein (eds.) *Extreme Speech and Democracy* (Oxford: Oxford University Press, 2009); Frederick Schauer, 'Social Epistemology, Holocaust Denial, and the Post-Millian Calculus', in M. Herz and P. Molnar (eds.) *The Content and Context of Hate Speech: Rethinking Regulation and Responses* (Cambridge: Cambridge University Press, 2012); and James Weinstein, 'Hate Speech Bans, Democracy, and Political Legitimacy', *Constitutional Commentary* 32 (2017): 527–83.

342 For alternative conceptions of what autonomy norms, epistemic norms, and legitimacy norms, not to mention dignity norms and norms of cultural recognition, might imply about hate speech laws, including Holocaust denial laws, see Brown, *Hate Speech Laws*, chs. 3–7; Lyrissa Barnett Lidsky, 'Where's the Harm?: Free Speech and the Regulation of Lies', *Washington and Lee Law Review* 65 (2008): 1091–101; and Alexander Tsesis, 'Genocide Censorship vs. Genocide Denial Laws',

in P. Grzebyk (ed.) *Responsibility for Negation of International Crimes* (Warsaw: Institute of Justice Press, 2020). To illustrate this wider point about reasonable normative disagreement, take the argument that Holocaust denial laws undermine legitimacy. This argument itself assumes a particular conception of legitimacy as democratic legitimacy. But while that conception may be the only game in town culturally speaking in the US, that is, given American legal and political culture, it is certainly not the only plausible conception in other cultures. As Julia Suk explains: 'In France, by criminalizing Holocaust denial, the state makes clear that racism has no place in collective self-determination. This exclusion enhances, rather than undermines, the state's legitimacy, because the state cannot govern legitimately unless it makes a strong, clear break with a past racist regime. The law against Holocaust denial participates in this legitimating rupture.' Julia C. Suk, 'Denying Experience: Holocaust Denial and the Free-Speech Theory of the State', in M. Herz and P. Molnar (eds.) *The Content and Context of Hate Speech: Rethinking Regulation and Responses* (Cambridge: Cambridge University Press, 2012), p. 145. Furthermore, conceptions of legitimacy which emphasise democratic procedures and processes are also not the only alternative philosophically speaking. Another viable alternative is legitimacy as political legitimacy based on hypothetical agreement. Put simply, it is far from obvious that citizens would reasonably agree to allow racists and Holocaust deniers to speak with impunity if they were placed under idealised conditions of freedom and equality. See Alexander Brown, 'Hate Speech Laws, Legitimacy, and Precaution: Reply to Weinstein', *Constitutional Commentary* 32 (2017): 599–617.

343 On the one hand, the executive, including but not limited to the State Department and the Office of the President, has the final say over America's foreign policy agenda including the American visions of what international free speech norms should be, and how it should go about shaping and responding to competing visions of international free speech norms. On the other hand, the Supreme Court along with other courts lower in the judicial hierarchy is the key architect of domestic US legal norms on free speech. Whilst Senate committees, civil rights organisations, social media platforms, and other norm influencers have an influence over both domestic free speech norms and foreign policy on international free speech norms, the separation of the executive and the judiciary means that the different free speech norms that come under their spheres of influence can, and sometimes do, diverge.

That is not to say there will not be read across from domestic free speech norms to foreign policy on international free speech norms: it is important not to overstate the separation of powers. Key figures in the State Department, the Office of the President, and the Senate Committee on Foreign Relations, for example, will be fully aware of what the judicial branch is doing and the current state of play with the domestic US free speech norm; they also have an obligation to respect this norm when generating foreign policy on these matters. In international negotiations over treaties or agreements relating to, or implicating, matters of free speech, representatives of the United States will often publicly affirm that they cannot commit the United States to international free speech norms which violate the First Amendment to the Constitution, as interpreted by them but more importantly as interpreted by the judiciary at home. The US can formally agree to but also enter reservations to agreements to ensure compatibility with the domestic free speech norm as articulated by the Supreme Court.

That said, there is not quite the same path dependency between what the Supreme Court says about free speech and US foreign on matters of free speech as compared to, say, when the Supreme Court make a decision on a case with important implications for the domestic US free speech norm, and this decision directly binds the executive's domestic policy agenda. While there is no strict obligation on governmental authorities to repeal laws that have been struck down as unconstitutional, for example, in reality the laws effectively become unenforceable from that point onwards. Moreover, the President cannot sign into law a bill, for example, that has been held as unconstitutional by the Supreme Court.

344 For an account of the militant democracy approach, see Karl Loewenstein, 'Militant Democracy and Fundamental Rights I', *American Political Science Review* 31 (1937): 417–32; Karl Loewenstein, 'Militant Democracy and Fundamental Rights II', *American Political Science Review* 31 (1937): 638–58; Brown, *Hate Speech Law*, pp. 196–7.

345 Suk, 'Denying Experience', p. 145.

346 See Brown and Sinclair, *The Politics of Hate Speech Laws*, pp. 172–3.

347 For a discussion of hate speech laws in general as they relate to the imminent lawless action test, see Kammy Au, 'Freedom from Fear', *Lincoln Law Review* 15 (1984): 45–52, p. 52; James Weinstein, 'An Overview of American Free Speech Doctrine and its Application to Extreme Speech', in I. Hare and J. Weinstein (eds.) *Extreme Speech and Democracy* (Oxford: Oxford University Press, 2009), pp. 88–9; and Brown, *Hate Speech Law*, p. 68.

348 See Stephen J. Roth, 'The Laws of Six Countries: An analytical Comparison', in L. Greenspan and C. Levitt (eds.) *Under the Shadow of Weimar: Democracy, Law, and Racial Incitement in Six Countries* (Westport, CT: Praeger, 1993); Bleich, *The Freedom to Be Racist?*, ch. 4; James Weinstein, 'Hate Speech, Viewpoint Neutrality, and the American Concept of Democracy', in T. Hensley (ed.) *The Boundaries of Freedom of Expression and Order in a Democratic Society* (Kent: Kent State University Press, 2001); Kevin Boyle, 'Hate Speech—The United States Versus the Rest of the World', *Maine Law Review* 53 (2001): 488–501; Edward J. Eberle, *Dignity and Liberty: Constitutional Visions in Germany and the United States* (Westport, CT: Praeger Publishers, 2002); Frederick Schauer, 'The Exceptional First Amendment', in M. Ignatieff (ed.) *American Exceptionalism and Human Rights* (Princeton: Princeton University Press, 2005); Frederick Schauer, 'Freedom of Expression Adjudication in Europe and America: A Case Study in Comparative Constitutional Architecture', in G. Nolte (ed.) *European and U.S. Constitutionalism* (Cambridge: Cambridge University Press, 2005); Anne-Marie Slaughter, 'A Brave New Judicial World', in M. Ignatieff (ed.) *American Exceptionalism and Human Rights* (Princeton: Princeton University Press, 2005); Eric Barendt, *Freedom of Speech, Second Edition* (Oxford: Oxford University Press, 2005); C. Edwin Baker, 'Hate Speech', in M. Herz and P. Molnar (eds.) *The Content and Context of Hate Speech: Rethinking Regulation and Responses* (Cambridge: Cambridge University Press, 2012); Floyd Abrams, *The Soul of the First Amendment: Why Freedom of Speech Matters* (New Haven: Yale University Press, 2017); and Brown and Sinclair, *The Politics of Hate Speech Laws*, p. 184.

349 See Brown and Sinclair, *The Politics of Hate Speech Laws*, pp. 67–72, esp. p. 70. See also Brown, *Hate Speech Laws*, chs. 2 and 10.

350 See Alexander Tsesis, 'Burning Crosses on Campus: University Hate Speech Codes', *Connecticut Law Review* 43 (2010): 617–72; Alexander Tsesis, 'Inflammatory

Speech: Offense Versus Incitement', *Minnesota Law Review* 97 (2013): 1145–96; Alexander Tsesis, 'Campus Speech and Harassment', *Minnesota Law Review* 101 (2017): 1863–917.

351 See Brown and Sinclair, *The Politics of Hate Speech Laws*, pp. 290–4. See also Scott D. Gerber, 'The Politics of Free Speech', *Social Philosophy and Policy* 21 (2004): 23–47.

352 Suk, 'Denying Experience', p. 144.

353 Alverez v. United States, Justice Alito dissenting opinion, at 739.

354 See Michel Rosenfeld and Andras Sajo, 'Spreading Liberal Constitutionalism: An Inquiry into the Fate of Free Speech in New Democracies', in S. Choudry (ed.) *The Migration of Constitutional Ideas* (Cambridge: Cambridge University Press, 2006), pp. 161–3; Peter Molnar, 'Towards Improved Law and Policy on "Hate Speech": The "Clear and Present Danger" Test in Hungary', in I. Hare and J. Weinstein (eds.) *Extreme Speech and Democracy* (Oxford: Oxford University Press, 2009); and András Koltay, 'The Clear and Present Danger Doctrine in Hungarian Hate Speech Laws and the Jurisprudence of the European Court of Human Rights', in R. L. Weaver et al. (eds.) *Comparative Perspectives on Freedom of Expression, The Global Papers Series, Volume Two* (Durham: Carolina Academic Press, 2017).

355 See *Jersild v. Denmark*, ECtHR, Strasbourg, 23 September 1994, No. 15890/89; *Garaudy v. France*, ECtHR, Strasbourg, 7 July 2003, No. 65831/01; *Soulas and others v. France*, ECtHR, Strasbourg, 10 July 2008, No. 15948/03; *Balsyte-Lideikiene v. Lithuania*, ECtHR, Strasbourg, 4 November 2008, No. 72596/01; *Féret v. Belgium*, ECtHR, Strasbourg, 16 July 2009, No. 15615/07; *Willem v. France*, ECtHR, Strasbourg, 16 July 2009, No. 10883/05; *Aksu v. Turkey*, ECtHR, Strasbourg, 15 March 2012, Nos. 4149/04 and 41029/04; *Vejdeland and Others v. Sweden*, ECtHR, Strasbourg, 9 February 2012, No. 1813/07; *Atamanchuk v Russia*, ECtHR, Strasbourg, 11 February 2020, No. 4493/11; *Sanchez v. France*, ECtHR, Strasbourg, 2 September 2021, No. 45581/15.

356 See *Erbakan v. Turkey*, ECtHR, Strasbourg, 6 July 2006, No. 59405/00; and *Stomakhin v. Russia*, ECtHR, Strasbourg, 9 May 2018, No. 52273/07.

357 Consider *Case of György Nagy*, Budapest-Capital Regional Court, 7 December 2012, No. 23.Bf.10.283/2012/4; and *Case of Kuruc.info*, Budapest Metropolitan Tribunal, 14 January 2015.

358 See *Sanchez v. France*; *Pastörs v. Germany*; and *Atamanchuk v. Russia*.

359 *Perinçek v. Switzerland*, para. 234.

360 See *Witzsch v. Germany*, at 8; *Pastörs v. Germany*, para. 48; and *Behar and Gutman v. Bulgaria*, para. 67.

361 Consider Joint Resolution S.J.RES.14, 30 April 2009.

362 For a critical discussion of normative arguments against the enactment of hate speech laws in general that rely on the idea of a slippery slope, see also Brown and Sinclair, *The Politics of Hate Speech Laws*, ch. 5.

363 See Matsuda, 'Public Response to Racist Speech', p. 2343; and Brown and Sinclair, *The Politics of Hate Speech Laws*, pp. 165–6.

364 Brown and Sinclair, *The Politics of Hate Speech Laws*, ch. 4.

365 See Alexander Tsesis, *Free Speech in the Balance* (Cambridge: Cambridge University Press, 2020).

366 Tsesis, 'Genocide Censorship vs. Genocide Denial Laws'.

367 See Brown and Sinclair, *The Politics of Hate Speech Laws*, pp. 172–3.

368 @ImranKhanPTI, Twitter, 17 April 2021.

369 Office of the United Nations High Commissioner for Human Rights, Rabat, 5 October 2012.

370 Laura MacInnis, 'Ahmadinejad Prompts Walkout from U.N. Racism Summit', *Reuters*, 20 April 2009. Available at: www.reuters.com/article/us-racism-un-id USLJ34980320090420.

371 See UNCHR Resolution 1999/82 on Defamation of Religions, 30 April 1999, E/CN.4/RES/1999/82; UNCHR Resolution 2000/84 on Defamation of Religions, 27 April 2000, E/CN.4/RES/2000/84; UNCHR Resolution 2001/4 on Defamation of Religions, 18 April 2001, E/CN.4/RES/2001/4; UNCHR Resolution 2002/9 on Defamation of Religions, 15 April 2002, E/CN.4/RES/2002/9; UNCHR Resolution 2003/4 on Defamation of Religions, 13 April 2003, E/CN.4/RES/2003/4; UNCHR Resolution 2004/6 on Defamation of Religions, 8 April 2004, E/CN.4/RES/2004/6; UNCHR Resolution 2005/3 on Defamation of Religions, 12 April 2005, E/CN.4/RES/2005/3; UNHRC Resolution 4/9 on Combating Defamation of Religions, 30 April 2007, A/HRC/RES/4/9; UNHRC Resolution 7/19 on Combating Defamation of Religions, 27 March 2008, A/HRC/RES/7/19; UNHRC Resolution 10/22 on Combating Defamation of Religions, 26 March 2009, A/HRC/RES/10/22; UNHRC, Resolution 13/16 on Combating Defamation of Religions, 15 April 2010, A/HRC/RES/13/16.

372 Brown and Sinclair, *The Politics of Hate Speech Laws*, pp. 172–3.

373 For detailed discussion of the merits of legal cases involving defamation of religion, See Joshua Foster, 'Prophets, Cartoons, and Legal Norms: Rethinking the United Nations Defamation of Religious Provisions', *Journal of Catholic Legal Studies* 48 (2009): 19–58; Kwame Anthony Appiah, 'What's Wrong with Defamation of Religion?', in M. Herz and P. Molnar (eds.) *The Content and Context of Hate Speech: Rethinking Regulation and Responses* (Cambridge: Cambridge University Press, 2012); Richard Moon, *Putting Faith in Hate: When Religion Is the Source or Target of Hate Speech* (Cambridge: Cambridge University Press, 2018); and Eva Hauksdóttir, 'Restricting Freedom of Expression for Religious Peace: On the ECHR's Approach to Blasphemy', *European Convention on Human Rights Law Review* 2 (2021): 75–118.

374 Art. 216 of the Penal Code (formerly Art. 312). For analysis, see Brown and Sinclair, *The Politics of Hate Speech Laws*, pp. 80–1, 172.

375 Art. 499bis of the penal code (as amended in 2021 by the Criminalization of Insulting Iranian Religions and Ethnicities Act).

376 See Brown, *Hate Speech Laws*, p. 26.

8 Epilogue

1 Snap Inc., Community Guidelines, Terrorism, Hate Groups and Hate Speech (as of 10 June 2023). Available at: https://snap.com/en-GB/community-guidelines.

2 See also Alexander Brown, 'What Is Hate Speech? Part 1: The Myth of Hate', *Law and Philosophy* (2017) 36: 419–68, pp. 447–9; Alexander Brown, 'What Is Hate Speech? Part 2: Family Resemblances', *Law and Philosophy* 36 (2017): 561–613, pp. 571–3.

3 Keith Bach, 'Loaded Words: On the Semantic and Pragmatics of Slurs', in D. Sosa. (ed.) *Bad Words: Philosophical Perspectives on Slurs* (Oxford: Oxford University Press, 2018), p. 62.

4 Interestingly, its Oversight Board has often taken evidence from Facebook about what the details of the authoritative internal policy on hate speech and then made

recommendations that aspects of the internal policy ought to be included in the public-facing version (community standard). See, for example, Facebook Oversight Board, Case Decision 2021-005-FB-UA, 20 May 2021. Available at: www.oversightboard.com/decision/FB-RZL57QHJ.

5 We note that Facebook has clarified this in some of its ad hoc public communications on hate speech. For example: 'While there is no universally accepted definition of hate speech, as a platform we define the term to mean direct and serious attacks on any protected category of people based on their race, ethnicity, national origin, religion, sex, gender, sexual orientation, disability or disease.' Marne Levine, VP of Global Public Policy, 'Controversial, Harmful and Hateful Speech on Facebook', *Facebook*, 28 May 2013. Available at: www.facebook.com/notes/344897590097197/.

6 We note that this same recommendation has been made by the Facebook Oversight Board in more than one case. See Facebook Oversight Board, Case Decision 2021-010-FB-UA, 27 September 2021. Available at: https://oversightboard.com/decision/FB-E5M6QZGA/. And Facebook Oversight Board, Case Decision 2021-011-FB-UA, 28 September 2021. Available at: www.oversightboard.com/decision/FB-TYE2766G/.

7 Facebook Community Standards (as of 10 June 2023). Available at: https://transparency.fb.com/en-gb/policies/community-standards/.

8 Office of the United Nations High Commissioner for Human Rights, Guiding Principles on Business and Human Rights, New York, 2011, Principle 11. Available at: www.ohchr.org/sites/default/files/documents/publications/guidingprinciplesbusinesshr_en.pdf.

9 See Alexander Brown and Adriana Sinclair, *The Politics of Hate Speech Laws* (Abingdon: Routledge, 2020), ch. 4.

10 Alexander Brown, *Models of Governance of Online Hate Speech* (Strasbourg: Council of Europe, 2020), p. 52.

11 For an overview on the silencing effect of hate speech, see Alexander Brown, *Hate Speech Law: A Philosophical Examination* (Abingdon: Routledge, 2015), pp. 84–5.

12 See Brown and Sinclair, *The Politics of Hate Speech Laws*, ch. 3.

13 Ibid, ch. 4.

14 Consider Arts. 3 and 6 of the Council of Europe Additional Protocol to the Convention on Cybercrime concerning the criminalisation of acts of a racist and xenophobic nature committed through computer systems, Council of Europe, Strasbourg, 28 January 2003, European Treaty Series No. 189.

15 Why would a state sign and ratify a treaty it does do not actually agree with and only consents to by entering reservations to the main treaty obligations? The answer is that states, and powerful states in particular, want to be part of treaty negotiations, even for treaties they do not support. This cuts both ways. Objector states, who want to water down a treaty, may find themselves outmanoeuvred by other states. Other states may not concede to the changes the objector state wants and then the objector has to decide whether to accept the treaty as it is or walk away. While it may seem obvious that a state would not sign a treaty it was not happy with, in practice this is less so because involvement provides influence. So, a state will often sign a treaty it is not completely happy with, enter reservations to it and hope that by retaining its place at the table, it can steer the future direction of the application of the treaty and the creation other similar treaties in a more favourable way.

16 United Nations International Law Commission, Report of the International Law Commission Seventy-First Session, *New York*, 2019, ch. 5. Available at: https://legal.un.org/ilc/reports/2019/.

17 See Brown and Sinclair, *The Politics of Hate Speech Laws*, ch. 4.

18 Ibid.

19 See, for example, the body of country monitoring reports produced by the European Commission against Racism and Intolerance (ECRI). Available at: www.coe.int/en/web/european-commission-against-racism-and-intolerance/country-monitoring. See also the Octopus Project, *Implementing the Protocol to the Convention on Cybercrime on Xenophobia and Racism: Good Practice Study*, 2023. Available at: www.coe.int/en/web/cybercrime/octopus-project.

INDEX

Printed in the USA
CPSIA information can be obtained
at www.ICGtesting.com
LVHW020624261223
767207LV00037B/97